Wood screw types and uses

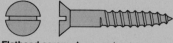

Flathead screw: A general-purpose screw for flush or countersinking installation

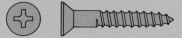

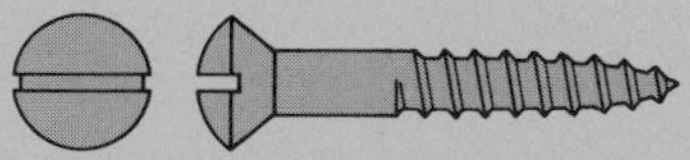

Oval head screw: Top of head protrudes, making screw easy to remove; ornamental applications

Round head: Utility screw, often used with washer, for fastening a thin board without splitting it

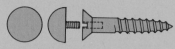

Dome head screw: Detachable cap makes this special order screw right for ornamental work

Phillips head screw: Cross-slot heads minimize screwdriver slip out; requires Phillips driver

Lag bolt (or screw): This heavy-duty screw is driven by turning its nutlike head with wrench

Metal screws

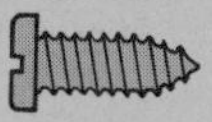

Pan head (pointed): For use in drilled sheet metal and also as a high strength fastener for plywood.

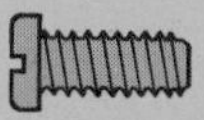

Pan head (blunted): For use in pre-drilled pilot holes, where a sharp point is not necessary for penetration.

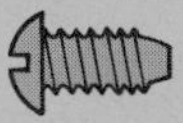

Roundhead (partial tapping): For use in pre-drilled holes; taps machine-screw threads for fastening strength.

Roundhead (self-tapping): For use in deeper thicknesses of metal than partial tapping roundhead screws.

Screw washers

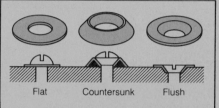

Flat   Countersunk   Flush

Lumber: Linear to board feet conversion table

Linear feet	5'	10'	20'	30'	40'	50'	100'	250'	1000'
Stock	Board feet								
1 x 2	.83	1.7	3.3	5	6.7	8.3	16.7	42.7	166.7
1 x 3	1.25	2.5	5	7.5	10	12.5	25	62.5	250
1 x 4	1.7	3.3	6.7	10	13.3	16.7	33.3	83.3	333.3
1 x 6	2.5	5	10	15	20	25	50	125	500
1 x 8	3.3	6.7	13.3	20	26.7	33.3	66.7	166.7	666.7
2 x 4	3.3	6.7	13.3	20	26.7	33.3	66.7	166.7	666.7
2 x 6	5	10	20	30	40	50	100	250	1000
2 x 8	6.7	13.3	26.7	40	53.3	66.7	133.3	333.3	1333.3
2 x 10	8.3	16.7	33.3	50	66.7	83.3	166.7	416.7	1666.7
2 x 12	10	20	40	60	80	100	200	500	2000
4 x 4	6.7	13.3	26.7	40	53.3	66.7	133.3	333.3	1333.3

Note: Conversions that do not appear in the table can easily be calculated by using multiples of the quantities given. Or, multiply the dimensions of the lumber in inches by the total length in feet and divide by 12; i.e.,a 1 x 8 that is 12 ft. long = 1 x 8 x 12 = 96 ÷ 12, or 8 board feet.

Nominal and actual lumber sizes*

Nominal size (in inches)	Actual size (in inches)	Nominal size (in inches)	Actual size (in inches)	Nominal size (in inches)	Actual size (in inches)
1 x 2	¾ x 1½	1 x 12	¾ x 11¼	2 x 12	1½ x 11¼
1 x 3	¾ x 2½	2 x 2	1½ x 1½	3 x 4	2½ x 3½
1 x 4	¾ x 3½	2 x 3	1½ x 2½	4 x 4	3½ x 3½
1 x 5	¾ x 4½	2 x 4	1½ x 3½	4 x 6	3½ x 5½
1 x 6	¾ x 5½	2 x 6	1½ x 5½	6 x 6	5½ x 5½
1 x 8	¾ x 7¼	2 x 8	1½ x 7¼	8 x 8	7¼ x 7¼
1 x 10	¾ x 9¼	2 x 10	1½ x 9¼		

*All sizes come in standard lengths of 8, 10, 12, 14, 16, and 20 feet.

Reader's Digest

HOME IMPROVEMENTS MANUAL

The Reader's Digest Association Inc.
Pleasantville, New York / Montreal, Canada

Home Improvements Manual

Project Director	John Speicher
Art Director	David Trooper
Art Production Editor	Dorothy R. Schmidt
Associate Editors	Paul Ahrens
	Valentin Chu
	Susan Parker
Copy Editor and Indexer	Elizabeth T. Salter
Art Editor	Virginia Wells Blaker
Section Designers	Gordon Chapman
	Larissa Lawrynenko
	Edward Lipinski
	Marta M. Strait
Assistant Artists	Lisa Grant
	Carol Waters
Editorial Assistant	V. Frederick Veader
Label typography	Grace Del Bagno

The credits and acknowledgments that appear
on the facing page and on other pages
throughout this book are hereby made
a part of this copyright page.

Library of Congress Catalog Card No. 81-84488
ISBN 0-89577-132-2

Printed in the United States of America

The editors are grateful for the assistance provided by the following individuals, manufacturers, and organizations:

Contributors

Chief Contributing Editor
Daniel Weiss

Contributing Editors
Linda Hetzer
Mort Schulz

Contributing Writers
Robert Bahr
Gene Balsley
Karen Bussolini
Mary Durant Harwood
Frank Latham
Joseph Morschauser

Independent Project Managers
Fred W. Bumiller, Jr.
Eric Chase
Linda Hammer
Alexander Russoniello
Tim Snider
Fred Ward

Contributing Artists
Dominic A. Colacchio
Jorge Hernandez
John A. Lind Corporation
Dominick Micolupo
Max Menikoff
Ken Rice
Jim Silks
Ray Skibinski
Robert Steimle
B. Anderson Strait
Eugene Thompson
Steve Turner
Bill Wilkinson
Lynn Yost

Commissioned Photography
David Arky
Joseph Barnell
Karen Bussolini
Irv Elkin (cover)
Linda Hammer
John R. Johnson
Lilo Raymond
Alexander Russoniello
Daniel Weiss

Consultants

Chief Consultant
Tim Snider

General Consultants
George Daniels
Marie Daniels

Architectural Consultants
Eric Chase, A.I.A.
Kenneth Kraus, A.I.A.
P. A. Marchetta, A.I.A.

Design Consultant
Gordon Chapman

Technical Consultants
Chris Anderson,
Builder
Fred W. Bumiller, Sr.,
Builder
Fred W. Bumiller, Jr.,
Builder
Stewart Cameron,
General Contractor
John Conway,
Electrician
Matthew G. Cusack, Jr.,
Builder
Steve Johnson,
Builder
David Novalis,
Roofing and Skylights
Larry Perry,
Builder
Pete Plaza,
Masonry Contractor
Duke Rhoades,
Roofing
Robert S. Robbins,
Plumbing and Heating
Levi Ross,
Builder
Peter Schnitzer,
Builder
Philip Sieb,
Electrical Contractors
Gaylord Stadshaug,
Builder
B. Anderson Strait,
Architectural Designer

Organizations

Aanensen's Cabinetmakers
Admiralty-Heritage Co.
Advanced Drainage Systems, Inc.
Alenco Div., of Redman
  Building Products, Inc.
American Olean Tile Co.,
  div. National Gypsum Co.
American-Standard Co.
Ames Stapling & Nailing
  Systems, Inc.
Andersen Corporation
Appropriate Technology Corporation
Arkansas Power & Light Company
Armstrong Cork Company
Benjamin Moore & Company
Big Timer Stove
Bird & Son, Inc.
Boise Cascade Corporation
Brammer Manufacturing Company
Bruce Hardwood Floors,
  div. Triangle Pacific Co.
Bryant Electric Company
Building Stone Institute
Burton Enterprises, Inc.
California Redwood Association
Carley's Plumbing and
  Electrical Supply
Carrier Air Conditioning Group
CertainTeed Corporation
Collins & Aikman
Coppes, Inc.
Da-Lite Screen Co., Inc.
Discovery Designs
Eccles Garden Shop
Elson (Sekisui Products)
Evans Products Company
Fireline, Inc.
Ford Products Corporation
Georgia-Pacific Corporation
Grant Hardware Co.,
  div. Buildex, Inc.
Halo Lighting
Heads Up, Inc.
Honeywell, Inc.
Howmet Aluminum Corp.,
  Southern Extrusions Div.
Hurd Millwork
Import Specialist
Intertherm, Inc.
The Iron Monger
Johns-Manville Sales Corporation
J & P Sales Company
Kelly Moore Paint Company
Kemper, div. of Tappan
Kohler Company
Kroin-Architectural
Lakeshore Industries, Inc.
Lawrence Kantor, Inc.
Lennox Industries, Inc.
Levolor Lorentzen, Inc.
Lightolier, Inc.
Lis King, Inc.
Marlan Lewis Designs

Martin Industries
Marvin Windows
Merillat Industries, Inc.
Miami-Carey, Jim Walter Company
Moen, div. of Stanadyne
National Woodwork Manufacturers Assn.
National Oak Flooring
  Manufacturers Assn., Inc.
Novalis Roofing Company
E. A. Nord Company
NuTone, div. of Scovill
Olympic Stain, div. COMERCO, Inc.
Owens-Corning Fiberglas Corporation
Port Townsend Lumber Company
Preway, Inc.
Quakermaid
Reynolds Metals Company
St. Charles Manufacturing Company
Shakertown Corporation
Simpson Timber Company
Sto-Cote Products, Inc.
Sub-Zero Freezer Co., Inc.
Sumner Rider & Associates, Inc.
Therma Tru, subsidiary of
  LST Corporation
U. S. Gypsum, Company
United States Mineral
  Products Company
Velux-America, Inc.
Ventarama Skylights Corporation
Vulcan-Hart Corporation
Wasco Products, Inc.
Westinghouse Electric Corporation
Wood Metal Industries, Inc.

Contents

Contents

About this book

The *Home Improvements Manual* is the newest of the Reader's Digest practical do-it-yourself guides. It was conceived to complement our *Complete Do-it-yourself Manual.* Millions of people have used that book to accomplish, at minimum cost, many home-improvement jobs and repairs that would otherwise have required the services of professionals. Over the years, many of these men and women have written or called to ask if we were planning to publish anything new and equally useful that would deal with the entire house, room renovations, additions, and plans and drawings.

This book is our answer. The *Home Improvements Manual* is a total book of the house. It applies equally to do-it-yourselfers and to those who intend only to plan or oversee their projects. Even if you never intend to pick up a hammer and saw, you can save time and money—and find inspiration—by using this book for reference.

The manual opens with a chapter on American house styles. Then comes an illustrated introduction to the subject of building codes that tells why and how a house must comply with established standards. Sections follow on architectural drawings, drawing your own plans, estimating costs, ordering materials, obtaining building permits, and dealing with contractors. Collections of color photographs show finished renovations—everything from new kitchens to solar retrofits—from all across the nation, in city, suburban, and rural homes.

All of the necessary how-to instruction is here, in the customary Reader's Digest clarity of presentation. We also tell the do-it-yourselfer what he cannot do—as, for instance, when a project involves extreme physical exertion. Chapters on restoring older houses will be significant to bargain hunters who long to transform a "fixer upper" into a dream house. There are pages on vacation houses and building houses from kits.

There are also pages for the reader whose immediate needs are simpler—a well-designed closet or an innovative design for a bunk bed. An extensive chapter on electrical wiring is not only up-to-date, it is illustrated down to the last terminal screw to assure clarity and safety. Plumbing instructions are covered; so, too, are bearing walls, roofing, siding, flooring, tiling, skylights, pre-assembled windows, pre-hung doors, decks, patios, home security systems—and much more. In a single winter the chapter on energy efficiency and solar design could pay back the price of the book many times over.

Here, then, is a concise reference library on your house and its possibilities, within one set of covers.

Planning an improvement

What is the architectural style
of your house? How is it built?
How can you finance an improvement? Should you act as your
own contractor, a difficult undertaking; if you do, how do you get
a zoning variance, draw plans,
estimate costs and order materials,
get a building permit and arrange
for required inspections?
All such matters, important to
planning, are covered in this
section. The pages on building
codes explain how and why your
work must meet the structural
standards established in your
community.

contents

American houses/Style and structure

Many peoples, many styles

In planning a home improvement you will want to consider the style and structure of your existing house. Aside from style, any improvement, addition, rehabilitation, or restoration will seek harmony between existing and new materials. The direction of an addition—to the side, the rear, or upward—will be determined, in part, by the function of the new space—whether a garage, a greenhouse, a bedroom, or a deck—and by whatever limits may be imposed by property lines.

It is the purpose of this opening chapter to treat such considerations. In the pages that follow, some 10 different architectural styles used in the construction of dwelling houses since the early days of Colonial history are discussed and illustrated. We begin with the first New England houses, the salt-box and the Cape Cod, which resulted when the Colonists' attempted to duplicate the houses they had known in England, using the materials available to them in North America. Georgian, Federal, Greek Revival, Victorian, Spanish style, Ranch, and Contemporary styles fill out the roster of this opening chapter. Traditional additions made to such houses are shown, and the original materials and construction techniques used to build the houses are discussed in every case.

American eclecticism

Many American houses are actually eclectic in style; that is, they are composed of elements and influences of two, three, or more different styles. If there is such a thing as the typical American house, it is probably just such an eclectic house, rather than a house of a pure historic style. This is partly because more than two-thirds of the country's existing 80-million-plus single-family homes, apartments, and other types of housing units have been built since 1940. In fact, about 15 million of today's housing units have been built since the year 1970.

Older American houses are also often eclectic in style. On these two pages are seven illustrations of houses that cannot be said to be expressions of any single style covered on ensuing pages. Yet these are among the most common seen on the American landscape. Why should this be so? Houses built in America during the last three hundred years always reflected the lives of the people who built them. These houses tell what materials the builders had available to them, the construction methods and skills they had to learn, the kind of social life they created, and the political climate in the country. And most houses were actually designed by

What style is this house? Like the majority of American houses, this house is eclectic in style: it incorporates architectural details from several different styles and periods. Many houses like the one shown were built in the first four decades of the 20th century.

carpenters not by architects. Thus they represented the popular and economical adaptations of local style.

Regional styles

Dutch colonists, settling mainly in what was to become New York, built houses of fieldstone with curved gambrel roofs. Eaves extended out over the front of the house and were supported by posts to create a portico or porch. This became the popular farmhouse style throughout the Middle Atlantic states.

French and Spanish influences were combined in many of the houses that were built in the Old South, especially in New Orleans. A prominent feature of these houses was a balcony enclosed by decorative wrought-iron railings.

Farmhouses in the midwest often were not built in any particular architectural style, but were simply practical houses erected by hardworking farmers to meet their immediate needs. The houses seldom had any ornament; if they did, it was usually an indication of the unusual prosperity of the owner.

The Germans and Swedes who settled in the Middle Atlantic and North Central States built simple three-room houses of rough fieldstone—stones found embedded in surrounding pastures. These houses were one or two stories high, some with an asymmetrical front elevation—the front door was set to one side. In early Swedish houses, the chimney was at one end and provided a corner fireplace in the living room.

The Victorian period is generally remembered for large, rambling houses of wood frame or brick. However, peo-

ple also built small cottages, decorating them with Victorian millwork. These small Gothic cottages had vertical wood siding to emphasize the steep gables, as seen in the drawing on the opposite page. The Gothic cottage is most common in the eastern part of the nation.

Making additions

With an addition, you can maintain the original style of the house, you can add on in a different but harmonious style, or you can change the style completely.

In very old houses, for example, you may want to match existing beams with fabricated modern alternatives; although huge timbers are not readily available at acceptable costs, except as salvage, girders and flitch plates can be finished with boards treated or distressed to resemble old beams. Where the original building materials—of say, brick or fieldstone—cannot be used for an addition because of cost, the proper choice of siding and roofing will result in a harmonious appearance. Authentic moldings and trim can often be found as salvage, or closely imitated at the neighborhood lumberyard.

When you decide to make an addition to your house, you will probably find there is more than one possible way to go. For example, you may be able to increase the attic space with dormers, move a bearing wall to gain space, or extend part of the house along its existing lines; you can add a story, add an entire wing, convert a garage or a porch into a room, or finish the basement.

Which way you actually go may also depend on the cost of the job.

The garrison house was built as early as the 1670s. Such houses often had an overhanging second story, created by extending the first-floor ceiling joists beyond the first-floor walls. Timber construction made the house almost impregnable to attack.

Dutch Colonial houses featured gambrel roofs—roofs incorporating a steep pitch on the lower flanks with a shallower pitch at the ridge line. The gambrel roof —particularly when combined with dormers—provided ample living space in the attic.

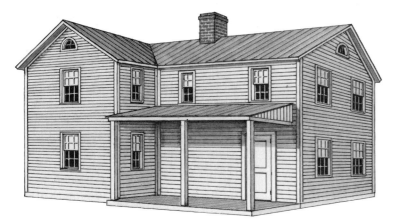
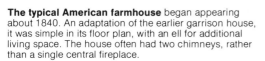

The typical American farmhouse began appearing about 1840. An adaptation of the earlier garrison house, it was simple in its floor plan, with an ell for additional living space. The house often had two chimneys, rather than a single central fireplace.

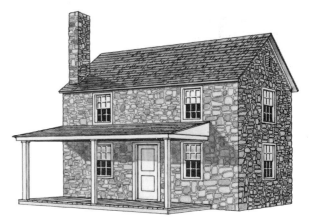

Swedish and German homesteads of the late 18th and early 19th centuries were similar in design. Stones removed from surrounding fields were the basic building materials for these houses.

The Gothic cottage appeared during the Victorian period. More modest than the large structures for which the era is noted, it had Victorian lines and decoration.

English Tudor-style houses have been built since 1920. Incorporating many influences, Tudor is not a pure style. Stucco and half-timber are its characteristic materials.

American Houses/Style and Structure

Saltbox

The profile of a saltbox house is its most distinctive feature. Its steeply pitched roof, short in front and sloping almost to the ground in back, gives the house the appearance of an old salt container.

These oldest of Colonial New England houses were often built in sections, according to the needs of the builder. The first section, the main body, consisted of two floors and an attic. A shed or lean-to, generally for the kitchen, was added to the back, resulting in the long rear roof line. On historic saltbox houses, the rear roof line often is indicative of when the lean-to was constructed. If the line is one unbroken pitch, the lean-to was part of the original building, while a break in the roof line usually indicates a later addition.

Saltbox houses were always built so that they faced south, to take advantage of sunshine coming in the front windows for warmth and light. The windowless design of the rear roof afforded protection from the weather and the north wind. Massive central chimneys made of stone or brick—often with molding along the top edge—furnished large fireplaces in each first-floor room.

The frame

The frame of a saltbox was built of large, hand-hewn timbers, normally oak but sometimes hard pine, held together with mortise-and-tenon joints. The structure was supported at the corners by angle braces and along the ceiling of the first floor by heavy timbers called girts, which were often as large as a foot square. These large beams were too heavy to be moved by the members of a single family, making "house raising" gatherings of friends and neighbors a necessity. The resulting house was extremely sturdy; in fact, such frames were stronger than necessary for dwelling-house construction.

For insulation, the spaces between studs were filled with a mixture of clay and straw, or with a rough brick masonry called nogging. Interior walls were plastered and most beams were

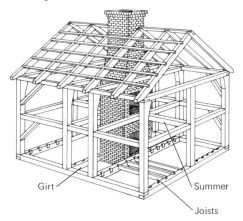

Girt
Summer
Joists

left exposed. The house exterior was covered with clapboards—thin, wedge-shaped boards, about 5 inches wide and 4 to 6 feet long. The ends of the clapboards were beveled so that adjacent boards could be overlapped at the

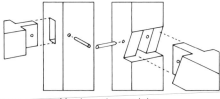

Mortise-and-tenon joint

studs. The clapboards, of oak, cedar, or white pine, were split, not sawed. They were left unpainted, to weather. The roof was covered with wood shingles.

Symmetrical front elevation

The front of the Colonial saltbox house was symmetrical. The first floor had a center door with one or two windows on either side of it; the second floor had three or five windows directly over the door and windows on the first floor. The original windows were double-hung sashes with small individual panes and large muntins, the supports between the panes. The placement of windows in the gable ends was not symmetrical; these windows seem to appear wherever they were needed.

There was little or no ornament on the inside or outside of saltbox houses constructed in the 17th century. Sometimes the house was built with an overhang; both the front and the gable ends—or often just the front of the second floor—were built out over the first floor by about 12 inches. The saltbox house changed very little in the 18th century; the overhang became nar-

rower and a cornice was added along the front of the house.

Additions

The Colonial builder often added rooms to the house as his family grew. These additions harmonized with the original and can often be used as guidelines for making improvements today. The additions were made to either side of the house or to the back and had steep shingled roofs and walls of clapboard. A room added to the side was set back so that it would not detract from the symmetry of the front elevation.

The placement of present-day additions will be determined by both the size of the addition and the shape of the surrounding property. Since a saltbox is an unadorned rectangle, additions of smaller rectangles can add to the geometry of the house and enhance it. To echo the unusual roof line, for example, a two-car garage with the same roof line can be added. Or skylights can be added to the roof in back to let light into the second floor.

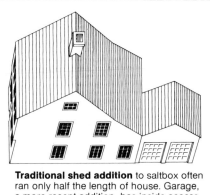

Traditional shed addition to saltbox often ran only half the length of house. Garage, a more recent addition, has inside access through the shed.

Cape Cod

Cape Cod houses are named for the peninsula of land that lies off the eastern shore of Massachusetts, where houses of this type were built in the 17th and 18th centuries. They are one and one-half story frame structures with regular gable roofs—as opposed to the two and one-half story saltboxes, with their irregular roof lines.

A Cape Cod house always had a good-sized brick or fieldstone chimney opposite the front door. The frame for the house was made of large hand-hewn timbers held together with mortise-and-tenon joints. The outside walls and roof were covered with long wooden shingles called shakes; made of pine or red cedar, the shakes were not painted, but allowed to weather. Several layers of shingles—sometimes as many as four or five—were applied to the roof for protection from rain. The walls, sheathed with planking about 3 inches thick, were covered with shingles on the outside. Inside, the planking was coated with plaster, which was made from pulverized clam shells and sand. The interior corner posts and ceiling beams were left exposed.

Size and floor plan

Cape Cod houses came in a variety of sizes. A full Cape had a center door, two windows on either side of the door, and a center chimney. A three-quarter

3/4 Cape   1/2 Cape

house had two windows on one side and one on the other side of the door, the front door and chimney were thus slightly off-center. A half house had the front door and the chimney at one end of the house with two windows beside the door.

The size of the house is not an indication of its age, but rather a statement of the needs of the builder. Sometimes a half house was built for an unmarried woman in the hope that a suitor would marry her and build the other half of the house. The floor plan of each of these houses was similar. The kitchen, running along the entire back of the house, was also used as a family room and a dining room. In full and three-quarter Capes, the parlor, in the front to the right of the front door, often had a paneled fireplace wall and wainscoting around the rest of the room.

The Cape Cod house was built low to the ground as protection against the weather and often faced south to utilize the sun's warmth and light. There were no dormers on the houses built in the 17th century; light for the attic sleeping areas came from windows in the gable ends of the house. These windows were irregular in both size and position. Dormers were an 18th-century addition to the house, as was the use of clapboards along the front elevation.

Roof variations

Variations of the common steeply pitched roof of the Cape were usually the result of the needs of large families for more sleeping space. One variation, a bowed roof, sometimes called a ship's bottom, was made with the same techniques used in shaping the hull of a ship. Green timbers were shaped over rocks and anchored at both ends. As the wood dried, it formed an arc. A gambrel roof, one with two slopes, was used because it afforded almost as much headroom as a full second story.

A Cape Cod house appears to be the New England adaptation of the simple country dwellings of many European cultures. Houses of similar size and shape but constructed of brick were

built in the South. Houses in the South were made of brick because the builders used the materials that were available, and clay and lime were abundant.

Bowed roof line   Gambrel roof line

In New England, wood was plentiful—oak, white pine, cedar, and spruce. Although the land was rocky, the stone was too difficult to work, and lime for mortar was scarce.

Additions

Most additions to Cape Cod houses in Colonial times were ells—rooms added in back at one end of the house, and perpendicular to it. Today, additions are made to either or both ends, according to the amount of space needed and the size of the surrounding property. Dormers, if none exist, offer a way of expanding and bringing more light to the upper floor. Simplicity of line is the key to preserving the country cottage charm of the Cape Cod Style.

In Colonial times, additions to Capes were ells, rooms perpendicular to the rear of the main house, dormers are later innovations.

Additions to the sides of Cape Cod houses traditionally were set back at the front and had a lower roof ridge.

11

American houses / Style and structure

Georgian style

Symmetrical in design, rather formal, and often opulent, the Georgian style flourished in Colonial America from the beginning of the 18th century until about 1780. The style is named for the three kings named George who reigned in England during those years. Georgian houses in America imitated British architecture of the period, which, in turn, looked back to classical Greece and Rome for inspiration.

Georgian houses in New England had a timber-frame construction, often with wood siding painted to look like masonry. Georgian houses in the South could be handsomely sheathed in true masonry because of the ready availability of the materials needed to make bricks. A slate-covered hipped roof—one in which all four sides slope up to meet a single ridge—was most common, although gable and gambrel roofs were also used. Sometimes a hipped roof had a flat deck on top that was enclosed with a balustrade, as in the large illustration on this page. A deeply carved decorative cornice ran along the front wall under the roof overhang.

The front entrance

The central front entrance, the most prominent feature of a Georgian house, was flanked by classical columns or pilasters—flat columns in shallow relief from the facade. The entrance was topped with a classical pediment. The

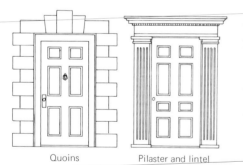

Quoins   Pilaster and lintel

columns and the pediment, with its decorative moldings, were based on Roman designs, which are more elaborate than earlier Greek designs.

Because glass became widely available in the Colonies in the 18th century, the central entrance often incorporated windows. Early Georgian houses had square-headed doorways with small rectangular panes over the door. Later, the well-known half-round fanlights came into use. In the more elaborate doorways, the pediment was built out from the house and rested on columns set a short distance from the door, creating a covered entrance or portico. The door was usually paneled either with four equal panels or with six

panels—the two center of which were generally smaller than the other four. Sometimes double doors were used, with each so narrow that both had to be opened to gain entrance.

Other Georgian features

The front of the house also featured quoins—heavy decorative blocks of masonry, or wood fashioned to simulate stone—which were set into the corners of the building. A belt course, a horizontal band projecting from the front wall at the upper floor level, marked the division between stories.

The windows were tall and narrow with broad muntins, the wood divisions between panes. The arch above the window was always pronounced, either a keystone arch of stone or a pediment of wood. If dormers were built, they often had such ornamentation as pilasters and pediment with rounded molding on the tops of the windows.

Because Georgian houses were larger than earlier Colonial houses, two chimneys, one at either end of the house, were necessary to heat all the rooms. The use of two chimneys allowed for a central entrance hall and a wider, more graceful staircase with two or three turns and decoratively carved balusters. In the interior, all the structural beams were covered over. In the wealthiest homes, walls were often decorated with paneling and cornices.

Cupolas, small domed structures situated on the tops of roofs, were popular during this time, but were built mostly on large houses or on public buildings.

Additions

An addition to a Georgian house looks best if it has the same stately proportions as the original and if it is sheathed with harmonious if not the same materials. Windows of the same size as those in the original house unify new and old.

The garage added to this Georgian house preserves the graciousness of its style. The balustrade on the garage roof echoes that on the original roof.

Federal style

Federal houses reflect the first indigenous architectural style to appear in America following independence from Britain. After the War of Independence, there was an effort to turn away from things British—an effort led by Thomas Jefferson. In architecture, the opulent, convoluted, highly decorated Georgian style was soon replaced by the clean, stoic lines of the Federal.

The fundamental Georgian building was actually modified slightly. The changes were primarily refinements in proportion and in scale. The Federal style was a development of rather than a revolt against Georgian; the rectangular house with a center front door continued to be built. The ornamentation inside and outside the house was more austere, purer, and more delicately scaled.

Materials, colors, and shapes became lighter as the decoration became more simple: no longer any quoins, belt courses, elaborately decorated cornices, or projecting pediment over the front door. The voluminous hipped roof covered with slate that marked the Georgian disappeared gradually with the introduction of the Federal style.

The center doorway

The lightening of the exterior led to larger windows with larger individual panes and smaller muntins. And the trim was less pronounced; in masonry

A delicate doorway was the hallmark of the Federal style. It is topped with a half-round or elliptical fanlight and flanked with side lights.

houses, the windows were usually topped with recessed semicircular arches made of brick. The design of the center doorway and windows was more delicate in detail than the Georgian; the door had a half-round or elliptical fanlight above it and side lights surrounding it, all of which let light into the hall. The door continued to have six panels, but the arrangement of the panels changed; the two smallest were at the top. This entrance has become a hallmark of the Federal style.

Above this entrance, there was often a Palladian window, consisting of three round-topped units; the middle sash was taller than those on either side. Palladian windows are named for Andrea Palladio, an Italian Renaissance

architect who employed classical forms and who provided the basis for Georgian architecture in England. These windows proliferated during the Federal period in America, and are distinctive of the Federal style.

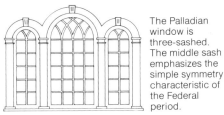

The Palladian window is three-sashed. The middle sash emphasizes the simple symmetry characteristic of the Federal period.

Interior changes

The houses were built of timber framing—covered most often with bricks, in the South, and with clapboards, in the North. The roof was steeply pitched and covered with wooden shingles.

Many changes also occurred in the interior. Paneling was de-emphasized—to just a baseboard—and walls were plastered. More delicate-looking plaster molding replaced the carved wooden molding. The interior was decorated in

pastels rather than dark colors. The fireplace was framed with a simple mantel, which replaced an entire wall of ornate paneling. Heavy cornices gave way to thin bands of delicate carving.

Additions

Although Federal-style houses were always at least two stories high, additions to them were often only one story. One typical addition (shown in box below) is an open porch built on one side of the house, with a door from the living or dining room opening onto it. Columns supporting the porch are in the same style as those flanking the front door. The slightly pitched roof covers a half-pediment that repeats the shape of the pediment over the door.

A two-car garage built as an addition on the other side of the house has the same shingle-covered pitched roof and clapboard siding as the main house and is congruous with it.

Many of the simplest Federal-style frame farmhouses were later given Greek Revival decorative accents in the mid-19th century.

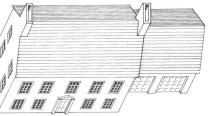

A modern addition to this Federal house is an open porch for outdoor living. The columns supporting the porch are the same style as those surrounding the door.

A two-car garage is supplied by an addition that has the same roof line and shingles as the original house; it is covered with the same harmonious clapboard siding.

American houses/Style and structure

Greek Revival

Benjamin Latrobe, considered the first professional architect in the United States, is credited with inaugurating the Greek Revival style in his design for the Bank of Pennsylvania in Philadelphia, in 1799. The style flourished throughout the first half of the 19th century. Asher Benjamin, a builder who in 1797 wrote the first American book on architecture, popularized the classical revival in his writings. It seemed fitting that America, as a fledgling democracy, should turn to the oldest Western democracy—that of ancient Greece—for inspiration for both public buildings and private homes.

Purest form

The main characteristics of Greek Revival were the use of pillars and a pediment to form a portico in the front of the house. The roof was shallow in pitch or even flat, and the chimney inconspicuous. Classical Greek architecture, the basis for the style, is both simpler and more solid than the Roman architecture that inspired the more ornate Georgian period.

In its purest form, the Greek Revival style attempted to re-create a Greek temple. To do this, the gable end of the

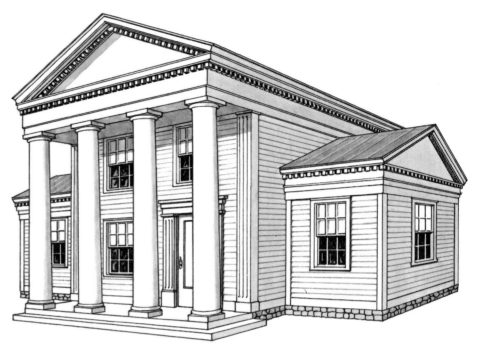

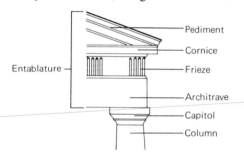

standard rectangular house (see *Federal style*, p.13) was turned forward and the front entrance was put under the gable. The gable became the pediment, and it was often built out from the house as an overhang and supported by columns to form a portico.

The doorway assumed a special importance. An imposing main entrance was placed under the portico at the garden level. The front of the house was sophisticated in proportion and detail. A desire for symmetry governed the placement of the columns, usually even in number, and also the windows, which were both taller and wider than windows had been previously. The front door was usually located at the very center of the facade in Greek Revival houses in the South; in New England adaptations, it was sometimes placed to one side.

The pediment and architrave, the molding immediately above the columns, were often decorated with dentils—relief blocks regularly spaced like a

row of teeth—and with simple geometric Greek fret and floral or foliated anthemion designs, also carved in shallow relief. Sometimes low, narrow windows that opened inward, called eyebrow windows or "lie-on-your-stomach" windows, were built in the architrave to let light into the upper floor.

Variations

In the South, an adaptation of the Greek Revival portico led to what is called Southern Plantation architecture. The usual portico, with its tall white columns, covered the front of a two-story house; the second story projected to meet the columns, creating a balcony on the second floor above a veranda on the ground floor. Sometimes the columned portico was built along one or both sides of the house, departing from a true re-creation of a Greek temple, which had columns only at the front.

On some smaller Greek Revival houses, neither pediment nor portico were used; instead, heavy pilasters

were built at the corners and flanking the doorway. The roof had a slight pitch but a high cornice above the architrave was used to hide the peak. The overall look was that of a flat-roofed house dominated by classical moldings—the architrave, cornice, and the heavily grooved pilasters.

All the country was caught up in Greek Revival. During the first half of the 19th century, furniture was decorated with Greek motifs. Many existing frame houses, built in earlier periods, were given Greek Revival entrances, corner pilasters, and decorative relief moldings with dentil, fret, and anthemion designs. Sometimes existing doorways were done over in the Greek Revival style; in other cases, entrances were built where none had existed, as in the gable ends of renovated New England Federal farmhouses. Thus the presence of Greek Revival features is not always proof of even the approximate age of an old house; its core may be of a greater antiquity than such features suggest.

Small Greek Revival-no portico   Southern plantation with French influence

Victorian

Stick

Italianate

Mansard or French

Shingle

Victorian Gothic or Queen Anne

The term "Victorian," as applied to American architecture, encompasses a variety of styles that have in common the use of irregular shapes flowing into a large form, patterns reminiscent of natural growth. In America, Victorian architecture was based largely on the medieval Gothic style. Flourishing mainly in the second half of the 19th century, it reflected a return to nature, to religion, and also a turn toward romanticism. It was a direct reaction to the austerity and formality of the classical styles that preceded it.

With central heating, electric power, gas, and running water available in city homes, the architect was suddenly free to develop a floor plan to suit the individual tastes of his clients. In effect, a house could be designed from the inside out. The massive fireplace formerly at the core of dwelling-house construction was replaced by a coal-burning furnace in the basement and a stove in the kitchen. Indoor plumbing made the outdoor privy obsolete. The new balloon or skeletal frame employed light lumber nailed together, rather than heavy mortise-and-tenoned timbers. This frame, which allowed for much greater flexibility in layout, had become practical because of the availability of mass-produced dimensioned lumber and machine-made nails after

1840. And the invention of the scroll saw encouraged the use of decoration.

A variety of styles

American Gothic or Carpenters' Gothic, the predominant Victorian style, was characterized by the millwork we call gingerbread. Gingerbread decoration began as an attempt to copy the stone-carved trim of medieval Gothic architecture. But wood was cheaper and easier to work and soon this millwork developed its own character. The Gothic house had steep gables with vertical siding to accentuate the height, arched windows with diamond panes and bay windows, towers with peaked roofs, cross gables, and porches or verandas on more than one side.

The Italianate Style was a conscious attempt to imitate the villas built in Italy. Italianate houses featured tall, arched windows, scrollwork, and prominent brackets under the roof holding up an elaborate cornice. The style was also called Carpenter Italianate and, in the northeast, Hudson River Bracketed. Smaller houses were square, flat roofed and sometimes had a cupola on top. Regardless of size, an Italianate house had heavy brackets, decorative eaves, and tall windows.

The most conspicuous French contribution to American Victorian was the

Mansard roof; this is a roof with two slopes—the lower one steeper than the upper, and usually containing prominent dormer windows. French windows were another Victorian adaptation. Used as first-floor windows, they reached the ground and were flanked by long louvered shutters.

The Stick Style favored by Andrew Jackson Downing, an architect of the period, overlaid the house with vertical and later horizontal and diagonal sticks or thin molding. Queen Anne Style, introduced in San Francisco in the 1880s, had a horizontal emphasis, with unrestrained arrangements of shapes and decorations.

The Shingle Style, a later Victorian development, arose in reaction to the unwieldiness of Victorian houses. Designs in this style were covered with shingles to create a single continuously flowing shape.

Additions

Victorian houses begat additions of almost every shape, stuck on at any place and in any direction. New bays, entire wings, or odd projections became part of the whole simply through a consistency in the use of exterior materials and trim. Additions made today, if they observe these principles, can blend harmoniously into the original.

American houses/Style and structure

Townhouses

Federal

Georgian

Brownstone

Bowfront Victorian

Townhouses were built as space-saving, family houses in North American cities as early as the end of the 17th century. The earliest houses were adaptations of similar houses in England; they had frames of hand-hewn timbers, walls of clapboard or brick, and pitched roofs with dormers in both front and back. A gambrel roof (pp.10–11) was sometimes used to increase the attic sleeping area. Generally two stories tall, they had a first-floor door, a window in both front and rear, an end chimney, and were one room wide and two rooms deep.

By the middle of the 18th century, the typical townhouse incorporated a bay window on the first floor. The house was still one room wide, with an interior stairway opposite the front door. The height had increased to three floors plus an attic. At the back of the house was a porch, or simply an overhang supported by columns that led to the privy. In some cities the house was built on a higher foundation, which necessitated an outside entrance stairway, or stoop.

Variations
Georgian townhouses, faced in brick, had a front door flanked by pilasters and topped by a pediment. Their small-paned windows had keystone lintels and their dormers had pediments. A belt course and an ornamented cornice also decorated the front elevation.

Federal townhouses, although they were similar to the Georgian, were more delicate, lighter, and more sophisticated in decoration.

In the Victorian period, many Eastern townhouses in the Italianate style were faced with brown sandstone quarried in Connecticut. These houses became very fashionable and were called brownstones.

Styled to fit the city
Townhouses varied according to the circumstances of the city and the neighborhoods in which they were built. Early townhouses in Boston were larger than those of other cities because building lots had greater frontage. The extra width permitted a center front door. The first floor was built close to the ground, and these houses seldom had a front stoop. Boston townhouses built in the Victorian period were narrower, but their bowed fronts increased interior living space.

Philadelphia houses were generally more crowded than those of Boston and were more severe in style. During the Victorian period when townhouses in Boston and New York were elaborate and faced with brown sandstone, Philadelphia continued to build modest red-brick rowhouses.

New York's townhouses were limited in width to one room plus a staircase because of an early ordinance governing the size of building plots.

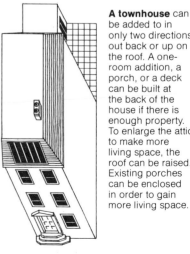

A townhouse can be added to in only two directions: out back or up on the roof. A one-room addition, a porch, or a deck can be built at the back of the house if there is enough property. To enlarge the attic to make more living space, the roof can be raised. Existing porches can be enclosed in order to gain more living space.

Spanish style

Spanish-style architecture of the south-western United States was influenced by both the native Pueblo Indians and the Spanish colonists. The building techniques used were in some measure the result of a poor economy and an inhospitable land that provided few building materials.

The traditional building material was adobe, a mixture of clay and straw or manure that was shaped into bricks. The bricks were dried in the sun and, with mud for mortar, they were used to make walls. The surface was covered with wet clay and smoothed by hand. Adobe is appropriate for an arid climate. It is dry porous, so that it insulates well, and if damaged by occasional rain, it is easily repaired. But in damp and rainy climates, adobe quickly deteriorates.

The houses built by the Pueblos were low and simple, with massive adobe walls; they made frugal use of wood, usually oak or cypress. There was no foundation; walls were built directly on the ground, tapering from a thickness of about 3 feet at ground level to 2 feet at the roof. There were few windows and no ornamentation. Surfaces were rough and corners were rounded.

The roof of a Pueblo house was supported on logs embedded in the top of the wall. The logs were in their original round shape, with the bark removed. Some of the logs projected beyond the wall, forming one of the most characteristic features of the Pueblo house. The roof, low-pitched because the small amount of rainfall made a steep roof unnecessary, was extended over the walls to create an overhang that kept the hot sun from the walls, windows, and doorways.

The Spanish contributions

The Spanish imposed a symmetry on the exposed posts, introduced curved roof tiles, and enlarged the roof overhang to form a loggia. The loggia was often given the added emphasis of curved arches. The Spanish also tiled the floors, enlarged windows and doors, and added such decorative elements as brackets, hand-carved wooden doors, wrought-iron window grilles, and assorted hardware. The inside of the house was much the same as the outside, with plain adobe walls, exposed ceiling beams, curved archways between rooms, and ornament limited to the windows and doors.

The house plan

The house was usually built with three wings set in a U shape to create a private inner courtyard or patio. The roof extended from the walls inside the U and was supported on posts to form the loggia, or arcade. The closed end of the U, the public side of the house, was plain, and often built right on the street. The patio, with its garden, was reserved for the family's use. If possible, the open end of the U faced south.

The loggia, the house, and the patio were all built on the same level; it was possible to walk indoors or out without climbing steps. The common level helped unify indoor and outdoor spaces, linking the dark interior rooms with the brightly lit patio. The loggia, often with benches built along the walls, served as an outdoor living room. It can rightly be called American architecture's first family room.

The base of the U contained the living room and dining room. The side wings, containing the bedrooms and the kitchen, pantries, and other service facilities, were only one room deep and had no inside hallways. All the rooms opened onto the loggia, which served as an outdoor passageway.

Additions

An addition to a Spanish-style house can extend the base of the U laterally, or one of the perpendicular wings. If the base is extended, a second partially enclosed patio will be created behind it.

Spanish Mission

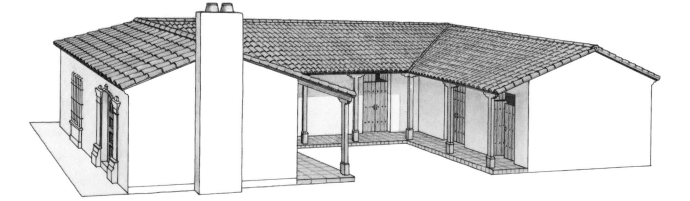

Ranch

The modern ranch house developed as the result of a number of architectural influences. Perhaps its most obvious predecessor was the Spanish house (discussed on the previous page), with its low-pitched roof, its low-slung profile hugging the land on which it was built, and its convenient arrangement of rooms on a single level.

The great appeal of the Spanish ranch house lay in its eminent livability together with its use of indigenous building materials. When the ranch style was adopted in northern areas, the plain adobe walls and curved tile roof were superseded by locally available materials—walls of vertical wood siding, fieldstone, or brick, and a wood shingle roof.

Wright's influence

A major contributor to the development of a ranch style was Frank Lloyd Wright. In the early decades of the 20th century, Wright designed houses in a style that became known as Prairie Architecture. He viewed his houses as an antidote to Victorian style, which he characterized as "the awful building in vogue at the time." Wright felt the attic of a Victorian house was not livable. In his view, it was a place for servants to swelter in. Moreover, he deplored the non-functional and artificial excesses of the style: Victorian dormers, for instance, which seemed to him to be elaborate enough to be buildings of their own, and to be simply stuck onto the exterior. And Wright was strongly opposed to basements—a basement dug into the earth was invariably damp.

So Wright dispensed with the stifling attic, the overdecorated dormer, and the unhealthy basement. He built a Prairie house that sat low to the ground on a cement or stone platform (which has evolved into the modern slab foundation). He wanted the house to associate with the terrain in ways that made it appear to be a natural, or organic, part of the land. His use of a low-pitched roof was combined with windows and door designed on a more human, more functional scale. Casement windows swung outward to integrate the house with the outdoors. Decorative trim was kept to a minimum on both the inside and the outside.

In designing his floor plan, Wright was also influenced by the practicality of Japanese houses. His arrangement of rooms included children's rooms large enough for both play and sleep, well-planned kitchens, servants' rooms adjacent to the kitchen, and a feeling of openness and comfortable scale.

The modern ranch

A ranch house is characterized by its compactness, its bringing together of services, and its lack of unnecessary rooms. There is no back parlor or library and the dining room becomes less important; it is often attached to the living room or the kitchen. The result is a house that is economical to build and practical for family living.

In modern ranch houses, the garage is usually attached to the house and both structures have the same roof line, emphasizing a continuous low profile with a horizontal look. If a ranch house

A high or split ranch house is the result of compressing the familiar low-slung ranch to fit within a standard city or suburban lot.

has to be compressed to fit within a standard city or suburban lot, the result is a split or high ranch. One common way of splitting the house places the garage and one room—such as a family room or a playroom—on the lower level, with the remainder of the house above.

Additions

An addition to a ranch house, if built perpendicular to it in back, can create a sheltered rear patio, an area for private outdoor living that is reminiscent of the enclosed patio of a Spanish–style house. If the addition is built at the living end of the house, it can house a deck, solarium, or family room. If it is built off the bedrooms, it can enclose a new master bedroom.

Where property lines are wide enough, an addition built to one side of the house will accentuate the long, low horizontal profile of the ranch. Any addition, to harmonize with the house, should be one story high (with the exception of a high ranch), have the same roof line, and be sheathed in the same or similar materials.

Low adobe house is an adaptation of indigenous Pueblo Indian, Spanish, and ranch styles that has recently seen a revival in the Southwestern United States.

Contemporary

Contemporary American house styles have been shaped largely by two demands: first, that the house be functionally efficient; second, that it be artistically imaginative not only in design but also in its use of materials.

To be functionally efficient, a house must be simple, pragmatic, and economical—economical in its initial cost as well as in its maintenance costs. To be artistically imaginative, a house should express the individuality of both the person who designs it and the people who will live in it, and it must harmonize with its surroundings.

Modern American houses have been heavily influenced by the ideas of four great architects of the 20th century: Frank Lloyd Wright, Walter Gropius, Ludwig Mies van der Rohe, and Le Corbusier.

Frank Lloyd Wright
Wright, an American born in 1869, was an individualist who designed open houses—as opposed to dwellings with many small, and compartmentalized rooms. Interior volumes flowed easily into one another and the low, horizontal lines of roof and eaves seemed to arise from the rhythms of the surrounding land. He designed houses with planes parallel to the ground, houses that often looked like natural outgrowths of the landscape. His earth-toned colors emphasized the nature and origin of materials. Wright reduced the number of rooms inside the house. He designed interior walls and ceilings as light, enclosing screens, not heavy, structural supports. His windows and doors were not mere apertures for light and egress, but openings through which interior volumes seemed to merge and inter-

change with the environment beyond. Wright minimized ornament in his houses, and his preferred decor emphasized the natural structure and texture of materials. He incorporated heating, lighting, and plumbing as integral parts of the architecture. By the time of his death in 1959, Frank Lloyd Wright had revolutionized the concept of residential architecture.

Walter Gropius
Gropius, founder of the post-World War I Bauhaus school of architecture in Germany, advocated an architectural style that was logical, socially responsible, and technologically aware. His architecture wedded modern design to modern technology.

Gropius used contemporary materials, such as steel, reinforced concrete, and plate glass, to create streamlined, functional designs. He held always that "form follows function," a phrase originally coined by Louis Sullivan, the seminal Chicago architect of the 19th century whose most famous pupil was Frank Lloyd Wright.

Ludwig Mies van der Rohe
Mies van der Rohe—who like Gropius left Germany, ultimately for America, in the years leading to World War II—designed houses with all unnecessary weight removed. His structural frameworks were usually unclad and visible. He used industrial materials and, following Wright's lead, separated structural supports from the space-defining curtain component of walls to create a flowing rather than compartmentalized space. Unlike Wright, Mies opposed any emphasis on personal expression and individualism in architecture. Mies van

der Rohe's designs are geometric structures—cold, crisp, and rational.

Le Corbusier
Le Corbusier ("The Crow") was the pseudonym of the 20th-century French architect Charles Edouard Jeanneret. His greatest influence has been on urban apartment-house and condominium construction. Le Corbusier believed that architecture should express the intellectual and socially advanced aspects of modern civilization. He was not a functionalist; although his designs were precise, they evinced his feeling for humanity and dedication to human scale. He, too, objected to rooms that were small boxes enclosed by structural supports. The walls he designed were partitions that could be placed wherever he wanted them. To admit natural light, he designed windows that ran the full length of a room. But Le Corbusier held that modern technology could be more than functional—that it could demand of architects a higher level of taste and a responsiveness to human proportion.

The result
These and other great modern architects have contributed to contemporary houses that are functional, economical, built of a wide variety of materials, and need not be limited by conventional structural methods. Most are efficient and many are also individualistic.

Individualistic contemporary expression is most readily indulged in building a vacation home. The ultimate in efficient functionalism in these times of increased energy costs is found in designs incorporating solar technology and principles.

Frank Lloyd Wright   Mies Van der Rohe   Le Corbusier

Financing home improvements

A variety of approaches

In today's economic climate, paying cash for home improvements may seem to be a prudent course, but this is not always the case. A well-planned loan leaves your savings intact for emergencies, and there may be tax advantages in borrowing. The best course is determined by the amount you will need and your personal financial situation.

Contracting, or doing it yourself: Cost, of course, depends on the size and complexity of the improvement. But the cost for a given job can vary considerably, depending on how much work you do yourself. The most expensive component of most projects is labor; if you do the work yourself, the only major expense will be materials. You can also save money by acting as your own contractor—dealing directly with the workmen and suppliers—but that can be a headache, especially for a novice. A number of vocational schools and college extensions schedule short courses in becoming a contractor that are designed for the do-it-yourselfer.

A persuasive financial argument can be made for doing all the work yourself: savings generally range from 50 percent to 75 percent of the cost of contracting the entire job. However, some home improvements may be beyond your skills. Others, such as electrical work, plumbing, heating, and major structural changes, require hiring a licensed professional to do the actual work or at least to inspect the finished improvement. Some jobs require such expensive tools that it is actually more economical to have the work done by a professional. Remember, a job need not be done entirely as a do-it-yourself project or by hired workers; you can divide the work in any way that suits your skills. If you plan to do the work yourself, prepare your own detailed estimates of costs, a subject covered in *Estimating costs/Ordering materials*, on page 48. Your work must meet your local building code requirements, as described on pages 21–37.

Even if you decide to hire a contractor for the whole job, you must furnish an exact description of what is to be done, including specifications for materials, quality, colors, etc. You should then get at least three estimates from reputable contractors (check references carefully). In addition, as a prudent homeowner you must continually check the work as it proceeds and be prepared to halt the project if it is deviating from your specifications.

Borrowing money: Generally, extensive home improvement projects are financed through conventional lending institutions—banks, credit unions, savings and loan associations, and thrift organizations. Inflation and deregulation of financial institutions have allowed the easing or lifting of interest ceilings, and it is now difficult to generalize about either the amount of money that lenders will supply or the interest they will charge. Before applying for a loan, investigate as many sources as possible to ensure getting the most advantageous terms.

FHA loans: The Federal government, through the Federal Housing Administration (FHA), guarantees certain home improvement loans. Such loans are restricted to permanent structural work on a dwelling; the FHA will not guarantee home improvements considered luxuries, such as swimming pools and tennis courts, nor will they guarantee non-structural improvements, such as kitchen and laundry appliances.

Contractor financing: Larger contractors can usually arrange loans through their banking connections, but since you will be repaying the loan, the contractor is unlikely to shop for the lowest rate of interest. He will also charge you for arranging the loan.

Unsecured loans: Most conventional loans are secured by liens on your property or other valuables that the lender believes can cover repayment if the loan is in default. However, a borrower with a good credit rating can sometimes obtain an unsecured personal loan on his signature alone. Some lenders, such as Federally chartered savings and loan associations, are forbidden by law to make this kind of loan. Banks (especially one where you have been a long-time customer) and consumer loan companies are possible sources of such loans.

Mortgage loans: You can get a new mortgage that would pay both the outstanding debt on your existing mortgage and the cost of the improvements you plan. However, many mortgages require a penalty if you pay your debt early; also, some lenders issuing a new mortgage consider that you are really buying the house afresh and require new appraisals, title search, and filing costs. While a new mortgage will doubtless carry a higher rate of interest than your current mortgage, it may still be fairly inexpensive when compared to the interest rates on other loans.

In some cases a second mortgage, which basically allows you to borrow against increased equity in your home, is your best source of funds for home improvements. Second mortgages are usually for less money than the original mortgage, may have a higher interest rate, and generally must be paid off in a relatively short period of time (usually 5 to 10 years).

If your existing home mortgage is an open-end mortgage, you can borrow money for home improvements without rewriting the mortgage. Generally, the new loan is limited to only as much money as would raise your total debt to the amount of your original loan.

Life insurance: You may want to borrow from life insurance. Your insurance agent can quickly tell you if this is possible and how much money is available to you. The interest rate is low, and the loan is almost automatic. However, until you repay the debt, the value of your insurance is reduced by the amount of the unpaid balance.

Passbook loans: Savings accounts are another quick and inexpensive source of money. Passbook loans require that you pledge the money you have in the bank (up to the amount of the loan) against the loan. The loan is inexpensive (1 percent to 3 percent over the rate your savings are earning). In theory, you could save interest costs by "lending" yourself the money out of savings and repaying the debt to your account each month, but this calls for great discipline and determination.

VA loans: Veterans Administration (VA) loan guarantees for home improvements require that you be a qualifying U.S. veteran who either owns his home or is in the process of paying for it under an existing GI mortgage.

Before undertaking a major project, consider that not all home improvements add to the resale value of your house, and only a few will actually recoup their full cost when the house is sold. As a rule, a house cannot be sold for much more than the average price of other houses in the neighborhood, so the cost of improvements that price your property far above that level are unlikely to be recovered.

The fine print: Before signing any home improvement loan or contract, be absolutely certain that you understand every word and that exactly what you want is specified in writing; never accept verbal guarantees or assurances. We repeat, do not sign *anything* until you have read the document and fully understand what you are signing. On expensive projects, have your lawyer draw up the contract—this could save you great trouble and expense later.

Remember that the lender is in no way responsible for the quality of the home improvement and that the guarantor, the FHA or other government agency, does not provide any guarantee that the work will be done right, only that the loan will be repaid. Getting the home improvements you desire the way you want them is in the last analysis up to you, the homeowner.

Building codes/Introduction to construction

Building officials, permits, and inspections

Before you pick up your hammer to make any additions, alterations, or repairs to your dwelling, you must familiarize yourself with the comprehensive laws governing construction that every community has. Zoning ordinances determine the type of buildings allowed in specific areas, and often control the location and size of the buildings. Building codes govern all aspects of actual construction. Zoning ordinances and building codes vary from town to town; in fact, they can vary dramatically in neighboring towns. You must abide by the laws of your community.

Zoning ordinances: The zoning ordinances restrict areas of a community to specific building uses, such as business, industry, multi-family dwellings, and single-family dwellings. These laws will not ordinarily affect additions and alterations. However, many zoning ordinances also require that buildings be set back a minimum distance from property lines. They can limit the proportion of a lot that can be covered by a building, and establish a maximum building height. All additions and alterations must conform to these laws.

You can get a copy of your local zoning ordinances from your local Planning or Building Department. Appeals of rulings by these departments are made to local boards of adjustments. If you are building an addition to a dwelling that was constructed near a property line before current zoning ordinances were enacted, you will have to file an appeal with the board to officially allow the addition to violate current set-back requirements.

Building codes: Building codes are the detailed regulations covering all aspects of construction, including alteration, repair, use, occupancy, and maintenance, to ensure that all buildings meet certain minimum standards of health and safety. The codes deal with building design, the quality and strength of materials, building techniques, electrical wiring and equipment, plumbing fixtures and sewage systems, furnaces, chimneys, air vents, fireplaces, cooling devices, large appliances, and so on. In each case, building codes establish minimum standards that must, by law, be met.

Most communities adopt, in whole or in part, one of the four comprehensive model codes developed by builders, architects, and building officials throughout the country. Communities are empowered to make any changes they want in these model codes. Therefore, even though you know that your community uses a model code, you must check for the particular amendments in force in your community.

Building officials: Building codes are administered and enforced by appointed local officials called building officials. The local building official has a copy of the local code that you can see. (Codes can sometimes be found at the public library as well.) You should consult the building official if you have any questions about the local code. The building official makes inspections (see below) to ensure that all construction is in accordance with the code.

Building codes were originally devised to prevent unscrupulous builders from constructing unsafe buildings. The original codes were specification codes, dictating that construction proceed in a certain way using the specified materials and techniques. They have largely given way to performance codes, which establish certain strength and safety standards for construction, and allow the use of any materials and techniques provided the standards are met. In the model codes, many specifications still exist. They are useful because there is much uniformity of design and technique in the construction industry. However, they are not intended to forbid the use of alternate materials and techniques. The building official is empowered to approve any designs, materials, and techniques not specified in the code if they meet the safety performance standards of the code. If he cannot determine this by examining your plans (see below), he can require you to present evidence to substantiate your claims. He can also allow deviations if standard practice causes you unusual inconvenience or hardship—for example, if you are altering a house constructed before there were building codes.

Penalties: Obey the building official. Each day your work violates the code you are guilty of a separate offense, a misdemeanor. You can be fined. The building official can force you to stop work, and can prevent you from inhabiting whatever you are building.

Permits: Before you start work, you must apply to the building official for a work permit. With your application you must supply a scale drawing clearly indicating what you are planning to do and the materials and techniques you will employ. These plans must indicate that you are conforming to the code. Communities require different types of drawings—ask your building official before you submit plans. For major work, certification by an architect can be required. There is a permit fee.

Permits are not required for minor repairs or alterations. If there is no cutting away of a wall, removal or cutting of structural support, or alteration or replacement of plumbing, gas, or electrical systems, then ordinarily no permit is required. If you have any doubt consult your building official.

Inspections: After the permit has been secured, you must arrange for the building official to inspect the work in progress. Building codes require inspections at specific times so that the building official can ascertain the safety of each phase of construction before it is obscured by additional work. An inspection is ordinarily required for the foundation, for the wood frame and masonry, for lath and wallboard, and for plumbing, electrical, and mechanical systems. Many communities require additional inspections as well, to assure compliance with particular local requirements. Never proceed until the necessary inspection is made; the building official can force you to tear down anything that obstructs his view of what must be inspected.

Certificate of occupancy: After the final inspection, when all construction is completed to his satisfaction, the building official issues a certificate of occupancy, legally allowing you to occupy what you have constructed.

Inspectors' schedules: Because your building official might have a limited inspection schedule, you should check with him well in advance of a necessary inspection. Coordinating your schedule with his can save you from having to sit around with an unfinished structure awaiting inspection; such delays can be costly if you employ subcontractors.

About this section: The following 16 pages are an introduction to the wide variety of construction details governed by building codes. This section does not cover every possible detail. It is absolutely essential that you always check your local code. Not only will the code explain everything from nailing schedules to inspection schedules, it will also alert you to any regional wind, water, soil, or earthquake condition that could affect your construction.

Building codes establish minimum standards for safety; they tell you how safe your structure must be. They do not tell you how to build. This section can serve as a general introduction to construction, but it is not intended to supplant the more detailed chapters that follow; these must be consulted before construction is started. This section covers the building codes governing foundations, floors and underfloor areas, wood frame, interior and exterior finish, and roof covering. Codes governing electricity and plumbing are discussed in later chapters dealing with house wiring and the installing of new plumbing and fixtures.

Building codes/Introduction to construction

Foundations and footings

As emphasized in the preceding discussion, the illustrations and captions on these pages are not meant to replace those specifications in your local building code that govern an addition to your house. You must follow your local code in any work you do. Neither are these pages meant as do-it-yourself instruction; such information comprises the bulk of other chapters in this book. The intent here is to give some typical examples of elements that are governed by code; in other words, these pages are an introduction to the facts of house construction that can affect the professional architect and contractor, as well as the do-it-yourselfer.

The foundation and footings are the substructure of the house—that is, the part that lies largely below grade (ground level.) A foundation must safely bear both its own weight and the weight of the superstructure of the house. Without a sound foundation, a house may settle unevenly, causing walls to crack, water to infiltrate, and a general disintegration. Building codes establish guidelines to insure that foundations are designed and constructed to provide adequate support.

Factors affecting design: The design of the foundation and footings depends on the superstructure of the house: How many stories will it have? How will it be constructed (wood frame, masonry, etc.)? The larger and heavier the superstructure is, the stronger the foundation must be to support it. The soil beneath the foundation is also a design consideration. Is the soil stable, able to support great weights, or is it unstable? (Silty-clay soils, for example, have an extremely poor bearing capacity.) Is the ground in question usually dry, or does it have poor drainage, has it a high water table, or does it lie in a flood plain? Is the house in a high seismic risk zone (an area of high earthquake danger)?

All such factors are reflected in local building codes. Unstable water or soil conditions may necessitate special construction; for example, deeper footings, thicker walls, or the use of reinforced concrete. Seismic risk exists in much of the western United States, especially in California and Nevada, and locally throughout the country. Construction in these areas is required to meet special code and design standards.

Footings. Footings are concrete volumes sunk into the ground to form a base for the foundation. They transmit the weight of the house to the soil below. Footings must distribute the weight of the house evenly, so the house will settle negligibly, or uniformly.

The dimensions of the footings are governed by the number of stories in the house and the materials to be used in building it. In temperate regions, most codes require footings at least 12 inches below grade. If the frost line—the greatest depth to which frost will penetrate—is more than 12 inches deep, the footings must be sunk below it to ensure that heaving of the soil caused by freezing will not disturb the foundation. In some places, footings must be sunk several feet below frost line.

Slab foundations: Slab foundations, which are generally used on houses without basements, consist of a slab of concrete poured at grade. The slab may have a separate footing along its perimeter, and sometimes interior footings designed to help support the load of the house above; or, the footings and slab may be poured at the same time as one solid unit, called a monolithic slab foundation, a procedure that is best left to the professionals. The slab itself is the ground floor of the house.

Pier foundations: Piers are short vertical supports that rest upon individual footings. Piers generally are constructed of concrete or masonry; the footings are concrete. Like slab foundations, pier foundations are used on houses without full basements, as well as for decks, porches, and other extensions of a house.

Perimeter foundations: A perimeter foundation usually consists of a contin-

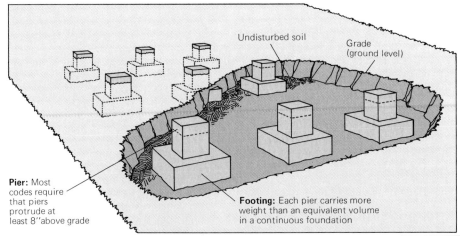

Pier: Most codes require that piers protrude at least 8"above grade

Undisturbed soil

Grade (ground level)

Footing: Each pier carries more weight than an equivalent volume in a continuous foundation

Pier foundation: A pier foundation consists of piers—short columns of either concrete block or cast concrete—that often rest on separately poured concrete footings. Frequently, pier and footings are poured as one unit. Wood posts are then anchored to the piers, and beams, in turn, are attached to the posts. The footings must lie at least 12 in. below grade (ground level) or beneath the frost line if the earth freezes to a greater depth than 12 in. in winter. The frost line may be several feet deep in northern sections of the United States.

Pier foundations are frequently used for additions to a house. The crawl space, between grade and the floor framing, must be well ventilated, as discussed on these pages.

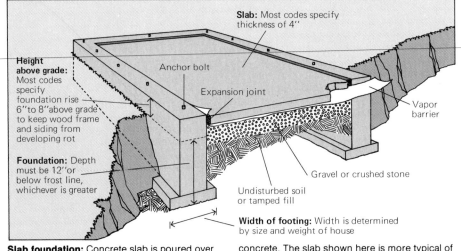

Slab: Most codes specify thickness of 4"

Anchor bolt

Expansion joint

Height above grade: Most codes specify foundation rise 6"to 8"above grade to keep wood frame and siding from developing rot

Vapor barrier

Foundation: Depth must be 12"or below frost line, whichever is greater

Gravel or crushed stone

Undisturbed soil or tamped fill

Width of footing: Width is determined by size and weight of house

Slab foundation: Concrete slab is poured over compacted fill, which is covered with a layer of gravel or crushed stone. Immediately beneath the slab is a vapor barrier, usually made of polyethylene sheeting. Developers generally employ "monolithic slabs," in which the slab and the footings are poured as a single block of concrete. The slab shown here is more typical of what a homeowner would do for an addition to his house: the footings and slab are poured separately, with an expansion joint between them and insulation to below frost line. Separate footings may be poured to support interior bearing walls in larger additions.

uous concrete footing supporting foundation walls made of masonry or concrete, which enclose a basement.

In soils with poor drainage, codes may require that perimeter foundations be provided with drains. Foundation walls enclosing basements must be damp-proofed in one of a number of ways, usually with a layer (parging) of Portland cement and/or a coat of bituminous material, such as asphalt or tar. Furthermore, if basement rooms are to be lived in—that is, not used just for storage, hallway, or utility space—the basement walls must be *waterproofed*. Building codes may require the application to the outside of the foundation of such materials as hot mopped felts, roofing material, and laminated polyethylene film.

Unbalanced fill: This is defined as the difference in height between the outside finished grade and the basement floor. Codes establish the allowable height of the unbalanced fill, depending on the construction of the basement walls.

Insulation: Many communities have recently adopted code provisions requiring the insulation of foundations. Such provisions come in response to mounting national concern over the need to conserve energy. In the case of perimeter foundations, some insulating board or foam is often applied to the outside surface of the foundation (basement) wall, where the waterproofing is applied. In slab designs, the insulating material is usually placed between the perimeter wall and the slab, serving also as an expansion joint, as well as under the slab.

Anchor bolts: In houses of wood-frame construction, codes require that anchor bolts be embedded in the foundation to secure the frame of the house to the foundation.

Materials: The minimum quality or grade of all construction materials is dictated by local building codes. This regulation extends beyond mere dimensions to the composition of foundation concrete (the proportion of cement, sand, and stone in the mixture), the composition of mortar for masonry, as well as other factors.

Many codes require that wood that is exposed to earth or water be protected against decay and termites.

Inspections: Inspections of foundations by a building official are usually made after excavations for footings are completed and forms and reinforcing are in place. This, however, is before the concrete is poured.

Building code regulation of house framing is discussed on ensuing pages.

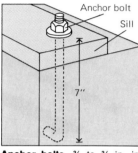

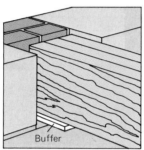

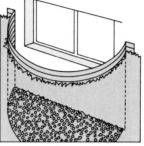

Anchor bolts, ⅜ to ¾ in. in diameter, are embedded at prescribed depths—usually at least 7 in.—in concrete every 6 ft. along the foundation perimeter.

Narrow air space must be left around a wood girder where it rests in foundation, to prevent rot. A metal or asphalt buffer is inserted at bottom.

Basements and crawl spaces must be ventilated, as described in text. Openings below grade for basement windows require a properly drained well.

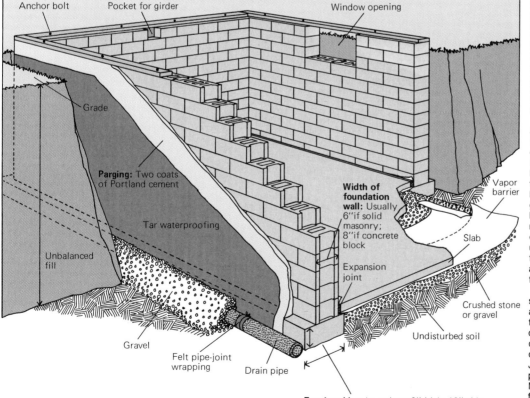

Perimeter footings support foundation basement walls made of masonry blocks or concrete. Basement walls are moisture-proofed with layers (parging) of Portland cement, layers of bituminous material, and/or plastic sheeting. (Many codes now require insulation of the foundation.) Drain tiles collect water and empty into a drainage system—for example, dry wells.

The specifications for footings are governed by the weight of the load they will bear, and the type of concrete used. Size of the basement wall is further governed by the height of the unbalanced fill— the difference in height between the outside finished grade of the earth and the basement floor. According to many codes, an 8-in.-thick wall of hollow masonry blocks can be used for 4 to 6 ft. of unbalanced fill; however, a professional should always be consulted in planning foundation specifications.

Expansion joints—tar-filled spaces about ½ in. wide all along the seam between the floor slab and foundation wall—diminish the danger of cracking caused by expansion and contraction in heat and cold. Joints can be filled with pre-molded bituminous strips. Niches for girders and spaces for windows are planned before foundation is laid.

Footing: Must be at least 6"thick; 12"wide for one-story wood-frame house, 15"for two stories and 18"for three stories

Building codes/Introduction to construction

Floors and underfloor areas

In most wood-frame houses, the floors are held up by joists—large, parallel wooden boards set on their edges. In a very small dwelling, the joists can run the entire length of the house, with their ends resting on wood sills anchored to the foundation walls. For most houses, however, this is impractical. To support the weight of the superstructure, conventional wood joists would have to be so long and thick that their cost would be prohibitive. Therefore, most houses have supporting girders that run perpendicular to the joists beneath the first floor. These girders are often supported by posts or piers, which in turn rest on concrete footings in the basement.

Protection of underfloor areas: Conventional wood girders and joists must be protected because they are susceptible to decay and termite infestation. Building codes require that these parts be protected by chemical treatment, or that special resistant woods be used. Codes often specify in which sites the wood must be protected: for instance, wood embedded in grade (a construction practice to avoid); wood in contact with masonry or concrete that is in direct contact with soil; and girders within 12 inches and joists within 18 inches of soil, as in crawl spaces.

Crawl space: The crawl space—the space between the bottom of the floor joists and the earth in a building with no basement—must be ventilated to help protect the wood against rot. Building codes often require a certain number of such openings and specify their size. The required ventilation area can be reduced if a vapor barrier is placed over the soil underneath the building. There must be an access to the crawl space—in many codes, an opening measuring 18 x 24 inches. All openings must be covered with corrosion-resistant wire mesh.

Girders: Wood girders are usually made of boards nailed, lagscrewed, or laminated together to form a heavy beam. Solid timber beams are generally too expensive and too difficult to work with; they are also more likely to shrink and split than built-up girders.

Specifications for wood members are usually given in nominal dimensions. For example, 2 x 4 inches (the nominal dimension) actually measures, after shrinkage and dressing, about 1½ x 3½ inches. A code calling for a board 2 inches thick really means 1½ inches.

Codes not only regulate the size of girders, but also the distance they can span without support and the spacing between them. These specifications will depend on the load of the house; the heavier the superstructure, the larger the girders, the shorter the unsupported

spans, and the closer the spacing between girders. Codes also set specifications for steel girders and trussed joists.

A girder entering a masonry wall for support must rest in a pocket deep enough to support it properly. Most codes require at least a 3-inch bearing surface and a ventilation space around the girder. Consult a professional.

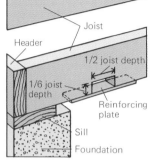

Notching: Notches for pipes and cables can be made in joists—for example, to gain headroom in a basement. However, the notch must lie within one-third the distance from joist's end, and cannot exceed size limits indicated above.

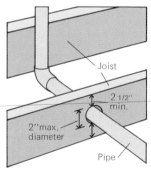

Bored holes: As with notching, no hole should be drilled farther than one-third the way out from a joist's end. A hole must not be closer than 2½ in. to either the top or the bottom edge of a joist. A hole's diameter should not exceed 2 in.

Posts and piers: In houses with basements, girders are usually supported by wood posts or by steel (hollow or concrete-filled) posts called Lally columns. In houses with crawl spaces, girders are often supported by concrete or masonry piers.

Posts and piers, as well as the footings they rest on, must safely support the

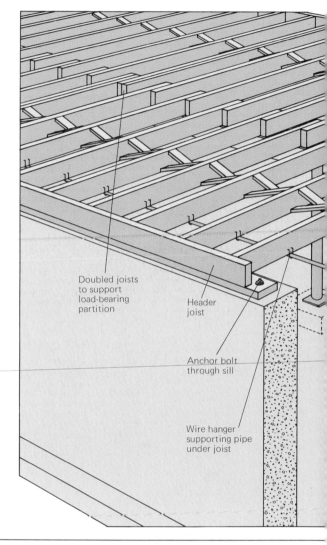

Planning the framing

Most building codes require that interior designs of houses meet minimum health and safety requirements. The codes regulate such matters as the lighting, ventilation, room dimensions, sanitation, and the size and location of exits. Although these factors pertain to the finished rooms of the house, they must be incorporated into the plans for the framing before construction is begun.

Lighting and ventilation: Many codes require habitable rooms—those used for more than just storage or utility space—to have window space of at least 10 sq. ft. (for example, 36 x 40 in.) or 10% of the floor

area of the room, whichever is greater. One-half of this window area must be openable, unless there is a mechanical ventilation system that changes the air in the room every 30 minutes.

Bathrooms and lavatories with toilets must have 3 sq. ft. of windows (for example, about 20 x 22 in.), one-half of it openable; however, this requirement can be met by substituting good artificial lighting and a mechanical ventilation system that changes the air every 12 minutes.

Glass that is subject to impact, such as in shower-stall doors, must meet shatter-proofing standards.

Room dimensions: Many codes require that every house have at least one habitable room with at least 150 sq. ft. of floor area (for example, 10 x 15 ft.). Other habitable rooms must have at least 70 sq. ft. of floor space; kitchens must have 50 sq. ft. or more. The floor plans of habitable rooms, other than kitchens, must measure at least 7 ft. in either horizontal direction.

Ceilings of habitable rooms must average no less than 7½ ft. in height over at least half their floor area. In some codes, no part of a room ceiling—as in a finished attic—can be lower than 5 ft. above the floor.

loads they carry. Most codes require that floors be able to withstand 40 pounds per square foot (40 lb/ft²) live load; sleeping rooms and attics must support 30 lb/ft². (The live load is the weight of whatever will go into the room. This is to be distinguished from the dead load, which is the weight of the materials making up the house.)

A typical code requirement for a three-story frame house is 6-x-12-inch supporting girders (or an equivalent in built-up lumber or steel). If girders are spaced 15 feet apart, the allowable span between posts or piers supporting the girders is generally 4 feet. Girders are usually evenly spaced, but their spacing may be varied to place them under

important load-bearing walls. The supporting posts must be no smaller than 3-inch steel pipes or 4-x-4-inch wooden beams. The concrete footings must be at least 2 feet square. The above specifications vary considerably in practice; consult your local code, building department, or a professional builder.

Joists: Floor joists usually rest on a sill. The sill is a piece of wood (usually 2 x 4 or 2 x 6 inches) that runs around the perimeter of the building and is bolted to the top of the foundation. Joists normally must rest several inches on the sill. To ensure that joists can support the necessary load, codes govern both their size and their unsupported span (the distance between girders or other supports). Joists are usually spaced 16 inches apart, but this can vary. For example, they can be spaced closer to provide extra support under load-bearing walls or bathrooms.

The ends of joists are usually nailed to a header or an adjoining stud, as illustrated on following pages. Joists that are not so attached must be supported so they do not turn or twist. Diagonal bridging or solid blocking between joists will prevent this. Many codes will also require blocking or bridging if the depth to thickness ratio of the joists is more than 6:1 (for example, joists 2 x 14 inches would require support). Bridging or blocking is usually attached every 8 feet along the length of the joists. Notches and holes in joists for pipes and cables must not weaken the joists.

Joists surrounding openings in the floor (for example, for a stairway) must be reinforced by doubling—the use of double headers and trimmers. Some codes require the use of metal fasteners called joist hangers or a post if the opening in the floor is more than 6 feet.

The construction of second- and third-story floors is similar to that of the first floor. However, there may be no girders for upper floors; intermediate support for the joists may be provided by the plates of load-bearing walls. Joists in the upper floors may be shallower than in the first floor, depending on design.

Subflooring: A layer of subflooring is attached to the top of the floor joists. Subflooring is usually made of 1-x-6-inch strips of wood laid diagonally across the joists, or of plywood sheets. Codes determine the grade and required thickness of the plywood and the allowable span between joists. The subflooring provides a base for the finished flooring, and also welds the joists into a single, rigid structure.

Fasteners: Attaching the frame is discussed on following pages.

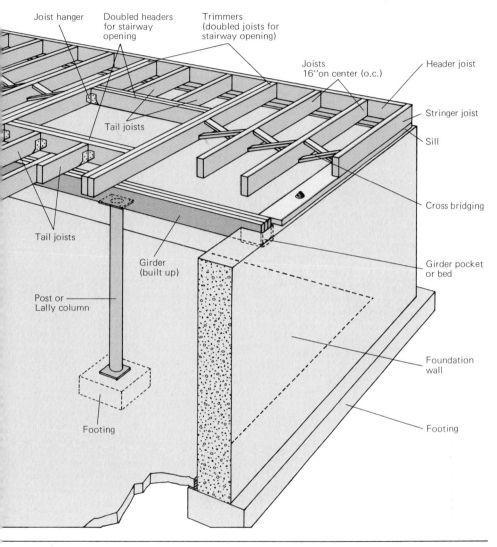

Joist hanger — Doubled headers for stairway opening — Trimmers (doubled joists for stairway opening) — Joists 16" on center (o.c.) — Header joist — Stringer joist — Tail joists — Sill — Cross bridging — Tail joists — Girder (built up) — Post or Lally column — Girder pocket or bed — Footing — Foundation wall — Footing

(See section on finishing attics, pp.163–170.) Ceilings in other rooms, including hallways, must be at least 7 ft. high.

Sanitation: Codes require that every house have a flush toilet, a wash basin, and a bathtub or shower. The bathtub or shower must be in a room that affords privacy to the user. Shower-compartment floors and walls must be made of a smooth, hard, non-absorbent material, to a height of at least 6 ft. above the floor. Any glass in bath and shower doors and panels must be shatter-resistant.

Most codes require that every house have a kitchen area

containing a sink made of a non-absorbent material. Dwellings must have both hot and cold running water. Plumbing fixtures must be connected to either a sanitary sewer or a private sewage disposal system, such as a septic tank.

Exits: All rooms used for sleeping must have one window or exterior door that can be used for escape. An escape window must be operable from inside. The sill must be no more than 44 in. from the floor. The window must have an area of at least 5.7 sq. ft. (about 2 x 3 ft.); the window cannot be less than 24 in. high or 20 in. wide.

Every room in the house must have access to an exit door that is at least 3 ft. wide and 6 ft. 8 in. high. No hallway between any habitable room and the exit can be less than 3 ft. wide.

Garages: Many codes prohibit direct openings between a private garage and rooms used for sleeping. Other openings between a garage and a residence must have solid wood doors, at least 1⅜ in. thick. Codes may require such doors to have a fire rating.

Smoke detectors: Many codes require new houses or additions to have at least one smoke detector to give warning in case of fire.

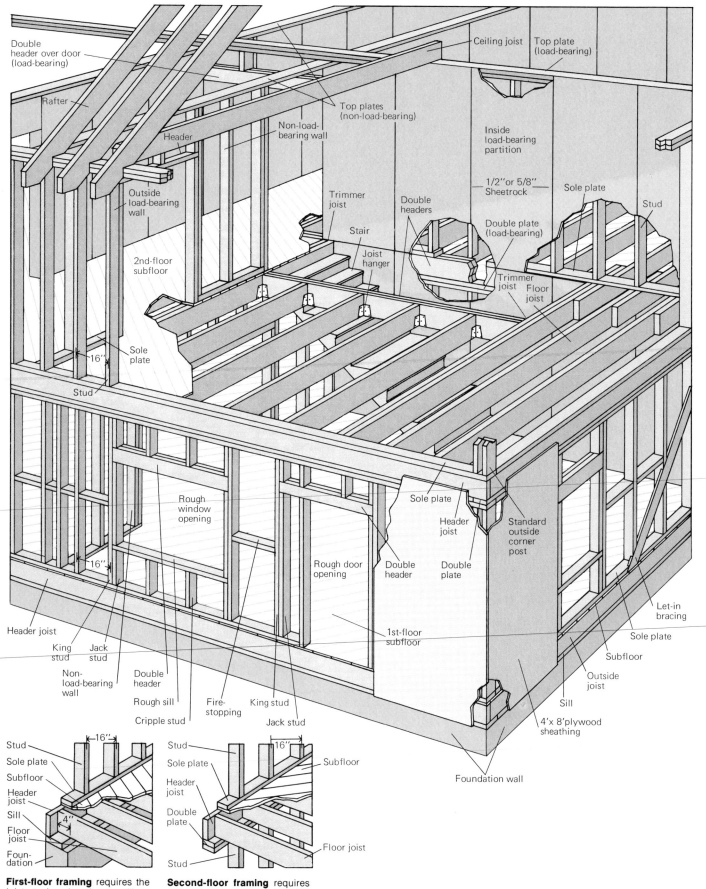

Double header over door (load-bearing)

Rafter

Header

Outside load-bearing wall

2nd-floor subfloor

Sole plate

16"

Stud

Header joist

King stud

Jack stud

Non-load-bearing wall

Double header

Rough sill

Cripple stud

Fire-stopping

King stud

Jack stud

Top plates (non-load-bearing)

Non-load-bearing wall

Trimmer joist

Stair

Joist hanger

Double headers

Ceiling joist

Top plate (load-bearing)

Inside load-bearing partition

1/2" or 5/8" Sheetrock

Double plate (load-bearing)

Trimmer joist

Floor joist

Sole plate

Stud

Rough window opening

16"

Rough door opening

Double header

Double plate

1st-floor subfloor

Sole plate

Header joist

Standard outside corner post

Let-in bracing

Sole plate

Subfloor

Outside joist

Sill

4'x 8'plywood sheathing

Foundation wall

Stud

Sole plate

Subfloor

Header joist

Sill

Floor joist

Foundation

16"

4"

First-floor framing requires the joists to be placed on a sill anchored to a foundation wall.

Stud

Sole plate

Header joist

Double plate

Stud

16"

Subfloor

Floor joist

Second-floor framing requires that joists be placed on a double plate on top of first-floor studs.

26

Wood-framing

Wood-framing is the skeleton of a house. It is the basic supporting structure—covered with walls, floors, and the roof. The framework is constructed of sawed lumber, generally softwoods, whose dimensions are governed by codes according to the structural function of each element.

The most common type of wood-framing in the United States is the *platform* or *western frame*, depicted on this and the following three pages. Other kinds of framing share most basic features of the platform frame, and code requirements are similar.

As noted elsewhere, specifications for lumber are usually given in nominal dimensions. A code calling for a board 2 inches thick means one that is actually about 1½ inches thick.

Sill: The sill is a horizontal piece of lumber that runs under the framework. It is fastened to the top of the foundation by means of bolts anchored in concrete, as shown on page 23. The sill transfers the weight of the house from the framework to the foundation. Codes usually require that a sill be at least a nominal 2 inches high and 4 inches wide. In practice however, a 2 x 6 is generally used to permit the placement on the sill of a continuous header joist that will allow a 4-inch bearing surface for floor joists.

Header joist: The header joist is a joist at right angles to floor joists. It is nailed to the top of the sill or, if on an upper floor, to the double plate. The ends of the floor joists rest on the sill or double plate, and are nailed into the header joists, as seen opposite and on preceding pages.

Stud: Studs are the vertical members that make up most of the wall-frame. Many building codes require that studs in exterior walls be 2-x-4 members spaced 16 inches apart from center to center. If the building is three stories high, studs in the first story must be 2-x-6 or 3-x-4 members.

Partition: Partitions or interior walls, either help support the joists of the floor above (and are called load-bearing partitions or load-bearing walls) or do not (and are non-load-bearing partitions or walls). Bearing walls are framed just as exterior walls are. Non-bearing walls can be less sturdy. Many codes allow studs in non-bearing partitions to be 2 x 4s spaced 24 inches apart, or 2 x 3s spaced 16 inches apart. (See the sections on working with load-bearing walls on pp.76–85 and working with non-bearing partitions on pp.86–87.)

Sole plate: The sole or sole plate is a piece of lumber, the same size as the studs, nailed to the subfloor, forming a base for the studs.

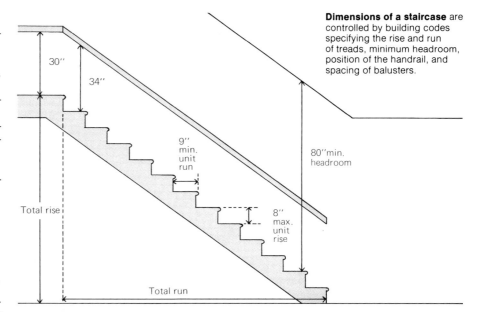

Dimensions of a staircase are controlled by building codes specifying the rise and run of treads, minimum headroom, position of the handrail, and spacing of balusters.

30"

34"

9" min. unit run

80" min. headroom

8" max. unit rise

Total rise

Total run

Top plate: The top plate is a member on top of and nailed to the upper ends of the studs. When it supports the joists for the upper story, it is usually a double 2-x-4 plate. It has the function for the upper floor that the sill has for the first floor. Top plates of the top floor support ceiling joists and roof rafters, as seen on pages 28–29.

Sheathing: Sheathing, usually made today of plywood sheets, is nailed to the outside of the studs of the exterior walls. This not only creates a barrier between the inside and outside of the house, but also gives stiffness to the wall-framing. If sheathing is not applied, many codes require that each end of the exterior wall be braced with a diagonal 1-x-4 member (let-in brace) extending from the foundation to the top plate.

Openings in the frame: Large openings in the wood frame, such as for doors or windows, make it necessary to cut some of the studs. To compensate for the support lost by this cutting, the opening is reinforced with vertical members called *trimmers* and horizontal members called *headers*. The wider the opening is, the greater the load the headers and trimmers must support. Codes determine the minimum size of trimmers and headers, depending on the span and the load above. For example, in a medium-size wood-frame house two stories high, a typical code requirement for a header on the first floor spanning a 4- to 6-foot opening in a load-bearing wall would be double 2-x-8 boards, to be supported by double trimmers the same size as the studs. This arrangement could also support a 10-foot span in a non-bearing partition.

Firestopping: Building codes require that barriers (firestopping) be placed in

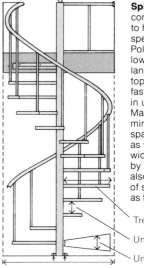

Spiral staircases come in kits made to homeowner's specifications. Pole is secured to lower floor; the landing plate at the top of staircase is fastened to joists in upper floor. Maximum rise and minimum horizontal spacing (unit run) as well as tread width are governed by code. Codes also restrict use of spiral stairs as fire exits.

Tread width (26"min.)

Unit rise (9 1/2" max.)

Unit run (7 1/2" min.)

Min. stair opening 2" wider than dia. of stair

concealed spaces that can act as flues to spread flames during a fire. Firestopping can be made of a non-combustible material, or of wood at least 2 inches thick. It is usually required in stud walls at ceiling, floor, and middle levels, and in any other openings that can facilitate rising columns of air and flames.

Fasteners: The strength of the wood-framing depends on the way the parts are attached to each other as well as on the strength of the members themselves. For this reason, building codes also dictate minimum standards for fastening the frame. Some examples of the required size and spacing of nails and other hardware in different joints of the frame are to be found on pages 36 and 37.

Staircase: The dimensions of the various elements in a staircase are governed by building codes, as illustrated in the two drawings above.

Building codes/Introduction to construction

Roof framing

A roof is subjected to more diverse loads than any other part of the frame. These loads include the dead load of the roof itself, snow loads, and wind loads. Traditionally, roofs in colder climates were designed with steeper slopes to shed snow, while lower-pitched and thus cheaper and simpler roofs have been used in warmer climates. Modern construction techniques have made this distinction less binding today.

Building codes stipulate that whatever roof is put on a dwelling must safely support the loads it will bear. Snow and wind load requirements are available from local building officials.

Gable roofs: There are many kinds of roofs, each with its own design peculiarities. Different roof types are sometimes combined in one large roof; thus roof engineering is complex, which explains why the building codes governing roofing are voluminous.

The most common design is the gable roof. The gable roof consists of two planes that meet at a central peak and slope down to opposite walls. The triangular sections of the wall (as seen from the sides) are called gables, hence the name gable roof.

The gable roof is a simple design. It is often built with protruding windows called dormers. Other, more complex roofs, the hip roof, for example, incorporate the gable design. Most roofs contain many of the elements used in the gable roof. Therefore the discussion of the construction of the gable roof in the following paragraphs applies, at least in part, to most other roofs as well.

Rafters, ridge board: The primary structural members of a gable roof are the rafters, which correspond to the joists in floors, and are usually about the same depth and thickness as the joists. Building codes control the grade of wood, spacing, unsupported span, and dimensions of the rafters, according to the design and load of the roof. Codes also control the unsupported span of the ceiling joists of the top floor, depending on the load—for example, the load imposed by the roof, and any significant live loads from attic use.

The rafters meet at the peak of the roof along a member called the ridge board. Codes usually require the ridge board to be at least 1 inch thick. The rafters are cut diagonally so that they rest flush against the ridge board, always in pairs, one directly opposite the other. Most codes require that the ridge board be as deep as the cut ends of the rafters. The lower ends of the rafters are also cut or notched diagonally so that they will lie flush on the top plate (the doubled 2 x 4s atop the exterior wall studs).

Downward loads on the roof tend to push the rafters out at the eaves (the lowest part of the rafters), forcing apart the rafters, the top plates, and the studs

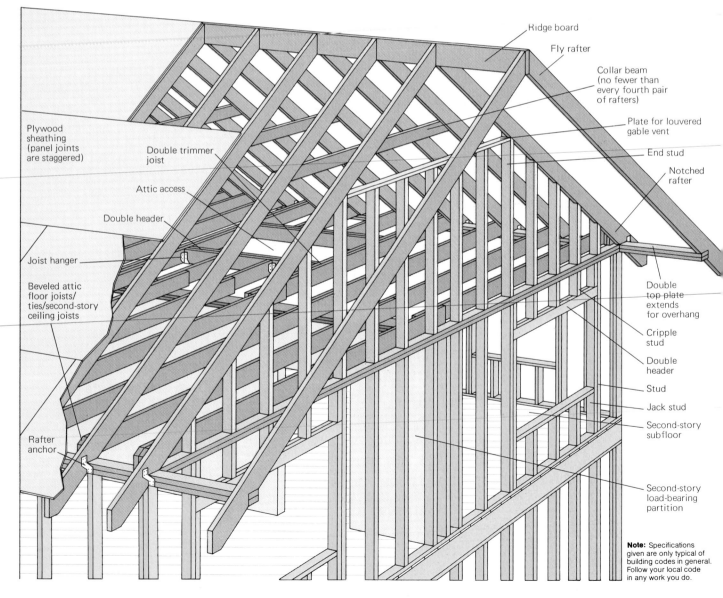

Ridge board

Fly rafter

Collar beam (no fewer than every fourth pair of rafters)

Plate for louvered gable vent

End stud

Notched rafter

Plywood sheathing (panel joints are staggered)

Double trimmer joist

Attic access

Double header

Joist hanger

Beveled attic floor joists/ties/second-story ceiling joists

Rafter anchor

Double top plate extends for overhang

Cripple stud

Double header

Stud

Jack stud

Second-story subfloor

Second-story load-bearing partition

Note: Specifications given are only typical of building codes in general. Follow your local code in any work you do.

below. This force is counteracted by the attic floor joists (upper floor ceiling joists), which usually run parallel to the rafters and supply the necessary tying strength. If the attic floor joists are perpendicular to the rafters, special ties must be attached to the rafters.

Collar beams: Wind blowing across a gable roof applies downward pressure on the side of the roof facing the wind while creating an upward lift due to reduced atmospheric pressure on the side away from the wind. Thus the roof must not only support downward and outward pressures, it must also be anchored against lift; moreover, the rafters must be supported so they will not pull apart at the ridge.

One way to provide lateral support is by connecting opposing rafters with short boards called collar beams or col-lar ties. Collar beams are usually made of 2-x-4, 1-x-6, or 1-x-8-inch lumber. They are attached somewhere below the ridge. Collar beams not only prevent the rafters from pulling apart in high winds, they also reduce the necessary size of the rafters by supplying an intermediate support. They also reduce the outward thrust of the rafters at the eaves. If the attic is finished, the collar beams may double in service as the attic ceiling joists.

Ventilation, access: Most building codes require attic ventilation open-ings, such as the soffit, ridge, and end vents illustrated on these pages. Most codes also require interior access into attics; this is usually an opening of at least 22 x 30 inches.

Roof boards: The rafters are clad with a layer of wood, which serves as the base for the roof covering (for example, shingles). In some, particularly older, houses, the roof boards are narrow parallel boards applied perpendicular to the rafters (not diagonally like subflooring). Codes usually require that roof boards be at least ⅝ inch thick, and have a 24-inch maximum unsupported span. Plywood sheathing is widely used today, usually in 4-x-8-foot sheets. Since rafters are normally spaced 16 or 24 inches apart, all joints can be made on the rafters. Plywood spanning 2 feet usually must be at least ⅜ inch thick.

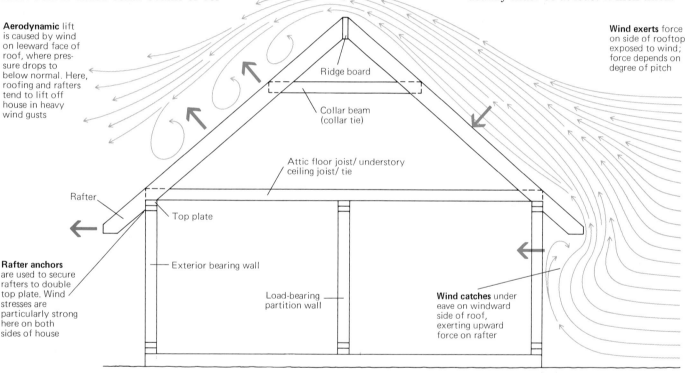

Gravity causes downward load at rafter peak

Aerodynamic lift is caused by wind on leeward face of roof, where pressure drops to below normal. Here, roofing and rafters tend to lift off house in heavy wind gusts

Wind exerts force on side of rooftop exposed to wind; force depends on degree of pitch

Ridge board

Collar beam (collar tie)

Attic floor joist/ understory ceiling joist/ tie

Rafter

Top plate

Rafter anchors are used to secure rafters to double top plate. Wind stresses are particularly strong here on both sides of house

Exterior bearing wall

Load-bearing partition wall

Wind catches under eave on windward side of roof, exerting upward force on rafter

Ventilation

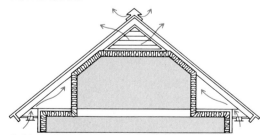

Gable roof over an occupied attic is especially prone to condensation problems because the air in the attic is warm and moisture-laden. Codes generally require a system of vents permitting free circulation of air in the spaces under ridge and rafters to protect the roof against condensation and resulting rot.

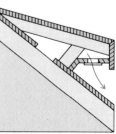

Roof vent can be placed near top of roof, as long as the vent is carefully shielded against rain, ice, and snow.

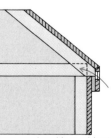

Eave vents with a midget louver are employed to ventilate the attic and roof where rafters do not over-hang enough to require the use of soffit vents.

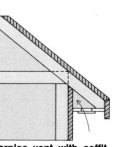

Cornice vent with soffit provides a greater air flow in space under the eaves and between attic rafters than does eave vent.

29

Building codes/Introduction to construction

Interior wall covering

The interior of the wood frame is finished with a covering to hide the rough construction beneath it, to help provide insulation, and to serve as a smooth interior surface for the rooms of the dwelling. By far the most common interior wall surfaces are plasterboard and plaster. (Plasterboard is also called drywall or gypsum wallboard, and is sold under such trade names as Sheetrock. Note that plaster is made of the mineral gypsum, sometimes with other additives; in these paragraphs, plaster and gypsum are synonymous.)

Plasterboard (drywall) construction: Plasterboard consists of a layer of plaster sandwiched between paper, with edges of various shapes. The wallboards are installed on the frame and their joints are smoothed over, giving a finished plaster wall with a paper covering. No additional plaster is applied. This technique is called drywall, or plasterboard, construction.

Types of plasterboard: There are several types of gypsum wallboard. The most widely used has one rough gray side and one smooth cream-colored side; the cream color faces the inside of the room. Gypsum wallboard with a layer of aluminum foil applied to the back is called insulating wallboard. The core of Type X wallboard includes fire-resistant ingredients, for use when high fire resistivity is needed. Special water-resistant backing board, with water-repellant surfaces and a water-resistant core, is used in bathrooms.

Walls are usually constructed of one layer of gypsum wallboard. Two layers increase the fire-resistance, sound insulation, and structural stiffness.

The boards are attached to the wood frame. The frame must meet certain structural requirements, like those that apply to gypsum lath, discussed below. It is essential that the members be installed accurately, creating one level plane, so the wallboards can lie flat against the frame. Most codes require that weather protection be provided before the gypsum wallboard is installed. Gypsum wallboards can be installed over a masonry surface, but furring is attached to the masonry to provide a gap that protects the gypsum from moisture.

Spans and fasteners: Codes dictate how the gypsum boards must be attached. Spacing of fasteners, and permissible unsupported spans, vary according to whether nails or screws are used, with or without a special adhesive; whether the gypsum surface is horizontal (ceiling) or vertical (walls); whether the long end of the board is parallel or perpendicular to supports; whether boards are ½ or ⅝ inch thick.

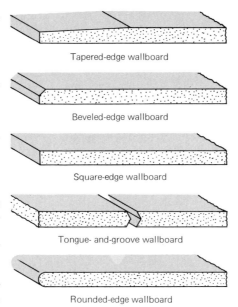

Tapered-edge wallboard

Beveled-edge wallboard

Square-edge wallboard

Tongue- and-groove wallboard

Rounded-edge wallboard

The edges of standard gypsum wallboard are slightly tapered. After wallboards are installed, spaces between them are covered with paper tape and smoothed with adhesive compound to make the joints less noticeable. Most building codes require that joints that are parallel to supports must be made right on the supports, not in between them. The adhesive compound is also applied over the heads of nails and screws in the boards.

Other drywalling: The term drywalling has come to apply to other types of wallboards. Plywood is often used, with a rough surface if it is to be covered, or with a fine finished surface, frequently Douglas fir, if it is to be left exposed. Different veneers are also available. Fiberboard, particle board, hardboard, and wood paneling are other common choices. The installation of these boards is similar to that of gypsum wallboard. Moldings are frequently used to cover the joints between the boards, though sometimes they are left exposed (wood paneling with vee notches, for example). All drywall construction is controlled by building codes.

Lath and plaster: The traditional way to construct plaster walls is to attach to the wood frame a base that will support plaster, and then apply the wet plaster over it. This base, to which the plaster adheres, is called lath.

There are two modern types of lath. The most widely used today is gypsum lath, made of a layer of gypsum sandwiched between sheets of thick porous paper. Gypsum lath is similar to gypsum wallboard, or plasterboard. It is sometimes perforated to improve adherence. The most common thickness is

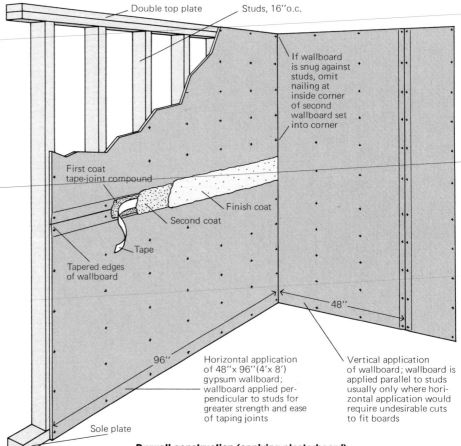

Double top plate

Studs, 16"o.c.

If wallboard is snug against studs, omit nailing at inside corner of second wallboard set into corner

First coat tape-joint compound

Finish coat

Second coat

Tape

Tapered edges of wallboard

48"

96"

Horizontal application of 48"x 96"(4'x 8') gypsum wallboard; wallboard applied perpendicular to studs for greater strength and ease of taping joints

Vertical application of wallboard; wallboard is applied parallel to studs usually only where horizontal application would require undesirable cuts to fit boards

Sole plate

Drywall construction (applying plasterboard)

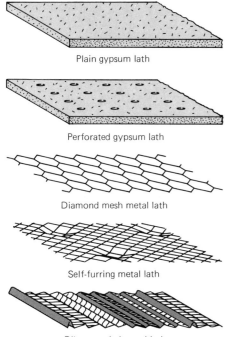

Plain gypsum lath

Perforated gypsum lath

Diamond mesh metal lath

Self-furring metal lath

Rib-expanded metal lath

⅜ inch, and a common panel size is 16 x 48 inches, but panels of longer lengths are also available.

The other common modern lath is metal lath, made of an expanded metal (an open metal pattern) or a wire fabric.

Installing the lath: Lath is installed on the inside of the completed wood frame. Codes normally require that vertical wood members—either studs or furring—support the lath. Furring consists of long strips of wood placed over a frame or wall. To support gypsum lath the furring should be at least 2 x 2 inches when over a frame, and at least 1 x 2 when over solid backing.

Gypsum lath is nailed or stapled to the studs or to the furring strips. Codes usually require that the long dimension of the panel run perpendicular to the supports (the studs, joists, or furring) to give the wall greater stiffness. End joints between panels must be staggered. Codes also specify that exterior roof and wall sheathing must be in place—or some form of weather protection must be provided—before gypsum lath is installed; the boards will swell if they get wet.

Building codes determine the type and spacing of fasteners for all lath. They also control its maximum unsupported span (the distance between supports, such as studs or furring).

Masonry surfaces can be used to support plaster without lath, but only if the surfaces never contain moisture, as in the case of an interior bearing wall that is not exposed to weather.

Applying the plaster: After the lath is installed, the wet plaster is applied. Codes usually require at least two coats of plaster, and three are frequently used (see illustrations, this page). Codes determine the composition of the plaster, and also set the minimum thickness of its application, usually ½ to ⅝ inch.

Each layer of plaster must dry before the next is applied. Drying time can be from one to several days. Even after the plaster has set, it is not until months have passed that most of the water has evaporated. To prevent blistering, paint and wallpaper should not be applied until about six months after plastering. These waiting periods make the lath and plaster method expensive. The method has other liabilities as well. It is a messy job. Water in the plaster can swell the members of the wood frame; when they dry, they shrink and can crack the plaster. As a result, the lath and plaster method is now rarely used. It is estimated that today only about one house in 5,000 is finished this way.

Inspection: An inspection by a building official is ordinarily made after all lathing is in place but before the plaster is applied. For drywalling, the inspection is made after the wallboard is in place, but before the joints and fasteners are taped and finished.

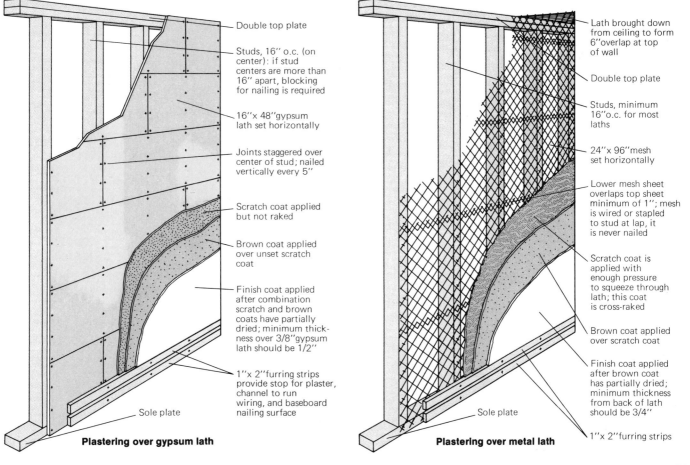

Plastering over gypsum lath

- Double top plate
- Studs, 16″ o.c. (on center): if stud centers are more than 16″ apart, blocking for nailing is required
- 16″x 48″gypsum lath set horizontally
- Joints staggered over center of stud; nailed vertically every 5″
- Scratch coat applied but not raked
- Brown coat applied over unset scratch coat
- Finish coat applied after combination scratch and brown coats have partially dried; minimum thickness over 3/8″gypsum lath should be 1/2″
- 1″x 2″furring strips provide stop for plaster, channel to run wiring, and baseboard nailing surface
- Sole plate

Plastering over metal lath

- Lath brought down from ceiling to form 6″overlap at top of wall
- Double top plate
- Studs, minimum 16″o.c. for most laths
- 24″x 96″mesh set horizontally
- Lower mesh sheet overlaps top sheet minimum of 1″; mesh is wired or stapled to stud at lap, it is never nailed
- Scratch coat is applied with enough pressure to squeeze through lath; this coat is cross-raked
- Brown coat applied over scratch coat
- Finish coat applied after brown coat has partially dried; minimum thickness from back of lath should be 3/4″
- Sole plate
- 1″x 2″furring strips

Exterior wall covering

The exterior covering of the wood frame of a dwelling protects the frame from the elements, keeps wind and dust from entering the dwelling, provides thermal and sound insulation, and gives the dwelling an attractive appearance. The common exterior coverings can be divided into four groups: siding, shingles, masonry veneer, and stucco.

Drop siding: This is the simplest kind of siding (also called novelty, or rustic siding). Horizontal boards that fit together (tongue and groove, or shiplap, for example) are driven tightly against each other as they are nailed to the outside of the studs.

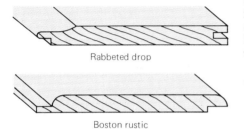

Rabbeted drop

Boston rustic

No sheathing is used beneath drop siding; in effect, drop siding combines sheathing and siding in one layer. It is not recommended for use on permanent structures that must be watertight, and generally is used only on sheds and unheated garages.

Lap siding, or bevel siding: This consists of overlapping horizontal boards, which are applied over sheathing covering the studs. When the boards are 8 inches or more in width, this is sometimes called bungalow, or colonial sid-

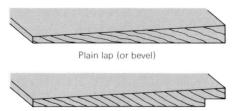

Plain lap (or bevel)

Rabbeted lap

ing; when the boards are less than 8 inches wide, this is called clapboard siding (though true clapboards, made by splitting rather than cutting the wood, are no longer made commercially). The boards are beveled—thicker at one edge than the other. They are installed with the thick edge facing down, overlapping the thin edge of the board just below, to make the siding waterproof.

Aluminum and plastic (polyvinyl chloride) siding: Usually designed to simulate wood lap siding, the upper and lower edges of the siding are crimped so that successive courses interlock. Nails (aluminum nails are frequently required in aluminum siding) are driven into horizontal slots at the top and bottom of the siding strips, allowing the strips to expand and contract with changes in temperature. Building paper is usually not required.

Plywood: Panels made with special waterproof adhesives are sometimes applied like lap siding. Plywood lap boards are available in many textures, and are usually wider than normal lap boards. Plywood offers an inexpensive way to create a strong, stiff lap siding.

Vertical boarding: The boards are installed with the long dimension running vertically, unlike drop and lap siding. This style is common on barns and sheds, but is used on houses as well. Sometimes the boards fit together tightly. More often, the joints between the boards are covered by nailing other, narrower boards, called battens, over them; this style is called board and batten. Aluminum siding that simulates board and batten is available.

Horizontal siding: This is much like drop siding, which was discussed earlier, except that the boards are applied over sheathing.

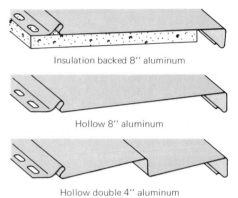

Insulation backed 8" aluminum

Hollow 8" aluminum

Hollow double 4" aluminum

Shingles: Wood, asbestos, and even asphalt shingles can be used as wall coverings. Shingles and shakes (wide, wood shingles) are usually applied with a double or triple overlap to make the covering waterproof. The application of shingles is discussed on the following two pages on roof coverings.

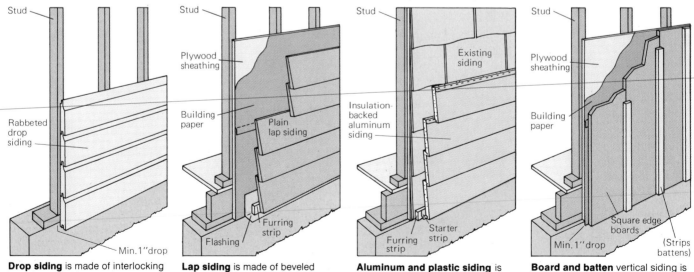

Drop siding is made of interlocking boards, up to 12 in. wide. Most codes require a thickness of at least ⅜ in. For all siding, codes require corrosion-resistant fasteners, and specify their size and spacing. For example, drop siding 8 in. wide requires two 8-penny nails per stud, penetrating at least 1 in. through the siding into the stud.

Lap siding is made of beveled boards, installed with the thick end facing down and overlapping the thin end of the board below. The lapping ranges from ½ in. to over 2 in., depending on the size of the boards. Building paper is applied over the sheathing before the siding is attached, to provide an additional weather barrier.

Aluminum and plastic siding is made of courses of interlocking strips. Because the insulating value of aluminum and plastic is negligible, insulating board can be attached to the inside of the siding; this also helps prevent denting. Openings in the bottom of the strips let the siding "breathe," preventing condensation in walls.

Board and batten vertical siding is usually made of 1 x 2 in. or 1 x 3 in. battens nailed over boards 4 to 6 in. wide. Weather-resistant woods, such as redwood, red cedar, or cypress, are used. The siding is nailed directly into the sheathing or into 2 x 4 in. blocking.

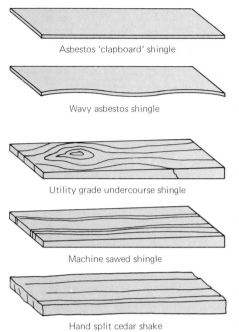

Asbestos 'clapboard' shingle

Wavy asbestos shingle

Utility grade undercourse shingle

Machine sawed shingle

Hand split cedar shake

Masonry veneer: Masonry veneer is a thin covering of brick or stone. Codes forbid the use of masonry veneer to support anything but the dead load of the masonry above.

The most common masonry veneer is brick, usually a 4-inch-wide facing, applied over sheathing and a thick layer of building paper. The building paper not only provides weather protection, it also protects the wood from the water in the mortar during construction. The veneer sits on the top of a recess in the foundation wall.

Because the veneer has little strength it must be supported by the wood frame. This is done with corrosion-resistant metal ties, one end lying in the mortar bed of the brick, the other nailed to the sheathing. The size of the ties is controlled by codes. They are usually required every four or five courses of brick, spaced approximately 24 inches apart along the mortar joint; in areas of high wind pressure or high earthquake danger, the spacing may be closer. Masonry veneer is usually allowed to extend 35 feet above grade, except in unstable wind and earthquake zones. (To reach such heights, the veneer must be much thicker than 4 inches.)

Masonry above such openings as doors and windows must be supported by lintels made of reinforced masonry or concrete or steel; codes establish minimum lintel size. Lintels must have at least a 4-inch bearing surface for support on each side.

A 2-inch space is ordinarily left between the brick veneer and the sheathing. This is done in order to allow water to condense on the inside face of the brick, run down, and then drain through "weep holes" that are left in the bottom course.

Stucco: Stucco is a Portland cement mixture that is used to give a dwelling a weather-resistant covering.

Stucco is applied over lath, a backing usually made of expanded metal or wire fabric that adheres to and supports the stucco; in effect the lath and stucco form a slab of reinforced cement.

Lath is normally attached over a heavy layer of building paper, which in turn is over sheathing. If there is no sheathing, a backing can be made by nailing parallel rows of heavy wire across the studs, no more than 6 inches apart vertically. Building paper is applied over the wires; then the lath is applied. Certain surfaces must have solid backing before stucco is applied. The wire, lath, and backing are all governed by codes.

At least three layers of stucco are ordinarily required over metal or wire lath, and at least two coats over solid masonry or concrete backing. The constitution of the stucco (the proportion of Portland cement, lime, and sand) is controlled by codes, and varies for each coat. Epoxies are sometimes used in the stucco mixture. Codes also establish the minimum thickness of the stucco, frequently between $\frac{5}{8}$ and $\frac{7}{8}$ inch.

After the first layer is applied, it must be sprayed periodically with water so that the stucco sets. Codes normally require that this process, called moist curing, last at least 48 hours. The second coat must moist cure for 48 hours, but the final coat cannot be applied for an additional five days.

Flashing: Corrosive-resistant flashing is required around all exterior door and window openings to make them waterproof. Flashing is also required in other locations susceptible to water entry, such as at the intersection between roof and walls, above projecting wood trim, around chimneys, and around all roof valleys and openings (see pp.34–35).

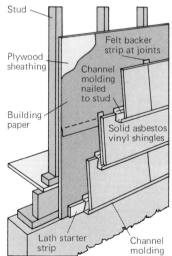

Solid vinyl and mineral fiber siding is attached with metal channel moldings. Channel moldings are nailed through sheathing and into studs, usually using ⅜-in.-head galvanized nails 1½ in. long. Mineral fiber siding is virtually fireproof, but local codes may preclude the use of such shingles that contain asbestos.

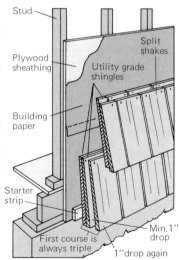

Cedar shakes and wood shingles are applied over building paper and plywood sheathing. Each course (row) of the shingles can be doubled for added weather protection, as indicated here.

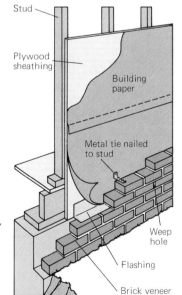

Brick veneer, the most common masonry veneer, is usually made of a single course of brick, about 4 in. thick. It is attached to the sheathing by metal ties.

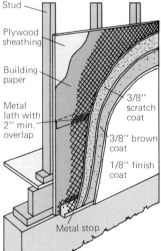

Stucco, or Portland cement plaster, is a mixture of Portland cement, lime, and sand, applied wet, usually over heavy metal lath. Three coats are ordinarily applied; the minimum thickness of each is controlled by local building codes.

33

Roof covering

The framing of the roof is given a watertight cover. In single-family dwellings, the cover is usually shingles made of asphalt, wood, slate, asbestos, or tile. Flat roofs are covered with sheet roofing or built-up roofing.

Roofing is applied over sheathing covering the rafters (see *Roof framing*, pp.28–29). An underlayment made of asphalt-saturated felt is installed under most roofing materials. Building codes specify the weight of the felt, depending on the material and slope of the roof; it is usually 15 or 30 pounds per roofing square (1 roofing square equals 100 square feet of roof surface area). The underlayment is waterproof, but allows vapor to escape, helping to prevent condensation inside the roof.

The slope or pitch of the roof, a crucial consideration in selecting and installing roof covering, is usually described as a ratio of the vertical rise of the roof to its horizontal run. For example, a pitch of 4 in 12 (or 4 over 12) means that the roof rises 4 inches for every 12 inches it runs horizontally (and the angle of the roof is about 18½°).

Shingles: Shingles do not provide an unbroken cover for a roof. The slope of the roof directs water over the overlapping shingles, thus making the roof watertight. Therefore, shingles usually are used only on roofs with a pitch of 4 in 12 or more (though sometimes as low as 3 in 12). The higher pitch also helps preserve the roof. The lower the slope is, the greater is the possibility that wind will lift the shingles off the roof, break them, or allow water to infiltrate. On shallow roofs the shingles stay wet longer, and disintegrate faster. For example, split cedar shingles that would

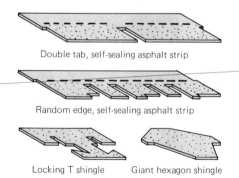

Double tab, self-sealing asphalt strip

Random edge, self-sealing asphalt strip

Locking T shingle   Giant hexagon shingle

last about 40 years on a roof with a slope of 4 in 12 would last about 60 years on a roof with a pitch of 8 in 12; on a wall they would last indefinitely. (Shingles and shakes are also discussed on pp.32–33.)

Asphalt shingles: Because of their low cost and relative ease of installation, asphalt shingles cover the roofs of about 90 percent of the houses in the United States. They are made of as-

phalt-impregnated felt covered with a layer of ceramic granules. They are applied so that the exposure, the part of the shingle exposed to the weather (not beneath the next course), is usually about 4 inches wide.

Underlayment is required beneath the shingles by most building codes. Most codes waive the requirement if the shingles are being applied over an existing roof, if the slope of the roof is greater than 7 in 12, or if there is triple thickness everywhere on the roof. (The lower the roof pitch, the greater the need for triple coverage.) Triple coverage, and the use of heavy shingles (above 235 pounds per square) help prevent wind damage. Specially shaped shingles whose exposed edges interlock with each other to prevent wind lift are sometimes applied atop existing roofs.

All roofing materials must be installed with corrosion-resistant fasteners, which are controlled by codes. Nail the shingle strips at each end and at least two intermediate points.

Wood shingles: Wood shingles are usually made of cedar or redwood, and are available in standard 16-, 18-, and 24-inch widths. They are usually installed with triple overlap (a 16 or 18 shingle has a 4- to 5½-inch exposure, depending on the pitch of the roof). Codes generally require that each shingle be attached with exactly two nails. A ¼-inch gap is usually left between shingles to allow them to swell when they are wet. The breaks between shingles must be staggered between successive courses to prevent water penetration.

Unlike other roofing, wood shingles (and shakes) can be installed over spaced sheathing made of strips of wood spaced apart, rather than strips pushed tight together or sheets of plywood (called solid sheathing). Most codes require the boards to be at least 1 x 3s spaced at most 4 inches apart. The shingles span the gaps, making a watertight cover, but the spacing allows air to circulate around the shingles. It is believed that this keeps the shingles drier, and therefore they last longer. Spaced sheathing can only be used on roofs with a pitch of 4 in 12 or more; roofs with a lower pitch must have solid sheathing and an underlayment. (See the diagram of wood shingles, p.33.)

Wood shakes: Wood shakes are split, not sawed as wood shingles are. Therefore they are not as uniform as shingles and do not lie as neatly on top of one another as shingles do. Installation of shakes is similar to that of shingles, except that the exposure of shakes is greater, and a strip of roofing felt or building paper is installed beneath each course of shakes.

Because of fire hazard, wood shakes and shingles are forbidden in many communities throughout the country.

Slate shingles: Slate is one of the best and most durable roofing materials; slate shingles, unlike wood and asphalt, should outlast the house they cover.

Natural slate shingle

Slate shingles range in size from 6 x 10 to 14 x 26 inches, and are at least ³/₁₆ inch thick but are often much thicker. Slate is heavy, and therefore the roof framing must be sturdy.

Asbestos cement shingles: Asbestos cement shingles, also known simply as asbestos shingles, are made of a mixture of Portland cement and asbestos fibers, formed under high pressure into different shapes. Codes generally require the roof supporting the shingles to have a pitch of at least 3 in 12.

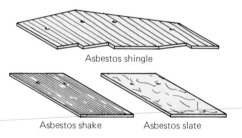

Asbestos shingle

Asbestos shake   Asbestos slate

Tile shingles: Most tile shingles are made of clay and have the familiar burnt-red color. They are heavy, require sturdy framing, and must be very carefully installed. Codes usually require a pitch of at least 3 in 12.

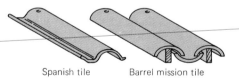

Spanish tile   Barrel mission tile

Flashing: Codes require that flashing (metal, plastic, or impregnated fabric) be installed to prevent water infiltration in any joint that can admit water.

Flashing is always required along valleys, where two planes of a roof meet. Sometimes the roofing ends in the valleys and the flashing is exposed, or open. Some roofing, such as asphalt shingle, is flexible and crosses the valley over the flashing (called closed flashing). Building codes specify the necessary dimensions and composition of flashing and the minimum distance it must extend up each roof plane, depending on the roofing material and slope of the roof.

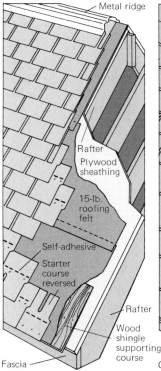

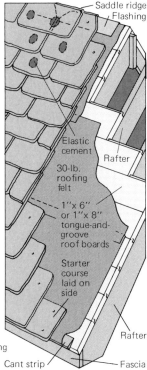

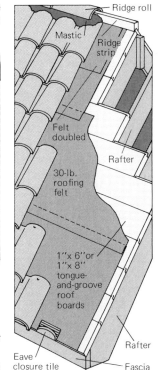

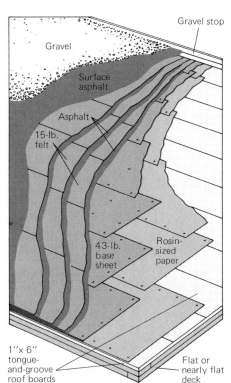

Asphalt shingles are applied in strips, usually 36 in. long, with at least a double overlap. Slots simulate separate 12-in. shingles. Adhesives help hold shingles down, and can be required in high-wind zones.

Slate shingles are attached by nails that pass through two holes drilled near top corners into heavy underlayment and sheathing. Pitch of a roof supporting slate shingles must be at least 6 in 12.

Clay tile shingles come in many different shapes, such as Greek, Roman, and Spanish (shown here). They interlock on the sides and have a small vertical overlap. One copper nail fastens each tile.

Built-up roofing is common on flat commercial buildings and dwellings with a pitch of 3 in 12 or less. It is made of layers of asphalt in which are embedded layers of roofing felts. Building codes usually require at least three layers of felt, and some minimum concentration of asphalt. Embedded ceramic chips are used to reflect sunlight.

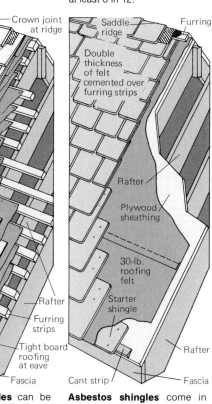

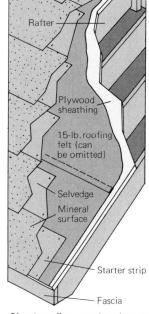

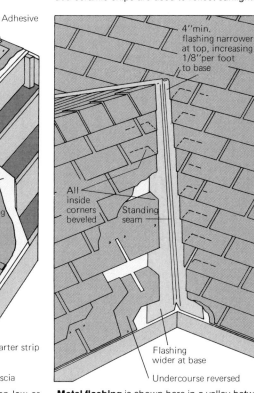

Split cedar shingles can be attached over spaced sheathing, to allow circulation and prevent rot. Felt is applied over furring strips or battens, which are nailed to the rafters. Overhang forms drip.

Asbestos shingles come in various shapes. "American," shaped like slate, is similarly applied. Other shapes, such as the diamond, hexagonal, and Dutch lap, are installed with less overlap, and thus are cheaper.

Sheet roofing, used on low or flat roofs, is made of the same material as asphalt shingles. The sheets overlap and are attached with nails and adhesives. New sheet roofing is made of synthetic rubber.

Metal flashing is shown here in a valley between roof faces of different pitches. Flashing gets wider as it approaches the eave. Splash diverter rib down the center prevents water from running from the steeper roof over onto and possibly beneath the shingles of the adjoining roof with its shallower pitch.

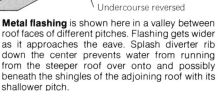

Building codes/Introduction to construction

Charts and tables

As discussed on pages 21-35, building codes specify the type and minimum size and spacing of fasteners used in construction. Below is a table of fasteners for construction of a wood frame. It is a composite of specifications from several national codes governing dwelling-house construction. Though these codes are in force in much of the country, remember that communities are empowered to make changes—always check your local code.

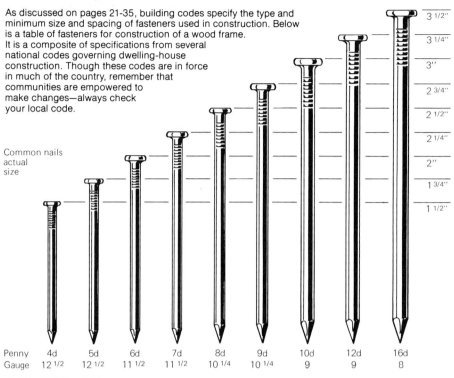

Common nails actual size

Penny	4d	5d	6d	7d	8d	9d	10d	12d	16d
Gauge	12 1/2	12 1/2	11 1/2	11 1/2	10 1/4	10 1/4	9	9	8

JOINING STRUCTURAL MEMBERS	METHOD	NO.	SIZE	PLACEMENT
Beams and headers				
Built-up girders and beams	Face-nail		20d	32" o.c. staggered
Ledger strip to beam	Face-nail	3	16d	At each beam
Continuous header	Face-nail		12d	12" o.c. staggered
Header to joist	End-nail	3	16d	
Joists and rafters				
Joists and rafters to sill, girder, or plate	Toenail	2	10d	
Joist to lap at partition or girder	Face-nail	4	16d	
Rafter to ceiling joist	Face-nail	5	10d	
Rafter to ridge board	End-nail	3	16d	
Rafter to valley or hip rafter	Toenail	3	10d	
Collar tie to rafter	Face-nail	2	12d	
Studs and plates				
Sole plate to joist or blocking	Face-nail		16d	16" o.c.
Top or sole plate to stud	End-nail	2	16d	
Stud to top or sole plate	Toenail	4	8d	
Doubled studs	Face-nail		10d	16" o.c. staggered
Built-up corner studs	Face-nail		16d	16" o.c.
End of stud partition to exterior stud wall	Face-nail		16d	16" o.c.
Upper top plate to lower top plate	Face-nail		16d	16" o.c.
Upper top plate, laps, and intersections	Face-nail	2	16d	
Diagonal let-in brace	Face-nail	2	8d	
Board sheathing				
1" x 6" and smaller boards	Face-nail	2	8d	At each bearing
1" x 8" and larger boards	Face-nail	3	8d	At each bearing
2" x 6" T&G decking	Face-nail	2	16d	At each bearing
Plywood sheathing				
3/8" thick and less plywood	Face-nail		6d	6" edge, 12" intermediate
1/2" to 1" thick plywood	Face-nail		8d	6" edge, 12" intermediate

Note: All nails are smooth-common, box or deformed shanks.
Nail is a general description and may be T-head, round, or modified round head.

Using building code tables

Codes require that such structural elements as beams, joists, and rafters be strong enough to bear their loads. They must meet minimum requirements for size and quality of wood, and have no more than a specified maximum unsupported span (the distance between supports). These requirements depend on the design of the house and the load the element must support.

Understanding table terminology: Building code tables controlling structural elements are voluminous. Two examples appear on these pages.

On the opposite page is a small part of a table titled "Allowable Spans for Floor Joists" from the *One and Two Family Dwelling Code*. To use the table you must know the anticipated dead load (the load, or weight, of the materials of the house itself) and the anticipated live load on the floor (the load of people, furniture, and whatever else goes into the house).

As indicated at the top of the table, the example given here pertains to a floor supporting 10 pounds per square foot dead load and 40 pounds per square foot live load (which is standard for wood-frame dwellings). If your floor has a different load, you would consult a different table in your code booklet.

You must also know the type and grade of lumber the joists are made of. By looking at the tables in your code book, or at an architectural reference book, you can find two numerical values for the wood, determined by scientific testing, which indicate its ability to withstand weight without bending or breaking. They are the "extreme fiber stress in bending" or "fiber stress value" (abbreviated Fb or simply F), and the "modulus of elasticity" (E).

Example: You are installing floor joists made of Douglas fir, standard grade. The live load on the floor will not exceed 40 pounds per square foot, and the dead load will not exceed 10 pounds per square foot. You want the joists to span 12 feet unsupported. How deep must they be?

By checking your reference source, you find that for this wood, the Fb is 1,200 pounds per square inch and the E is 1,760,000 pounds per square inch. (The fiber stress value varies significantly with the grade of wood, the modulus of elasticity much less so.)

Look down the column in which E = 1.7 million. The modulus of elasticity of this wood is great enough to meet the requirements of this column or any column to the left of it, where E is lower. Find the first row where the joist spacing is 16 inches. Follow this row to where it intersects the column E = 1.7 million. The top number in this box says that the maximum unsupported span of joists of this spacing (16 inches), size (2 x 6), and E value (1.7 million) is 9 feet 11 inches. Thus this joist size is not sufficient for your required 12-foot span. (The bottom number in the box, here 1,310, is the Fb value. It does not matter in this case because the joist is already shown to be too small.)

Look down to the next joist size, 2 x 8. Read across the row in which the spacing is 16 inches to where it intersects the column E = 1.7 million. This box says that joists 2 x 8 spaced 16 inches apart made of wood with an E of 1.7 million or greater can span 13 feet 1 inch, if the wood has an Fb of 1,310. However, the wood you have selected has an Fb of only 1,200. Look back across the row to the left to find the first box in which the Fb is 1,200 or lower. This box says that joists 2 x 8 spaced 16 inches apart with an Fb of 1,200 can span 12 feet 7 inches, if the E is at least 1.5 million (which it is). This is your solution: Your joists must be at least 2 x 8s.

You can increase joist spans and spacing by using higher-grade woods (those with higher fiber stress values). Generally, construction and standard grades are adequate for residential use.

Deflection: The table on page 37 also assures that if the values are met, the deflection of the joists will be 1/360 of the joist span or less. This means the floor will not bounce or shake unduly.

Allowable spans for floor joists

Design criteria: Deflection—for 40 pounds per square foot live load, limited to span in inches divided by 360. (All rooms except those used for sleeping areas and attic floor.) Strength—live load of 40 pounds per square foot plus dead load of 10 pounds per square foot determines the fiber stress shown.
Note: The extreme fiber stress in bending (F_b), in pounds per square inch, is shown below each span.

Joist Size	Spacing	Modulus of elasticity in millions of pounds per square inch (E)													
		0.9	1.0	1.1	1.2	1.3	1.4	1.5	1.6	1.7	1.8	1.9	2.0	2.2	2.4
2" x 6"	12"	8'-10" 780	9'-2" 830	9'-6" 890	9'-9" 940	10'-0" 990	10'-3" 1040	10'-6" 1090	10'-9" 1140	10'-11" 1190	11'-2" 1230	11'-4" 1280	11'-7" 1320	11'-11" 1410	12'-3" 1490
	16"	8'-0" 860	8'-4" 920	8'-7" 980	8'-10" 1040	9'-1" 1090	9'-4" 1150	9'-6" 1200	9'-9" 1250	9'-11" 1310	10'-2" 1360	10'-4" 1410	10'-6" 1460	10'-10" 1550	11'-2" 1640
	24"	7'-0" 980	7'-3" 1050	7'-6" 1120	7'-9" 1190	7'-11" 1250	8'-2" 1310	8'-4" 1380	8'-6" 1440	8'-8" 1500	8'-10" 1550	9'-0" 1610	9'-2" 1670	9'-6" 1780	9'-9" 1880
2" x 8"	12"	11'-8" 780	12'-1" 830	12'-6" 890	12'-10" 940	13'-2" 990	13'-6" 1040	13'-10" 1090	14'-2" 1140	14'-5" 1190	14'-8" 1230	15'-0" 280	15'-3" 1320	15'-9" 1410	16'-2" 1490
	16"	10'-7" 850	11'-0" 920	11'-4" 980	11'-8" 1040	12'-0" 1090	12'-3" 1150	12'-7" 1200	12'-10" 1250	13'-1" 1310	13'-4" 1360	13'-7" 1410	13'-10" 1460	14'-3" 1550	14'-10" 1640
	24"	9'-3" 980	9'-7" 1050	9'-11" 1120	10'-2" 1190	10'-6" 1250	10'-9" 1310	11'-0" 1380	11'-3" 1440	11'-5" 1500	11'-8" 1550	11'-11" 1610	12'-1" 1670	12'-6" 1780	12'-10" 1880
2" x 10"	12"	14'-11" 780	15'-5" 830	15'-11" 890	16'-5" 940	16'-10" 990	17'-3" 1040	17'-8" 1090	18'-0" 1140	18'-6" 1190	18'-9" 1230	19'-1" 1280	19'-5" 1320	20'-1" 1410	20'-8" 1490
	16"	13'-6" 850	14'-0" 920	14'-6" 980	14'-11" 1040	15'-3" 1090	15'-8" 1150	16'-0" 1200	16'-5" 1250	16'-9" 1310	17'-0" 1360	17'-4" 1410	17'-8" 1460	18'-3" 1550	18'-9" 1640
	24"	11'-0" 980	12'-3" 1050	12'-8" 1120	13'-0" 1190	13'-4" 1250	13'-8" 1310	14'-0" 1380	14'-4" 1440	14'-7" 1500	14'-11" 1550	15'-2" 1610	15'-5" 1670	15'-11" 1780	16'-5" 1880
2" x 12"	12"	18'-1" 780	18'-9" 830	19'-4" 890	19'-11" 940	20'-6" 990	21'-0" 1040	21'-6" 1090	21'-11" 1140	22'-5" 1190	22'-10" 1230	23'-3" 1280	23'-7" 1320	24'-5" 1410	25'-1" 1490
	16"	16'-5" 860	17'-0" 920	17'-7" 980	18'-1" 1040	18'-7" 1090	19'-1" 1150	19'-6" 1200	19'-11" 1250	20'-4" 1310	20'-9" 1360	21'-1" 1410	21'-6" 1460	22'-2" 1550	22'-10" 1640
	24"	14'-4" 980	14'-11" 1050	15'-4" 1120	15'-10" 1190	16'-3" 1250	16'-8" 1310	17'-0" 1380	17'-5" 1440	17'-9" 1500	18'-1" 1550	18'-5" 1610	18'-9" 1670	19'-4" 1780	19'-11" 1880

Source: One and Two Family Dwelling Code

Allowable stresses for wood (psi), for 2"-4" thick, 6" and wider, #2 grade

Species	Modulus of elasticity (E)	Extreme fiber stress in bending (F_b)	Compression parallel to grain (c‖)	Horizontal shear (h)
Western hemlock	1,400,000	1,250	975	90
Lodgepole pine	1,200,000	1,050	750	70
Douglas fir/larch	1,700,000	1,450	1,050	95
California redwood	1,200,000	1,400	1,200	80
Hem-fir	1,400,000	1,150	850	75
Eastern spruce	1,200,000	1,000	750	65
Eastern hemlock	1,100,000	1,200	900	85
Eastern white pine	1,100,000	950	700	70
Southern pine	1,400,000	1,200	900	75

Source: The National Design Specification for Stress-Grade Lumber and Its Fastenings, National Forest Products Association

Table (above) and chart (left) are presented here to help you read code tables. In planning any job always consult your local building code, an architect, or local building officials.

The factors affecting joist selection are the distance spanned without intervening support; spacing between joists; the loads the joists will carry; joist size and wood.

To use the table, first find in the chart the fiber stress (F, or Fb) and modulus of elasticity (E) values for the wood of the joists; with these figures, use the table as described in the text to determine joist specifications. Note that the chart is for #2 grade lumber; lower grades (e.g., construction grade and standard grade) are somewhat weaker, higher grades stronger.

For most wood-frame dwellings, fiber stress and modulus of elasticity alone need enter your figuring. Shear and compression, also listed in the chart, are not normally considered relevant to family residences.

Architectural drawings

Buildings on paper

The architectural drawings of a building are a series of related two-dimensional views that, taken together, depict in its entirety a complex three-dimensional structure. The drawings provide all the necessary information to the builder and subcontractors as to exactly how the building is to be constructed; they show the owner what he is buying; and they indicate adherence to zoning and building ordinances for local officials.

The principal drawings: There are three principal types of drawings.

The floor plan (see pp.40–42) is a bird's-eye view of a full floor of the house (one plan for each story) after an imaginary horizontal slice has been made through the building. The floor plan shows all of the horizontal dimensions, the size and shape of the spaces, accesses, doors, windows, built-in fixtures, appliances, etc. Usually the design process begins with the floor plan.

The other drawings, elevations and sections, are vertical views, and usually derive from the floor plan. Elevations (pp.44–45) are drawings of the exterior walls of the structure, one straight-on view of each wall. Their purpose is to illustrate the vertical surfaces as they are to appear when the structure is completed. Sections (pp.42–43) are views of the structure after imaginary vertical slices have been made through it. Sections illustrate the major supporting structures of the building; they show how everything is supported.

The way a floor plan, a section, and two elevations relate to a building are shown in the diagram below. These drawings are based on those done by an architect for the house addition chapter beginning on page 241, where the construction work is depicted in detail.

Other drawings: Other common architectural drawings include the site plan (opposite page); interior elevations (p.45); views of portions of walls taken from the inside, used to illustrate built-in fixtures and finishes; special-purpose drawings (p.46), such as framing, foundation, and electrical drawings; and details (p.42), which are large scale drawings of elements whose complexity requires them.

Orthographic: Most architectural drawings are orthographic. The line of sight for each drawing is perpendicular to the plane of what is being shown. Consequently, all elements in the plane of the drawing are depicted in their true proportions (in scale); there isn't any foreshortening of these elements.

Using a set of drawings: A complete set of architectural plans for a dwelling or large addition usually runs from 4 to 15 or more pages, each about 24 x 36 inches in size. Along with the drawings (each copiously annotated) are pages of "specifications," in which the architect specifies the materials and techniques the builder and subcontractors are to use. Together, the drawings and the specifications constitute a complete description of the building; if the house is being contracted for by a buyer, the drawings and specifications become part of the legal agreement.

Architectural drawings are technical and complex, but they are not impenetrable. You must study them, familiarize yourself with their terminology and conventions. Look at the plans on the following eight pages; compare them with their actualization starting on page 241. If you can secure plans of your house, follow them as you look around; notice the correspondence between depictions and real structures. If you are going to draw plans yourself, see *Drawing your own plans*, page 47.

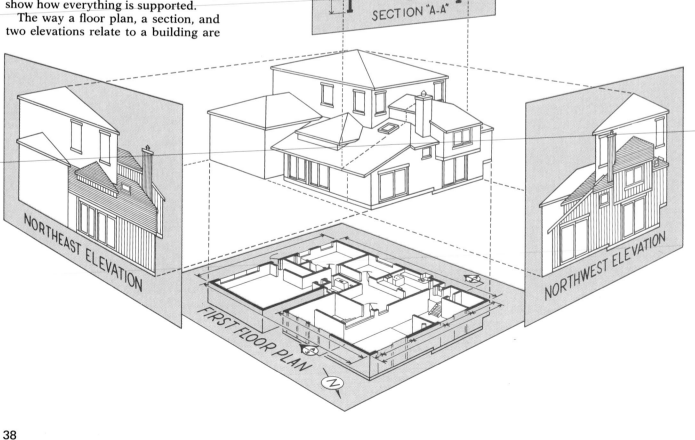

SECTION "A-A"

NORTHEAST ELEVATION

NORTHWEST ELEVATION

FIRST FLOOR PLAN

Site and landscaping plans

A site plan is a bird's-eye view of construction and the plot on which it stands. The site plan shows the property lines, gas, water, sewer, and electricity lines leading from outside the property, the main structure and all outbuildings, the planned additions, roadways, and walkways on the property.

Site plans ordinarily must be submitted to local zoning and building departments before any construction on the site is begun (see *Introduction to construction*, p.21); the plans must include a survey (an accurate measurement of the elements of the plot done by a professional surveyor) to show adherence to zoning and building regulations. You are usually given a site survey with the deed when you purchase property. If you lose it the surveyor who prepared it or his successor can probably replace it. Your own drawings of planned additions can often be added to the survey, though some communities insist that any amendment of the survey be done by a licensed surveyor.

The site plan of the addition covered on page 241 and ensuing pages is shown on this page. It includes many of the standard features of site plans. Other common features not shown here include setbacks (the distance zoning ordinances require buildings to be set back from property lines; here they are not in force because ordinances were enacted after the house was built), rights of way, septic systems, and sidewalks. If you are drawing plans you should include all features, however irrelevant they may seem. This can help

prevent difficulties, such as an inadvertent hole dug through your gas line, or a pile of bricks deposited over the filler pipe to your oil tank in the winter.

Landscaping plans: A landscaping plan is a site plan that includes elements of the natural environment. It shows how construction (such as a building or addition) will look in its immediate natural setting. It indicates

topographical contours and helps show what views will be like from inside the building and where shade will fall. A landscaping plan of the same house and addition placed in a more rural setting is shown below.

Site and landscaping plans are generally oriented in the same compass directions as the other drawings to facilitate referral from one to the others.

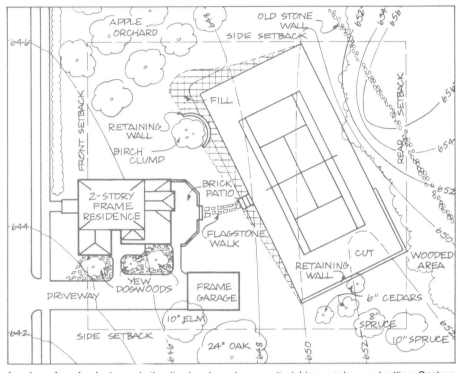

Landscaping plan for house in the site plan shows house as it might appear in a rural setting. Contour lines indicate elevations, measured in feet. Earth is removed (cut) or filled in at site where indicated.

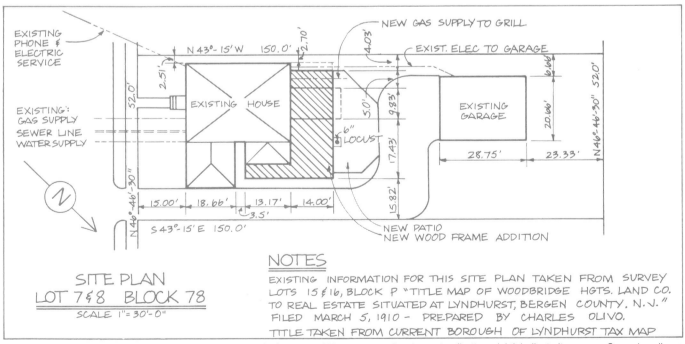

This site plan for the house and addition shown beginning on p.241 includes many standard features of site plans. Dimensions are taken from a survey; site plan notes (bottom right) indicate its source. Surveying dimensions are always in decimals of feet, not in feet and inches.

Architectural drawings

Floor plans

A floor plan is a bird's-eye view of a floor after a horizontal slice has been made through the building about halfway up the wall (see diagram, p.38). The floor plan conveys more information about the building than any other view. It shows the entire layout—all walls, openings (windows and doors), stairways, and their dimensions, which are necessary for constructing the wood frame. It also shows built-in structures, such as counters, cabinets, and major appliances.

Floor plans are covered with the architect's writing, which identifies the elements of construction and provides instructions for the builder. Plans are frequently far more cluttered than the two shown here. Do not be intimidated; they simply require careful attention. Floor plans can also include electrical drawings. For purposes of clarity the electrical drawing for this addition is shown separately on page 46.

Floor plans (one for each story) are oriented the same way, in line, so that by moving one sideways, over the other, elements line up exactly as they do in the structure itself. (The two floor plans shown here, based on those for the addition beginning on p.241, are only partial plans; architects' complete plans illustrate all floors in their entirety.) The scale of floor plans is usually at least ¼ inch per foot. The scale is indicated on the drawing.

Graphic symbols: Several standard architectural symbols are employed on these floor plans: brick (diagonal lines), insulated stud wall (wavy lines), and uninsulated stud partitions (open, no lines). The architect chose to fill walls in the existing building with parallel lines, so as to distinguish it from the new addition. Symbols that are chosen arbitrarily (rather than by established convention) are usually labeled, or a symbol legend is provided.

The weight of the lines on the floor plan also conveys information. The heaviest lines depict walls, girders, and section cuts. Intermediate lines depict such elements as doors, windows, stairs, counters, and dimensions. Light

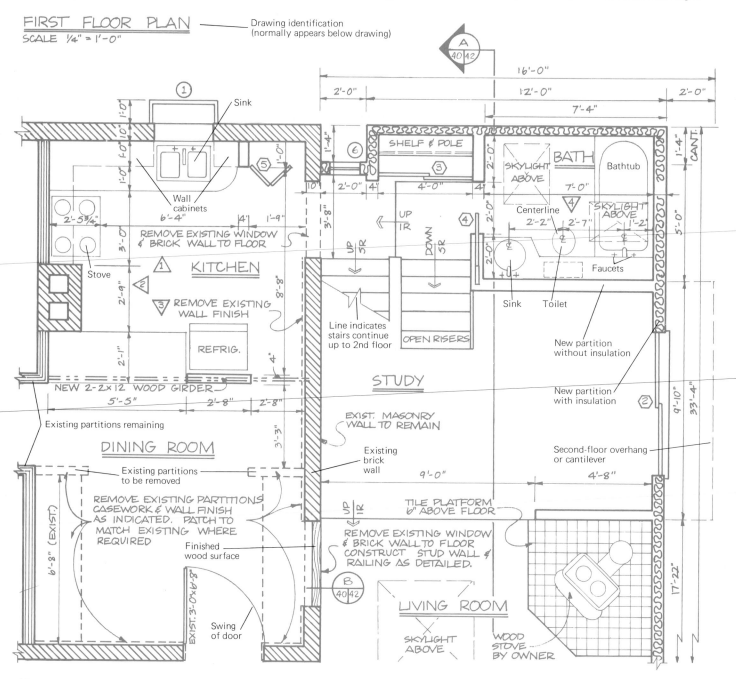

FIRST FLOOR PLAN
SCALE ¼" = 1'-0"

Drawing identification (normally appears below drawing)

40

lines show surface features, such as tile.

Broken lines in the floor plan depict elements that would not in fact be visible. For example, the closet pole (obscured by the shelf) and the toilet tank (obscured by the counter) are represented by short broken lines. Overhead elements, such as skylights, roof overhangs, and wall cabinets in the kitchen, appear as longer broken lines. (Notice that the skylights and the second-floor overhang, or cantilever, appear in broken lines on the first-floor plan, and as unbroken lines on the second-floor plan.) Elements that are to be removed by the builders, such as the partitions in this dining room, are also shown in broken lines.

A line shaped like a sharp sine curve or hook indicates that a broken element continues, but its continuation is not shown in the drawing (see, for example, the walls on the left side of the first floor in the drawing on p.40).

Doors and windows: Doors and windows are drawn as accurately as the scale allows; this can aid in identifying their type—for example, bifold, sliding, swinging. Doors on hinges are drawn in the open position, with arcs delineating their total swing. Doors and windows are usually keyed to separately prepared schedules (see p.45), which provide their complete specifications.

Even if the windows or doors are positioned so that no single horizontal slice through the building will intersect them all, they are still all shown on the floor plan.

Stairways: A stairway running down from the floor depicted in a plan is shown in its entirety because it can be seen from the plane of the building slice. A stairway running up is cut off by a line indicating that the stairway continues but that the continuation is not drawn (it is above the plane shown). Stairways are sometimes labeled "up" or "down"; this means up or down starting from the floor illustrated in the plan. The number of risers in each stairway is indicated on the drawing; for example, "5R" means there are five risers in the stairway.

Fixtures: Fixtures are depicted as they look from overhead. Those fixtures with distinguishable shapes, such as stoves, sinks, and bathtubs, are usually not labeled.

Section, elevation, and detail indicators: Symbols on the floor plan indicate the exact orientation of the building section drawings (pp.42-43), interior elevations (pp.44-45), and detail drawings (p.42). Sections are indicated by heavy broken lines that run across the floor plan (one is shown here; others also would be drawn). Letters and numbers in the circle at the end of the section line tell where the section drawing can be found. The arrow shows the direction of the section view (with respect to the section line).

The indicators for detail drawings are the same as for sections, but without the arrow.

Interior elevations are indicated by small numbered wedges. Interior elevations, numbered 1 and 4 on the first-floor plan, are shown on page 45.

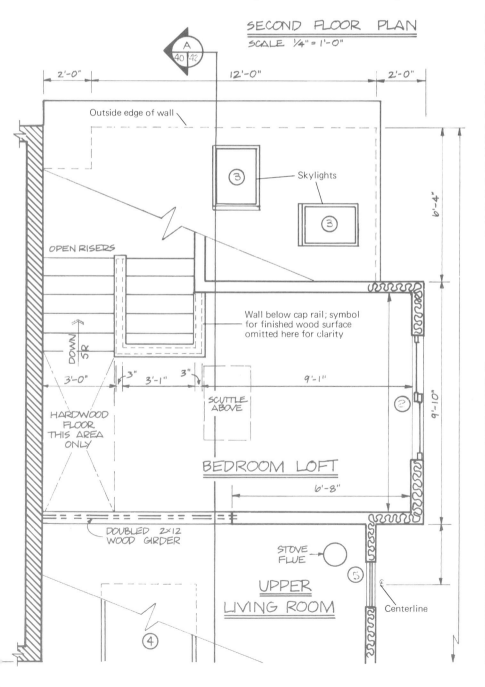

SECOND FLOOR PLAN
SCALE ¼" = 1'-0"

Outside edge of wall

Skylights

OPEN RISERS

Wall below cap rail; symbol for finished wood surface omitted here for clarity

DOWN 5R

HARDWOOD FLOOR THIS AREA ONLY

SCUTTLE ABOVE

BEDROOM LOFT

DOUBLED 2×12 WOOD GIRDER

STOVE FLUE

Centerline

UPPER LIVING ROOM

Symbols legend

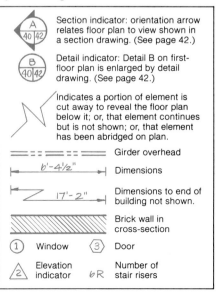

Section indicator: orientation arrow relates floor plan to view shown in a section drawing. (See page 42.)

Detail indicator: Detail B on first-floor plan is enlarged by detail drawing. (See page 42.)

Indicates a portion of element is cut away to reveal the floor plan below it; or, that element continues but is not shown; or, that element has been abridged on plan.

Girder overhead

Dimensions

Dimensions to end of building not shown.

Brick wall in cross-section

① Window   ③ Door

② Elevation indicator   6R Number of stair risers

Architectural drawings

Sections and details

A section is a view of a building through which a vertical slice has been taken. Its purpose is to illustrate major supporting structures for approval by building officials and as instruction for builders. Such structures include: the footings, foundations, girders, bearing walls, and rafters. Sections also illustrate the various layers that constitute the roof and exterior walls.

The architect chooses the locations of section cuts (slices) to illustrate as many of the supporting structures as possible. A building often has several section views   'cause the structures often vary in different parts of the building. The large section shown below is one of two the architect chose for this house and addition. The exact location of the section slice is indicated on the floor plans (pp.40–41); a symbol keys the slice to this and other drawings. As in the floor plan, the architect will often take a small amount of license in depicting an element in the section drawing though it is not in fact intersected by the section slice. For example, two skylights are illustrated in this section. Two exist in the roof, but if you look at the floor plans on pages 40–41, you will see that only one actually lies on this section cut.

Graphic symbols: Conventional architect's symbols for such elements as brick, insulation, earth, gravel, and finish lumber are employed in this section drawing. The large X's indicate wooden framing members that are cut by the section slice.

Labels and instructions: The architect writes on the drawing to identify the elements of construction and to provide instructions to builders. Some of the common abbreviations that architects use are identified in the legend.

Because too many labels and instructions can clutter a drawing beyond comprehensibility, other shortcuts are used. Labels and instructions sometimes appear only on one part of the drawing, though they apply to other parts as well. For example, the instruction "metal joint reinforcement every other course" appears only once below to save space. Sometimes information that applies to many parts of a building is separated into smaller "typical" drawings. For this house the architect supplied such drawings as a typical footing, anchoring at the exterior wall, and typical perimeter slab insulation.

Only large or unusual members of the wood frame are labeled. For example, the double 2-x-12 headers are labeled, whereas the 2-x-4 studs and plates are not labeled.

Scale: The scale of section drawings is usually at least ¼ inch per foot, but may be larger.

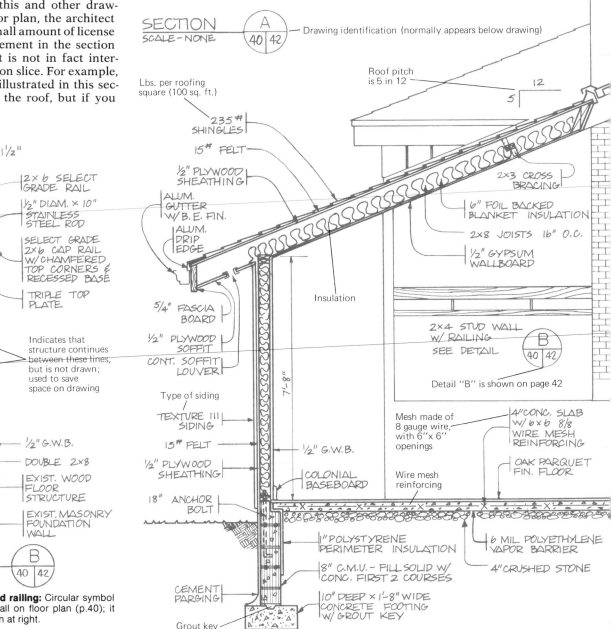

SECTION SCALE–NONE (A) 40 | 42 — Drawing identification (normally appears below drawing)

Roof pitch is 5 in 12

12
5

Lbs. per roofing square (100 sq. ft.)

235# SHINGLES
15# FELT
½" PLYWOOD SHEATHING
ALUM. GUTTER W/ B.E. FIN.
ALUM. DRIP EDGE
5/4" FASCIA BOARD
½" PLYWOOD SOFFIT
CONT. SOFFIT LOUVER

Type of siding
TEXTURE III SIDING
15# FELT
½" PLYWOOD SHEATHING
18" ANCHOR BOLT

Insulation

2×3 CROSS BRACING
6" FOIL BACKED BLANKET INSULATION
2×8 JOISTS 16" O.C.
½" GYPSUM WALLBOARD

2×4 STUD WALL W/ RAILING SEE DETAIL (B) 40 | 42

Detail "B" is shown on page 42

Mesh made of 8 gauge wire, with 6"x 6" openings

Wire mesh reinforcing

½" G.W.B.

COLONIAL BASEBOARD

4" CONC. SLAB W/ 6×6 8/8 WIRE MESH REINFORCING
OAK PARQUET FIN. FLOOR
6 MIL POLYETHYLENE VAPOR BARRIER
4" CRUSHED STONE

1" POLYSTYRENE PERIMETER INSULATION
8" C.M.U. – FILL SOLID W/ CONC. FIRST 2 COURSES
10" DEEP × 1'-8" WIDE CONCRETE FOOTING W/ GROUT KEY

CEMENT PARGING
Grout key

5 ½"
1 ½"
2×6 SELECT GRADE RAIL
½" DIAM. × 10" STAINLESS STEEL ROD
SELECT GRADE 2×6 CAP RAIL W/ CHAMFERED TOP CORNERS & RECESSED BASE
TRIPLE TOP PLATE
5 ½"
3"
½"
5'-0"
2'-2"

Indicates that structure continues between these lines, but is not drawn; used to save space on drawing

½" G.W.B.
DOUBLE 2×8
EXIST. WOOD FLOOR STRUCTURE
EXIST. MASONRY FOUNDATION WALL

DETAIL SCALE 1"=1'-0" (B) 40 | 42

Detail of stud wall and railing: Circular symbol refers to location of wall on floor plan (p.40); it also appears on section at right.

7'-8"

Detail drawings: A detail drawing is usually a section drawing of a specific element drawn in a large scale; it has a smaller scope and a larger scale than a building section. Details can take other forms, such as exploded views, or perspective views—whatever illustrates the element most clearly. Architects draw details of things that cannot be adequately illustrated on a smaller scale.

The scale for detail drawings is usually at least ½ inch per foot and frequently much larger.

The location of the element illustrated in a detail drawing is indicated on the floor plan, on a section drawing, or both. The detail drawing shown below, left, is located both on this section and on the floor plan found on pages 40–41 of this chapter.

Symbols and abbreviations

Finished lumber

Insulation

Concrete

Concrete block

Gravel

Earth

F.B —Foiled backed
O.C. –On center
O.H. –Overhang
w/B.E. FIN.–With baked enamel finish
G.W.B.–Gypsum wallboard, or "Sheetrock"
C.M.U.–Concrete masonry unit (concrete block)
BY OWNER–Contractor not responsible for purchase or installation

CONC. –Concrete
CONT. –Continuous
EXIST. –Existing

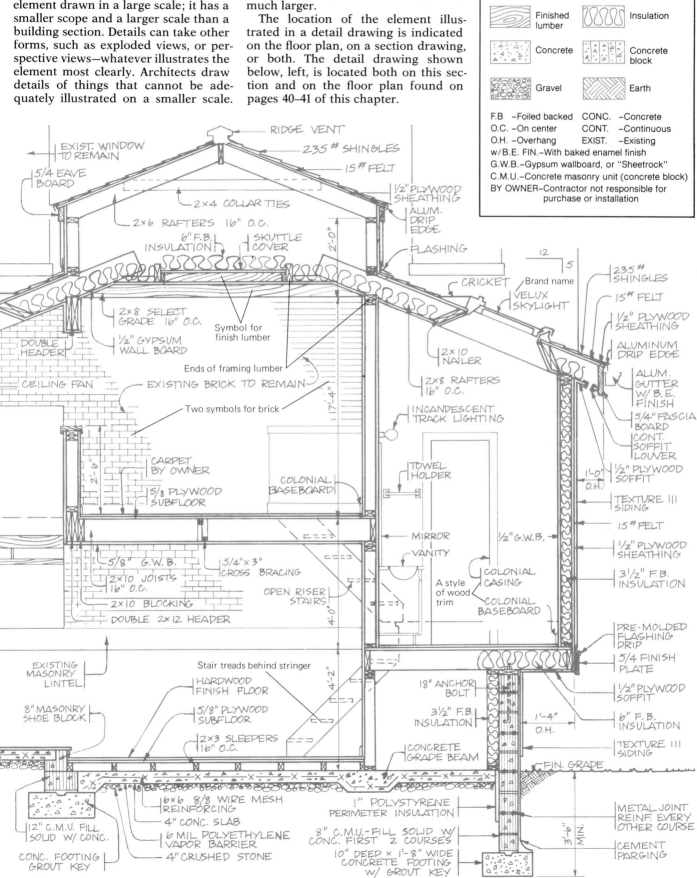

Architectural drawings

Elevations

Building elevations are drawings of the vertical surfaces of a building; they show the sizes and locations of the elements of construction that are visible when construction is complete. They differ from the building sections (see pp.42–43) whose function is to show cutaway views of structural elements—that is, to show how things are put together rather than how they look when they are assembled. There are two types of elevations: views from the outside of the building, called exterior elevations, and views from the inside, called interior elevations.

Exterior elevations: Exterior elevations are views of the outside of a building. Each view is taken along a line of sight that is perpendicular to the wall it depicts (thus it is an orthographic view; see p.38). A building normally has four exterior elevations, one for each wall. But an addition will often have only three elevations because one of its

sides lies unseen against an adjoining wall of the existing building.

Exterior elevations illustrate the wall covering, the sizes and types of doors and windows in the walls, the roof pitch, the flashings, moldings, and any other exterior finishing details, and usually the overall vertical dimensions of the house. Each elevation is identified by the direction it faces. Below is the northwest elevation of the house and addition covered on page 241 and ensuing pages (see also diagram, p.38). The architect's plans usually include all of the exterior elevations.

The scale of exterior elevations is usually ¼ inch per foot, or ½ inch per foot or larger if necessary to clearly illustrate details. The scale is indicated beneath or beside the elevation identification. (The ⅜ inch per foot scale is used here because of the size of the page; it is irregular.) The broken line demarks the foundation; this is often

omitted from elevations. The two small perpendicular lines above portions of the roof indicate the roof pitch; here it is 5 in 12—the roof rises 5 inches for every 12 inches it runs horizontally. (This is a 37.5° slope, but pitch is always expressed as a ratio of vertical rise per foot of horizontal run.)

Because the drawing is concerned mostly with the new addition, little detail is shown on the existing house. The distinction between the two is accentuated by the heavy line used by the architect to outline the addition.

Interior elevations: Interior elevations are views of areas of walls taken from the inside of the building. They are used to illustrate the locations and heights of fixtures that are built-in, such as wall cabinets, countertops, and plumbing and electrical fixtures. They also indicate interior surface finishes. Interior elevations of the kitchen and bathroom are shown on these pages.

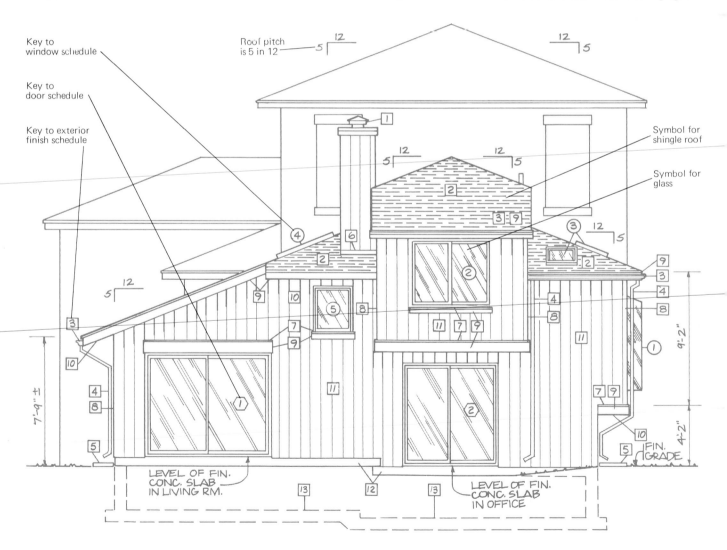

NORTHWEST ELEVATION
SCALE 3/8" = 1'-0"

Interior elevations are identified by numbered arrows or wedges; a similarly numbered sign on the floor plan (see pp.40–41) points to the wall pictured in each elevation.

The scale of interior elevations is usually ½ inch per foot; it is indicated beneath the drawing. "Scale—none" means the scale is extremely irregular, not a multiple of ¼ inch.

Schedules: Regardless of how large the scale of an elevations drawing is, some important information usually cannot practicably be drawn. Because of this, architects key parts of their drawings to lists, called schedules, which describe undrawable details. Schedules also provide information about items that are drawn but require further specification, such as siding, doors, windows, and fixtures, and even such equipment as air-conditioning.

Other schedules provide a list of the major prefabricated components in-stalled in a building. Finish schedules specify finishing materials and techniques for the different interior and exterior surfaces. When schedules are comprehensive (in simple jobs they often are not) they are valuable aids in ordering materials and estimating costs (see p.48); even if you are building from your own drawings, it is good to make up schedules.

Four schedules pertaining to the interior and exterior elevations illustrated on these two pages (as well as to the other plans in this chapter) are shown here. They are not complete; other materials not listed will be included in the finish of the addition; the schedules have been abbreviated for purposes of clarity.

Architects often include more information in their schedules, such as makes and model numbers for windows, doors, and plumbing and electrical fixtures (and the quantity of each); identification of the drawing on which the schedule item is keyed (they will not all appear on the elevations); and such comments as "installed as per manufacturer's instructions."

EXTERIOR FINISH SCHEDULE

ITEM	DESCRIPTION
1	CHIMNEY FLUE & CAP AS PER MFR'S. SPEC.
2	235 # ASPHALT SHINGLES - BLACK BY BYRD
3	ALUMINUM GUTTER W/B.E.FIN. BY REYNOLDS
4	ALUMINUM LEADER W/B.E. FIN BY REYNOLDS
5	PRE-CAST CONCRETE SPLASH PAD
6	FLASHING
7	PRE-MOLDED FLASHING DRIP
8	PRE-MOLDED CORNER BEAD
9	5/4" RAKE, EAVE, OR FASCIA BOARD- STAINED
10	½" PLYWOOD SOFFIT
11	T- III SIDING
12	CEMENT PARGING
13	10" CONCRETE FOOTING

WINDOW SCHEDULE

WINDOW	SIZE	DESCRIPTION
1	3'-0"x4'-0"x1'-0"	GREENHOUSE WINDOW BOX
2	4'-11½"x 4'-11"	ALUMINUM SLIDER
3	21 5/8"x 27½"	SKYLIGHT BY VELUX
4	44 7/8"x 46½"	SKYLIGHT BY VELUX
5	2'-0"x 3'-0"	FIXED GLASS
6	1'-6"x 6'-0"	FIXED GLASS

DOOR SCHEDULE

DOOR	SIZE	DESCRIPTION
1	8'-0"x 6'-9"	ALUMINUM SLIDING
2	6'-0"x 6'-9"	ALUMINUM SLIDING
3	4'-0"x 6'-8"	BY PASSING HOLLOW CORE
4	2'-0"x 6'-8"	POCKET HOLLOW CORE
5	1'-9"x 6'-0"	BI- FOLD LOUVERED

ROOM FINISH SCHEDULE

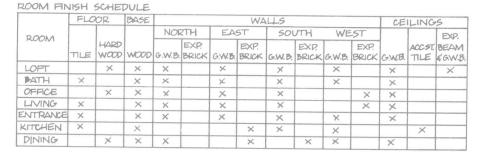

| ROOM | FLOOR | | BASE | WALLS | | | | | | | | CEILINGS | |
| | TILE | HARD WOOD | WOOD | NORTH | | EAST | | SOUTH | | WEST | | | |
				G.W.B.	EXP. BRICK	G.W.B.	EXP. BRICK	G.W.B.	EXP. BRICK	G.W.B.	EXP. BRICK	G.W.B.	ACCST. TILE	EXP. BEAM & G.W.B.
LOFT		×	×	×		×		×		×		×		×
BATH	×		×	×		×		×		×		×		
OFFICE		×	×	×		×		×			×	×		
LIVING	×		×	×		×		×			×	×		
ENTRANCE	×		×	×		×		×		×		×		
KITCHEN	×		×			×		×		×			×	
DINING		×	×	×		×		×		×		×		

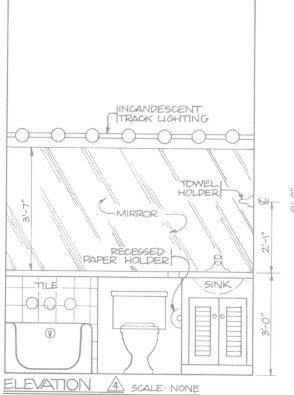

ELEVATION ④ SCALE- NONE

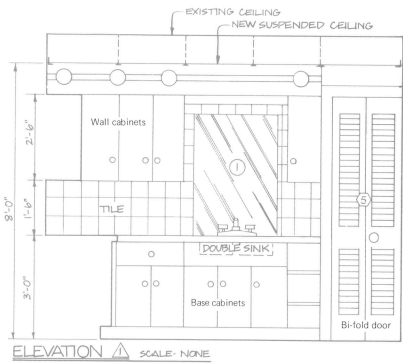

ELEVATION ① SCALE- NONE

These interior elevations of the bathroom and kitchen show the location and heights of the major built-in elements, and the type of surface finish. The wedges numbered 4 and 1 on the floor plan, pages 40–41, point to the walls pictured above.

Architectural drawings

Special purpose plans

Special purpose plans are drawings architects use to illustrate complete systems that are integral to a building. Sometimes these drawings are incorporated into one of the other plans (for example, the electrical system sometimes is depicted in the floor plan).

The electrical plan, foundation plan, and roof framing plan of the house and addition covered on page 241 and following are in part shown here. Other common special purpose plans are the floor framing plan, the heating system plan, and the plumbing schematic. Scale for special purpose plans is usually ⅛ or ¼ inch per foot, though it is frequently irregular ("scale—none").

Drawings of mechanical systems (heating, plumbing, electrical) are usually accompanied by legends that explain the symbols; though many symbols have become established by convention, architects usually will not risk misinterpretation.

Electrical symbols

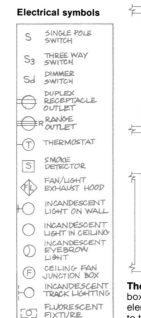

S	SINGLE POLE SWITCH
S₃	THREE WAY SWITCH
Sd	DIMMER SWITCH
	DUPLEX RECEPTACLE OUTLET
R	RANGE OUTLET
T	THERMOSTAT
S	SMOKE DETECTOR
FL	FAN/LIGHT EXHAUST HOOD
	INCANDESCENT LIGHT ON WALL
	INCANDESCENT LIGHT IN CEILING
	INCANDESCENT EYEBROW LIGHT
F	CEILING FAN JUNCTION BOX
	INCANDESCENT TRACK LIGHTING
	FLUORESCENT FIXTURE

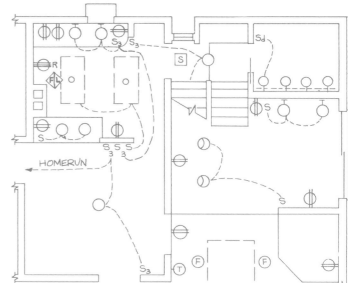

The electrical plan shows the electrician where to install such things as boxes for lights, outlets, and switches; wiring connecting these and other elements; special capacity for ranges and other appliances; and the lines back to the fuse box. Legend at left explains the symbols.

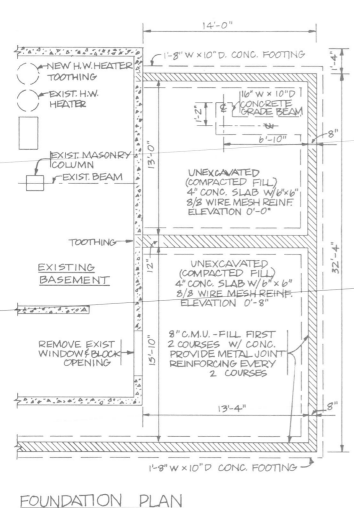

FOUNDATION PLAN
SCALE ⅛" = 1'-0"

Foundation plan gives excavator and mason instructions for foundation and footings. Water heaters are included here only to obviate another drawing. Like the other plans on this page, this shows only part of the house; true architect's plans cover the entire area of planned construction.

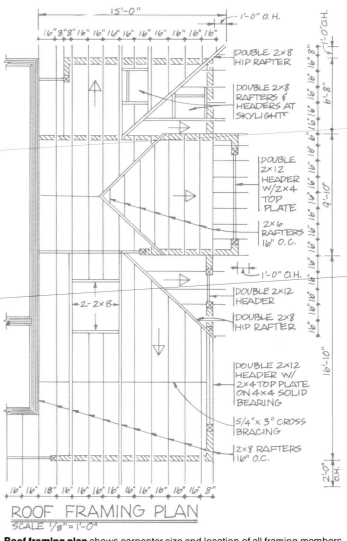

ROOF FRAMING PLAN
SCALE ⅛" = 1'-0"

Roof framing plan shows carpenter size and location of all framing members. Arrows indicate where roof slopes downward. From this plan carpenter determines final measurements, which are worked out at the building site. Floor and wall framing plans are similar.

Drawing your own plans

If you intend to do your own drawings for an alteration or an addition to an existing building, first decide exactly what you want to achieve by your construction. What kind of space do you need? For what use? What characteristics must it have—size, shape, accesses, light, sound properties, storage, special fixtures, appliances, etc.?

It is a good idea to sketch rough plans for a project even if you intend to hire an architect. The drawing process can give you a better understanding of your ideas and help you to convey them to the architect.

Materials: A few basic materials should be used for architectural drawings. Choose tracing paper with a blue line grid, preferably with ¼-inch squares. Tracing paper facilitates the transfer of information from one drawing to another. Also, your final drawings must be on tracing paper to be blueprinted (copied). In addition you should have a roll of tracing paper that is thinner, and thus easier to see through, which you can put over other drawings to make quick sketches.

Hard pencils are always preferable to soft ones because they do not smudge as easily and retain a fine point longer. You will also need a good pencil sharpener. Instead of ordinary rulers, most architects use scales, which are triangular rulers that can be rotated to any of six differently scaled straight edges.

Templates are drawing aids—stencil-like pieces of plastic with small cutout patterns used to draw various types of regular lines and shapes. Available in different scales—¼ and ⅛ inch are the most common—they allow for quick, easy tracing of door swings, roof pitches, circles of different diameters, and kitchen and bathroom fixtures. Some include an edge for tracing stair treads, and some have a scale to facilitate drawing framing diagrams and estimating framing materials.

Good erasers are essential. Eraser shields, thin pieces of metal with cutout areas, allow you to mask a drawing and erase small portions of it without disturbing the rest.

A drafting board usually has a metal edge to guide the movement of a T-square in drawing horizontal lines perpendicular to true vertical as well as parallel lines. A right triangle moved along the arm of the T-square can be used to draw vertical lines perpendicular to true horizontal, and so on. A normal desk surface is adequate, but requires special effort to keep lines accurate. Use masking tape to secure the paper to your drawing surface. A tape measure is used to take measurements on the existing building; these mea-

Materials

Drawing board
T-square
30° –60° –90° triangle
45° triangle
Adjustable triangle
Tape measure
Architect's scale
House plan template
Pencils
Pencil sharpener
Eraser
Erasing shield
Masking tape
Tracing paper (plain)
Tracing paper with blue line grid

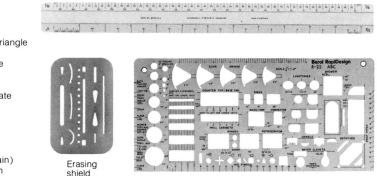

Erasing shield

House plan template—¼″ scale

---

surements are then written in the corresponding positions on the plan.

Drawing an existing building: Before making any drawings of additions or alterations, you should first draw the existing structure, or that part of it that bears on the projected new work. Draw a floor plan (see pp.40–41) and also a section (pp.42–43). It is crucial to determine in the section drawing how the structure is supported; to draw an accurate section you should examine posts, girders, first-floor joists, etc., in the basement; look at the attic framing elements, removing electrical fixtures, and so on, if necessary, to determine the location and orientation of the supporting structures. Also draw all the necessary elevations (pp.44–45). Make these drawings as accurate as possible, or you may find that your new construction and the existing building do not fit.

Drawing the alteration or addition: There is no simple formula for designing an alteration or addition. Look over the other chapters in this book and at architectural reference books and magazines to get an idea of what is involved in designing and building new spaces.

Consider these factors: The new space must fit the use it is intended for. You might want to cut paper templates of your furniture (in scale) to see how they fit in the new space. Think about accesses to the space, and anticipate how people will move through it. What will the views from windows be like? Check the availability and exact dimensions of pre-constructed elements (such as windows and pre-hung doors) before incorporating them into your plans. The new space must be structurally consistent with the existing building. Keep in mind the location of such elements as underground pipes, wires, septic systems, and oil tanks. If the work requires the use of heavy equipment, the site must be accessible. All work must adhere to zoning and building regulations.

The first steps: If you are redesigning an existing space, lay a piece of light tracing paper over the existing floor

plan, and start drawing your renovation. After many rough trials, the plan will begin to take shape. Collect, digest, and simplify the material into one floor plan. You can use this drawing to calculate the new surface area in square feet; by consulting a local expert you can get a rough cost estimate for your project, based on current average construction costs per square foot of renovation or new construction.

After the floor plan is complete, draw all of the exterior elevations of both the new space and existing building. This will allow you to ensure that the architectural style (for example, roof pitch, window heights, surface covering) of an addition blends with the house.

Draw a section of the new space. This will help you to plan adequate support for all elements of the space.

Draw interior elevations of kitchens and bathrooms. If you are not experienced at constructing a wood frame, it is a good idea to draw a complete framing plan. (Framing is covered in several chapters of this book, including *Building codes*, pp.21–37, *Interior bearing walls*, pp.76–85, and *Non-bearing partitions*, pp.86–87.) This will give you a better idea of what is involved in the work, and also a more accurate idea of the necessary materials. Similarly, you should draw details of elements you are not familiar with; the drawing will make the construction easier. It is always easier to erase and redraw than to pull apart and rebuild. Create materials schedules (p.45) as detailed as possible, to use when ordering materials.

When you have finished all of the drawings, redraw them on final pages, with their schedules, labels, directions, and keys, all in a logical arrangement. Take the finals to a blueprinter for copies (for yourself, the zoning department, the building department, the plumber, electrician, etc.). Remember that blueprints can only be made from tracing paper; drawings on other types of paper must be copied by a more expensive photographic process.

Ordering materials and estimating costs

A painstaking task

From your completed plans (see pp.38–47) you can make a list of all the materials you will need for your job. A materials cost estimate can be reached by taking this list and increasing it by a fudge factor (say, 20 percent) to cover waste (both necessary and accidental), and then submitting it to several local suppliers for price quotes. To this add the cost of labor and subcontractors.

Compile the list in the order of the actual construction; this reduces the chances of omitting anything. It also makes clearer at which points you will require the aid of laborers and subcontractors. You can get an accurate materials list from your plans with proper diligence. Getting accurate estimates for labor costs is always more difficult.

Before construction begins: Some costs are incurred before work starts. These include the price of demolition of structures or parts of structures that must be removed; garbage removal from the site; protection of the living area from dirt; protection of passersby from dangers of construction; building and electrical permits; tool rental; interest on a bank loan (see *Financing a home improvement*, p.20); insurance (this may be required if you have a bank loan); architect's fee (which can run from 7 to 15 percent of the job); soil testing; and consultants fees. Anticipate additional labor costs if the site is not accessible to trucks for normal delivery of materials, or to heavy equipment for work. Any landscaping or site preparation should be considered.

Excavation: Any large excavation work should be done by a subcontractor. The size of the excavation is determined by the volume of earth removed, measured in cubic yards. (To calculate an irregular volume in cubic yards, multiply the width by the length by the depth of the excavation, in feet, and divide the product by 27. Present this number to an excavator for an estimate.) You can rent tools to do a small job yourself. You may also have to rent a pump to keep the excavation dry.

Foundation: For large jobs, it is always best to contract with a mason to handle excavation forms and pouring of foundations and footings, or at least to buy concrete from a cement company and have it poured directly from the truck into your pre-built forms. You can rent formwork for pouring concrete; it is measured in square feet. You need form ties, anchor bolts, and reinforcing rods and/or mesh.

If you want to prepare your own concrete you may have to rent a mixer; even if you mix it by hand you will need a wheelbarrow, hoe, and other tools. Determine the amount of concrete for the foundation, in cubic yards, from the volume of the formwork; add the volume of the foundation floor. Gravel for the concrete is measured by the ton.

For masonry work, figure the number of blocks or bricks needed by multiplying the number of blocks per course by the number of courses. Estimate the amount of mortar you will need. For example, for every 100 common stretcher blocks (8 x 8 x 16 inches each), you will need about 2½ 70-pound bags of mortar and 667 pounds of sand. Estimate about 6.16 bricks per square foot for a 4-inch-thick course. Rough stone is measured by the cubic foot.

The vapor barrier and cement parging (several layers) are estimated in square feet. Building paper is sold in rolls of 500 square feet each.

Drainage pipe is sold by the linear foot. Any backfill needed for the foundation is measured in cubic yards.

Framing: Unless you are experienced at framing, use a complete framing diagram to estimate and order materials. You can get an approximation of the number of studs (spaced 16 inches o.c.) by multiplying the wall's length, in feet, by 0.8; add three studs per corner.

Determine the sizes of such large members as the joists, rafters, and headers; remember that some are doubled. Write down all of the framing members in one list, arranged by size and linear feet. Lumber is sold in lengths ranging from 8 feet to 16 feet, in 2 foot increments. Longer sizes may have to be specially ordered, and cost extra. Order the sizes that require the least labor and cause the least waste.

Calculate the total surface area of the building or addition, in square feet, for sheathing. If you use 1-x-8 boards, figure on 20 percent waste. If you use plywood, lay a 4-x-8-foot template (in scale) over your plans. This will show how the pieces fit together; you can see the size and shape of pieces cut away for openings, and determine if they can be used elsewhere. Your estimate should be closer than with boards. This presents a typical dilemma, which should be resolved in the planning stage: plywood is generally more expensive than boarding, but the estimate can be more accurate. Plywood requires far less time to install, but unlike boarding, it is almost impossible to install without help.

Subflooring is figured similarly to sheathing.

Board feet: Sometimes a lumberyard will only give an estimate if wood is measured in units called board feet. A board foot is the amount of wood in a board 1 x 12 x 12 inches. The formula is: dimensions of the board in inches x length of the board in feet ÷ 12. For example, a 2 x 4 that is 1 foot long is ⅔ of a board foot. A 2 x 6 that is 2 feet long is 2 board feet. A 2 x 4 that is 6 feet long is 4 board feet; a 2 x 8 of the same length is 8 board feet.

Exterior covering: To order roof covering, use the area figure you calculated for the roof sheathing. Roofing is usually sold in units called roofing squares, each sufficient to cover 100 square feet of roof area. Figure about 5 to 20 percent waste for shingles, depending on how many edges the roof has. Metal drip edge is sold in 10 foot lengths. Gutters and flashing are sold in linear feet; choose the stock size that will result in the least waste. Building paper is sold in rolls, each 250 square feet; because of overlapping, figure 200 square feet per roll.

When you order windows and doors, check to see if jambs (and hinges and stops for doors) are included; if they are not, they must be figured separately.

Molding for trimming around doors, windows, gables, and eaves, is measured in linear feet. Allow 20 percent for waste. Remember boards or plywood for soffits and the various vents (p.29). Order caulking. Figure paints, stains, and preservative by the area of coverage, in square feet.

Mechanical systems: Determine the number of outlets, switches, and light boxes you will need. Remember other devices, such as door bells, thermostats, and heating units. Estimate the necessary length of wiring for all new branch circuits. Hookups for large appliances require special outlets (and additional labor, if you hire an electrician). Include the cost of installing a fuse box or circuit breaker panel.

Plumbers usually provide their own materials; it is understood that part of their profit derives from your purchase of their materials. If you buy the supplies yourself, many plumbers will not take the job. Check ahead.

Interior covering and finish: Base your estimate for insulation of the area on the figure you calculated for sheathing. Interior wall covering is figured in square feet (the length of the wall times its height, minus the area of the openings for doors and windows). As with sheathing, the use of a paper template on the plans can make the estimate more accurate. If you are using gypsum wallboard, include the cost of tape, compound, and corner bead. Include accessories for other surfaces. For example, the suspended ceilings require metal grids; some wood panels require special trim; some floors require special adhesives and fasteners; wood floors must be sanded, stained, varnished.

Interior renovations

The color photographs that introduce this section are a collection of renovations made by homeowners and apartment-dwellers across the country. Do not expect the glamorized studio pictures that you usually see in books and magazines —projects you could not afford to do yourself, or which are not suited to your lifestyle. Kitchen, bathroom, attic, and basement renovations, solutions to storage and shelf-space problems, and a great deal more, are shown here.

contents

Kitchens

A rustic look, or gleaming modern

A kitchen renovation can be as simple as installing new appliances or new cabinets in an existing space, or as complex as building a new room. How you renovate depends on your needs and tastes. Kitchens run the gamut from rustic to gleaming modern.

According to your particular needs, you will want to create a kitchen that is efficient, probably one that minimizes walking distances between appliances and countertops, yet has large enough work areas and well-organized storage space. The kitchen should be comfortable and esthetically pleasing to you.

To take advantage of the unique interior space of the top floor of a San Francisco Victorian townhouse (top, left), the old ceiling was removed to reveal the roof beams; the ceiling now peaks to 18 feet. Modern appliances were installed and custom-built cabinets provide storage and work space. To add a glass-enclosed eating area to a ground-floor kitchen (above, right), a load-bearing wall was removed (pp.76–85; 276–283) and a cross beam, a 2 x 10, was installed on top of the new opening; the eating area, built onto an existing patio that now forms the floor, has a rear wall of solid glass and sliding glass doors on either side.

To express a warm and rustic feeling in a modern kitchen (right) ready-made oak cabinets were combined with a ceiling of Eastern white pine featuring exposed beams.

Existing features in the older kitchens at right presented problems that were solved by imaginative design.

The large arcade (near right) in a turn-of-the-century kitchen, housed a large coal stove. In modernizing the kitchen, wall ovens and a cooktop were combined with prefabricated cabinets to fill the unusual volume. The inside of the arcade was tiled for easy cleaning and the Formica surrounding the cooktop was extended to form a counter for eating. When the small kitchen (far right) was renovated, the old flue was used with a new stove and new hood. The old brick chimney in the corner was covered over with paneling to form a diagonal wall. The stove was placed against this wall, a dishwasher was installed, and the old cabinets were repositioned for maximum counter space. Open shelves were built for additional storage space.

Brammer Manufacturing Company

David Arky/Designed by Jose A. Pulido

Manufacturer's cabinets are available in many styles and offer a uniform, custom-made appearance (top left photo). A kitchen in a 1925 suburban house was redone with a selection of such cabinets (top right); in the process, a seldom used back stairway was removed to make room for the refrigerator. New cabinets and appliances, conveniently arranged on three walls, form a large U providing ample work space. The countertop is Formica and the floor is covered with sheet vinyl. The result is a simple, varied, informal look.

Allmilmö Corporation

Kemper/Tappan

A new, more efficient kitchen does not have to involve structural changes. A kitchen can be renovated, modernized, or simply changed in style by installing in the existing space prefabricated cabinets designed by manufacturers. If you want to create a gleaming modern kitchen, such as the one pictured above, or a rustic kitchen, you can choose from a wide variety of kitchen cabinets, materials for countertops, and flooring materials. The choice depends on the style you prefer, and how maintenance-free you want the room to be. You can install the cabinets, countertop, and flooring yourself or have the job done at a much greater cost by professionals.

Space-saving storage devices and organizers provide a place for everything. The manufacturer's cabinetry shown is, clockwise from the top right, a narrow cabinet designed to store trays, drawer dividers to organize flatware and cooking utensils, shallow hinged cabinets for canned goods, and a Lazy Susan for spices and other condiments.

Kitchens

Owner-designed and renovated spaces

David Arky / Designed by David Trooper

This cheerful suburban kitchen belies its origin as a dark, cramped room. The space was gutted and the back wall was extended 3 ft. while the ceiling was brought down from 8½ to 7½ ft. and fitted with down lighting. Sheetrock was applied over the old plaster walls, and appliances were arranged for maximum efficiency; the stove was placed against the back wall, where it vents directly to the outside.

To brighten the room, a larger window was installed and additional down lights were positioned in the soffit above the countertop work area. Custom-built cabinets were finished by the owner to match the frames of the window and door. A butcher block countertop has a backsplash of Portuguese tiles.

Philip MacMillan James / Courtesy of HOME

Stephen Marley / Designed by Sarah Lee Roberts, ASID

In this renovation, the owners were restricted in terms of horizontal space. Thus they went upward—not outward—to achieve a new sense of light and spaciousness in what had been a cramped, dark kitchen. The room was gutted and the ceiling removed, opening up the attic crawlspace; this raised the kitchen ceiling to the height of the roof above—some 11 ft. A large skylight was then cut into the roof over the work area, flooding the entire kitchen with light.

What had been a narrow galley kitchen in a 55-year-old tract house was given a new look, and a new sense of openness, largely through the elimination of old walls. Formerly compartmentalized into small rooms, the entire volume of entry hall, eating nook and kitchen now flow freely as the result of the use of partial walls at floor and ceiling levels; spaces are still defined, but communicate. Like the tongue-and-groove ceiling, cabinets and parquet were installed by professionals. Note that the direction of the tongue and groove emphasizes the original galley sweep of the renovated space.

Randall Fleming, photographer & architect / Built by H.L. Falk, Inc.

Lilo Raymond / Designed by Felix Arbeo

Owner-designed cabinetry provides a light rustic motif for this newly built kitchen in what were formerly maid's quarters in a rambling 1920s house. The cabinet doors have solid oak frames, with panels of oak veneer. The veneer was rift cut to produce a vertical grain, giving a suggestion of height to the ceiling. Note the enclosure of the window by the cabinets on the wall at left, a unique touch. The old Douglas fir tongue-and-groove subfloor was exposed, sanded and stained, and covered with islands of carpet. Hanging lamps accent an airy, Early American atmosphere.

This kitchen was created in an urban industrial loft renovated as a residence. The work island, with a sink, dishwasher, and storage drawers, defines the kitchen area with respect to the large, open space surrounding it. (For a view of the entire loft, see p.322.) A tiled archway backs a professional range beyond the island.

© 1978 Robert Perron / Designed by Myles Weintraub

When a cabin in the woods was renovated for year-round use, three rooms were gutted to create space for a large eat-in kitchen. To accentuate the cabin's rough-hewn flavor, stock cabinets of solid oak and a dishwasher in matching oak veneer were chosen; countertop and backsplash were fashioned of maple butcher block. Across the kitchen, glass sliding doors lead to a deck. Additional light enters the kitchen through the newly installed large windows.

A professional restaurateur designed this roomy home kitchen in what had been an extra bedroom. The old kitchen became an enlarged hallway and a pantry. The new kitchen has room for restaurant equipment, and ample space for preparing meals on the counter next to the sink and on the butcher block-topped center island. To provide natural light and to increase the work space, a bay window was installed. Small electrical appliances are kept on the window ledge and extra outlets were installed on the wall below the window.

© 1979 Karen Bussolini / Designed by Eric Epstein of Gilvarg-Epstein Design

53

Bathrooms

Modernizing for efficiency or a sense of luxury

Bathrooms are the second most popular rooms (after kitchens) for remodeling, and for a number of good reasons.

Bathrooms often do not function well. The fixtures do not work well together. Many bathrooms lack storage space. The usual medicine chest and the occasional vanity do not provide sufficient space for towels, toiletries, cleaning materials. Bathrooms wear out. Constant use and high humidity take their toll of the materials used.

Many bathrooms are not luxurious so they are renovated to create a sybaritic retreat in what was just a dingy room.

The photographs on these two pages show some renovated bathrooms and some newly added bathrooms.

This small bathroom under the peak of the roof of a Victorian house was enlarged by raising the roof 2 ft. and extending a small back dormer. A skylight was installed in the sloping back wall, a new shower was added, insulation was increased, and the original tub was repositioned. An old sink salvaged from a barber shop was installed under the existing front window. The toilet, to the right of the sink, remained in its original position. (The step-by-step wallpapering process is shown in photographs on pp.103 to 105.)

© 1980 Karen Bussolini / Designed by Eric Chase

Hedrich-Blessing / Designed by Joseph E. Kinnebrew IV

© 1979 Robert Perron / Designed by Habitat, Inc. South Deerfield, Mass.

Lilo Ra

This bathroom off a master bedroom was created with recycled bathroom fixtures and cedar paneling. The vitreous china sink with its oversized bowl and large pedestal has a laboratory faucet. The extra-long, claw-footed tub, a rare find, was installed on a step so the bather could enjoy the view. The shower stall, enclosed in cedar, has a shower curtain inside the louvered door.

On the second floor of a kit house, the bathroom (left) is located under a sloping ceiling of cedar roof decking. The kit uses standard post-and-beam construction—it is flexible and can be adapted to the owner's needs. Here, a skylight was strategically placed to provide light for the enclosed bathtub as well as for the rest of the room.

A modular fiberglass bathtub and shower (above) is a convenient fixture to use if you are building a new bath, because it is quicker to install than a conventional tub surrounded by tile. Modular tubs and showers come in single units or in pre-fitted sections that can be installed over drywall or tile.

The limited amount of space in this bathroom inspired the owner to build the storage vanity that surrounds the molded synthetic Corian countertop and sink. The vanity is made of birch plywood that was kerfed so it would curve to fit the countertop. The curve was necessary because the door opens into the room.

For added privacy, the toilet is separated from the sink by a wallboard partition. A stackable washer and dryer are located on the wall to the right of the tub.

To avoid the expense of moving large drain pipes, this bathroom was designed on two levels. The first level containing the sink is one step up from the floor of the hall immediately outside. A second level containing the toilet and bathtub was created to accommodate an upturn in the pipe leading to the toilet. The floor, the walls surrounding the bathtub, and the top of the vanity are all covered with the same square ceramic tile for a unified look.

To bring daylight into a bathroom built in one corner of a bedroom, a panel of translucent glass was installed in one wall and across the ceiling, which is lower than the bedroom ceiling. Shelves in the glass wall hold toiletries. The shower area, which takes up half the bathroom, has a slightly lower floor that slopes toward the center drain. The shower is separated from the toilet and sink by a ceramic-tile-covered partition. The walls and floor are covered in the same ceramic tile.

An attic was renovated to make a new master bedroom, a study, and a bathroom between the two rooms. The renovation entailed installing skylights to take advantage of the southern exposure and increasing the insulation: fiberglass, and 1-in. thick solid board insulation. The chimneys in the center, one for the furnace and the other for the fireplace, were painted white.

In the new bathroom, the sunken tub was located directly above the tub in the bathroom below to save on plumbing costs. The tub was sunk into the floor so that a person could stand up in the shower. The sink is enclosed in a Masonite vanity covered with Formica.

Shelving and storage

Imaginative solutions to a common problem

Some people consider ample storage space an amenity while others view it as an absolute necessity. But most people when they buy a house or rent an apartment look at the closets first. If you yearn for shelving for stereo equipment, space to hang out-of-season clothes, a display cabinet for dishes, or a place for children's toys, you can build to suit your special needs.

The photographs on these two pages show a variety of storage units, some entirely custom-made and others built around stock cabinets. Each provides much storage space in small areas.

Shelves for storing books, records, and treasured mementos are necessary in a house (above, left) and in an apartment (above, right). In the house, 1-ft.-deep oak shelves were built into one wall and right across the back of the bedroom door, which is on wheels so it can be opened easily.

In the apartment, plywood shelves and metal supports cover an entire wall. These shelves are 1¼-in. birch plywood, with a veneer strip glued to each edge. Twice the number of necessary supports were used—only half are structural, having been nailed into studs—creating a vertical counterpoint to the long horizontal shelves.

This kitchen storage wall was built to hold cookbooks, serving dishes, and other items not used every day. The open area in the center of the cabinet has a pull-out desk top and a wall telephone. The cabinet is made of solid oak that has been painted white. The doors are white oak with a natural stain. The top doors have center panels of tinted glass.

In a renovated loft, floor-to-ceiling kitchen shelving was built of 1⅛-in. birch veneer plywood. A staircase of 1⅛-in. solid birch was built to provide access to the topmost shelves. Both stairs and shelves are finished with clear lacquer. Half of the shelves have sliding glass doors to protect the dishes while the other half have been left open.

Although building a staircase just for shelving might not be practical, building shelves along an existing staircase can provide storage space in what otherwise would be an unused area.

56

Norman McGrath / Designed by Noel Jeffrey

David Arky / Designed by David Trooper

A large unit housing two beds, two desks, and lots of bookshelves divides a bedroom into semiprivate areas for two young boys. The unit (seen here from one side) is made of birch plywood that has been finished with clear lacquer in some places and painted with high-gloss enamel in others. The sliding round panel above the bed covers a window-like opening. The standard library ladder, cut down to a desired size, is on wheels and runs on a track.

A small home office was created under the eaves in a second-floor room of a 1925 house. Shelves designed around a metal file cabinet were built into the sloping wall. The shelves surrounding the file cabinet are enclosed in standard louvered doors painted white.

© 1979 Robert Perron / Designed by Sunshine Design

Norman McGrath / Designed by Leonard Colchamiro

The solution to a storage problem in a small, closet-less bedroom was to build a storage unit of birch plywood. There is an area for hanging clothes behind the full-length curved doors, and there are shelves above the clothes closet and in the smaller section to the left. Instead of handles, cut-outs were made in the doors.

For ample storage in a master bedroom, one entire wall was designed to store diverse items while still presenting a unified look. The unit is made of Sheetrock over metal studs and encloses a mirror and oak chests of drawers; it has Formica-topped shelves, and was built to the owner's specifications. A similar unit could be designed to fit around standard stock cabinets or bookcases.

Attics

New rooms with unique lines

An attic is often used as a large closet, but all it takes to make it a functioning room is a light source and insulation.

An attic renovation can include raising the roof or adding a dormer (see pp.284–291). An attic remodeling can also involve cutting windows in the gable end of the roof to bring light into a cozy room. Whether the roof line is original or raised, the angles of rafters, gables, hips, eaves, and the ceiling make an attic room unique, as shown by a variety of renovations in the photographs on these two pages. (See also *Finishing attics*, pp.162–169.)

The gable end of an attic (left) was opened up and a deck was added to the exterior atop an existing porch. French doors and windows were put in first, and then triangles of glass were cut to fit remaining space. The new master bedroom has fiberglass insulation and Sheetrock walls.

The attic of an 1820 farmhouse (above) has one large fixed window and three awning windows in the gable end. Window treatment is the same in other half of gable end. Ceiling and walls are covered with textured plywood.

A master bedroom and bath, whose anteroom is accessible through an irregular archway, were created in the attic of a turn-of-the-century farmhouse. The ceiling was temporarily removed and insulation was added under the roof; walls were covered with salvaged redwood.

The attic in a Victorian house (above) was made into a sitting room. Insulation was added to the ceiling, and walls and ceiling were covered with rough-cut Douglas fir. Custom-built bookcases surround the original chimney.

All photographs on this page show the conversion of a large attic (below) in a 1906 house, into a studio/guest apartment (right). The main room has the original window in the gable end plus a new skylight. The walls are Sheetrock except for the end wall of oak flooring. The collar beam was enclosed with a plywood box large enough for a fluorescent light fixture. For how-to photographs of attic, see pages 162–169.

The stairs (right) and the bed platform, made of plywood and 2 x 4s, are covered with the same carpet as the main room. One side of the stairwell is sheathed in oak strip flooring to match the gable end wall; the exposed beams are covered with oak plywood. The original window over the stairwell was replaced with a larger window. The kitchenette (far right), opens to the main room, has a sink, a small refrigerator, and a storage cabinet. The countertop and cabinet doors are covered with Formica.

The new bathroom (right) and the kitchen were built at one end of the attic on either side of the chimney (above, left). The center photograph shows the studs and doorframe in place. The new bathroom (right) has a floor 8 in. higher than the main floor to accomodate the plumbing pipes. The floor and lower half of the walls are covered with 2-in.-square mosaic tiles. The window is original; the skylight was added.

Photographs on this page by Linda Hammer / American Olean Tile Company (bathroom tile) / Andersen Corporation, Bayport, Minn. (windows) / Bruce Hardwood Floors (wall paneling) / Colonnade™ Carpet from Collins & Aikman / Halo, Lighting Products Division, McGraw-Edison (light fixtures) / Lighting Products Division, McGraw-Edison (light fixtures) / St. Charles Manufacturing Co. (kitchen cabinets) / Sub-Zero Freezer Co., Inc. (under-counter refrigerator). Kohler Company (bathroom fixtures) / Levolor Blinds by Levolor Lorentzen, Inc. / Moen®, A Division of Stanadyne (kitchen sink and faucet) / Benjamin Moore & Co. (paint) /

Porches

Practical and economical conversions

A porch evokes an awareness of days gone by, a time when a glass of lemonade and a rocking chair offered a brief respite from the summer's heat. But porches can be brought into the present by converting them to year-round use as a much-needed extra room—a family room, a home office, a greenhouse.

It takes less work to convert a porch than to add a new room because the frame and foundation are already there. The conversion entails adding windows, insulation, and a heating system, plus the personal features that make rooms unique.

One part of the sweeping porch surrounding this Victorian house was converted to a sunroom by enclosing it with large windows. The section that encircles three sides of the house was left open. The house is on Mackinaw Island in Northern Michigan. In this conversion, tall, mostly uncurtained, paned windows were used so that a view of Lake Huron would not be obscured.

A large family needed an informal place where everyone could relax together in the warm weather. They enclosed their open back porch with tall, almost floor-to-ceiling windows. A sliding glass door leading to the kitchen makes this room convenient for family meals. For easy maintenance, ceramic tiles cover the floor and continue up the wall beneath the windows.

This back porch of a Texas house was enlarged and enclosed with screens in the 1920s. The present owners winterized the porch by installing removable Plexiglas panels over the screens and adding hot-air heating. A rug was laid over the original wood floors.

For summer use, the owners can remove the panels, let down the awning, and use the ceiling fan to keep the air circulating.

Three doors on the porch lead to the dining room, to the center hall, and to a bathroom built in what had been a storage room.

Dudley Witney

Tom Ebenhoh / Courtesy of HOME

The front porch of a century-old farmhouse was transformed into a passive solar greenhouse. The glass porch, warmed by the sun, makes winter living comfortable.

To build the greenhouse, the wall between the living room and porch was removed and a steel beam boxed in wood was added for support. The walls are glass door replacements, which cost less than standard window panels; the room has glass doors at either end. The brick floor has drainage holes for water from the plants.

Jim Norris / Courtesy of HOME

Vern Green / Designed by Arne Bystrom, AIA / Courtesy of HOME

A second-story sleeping porch was converted into a home office used year-round by adding floor and ceiling insulation, a gas-fired heater, and storm windows. The only other additions were a new paint job, and, for added protection from the cold, a sisal rug with an extra-thick backing. To take advantage of the natural sunlight, none of the windows on the three exterior sides of the porch has curtains. Shelves were built along part of one interior wall for storage.

This impressive glass-enclosed room provides the owners with a place for year-round entertaining and at the same time enhances the facade of their house.

What was a screened-in porch was remodeled by replacing the screens with glass on all three sides, laying a new brick floor, and installing baseboard heating. To create an unobstructed view of a nearby lake from the living room, one section of the wall between living room and former porch was removed and replaced with glass.

61

Garage conversions

New living space at first-floor level

Converting a garage to a new room adds an enormous amount of living space to a house and takes advantage of an existing framework. A garage can become a family room, a living room, a kitchen, or even a poolside cabana, depending on where it is situated in relation to the rest of the house.

Often, the changes on the outside of a renovated garage are as dramatic as those on the inside and entail much more than just replacing the garage doors. The photographs on these pages show exterior and interior views of converted garages.

© 1978 Robert Perron / Designed by Robert Nevins

The garage and the breezeway that connect the garage to the house (left, top) were converted into a new living room and an entry hall. The old living room became a formal dining room. In the photograph of the interior (left, bottom), the wall that separates the entry hall from the living room is shown. The dining room can be seen through the doorway on the left.

The wall between hall and living room is a supporting wall; the openings were cut out to permit a view of the living room from the hall. On the bar the panels inside the semicircle are cabinet doors with concealed hinges; the cabinet is used for bar storage. The original hip roof of the garage was retained in the new living room except for the area just above the bar unit where the ceiling was lowered to accommodate heating ducts and lighting fixtures.

Karl H. Riek, Photography / Designed by John Hughes, Architect

A new garage was added on the right of the house.

A two-car garage on the left of the house (above) was converted to a family room (right) by adding insulation to the walls and ceiling and installing large fixed windows in the front wall in place of the garage doors. Additional windows, cut in the side walls, have fixed curved portions above awning windows.

On the floor, the original concrete slab was leveled and covered with plywood before a hardwood parquet flooring was installed. On the ceiling, the beam that runs along the peak of the ceiling was installed and 2 x 8s were used to box in the original rough trusses. To finish, ⅜" redwood tongue-and-groove paneling was applied over insulation.

Part of a large garage was converted into a poolside cabana (left) leaving parking space for two cars. The sloping tile roof was extended over the existing bathroom and dressing rooms at the far end to give the renovation a longer, unified look.

To open the large entertainment area to the pool, this central room carved out of the garage has large glass doors that slide back into concealed pockets. In the interior of the room, easy maintenance was a prime consideration so the floor was covered with water-resistant seamless vinyl flooring. The room is equipped with a bar, sink, and refrigerator but has no facility for cooking. Redwood latticework painted white decorates both the interior and exterior of the cabana.

The garage (left) was converted into a second living room with easy access to the outdoors. The garage doors were replaced with sliding glass doors that have stationary glass panels on either side. The original driveway became a brick-covered patio and was surrounded with a hedge for privacy. The original concrete garage floor was covered with vinyl travertine tile.

The one-car garage (above) adjacent to the kitchen was converted to a family room that doubles as a den or study. The door between the kitchen and garage was removed and doorway was enlarged to form a great arch. The garage door was replaced with a sliding glass door. The decor of the large, sunny rooms brings the outdoors in; the walls are covered with wood siding that matches the siding on the house's exterior and the floor is covered with a slate-patterned vinyl.

Basements

Habitable space awaiting exploitation

Basements are often rooms without a fully realized function—at best, musty storerooms. But any basement can be made into a warm, inviting room.

A basement renovation sometimes entails more cosmetic than structural changes. Ceilings are lowered to hide heating and plumbing pipes, and the basement windows are given ingenious treatments. These photographs show a variety of renovations that resulted in eminently livable rooms. (See also *Finishing basements*, pp.158–161; and *Waterproofing basements*, pp.66–69.)

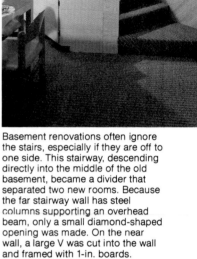

This basement was converted into a bedroom and study for a teenage boy. But should the family's needs change, it could easily become a den or family room. Because the bedroom was designed to be maintenance-free, the built-in drawers, shelves, and desk are covered with Formica. The small basement window above the couch was enlarged to meet the fire codes and to allow more light into the room. Redwood planks set in the ceiling act as a room divider as do the thin strips of redwood that reach from floor to ceiling.

Basement renovations often ignore the stairs, especially if they are off to one side. This stairway, descending directly into the middle of the old basement, became a divider that separated two new rooms. Because the far stairway wall has steel columns supporting an overhead beam, only a small diamond-shaped opening was made. On the near wall, a large V was cut into the wall and framed with 1-in. boards.

For a dramatic effect, the bottom step was replaced with a platform of lumber and ¾-in. plywood. The partition was covered with paneling set at an angle that echoes the angles of the structure.

An entertainment center in the basement of an 1830 house was given a country look by using 200-year-old barn siding to build the cabinets and corner posts that form a small but complete galley kitchen. The countertop is Formica. The same barn siding was used to cover the end wall on either side of the fireplace; it contrasts with the white plaster side walls. The floor is composed of handmade, 8-in.-square, sun-dried bricks that have been protected with a coat of semigloss polyurethane seal.

A large room divider was created by placing bookcases on either side of the boxed-in supporting post in this basement renovation. A ladder-like rack just above the bookcases extends from wall to wall to give the unit a built-in look. The walls are covered with exterior grade plywood. Lumber used to cover the seams is decorated with a stenciled pineapple motif. The new basement ceiling is suspended, for easy access to plumbing and heating pipes. Floor is vinyl.

Restoring stone foundations

A cure for an old house

Restoring the stone foundations found in older farmhouses and vintage homes is a unique problem. All foundations are subject to forces of weathering, water infiltration, and to subsidence and upheaval of the earth in which they rest. But stone foundations are the most vulnerable to such forces.

Foundations may have been constructed on ground that does not evenly support their weight. Settling and cracking occur. Footings may be inadequate or non-existent.

Moisture from underground sources often can cause foundation problems. Frost tends to attack the weakest parts of foundations. Water penetration and alternate cycles of freezing and thawing cause an upheaval of the stones periodically, resulting in damage.

Loose mortar can be a consequence of too little mortar having been applied when the foundation was laid—or the mortar may have expanded, losing its bonding power as the result of water saturation. Mortared stone walls are especially apt to develop bonding problems. The characteristics of mortar and stone are so different that traditional builders laid foundation walls of cut and fitted stones in such a way that the mortar, if used at all, was more sealer than bonding agent.

Crumbling stones: In the case of a crumbled stone foundation, whatever rests on a damaged section of the foundation wall—the sill and/or the floor joists—will sag from loss of support. The main job therefore is in raising the affected floor joists to permit restoring the foundation to proper height. Jacking up the affected joists should be done gradually until they are level with the rest of the underfloor framing. The object is to avoid sudden stress on the old house (see *Posts, beams, and floor joists*, pp.70–75).

The illustrations at right show the typical order of work entailed in restoring an old stone foundation. Before undertaking the repair, check the basement to determine whether walls are badly cracked, with damage extending below ground level. Such extensive damage calls for evaluation by a structural engineer and repair by professional workmen.

Jacking up the floor above the foundation wall is a major project that some homeowners may also want to leave to professionals. However, if the wall is structurally sound, and the repairs are carefully carried out, you can approach the job of restoring stone foundations with confidence. You also have the option of pouring a new concrete foundation under the joists, as seen in our chapter on restoring an old house.

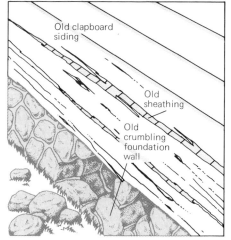

1. To repair a crumbling old stone foundation wall, first remove enough siding from the wall above the damaged section to expose the ends of floor joists and the cracked sill. Some old foundations may be without a sill.

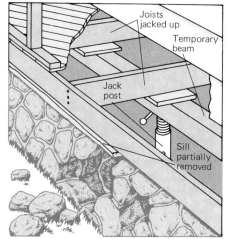

2. A temporary beam and jack posts are installed to gradually lift joists from sill and foundation wall (see *Posts, beams, and floor joists*, pp.70–75). Use chisel and hammer to remove damaged sill without breaking anchor bolts.

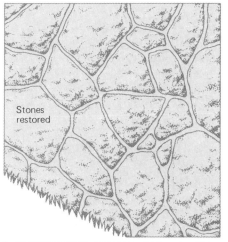

3. All broken stone and loose mortar should be pried and chiseled out, and crevices brushed clean. Check the condition of stones and replace any that seem to be disintegrating. Fit new stones carefully; make sure they are solidly positioned.

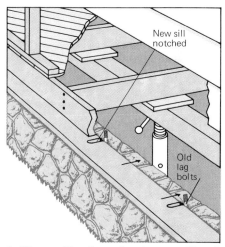

4. After repairing the wall, cut a new sill to fit. Position the sill as it is to be installed. Mark the sites of the foundation lag bolts on the sill, and notch the board as shown. Slide it between the foundation and the floor joists.

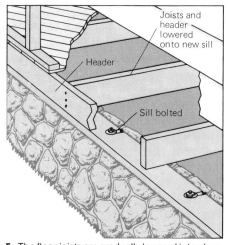

5. The floor joists are gradually lowered into place over new sill. Toenail a replacement header joist if needed, and the joists, onto the sill, which has already been fitted tightly to the foundation using oversize washers on lag bolts.

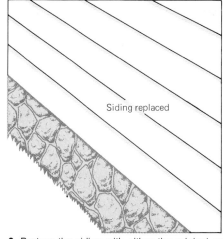

6. Restore the siding with either the original or new matching boards. Nail siding back in position with new nails in new nail holes. If authenticity of old construction details is important, antique-style "cut" nails can be used.

Waterproofing basements

Causes and remedies

Any finishing improvement planned for a basement should not be attempted until the basement is waterproofed.

The initial task in waterproofing a basement is to define the exact cause of the dampness. The problem may simply be one of high humidity and the resultant condensation on water pipes and walls. However, moisture may be seeping through porous foundation walls—or through cracks in the walls or floor.

In some cases, the foundation may not have been adequately waterproofed when it was built. Or, even worse, when the builder was completing the house, the trench around the foundation walls might have been used to dispose of unwanted construction leftovers. Such slipshod landfill can dam up pockets of water, preventing its free flow away from the foundation walls. Another source of water infiltration may lie in a high groundwater table, or gutters and downspouts may need repair to prevent the build-up of runoff from the roof at the foundation during periods of rain.

Water condensation is a fairly simple problem. Often it can be controlled merely by wrapping insulation around dripping cold-water pipes. You can install a dehumidifier, or improve the ventilation in the basement. Wet walls can be caused either by condensation or by seepage. Tape a square piece of plastic over a damp area. If in two or three days the wall underneath the plastic is dry, condensation is the culprit. If the wall is damp beneath the plastic, water seepage is the cause. Seepage can be stopped with the masonry sealing techniques described on the opposite page. Cracks can be sealed using various techniques; but active cracks and stationary cracks require different patching methods. Methods of identifying the types of cracks, and remedies for these cracks are discussed on pages 68 and 69.

Outside or inside: It is far more effective to waterproof a basement on the outside of the foundation wall. One reason is that water and moisture are stopped *before* they enter the foundation. Another is that hydrostatic pressure, or underground water pressure, tends to press against and tighten waterproofing on the outside of the foundation, but to loosen and push it off the insides of the walls.

If your problem can be eliminated by waterproofing inside the basement, consider yourself fortunate. If inside waterproofing fails, you may have to take the more expensive step of having the affected area of the foundation excavated and waterproofed as shown on the opposite page.

In some cases, waterproofing a basement may prove too difficult or too expensive for your budget. In such situations the best solution may be to install a drain at the lowest point of the basement floor, if the terrain and character of the earth allow groundwater to percolate away easily. If not, install a sump pump that automatically pumps the water out of the basement.

No technique can help a house if it is a victim of overwhelming forces, such as underground springs, extremely poor drainage, or improper grading. In these cases the basic remedy is to drain the earth around the house (see the chapter on dry wells and drainage).

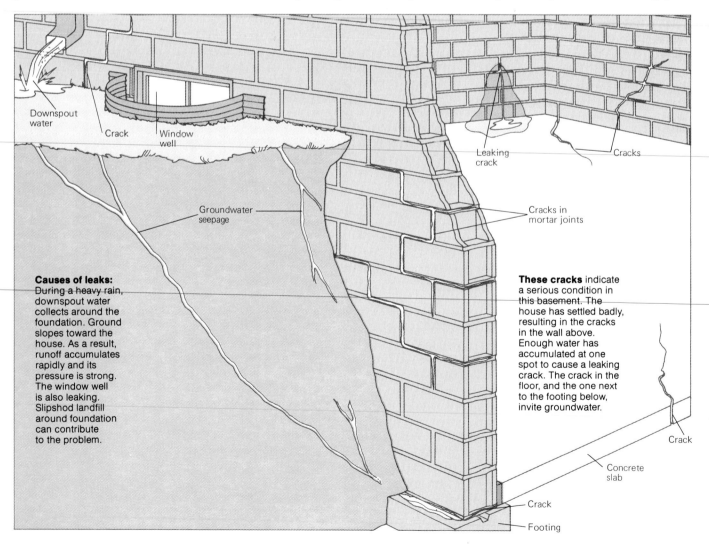

Downspout water

Crack

Window well

Leaking crack

Cracks

Cracks in mortar joints

Groundwater seepage

Causes of leaks: During a heavy rain, downspout water collects around the foundation. Ground slopes toward the house. As a result, runoff accumulates rapidly and its pressure is strong. The window well is also leaking. Slipshod landfill around foundation can contribute to the problem.

These cracks indicate a serious condition in this basement. The house has settled badly, resulting in the cracks in the wall above. Enough water has accumulated at one spot to cause a leaking crack. The crack in the floor, and the one next to the footing below, invite groundwater.

Crack

Concrete slab

Crack

Footing

Masonry sealers

Masonry sealers are most effectively and most easily applied during dry weather. Before you begin sealing, reduce the groundwater pressure on the foundation. Clean gutters and downspouts. Repair or replace them if they are not in good condition. Install splash blocks to help divert downspout water away from the foundation.

Waterproofing on the outside surface of foundation walls is more effective than inside because groundwater pressure forces sealers into the pores of the foundation. When seepage occurs on all sides of the basement, it will be necessary to dig a ditch all the way around the foundation down to the level of the footings—if the use of dry wells or some other simple system of draining the land doesn't work. Sealing a foundation from outside is hard work, and expensive if it is done by a professional.

Whether inside or outside, all surfaces to be treated must be free of paint, whitewash, or dirt. Oil and grease can be removed with a scrub brush and detergent. Finally, hose down the wall or floor that is to be sealed, so as to remove the detergent used in cleaning.

Types of sealers: The waterproofing sealers fall into three broad categories: waterproof sealers containing such additives as silicone, acrylic, or paraffin, usually used inside the basement; Portland cement mortar, with or without the additives, used on either the inside or the outside of the walls; and bituminous sealers, based on asphalt or coal-tar pitch, usually used outside.

Cement-based sealers are applied with a trowel or a heavy brush. Thin sealers work best if you apply them with a large brush. The bituminous sealers go on with a roofer's brush or a roofer's mop. Cement mortar sealers require a surface that is wet almost to saturation but not dripping wet. The first coat of sealer is then brushed or troweled on the foundation. A second coat goes on while the first coat of sealer is still wet. Manufacturer's instructions vary and should be followed strictly.

Thin sealers containing silicone are popular because they are transparent and easy to brush on, but they decompose faster than cement or the bituminous variety.

Membrane sealing is an exterior waterproofing technique that wraps the entire foundation in roofing paper, and then seals it with a bituminous sealer. It is virtually impossible to seal a foundation in this way in a finished structure. However, leaks may indicate a damaged *part* of the membrane in an existing house, and repairs to small areas can be made using tar paper and two coats of bituminous sealer.

Types of sealers

Cement mortar	An economical and durable mixture of one part cement and two parts water.
Cement latex	A cement-based sealer with synthetic rubber additives.
Bituminous sealers	Used in exterior sealing, they can be applied hot or cold. Hot application is messy, but the sealer penetrates the wall deeply.
Epoxy resins	They are synthetic, quick-setting, with a tough, water-resistant surface.
Silicone sealers	Popular and easy to use, their service-life ranges from four years with a 5% additive, to eight years with a 10% additive.
Xypex	This cement with silica powder penetrates and crystallizes in foundation pores.

Sealing from the outside

1. Waterproofing from the outside requires access to the foundation from ground level down to the footings. A back-hoe operated by a professional saves a lot of digging by hand and insures a trench of the correct width.

2. After a thorough cleaning of the foundation wall, bituminous sealer is applied with a brush or roller. Thicker, more viscous varieties can require use of a trowel, coarse brush, or roofer's mop. Sealers are applied either hot or cold.

3. While the bituminous coating is still wet and sticky, sheets of tar-treated roofing paper are applied over the foundation wall, pressed and smoothed over with a clean brush. This is effective in repairing previously treated foundations.

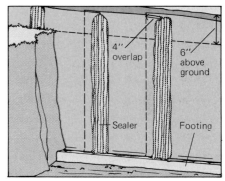

4. Where the wall meets the footing, the sheets of tar paper should overlap each other and curve away from the wall. The top of the membrane should extend at least 6 in. above grade (ground level). Another coating is applied over the paper.

Sealing from the inside

Thick sealing compound, such as cement mortar, can be applied to the inside of walls. If there is no strong external groundwater pressure, this technique will usually successfully control dampness and light seepage.

Thin sealers containing silicone or epoxy are best applied with a large brush. Any sealer should be applied broadly over the surface being treated. Work the sealing compound well into the pores of the wall or floor.

Waterproofing basements

Fixing cracks in walls and floor

Cracks in the basement walls and floor often come to the attention of the homeowner in the aftermath of a heavy rainstorm or during a spring thaw when the ground is saturated with water. Basement flooding not only ruins stored household items, it also makes any improvement there impossible.

Basement walls and floors crack for a variety of reasons. Mortar may have shrunk since the building was completed, or become saturated with moisture and crumbled away. Sometimes very strong hydrostatic pressure from groundwater, pressing against foundation walls, may pop out the joint mortar between concrete blocks or between the wall and the floor. The builder's poor workmanship or use of substandard materials can also be at fault. The resulting crack or cracks in basement walls, if below grade (ground level), often become leaky in the wet season.

Locating leaks: It often happens that water entering the basement from a crack at one location in the foundation wall originates from quite another place outside the house. It may be troublesome to find the real source of the leak; but it is necessary if the flooding problem is persistent and severe.

Some basement cracks are structural in nature: they are due either to major flaws in the original construction, or to the uneven settling of the foundation over the years. Basement walls or floors that are riven with cracks and leak substantial amounts of water may be warnings of serious problems in your house. A structural engineer should be consulted to ascertain the cause of such cracks. You may end up replacing an entire foundation wall or pouring a reinforced concrete floor over the existing floor where major damage has occurred with the passing years.

Fill and drainage: Fortunately, most cracks in the basement can be repaired reasonably well employing the techniques illustrated on this and the opposite page. But repairs will only be as good as the ability of the soil around the foundation to shed water quickly. Surface water should be diverted and carried away from the foundation.

If the soil around the house appears to have an unusual affinity for water, make a check on the quality of your landfill. Dig down a few feet outside the basement wall. If you discover broken bricks and left-over construction materials, the landfill should be dug out and replaced. Use a layer of gravel, a layer of sand, and fill the trench with earth. After one or two heavy rains, level the fill with topsoil.

If the drainage and landfill at the site present no apparent problems, you can attempt to repair the cracks from inside the basement or by excavating and sealing the outside of the foundation (see pp.66–67). First, determine the characteristics of the crack or cracks—for example, are they stationary, do they shift with the season—as the soil thaws and freezes; or are the cracks continuously active?

You must distinguish among these kinds of cracks because different types of cracks are treated in different ways. Among the shifting cracks, those that wax and wane during the seasons are quite different from those that continuously, though gradually, widen in size. Such cracking may hint at serious structural problems requiring professional consultation.

Testing cracks

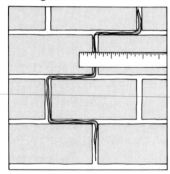

Testing cracks to determine if they are stationary or active can be done by taking periodic measurements in different seasons. Record and compare measurements.

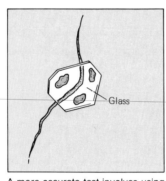

A more accurate test involves using epoxy to glue a flat glass plate to the wall so it bridges the crack. Movement will shatter the glass, showing the crack is active.

Stationary cracks

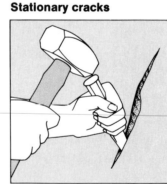

1. Stationary cracks are slightly enlarged below the surface with a cold chisel to provide "tooth" for the patching material. Minor cracks need not be undercut.

2. Brush and vacuum the chiseled crack, then wash it with a hose. Fill the crack half full with patching mortar. When dry, fill all the way and smooth the surface.

Active cracks

Clean active cracks of debris and dirt; then, undercut crack with a cold chisel so that the bottom is slightly wider than the top. Clean again and wash before sealing.

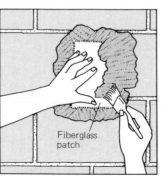

Minor active cracks can be covered with fiberglass patches. Apply asphalt sealer, stick the patch on and cover with additional asphalt. The sealer can be applied cold.

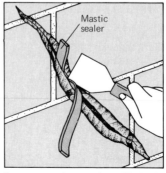

Larger cracks are best filled with mastic joint sealer that has been heated until pliable and pressed into the crack to about half its depth. The sealer will remain elastic.

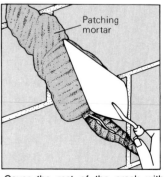

Cover the rest of the crack with patching mortar, which protects the mastic joint sealer. In time the patching mortar may break and fall away. A new patch can be applied.

Leaky cracks

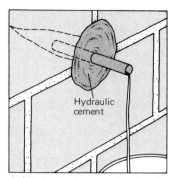

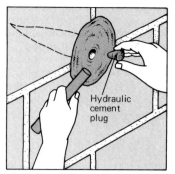

1. Seasonally, or after a downpour, water may pour through a crack. Even such an active water spout can be stopped with hydraulic cement, which quickly hardens and expands.

2. Chisel the crack wider, so that a short length of bleeder hose or tube can be inserted into it. Now most of the water goes through the hose, reducing pressure around it.

3. Mix hydraulic cement with water according to package instructions. Trowel the mix into the crack around the hose. Press on it firmly until it sets in a few minutes.

4. Mold a stiff hydraulic cement mix into a plug. Pull off the bleeder hose and insert the plug tightly into the hole. Hold it for a few minutes until the water is stopped.

Cracks between floor and wall

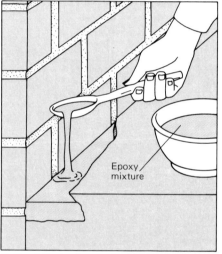

1. Cracks between basement floor and the foundation are apt to leak because separate construction surfaces meet along these lines. Undercut and widen the crack with a cold chisel.

2. Carefully dry the crack with a propane torch. Line the joint with a mastic sealer pad and fill the crack with epoxy resins to about ¾ of its depth. Fill and finish with patching mortar.

Installing a sump pump

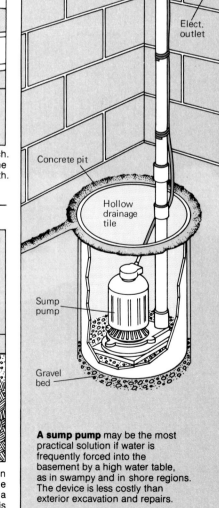

A sump pump may be the most practical solution if water is frequently forced into the basement by a high water table, as in swampy and in shore regions. The device is less costly than exterior excavation and repairs.

Installing a drainage system

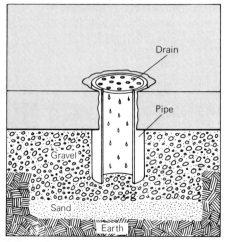

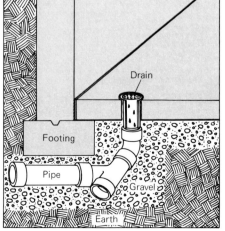

A floor drain with a dry well, under certain circumstances, may cure a chronically flooded basement. Water coming from one area will flow into the dry well and be drained off, if the house is situated on sloping ground.

A more elaborate set-up, involving a floor drain that pipes basement water all the way under the floor and the foundation footing, also requires a sloping site to let the water run off once it is outside the house.

Posts, beams, and floor joists

Identifying structural defects

As a homeowner you may be aware of floor problems in your house. Warped, loose, or squeaking floor boards are annoying reminders that all is not perfect. Floors that sag, slope, or shake when walked on are symptoms that should not be ignored. It's important to distinguish between indications of harmless warping or shrinking, and those of more serious problems.

Nearly all wooden floors are built and supported in the same way. The finished flooring is laid atop a subfloor. The subfloor rests on joists. The weight of floor, subfloor, and joists is carried down by beams, posts, and bearing walls to the footings or foundation. Structural faults in any part of this system are reflected upward and appear as problems in the finished flooring of a dwelling.

If a table or chair rocks on its legs, if the floor moves when someone walks across the room, or if you live with squeaking boards underfoot, you know there is something wrong. If doors and windows stick and plaster on walls or ceilings is cracked, you should suspect structural problems. But even without any of these indications, it is worthwhile to make occasional checks of the floors and their underlying supporting elements.

The drawing below is a catalog of some common structural problems that can exist in a frame house and show up in the flooring above. Obviously some

of the situations depicted are unlikely to be found in a normally well-built house, unless a house has deteriorated seriously with age.

What follow on this and ensuing pages are diagnostic methods and remedies for dealing with these common problems in floors and their support system in a typical house. By and large, the remedies consist of re-establishing a solid connection between the floor and the structural elements—the joists, posts, etc.—employed to support the floor and other parts of the house.

Most diagnoses and some cures can be accomplished from above the floor. Others should be performed from beneath the floor joists and similar elements. In many cases this is done easily from a crawl space or an unfinished basement. But on upper floors, or if the basement is finished, it may be necessary to remove a few floor boards, or a part of the ceiling below, to spot or deal with a problem.

Finding the problems: Squeaking floor boards are the easiest to check. You need only walk back and forth to locate the noise. Squeaks alone usually indicate loose flooring.

Jump up and down on the floor. If it shakes underfoot or if doors and windows rattle, the floor joists are most likely too weak for the load they carry. The joists may be undersized, they may span too great a distance, or they may have cracks, or rot, or sizable notches.

Roll a marble or a rubber ball across the floor. If it always heads for the center of the room, you have sagging joists. If it repeatedly ends up in one corner or by a particular wall, you have sloping joists. Sagging and sloping joists, especially near an exterior or interior bearing wall, can indicate a major problem. They probably mean that the joists are not properly supported by a beam or the foundation wall.

While these last are major problems, they are by no means incurable. You can usually confirm your diagnosis by physically inspecting and probing the joists, the beams, and the foundation wall on which the joists rest. Frequently, the problem is simply that the joists have shrunk with age, or a plumber or an electrician has notched too liberally into several joists to install a pipe or other utility connection. It may be that the cross-positioned bridging strips for bracing the joists are loose, worn, or absent altogether.

Use the diagram below as a guide to trace the path of load downward. The finished floor should be in close contact with the subfloor, which in turn should be firmly secured to the floor joists. The joists should rest solidly on the sills of the foundation wall, or on beams supported adequately by strong posts. As you trace downward, watch for play or movement at each link of the structural chain that carries the load down to the foundation and post footings.

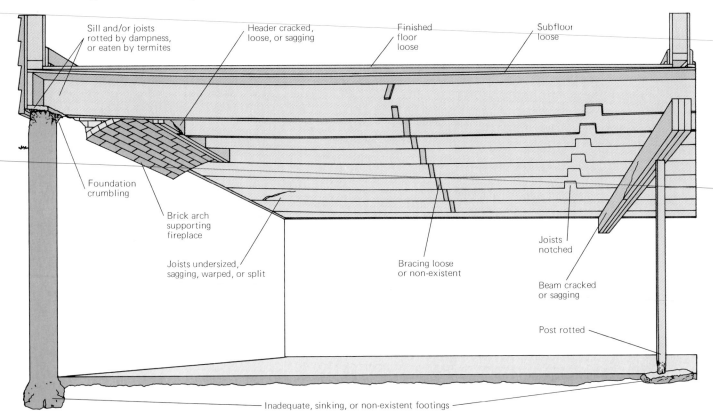

Sill and/or joists rotted by dampness, or eaten by termites

Header cracked, loose, or sagging

Finished floor loose

Subfloor loose

Foundation crumbling

Brick arch supporting fireplace

Joists undersized, sagging, warped, or split

Bracing loose or non-existent

Joists notched

Beam cracked or sagging

Post rotted

Inadequate, sinking, or non-existent footings

70

Repairing squeaking floors

In many cases you can fix squeaking floors by working directly on them from above. Squeaks caused by slight rubbing between boards can be silenced by lubricating with graphite or talcum powder. Glazier's points (the small metal triangles used to secure window panes) can be driven between boards to anchor a loose member more securely to its stable neighbors.

Boards that have loosened, and buckled upward, can be nailed back into place. Finishing nails hammered in diagonally often stop such squeaks. Drill pilot holes and use a nail set to recess the nail heads. Another method is to glue down loose boards.

Wood screws have much more holding power than nails. They should be used in areas of heavy foot traffic. Drill a pilot hole and countersink the screw. Fill the countersink with a plug cut from a length of dowel.

Loose floors can sometimes be corrected from below the floor. For instance, boards that have lifted from the subfloor can be drawn down and secured with wood screws as illustrated at the bottom of this page. When you find that a joist has shrunk away from the floor, firm contact can be restored by driving wooden shingles as shims between subfloor and joist. Try for a snug fit, remembering that over-driving the shim may lift the flooring and create new problems. Where the distance between the floor and a shrunken joist is considerable, or where a large area is unsupported, nail a hardwood batten (bottom illustration) to the joist after making sure the batten is in firm contact with the subfloor above.

All of these remedies assume that the joists themselves are solid and firmly supported by their posts and beams.

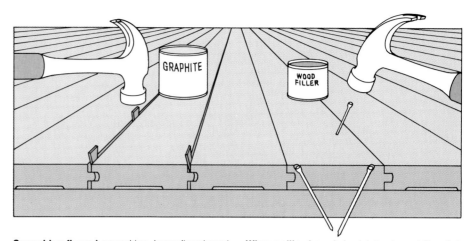

Squeaking floor: A squeaking, loose floor board can be shimmed tight by driving glazier's points at 6-in. intervals. Use a nail set to drive points below the surface of the floor. Powdered graphite or talcum powder forced between loose boards often eliminates squeaks.

When nailing boards back into place, drill a pilot hole three-fourths the diameter of the nail to be used. Drive finishing nails diagonally in pairs. Recess the nails with a nail set. Use wood putty to plug hole and to fill cracks between boards. Sand and finish to match the floor.

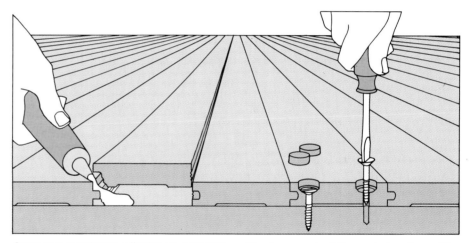

Other methods: Wood adhesive or carpenter's glue offers a quick way to refasten a loose and squeaky board. Good adhesives will do the job, and they require no tools. After you have applied the glue, weight the board in place for the length of time that is recommended by the manufacturer.

Wood screws should be used where there will be heavy traffic. Countersink flat-head screws in pilot holes. Soaping the screw threads will ease the friction of getting the screws through hard or old wood. Glue in a wood plug to complete the repair. Stain and finish plug to match existing floor.

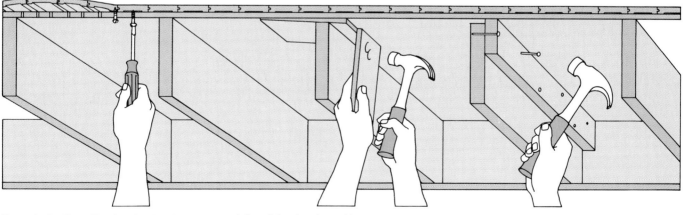

Beneath the floor: Flooring that has lifted from the subfloor can be drawn back in place with wood screws from below (left); a 1¼-in.-long screw will generally give good purchase on the loose board without breaking through it (check thickness of subfloor and floorboards to determine the proper screw length).

A floor joist shrunken with age is shown in the center illustration. Contact between the subfloor and the joist is restored by driving wooden shingles in place as shims. Achieve a snug fit, but do not drive the shim so far as to raise a bump in the floor. This approach can be used to correct first-floor problems from the basement.

A large gap between shrunken joist and subfloor (right) is closed using a wooden batten—either a 2 x 4 or 2 x 6. Nail the batten to the joist, with the batten firm and flush against the subfloor. After installing the batten, replace the bridging between it and the neighboring joist, as illustrated elsewhere on these pages.

Posts, beams, and floor joists

Bridging and bracing unstable floor joists

Floors that bounce and shake under the weight of human traffic may be missing adequate bridging between floor joists. Bridging is a system of small wood or metal braces attached diagonally between the joists, preventing them from twisting under shearing stresses and re-distributing loads evenly throughout the underfloor structure.

Loose bridging can sometimes be nailed back in place. If the wood has rotted, you will have to install new bridging. Making new bridging from

wood involves miter cuts and small clearances for hammering, and may be more of a carpenter's chore than you want to take on. Ready-made metal bridging is an excellent alternative. It can be installed without driving nails or screws through the metal.

Old bridging need not be removed, except for esthetic reasons.

Prefabricated metal bridging is installed by driving the forked end of the piece into the upper part of a joist, then hammering its serrated lower end

tightly against an adjacent joist. Avoid driving the bridging member so tightly that the joists are forced out of shape.

Solid wooden braces of the same size as the joists can also be nailed between joists to provide stability. Areas under such heavy loads as bathroom fixtures, new tile floors, and pianos can be reinforced in this way, as seen in the illustrations below. Use 16-penny nails to secure the new braces. Use a staggered arrangement so you can nail directly into the boards without toenailing.

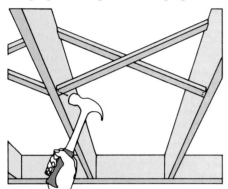

Loose bridging, often the cause of a bouncing floor, may simply be toenailed snugly back in place if the wood is still in good condition. Use rosin-coated nails and stagger them to avoid splitting the bridging member.

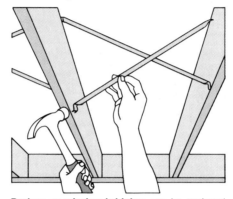

Broken or missing bridging can be replaced with prefabricated metal bridging. Hammer the forked, flat end of the bridge into the upper part of a joist, and the serrated, bent end tightly against the adjacent joist.

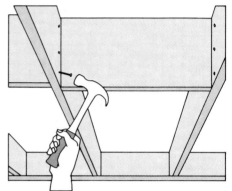

Blocking or solid bridging, the same dimensions as the joists, strengthens weak joists bearing heavy loads. Install blocks about 8 ft. apart, staggered so they can be nailed directly into the joists from behind.

Strengthening weak joists

Strengthening individual joists is necessary under certain circumstances: the joist may be undersized for its load, cracked, rotted, or simply sagging a bit because of age. Floor joists in older buildings were never intended to carry the weight of a modern bathroom.

Installation of new plumbing, in fact, is often the source of a dual problem. Not only has the load increased, but plumbers will often notch several joists to make it easier to install pipes. Such notching can considerably weaken joists. For example, if a 3-inch notch has been cut into a 2 x 8 joist, the load-carrying capability of the joist is reduced to that of a 2 x 5. If a notch must be cut into a joist, it is better to cut into its top rather than its bottom edge—better still to drill and cut a hole midway between the top and bottom edges. A notch near an end of a joist will weaken it to a lesser degree than one near its middle. (For more information on notching joists, see pp.24–25.)

Whatever the cause of a weakened joist—notch, crack, or dry rot—the cure is the same: reinforce the joist.

Before beginning the actual work of reinforcing a joist, you will have to remove the old bridging completely. Then, if a weakened joist sags downward, you should realign it with the

help of one or two jack posts—or a contractor's or house jack, if you are working in a crawl space. (See pp.73–75 for instructions on jacking up joists.) Make sure that there is nothing attached to the joist that can be damaged, such as a utility pipe.

When you are satisfied that the joist is back in proper position, nail a generous length of 2 x 4 on both sides of the defect to stiffen the joist. Rosin-coated,

16-penny nails insure a lasting repair.

Avoid distorting the floor joist. Instead of bowing the joist upward in an attempt to force it against the subfloor, stop when the joist is aligned and then reinforce it. If there is still a gap between the subfloor and the newly straightened joist, use shims or hardwood battens to fill the gap (see pp.70–71). Installing new metal bridging completes the job.

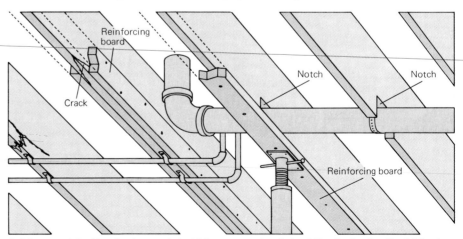

Joists are notched by plumbers and electricians to give access to pipes and electrical cable. This, like a crack, weakens the joists. The effect can be partly offset by nailing boards either on both sides of a notch (left) or under it (right). If a joist is

sagging, it should be slowly raised back into place with a jack post before reinforcing it (see pp.73–75). When a reinforcing board is to be attached to the bottom of a joist it should be put in place before jacking the joist.

Installing a new joist or header

Occasionally, you may find after a detailed examination that one or more of your joists require not just reinforcement but replacement. Often the existing joist, whatever its condition, can be left in place and a new joist can be added alongside it, using a technique known as "doubling."

Doubling a floor joist is a simple process in theory. The sagging old joist is jacked up into proper position and the new joist is nailed in place next to it, as seen in the drawing at top right on this page. The jack is then removed. In practice, however, the job calls for patience and close attention to detail. You must, first of all, remove the bridging, if any, between the joist to be doubled and the joists at either side.

Clearance for new joists: Depending on the number of joists to be supplemented, you will need: one or more jacking posts, some 4 x 4s, 2 x 6s, and 2 x 8 replacement joist lumber.

In older homes, joists were cut at the lumber mill to actual size; that is, a 2 x 8 actually measured 2 x 8 inches or very close to it. Today lumber is always cut to what is known as nominal size. The 2 x 8 you buy actually measures 1½ x 7½ inches. Consequently, if your existing joists are old enough to be of actual dimensions, your new joist can easily be inserted in the existing space between the girder and the sill and the flooring above. But if the existing joists are also of nominal dimensions, it is easier to install a new joist by first chiseling an end slightly to gain clearance, then shimming that end tightly after inserting the joist in position.

Jacking procedures: Place the foot of the jack on a piece of 4 x 4 lumber and support the floor joist above with a second piece. If you are raising several old joists at the same time, as shown on page 74, you can shim the space between the 4 x 4 and the old joists with 2 x 6 spacing blocks; this gives additional room to maneuver the new joist or joists during installation.

Jacking a floor joist requires patience and special care to avoid damaging the structure of the house. Previously patched wall cracks can open up. Soil and service pipes can be damaged.

Take these factors into consideration before you operate the jacks. Many contractors advise raising a joist—and lowering the jack after the work is done—over a period of days. They suggest a maximum of a quarter turn of the jack handle every three or four days, or ⅛ turn every two days. Lifting any joist or beam much more than a quarter inch should be done only after consulting a structural engineer.

With these warnings in mind, proceed as follows: Jack the old floor joist into proper position. Obtain a new joist that is as close a match to the old joist as possible. Maneuvering the new joist into place can be done by one person,

but having a helper will simplify the job considerably. When you are satisfied the new joist fits correctly and will support the load overhead, shim the end at the wall snugly. The other end of the joist, probably resting on a beam or steel girder, should also be shimmed tightly in place. Nail the new joist to the old one. Use 16-penny, rosin-coated nails. Set the nails at about 1-foot intervals, staggered, as shown in the drawing at top on this page.

Lower the jacks a little every few days, so that the new joist takes up the load gradually. When the jacks have been removed, install the metal bridging (see opposite page).

In replacing joists that terminate at headers, or the headers themselves, use the same doubling technique described above. Prefabricated fasteners, such as the joist hangers shown below, greatly strengthen the connections at critical points. Since headers are usually located under such heavy structures as fireplaces or staircases, a cautious approach to their repair is advisable.

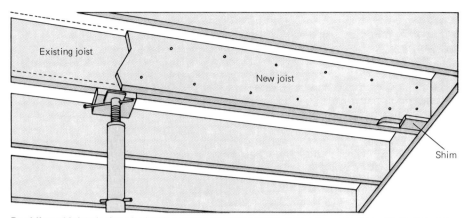

Doubling of joists is done by jacking up the old joist and inserting a new one alongside it. Chisel the end of a new joist for easy insertion. If the old joist has actual rather than nominal dimensions, chiseling may not be required. Shim the chiseled end tightly in place, then nail the new joist firmly to the old one.

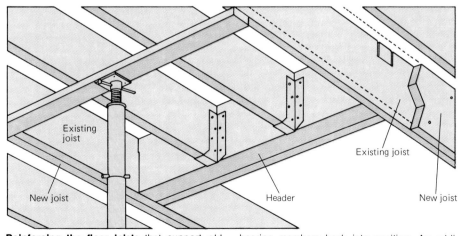

Reinforcing the floor joists that support old headers, or reinforcing the headers themselves, is only marginally different from doubling a joist as described elsewhere on this page. One or more jacking posts are employed to lift sagging load-bearing members back into position. An additional joist is positioned directly alongside the existing joist and nailed firmly to it. The difficulty of nailing through double or triple headers can be avoided by using joist hangers as shown.

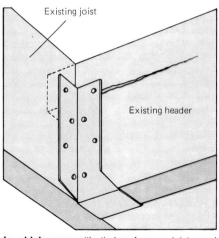

In old houses with timber frames, joists and headers were often notched to make interlocking joints. Cracks develop in such joints. Here, a joist hanger is shown being used to repair a crack; alternatively place a post under sagging element.

Posts, beams, and floor joists

Repairing sills, beams, and posts

Sometimes floor problems go beyond the defects in flooring and joists discussed on previous pages. The causes can lie deeper, in the structural elements on which floor joists rest: beams, their supporting posts, the foundation sill, and even the foundation wall itself.

The drawing below suggests some solutions to a number of typical problems that can develop in sills, beams, and posts. The basic remedy, in each case, requires taking the load off the damaged part so that repairs can be made. Once the repair restores the structural part to its proper function, the temporary supports can be removed. As in other major structural improvements, when in doubt—or if the problem turns out to be more complex than it appeared to be at first—do not proceed without professional evaluation.

At the left in the drawing below is a rotted sill; the ends of the joists illustrated have been damaged by moisture seeping in at the sill. The result is a sloping floor. This condition is common in older houses where the sill is near ground level (or as the result of subsidence, below it) and therefore vulnerable to water and dampness in the soil.

Alternatives: The alternatives are either to put in all new joists—or to install an additional beam under the existing joists close to the foundation wall. The new beam props up the failing joists inside their rotted ends.

Put up a temporary support system, consisting of a beam and two jack posts on load-distributing 4-x-8 pads, as illustrated, then install the new framing elements. If you are dealing only with a rotted sill, the sill alone can be replaced. Generally, water damage to a sill will spread to the ends of the joists as well, so the joists are usually also replaced or "doubled." See page 73. After repairs the entire temporary supporting system is removed.

Instead of replacing the sills, and doubling or replacing all the joists, you might prefer a compromise solution. Use the same temporary support sytem, but erect a permanent beam to support the joists as shown at far left in the drawing below. The load in this case is held up independently of the foundation. Such a method of restoring floor joists is admittedly a half-way measure. You will be saved the trouble and expense of tearing out the old floor and installing new joists; however, the new beam diminishes headroom in the basement and the posts take up space.

If you discover that the post or posts supporting a load-bearing beam in the center of the basement have decayed due to dampness, or have been damaged by termites, you should replace the posts with Lally columns—steel columns filled with concrete. Shown on either side of the Lally column in the drawing below are temporary support posts; these supports carry the load until a Lally column can be installed to replace the defective posts. In the drawing, the defective posts have been removed from beneath the beam.

New footings: When you have temporarily supported the beam and removed a defective post, carefully inspect the post's footing. When in doubt, installing a new footing is good insurance against future trouble. If your floor is concrete and at least 6 inches thick, and the post is not required to carry a heavy load, you can use a metal plate fixed to the concrete to support the load. A steel plate ½ inch thick and at least 6 inches square will be adequate. Installing a load-supporting plate requires drilling the concrete to accept metal screw anchors. The plate is drilled and then attached with heavy-duty lag screws, tightened into the screw anchors with a wrench. Order a load-bearing plate pre-drilled by the

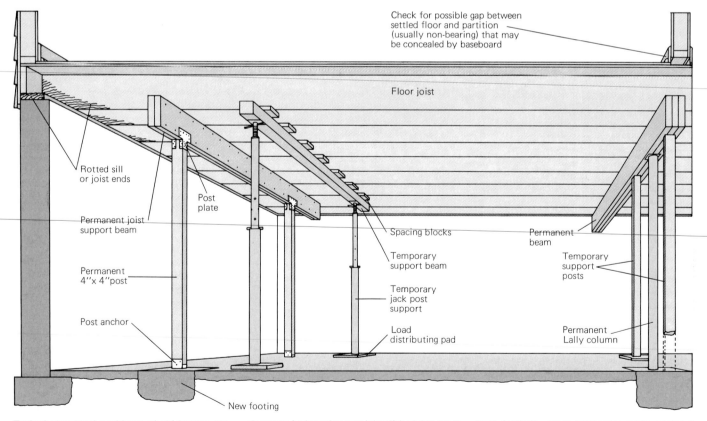

Check for possible gap between settled floor and partition (usually non-bearing) that may be concealed by baseboard

Floor joist

Rotted sill or joist ends

Post plate

Permanent joist support beam

Permanent 4"x 4"post

Post anchor

Spacing blocks

Temporary support beam

Temporary jack post support

Load distributing pad

New footing

Permanent beam

Temporary support posts

Permanent Lally column

Typical structural problems of old houses are found in foundation sills, beams, posts, and post footings. Repair of rotted sill or joist ends (top left) requires a temporary support of jack posts and a beam (near center). The spacing blocks provide clearance for inserting new joists if the joists are to be doubled. An alternative to the installation of new sills and joists is a permanent support consisting of a new beam and posts (left). When it becomes necessary to repair damaged posts or post footings, erect temporary posts under a beam; replace old posts with Lally columns (right). New concrete footings are required for additional permanent posts. The concrete can be bought in small, ready-mix bags.

Useful tools and hardware

supplier. The lag screws themselves should be the tempered variety to avoid destruction by the wrench.

In most cases it is more workmanlike to put in a new concrete footing. A footing 2 feet square and 22 inches deep is usually adequate. However, consult your local building code for exact dimensions before setting to work.

A new footing will require about 1 cubic yard of concrete. You can prepare this amount without a cement mixer; save yourself some time and effort by using bags of ready-mixed concrete. More or larger footings will require greater amounts of concrete and in such cases it is less expensive to buy pre-mixed concrete from a contractor who will deliver and pour it into the space you have provided.

Whether you select a structural 4 x 4 wooden post or a steel column, you must make provision for securing the post solidly in place top and bottom.

Crumbled foundation: If you find a portion of an old stone or brick foundation wall has crumbled, causing joists that are otherwise sound to slope, you can use the same approach to the repair job. Jack up and support the joists and then repair the foundation (see *Restoring stone foundations*, p.65).

Replacing unsound posts and beams can be greatly eased with the help of some useful tools and hardware, available for rental or purchase from the local lumberyard.

Prefabricated steel plates may be applied to reinforce beams with minor cracks, which would otherwise have to be replaced. The plates sketched (lower left) are good choices for strengthening an exposed beam that is a decorative as well as a structural element in your home. The flat and the L-shaped steel plates should be used in pairs for maximum strength. The L-shaped plates are stronger, but they can easily be seen from below, which is a shortcoming from a decorative point of view.

As shown in the bottom drawing, the beam can be grooved by using a router and straight router bit of the appropriate size. It is possible to cut away parts of a beam to fit a T-plate that is flush with the surface of the beam. The reinforced beam can then be stained or painted, or encased in wood veneer.

The hardware shown at right of the beams comprises a metal anchor set for a wooden beam. The T-shaped plate on top secures the post to the beam. The assembly below it fastens to the bottom of the wooden post and anchors the

post to a concrete footing. It not only secures the post firmly, but also keeps its bottom from groundwater.

Types of jacks: For temporary support of joists and beams, you need jacks (lower right). Selecting the type of jack depends on the amount of extension needed and the amount of space you have to work in. Jack posts are generally used in basements where there is room to work and where a considerable "reach" is called for. For a confined area, typically a crawl space, a contractor's jack or house jack should be selected. Like the jack post it is a screw-operated mechanism. Occasionally, a well-made general-purpose hydraulic jack can be pressed into service. You may have to use cement blocks or other solid supports such as railroad ties to raise a hydraulic jack to working height. Hydraulics may have the advantage of being available around a home or garage, but their lifting range is somewhat limited. The possibility of leaking hydraulic fluid or accidental release of the locking mechanism make them unsuitable for major projects.

While heavy jacks are admittedly clumsy and hard-to-handle, you can be sure that they will stay securely in place while repairs are being done.

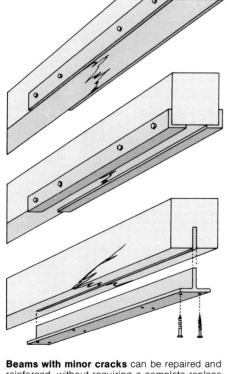

Beams with minor cracks can be repaired and reinforced, without requiring a complete replacement, by using prefabricated steel plates. These plates come in various types, including flat, L-shaped, and T-shaped.

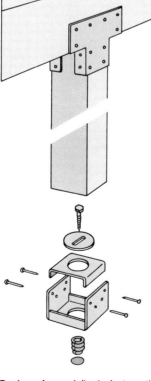

Post anchor set firmly fastens the top of a wooden post to a beam (top); and its lower assembly (bottom) anchors the bottom of the post in a concrete footing.

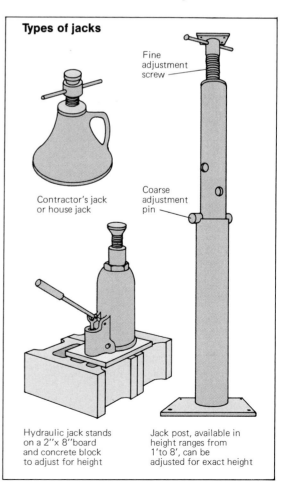

Types of jacks

Fine adjustment screw

Contractor's jack or house jack

Coarse adjustment pin

Hydraulic jack stands on a 2"x 8"board and concrete block to adjust for height

Jack post, available in height ranges from 1'to 8', can be adjusted for exact height

Interior bearing walls

Identifying load-bearing walls

Interior load-bearing walls are an essential structural element of most houses. To see why this is so, look at the cutaway drawing below; it shows how a typical private home is engineered. A central steel girder or wooden beam, supported at its ends by the foundation and along its length by posts on footings in the basement floor, runs the entire length of the longest dimension of the house.

At right angles to the central girder are the wooden floor joists. In the completed house, the joists support flooring and everything that may be on the floor, such as fixtures, furniture, occupants.

Since a single length of joist is neither long enough nor strong enough to span from wall to wall, two joists are usually employed. The outer end of each is supported by the exterior wall. The inner ends of the joists overlap each other atop the girder or beam.

All exterior walls that parallel the girder, or the roof line, are load-bearing walls. They support one end of the joists on every floor of the house. The central

girder supports nearly twice the weight carried by the exterior walls. It bears the load of two joists at every point along its length.

The ceiling of the first floor, additional floors, and in part the roof structure are also supported by joists. All the joists on upper floors are carried by the exterior walls at their outer ends. But instead of being supported by a central girder, the inner ends of these joists usually overlap on top of a supporting central wall. This is a load-bearing wall. Such interior walls—and there may be more than one—carry a major part of

the weight of the house and its contents. Interior alterations that weaken a bearing wall will seriously affect the structural soundness of the house.

In fact, the only way to eliminate a bearing wall entirely is to replace the wall with a specially fabricated truss, a built-up beam or a steel girder, such as the girder shown below. This usually is a job for a structural engineer and professional workmen.

If you look at the drawing again, you will notice that most interior walls are not bearing walls. They are identified as non-load-bearing, or partition, walls.

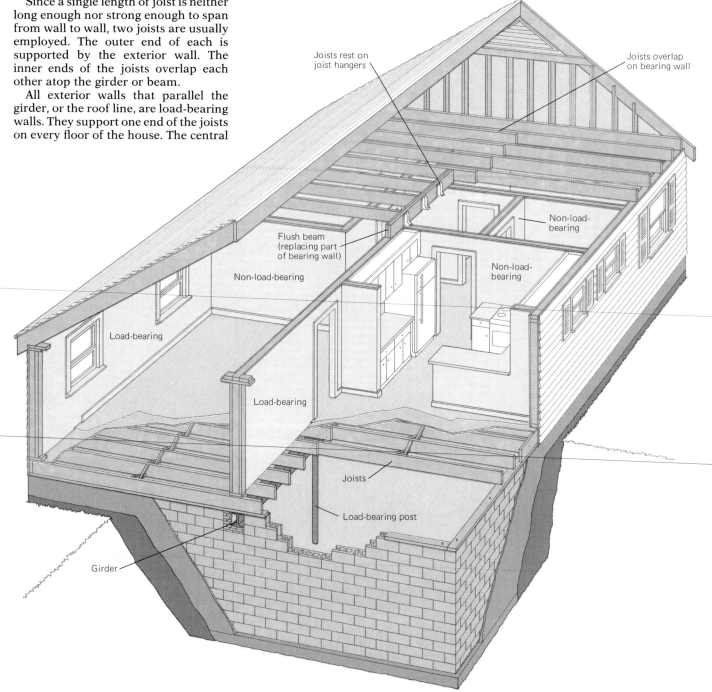

And you can see by the drawing, removing, relocating, or altering these non-bearing walls would have no effect on the soundness of the house.

With this basic understanding of how most houses are engineered, identifying bearing walls can often be a relatively simple task. For example, the typical house shown in the diagram has a central bearing wall that could be located by going down into the basement and measuring the distance from the load-bearing posts to the outside foundation walls. Unless you find any special bracing and doubling up of joists to form headers and trimmers (see *Building codes*, pp.21–37) in the exposed basement ceiling, the main load-bearing wall on the floor above will generally be an equal distance from the exterior wall as the girder in the basement is from the coinciding foundation wall.

Simpler methods: A simpler way to identify interior bearing walls is based on the direction in which the joists run. In the type of house shown, bearing walls are almost always found at right angles to the joists. Not all such walls are load-bearing, however; note that near the center of the house shown there is a non-bearing partition at right angles to the joists. Conversely, a bearing wall may sometimes run parallel to joists in the basement ceiling; the presence of heavy beams, girders, or headers signal load-bearing walls.

On these pages some simple methods are illustrated to show you how to determine the direction of joists and to find the places where ceiling joists overlap bearing walls. Use more than one test to confirm the evidence. Older houses that have undergone renovation may not be easy to analyze. If you have doubts, consult a professional.

Loads and other considerations

In planning the construction of any building, the architect or structural engineer must include in his calculations two types of loads, or downward forces.

The first of these is the *dead load*. It consists of the weight of the building itself, including all interior and exterior walls, joists, floors, ceilings, the roof, and various fixtures and equipment permanently attached to the house.

In addition, the structure must also be able to carry its *live load*, which includes furniture, appliances, movable equipment, people, and pets.

By being aware of how these loads are supported and distributed in his house, the homeowner will learn how best to position heavy loads, such as a grand piano or large bookcases, where they can be adequately supported by the load-bearing elements of the structure. For instance, a large bookcase containing heavy volumes should not be placed parallel to the floor joists. It should be at right angles to the joists so that several will share its weight. The same knowledge will also help in making decisions about removing part of a bearing wall.

Once a wall has been identified as bearing or non-bearing a related check should be made before it is actually opened. The reason for this: Some walls or partitions contain electric or plumbing installations. Rerouting electric cables and conduits may not be a major project, but relocating water pipes may prove to be a sizable problem. A waste pipe from a toilet cannot be relocated without redoing the bathroom. Tracing pipes and cables in the vicinity of a wall may save wasted effort.

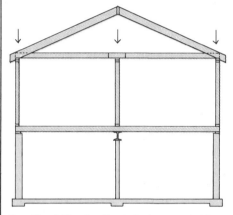

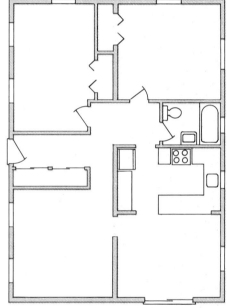

Dead load: The dead load of a house consists mainly of the weight of the structure itself. In a house (above) most of the roof and part of the attic press down on the front and back exterior walls. The interior bearing walls share the floor and attic weight. Included in the dead load are the permanent fixtures that are in the kitchen, in the laundry room, and in the bathroom (right).

Locating joists

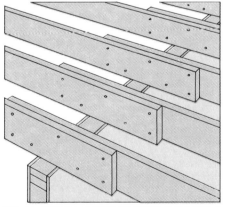

Visual evidence: If joists are visible in the attic, a quick glance usually will reveal if a wall is load-bearing. Overlapping joist ends are proof of a bearing wall. Such a wall will be located in a position directly underneath and at right angles to the overlapping joist ends.

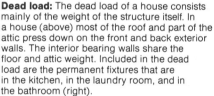
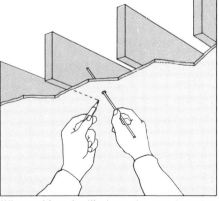

Wire probing: A stiff wire probe, run through a small hole drilled in the ceiling, will reveal the direction of the joists above. Walls running parallel to the joists are usually not load-bearing. This method is useful when an upper floor conceals the joists in question.

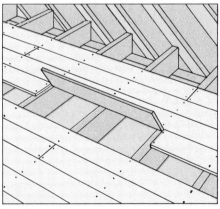

Floored attic: Usually the joists run parallel to the direction of the rafters. If the attic floor is completely covered so that no ends of joists are visible, and you suspect the joists may not parallel the rafters, you can lift up a piece or two of the flooring and inspect the joists.

Interior bearing walls

Basic procedures

The drawing to the right is a highly schematic illustration of post and lintel construction used to replace part of an interior bearing wall. As you can see from the cutaway plan, the weight-carrying function of the wall has been preserved by using a lintel, which is a beam over an opening, to span the archway. The lintel carries the load from above. In turn it is sturdily supported by posts at both ends. The posts then transfer the load to the floor joists and beam immediately below. Finally, the cumulative weight on the basement beam is distributed among the steel posts and the foundation wall.

You should consider several points before beginning work. The first: How will the proportions of the room be affected after the wall has been removed? Second: A span of more than 8 feet presents risks and potential problems for the nonprofessional; therefore, do not plan on completely eliminating a wall more than 8 feet in length without professional help. Third: You will have constructed an archway. Will there be enough headroom, after allowing for dimensions of the load-bearing lintel?

The approach to removing a bearing wall is simple and easily understood. It involves first supporting the overhead load, then removing the wall. The task is completed when the lintel and posts are installed, so that they carry the load of the old wall. Such a project is within the capabilities of homeowners with carpentry experience.

Professional consultation: The methods suggested here are for an average frame house with two stories and an attic. It may be that your house is structurally different from our model, with its loads supported differently. When in doubt, consult a structural engineer or an experienced builder. It may still be possible for you to do the actual work yourself by modifying our suggestions to fit your situation.

Other conditions may necessitate professional help, or preclude removing a bearing wall altogether. It may be that the weight above such a wall is too great to be supported using the techniques presented. Heavy loads above, such as an elaborate bathroom, or a giant refrigerator, are clearly more-than-average loads that would affect your decisions. Furthermore, if a bearing wall supports a third or fourth story, or the house frame has shifted because of foundation problems or old age, the job could be complex and even hazardous.

Taking into account the structural individuality of your house and the limitations of these techniques, the methods suggested in following pages should help you carry out your project.

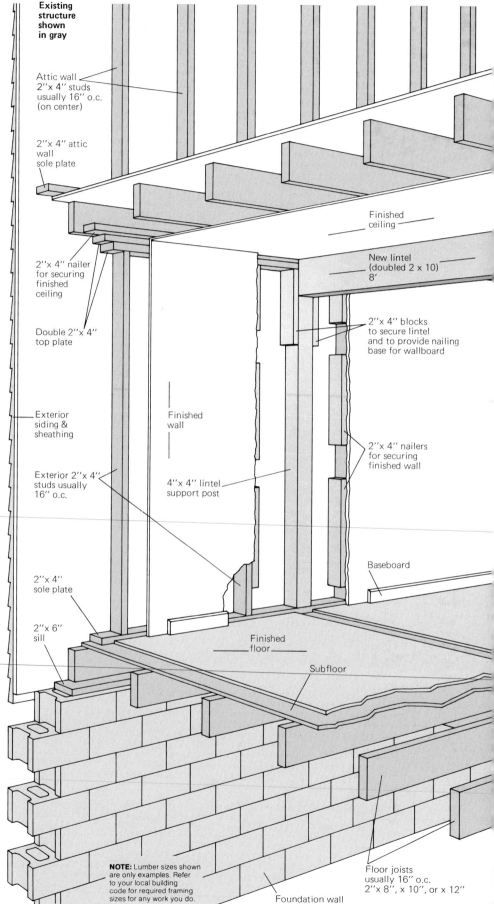

Existing structure shown in gray

Attic wall 2″x 4″ studs usually 16″ o.c. (on center)

2″x 4″ attic wall sole plate

2″x 4″ nailer for securing finished ceiling

Double 2″x 4″ top plate

Exterior siding & sheathing

Exterior 2″x 4″ studs usually 16″ o.c.

2″x 4″ sole plate

2″x 6″ sill

Finished ceiling

New lintel (doubled 2 x 10) 8′

2″x 4″ blocks to secure lintel and to provide nailing base for wallboard

Finished wall

2″x 4″ nailers for securing finished wall

4″x 4″ lintel support post

Baseboard

Finished floor

Subfloor

Floor joists usually 16″ o.c. 2″x 8″, x 10″, or x 12″

Foundation wall

NOTE: Lumber sizes shown are only examples. Refer to your local building code for required framing sizes for any work you do.

Selecting the lintel

In planning for a lintel to replace part of an interior bearing wall, first compute the load the lintel will support. This is the total weight of the house directly over the lintel. The longer the lintel's span, the greater is this load.

The examples below will help you calculate what size lintel you need for a standard wood-frame house. One chart covers built-up wooden lintels—doubled or tripled 2 x 6s, 2 x 8s, etc. The second chart is for a flitch plate lintel—a steel plate sandwiched between boards. If headroom under the lintel is a problem, a flitch plate may be the answer, since it can support a greater load with less depth than lumber alone and is easier to work

with than a steel girder. Flitch plates are made by metal fabricators.

Use the small table at the end of this caption to find the estimated load in pounds per square foot for each part of the house above the lintel. Multiply this figure by the relevant dimensions as shown in the examples. One of these is always the span of your lintel. The other varies with the nature of the component. For the roof, project one of its slopes down onto the attic floor and measure the horizontal distance. For the attic and any other upper floor, take half the distance from your lintel to the next bearing wall, if the lintel is in an exterior wall. For lintels replacing interior bearing walls, as

in our large drawing, this measurement includes floor on both sides of the lintel. The key dimension for any wall above the lintel is the wall's height.

Locate your total load in the row for your lintel's span in one of the charts at the bottom of this page; the top of the column gives the proper lintel size. If your lintel span does not appear in the chart, use the next longer span.

Roof	= 40 pounds/square foot
Attic (low)	= 20 pounds/square foot
Attic (full)	= 30 pounds/square foot
2nd Floor	= 30 pounds/square foot
1st Floor	= 40 pounds/square foot
Wall	= 12 pounds/square foot

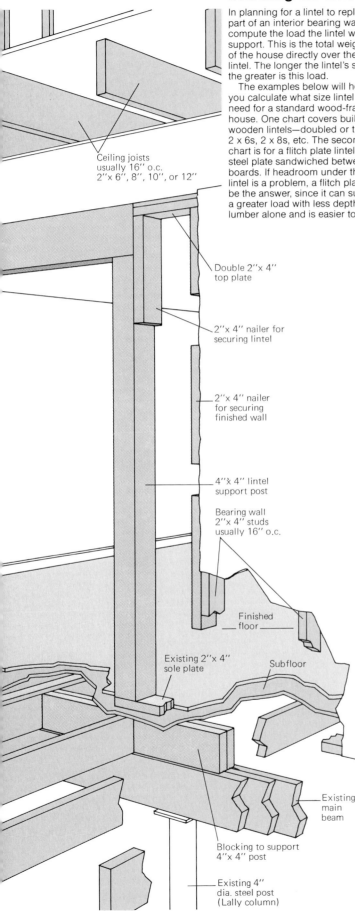

Ceiling joists usually 16″ o.c. 2″x 6″, 8″, 10″, or 12″

Double 2″x 4″ top plate

2″x 4″ nailer for securing lintel

2″x 4″ nailer for securing finished wall

4″x 4″ lintel support post

Bearing wall 2″x 4″ studs usually 16″ o.c.

Finished floor

Existing 2″x 4″ sole plate

Subfloor

Existing main beam

Blocking to support 4″x 4″ post

Existing 4″ dia. steel post (Lally column)

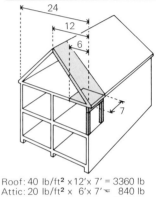

Attic: 20 lb/ft² x12′x 7′ = 1680 lb
Total load: 1680 lb

Roof: 40 lb/ft² x12′x 7′ = 3360 lb
Attic: 20 lb/ft² x 6′x 7′ = 840 lb
Total load: 4200 lb

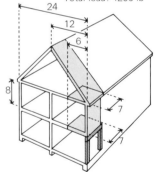

Attic: 20 lb/ft² x12′x 7′ = 1680 lb
Wall: 12 lb/ft² x 8′x 7′ = 672 lb
2nd fl: 30 lb/ft² x12′x 7′ = 2520 lb
Total load: 4872 lb

Roof: 40 lb/ft² x12′x 7′ = 3360 lb
Attic: 20 lb/ft² x 6′x 7′ = 840 lb
Wall: 12 lb/ft² x 8′x 7′ = 672 lb
2nd fl: 30 lb/ft² x 6′x 7′ = 1260 lb
Total load: 6132 lb

Built-up wood lintel (double or triple header*) on two 4″ x 4″ posts

Span	Weight (in pounds) safely supported by:							
	2-2x6	2-2x8	2-2x10	2-2x12	3-2x6	3-2x8	3-2x10	3-2x12
4 Feet	2,250	4,688	5,000	5,980	3,780	5,850	7,410	8,970
6 Feet	1,680	3,126	5,000	5,980	2,520	4,689	7,410	8,970
8 Feet		2,657	3,761	5,511		3,985	5,641	8,266
10 Feet		2,125	3,008	4,409		3,187	4,512	6,613
12 Feet			2,507	3,674			3,760	5,511
14 Feet				3,149				4,723

*with fiber stress (f) 1,000, see pp.36–37.

Steel flitch plate lintel supported by two 4″ x 4″ posts

Plate / Span	Weight (in pounds) safely supported by wood sides and plate								
	2-2x8 + 7½″x . . .			2-2x10 + 9½″x . . .			2-2x12 + 11½″x . . .		
	⅜″	⁷⁄₁₆″	½″	⅜″	⁷⁄₁₆″	½″	⅜″	⁷⁄₁₆″	½″
10 Feet	6,754	7,538	8,242	10,973	12,199	13,418	15,933	17,729	19,604
12 Feet	5,585	6,216	6,827	9,095	10,131	11,106	13,224	14,517	16,265
14 Feet	4,756	5,293	5,811	7,751	8,623	9,463	11,295	12,561	13,876
16 Feet		4,481	5,036	6,746	7,494	8,221	9,815	10,953	12,086
18 Feet				5,942	6,606	7,158	8,675	9,652	10,647
20 Feet					6,466	7,746	8,618	9,408	

Interior bearing walls

Temporary supports

Alterations in a bearing wall cannot begin until you have provided a means of temporarily supporting the weight carried by the wall. On this and the facing page, two generally accepted ways of solving this problem are illustrated and discussed.

Jack posts: Jacking columns, or jack posts, shown below, can often be rented from a tool supplier, lumberyard, or home center. They offer a quick and convenient temporary support system. However, they are heavy, and you will probably need help in loading and transporting them to and from your home. Jack posts come in a range of sizes; a post that measures 8 feet 4 inches when fully extended can be compressed to about 5 feet for transporting and storing. You can move them in a large station wagon or small truck.

You and your helpers should set up the jack posts as shown on this page at a distance of about 30 inches on both sides of the bearing wall to be altered. Note that built-up beam of 2 x 4s is placed across the jack tops to support the load from the ceiling joists. A single 1 x 6 under the bases of the posts transmits the weight to the floor joists below.

With two helpers, you can generally make quick work of erecting these temporary supports. You must, of course, make sure your jack posts are vertical and firmly secured by a tight fit at floor and ceiling. Finding the exact location of the floor and ceiling joists is not essential because the wooden beam and baseplate you have used will absorb the load from above and redistribute it evenly across the floor joists below.

Double supports: Remember that you cannot support the load carried by the bearing wall with a single set of jack posts and wooden supports. After setting up the first support system, as shown here, you and your helpers must go to the other side of the bearing wall and use a second set of jack posts and timbers to create a second temporary support. This is essential because joists usually overlap above a bearing wall, as discussed earlier in this section. Supports must therefore be erected on both sides of the wall to assure that both banks of ceiling joists are secured be-

fore any part of the existing wall is removed. If this is not done, the set of joists left unsupported will break through the ceiling, severely damaging the structure of the house.

Once you are satisfied that the jack posts you have put in place are securely supporting the overhead load, you and your helpers can begin work removing the portion of the bearing wall you have selected for alterations.

Wood-frame supports: An entirely workable alternative to the use of jack posts is illustrated on the facing page. Most, if not all of the work can be done without the aid of a helper, which may be an advantage. But the main reason for using wood-frame supports is that they provide an alternative to jacking columns. If you live away from a metropolitan area, jack posts may be difficult to rent or purchase. In either case, consider building your temporary supports out of 2 x 4s.

Wood-frame temporary supports are built in much the same way any bearing wall would be framed—with a sole plate on the bottom and a top plate on top. But the vertical studs must be deliberately cut slightly shorter to allow the frame to be built on the floor and swung up into position. (If the frame was built to exact ceiling height, the top plate would not quite clear the ceiling in rotating up from the floor to a vertical position.)

Refer to the drawing and you will see that the temporary support has been shimmed up against the ceiling joists—with wedges of scrap wood or spare roof shingles. Note that these shims are placed directly under the ceiling joists overhead, a necessary measure whose significance is discussed in the following paragraphs.

As in the case of jack posts, your wood-frame 2-x-4 supports are installed on both sides of the wall to be removed. The supports should be at least as long as—preferably a bit longer than—the section of wall you are remodeling.

Locating ceiling joists: Before beginning to build your 2-x-4 frames, you must locate the center of each ceiling joist and transfer this mark to your top plates. This procedure is illustrated in the small drawings on page 81. It is essential that your vertical 2 x 4s—the studs—are located directly under the ceiling joists. Therefore these markings dictate the position of the studs and shims in your temporary support.

Despite the fact that your supports are to be temporary, make every effort to do a workmanlike job. The studs and top and bottom plate must be square, securely nailed, and positioned directly beneath the ceiling joists.

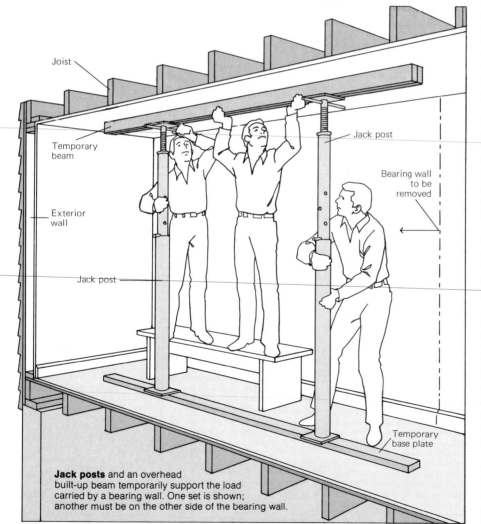

Joist

Temporary beam

Exterior wall

Jack post

Jack post

Bearing wall to be removed

Temporary base plate

Jack posts and an overhead built-up beam temporarily support the load carried by a bearing wall. One set is shown; another must be on the other side of the bearing wall.

Ceiling damage: As you rotate the 2-x-4 frame into position and drive the shims into place, you can expect some slight damage to the ceiling material. If your work is accurate, this will almost always be a minor problem. Repair the ceiling by patching the plaster and re-painting after the job is done.

You can minimize damage to the ceiling by buffering your shims with cloth. Either wrap the shims with cloth, or tape pads of cloth to the tops of the shims. The temporary supports are unlikely to mar the floor.

Exterior bearing walls: The temporary support structures described on these two pages can be adapted for use when working with exterior bearing walls, covered in a later section of this book. The main difference is that only one support system is necessary for an exterior wall. Whereas interior bearing walls are generally modified to give more spaciousness to a room, exterior walls are often moved in order to expand a house or they are opened up to provide new doorways, windows, or glass wall surface.

Locate joists from above if the area is accessible from the attic. Mark the centers of the joists on a 2 x 4; they will correspond to nail heads in unfinished attic subfloor.

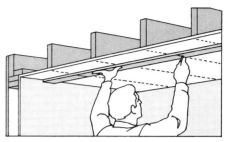

Transfer attic measurements to the ceiling below so that the temporary wood-frame support will have its studs located directly below each of the ceiling joists.

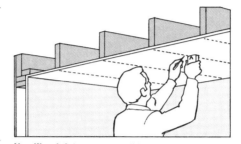

If ceiling joists are accessible only from the room below, you can use a magnetic or electronic stud finder to detect the nails. You must then mark the location of the joists.

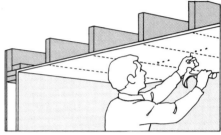

A long nail or stiff wire can be used to probe for joists; where the probe encounters a joist, mark it. These marks will provide the pattern for the spacing of your studs.

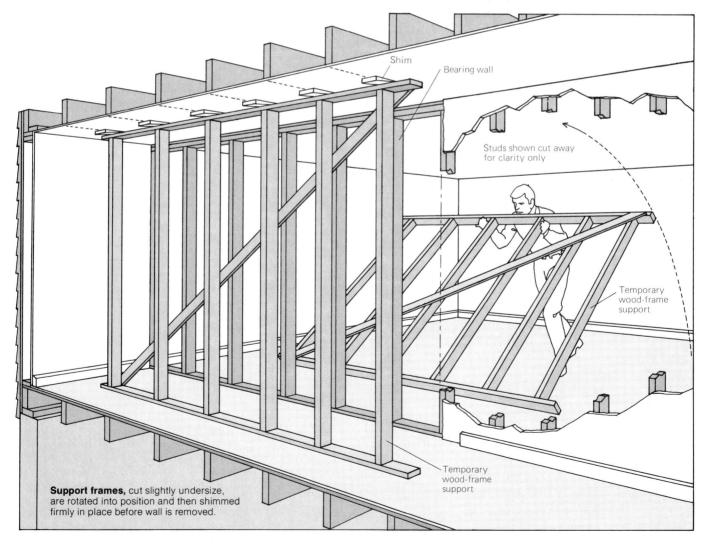

Shim

Bearing wall

Studs shown cut away for clarity only

Temporary wood-frame support

Temporary wood-frame support

Support frames, cut slightly undersize, are rotated into position and then shimmed firmly in place before wall is removed.

Interior bearing walls

Dismantling studs

Before removing the studs as shown below, you must take several preparatory steps: first, satisfy yourself that your temporary supporting walls are tightly in place. Then moldings, baseboards, and trim are removed. Generally these items are well worth saving. Remove all nails from the dismantled woodwork as you go. This makes handling and stacking trim simple and reduces the danger of stepping on a nail.

Wallboard (Sheetrock) is stripped from the wall frame to give access to the studs shown. This can be initiated by drilling a hole in the wallboard to ac-cept a saw blade and then cutting between the studs with a handsaw, although a power saber saw is easier and quicker to use.

Studs can be removed by knocking them out with a sledgehammer, as shown. Some workers saw the studs in half. Removal is easier, but valuable lumber is cut into shorter lengths.

The man depicted at left, below, is using a handsaw to aid in removing the last stud, which is usually adjacent to a built-up pair of studs within the exterior wall running at right angles to the bearing wall. Depending on the load on this particular end stud, a power saw could bind suddenly, thereby creating an unnecessary hazard to the operator. Once the last stud is cut through with a handsaw, it is pried from the wall with a crowbar inserted in the saw-cut. Do not try to save a piece of lumber by knocking this last stud off with a sledgehammer, as you might damage the adjacent wall surface inadvertently. A narrow section of the wallboard on the inside of the exterior wall nearest to the bearing wall has to be cut away in this process. This gap is later mended with new Sheetrock and wallboard plaster.

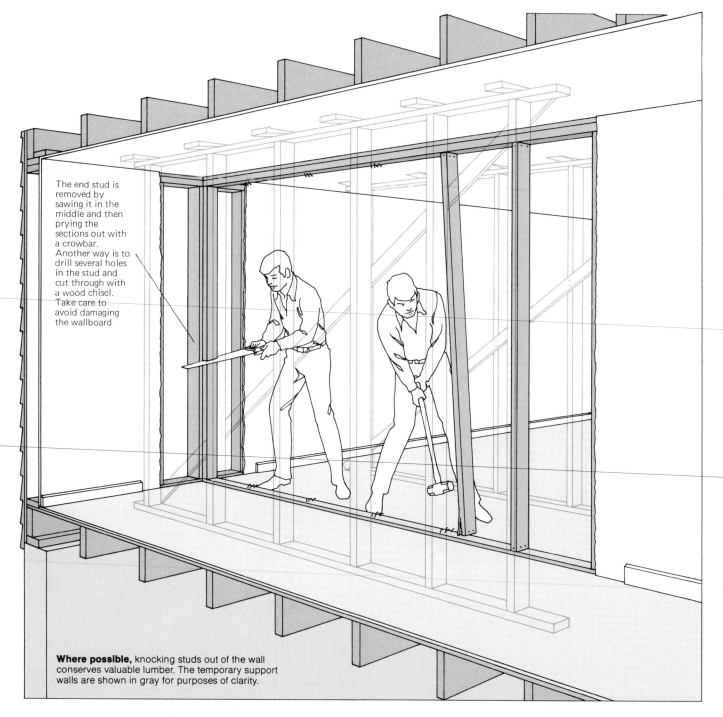

The end stud is removed by sawing it in the middle and then prying the sections out with a crowbar. Another way is to drill several holes in the stud and cut through with a wood chisel. Take care to avoid damaging the wallboard

Where possible, knocking studs out of the wall conserves valuable lumber. The temporary support walls are shown in gray for purposes of clarity.

Removing top and sole plates

After all studs are removed, you will remove the plates in the floor and ceiling. The bottom or sole plate can usually be pried up with a claw hammer and crowbar. If the sole plate proves stubborn, make parallel cuts, about 2 inches apart near its center, then knock out the cut sections. Or you can use the method shown at right. Once a segment of the sole plate is removed, it is easy to pry up the rest of the plate.

If headroom is not a problem, you need not remove the top plate from the ceiling—simply install the new lintel beneath it. The top plate can be taken out by one person, but it is usually made of built-up lumber and nailed into the plate of the adjoining wall. If your assistant can get above the top plate, it's a simple matter to ram the board down with a 2 x 4 as shown. Otherwise, you may have to chisel or saw off a piece first, as in the case of the sole plate.

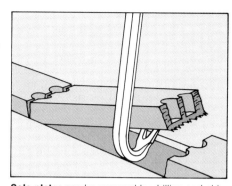

Sole plates can be removed by drilling and chiseling first, and then prying out the sections of the plate with a crowbar.

Attic access enables helper to push down top plates with a 2 x 4 through the ceiling slit

Top and sole plates can be dismantled by a variety of methods, as can be seen in the illustration above. Remove the top plate only if additional headroom is needed.

83

Interior bearing walls

Measuring lintel and posts

By placing the lintel on the floor as seen in the drawing below, one can determine the exact length of the posts that will support it. At this point the temporary supporting frameworks (only one of which is shown) still carry the load.

The new supporting posts will carry all the load on the lintel. They will transmit this load downward through various structural elements to the basement floor. The posts selected must be of appropriate size and quality, ranging from 3 x 4 all the way up to 8 x 8 if they are wooden (see pp.78–79). This selection is crucial because in the original wall, the load was distributed among a number of studs spaced fairly close together, while the two new posts holding up the lintel will now bear the entire burden formerly spread along the missing section of load-bearing wall. Avoid using steel posts except in the basement or on the first floor; they are heavy and need strong footings.

Refer to the detail at right for underfloor structure suggestions. All lumberyards sell ready-made hardwood thresholds that can be used to cover the gap where the section of sole plate was removed from the floor.

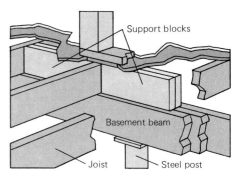

Double support blocks are driven in tightly under the new post. If there is no beam or bearing wall below, consult a professional.

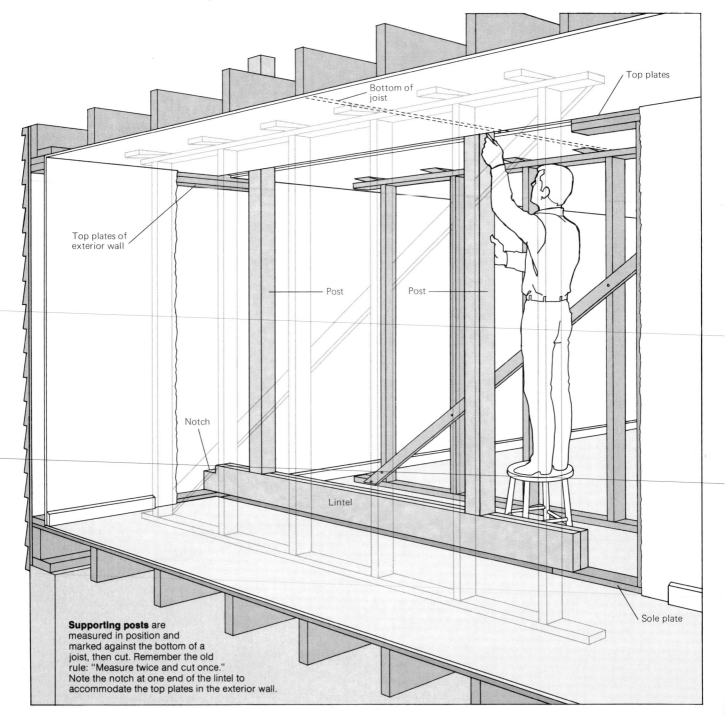

Supporting posts are measured in position and marked against the bottom of a joist, then cut. Remember the old rule: "Measure twice and cut once." Note the notch at one end of the lintel to accommodate the top plates in the exterior wall.

Installing lintel and posts

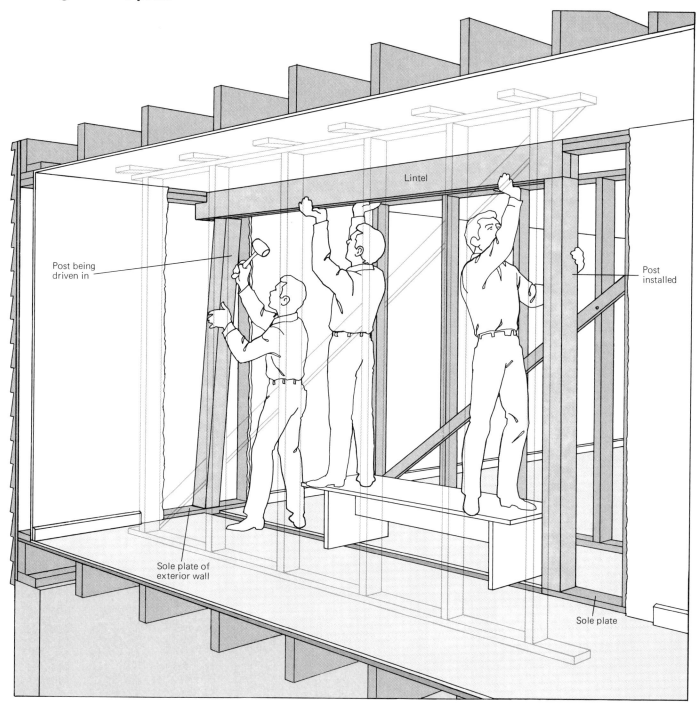

Lintel

Post being
driven in

Post
installed

Sole plate of
exterior wall

Sole plate

When the posts have been cut as marked, the lintel is raised and positioned against the joists above by your helpers. The posts are driven in tightly between the lintel and sole plates, shimmed if necessary. They are then toenailed to the lintel and plates, and secured with nailing blocks.

Now the temporary supports can be removed. The next steps are to finish the walls (see *Working with wallboard,* pp.88–91), and the floor (see *Installing hardwood flooring, baseboards, and moldings,* pp.156–161.) The lintel may be stained as an exposed beam.

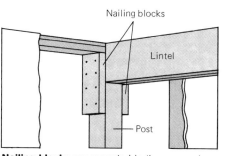

Nailing blocks

Lintel

Post

Nailing blocks are mounted in the areas where the posts meet the lintel. These blocks help to secure the joists and also provide nailing bases

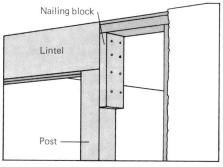

Nailing block

Lintel

Post

for the wallboard. The blocks are attached in the manner shown above, with sides facing the back of the wallboard to be installed.

Non-bearing partitions

Planning the job

Non-bearing partitions are used to divide a house's large open interior spaces into smaller rooms. These walls carry none of the load of the house (see *Interior bearing walls*, pp.76–85). Existing partitions can thus be removed to open up small rooms into larger ones; or, conversely, new partitions can easily be built to subdivide open expanses—for example, to create bedrooms in a finished attic.

As shown by the large illustration at bottom of this page, a non-bearing partition usually has a light wood-frame skeleton. Double sole plates—typically, 2 x 4s—form the base of the frame. First, the lower sole plate is nailed to the floor; then, the fully fabricated frame—consisting of the second sole plate, the top plate, and the vertical connecting members called studs—is raised onto the bottom plate and nailed into place. Partition frame construction is illustrated on the opposite page.

Once in place, the partition framework can be covered with a variety of wall coverings. The application of plasterboard, or gypsum wallboard, is described on the following pages; paneling is the subject of a subsequent chapter.

Studs and fire stops: Although partition construction is comparatively simple, you should check your local building code before ordering materials. Your local code may give you options for stud size and spacing (although for walls to be covered with plasterboard, 2-x-4 studs spaced 16 inches on center will facilitate the nailing of the plasterboard and provide a properly rigid wall). Building codes commonly require the inclusion of fire stops in the frame (see *Building codes/Introduction to construction*, pp.21–37). Fire stops prevent a wall from acting as a flue.

Nailing to joists: In framing for a new room, one or two of the partitions will typically run parallel to existing floor and ceiling joists; the remaining partition or partitions will run perpendicular to these joists. Partitions parallel to joists should be located directly under a joist in the ceiling so that the top plate can be nailed through the ceiling into it. (Methods of locating joists are described on pp.77 and 81. If for any reason you are forced to place a partition between two parallel ceiling joists, you can install nailing blocks every few feet between the joists; however, this entails ripping up the existing ceiling or the floor above to reach the ceiling joists, a difficult job.)

A partition running perpendicular to the joists poses no special problem once the joists are located and their positions are marked; the top plate of the partition is simply nailed through the ceiling into each joist at its point of intersection. The lower sole plate is nailed to the flooring and subfloor, and need not center on a floor joist.

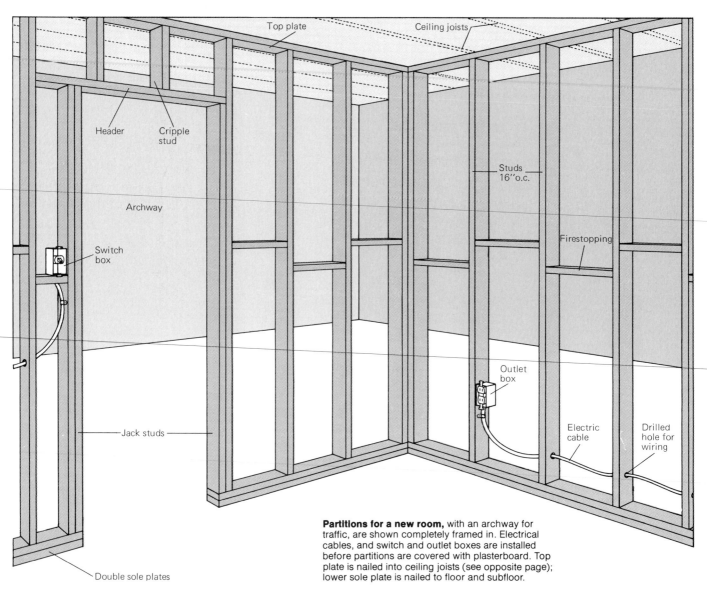

Partitions for a new room, with an archway for traffic, are shown completely framed in. Electrical cables, and switch and outlet boxes are installed before partitions are covered with plasterboard. Top plate is nailed into ceiling joists (see opposite page); lower sole plate is nailed to floor and subfloor.

Framing the partition

1. Mark location of the partition under a joist in the ceiling (see pp.77 and 81); then have your helper drop a plumb line at several points along the joist. In this manner, transfer the line from the ceiling to the floor. Use a chalk to mark the floor.

2. When position of partition has been marked on the floor, nail a 2 x 4 of the appropriate length on top of the chalk line to serve as the lower sole plate. Do the same for other walls. For the time being, ignore the archway.

3. Take accurate measurements for the dimensions of the partitions. (The length of the studs should be the height of the ceiling minus 4½ in., to make room for the one top and two sole plates.) The exact positions of the studs are marked on plates before nailing. Brace studs against baseboard when nailing.

4. With the aid of a helper, lift the partition and slide it into position over the sole plate nailed to the floor. Nail the top plate to the ceiling joist(s). Nail end studs to an existing wall stud, where applicable. Finally, nail the upper sole plate to lower sole plate (any gaps resulting from inaccurate measurement can be filled with shims). Saw out and remove sole plates at the archway.

Framing details

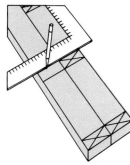

Mark top and sole plates side by side for studs. Begin at an end, following code intervals. Allow ¾ in. on either side of center for thickness of studs.

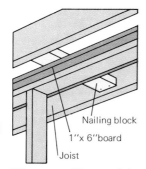

Where a partition parallels ceiling joists but cannot be located beneath one, open ceiling and anchor top plate to 1 x 6 and blocks added every few feet.

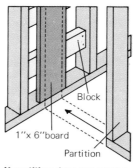

If partition does not meet a stud in the existing wall, open wall and add blocks between two studs; attach a 1 x 6 to blocks for nailing partition and wallboard.

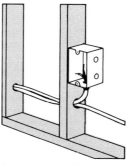

An outlet or switch box is first mounted in position on a stud; ¾-in. holes are then drilled in the studs to run cables (see *Electrical wiring*, pp.172–201).

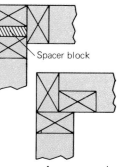

Corner posts are used where two partitions meet. Either shape combines three 2 x 4s for strength and to provide wallboard nailing surfaces.

87

Working with plasterboard

Covering a wallframe with gypsum board

Walls made of lath and plaster have largely become a thing of the past. Drywall, or walls covered with panels of plasterboard (gypsum wallboard) have taken their place because this construction is easier, faster, and more economical. Nails, special fasteners, and stapling machines are all used to attach the panels; but inexpensive annular nails are used most often.

Standard thicknesses of wallboard are 3/8 inch, 1/2 inch, and 5/8 inch. Panels are customarily sold in 4-x-8-foot sheets, 1/2 inch thick. Some building codes specify the type and finishing method for plasterboard (see *Building codes,* pp.30–31). Wallboard is manufactured in lengths up to 16 feet. The sheer weight and bulk of such large panels, however, makes them difficult to handle. Do-it-yourselfers generally work with 4-x-8-foot sizes.

Most plasterboard has a smooth side of white or cream-colored paper, a backing of kraft paper, and a central core of gypsum. The core is incombustible, and the paper facings are insignificant as a fire hazard. Some wallboard is made with decorative surfaces of various designs, including simulated wood grain. Plasterboard is sold with half a dozen kinds of edges: straight, tapered, squared, beveled, rounded, and tongue-and-groove.

Handling: Handling and storing of plasterboard requires skill and care.

The gypsum core, faced on both sides with paper, is dense, soft, and crumbly. A full-size panel is both heavy and brittle; it should be carried vertically, not horizontally, by one person—horizontal stresses can cause a panel to break under its own weight. Plasterboard should be stored in stacks on dry, flat surfaces to prevent cracking.

Application: If both the ceiling and the walls are to be covered, the ceiling should be done first. When the room is completed the panels on the walls will act as pilasters to help support panels on the ceiling. Wall panels butt snugly against the ceiling; any gap at the bottom will be covered by the baseboard. The panels can be attached either vertically or horizontally to the wallframe, depending on the wall's dimensions.

Double layers: In certain parts of the house, double layers of plasterboard may be advisable, as in a bathroom, kitchen, or a busy hallway. The extra layer will result in a wall that has better sound-absorbing qualities, is stronger, and more fire-resistant. In a double installation, the first layer—of ordinary plasterboard, 3/8 inch backer panels, or sound-deadening panels—is usually nailed over the wallframe. The second layer is then attached to the first with adhesive, mastic, or adhesive strips.

Basic techniques for cutting, installing, nailing, and taping plasterboard appear on this and following pages.

Wood vs. metal studs

An alternative to using conventional wood studs is the use of prefabricated metal studs, gauged for both bearing and non-bearing walls. Widely used by professionals in commercial buildings, they are beginning to attract do-it-yourselfers (but may not be available at all home centers).

The studs, ranging in length from 2 to 30 ft. and in width from 1 to 6 in. are assembled into floor and ceiling tracks. A power screw-gun is used to fasten the studs and plasterboard with self-drilling, self-tapping screws. The metal framing system is fireproof and easy to install, but less well insulated acoustically than traditional wood framework.

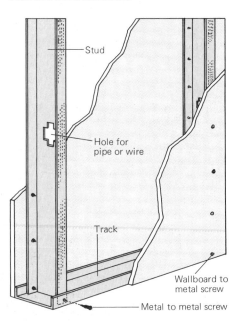

Stud

Hole for pipe or wire

Track

Wallboard to metal screw

Metal to metal screw

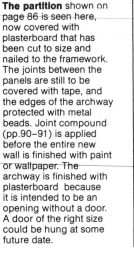

The partition shown on page 86 is seen here, now covered with plasterboard that has been cut to size and nailed to the framework. The joints between the panels are still to be covered with tape, and the edges of the archway protected with metal beads. Joint compound (pp.90–91) is applied before the entire new wall is finished with paint or wallpaper. The archway is finished with plasterboard because it is intended to be an opening without a door. A door of the right size could be hung at some future date.

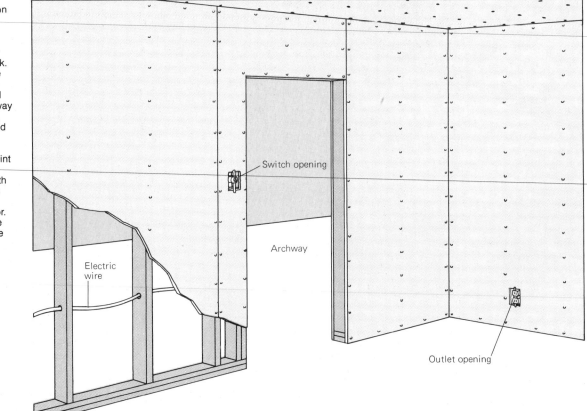

Electric wire

Switch opening

Archway

Outlet opening

Cutting panels

Plan the placement of your 4-x-8-foot plasterboard panels to minimize the need for cutting. But prepare to cut pieces to fit corners, areas above doorways, and other special spaces.

Cutting a plasterboard panel to a smaller size is relatively easy once you understand the unique nature of this hefty but crumbly material. The first step is to measure accurately for a piece that is to fill a particular area. For se-

cure fastening, the vertical edges of any panel should cover at least half the thickness of a stud; its top or bottom edge—where applicable—should lap far enough over the frame's top plate or sole plate to provide nailing space.

For a straight-line cut all the way across a panel, score the board using a knife with a sharp, stiff blade. The knife point should cut through the paper and part way into the gypsum core. Then,

position the panel over a firm support; with the scored line facing up, snap the cut section downward. To avoid a ragged tear on the other face, score its paper before separating the pieces.

Both hand and power-operated saws can be used to cut plasterboard. But a long straight line may be difficult for an inexperienced person, and saws throw off a messy fallout of gypsum dust. Use a saw only for irregular cuts.

 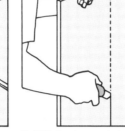 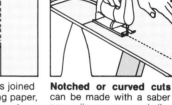 

1. For a straight cut, mark line with pencil and straight-edge. Score with a sharp knife along pencil line.

2. Align the scored portion with a table edge or a 2 x 4 placed on the floor. Snap excess portion downward.

3. With the two parts joined only by the remaining paper, hold at right angles; cut upward to separate.

Notched or curved cuts can be made with a saber saw, a jigsaw, or any similar small power or hand saw.

To cut an opening, first drill a hole or two inside the marked shape, then insert a keyhole saw to cut.

Fitting panels on the frame

You can apply plasterboard either parallel or perpendicular to the joists or studs. The best plan is the one that results in the fewest cuts, and the least number and shortest lengths of joints. Joints in the lower half of a wall are easier to nail and tape than are those in the upper half. Planning and some simple calculations can make your task considerably easier.

Attaching heavy, brittle sheets of plasterboard to a ceiling requires at

least one helper. A T-shaped brace made of scrap lumber, slightly longer than the height of the ceiling, is an essential tool. After the panel has been raised to the ceiling, the brace is wedged securely with a bit of foot pressure, so that the helper can either leave the scene while the panel is being nailed or help with the nailing.

Plasterboard can be installed on walls without the assistance of a helper if you install the panels vertically. Hori-

zontal installation calls for at least part-time help in installing the upper course of panels (see p.90).

Keep in mind when installing plasterboard never to cut a panel even slightly larger than the space allotted to it: edges or corners will crumble when the panel is forced into place. A board cut slightly smaller than proper size presents only minor problems. Any small gap can be filled and made invisible with tape and joint compound.

 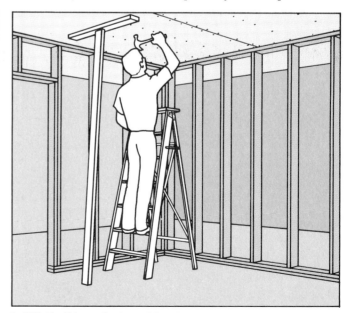

1. At least two persons are required to place a 4-x-8-ft. panel on the ceiling. With one person raising the panel overhead and ascending the ladder, the helper raises the T-brace, keeping panel level at all times.

2. With the T-brace firmly wedging the panel, one person can begin the nailing while still partly supporting one end of the panel. Typically, panel would be nailed to exposed attic or basement ceiling joists.

Working with plasterboard

Fitting panels on the frame

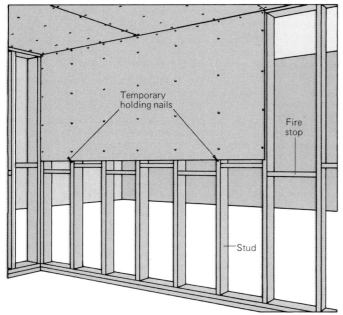

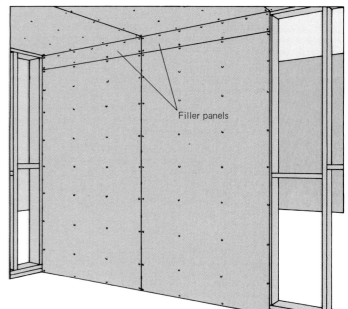

Horizontal Installation, requiring fewer joints than vertical panels, is customary where ceilings are not more than 8 ft. A helper positions top panel snugly against ceiling (see text, p.88), while 6d (2-in.) nails are driven temporarily into a pair of studs to hold the panel for nailing (opposite page); temporary nails are then removed.

Vertical Installation, has an advantage. It can be done by one person without a helper, because the panels are supported during nailing by the floor or blocks placed on the floor. Vertical installation is also used for rooms with extra high ceilings; spaces above panels can be filled with sheets cut horizontally, with joints above eye level.

Fitting details

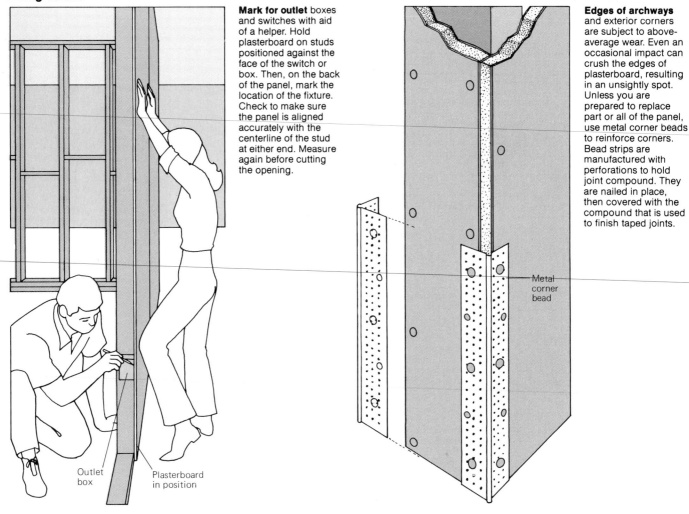

Mark for outlet boxes and switches with aid of a helper. Hold plasterboard on studs positioned against the face of the switch or box. Then, on the back of the panel, mark the location of the fixture. Check to make sure the panel is aligned accurately with the centerline of the stud at either end. Measure again before cutting the opening.

Edges of archways and exterior corners are subject to above-average wear. Even an occasional impact can crush the edges of plasterboard, resulting in an unsightly spot. Unless you are prepared to replace part or all of the panel, use metal corner beads to reinforce corners. Bead strips are manufactured with perforations to hold joint compound. They are nailed in place, then covered with the compound that is used to finish taped joints.

Nailing and taping panels

In nailing plasterboard panels, use nails long enough to penetrate the thickness of your size panel (see text on page 88) and that extend about 1 inch into the studs. On 2-x-4-studs where two panels meet, nailing space of about ¾ inch will exist for nailing the end of each panel. Annular ring nails are a good choice for nailing. Drive them with a crownhead hammer (it has a rounded head); first drive the nails flush with the surface of the plasterboard, then dimple them slightly into the plasterboard, being careful not to rupture the paper covering of the panel. The small depression will hide the nail head and hold joint compound uniformly.

Joint compound and tape: The application of the joint compound and the taping begin once all panels are nailed in place. Mix the compound with water according to manufacturer's directions. Begin taping by applying a layer of compound about 3 inches wide along a joint, using a 4-inch joint knife.

Fill up all the nail dimples and the cracks where panels meet. Cut an appropriate length of joint tape and press it into the wet compound, working the tape into the compound with the joint knife so that the cement oozes out of the tape holes and along the tape edges. Then, smooth the compound on the tape and feather it at the edges to make a uniform transition with the wall.

At inside corners the tape is creased lengthwise to fit into the cemented joint. Outside corners can be finished with tape, but it is much better practice to nail on the metal corner beads that are manufactured for this purpose. Use this metal edging wherever corners might be damaged by frequent traffic, as in a hallway or an archway. The beads are also finished with compound.

Successive coats: The first coat of compound was applied slightly wider than the tape, and under the tape. Successive coats are applied over the tape and to a much greater width.

After the first coat has dried for 24 hours, apply a second coat over the tape and feather it to a width of about 6 inches. As you work, also apply the compound to any nail holes and accidental dents in the surface. Fill these areas flush. Smooth the compound with the knife, and with a wet paint brush or sponge. When the second coat dries, sand it with a medium-grit sandpaper and then a fine grade of finishing paper. Do not apply excessive pressure, or you risk marring the plasterboard surface.

The second coat of compound may shrink in drying, so that dents remain slightly visible. Apply a third coat of compound, feathering it out to about 10 inches to achieve a smooth transition with the surface of the plasterboard. This final coat is usually applied more thinly than previous coats, making it easier to smooth and finish. Again, allow 24 hours drying time and sand the last coat with a fine-grit finishing paper.

Priming: Prepare the plasterboard walls for painting by applying a primer or base coat of paint. Prime with shellac or varnish if you intend to wallpaper.

Nail and dimple using crownhead hammer.

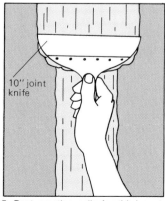

1. Apply first coat of joint compound with a 4-in. joint knife, to a width of about 3 in. Spread the cement generously with the knife.

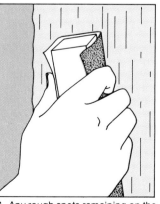

2. Cut off full length of tape and press it evenly over the joint. Work the tape well into the wet cement; smooth surface and feather edges.

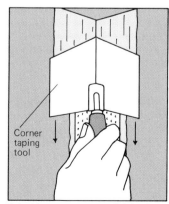

3. Alternate method of taping involves unrolling the tape along the joint while working it into the compound; this requires dexterity.

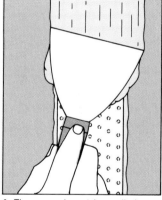

4. The second coat is applied over tape 24 hours after the first. Spread the compound about 6 to 8 in. wide. Feather the edges well.

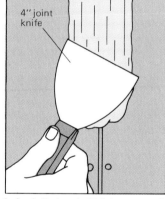

5. Best practice calls for third coat applied 24 hours later. A 10-in. joint knife spreads compound 10 in. wide. Feather edges finely.

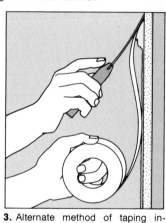

6. Any rough spots remaining on the third coat of the compound are smoothed with fine-grit sandpaper after the cement has dried.

7. Inside corners are finished by creasing the tape along its length before pressing it into the cement. Work tape in with corner taping tool.

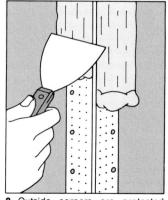

8. Outside corners are protected with perforated metal corner beads. They are nailed in place, and compound is worked onto the beads.

New ceilings

Acoustical tile ceilings

Acoustical tiles can create an attractive ceiling that is acoustically and thermally insulating, fire resistant, washable, inexpensive, and easy to install.

If there is an existing ceiling made of plaster or wallboard that is sound and with unbroken, level surface, acoustical tile can be attached to it with cement. If the surface of the ceiling is weak, uneven, or deteriorated, or if there is no ceiling over the joists, parallel rows of furring strips are installed as supports.

A careful plan of the ceiling is drawn to determine the exact configuration of the tiles. Most tiles measure 12 x 12 inches; but 12-x-24- and 16-x-16-inch tiles are also available (the latter require that the furring strips be spaced accordingly). Because the dimensions of a ceiling rarely come out to an exact number of feet, border tiles must be calculated and cut for each edge of the ceiling, as explained below.

From the plan the number of tiles can be accurately determined (5-10 percent waste should be allowed). You need 100 linear feet of 1-x-3 furring and 1¾ pounds of ⁹/₁₆-inch coated staples for every 100 square feet of ceiling.

Furring strips are installed according to the plan, so that each will be centered directly under the stapling flanges of a row of tiles. The furring runs perpendicular to the joists, nailed to the joists with two 8-penny nails at every juncture. If the joists are concealed by an existing ceiling, they are located by tapping the ceiling, and marked before the furring is nailed in. The furring is checked for level and shimmed where necessary to provide a level surface. Furring is also installed around projecting vents; the entire ceiling can be lowered to cover projections or simply to improve the proportions of the room with a lattice of furring strips.

Chalk lines are snapped down and across the furring strips to guide the placement of the tiles. Boxes containing the tiles are opened in the room at least 24 hours before they are installed, so they can acclimate to the local temperature and humidity. The border tiles are cut and installed according to the plan, leaving a small space next to the wall. The tiling proceeds outward from the corner and across the ceiling. The tongue-and-groove tiles fit neatly into each other, and should not be forced together. (Butt end tiles are sometimes used for gluing to an existing ceiling.) Each tile is stapled through its flange in three places on its exposed edge and once in the corner into the furring. Hands should be coated with talc to prevent smudging the tiles. Finally, wood trimming (already stained to prevent discoloration of the tiles) is nailed around the perimeter.

Ceiling furring layout

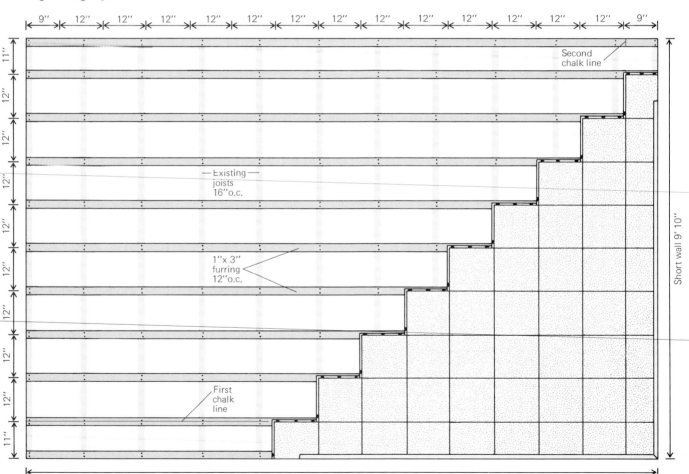

Planning the ceiling: The ceiling is measured and a plan drawn to scale on a piece of graph paper. Standard acoustical tiles are 12 in. squares. For the best appearance, the border tiles (which may be shorter than 12 in.) should be even on both sides of the room. Border tiles should be as large as possible, never less than 6 in. in width or length. For example, if a room is 15 ft. 6 in. long, each row of tiles should be designed to run 14 complete tiles, with one 9 in. border tile on each end. If the room is 9 ft. 10 in. wide,

each cross row should have 8 complete tiles and an 11-in. border tile on each end. The furring strips are installed (see large drawing, top of facing page) according to the plan you have drawn.

A chalk line is snapped down the center of the second furring strip. A steel square or a 3-4-5 triangle is used to snap a second chalk line perpendicular to the first, across the furring. These lines guide the placement of the initial rows of tile.

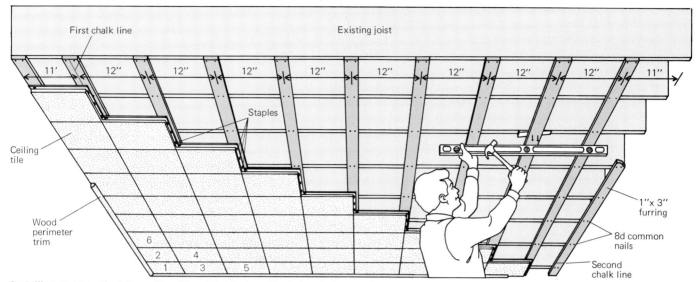

Installing an acoustical tile ceiling: The grid of furring strips is installed according to the ceiling plan. The strips generally run perpendicular to the ceiling joists. The first 1-x-3 furring strip is flush with a wall. The second is placed so the edge of the border tile will center on it; for the plan shown on the facing page, the strip would center 11-11½ in. from the starter wall (the stapling flange extends ½ in. from the tile). Furring is then nailed every 12 in. o.c. across the ceiling. The second to last strip should be as far from the end wall as the second strip is from the starter wall. The last strip is flush with the end wall. Each furring strip is attached with two 8-penny nails to each joist. Shims are installed where necessary so the furring surface is flat. When furring is completed, the tiles are installed, working outward from the corner, as indicated by the numbers above. Tiles are attached to the furring with 9/16 in. coated staples, three staples on the leading edge of each tile, one in the back corner. Trim perimeter with stained wood.

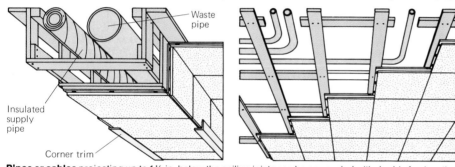 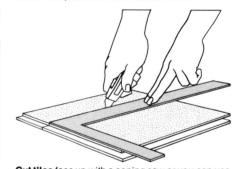

Pipes or cables projecting up to 1½ in. below the ceiling joists can be concealed with double furring, the second course running perpendicular to the first (above, right). Large vents or pipes can be boxed with furring strips, spaced as they are in the rest of the ceiling. Where there is danger of sweating, pipes within the ceiling should be insulated.

Cut tiles face up with a coping saw or you can use a very sharp fiberboard knife. Be sure that the tongue edge and the flange for stapling remain intact as the border tiles are cut.

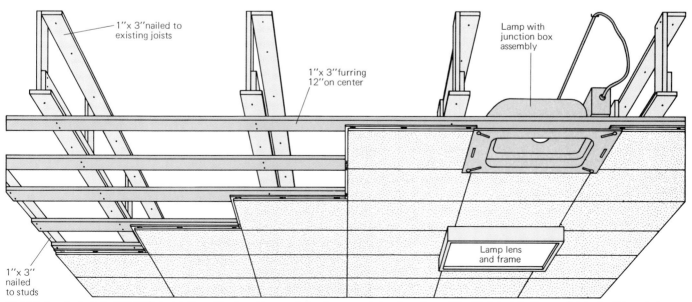

Light fixture in suspended ceiling: A lattice of furring strips can bring the nailing surface for tiles down to any height (see also *Suspended ceilings,* pp.94–95). Incandescent light fixtures, which are the same size as the ceiling tile (usually 12 in. square) can be laid into the ceiling where there is no obstruction above. If the tile is installed over a finished ceiling, a hole must be made to the depth of the light fixture. The fixture is held in place by an adapter plate that is screwed into the furring strips. The junction box assembly and reflector pan are recessed.

New ceilings

Suspended grid systems

Suspended ceilings are composed of a lightweight fiberglass or of acoustical panels laid into a metal interlocking grid that is suspended from the ceiling joists with wires. Suspended ceilings are often used to lower high ceilings, or over unfinished ceilings with exposed pipes, wiring, or ducts. Because the panels are laid atop the grid, and not attached to it, suspended ceilings allow permanent easy access to the mechanical systems in the ceiling.

As with acoustical tile ceilings, suspended ceilings require planning to figure the configuration of the panels and the size of the border panels (see below).

The height of the finished ceiling is determined, and a metal molding is attached to the walls at that height around the room; this supports the ends of the border panels and the ends of the pieces of the metal grid. The metal grid is composed of two elements: the main runners, which run the entire length of the room (made of interlocking segments), usually perpendicular to the ceiling joists; the cross tees, short pieces that lock between the main runners.

The installation of the grid is guided by strings strung across the room at ceiling height, carefully measured from the walls. Wires are attached to the ceiling's joists with screw eyes; after these are bent at a prescribed height (guided by another guide string), they are attached to the main runners. Cross tees are snapped into place; the outside tees are cut with tin snips so they lie in the flange of the outside molding. Tees are installed laterally, wall to wall, to lock the grid together, then proceed down the length of the ceiling.

Border panels are measured and cut one at a time. They and the complete panels are laid in, resting on the flanges of the grid. Three inches of clearance between the grid and any ceiling obstructions are required to install panels.

Ceiling grid layout

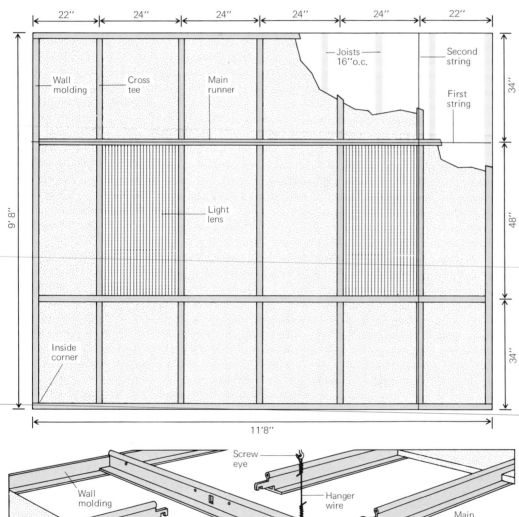

Planning the ceiling: The ceiling is measured and drawn in scale on a piece of graph paper. The most common suspended panels measure 24 x 48 in.; the long dimension of the panels generally runs parallel to the ceiling joists, usually the short dimension of the room. As with acoustical tiles, border panels, which are measured and cut to finish each row, are symmetrical at each end and as large as possible. For the 48 in. dimension, no panel should be less than 24 in.; in the 24 in. dimension no panel should be less than 12 in. For example, each row in a room 10 ft. 8 in. wide (the short direction) would consist of one 48-in. panel and two 40-in. border panels. If the room is 11 ft. 8 in. long, each course would consist of four 24-in. panels and two 22-in. borders. After the height of the ceiling is determined and marked with a chalk line (see below, left), the width of the first border panel is measured in from the short wall (here 22 in.) on both ends of the room. A reference string is strung across the room between these points at the ceiling height. The length of the first border panel (here 34 in.) is measured in from the long walls; a second string, perpendicular to the first, is strung across the ceiling. The first main runner will sit above the first string; the first cross tee will sit above the second.

A level chalk line is snapped around the room, and a wall molding is attached to the wall over it so its lip is at the desired height of the ceiling. The molding overlaps or butts at inside corners, and is miter cut for outside corners. When the main runners and the outside cross tees are installed, they are cut so one end will sit on the molding. Main runners are made of segments that slide together, locking with tabs in their ends. The cross tees lock into slots in the runners, which must be positioned correctly to accept them.

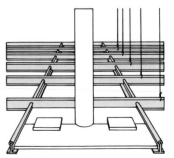

A panel is cut in half with a sharp fiberboard knife, and two semicircles are cut to accommodate a column. Scrap pieces of panel are glued atop the re-joined panels.

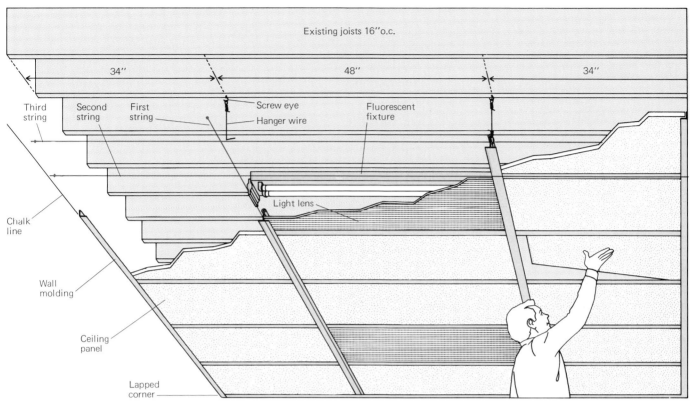

Existing joists 16″o.c.

34″   48″   34″

Third string
Second string
First string
Screw eye
Hanger wire
Fluorescent fixture
Light lens

Chalk line
Wall molding
Ceiling panel
Lapped corner

Installing the ceiling: After the wall molding is installed, the first main runner is cut so that a slot for accepting the first cross tee is directly above the second reference string (see illustration, opposite); this ensures that the border panel will be the proper width. Hanging wires for the main runner are attached with screw eyes into the ceiling joists every 4 ft., directly above the first reference string. A third reference string is strung tightly above the first string at the height of the holes in the main runner. The hanging wires are bent along this string; this ensures that the runner will hang exactly level.

The runners are all assembled and hung with wires across the ceiling. The first cross tee is cut to fit between the first main runner and the wall (here 34 in. long). The first row of tees is installed, wall to wall, then the other rows are similarly installed. When the grid is complete, the border panels are cut with a coping saw or a very sharp fiberboard knife; each panel is measured and cut individually. Panels are pushed through the grid at an angle and laid on the flanges of the grid. Panels should be handled from the edges, fingers touching the finished side as little as possible.

Lighting fixtures

Incandescent and fluorescent lighting fixtures can be used with acoustical tile and suspended ceilings. Most incandescent and fluorescent fixtures require only a normal 110-120-volt line, run from an outlet above the ceiling to the fixture.

The most common incandescent fixture is the same size as an acoustical tile, and is attached to the furring strips that support the tiles, as shown on page 93. These fixtures can also be used with suspended panels; each is set into a

12-inch-square hole cut into a panel, supported by two 23½-inch-long furring strips atop the panel running in the 24-inch dimension (first diagram below).

Fluorescent fixtures are often used with suspended ceilings. One type is completely recessed into the ceiling. It sits upon the main runners, near a supporting wire, and can be placed where there is at least 5 inch overhead clearance (above; second diagram below).

Another type of fluorescent fixture

attaches to the grid with mounting clips on its top and projects below the ceiling (third diagram below). It too must be placed near a hanging wire, but does not require overhead clearance. Fluorescent fixtures can often hook up to each other end-to-end, so a row can run the length of a ceiling.

This second design can be attached to acoustical tile ceilings with screws into the furring strips or joists: molly screws are used with plaster ceilings.

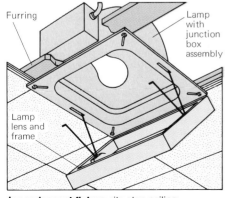

Furring
Lamp with junction box assembly
Lamp lens and frame

Incandescent fixture sits atop ceiling.

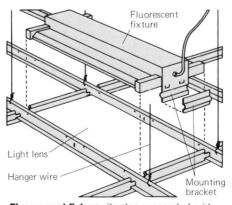

Fluorescent fixture
Light lens
Hanger wire
Mounting bracket

Fluorescent fixture sits atop suspended grid.

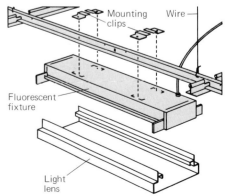

Mounting clips
Wire
Fluorescent fixture
Light lens

Fluorescent fixture projects from ceiling.

Paneling

Wall paneling

Wood paneling is an easy way to create an attractive interior wall surface. Wood paneling can be installed over an existing wall or unfinished wood frame or over a masonry surface that is prepared with furring strips. The three popular kinds of wood paneling are veneered plywood sheet, coated hardboard sheet, and solid board panels.

Veneered plywood sheet: These are made of a thin piece of plywood, usually ³/₁₆- to ³/₈-inch thick, with a very thin veneer of an attractive wood (usually a hardwood) glued to the face. Chemically produced veneers that simulate more expensive hardwoods have become popular. Other effects, such as barnwood and driftwood, are also chemically simulated on plywood sheets. The panels measure 4 x 8 feet, ordinarily, but other lengths are available.

Plywood sheet panels can be installed over an existing wall covering if it has a sound, flat surface. The wall studs behind the wall are located and marked; the nails holding the plywood panels are driven through the existing wall covering into the studs. Panels are installed to adjoin over the studs.

Plywood panels can be installed over open frame walls or over masonry walls if parallel rows of furring are installed (framing is suggested over masonry walls if there is much moisture present). Furring is also used if an existing wall covering is uneven or unsound. Because the panels are thin and flexible, a layer of gypsum wallboard is often installed first to make the wall stiffer, and to enhance its thermal and acoustical insulation qualities.

Place the panels in the room 48 hours before installation. They should be piled flat with furring strips separating them, to acclimate them to the local temperature and humidity. Because the panels differ slightly in color and grain pattern, they are set up against the wall and

Installing furring

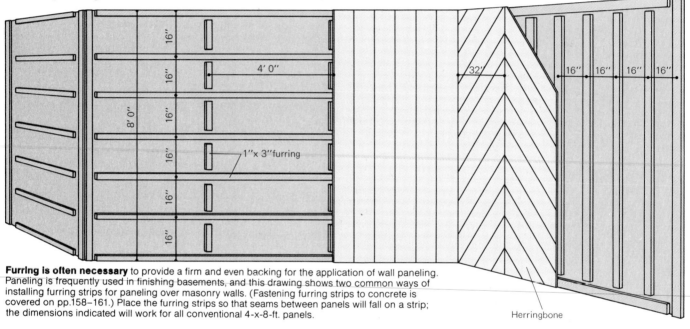

Furring is often necessary to provide a firm and even backing for the application of wall paneling. Paneling is frequently used in finishing basements, and this drawing shows two common ways of installing furring strips for paneling over masonry walls. (Fastening furring strips to concrete is covered on pp.158–161.) Place the furring strips so that seams between panels will fall on a strip; the dimensions indicated will work for all conventional 4-x-8-ft. panels.

Application with adhesives

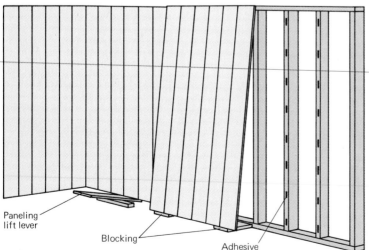

Applying panels with adhesives varies with the manufacturer. One technique, shown above, is to apply the adhesive to the furring or studs, temporarily attach the panel with nails across the top, and press it in. It is pulled back and blocked out a few inches until the adhesive becomes tacky. The panel is then pressed in permanently. The nails are countersunk or removed.

Herringbone pattern

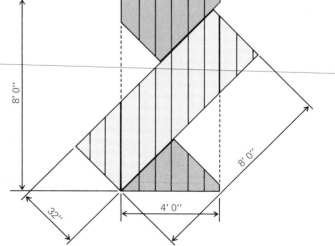

If planned properly, a 4-x-8-ft. plywood panel can be cut so that it can be installed diagonally (herringbone pattern) with minimal waste. One plan is shown above. The panel is cut from the center point at a 45° angle. A rectangle 32 in. wide is cut down the middle. The pieces cut off the top and bottom can fit against the ends of the cut panel.

arranged in the most attractive sequence before installation is begun.

Holes are cut to accommodate outlets, doors, and windows; the panels are cut with a fine-toothed saw to prevent the veneer from splitting. The panels are attached with finishing nails that are countersunk and covered with putty, or with special colored nails whose heads match the panels. Plywood panels can also be installed with special adhesives.

Coated hardboard sheet: These are made of compressed wood pulp and fibers, usually ⅛ to ¼ inch thick, which have an enameled or plastic laminated decorative surface. Like the plywood

panels, they generally measure 4 x 8 feet, but longer sizes are available.

Stiffer and stronger than plywood, hardboard panels do not need a backing of gypsum wallboard. They are nailed, or attached with adhesive, to an existing flat wall surface or to furring. When they are installed over a sound wall covering, vinyl or aluminum molding is attached first at 4-foot intervals, and the panels are slipped in between the molding.

Solid board panels: These are solid planks of softwood or hardwood, which are generally ½ to ⅞ inch thick, 3 to 12 inches wide, and almost any length. They come in clear or knotty grades,

smooth or rough finish, depending on the desired effect. The panels can run vertically or horizontally, the wall composed of all the same width or of several widths, in a regular or a random pattern.

Solid board panels can be installed over an existing wall, over furring strips, or directly over studs (if the panels run horizontally). The boards are usually matched—tongue-and-groove or shiplap. Butt-ended boards can be installed flat or in decorative surfaces, such as board-and-batten or board-on-board.

Plywood and solid board panels can be installed diagonally, in herringbone patterns, as shown on page 96.

Molding

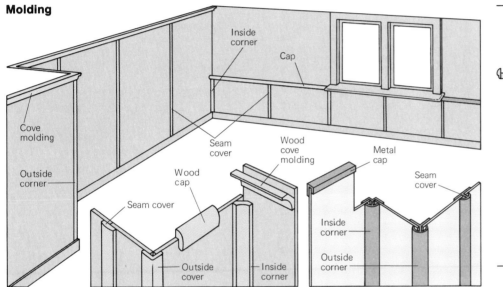

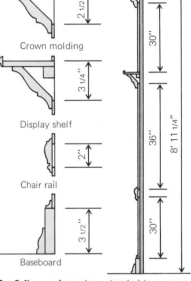

Molding is an important element in the finished appearance of a paneled room. It is generally used at the ceiling, around beams and columns, in corners, and around windows and doors. It can also be used over the joins between panels. Wood trim is used over wood paneling, installed after the panels are in. For hardboard paneling, vinyl or aluminum trim is installed first, and the panels are then slipped in.

An 8-ft. panel can be extended to cover a wall nearly 9 ft. high with baseboard and crown molding, and intermediate decorative trim, as shown above.

Ceiling paneling

In rooms with walls covered with veneered plywood sheet panels, the ceiling can be covered with the same, the channels in the panels running continuously from wall to ceiling. Plywood sheet panels should be nailed into furring or ceiling joists, not applied with adhesive.

Solid board panels and hardwood flooring planks can also be used on ceilings. They should be tongue-and-groove boards, nailed into furring or directly into ceiling joists.

Also available are artificial planks that simulate solid wood planks. They are designed and installed much like acoustical ceiling tiles (pp.92–93): they can be glued directly to a flat, sound ceiling surface, or stapled through their flanges to furring. They are installed so their joints stagger, joints always falling over furring. The three available widths can be used individually or together, in a regular or in a random pattern.

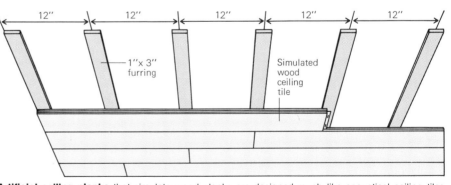

Artificial ceiling planks that simulate wood planks are designed much like acoustical ceiling tiles (pp.92–93). The planks are 4 ft. long, and vary from 5³⁄₁₆ to 8³⁄₁₆ in. wide. They are glued or stapled to a sound, flat ceiling surface, or stapled into furring. A ceiling can be composed of planks of one width, or of three widths, in a regular or a random pattern. The lengths are staggered.

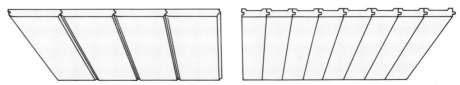

Solid wood panels, left, and hardwood flooring planks, right, both make attractive ceiling covering.

Wallpapering

Choosing and hanging wallpaper

The term "wallpaper" is often used interchangeably with "wallcovering"; it includes not only paper, but fabric, burlap, grasscloth, metallic foil, cork, and a growing number of synthetics. The synthetics include wetlook vinyl and fuzzy nylon flock, filmy Mylar, and a new breed of strippable materials with such exotic names as Tyvek, Fastbac, and Remay. A few of the new materials are hard to hang; but most are more durable and are easier to handle than the traditional papers.

Decor and design: The multitude of choices of color, pattern, texture, and material represented in dealers' sample books can be narrowed down according to the function of the room. Color can accentuate or tone down the features of a room. Patterns and colors should not clash either with one another or with the style of the house or your furniture. A busy pattern may suggest too frenetic a mood; striped patterns alter the perception of room size and ceiling height. Murals depicting landscapes, striking graphics, and the like, are usually used only on one uninterrupted wall.

The rough texture of grasscloth can lend a touch of warmth to any room, while the brilliant luster of foil has an electric effect. Tough vinyl (pure, cloth-backed, or paper-backed) is ideal for bathrooms, kitchens, and playrooms.

Delicate prints, velvety flock, and fragile grasscloth are for minimum-traffic areas, such as bedrooms and studies.

Buying wallpaper: Wallpapers are generally priced by the roll and sold in double- or triple-roll bolts. Rolls vary in width from 20½ to 28 inches (some textured or vinyl materials may come in widths of 36, 45, or 54 inches) but contain 36 square feet regardless of width.

Because of matching and trimming waste, each roll actually has about 30 square feet of usable paper. To estimate the amount required for a room, first calculate the area to be covered in square feet, then divide this figure by 30. For every standard-size window or door, deduct half a roll. The final figure is the number of rolls needed. Throw in an extra roll as a safety margin, especially if all of the walls of a room are to be papered. If the ceiling is also to be covered, remember to include its area in your calculations.

Mass-produced wallpapers can vary in color, unless the rolls are from the same printing run. Each roll is labeled with a run or lot number. Buy enough rolls with the same lot number initially, or you may later find yourself buying additional rolls that are noticeably different in color.

Handprints, fabric, and grasscloth usually come with a selvage—an un-

printed edge, which should be trimmed with a straightedge and razor knife.

Preparation: Many of today's papers are pre-pasted; so all one needs to apply them is a waterbox (shown upper right, facing page). For the unpasted papers, various types of adhesives are available: wheat paste, cellulose paste, vinyl compound, and vinyl-to-vinyl adhesive. Use the adhesive recommended by the manufacturer of the wallpaper.

Success in wallpapering depends on preparing a sound base. All holes and cracks in the wall must be patched, and irregularities sanded smooth. New plaster and new wallboard should be sealed first with an oil-base enamel paint, then brushed over with sizing. Latex paint, being porous, should be treated with a primer-sealer before wallpaper is applied.

Existing wallpaper should be used as a base only if it is tight and sealed with oil-base enamel and sizing. Never put airtight vinyl over old wallpaper, as this may induce mildew in the old paper's wheat paste. Never paper over an existing vinyl, foil, flock, or textured wallcovering. Foil, Mylar, unbacked fabric or grasscloth should be hung over a layer of lining paper, which is a blank wallpaper for improving adhesion, minimizing surface roughness, and preventing mildew. A great conve-

Locating the first strip

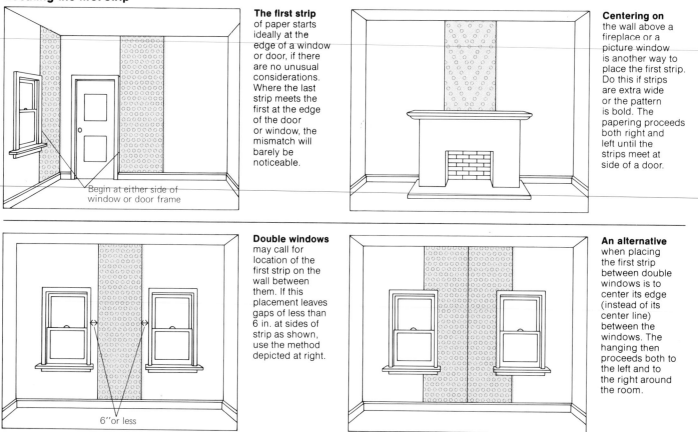

The first strip of paper starts ideally at the edge of a window or door, if there are no unusual considerations. Where the last strip meets the first at the edge of the door or window, the mismatch will barely be noticeable.

Begin at either side of window or door frame

Centering on the wall above a fireplace or a picture window is another way to place the first strip. Do this if strips are extra wide or the pattern is bold. The papering proceeds both right and left until the strips meet at side of a door.

Double windows may call for location of the first strip on the wall between them. If this placement leaves gaps of less than 6 in. at sides of strip as shown, use the method depicted at right.

6" or less

An alternative when placing the first strip between double windows is to center its edge (instead of its center line) between the windows. The hanging then proceeds both to the left and to the right around the room.

nience to do-it-yourselfers is the availability of synthetic, strippable wallcoverings. To remove them, pull at a corner and peel off an entire strip.

Working from the top down: Always check wallpaper for defects before cutting it. Each strip is cut some 4 inches longer than the height of the wall so that there is about a 2-inch overlap at both ends. These are trimmed with scissors or a razor knife along the ceiling and floor line after the paper is applied. Use butt seams between strips, except at inside corners.

Each pasted strip is booked (folded) as shown below and carried to the wall. Position the upper part of the pasted and booked strip on the wall and, with the smoothing brush, give the top part a few horizontal strokes. Then stroke downward and outward from the center line. Next, position the lower part of the strip against the wall, checking for alignment and sliding the paper into position with your palms, if necessary. Brush the rest of the strip, eliminating any air bubbles. Where wrinkles develop, pull the affected part away from the wall and reposition it.

On these and following pages basic wallpapering techniques are shown, together with photographs of an actual project notable for its difficulty and the special techniques that were required.

Matching the strips

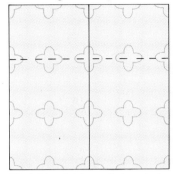

Straight match is used when design runs horizontally. Every strip is applied at the same level.

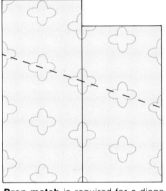

Drop match is required for a diagonal design. The trimmed waste of every other strip is the same.

Using a waterbox

A waterbox with tepid water is useful for pre-pasted wallpaper. Each strip is rolled pasted side out, soaked for the required time, and is applied directly from the box onto the wall.

Booking a pasted strip

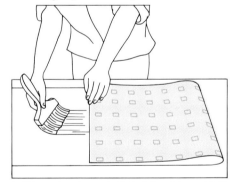

1. Using a brush, paste 2/3 of the strip and fold this portion paste to paste. Then paste the remaining 1/3 of the strip.

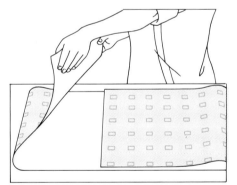

2. Fold the last 1/3 of the strip over on itself in the same manner. Take care not to crease the folds, as creases will show on the wall.

3. Smooth book at middle; wait 5 minutes. Booking eases handling and relaxes wallpaper by letting it shrink or expand before hanging.

Making seams

Small ridge for non-vinyl

Butt seams are widely used today. A strip is hung next to previously hung strip; slide it by hand toward the first strip until two meet. With non-vinyl paper, push the edges into a tiny ridge; it disappears when the paper shrinks upon drying.

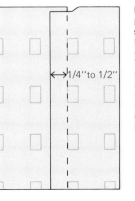

←1/4" to 1/2"→

Lap seams, once popular, are now seldom used because of their obtrusiveness. They are still used in corners and where narrow strips of paper must be joined to cover damaged or serrated edges.

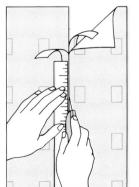

Double-cut seams are used for vinyl wallpaper, which does not adhere to itself well but requires snug, watertight joints not attainable with butt seams. Cut lap seams with a straightedge and razor knife, and pull off the two loose strips.

Wallpapering

Hanging special areas

In papering all the way around a room, the procession of wallpaper strips will be interrupted by such obstacles as windows, doors, fireplaces, corners, and built-ins. Such areas are not skipped and then covered later; this procedure would result in many mismatches of pattern. The specific techniques illustrated on these two pages are used to work with these obstacles so that the entire room has a sense of harmony.

Since no wall or ceiling is geometrically perfect, a plumb line is used to align the strips vertically, as shown below. Plumb the first strip on a wall and also plumb the first strips beyond the corners of intersecting walls.

First, the standard-size windows and doors are papered over; then the overlapping paper is trimmed away. Wide picture windows (and fireplaces) are treated differently, as are casements.

Papering around electric fixtures is covered on page 102; working around plumbing pipes is discussed on page 105. If you are using a wallcovering of metallic foil, which conducts electricity, be certain to trim off enough foil under the cover plate so that the foil does not make contact with wires or terminals.

Double-hung and picture windows

Double-hung windows, like doors, are usually papered over. The overlapping portion is then cut to the corners diagonally with scissors, and trimmed away on the wall with a razor knife.

Picture windows: 1. Cut, match, and hang middle strips in separate top and bottom panels (A, A^1, B, B^1). Do not trim them. Hang and trim strip C as described above.

2. Adjust small strips slightly up or down with palms so that any mismatches are minimized. Brush all strips to secure them to the wall, and trim off excess paper with razor knife.

Corners

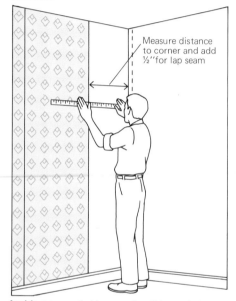

Measure distance to corner and add ½" for lap seam

Inside corner: 1. Measure the distance between the preceding strip and the corner at 3 points and add ½ in. Mark and cut next strip to this width so that it will lap ½ in. around corner.

Chalked plumb line

Width of remaining piece

2. Hang strip prepared in Step 1. If the cutaway piece is wide enough to use, mark its width from the corner. Drop a plumb line at this mark. A chalked line can be snapped to mark wall.

Lap seam

3. Hang the strip along the plumb line, overlapping the ½-in. corner strip. For vinyl wallpaper use vinyl-to-vinyl adhesive to secure the lap seam. Do not double-cut the seam.

Lap seam

Outside corner: Cut strip to width that wraps around corner 1 in. Hang it, and plumb and hang leftover piece, as described in Step 2. Make lap seam ½ in. from corner.

Casement windows

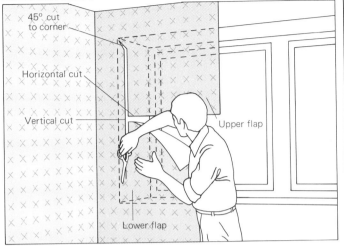

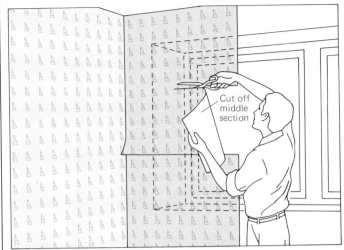

Traditional wallpaper: 1. Hang strip over the casement. Cut middle of strip horizontally to 1 in. from the casement edge. Then make vertical cuts toward the upper and lower corners; finish with a short 45° cut at each corner. Use scissors, not a razor knife, which may tear the paper.

Vinyl wallpaper: 1. Hang strip over the end of the casement and cut out a section from the middle with scissors. Make sure that enough material is left in the upper and lower flaps to cover the top and bottom of the recess casement with some trim allowance.

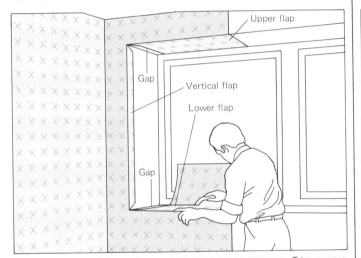

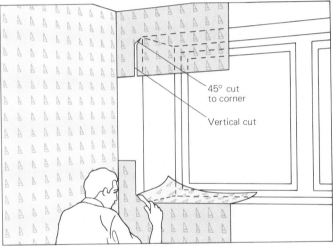

2. Brush upper and lower flaps onto the casement recesses. Trim excess paper at window frame with a razor knife. The 1-in. gap between the edge of each flap and the side wall will be covered later with lap seams. Press and brush the narrow vertical flap onto the casement side wall.

2. Make a vertical cut in the top flap 1 in. outside the casement edge, then a 45° cut to the casement corner. Make corresponding cuts in the bottom flap. Brush the flaps in over the recess. Trim them at the window frame only. Do not trim the edges at the side wall.

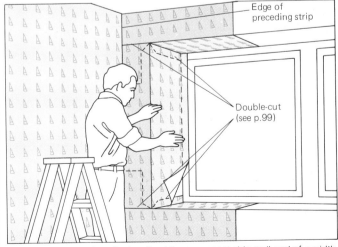

3. Measure and cut a matching piece to cover the casement side wall. Make sure the piece is long enough to cover the gaps and overlap ¼ in. with top and bottom flaps. The vertical lap seam should be set back ¼ in. from the corner of the recess to prevent fraying.

3. Cut a matching piece the length of the casement side wall and of a width equal to the distance from the edge of the preceding strip to the window frame, plus 1 in. Trim at the frame. Double-cut all the four overlaps as marked, and remove all pieces.

Wallpapering

Papering at outlets, switches, and fixtures

Outlets, switches: 1. Remove face plate, then paper over outlet; cut and remove paper inside plate line.

2. Press cut wallpaper edges firmly to the wall around the outlet, then replace the face plate.

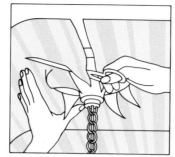

Light fixtures: 1. To paper around a ceiling light, cut a hole with a slit, then slide the paper in place.

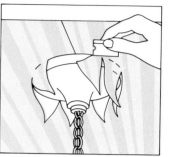

2. Trim closely around the light canopy. Brush on the paper and match the butt seam at the slit.

Ceilings

Wallpaper the ceiling before you start on the walls. For ease in handling, apply ceiling strips parallel to the shorter walls of the room. Mark a guideline for the first strip as shown in the illustration at right. Figure 2 inches at each end of a strip as trim allowance. If only the ceiling is to be papered, trim the excess after hanging; otherwise leave ½ inch on the walls for a lap seam with the wall strips. If you do not have a helper, use a homemade pedestal to hold the folded strips for hanging (see bottom right).

Where paper of the same pattern is used for ceiling and walls, matching may be a problem. For most patterns, the ceiling can only match one wall, which should be the wall most frequently looked at. Patterns that cannot be turned upside down, such as houses, trees, and animals, will run nicely up one wall and continue along the ceiling to the opposite wall, where you will have a glaring mismatch. The problem can be avoided by choosing plain or striped paper for the ceiling, or perhaps a subtle geometric pattern. Or simply paint the ceiling.

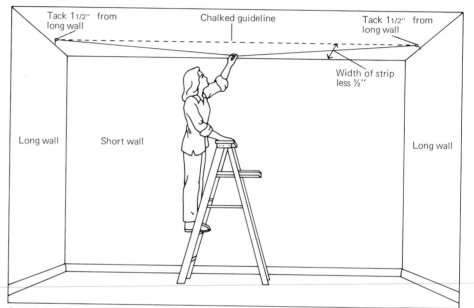

A guideline is marked for the first ceiling strip: from a short wall, mark two points, each a distance equal to the width of a strip minus ½ in. (for overlap on wall). Put tacks at these points. Stretch chalked string between tacks and snap string to mark the ceiling.

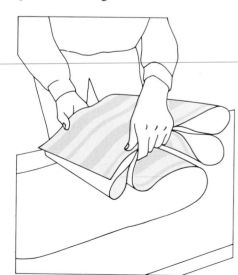

Each cut and pasted ceiling strip is folded accordion-fashion, paste-to-paste and pattern-to-pattern, for easier hanging.

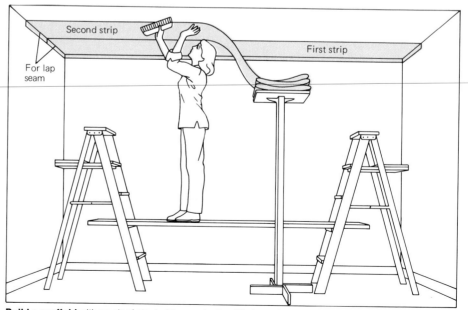

Build a scaffold with a pair of stepladders and a 2-x-10 plank. Strips (folded as shown in the drawing at left) can be supported near ceiling height by a homemade wooden pedestal, or held by a helper. Work with your supporting hand close to the smoothing brush.

Special techniques

The photographs here and on the following two pages show the wallpapering of an attic bathroom with odd-shaped wall and ceiling surfaces. The room had been created by raising a roof and adding knee walls. The papering was done by a professional paperhanger whose long experience has enabled him to develop effective techniques and shortcuts that often deviate from the standard practices described on previous pages. You may find many of his techniques applicable to difficult spaces in your own house. Beginning do-it-yourselfers may prefer initially to follow the standard procedures, but eventually anyone who wallpapers more than one room will develop techniques based on personal experience.

Order of work: The hanging started at a corner and moved clockwise around the room. At first the homeowner planned to leave the ceiling unpapered; thus the paperhanger chose to hang the strips flush with the ceiling and leave a trim allowance only at the bottom of the strips.

When the papering reached the area above the bathtub, a decision to paper the ceiling was made. From then on a trim allowance was also left at the top of the strips. This permitted a lap seam at the ceiling line (where a butt seam may result in gaps if the ceiling line is not true). Because of the unusually narrow wall spaces next to the windows, the procedure for papering at the windows differs from that illustrated on pages 100-101. The skylight was papered according to standard practice.

The material used is traditional unpasted wallpaper, which is usually applied with wheat paste. Our paperhanger used a vinyl adhesive because the room is a bathroom and vinyl adhesive is moisture resistant.

1. The newly finished bathroom is ready for wallpapering. All trim has been painted. The new plasterboard, including that on the ceiling, has been primed and sized for better adhesion.

2. A pasting table, made of a plywood board and a pair of sawhorses, holds paperhanging paraphernalia and a roll of wallpaper ready for cutting the first strip.

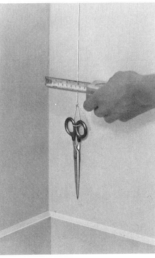

3. Measuring at two points from an improvised plumb line shows that the corner is true vertical. Paper can now be aligned with corner.

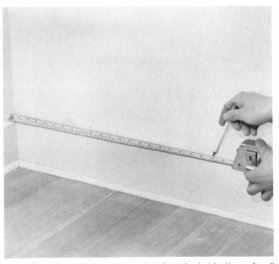
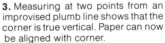

4. Width of first strip is measured and marked at bottom of wall. Vertical distance to top of wall (here under a sloping ceiling) is measured at the corner and at the point corresponding to strip's width.

5. Using vertical measurements made in Step 4, the ceiling slant is marked on wallpaper with pencil and straight-edge. The top of the strip is then cut with scissors to fit slope of ceiling.

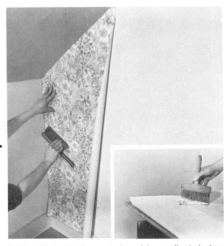

6. The first strip is pasted and hung flush below the sloping ceiling. A smoothing brush is used to press the wallpaper firmly to the wall and to brush out air bubbles.

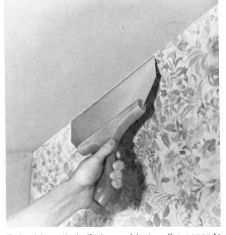

7. A wide putty knife is used to jam the paper to the ceiling line. No trim allowance is left at top since at this stage the ceiling was not to be papered. *(continued)*

Wallpapering

Special techniques (continued)

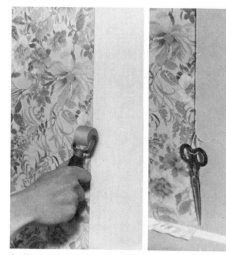

8. To make sure the edge of the strip adheres to the wall surface, a seam roller is run along it. The edge of the wallpaper is then checked with a plumb line for true vertical.

9. Bottom of strip is scored, using a serrated-edged trimming wheel, along the junction of the wall and the baseboard. The perforated line is then trimmed with scissors.

10. Before cutting second strip, paperhanger matches roll against first strip and finds that the drop match would mean much wasted paper. A new roll is matched and cut, with little waste.

11. A strip from the second roll is hung. Its upper portion is affixed to the wall, then the remainder is roughly positioned. It meets the first strip neatly along a straight butt seam.

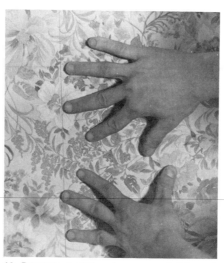

12. Because butted edges are slightly mismatched, paperhanger wets his fingers, presses second strip, and slides it into alignment. The seam is pressed with roller.

13. Wall switch was papered by removing face plate and pasting strip over entire wall; an area a bit smaller than perimeter of face plate was then cut out to uncover the electrical box.

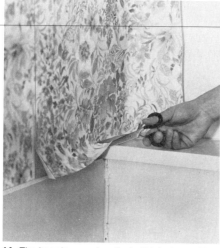

14. The hanging reaches the bathtub alcove. The bottom of a strip meets a splashboard and a ledge, and the paper is contoured with scissors to fit the space exactly.

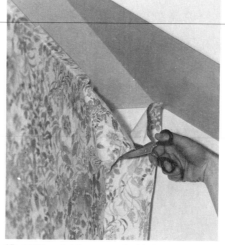

15. At this point the owner decided he wanted the ceiling wallpapered; paperhanger allows about 1 in. of overlap at the top of the wall for a lap seam. Overlap is cut to fit at corner.

16. The entire alcove has been papered. Note the overlap along the front edge of the sloping ceiling; seam was located here so that a person sitting in the tub would not notice it.

104

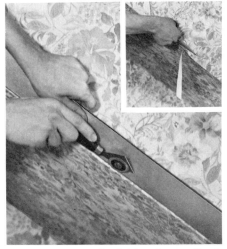

17. When sloping wall adjoining alcove ceiling is papered, a trimming wheel is run along a straight-edge ⅛ in. from edge; the edge is then trimmed with scissors and rolled down.

18. Paperhanger places a pre-cut L-shaped strip in narrow space around window; he trims it to fit, using a trimming wheel and razor knife. This is a difficult piece to fit precisely.

19. Wall behind washbasin comes next. To cut opening for hot-water pipe, paperhanger folds the paper back against a piece of scrap wood and makes a slash with the razor knife.

20. A jagged hole is cut at the end of slit made in Step 19; excess paper is pushed into pipe hole. Strip is smoothed onto wall and pipe escutcheon is slid back in place to cover pipe hole.

21. In preparing the knee wall and ceiling, a helper holds upper part of a long strip. Paperhanger matches strip first on the short knee wall, then moves upward over sloping ceiling.

22. A slack has developed in the paper because the ceiling slope is not true. If the entire strip were hung as is, the slack would result in hopeless wrinkles in the paper's surface.

23. To take up slack, the paperhanger slits the long strip at top of wall. The two flaps are pressed one over the other, making a wedge-shaped overlap. The mismatch is less noticeable.

24. A skylight is covered half way; overlap is then cut away. Rough edges are trimmed to fit skylight frame precisely, then rolled with a seam roller. Do the same with second half of skylight.

25. Wallpaper now completely covers the attic bathroom, including all the irregularly contoured areas resulting from the interplay of the walls and the sloping roof line of the house.

Hardwood floors

A base for a sound floor

To install a hardwood floor, you must adapt the construction to the existing base, which may be exposed joists, an existing floor, or concrete slab. A good base is essential for a sound floor free of such problems as boards that are moisture-warped, loose or squeaky, or that become excessively cold in winter.

Subflooring: If the room you want to floor has exposed joists and no flooring of any kind—as in an unfinished attic or in a new addition—a subfloor must be installed before laying the finish floor. Normally, ⅝- or ½-inch plywood is used for subflooring, but softwood boards, dressed and square-edged (not tongue-and-groove), ¾ inch thick and up to 6 inches wide, are considered suitable.

A board subfloor is laid diagonally across the joists, so that the finish floor may be laid in either direction—parallel with the joists or perpendicular to them. If joists are more than 16 inches apart, or are smaller than 2 x 8 inches, they must be covered with a ¾-inch plywood subfloor or reinforced (see *Posts, beams, and floor joists,* pp.70–75).

Existing floors: A hardwood floor can be installed directly over an existing wood floor or a floor covered with resilient or vinyl tile flooring. The old floor serves as the subfloor. But it must be in good condition, with all loose parts secured. An old ceramic tile floor should be removed, however; it will crack under stress even if covered with a new plywood subfloor.

Slabs, screeds, vapor barriers: If the room has an existing concrete slab floor, hardwood flooring may be laid over it in one of several ways, and without the use of a vapor barrier, provided the slab is dry. To test for moisture in a slab, cut a piece 1-foot square of polyethylene sheet; tape its edges to the slab to make an airtight seal. After one or two days, if the sheet shows no condensation droplets or cloudiness on its underside, the slab is dry.

An alternative test involves building a small putty ring a couple of inches in

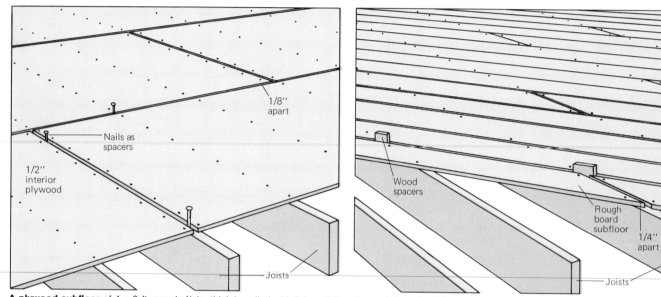

A plywood subfloor of 4-x-8-ft. panels ½ in. thick is nailed with 8d or 10d common nails on joists spaced 16 in. (o.c.). Drive nails at 6-in. intervals. Note that the panels are staggered. A ⅛-in. space is left between panels, using nails as temporary spacers.

A rough board subfloor is laid diagonally on joists. Boards are No. 1 or No. 2 common pine, dressed and square-edged; they are ¾ in. thick, and either 4 or 6 in. wide. The boards are face-nailed with 10d common nails at least twice at each bearing, and spaced ¼ in. apart with wood spacers.

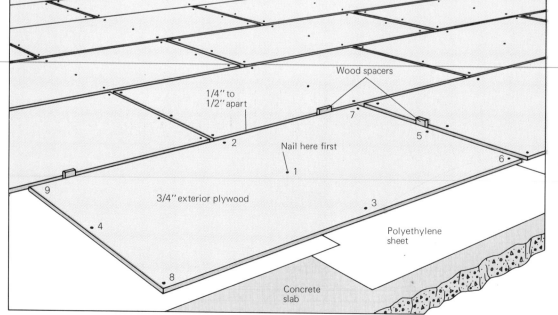

Plywood is laid directly on concrete slab, which is first covered with a vapor barrier of 4-mil polyethylene sheets. The ¾ in. exterior-grade plywood panels are positioned with end joints staggered, and spaced ¼ to ½ in. apart with wood spacers. A ½-in. expansion space is left at the walls. Each panel is nailed to the slab with 9 or more concrete nails, starting from the center. Nailing can be done with a heavy hammer, or a powder-driven concrete nailer that shoots out steel studs like bullets.

diameter on the concrete floor. A quarter teaspoon of dry (anhydrous) calcium chloride (available in drug stores) is put inside the ring, which is then covered tightly with a piece of glass so that the chemical is completely sealed off. If the crystals dissolve in 12 hours, the slab is too moist. Such tests should be performed at several spots during wet seasons to ensure their accuracy. Any moisture in the slab will require the use of a vapor barrier between the new flooring and the slab.

If a slab is not level, and the ceiling is more than 8 feet high, you might want to install a leveling joist system. A plywood subfloor may be laid without using joists, as is shown at bottom on the facing page. This involves driving nails into the concrete slab—a rather arduous task if done by hand. You can rent a powder-driven concrete nailer that, using powder charges similar to a .22 caliber long rimfire blank charge, shoots studs of hardened steel into the concrete with great ease.

You can also lay hardwood flooring on concrete slab without a subfloor. This is done using the screed method. The basic principle is to lay strips of floor board across sturdy ribs of 2 x 4s, called screeds or sleepers. The screeds are glued to the slab with hot-poured asphalt mastic. Although this method bypasses the installation of a new subfloor, it requires vapor barriers; and the screeds must be of treated lumber. The preservative should not be creosote, which might bleed through and stain the finish floor.

Hardwood floor strips are always laid perpendicular to joists or screeds, and preferably parallel to the longer dimension of a room. Plywood panels are laid as subfloor with their surface grains perpendicular to joists or screeds. You may want to lay insulation in the spaces between screeds—in addition to laying the vapor barriers shown on this page. Use perlite, vermiculite, or rigid, moisture-resistant polystyrene boards.

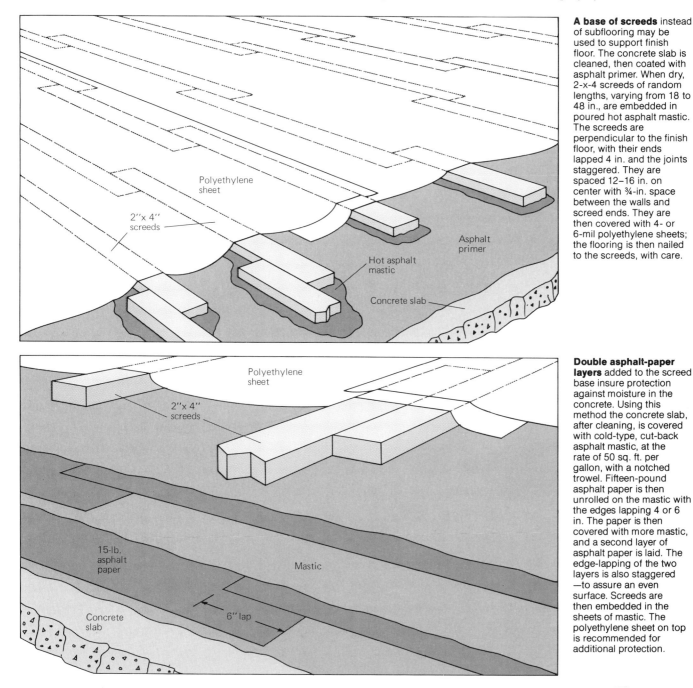

A base of screeds instead of subflooring may be used to support finish floor. The concrete slab is cleaned, then coated with asphalt primer. When dry, 2-x-4 screeds of random lengths, varying from 18 to 48 in., are embedded in poured hot asphalt mastic. The screeds are perpendicular to the finish floor, with their ends lapped 4 in. and the joints staggered. They are spaced 12–16 in. on center with ¾-in. space between the walls and screed ends. They are then covered with 4- or 6-mil polyethylene sheets; the flooring is then nailed to the screeds, with care.

Double asphalt-paper layers added to the screed base insure protection against moisture in the concrete. Using this method the concrete slab, after cleaning, is covered with cold-type, cut-back asphalt mastic, at the rate of 50 sq. ft. per gallon, with a notched trowel. Fifteen-pound asphalt paper is then unrolled on the mastic with the edges lapping 4 or 6 in. The paper is then covered with more mastic, and a second layer of asphalt paper is laid. The edge-lapping of the two layers is also staggered —to assure an even surface. Screeds are then embedded in the sheets of mastic. The polyethylene sheet on top is recommended for additional protection.

Hardwood floors

Choosing your flooring

Before the days of wall-to-wall carpeting, vinyl tiles, and resilient sheet flooring, hardwood boards were standard for residential flooring. Today, this traditional flooring is still quite popular; it is often preferred for its natural elegance and durability.

Hardwood flooring comes in three major varieties. The most common is strip flooring, consisting of narrow boards of the same width but random lengths. The second type is plank flooring, wider than strip flooring and installed in varying widths and lengths to create a casual country look. The ends of the planks are countersunk with screws and covered with wood plugs. Parquet flooring, the third type, consists of wood blocks laid with the grains of the blocks perpendicular to those of adjacent blocks, resulting in an intricate mosaic.

Board sizes and grades: Floor boards are available in a variety of dimensions. Strip flooring has a standard thickness of ¾ inch with widths of 1½, 2, 2¼, and 3¼ inches. The strips come in random lengths from 9 inches to 8½ feet. The strips are bundled by approximate average length. Strips must be laid on a sturdy subfloor. Plank flooring also has a standard thickness of ¾ inch, with widths that vary from 3 to 8 inches. Planks are usually supplied with wood plugs ¼ inch thick and ¾ inch in diameter. Parquet comes mostly in blocks 10 to 36 inches square, but also in rectangles, and sometimes in strips.

Flooring comes either unfinished or prefinished. Do-it-yourselfers will find that they can save time and effort if they use the prefinished boards.

Hardwood flooring is mostly oak, but beech, birch, hard maple, and even pecan are available. The flooring industry's grading system may be confusing to the uninitiated. Unfinished oak strips range from the best, designated as "Clear," through "Select and Better," "Select," "No. 1 Common," and "No. 2 Common." Some of these grades are subdivided into "Red" and "White," and also "Plain Sawn" (flat-grained), and "Quarter Sawn" (edge-grained). Beech, and other hard woods are graded, in descending quality, as "First," "Second," and "Third Grade," with subdivisions in some of the grades. Prefinished oak flooring is graded "Prime," "Standard and Better," "Standard," "Tavern and Better," and "Tavern."

Storing and handling: Great care should be taken in receiving and storing flooring; the kiln-dried flat boards and blocks may warp and twist out of shape. Flooring for a newly constructed house or room should be delivered only after the outside windows and doors are installed. Concrete and plaster work emit large amounts of moisture during drying, so flooring must not go into a house until these have dried. In winter, the room in which the flooring will be stored or installed should be heated for five days before the delivery, at a temperature of 65-70°F. It is advisable to store flooring in the room in which it will be installed, for at least two or three days beforehand to acclimate it. When hauling flooring on humid summer days, cover it with tarpaulin or vinyl sheet. Never unload flooring in rain.

Fastening: Strips and planks, most of which are tongue-and-groove, are blind-nailed and also screwed down. Parquet blocks are usually glued to the subfloor or slab with asphalt mastic.

The basic procedures for installing various types of hardwood flooring are described on this and following pages.

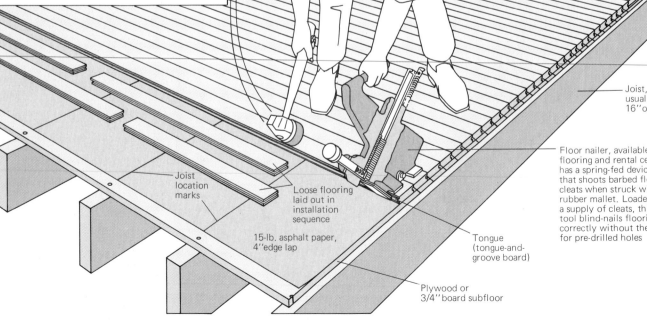

Strips of flooring are installed here with a floor nailer that shoots 2-in. barbed cleats through the floor boards and the plywood subfloor into the joists. Additional nails are driven into the subfloor between the joists, but not into the seams between panels. Behind the figure is a reducer strip (a strip of flooring with a sloping top). It is installed at the threshold of the doorway to give a transitional surface between the new floor and the slightly lower existing floor of the next room.

Reducer strip

Joist, usually 16" o.c.

Floor nailer, available from flooring and rental centers, has a spring-fed device that shoots barbed floor cleats when struck with a rubber mallet. Loaded with a supply of cleats, this tool blind-nails flooring correctly without the need for pre-drilled holes

Joist location marks

Loose flooring laid out in installation sequence

15-lb. asphalt paper, 4" edge lap

Tongue (tongue-and-groove board)

Plywood or ¾" board subfloor

Aligning and applying flooring

Wood flooring is best installed on vapor barriers because the boards are vulnerable to moisture. In addition to the protection below the subfloor (pp.106-107), a layer of 15-pound asphalt paper, lapped 4 inches at the ends, is laid between the finish floor and subfloor.

Pre-mark the positions of the joists or screeds on the asphalt paper. Whenever possible, drive nails through the subfloor into the joists or screeds below. Leave a ¾-inch gap between the floor boards and the wall for expansion. This gap is filled with cork strips and is later concealed by baseboard molding. Floor boards usually run parallel to the long side of a room.

Rental tools: In hand-nailing, you pre-drill holes and countersink the nails with a nail-set. This laborious task can be avoided if you rent a floor nailer, which blind-nails automatically at the correct angle with a minimum effort.

The first boards or strips should be aligned with a room-length line drawn several inches out from the starting wall; near a corner, place a strip ¾ inch from the wall, with the groove facing the wall. Then mark a point on the floor at the edge of its tongue. Do the same at the other corner, and draw a straight line between the two points. The first row of strips are laid along this line and face-nailed (nailed through the top of

the board, not the base of the tongue) into the subfloor and the joists or screeds beneath.

Random appearance: Lay out seven or eight rows of boards loosely with their ends staggered so that the joints are scattered randomly. Fit the grooves of the next row to the tongues of the first row. Face-nail the first three rows; blind-nail the rest (see illustrations) until you reach the last several rows when you again must face-nail.

Use 8-penny (2½-inch) finishing nails (or 2-inch cleats in floor nailer) in most cases. If the finish floor is on a plywood subfloor that is fastened to a concrete slab, use shorter nails or cleats.

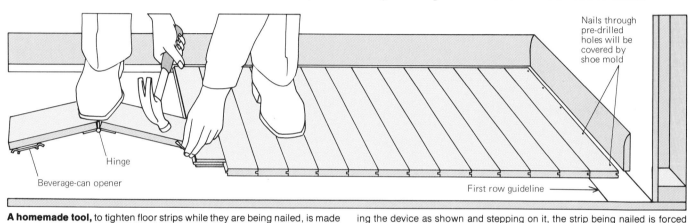

A **homemade tool,** to tighten floor strips while they are being nailed, is made of two hinged boards with a beverage-can opener as an anchor. By position- ing the device as shown and stepping on it, the strip being nailed is forced into a tight fit with the finished row.

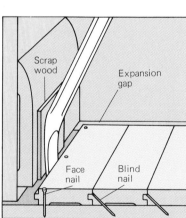

A **pry bar** may be used to hold the strips of flooring in the final row for secure nailing. Protect the wall or the existing baseboard with a piece of scrap wood. Face-nail the strip and leave an expansion gap of ¾ in.

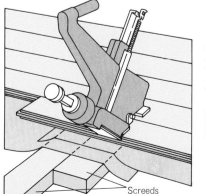

On a screed base (over a concrete floor), the finish flooring is nailed directly to the screeds through a vapor barrier. Ends of strips should rest on or near a screed. Nails are driven at every intersection with a screed.

Installing a plank floor

Plank flooring should be blind-nailed in manner similar to strip flooring. In addition, it is countersunk at the ends with No. 9 or No. 12 wood screws, and at intervals in between on very long planks. Some planks may come with countersunk holes and wood plugs. If not, drill holes ¾ in. in diameter and ¼ in. deep with the special bit shown. After the screws are installed, cover them with glue-on wood plugs, which can be bought from flooring distributors, or made from ¾-in. dowels of identical or similar hardwood.

A **plug cutter** is another possible means of making wood plugs for plank flooring. Attach a ¾-in. plug cutter to a drill press and cut plugs out of a ¼-in. board of the same kind of wood as the flooring.

Hardwood floors

Installing a parquet floor

A parquet floor is an inlaid mosaic of wood, consisting of solid or laminated wood blocks, usually prefinished. It can be laid by a homeowner with relative ease if the floor base is smooth.

Parquet blocks come in squares of various sizes, as well as in rectangular and random-strip shapes. These blocks, usually ranging from $5/16$ to $3/4$ inch thick with tongues and grooves, are glued with asphalt mastic to a subfloor or concrete slab. Other varieties, thinner, foam-backed, and the self-sticking type, are similar to vinyl floor tiles in application. Parquet applied with mastic is more durable than adhesive blocks.

Subfloor, or existing wood or resilient vinyl sheet floor, can serve as a base for parquet blocks if such surfaces are clean, smooth, and tight. On concrete slab, the blocks must be laid over a vapor barrier of either asphalt building paper or polyethylene sheets (p.107). The base surface must not be bumpy; irregularities on a slab can be ground off with a rented grinding machine, or an uneven subfloor can be covered with thin plywood.

The square blocks are laid in one of two patterns: square with the walls, or in sequences at a diagonal to the walls. The square pattern is more common and involves less cutting of blocks, but the diagonal pattern minimizes distorting visual effects.

Laying out the pattern: Once the pattern has been chosen, accurate planning can be done on graph paper, with each square on the paper representing one block. The room and the exact positions of the walls and doors are drawn to scale; the layout should minimize the amount of cutting of blocks at borders.

The diagrams on this page show traditional ways of laying out the pattern. Because walls are seldom perfectly straight, a reference line is drawn and the blocks are aligned with respect to it. Parquet blocks have small differences in size, so they should never be laid in rows; the small discrepancies would be increasingly magnified as the rows increased in number, throwing the pattern out of alignment. The blocks are always laid in pyramid or staircase-step sequence. Wooden blocks expand and shrink, so an expansion space of about $3/4$ inch is left between the flooring and the walls. This space is filled with cork strips and covered by the baseboard.

Working with mastic: Parquet blocks can be laid in several types of mastic. The National Oak Flooring Manufacturers' Association recommends a cold, cut-back asphalt mastic, applied with a notched-edge trowel at the rate of one gallon for each 50 square feet. This mastic hardens slowly so that the laying

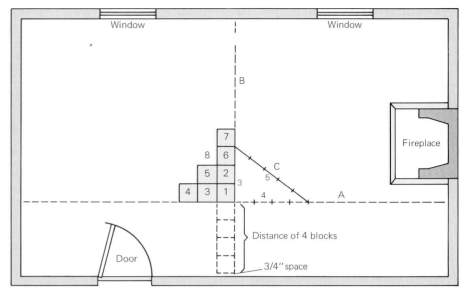

Square pattern parquet flooring procedure starts with the snapping of a line (A) on the mastic-covered floor. Locate line at a distance from a long wall of room of exactly four blocks plus $3/4$ in. At mid-point, snap a second line (B) perpendicular to the first. To assure a right angle, mark a point 4 ft. from the intersection point on one line and 3 ft. on the other; link two points with a test line (C). This line should be exactly 5 ft. long. Lay blocks in one quadrant of pyramid sequence in order indicated by numbers, then lay the next quadrant.

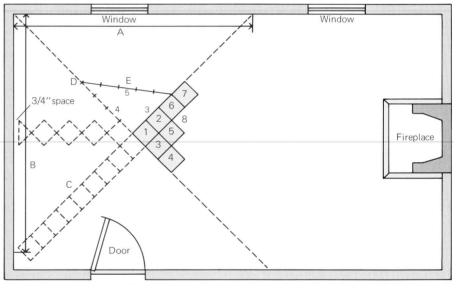

Diagonal pattern parquet flooring procedure starts with the snapping of two chalk lines (A,B) of equal length from one corner of the room. The ends of the lines are connected by a line (C), whose mid-point is used to snap a line (D) bisecting the corner. Lines C and D are at 45° angles to the walls and perpendicular to each other. To check the 90° angle, draw test line (E) as described in caption above. Lay blocks in one pyramid quadrant, then lay adjacent quadrants. Squares with dots indicate dry-run blocks placed lightly on mastic to determine border cut.

can be done anytime up to 48 hours after application. After 12 hours, it is hard enough for snapping chalk reference lines. (Procedure for snapping chalk lines is seen in the chapter on dormers.) Because the mastic is not completely hardened, however, temporarily position blocks as walkways and move about on these.

Each block is covered with a piece of smooth wood and tapped gently into the mastic with a mallet. Do not put heavy furniture on newly laid parquet block for 24 hours.

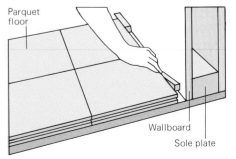

Cork expansion strips, $3/4$ in. wide and in 3-in. lengths, are laid in the expansion space left between the flooring and the walls.

Baseboards and baseboard moldings

Trimming the floor line

Baseboard molding and trim are installed to conceal the gap between the finish floor and the wall. In a room with hardwood flooring, the gap is usually in the form of a cork-filled expansion joint about ¾ inch wide. Baseboard molding consists of the baseboard itself, and the base shoe, which is a narrow strip of molding at the foot of the baseboard, as shown in drawings on this page. As the illustrations show, the trim found in old houses is often a 1-x-3 strip topped with a base mold and edged at the foot by a similar mold as the base shoe.

Baseboards run along the foot of walls. They are omitted at door openings and wall sections where baseboard heating elements are present. Baseboards are nailed through the wallboard into either a stud or the sole plate, never into the floor, which expands and contracts independently of the baseboard. The base shoe is nailed through the baseboard to the sole plate. Finishing nails, usually the 6-penny (2-inch) size, are used with a nail set. The holes are filled with wood filler.

Baseboard joints: At times it is necessary to join two boards along a straight section of the wall. This is done by mitering the board ends for a lap or scarf joint, as shown below. Such a joint must be made in front of a stud, so that nails can be driven into the stud.

Studs and corners: When installing baseboards it is important to pre-mark the stud positions for proper nailing. Place alongside the walls for a dry run before beginning nailing. At external corners of the wall, the baseboard joint is mitered. The mitering is normally at a 45-degree angle. Wall corners are not always true, thus it is good practice to check the angle before the actual cutting, modifying it if necessary. At internal corners, the baseboards meet at what is called a coped joint: this is made by cutting the end of one molded baseboard with a coping saw, so that the cut surface fits the contour of the other baseboard.

Bird's-eye view detail

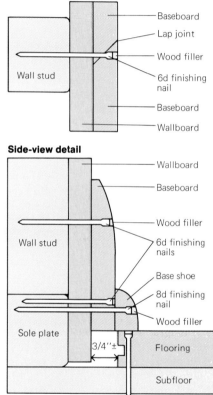

Side-view detail

Baseboard construction details are seen in upper drawing in cross section, as viewed from above looking down the length of a stud. Lower drawing shows the relations of baseboard, base shoe, and flooring.

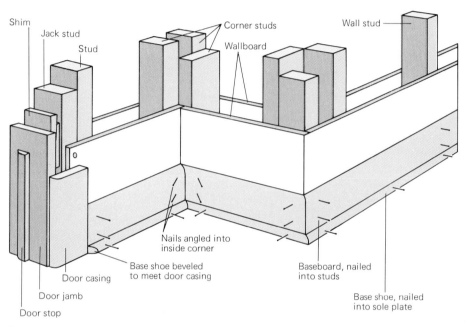

A cutaway view of a section of a wall near a door, showing studs, baseboards, and base shoes.

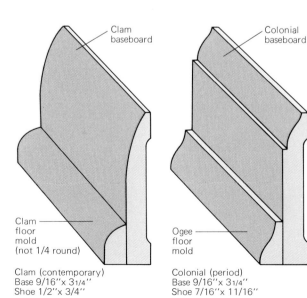

Clam (contemporary)
Base 9/16''x 3¼''
Shoe 1/2''x 3/4''

Colonial (period)
Base 9/16''x 3¼''
Shoe 7/16''x 11/16''

Built-up (old style)
Base 11/16''x 1 3/8''
Shoe 11/16''x 1½''

Three common types of baseboards and base shoes used in contemporary and traditional houses.

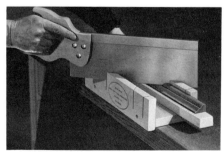

A miter box and a backsaw are used to cut baseboards and other moldings at a 45° angle. These cuts are made at wall corners and also for contoured lap joints along the length of a wall.

Ceramic tile

Ceramic tile, setting materials, and grout

Ceramic tile is a popular material for covering floors and walls, especially in bathrooms and kitchens. Similar to ceramic in qualities and installation procedures is vinyl tile (see p.119).

Glazed ceramic tile, with shiny or matte surface, comes in standard 4¼-inch squares and 6-inch squares, or 4¼-x-6-inch rectangles; all are 5/16 inch thick. These are nominal dimensions; actual dimensions are about 1/16 inch less. Octagonal and other interlocking shapes are also available (see pp.118–119). Traditionally, ceramic tiles were installed one at a time. Sheets of up to 64 connected tiles with uniform joints are used to speed installation of smaller tiles. Some sheets are pre-grouted with elastomer, or PVC rubber.

Ceramic mosaic tiles are smaller. They come in 1-inch squares, 2-inch squares, or 1-x-2-inch rectangles, all ¼ inch thick. Some other shapes are available. Mosaic tiles are usually installed in prearranged regular or random pattern sheets, generally 1 foot square; each sheet is installed much as is a single large ceramic tile. Each sheet of mosaic tile is held together either by a film of paper over its face (which is taken off after installation), or by small tabs of tape or rubber connecting individual tiles. The latter type has the advantage of allowing you to see the pattern of the mosaics as you proceed. Standard ceramic tiles that are scored to look like many smaller mosaic tiles are also available from tiling suppliers.

Quarry tile is made of natural clays, earthy red, brown, or gray in color. They are usually larger and more porous than glazed ceramic tile. Primitive tile (p.119) is a porous ceramic tile with irregular surfaces and borders; it is often coated with a sealer after installation.

Materials for setting ceramic tile: The traditional method of setting ceramic tile is to embed it in a ¾- to 1¼-inch-thick layer of Portland cement mortar (premixed Portland cement, sand, and hydrated lime) over a previously poured mortar bed. This is called a thick-set method, which is a difficult procedure and requires sturdy backing (see below) and a fair degree of skill.

Thin-set methods involve a much thinner layer of mortar or adhesive to

Backings for ceramic tile

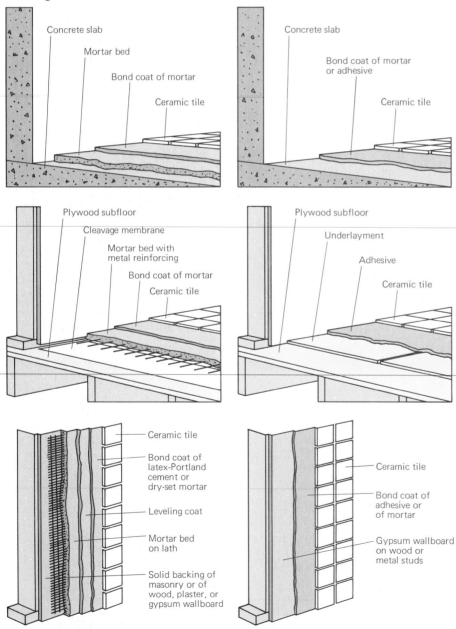

Concrete slab
Mortar bed
Bond coat of mortar
Ceramic tile

Concrete slab
Bond coat of mortar or adhesive
Ceramic tile

Plywood subfloor
Cleavage membrane
Mortar bed with metal reinforcing
Bond coat of mortar
Ceramic tile

Plywood subfloor
Underlayment
Adhesive
Ceramic tile

Ceramic tile
Bond coat of latex-Portland cement or dry-set mortar
Leveling coat
Mortar bed on lath
Solid backing of masonry or of wood, plaster, or gypsum wallboard

Ceramic tile
Bond coat of adhesive or of mortar
Gypsum wallboard on wood or metal studs

Concrete subfloor: The traditional thick-set cement mortar method (far left) used a mortar bed ¾ to 1¼ in. thick, made of Portland cement, sand, and hydrated lime. The overlying bond coat is a Portland cement paste if laid over mortar when mortar is still plastic; dry-set or latex-Portland cement mortar is used over cured mortar. The concrete base for both thick-set and thin-set applications must be well cured and have no cracks, waxy or oily films, or curing compounds. Thin-set application over concrete (near left) can use either dry-set or latex-Portland cement mortar, or an organic or an epoxy adhesive. The slab beneath thin-set applications should have a steel trowel or fine broom finish. The thin-set mortar coat is at least 3/32 in. thick; adhesives are usually thinner.

Wood subfloor: Wood subfloor backing for ceramic tiles must be stiff, with little deflection or bending. The cement mortar method (far left) requires reinforcing and use of a cleavage membrane, made of polyethylene or roofing felt, over a floor that is structurally sound (⅝-in. plywood or 1-in. boards minimum over joists spaced 16 in. o.c.). Organic adhesive (near left) must be laid over a double wood floor, made of a subfloor as described above with an overlay of ⅜ in. minimum plywood (exterior grade), with ⅛-in. expansion gaps left between the sheets. Adjacent sheets cannot vary in height more than 1/32 in. Epoxy adhesive, unlike organic adhesive, can be used in wet areas; it requires a thicker wood overlay, with gaps between the plywood sheets filled with adhesive.

Solid interior walls: Cement mortar can be applied on metal lath (far left) if a wall surface presents bonding difficulties, as do old plaster and wallpaper. The lath is anchored to the studs behind the wall. On an irregular wall surface with good bonding properties, a leveling coat of mortar can be directly applied to smooth the surface, just as in thin-set application (near left). Dry-set mortar or latex-Portland cement mortar can be applied over suitable concrete (see *Concrete subfloors*, above), and can also incorporate a leveling coat. Dry-set mortar can be used over gypsum board, but not if the board is water-resistant; organic adhesive is used over all gypsum board, as well as over plaster, plywood, wallboard, and other smooth surfaces.

hold the tile (pp.116–119). Dry-set mortar is a Portland cement mortar that can be applied as thin as $3/32$ inch. Latex-Portland cement mortar has similar uses as dry-set mortar, and is less rigid. Organic adhesive, usually applied in a $1/16$-inch-thick layer, is the most common for do-it-yourself work. Epoxy adhesive is a high-strength setting material. The backing for all installation must be rigid and smooth, although the thicker mortar beds can accommodate a slight unevenness in underlying surfaces. The choice of adhesive is affected by the backing (see below), the use of the room, the type of tile, and the grout. Always follow the manufacturer's instructions.

Grouting materials: Grouting materials, which fill the spaces between the tiles once they are installed, must be compatible with the tile and setting material. Portland cement grout, dry-set grout, and latex-Portland cement grout are all mixed with water to a pasty consistency; they require damp curing (wetting while they set). Mastic grout, more flexible and stain resistant than cement grout, comes as a pre-mixed paste. There are also epoxy grouts and silicone rubber grout. Some are better than others in wet areas; silicone should not be used on kitchen countertops. Follow manufacturer's directions.

Backing for tile: Ceramic tiles can be attached over almost any sound, dry, clean, level surface, such as steel-troweled concrete, wallboard, hardboard, plywood (exterior grade), or an existing tile surface in good condition.

Concrete surfaces that are unsmooth should be leveled with a layer of mortar (for mortar application), and must be well cured. New plaster must be cured at least a month before accepting tile. Any weak parts in a plaster wall should be patched and sealed with shellac. Old paint should be removed, or mostly scratched away. Wallboards and subfloors must be firmly supported, with no loose or springy sections. An unsound surface can be covered with an underlayment of exterior grade plywood, at least $3/8$-inch thick. Existing tiles should be ripped out if they are loose or uneven. Sound tile walls should be cleaned with a strong detergent and sanded with carborundum paper to promote adhesion.

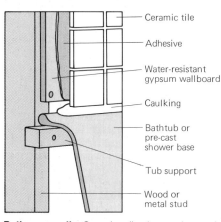

Ceramic tile

Adhesive

Water-resistant gypsum wallboard

Caulking

Bathtub or pre-cast shower base

Tub support

Wood or metal stud

Bathroom walls: Organic adhesive can be used over water-resistant gypsum board, which should be at least ½ in. thick, installed horizontally, and should stop at least ¼ in. above the lip of the tub. Taped joints should be coated with sealer to prevent water damage. Bathtub walls can also be prepared for tiling with the mortar and lath method over open wood or metal studs.

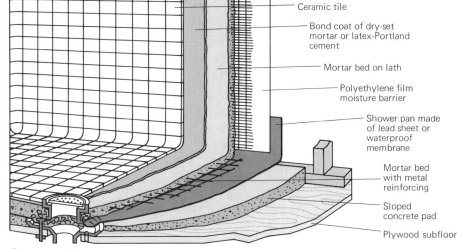
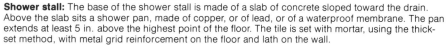

Ceramic tile

Bond coat of dry-set mortar or latex-Portland cement

Mortar bed on lath

Polyethylene film moisture barrier

Shower pan made of lead sheet or waterproof membrane

Mortar bed with metal reinforcing

Sloped concrete pad

Plywood subfloor

Shower stall: The base of the shower stall is made of a slab of concrete sloped toward the drain. Above the slab sits a shower pan, made of copper, or of lead, or of a waterproof membrane. The pan extends at least 5 in. above the highest point of the floor. The tile is set with mortar, using the thick-set method, with metal grid reinforcement on the floor and lath on the wall.

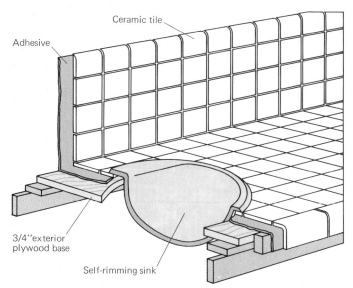

Ceramic tile

Adhesive

3/4" exterior plywood base

Self-rimming sink

Countertop: Ceramic tiles on countertops can be set with either organic or epoxy adhesives. The counter should be made of exterior grade plywood, at least ¾ in. thick. If the counter is well supported, the thick-set mortar method can be used. Certain grouts, such as the latex and silicone grouts, should not be used on kitchen counters.

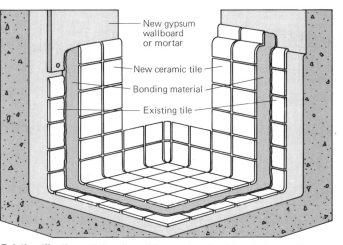

New gypsum wallboard or mortar

New ceramic tile

Bonding material

Existing tile

Existing tile: If an existing tile wall is sound and well bonded, new tile can be applied directly over it; if the old tile is faulty it should be torn out, or a structurally sound surface, such as lath or wallboard, should be installed over it to support the new tile. Wash the existing tile and abrade it with carborundum to enhance adhesion. Almost any mortar or adhesive can be used. An area above an existing tile wall can be filled with gypsum board or mortar and lath if the new tile wall is to extend higher. Existing tile floors can be covered with new tiles in a similar way if the surface of the floor is sound, level, and well bonded.

Ceramic tile

Using basic tile shapes in a typical room

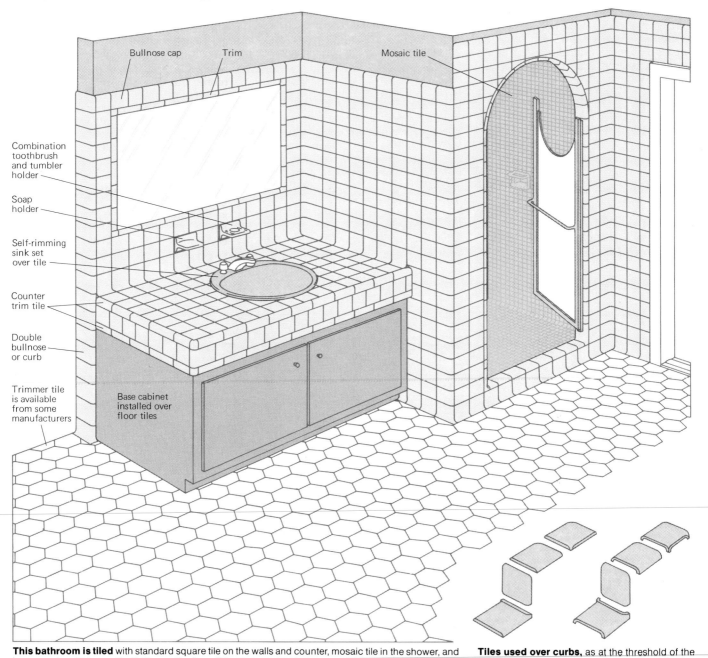

Bullnose cap

Trim

Mosaic tile

Combination toothbrush and tumbler holder

Soap holder

Self-rimming sink set over tile

Counter trim tile

Double bullnose or curb

Trimmer tile is available from some manufacturers

Base cabinet installed over floor tiles

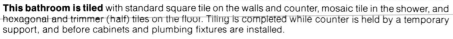

This bathroom is tiled with standard square tile on the walls and counter, mosaic tile in the shower, and hexagonal and trimmer (half) tiles on the floor. Tiling is completed while counter is held by a temporary support, and before cabinets and plumbing fixtures are installed.

Tiles used over curbs, as at the threshold of the shower above, vary depending on the adhesive material, thin-set (left) or thick-set (right).

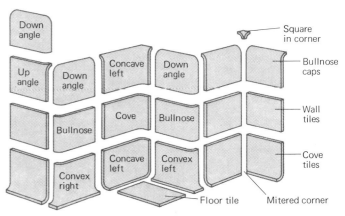

Down angle

Up angle

Down angle

Concave left

Down angle

Bullnose caps

Bullnose

Cove

Bullnose

Wall tiles

Convex right

Concave left

Convex left

Cove tiles

Mitered corner

These basic tile shapes are used with thin-set application (pp.112–113).

Down angle

Square in corner

Up angle

Down angle

Concave left

Down angle

Bullnose caps

Bullnose

Cove

Bullnose

Wall tiles

Convex right

Concave left

Convex left

Cove tiles

Floor tile

Mitered corner

These basic tile shapes are used with thick-set application (pp.112–113).

Planning a tiled room

Successful tiling depends on good planning. The basic planning strategy is to divide the walls and floors into large rectangular areas, which are easily tiled, leaving symmetrical border areas at the sides. Ideally, after measurement—allowing for the width of the joints between the tiles—border areas that remain will be exactly equal, and each no less than half the width of a tile (see *Measuring for ceiling tile*, pp.92, 94). In practice it rarely works out this well because room dimensions are seldom perfect in the average house.

The simplest area to tile is the floor of a rectangular room. Measurements are made using a board marked to your tile size; the sizes of the borders are calculated, and strings run perpendicular from the walls, intersecting in the middle of the room, guide the placement of the first tiles (see diagram, p.110). This is especially simple if the tiles are of an easy to cut material such as vinyl.

Where to place cut tiles: Ceramic tiles are most often used in kitchens and bathrooms—rooms with many built-in cabinets, plumbing, and other obstructions. This means cutting tiles to accommodate the changing dimensions of the room. You must decide where cut tiles or uneven borders will be least noticeable and how to improve your design to place them appropriately. On the other hand, tiles often fall behind fixtures, or in corners of a room where there is dim light and little traffic. In these cases, it makes sense to plan to install areas of uncut tiles where they will be seen, placing cut tiles and any uneven borders where they will not. Sometimes it is attractive to have ceramic wall tiles align with the floor tiles; in this case, tiling would begin at the juncture with the wall and proceed into the room. The tiling of a bathroom floor often begins at the doorway, especially if there is no threshold. Whole tiles greet the eye, and bear most of the traffic in and out of the room. Cut tiles then fall in the far corners. All measurements must take into account the shape and dimension of the special tiles that are used in corners, over curbs, and as trim, as shown in the small drawings opposite.

The large diagram on the facing page shows a tiled bathroom, involving standard ceramic tiles on the walls and countertop, hexagonal floor tiles (installed starting at the passageway at far left), mosaic tiles in the shower, trim and corner tiles, and special tile inserts (soap and toothbrush holder). Planning the tiling for such rooms is discussed in the caption accompanying the drawing at the bottom of this page.

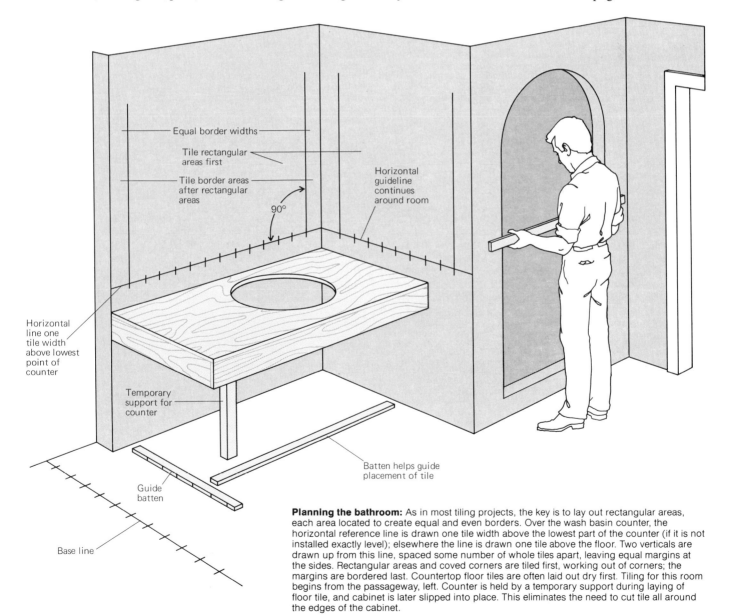

Equal border widths

Tile rectangular areas first

Tile border areas after rectangular areas

90°

Horizontal guideline continues around room

Horizontal line one tile width above lowest point of counter

Temporary support for counter

Guide batten

Base line

Batten helps guide placement of tile

Planning the bathroom: As in most tiling projects, the key is to lay out rectangular areas, each area located to create equal and even borders. Over the wash basin counter, the horizontal reference line is drawn one tile width above the lowest part of the counter (if it is not installed exactly level); elsewhere the line is drawn one tile above the floor. Two verticals are drawn up from this line, spaced some number of whole tiles apart, leaving equal margins at the sides. Rectangular areas and coved corners are tiled first, working out of corners; the margins are bordered last. Countertop floor tiles are often laid out dry first. Tiling for this room begins from the passageway, left. Counter is held by a temporary support during laying of floor tile, and cabinet is later slipped into place. This eliminates the need to cut tile all around the edges of the cabinet.

Ceramic tile

Tiling a shower stall

The tiling of a newly constructed shower stall, involving tiling of both walls and a floor, is shown in the illustrations on this and the facing page.

Backing: The walls in this stall are made of water-resistant gypsum board. A water-soluble adhesive (waterproof after it sets) was chosen as the setting material for the wall. The shower base, poured by a professional, is made of a slab of concrete, sloped to direct water toward the drain. Dry-set mortar was chosen by the do-it-yourselfer for the shower floor. Dry-set adheres to concrete, and because it is applied thicker than adhesives, it is better for smoothing small imperfections in the slab.

Planning: Tiling from the floor up is the standard procedure. But the walls of this shower stall slope in slightly at the bottom. Because of this, our do-it-yourselfer decided that installing the sheets of tile from the top down would make it easier to align the tiles than would tiling from the floor up. He had a perfect fit of tiles at the top, and simply cut the lower sheets to match as he installed them. Finally, he cut individual tiles to fill the small gaps at the sides.

After the wall was installed, the tiles for the floor were laid out dry. The finished shower contains a wooden bench opposite the shower head; the cut tiles were planned to fall beneath the bench, where they would not be seen.

Installing the wall: The measurements were carefully made, marked on the wall, and checked for level. The first piece to be installed was the upper corner piece, made of connected cove tiles. This served as a guide for placement of the other tiles.

The adhesive was applied with a toothed trowel, pushed in on the toothed edge to make ridges in the adhesive. A

coating 1/16 inch thick (following manufacturer's directions) was applied, as much at a time as would fall under the next sheet of tiles. After pushing each sheet against the adhesive, our man hammered through a carpet-covered board to make every tile set into the adhesive and to level the surface.

The gaps between the sheets of tile are made the same as the joints between the tiles on each sheet, preserving the uniformity of the wall. (Individual ceramic tiles are manufactured with edge tabs that serve as spacers to assure uniform joint width.) Tiles were removed from sheets to make openings for the shower pipe and the hot and cold water faucets; the removed tiles were shaped with nippers to fit around these obstructions, and installed individually with adhesive applied to the back (see illustration, below right). Tiles were cut to fit the gaps at each end of the wall. Straight cuts along the entire length of a tile are made with a tile cutter, which can be rented from a hardware store, or by scoring the glazed side with a glass cutter, and pressing along the break over a pencil or nail. Measuring and cutting border and corner tiles and irregularly shaped tiles is illustrated on page 119. Cut edges should be smoothed with a whetstone.

After the walls were completed they were carefully washed to remove the adhesive, then left to set for 24 hours.

Installing the floor: The floor tiles were laid out dry because the sloping concrete base made planning by measurement very tricky. The mortar was then mixed according to manufacturer's specifications. A screw cap was placed in the drain to protect it from mortar. The mortar was applied with a toothed trowel, much like the wall adhesive, but in a thicker bed. Mortar covered the

floor, a portion at a time, and as far up the walls as necessary to set the cove tile connecting the wall and floor. The sheets of tile were pressed into the mortar, then hammered in through a carpet buffer so every tile set and the surface was flat. A double row of smaller contrasting tiles filled the gaps running the length of the floor.

Grouting: The grout, mixed to manufacturer's specifications, was applied to the walls and floor with a rubber-surfaced trowel and forced into the joints between the tiles. After it sat for a while, but before curing, it was compressed into the joints with the handle of an old toothbrush. The excess was then carefully washed off the tiles with a sponge and water, and then with a clean cloth; if not removed before it sets, grout stays on the tiles forever. After cleaning, the tiles were wetted periodically for the next 72 hours until the grout set.

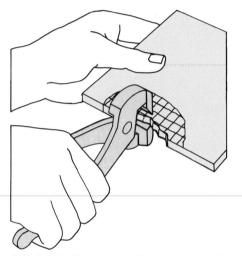

A tile is cut with nippers to allow for passage of a pipe. The area to be cut away is first scored with a glass cutter to facilitate cutting.

1. The corner strips, each made of six connected cove tiles, are installed first, to guide the placement of the other tiles.

2. The white, water-soluble adhesive is applied with a toothed trowel, only as much at a time as is needed for each sheet.

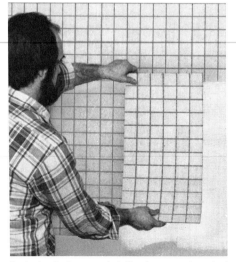

3. A sheet of connected tiles is pressed against the adhesive. The joints between the sheets are as wide as the joints between the tiles on the sheets.

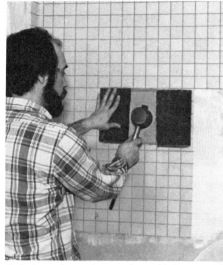

4. A piece of carpet-covered wood is hammered over each sheet so that each individual tile sets properly and the surface is flat.

5. Two tiles are removed from a sheet to accommodate the shower pipe. Later, pieces are cut and attached around pipe, (see illustration, facing).

6. The shower base, made of well-cured concrete, slopes toward the drain. It is brushed clean to promote adhesion to the cement mortar.

7. A ¼-in.-layer of dry-set mortar is applied to the floor and one tile-length up the wall. A screw cap protects the drain from dripping mortar.

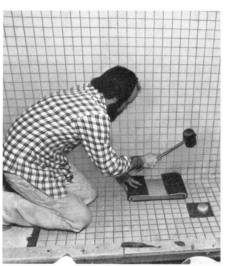

8. The sheets of tile are laid atop the mortar and hammered in. Mortar application requires that the tiles are carefully leveled.

9. Tile cutter blade is drawn along cut line on border tile. Tiles can also be cut with tile nippers, or they can be scored with a glass cutter.

10. Cut tiles are coated with adhesive and pressed individually into the gaps in the wall. A double row of smaller tile fills the gaps in the floor.

11. Grout is mixed and forced between the tiles in both the floor and wall with arc-like sweeps of a rubber-surfaced trowel.

12. Excess grout is washed from the tiles with water and a sponge. The grout is kept wet for three days so that it sets completely.

Ceramic tile

Common shapes and patterns

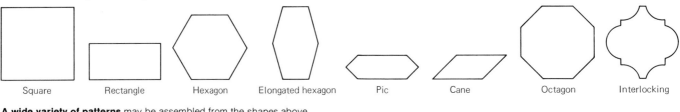

Square	Rectangle	Hexagon	Elongated hexagon	Pic	Cane	Octagon	Interlocking

A wide variety of patterns may be assembled from the shapes above.

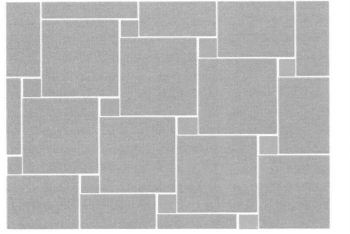

Large and small squares

Squares and rectangles

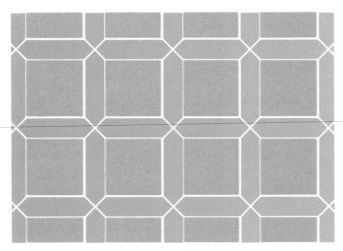

Squares and pics

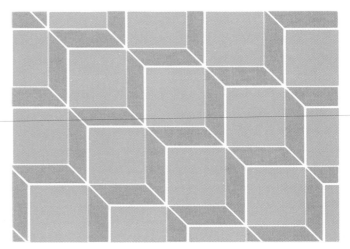

Squares and canes

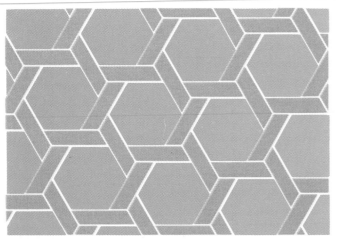

Hexagons and canes

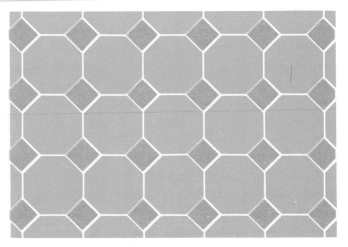

Octagons and squares

Laying a floor of primitive tile

Primitive tile has irregular edges and surfaces, and thus presents difficulties that regular ceramic tile and vinyl tile do not. The illustrations show one way a primitive tile floor can be installed.

Measurements were made, and the width of the border and intersecting center lines (p.115) determined by considering the size of the tile and the width of the joints between tiles (here wider than for standard ceramic tile). Our do-it-yourselfer decided to install a border made of smaller tiles in a railroad pattern, rather than larger cut tiles. Spacers, small pieces of wood tile or linoleum used to produce joints of regular width between standard ceramic tiles, were used to space the border tiles.

As the border sections were installed the interior of the floor was tiled outward with 8-x-8-inch tiles from the centerlines laid out earlier. The slight variations in the sizes of the tiles were accommodated by slightly varying the width of each joint. Spacers were not used between the 8-x-8-inch tiles. Better results were attained by laying them by sight, or "eyeballing." The corners were planned by first laying the tiles out dry.

Because of the irregular surfaces, mortar was used as the setting material, also a good material to use over this concrete subfloor. A small area of mortar was spread at a time with a toothed trowel. After each tile was laid it was hammered in with a rubber mallet to be sure it set into the mortar. After installation was complete and the mortar set, the entire floor was grouted.

1. After the room was measured and the width of the border determined, the border was installed. It is made of smaller tiles, installed in a staggered railroad pattern. Spacers between the tiles maintain a uniform joint.

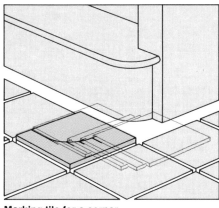

2. The regular 8-x-8-in. tile was installed from the centerline outward. Each tile was hammered into the mortar with a rubber mallet. Spacers were not used with these tiles because of their irregularity; they were installed by sight.

3. Because of the different sizes of tile, and the unusual angle, this corner was planned by first laying out the tiles dry. The large cut tiles were installed last. As in the rest of the floor, each tile was hammered in to set properly.

Cutting tiles for corners and borders

Accurate cutting of tiles is essential for an attractive tile surface. Accurate cuts for borders and corners or for fitting around irregular obstructions can be made by laying a tile over those already installed and making reference marks, as shown. Flexible tile, such as vinyl, can be cut with a sharp knife along almost any line. A cut on a ceramic tile usually goes all the way across the tile, whether or not that is desired; but it can be broken into small pieces and fitted together in place. An irregular shape can be cut into a ceramic tile by removing many small pieces from it along the cut line with tile nippers (p.116).

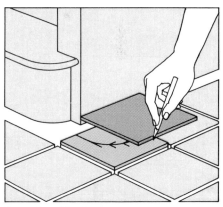

Marking tile for a corner.

Second marking for a corner.

Vinyl tile

Vinyl tile comes in two standard sizes, 9-inch and 12-inch squares, $\frac{1}{8}$ or $\frac{1}{16}$ inch thick. It is applied over backing suitable for ceramic tile (see pp.111–113).

Vinyl tile is usually applied from the center of a room outward. The room is measured, and after the sizes of the borders are determined (each more than half the width of an uncut tile, if possible), a string is stretched across the room to guide placement of the tiles (see diagram, p.110). A thin layer of adhesive is applied, as directed by the manufacturer. Over-application is a common problem, causing adhesive to ooze up between tiles (remove it with a cloth and solvent). The adhesive is applied over areas that permit installing the tile outward from the guide string in pyramid fashion. No spaces are left between vinyl tiles. They are laid, not slid, into place abutting each other. Marbleized or grained tile is laid so that adjacent tiles run in opposite directions.

Sheet vinyl flooring

Modern resilient flooring

Sheet vinyl flooring is commonly used in kitchens, and is also used in bathrooms, basements, and foyers. Sheet vinyl flooring is attractive, easy to install, easy to maintain, and water-resistant. Linoleum flooring, which is not water-resistant, is no longer manufactured in the United States.

Sheet vinyl flooring has some distinct advantages over vinyl tile flooring: it is easier to install, comes in a greater variety of surfaces and patterns, and once installed has far fewer (if any) seams in which dirt can accumulate.

Inlaid vinyl flooring: The thickest and heaviest vinyl floorings are the inlaid vinyls. The design of inlaid vinyl penetrates its entire thickness. It is thick, and feels heavy and sturdy underfoot; it comes in deep colors. Inlaid vinyl costs more than other vinyl flooring, and be-

cause of its weight inlaid vinyl should be installed by professionals.

Rotovinyls: This second type of vinyl is thinner and lighter, with designs that are printed on the surface and covered with clear vinyl. Rotovinyls contain a core of foamed or expanded vinyl, which makes them comfortable to walk on, and muffles noise.

Rotovinyls are flexible enough to be installed by the do-it-yourselfer. A careful plan drawn, the vinyl flooring is unrolled in another room and cut to the required sizes. It is then installed over adhesive applied either along the perimeter of the room or beneath the entire flooring, depending on the vinyl and the type of backing.

Stretch cushioned vinyls: The newest type of vinyl flooring is a light, cushioned vinyl that is also elastic. This elas-

ticity causes the flooring, after being installed by stapling or gluing around the perimeter, to contract, tightening the surface and eliminating wrinkles or looseness. The flooring can span small imperfections in the subfloor or backing and still allow for movement during change of seasons without showing gaps or cracks. The installation of this type of flooring is illustrated on this and the facing page.

Backing: Sheet vinyl flooring can be installed over almost any backing: for example, wood, plywood, particleboard, concrete, tile, or existing resilient flooring. The backing should be sound and flat; gaps or depressions can be filled with pieces of flooring. If the existing flooring is in woeful disrepair, it is usually easier to cover it with a new underlayment of plywood or particle-

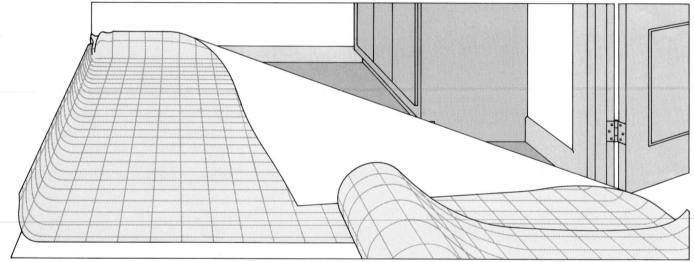

1. Baseboard moldings are removed. Flooring is unrolled, edges extending up the walls and cabinets. Enough material is unrolled to cover all of the room including bays and alcoves.

2. A second piece of flooring (if necessary) is laid like the first, covering the remainder of the room. The second piece is laid slightly overlapping the first, the patterns of the vinyl carefully aligned.

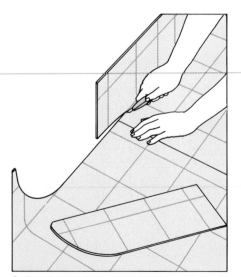

3. Two U-shaped pieces are cut away at the ends of the seam so the flooring fits exactly against the walls and lies flat on the floor. The two pieces of flooring are not allowed to slip.

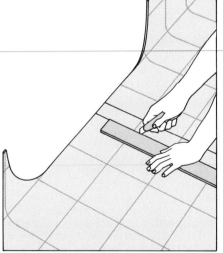

4. A sharp-bladed utility knife, guided by a metal straightedge, is used to cut down the seam through both layers of flooring. On simulated tile flooring the cut is made on a grout line.

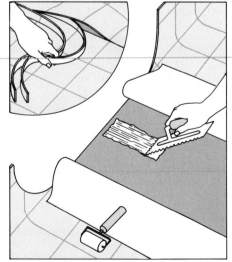

5. The waste strips cut in Step 4 are removed, and adhesive is applied to floor below seam; flooring is flattened with a hand roller. A sealing adhesive is then applied over seam.

board than to remove it. Existing sheet or tile flooring should only be removed for compelling reasons.

Preparing the surface: Vinyl flooring will bond to almost any porous material, including concrete (which, however, must not be moist, as in a damp basement). Non-porous surfaces, such as tile, should be roughened around the perimeter and wherever adhesive will be applied. Existing resilient flooring, backing, and lining felt should not be roughened by sanding because these old materials may contain asbestos fibers; if inhaled, asbestos is very dangerous. If a resilient floor must be removed, it should be sliced into strips and pulled up. Lining felt is then scraped up.

All perimeter floor trim must be removed. Clean the floor thoroughly; floor adhesives will not bond well to floors that are oily, dirty, cold, or wet. There are special cleaners that remove built-up dirt, grease, and wax.

Preparing the vinyl: The flooring is rolled up face-outward for 24 hours before installation. This stretches the elastic surface, which contracts after installation. Room temperature should be at least 65° F.

Installation: Bathrooms and kitchens that are less than 12 feet wide can be covered with vinyl flooring without seams (the flooring comes in 6- and 12-foot widths). If a seam is needed, it is cut and joined first. The two pieces of flooring are laid in place in the room overlapping at their edges with the patterns matching. A straight cut is made through both overlapping layers. The waste is removed and the trimmed pieces are attached with adhesive to the floor along the seam; the seam is covered with a sealing compound.

Once the seam is made, or if no seam is necessary, the flooring is fitted into each corner and the excess is sliced from the apex to eliminate wrinkles. The rest of the perimeter is then trimmed. The flooring is attached where possible with a staple gun; adhesive is used over concrete, or under toe-kick overhangs of kitchen cabinets, where a staple gun will not fit. Staples and adhesives can be used together. Complete work within two hours of fitting and trimming, before the flooring starts to contract.

Metal or vinyl molding is installed to cover the perimeter of the flooring. Metal thresholds cover the flooring at doorways. The flooring should be allowed to contract for a day before heavy furniture is moved back into the room.

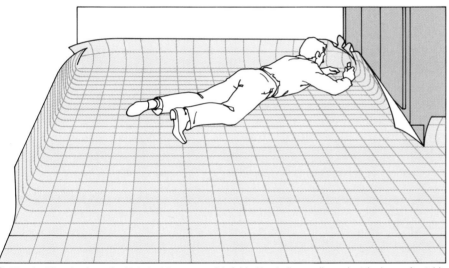

6. The vinyl flooring is pushed into inside corners; it is folded back diagonally against the base of outside corners. At all corners utility knife is punched through excess flooring at floor level and drawn upward, cutting vinyl to ensure tight fit and allowing flooring to lie flat.

7. Flooring is pushed firmly against the walls with a steel carpenter's square, and the excess vinyl is trimmed away with a utility knife.

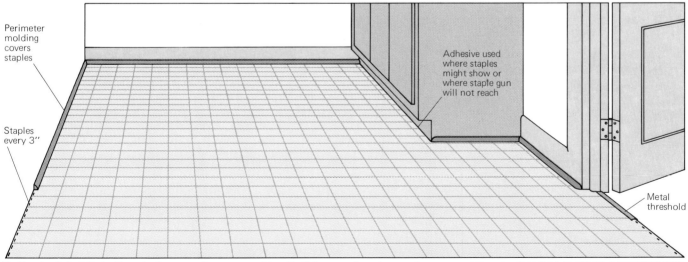

Perimeter molding covers staples

Staples every 3″

Adhesive used where staples might show or where staple gun will not reach

Metal threshold

8. Flooring is installed with a stapling gun wherever possible with ⅜-in. or ½-in. staples applied every 3 in. along the perimeter. Adhesive is used over concrete subfloors or where a stapling gun cannot reach, such as beneath toe-kick overhangs of kitchen cabinets. Adhesive is applied around perimeter; clean and prepare subfloor as described in adhesive manufacturer's instructions. Baseboard molding removed earlier, is replaced, covering the stapled edges of the completed floor. Allow the new flooring to contract for 24 hours before returning furniture.

Wall-to-wall carpeting

Kinds of carpet

Wall-to-wall carpeting, once made predominantly of wool fiber, is now also available in a variety of synthetic fibers that have many of the assets of wool without some of its liabilities. Acrylic, handsome and long-wearing, nylon, strong and stain-resistant, and polyester, shiny, bright and colorful, are less prone to cause static electrical shock, are easier to clean, and are far less expensive than wool.

Carpet composition: Unlike the traditional (and expensive) woven carpets made on looms, most modern carpets are tufted; that is, they are made of fibers stitched into a backing made of open fabric. This primary backing is attached to a second fabric backing, which rests on the floor, with an intermediate layer of latex. If the fibers stitched into the backing are left uncut, forming loops, it is loop-pile carpet. If the loops are split or cut off, it is cut-pile carpet. Traditional woven carpeting is still made, but it is very expensive and should be left to professionals to install.

Most good carpeting is laid over a

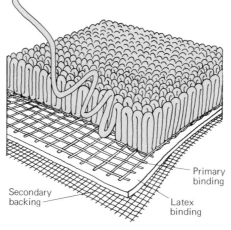

Elements of loop-pile carpet

Secondary backing

Primary binding

Latex binding

layer of padding, which cushions the carpet and helps muffle noise. Some less expensive carpeting is available with its own padding attached.

Cushion-back carpet: Cushion-back carpet, carpet that comes with its own padding already attached, is installed without stretching or using tackless strips. It is cut according to a floor plan,

like normal carpeting, and then installed either on adhesive troweled over the entire floor, or with tape placed around the perimeter.

The ease of installation and lower price of cushion-back carpet are balanced by some unfortunate qualities. Because the carpet is attached with adhesive, it can only be removed by ripping it up; the padding remains stuck to the floor and must be scraped up, and the carpet cannot be reused. The padding of cushion-back carpet is often of lower quality than separate padding, and can decompose quickly. Carpet installed with the perimeter tape does not hold well, and will also wrinkle, and pull up entirely if there is much traffic on it.

Carpet squares: Carpeting is also available in squares with adhesive-coated backs. The squares are installed much like vinyl or parquet floor tiles, with the pile directions of adjacent squares of carpet arranged to obscure the seams. Installation is easy; if a portion of a carpet is damaged or soiled, only those squares need be replaced.

Planning to carpet a room

Wall-to-wall carpeting is stretched tautly across the floor from tackless strips placed around the room's perimeter. Carpeting in rooms wider than 12 feet, the standard width of rolls of carpet, is seamed; determining the location of seams is a major consideration.

The pile fibers of a carpet all lean the same way, a result of the carpet being rolled up immediately after its manufacture. This pile direction, which affects the appearance of the carpet and thus influences how it is installed, remains the same for the life of the carpet. If you stroke a carpet and raise its nap, you are stroking against the pile. When

the pile direction faces you, the carpet gives its fullest, deepest appearance.

Pile direction and seams: In general, carpet should be installed so its pile direction faces the main entrance to the room. The longest seam of the room should run toward the main source of light in the room, usually a window; a seam is harder to detect running with the light. A seam should not run into a doorway, since heavy traffic over it could pull it apart.

Scale drawing: Draw the room in scale on graph paper. Include doorways, windows, and any bays or other offsets into which the carpet will extend.

Make no assumptions about the squareness of walls; take all measurements. Increase all dimensions by 3 inches to allow for error and final trimming.

From the drawing you can estimate the amount of carpeting and padding you need. (Padding does not have to be installed in continuous pieces.)

You will need tackless strips equal to the perimeter of the room plus waste. Metal strips are installed at doorways.

Cut a piece of paper to scale to simulate the 12-foot carpet width and move it over your drawing. If the carpet has a pattern, leave enough so that you will be able to match along the seams.

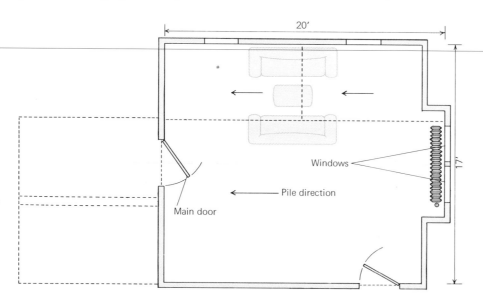

20'

Windows

Pile direction

Main door

17'

The principles of carpet planning, discussed above, are illustrated in this typical living room floor plan. The main source of light, the bay window at the far right, determines that the main seam of the carpet should run directly toward the window. This main seam is placed to the side of the doorway to the left, so it is not subjected to heavy foot traffic; there is no seam at all between the two doorways. The pile direction is toward the main door, so the carpet puts its best face forward to someone entering.

During cutting, the single 12-ft. wide length of carpeting that covers most of the room is rolled out an extra 10 ft. (plus a bit for trimming), and two pieces are cut from it (as shown by the dotted lines) to fit over the upper section of the room. Though this causes an extra seam, it will be mostly covered by furniture, as seen in the floor plan. This economy measure saves an extra 10 ft. of 12-ft.-wide carpet that would otherwise be needed to finish the room.

Basic preparations and preliminary procedures

Carpeting can be difficult work, but one of its advantages is that it requires little preparation of the floor beneath it. Loose boards should be nailed down, and gaps in the floor should be filled. Clean the floor, so dirt and grease don't pass through and discolor the carpet. Baseboard moldings are usually removed, and replaced after the carpet is installed. Place a scrap of carpet and padding over the floor and swing each door in the room over it; if a door sticks on the carpet, take the door down and trim it to clear.

Tackless strip: Carpeting is secured to the perimeter of the room with tackless strips, thin strips of wood with projecting sharp pins. (Tackless strips are so named because they replaced installation procedures in which tacks were nailed through the carpeting; the tack heads were visible after installation.) There are three types of tackless strips, with the pins ranging up to 1/4 inch in height; the strip to use depends on the thickness of the carpet. When carpet is placed over the proper tackless strip, you should be able to feel the pins through the carpet, but you should not be pricked by them.

Tackless strip comes in 4-foot lengths. Nails in the strips are used to attach them to the floor. Strips are available with masonry nails for use on concrete floors. Over surfaces that cannot be nailed, such as tile, the strips are cut into sections and cemented down. The tackless strip is attached around the entire perimeter of the room. Special metal strips used at doorways have a lip that is bent over the carpet after the carpet is installed. The strips are installed in front of such obstacles as radiators that prevent stretching the carpet all the way to the wall; the carpet is cut so its loose edges can be pushed back under the

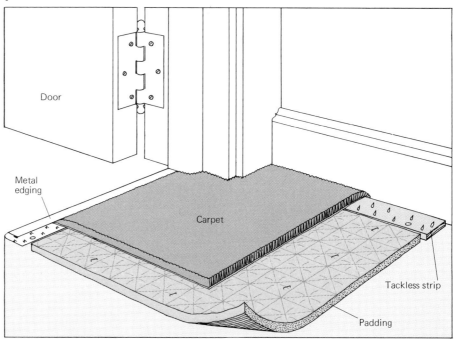

Wall-to-wall carpeting is stretched tautly between tackless strips installed around the perimeter of the room. The strips are nailed (or cemented) to the floor so that the pins lean toward the wall, with a small gap next to the wall so that the cut carpet can be tucked behind the strips. A metal edging strip at each doorway has points to hold the carpet, and a lip that is hammered over the carpet. Padding is attached, usually with staples, over the entire area of the floor within the tackless strips. Before installation begins, shoe molding or baseboard molding is removed.

obstacles (see diagram, p.124). Cut a piece of cardboard to a width of two thirds the thickness of the carpet; use it as a spacer to establish a constant gap between the wall and the tackless strip. The edges of the installed carpet are tucked into this gap.

Padding: Padding is installed beneath all carpeting, except cushion-back carpet. There are two types: foam and felt (which is more durable). Padding is cut from rolls and installed to cover the entire floor inside the tackless strips. It is stapled into wood floors and cemented over concrete. Padding has different

surfaces on each side; the manufacturer specifies which side should face up.

Rough cutting the carpet: In a room near the room to be carpeted, the carpet is unrolled and allowed to sit until it flattens and attains room temperature. It is then cut according to the scale drawing of the room. Cut-pile carpet is cut on the cloth backing: after the measurement is made, a chalk line is snapped, and the cut is made with a knife and straightedge. Loop-pile carpet must be cut on the face, either along a row of loops, if they are straight, or along a straightedge placed as a guide.

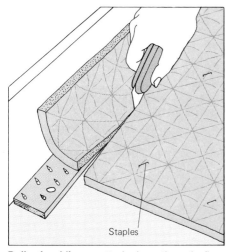

Rolls of padding are attached over the entire floor with a staple gun. A utility knife trims off excess along the tackless strips.

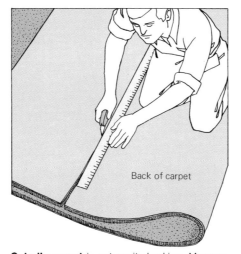

Cut-pile carpet is cut on its backing. Measurements are marked with chalk line; cut is made with a utility knife along a straightedge.

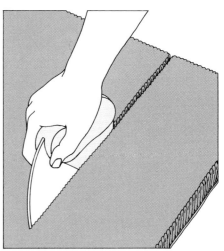

Loop-pile carpet is cut on the face, along straight row of loops or straightedge, with a utility knife or a special carpeting row-running knife.

Wall-to-wall carpeting

Installation

The carpet is moved into the room, pushed roughly into place, then kicked into the corners and against the walls so that a few inches of excess carpet turn up against the walls all around. Cuts are made with a utility knife to fit the carpet at corners and around obstacles.

Seaming: Seams between the different pieces of the carpet are made before the carpet is stretched and installed. The pieces are overlapped 1 inch at the seam; they are arranged so their pile direction is the same—to hide the finished seam.

A special row-running knife cuts along the edge of the top piece of carpet through the bottom piece. The cut strip is removed from the bottom piece. Both edges of carpet are then peeled back, and a strip of hot-melt seaming tape is placed on the floor beneath the entire length of the aligned edges. As the strip is activated with a hot iron, a short section at a time, the edges are rolled back together and carefully butted.

Installing the carpet: The seamed carpet is stretched across the room and

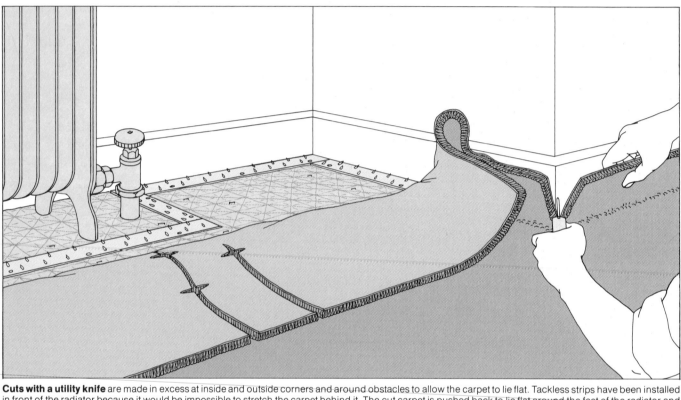

Cuts with a utility knife are made in excess at inside and outside corners and around obstacles to allow the carpet to lie flat. Tackless strips have been installed in front of the radiator because it would be impossible to stretch the carpet behind it. The cut carpet is pushed back to lie flat around the feet of the radiator and meet the base of the wall behind the radiator.

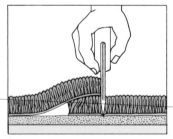

Seam is cut by overlapping pieces of carpet 1 in. and using top edge as a guide for knife.

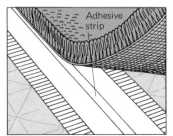

Hot-melt seaming tape is placed beneath the centerline of the seam atop the padding.

Hot iron activates hot-melt seaming tape. The iron, set at 250° F., is slowly drawn down the length of the tape to make it adhere to the carpet backing.

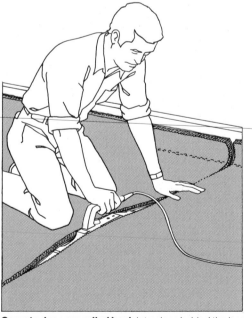

Carpet edges are rolled back into place behind the iron and carefully butted to form a smooth seam. Weights can be placed over seam til it sets.

then given its final trimming. The carpet is worked against the wall and set securely on the pin points of the tackless strips with a tool called a knee-kicker. A much longer tool, up to 26 feet long when fully extended, called a power stretcher is used to stretch and secure the far end of the carpet once the near end has been secured with the knee-kicker (see large drawing, this page). Both tools are at tool rental stores.

The procedure for installing a carpet usually begins at two points in a corner, with the knee-kicker. The power stretcher then secures the points on the two far walls directly opposite. The knee-kicker affixes the carpet all the way along the walls extending from the first corner. The stretcher then sets the carpet along the opposite walls. A hammer is used to force the carpet onto the tackless strip all around the room.

The stretched and installed carpet is given its final trim with a utility knife or a special carpet trimmer. The cut edges are tucked between the tackless strip and the wall with a screw driver.

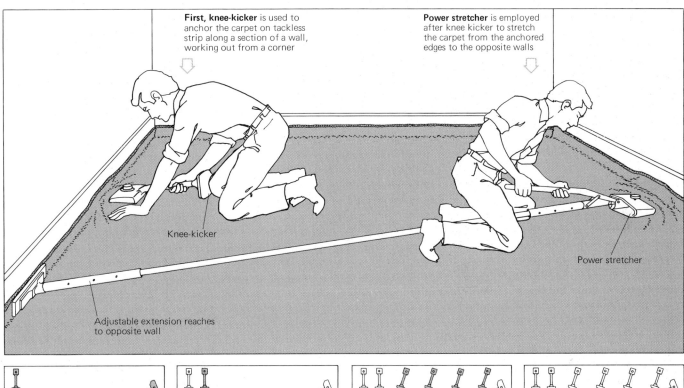

First, knee-kicker is used to anchor the carpet on tackless strip along a section of a wall, working out from a corner

Power stretcher is employed after knee kicker to stretch the carpet from the anchored edges to the opposite walls

Knee-kicker

Adjustable extension reaches to opposite wall

Power stretcher

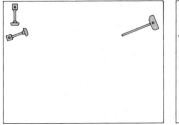

Using the knee-kicker and power stretcher: 1. Begin by using knee-kicker to attach carpet to tackless strip at two points on adjacent walls at an inside corner.

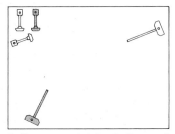

2. Use power stretcher to fix carpet at walls directly opposite the points set with a knee-kicker. The power stretcher has an adjustable extension to reach across room.

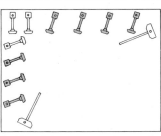

3. After fixing carpet at opposite walls with power stretcher, use knee-kicker to set the carpet at all points along the two walls that extend from the first corner.

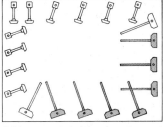

4. Use power stretcher to set carpet along two remaining walls of room. As the carpet is installed it is set securely in the pinpoints of the tackless strips with hammer.

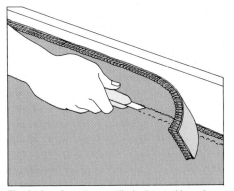

Final trimming along walls is done with a sharp utility knife. The carpet has been stretched on the tackless strips before this trimming.

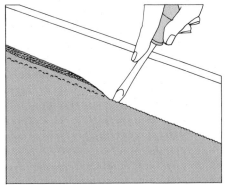

Screwdriver is used to tuck trimmed edges of carpet into the gap that is left between the tackless strip and the adjacent wall.

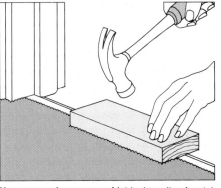

Hammer and scrap wood folds down lip of metal edging at doorway thresholds where door or people's feet might catch in carpet.

Interior doors

Standard and pre-hung doors

Lumberyards, home centers, and door stores sell "pre-hung" doors—doors that come already assembled in their frames and hung on their hinges. Pre-hung doors are usually more expensive than standard doors, but they are well worth the extra cost because hanging a standard door can be a tricky and time-consuming chore if you have never done it before. Manufacturers provide specifications for a door's rough opening (r.o.)—the framed space into which the assembled door fits. Generally, the rough opening for any door is about 2½ inches wider than the door at the side jambs, with a 3-inch margin at the top. Installing a pre-hung door entails framing the rough opening; shimming and nailing the jamb; and attaching the casing, as in steps 5, 8, 11, and 12, opposite.

Pass set: You can buy a door that includes an installed knob, latch, and lock. If you prefer to save money by installing the pass set yourself, buy a door with the holes for the lock and latch-bolt assembly and the mortise for the faceplate already drilled and cut, unless you have a set of drill bits ranging up to 2⅛ inches in diameter—a bit size used mostly by professionals.

Hanging a standard door: The step-by-step illustrations on the opposite page show how to install a standard door. (As noted above, only a few of the steps shown are required to hang a pre-assembled door.) The standard height for an interior door is 6 feet 8 inches. In most instances, clearance at the bottom of the door for the threshold or a rug can be obtained by making adjustments when cutting and shimming the top and side jambs. If it is necessary to cut away part of the door, and you are working with a hollow-core door, take a little bit off both the top and the bottom rather than all off the bottom. If for some reason you must cut more than 4 inches from a hollow-core door, make the cut entirely from the bottom; then re-fit the spline in the exposed channel in the door bottom.

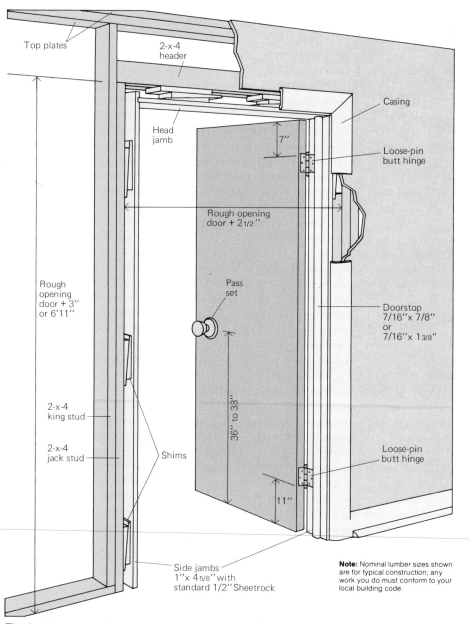

The doorframe assembly: Pre-hung doors are purchased fully assembled by the manufacturer, and are therefore less difficult to frame and hang than standard doors. But the elements of either type of door are the same, as shown here. The rough opening for the door in the wall frame consists of king studs, jack studs, and a header—2½ in. wider than the door at the sides and about 3 in. higher at the top. Jambs are positioned in the rough opening and shimmed square and plumb; hinges are hung on a side jamb; the gap between the jambs and the wall frame is covered with casing.

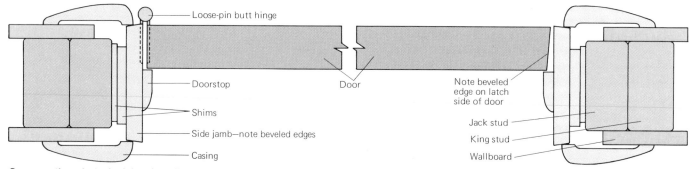

Cross section of a typical door installation: All parts are seen in position in this horizontal section drawing. Note that the hinge pin protrudes about ⅛-in. beyond the door; there are both left-hand and right-hand hinges for doors that open from either the left or the right. Doorstops fit snugly against the closed door (they are installed with the door in the closed position). The casing is set back slightly from the edge of the jamb to allow removal of the hinge pin. The leading edge of the door is beveled to give the door clearance to swing without leaving a visible gap between the closed door and the jamb on the outside. Side jambs are beveled for a neat fit with casings. Pre-hung doors come hinged to their jambs.

Hanging a standard door

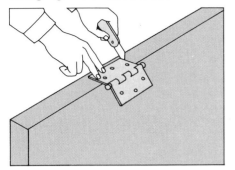

1. Position the hinges on your door (see drawing, opposite page). Mark the mortise areas with a utility knife; the barrel of each hinge should extend at least ⅛-in. outside the surface of the door at its inside edge, as shown at bottom, opposite.

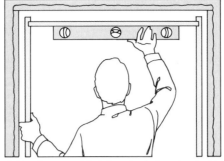

2. Set the assembled door jamb (head and side jambs) in the rough opening of the doorframe and check that it is level. Adjust by trimming the bottom of the longer side jamb. Shims will be placed between the jamb and frame.

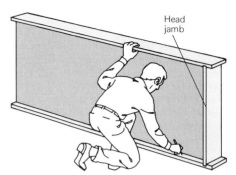

3. Place the door temporarily in the assembled jamb allowing about 1/16-in. clearance under the head jamb; transfer the markings for the hinge mortises from the door to the appropriate side jamb, left or right.

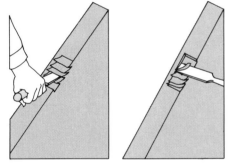

4. Chisel mortises in both jamb and door to a depth that will allow hinges to lie flush with adjacent surfaces. Make the recesses by first cutting small sections (left), then chiseling across the grain to remove chips (right).

5. Shim the hinged side of jamb first (using wood scraps or shingles). With a level, check that jamb is vertical, then nail it in place with 8-penny finish nails through the shims and into the frame. Leave nails protruding about ½-in. until Step 8.

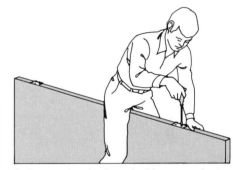

6. Remove the pins from the hinges, a pair at a time; install each hinge-half in its mortise bed on the door and on the jamb, making certain that the halves are properly matched. Drive the screws all the way in so the heads are flush.

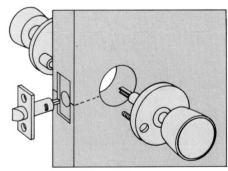

7. With the aid of a helper, install door by slipping top hinges together and inserting pin part way. Then slip lower hinge-halves together (or center, in a door with three hinges) and pin them. Do not set pins all the way until job is finished.

8. Shim and nail head and side jambs, allowing 1/16-in. clearance between the door and the jamb on all three sides. Swing the door to make sure that it works smoothly. After making any necessary adjustments, drive all the nails all the way in.

9. If you did not buy a door with knob and latch already installed or with pre-drilled holes, drill and chisel openings to accept the pass set. All pass sets come with instructions; most require a 2⅛-in. hole for knob assembly.

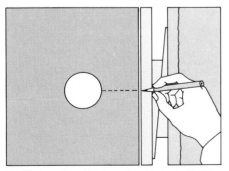

10. Mark center of latch on the side jamb. Position the strike plate on the jamb with front of opening set back equal to the distance from latch face to the edge of door. Drill out latch recess, mortise and install the strike plate.

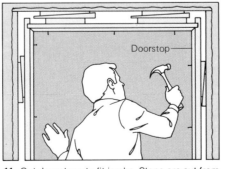

11. Cut doorstops to fit jambs. Stops are cut from standard 7/16 x 7/8 or 7/16 x 1 3/8-in. stock. With door closed and latched, install stops snugly (but not overly tight) against the door and nail them in place with 4-penny finish nails.

12. Cut and install casing around door. Set casing about ⅛-in. back from edge of jamb to allow clearance for removing hinge pins. Use 6-penny finish nails, driving them all the way in only after checking for needed adjustments.

Staircases

Planning a main staircase

Building the main staircase of a residential house requires both the technical precision of structural carpentry and the craftsmanship of cabinet-making. This is true even if the staircase is assembled from prefabricated parts ordered from a manufacturer or lumberyard. Each staircase poses a unique problem. The stairbuilder must construct a sloping bridge between two points on different floors, with uniform and well-proportioned treads and risers that are comfortable and safe to climb and descend. Such factors as minimum headroom at all points above the stairs, including the edge of the stairway opening on the higher floor, must be considered. Stairs must not sway or squeak.

These pages provide information useful in planning a new main staircase for your house; however, the actual work should be done only by someone with experience. Service stairs for basements and attics, and exterior stairs for decks, are simpler to build (see p.307). Spiral staircases (p.27), including kits, should be installed by professionals.

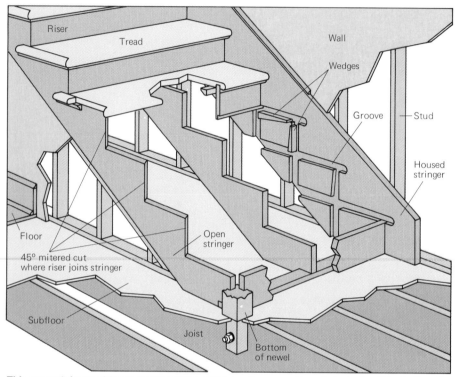

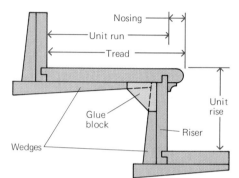

Cross section drawing shows how risers and treads are joined and supported in typical main staircase. The rabbet-and-groove joints, gluing blocks, and wedges make construction sturdy.

This open staircase (shown in cutaway view) has a wall on one side; a balustrade will be built on the other. On the closed side the treads and risers are set in the precision-routed grooves of a housed stringer secured to the studs in the wall frame; on the other side the treads rest on a plain open stringer supported by its own studs. All treads are notched into the risers.

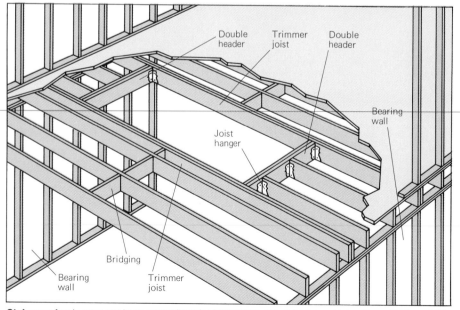

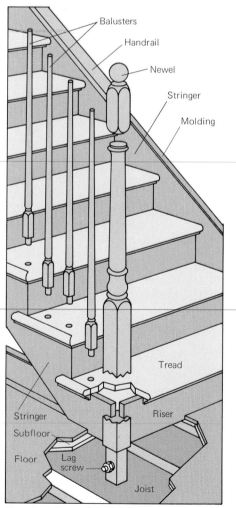

Stair opening is seen cut in an upper floor for installation of a staircase, which will parallel floor joists. Opening is reinforced with double-headers and trimmer joists fastened with joist hangers. Bridging appears between joists. Temporary supports (see p.74) are required during cutting—and permanent supports must be built if there is no adjacent bearing wall to tie into.

Newel posts anchor the balusters and handrails. They must support the full weight of an adult. The starting newel shown here is secured to the joist below the floor with a lag screw.

Staircase design: The simplest shape in staircases is the straight ascent, with at least 13 or 14 uninterrupted steps. A stair with a landing platform allows a climber to pause on his way. If a staircase turns 90° after a landing, it is called an L-type (including the long-L and wide-L types). When a staircase turns back on itself with a double landing, it is a narrow-U type. Wide-U stairs are found in bigger houses.

An enclosed staircase has walls on two sides, with a handrail on one or both walls but no balustrade. Moving large furniture up or down such a staircase is a problem. A stair with a wall on one side and a balustrade on the other is called an open staircase. It lends a decorative touch to a house.

Structural elements: The steps in a main staircase consist of treads and risers. To increase the toe room, treads usually have an overhang called a nosing. The steps are supported by two or three stringers. Smaller houses usually have plain stringers, but for a sturdy, squeak-free stair, a housed stringer is often used on the wall side. It has precision-routed ½-inch-deep grooves that snugly grip the ends of treads and risers. The balustrade, where used, has newel posts at both ends and on any intermediate landing. Each tread has usually two and sometimes three balusters, which are topped with a continuous handrail, as seen opposite.

Dimensions: Minimum dimensions for staircases are specified by building codes (see pp. 21–37). Most codes require that a staircase be at least 3 to 3½ feet wide, so that two persons can pass each other without collision, and bulky objects can be moved upstairs or down. The minimum headroom specified is 6

feet 8 inches (6 feet 4 inches for a basement stair), but 7 feet 4 inches to 7 feet 7 inches is generally recommended. The traditional standard height of the handrail is 30 inches at the rake (top of handrail to top of nosing on tread) and 34 inches at the landing. More recent thinking suggests 36 to 42 inches, respectively, for a more secure balustrade. For an easy grip, it is recommended that the width of the handrail not exceed 2⅝ inches. The space between balusters must be less than 5 inches (to block the passage of a child's head). For a main staircase, recommended riser height ranges from 7 inches to 7⅝ inches; the recommended tread width (not including the nosing) is from 10 to 11 inches. The nosing is usually 1¼ inches.

Staircase opening: When a staircase is built where none existed, one tricky problem is cutting an opening in the upper floor (illustration, lower left, opposite page). The width of the opening depends on the width of the stair, but its length is determined by the angle of the stair and the headroom required. If the length of the opening is perpendicular to the floor joists, it may be necessary to cut half a dozen joists—a major project requiring strong shoring of the upper floor both temporarily during the work and permanently in the finished frame. Thus, your location of a new staircase may be restricted by the existing structural elements of the house, as well as by floor space available on both the upper and lower landings. Minimum landing space is required at both ends of the new stairway.

Critical calculations: Planning requires calculating the angle of the climb, the tread width (unit run) and riser height (unit rise), so that the finished

stair fits the exact floor-to-floor height, with all the steps level and uniformly sized and spaced, as required by code.

To check if the unit rise, or riser height (R), and the unit run, or tread width (T), of a given staircase meet established standards, carpenters can employ any of the three following formulas:

(1) $2R + T = 24''$ to $25''$
(2) $R + T = 17''$ to $18''$
(3) $R \times T = 70''$ to $75''$

If the computation works out by any of the above formulas the staircase is safe and comfortable; it need not satisfy all three formulas.

The graph on this page plots various stair angles. The accompanying table gives examples of stair designs that meet requirements for given total rises and total runs—floor heights and horizontal distances covered by the stairs. To order a prefabricated staircase, you must provide a dealer with the following three accurate measurements: the total rise, total run, and stair width you desire. Rely on professional advice.

80''min. headroom

Headroom for a staircase is the vertical clearance between the lowest point on the ceiling and the edge of the tread or nosing immediately below it. Codes establish minimum standards.

Graph of stair angles

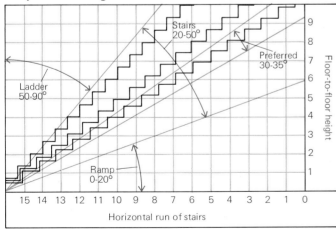

Stairs 20-50°
Preferred 30-35°
Ladder 50-90°
Ramp 0-20°
Floor-to-floor height
Horizontal run of stairs

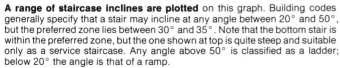

A range of staircase inclines are plotted on this graph. Building codes generally specify that a stair may incline at any angle between 20° and 50°, but the preferred zone lies between 30° and 35°. Note that the bottom stair is within the preferred zone, but the one shown at top is quite steep and suitable only as a service staircase. Any angle above 50° is classified as a ladder; below 20° the angle is that of a ramp.

Table of risers and treads

Floor-to-floor height	Unit rise	Unit run	Number of risers	Number of treads	Total run
9'	7¾"	10¼"	14	13	11'
9'	7¼"	10¾"	15	14	12'6"
9'	6¾"	10¾"	16	15	13'
9'	6"	11"	18	17	15'8"
8'6"	7¼"	10½"	14	13	11'4"
8'6"	7¼"	11½"	14	13	12'6"
8'6"	6⅜"	10⅜"	16	15	13'
8'6"	6⅜"	11"	16	15	13'9"
8'	7⅜"	10"	13	12	10'
8'	7⅜"	11"	13	12	11'
8'	6"	10⅜"	16	15	13'
8'	6"	12"	16	15	15'

Typical combinations of unit rise and unit run are given in this table, to fit common floor-to-floor heights (or total rise, the distance between the upper and lower floors). The number of risers multiplied by unit rise equals total rise. The number of treads multiplied by unit run equals total run. Building codes require that the risers and treads be uniform throughout the stair. Unit runs and rises are calculated to the nearest ⅛ in.

Shelves and closets

Planning storage space

A kitchen pantry, a clothes closet, a stereo center, and a bookcase may differ markedly in appearance and design. But they share the common function of providing storage space for household items that will be retrieved for regular or intermittent use by members of your immediate family.

As with any other project, begin by drawing plans of storage space to scale, taking into account the considerations discussed in the following paragraphs and illustrated on these pages.

Convenience, accessibility: Design and organize storage in a convenient, accessible way. Other chapters—notably those on bathrooms and kitchens—dwell on the convenient location of storage space in given rooms of the house. For any type of storage, however, a primary consideration is the height of those family members who will be using the closets, shelves, and cabinets most frequently. Objects should not be stored where they cannot be reached by the primary users, whether in the kitchen or

in a child's playroom. In vertical shelving, the most frequently retrieved items should be stored in the most conveniently reached central zone (see diagram below), with items used less often immediately above, and seldom-used objects at the lowest level.

Design bookshelves to be about the same depth as your books or only slightly deeper; you thereby reduce the amount of open shelving to be dusted, and avoid the problem of books slipping into open spaces behind other books.

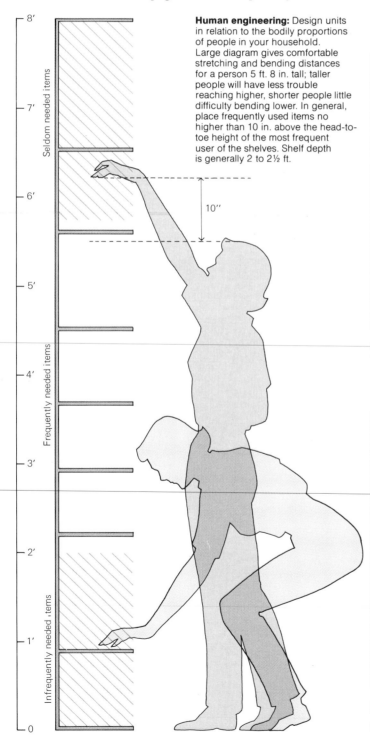

Human engineering: Design units in relation to the bodily proportions of people in your household. Large diagram gives comfortable stretching and bending distances for a person 5 ft. 8 in. tall; taller people will have less trouble reaching higher, shorter people little difficulty bending lower. In general, place frequently used items no higher than 10 in. above the head-to-toe height of the most frequent user of the shelves. Shelf depth is generally 2 to 2½ ft.

Seldom needed items

Frequently needed items

Infrequently needed items

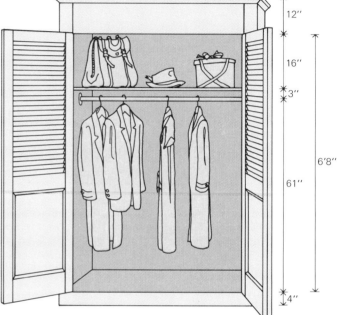
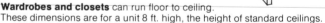

Wardrobes and closets can run floor to ceiling. These dimensions are for a unit 8 ft. high, the height of standard ceilings.

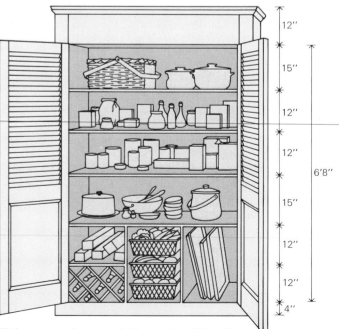

Kitchen pantry shown is height of standard 8-ft. ceiling. Typically, pantry would be built shorter in a work area, put up in the kitchen, then trimmed with 1-x-6 to 1-x-12 stock at the top after pantry is installed.

Constructed shelves

Bookshelving is usually made from boards 8 to 10 inches wide, spaced 10 inches apart; one or two shelves should have an 11- or 12-inch vertical clearance to accommodate large volumes. Bookcases can be designed so that shelf heights are easily adjusted at any time; use clip and track supports (illustrations, p.134) or drill a series of vertical holes 1 or 1½ inches apart in the sides of the case to accept movable pin, plug, or dowel shelf supports.

Solid wood boards, such as pine, are your best choice for most shelving. Plywood's cut edges are messy, requir-

ing the attachment of molding strips. Pine shelving and casing is cut to length from 1-inch stock (generally 1 x 8, 1 x 10, or 1 x 12); utility shelving for heavy objects may require 2-inch stock.

Calculate shelf loads before designing your projects and buying lumber. A typical shelf is 24-30 inches in length; 10 pounds of weight per linear foot represents a light load, 30 pounds a heavy load. Big books and stacks of phonograph records make a heavy load. Heavy loads can be compensated for by adding intermediate shelf supports or designing shelving with short spans.

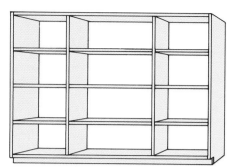

Frame is locked together with simple butt joints using wood screws. A back panel will make the case heavier but more rigid. Shelves are supported in the various ways shown below.

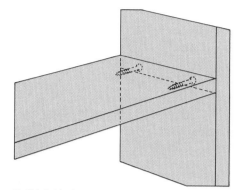

Butt joint is simplest method of assembling frame; if used internally to attach shelves, drill holes and drive screws at angles.

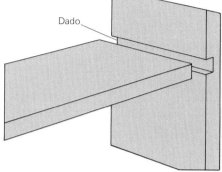

Dado groove is a more professional joining method; use a router or chisel to cut channels to widths of shelves, then glue shelves in place.

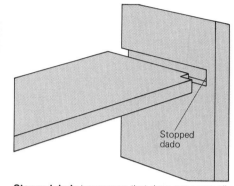

Stopped dado is a groove that does not come all the way through to front of vertical support; opening does not show from the front of unit.

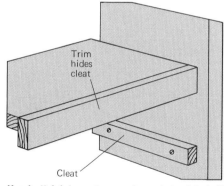

If a butt joint must support a substantial shelf load, reinforce it with a wood cleat cut from square or quarter round stock.

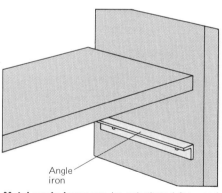

Metal angle irons can be substituted for wood cleats, As with cleats, measure carefully to establish positions so shelves will be level.

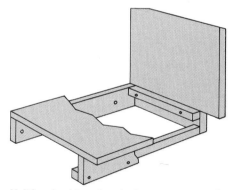

Unit is raised from floor by toe recess; recess is framed and trimmed with 1-in. stock as seen in this cutaway through bottom shelf.

Other shelf supports

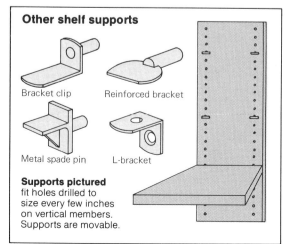

Bracket clip   Reinforced bracket

Metal spade pin   L-bracket

Supports pictured fit holes drilled to size every few inches on vertical members. Supports are movable.

Sags and bulges

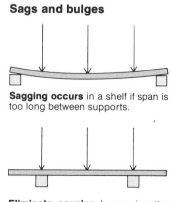

Sagging occurs in a shelf if span is too long between supports.

Eliminate sagging by moving the supports closer together.

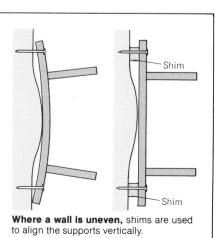

Where a wall is uneven, shims are used to align the supports vertically.

131

Shelves and closets

Adjustable standards and brackets

Adjustable standards, with brackets or clips, can be used to install shelves in a case (p.133) or directly on a wall. If used as the mounting for case shelves, the standards can be recessed in grooves in the wood, resulting in an installation that lies flush with the walls of the case, giving a finished, professional look. The grooves are cut with a router bit slightly wider than the standards.

Standards are attached with long screws or one of the variety of fasteners shown on page 139—toggle bolts, Molly bolts, screws, anchors, etc.,—depending on the type of backing, whether wall studs, masonry, or plaster.

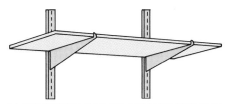

Locate bracket supports well inside shelf ends.

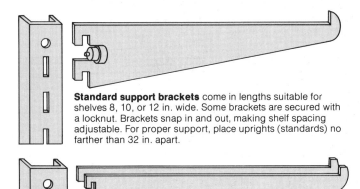

Standard support brackets come in lengths suitable for shelves 8, 10, or 12 in. wide. Some brackets are secured with a locknut. Brackets snap in and out, making shelf spacing adjustable. For proper support, place uprights (standards) no farther than 32 in. apart.

Keyhole slotted track is for heavy-duty installations. It differs from the heavy-duty standard shown (left) in being a single, not a double, track. The extra strength it has comes from the reinforcing gusset.

Heavy-duty brackets are used with double-track uprights (standards). These brackets are made for shelves that are between 12 and 24 in. wide. Because of the extra load, strain on uprights will be greater than with standard brackets; therefore, tracks should be anchored firmly.

Metal clips come with tracks slotted at 1-in. intervals. Clips and tracks are used to support shelves at their ends, rather than extending under the width of the shelf; thus they are the right choice for installing track shelves within a case or narrow closet. The tracks—a pair at each end of the shelving—can be recessed in grooves routed in the side walls of the case for a flush, professional look.

Stationary brackets

The adjustable standards (described above) are ideal as shelving for bookcases in which shelf spacing should be movable to accommodate changing uses and needs. Stationary brackets, much simpler to install, are excellent for shelving that can remain in the installed position—the single storage shelf typically found at the top of a closet, kitchen pantry shelving, and workshop and basement storage.

Wherever possible screw the support mounts into the studs behind the wall (studs are usually located every 16 inches) or into firmly mounted masonry or plaster anchors (see p.139).

Stationary supports are ideal for single shelves.

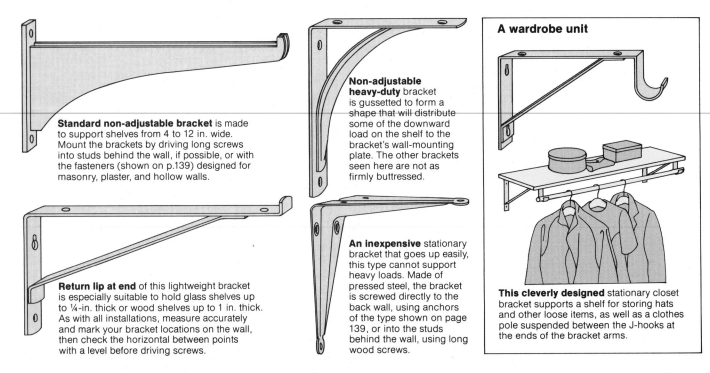

Standard non-adjustable bracket is made to support shelves from 4 to 12 in. wide. Mount the brackets by driving long screws into studs behind the wall, if possible, or with the fasteners (shown on p.139) designed for masonry, plaster, and hollow walls.

Non-adjustable heavy-duty bracket is gussetted to form a shape that will distribute some of the downward load on the shelf to the bracket's wall-mounting plate. The other brackets seen here are not as firmly buttressed.

A wardrobe unit

This cleverly designed stationary closet bracket supports a shelf for storing hats and other loose items, as well as a clothes pole suspended between the J-hooks at the ends of the bracket arms.

Return lip at end of this lightweight bracket is especially suitable to hold glass shelves up to ¼-in. thick or wood shelves up to 1 in. thick. As with all installations, measure accurately and mark your bracket locations on the wall, then check the horizontal between points with a level before driving screws.

An inexpensive stationary bracket that goes up easily, this type cannot support heavy loads. Made of pressed steel, the bracket is screwed directly to the back wall, using anchors of the type shown on page 139, or into the studs behind the wall, using long wood screws.

Utility storage

Give any family an empty garage or a basement floor and over the years they will fill it with possessions. Most families seem unable to avoid collecting everything from newspapers and old furniture to tools, toys, broken lawnmowers, remnant carpeting, and you name it. Very soon utility storage space gets so cluttered and disorganized no one can find anything. The best solution is to make more room, and organize it properly, by using vertical space. Put up shelves, either on walls or as space dividers in the middle of the room.

These shelves need not be costly, nor examples of fine carpentry. Basement or garage shelves need only be strong enough to hold what you put on them. Start by erecting pairs of 2-x-4 posts, one on either side of a ceiling joist or rafter. Attach them at the bottom to a 2-x-4 base lag-bolted to the concrete floor. Then bolt the shelf supports cut from 2-inch pine stock, or ¾-inch plywood, between the posts. Fasten plywood, particle board, or 1-inch pine shelves of your desired width, to the top edges of the supports, using small nails. The nails keep the shelves from sliding. Also nail facing cut from 1 x 2 pine stock to the outer edges of the shelves; the facing stiffens and improves the appearance of the shelves.

The height between shelves is a matter of choice. A distance of about 1½ feet is a good average interval; it provides enough clearance for most storage cartons and cans. Painting the shelves seals them against moisture. Use a matte finish paint; enamels stick to cardboard.

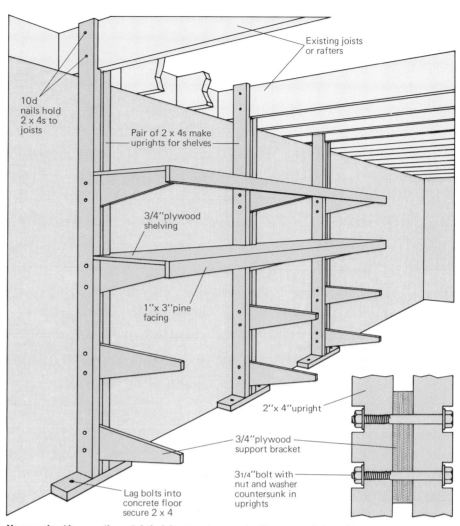

You need not buy costly metal shelving to put up good utility storage shelves. Shelves like those shown can be located in any basement or garage and are easy to construct from inexpensive materials.

Hooks and other space-saving devices

Where permanent shelving is not practical, long, square-bend screw hooks will hold a bicycle, wagon, or sled on a wall. A fold-up work table can be hinged to studs and supported by a retractable leg. A length of ¾-inch plywood cut 12 inches or so wide makes a hinged, retractable shelf. (Bolt the hinges through the plywood; use long screws to attach the hinges to the studs.) For wall-storage for small garden, shop, and craft tools, use a piece of commercial pegboard, nailing or screwing it securely to exposed studs. Hooks inserted in the pegboard holes hold the items.

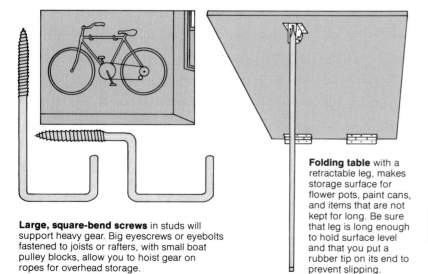

Large, square-bend screws in studs will support heavy gear. Big eyescrews or eyebolts fastened to joists or rafters, with small boat pulley blocks, allow you to hoist gear on ropes for overhead storage.

Folding table with a retractable leg, makes storage surface for flower pots, paint cans, and items that are not kept for long. Be sure that leg is long enough to hold surface level and that you put a rubber tip on its end to prevent slipping.

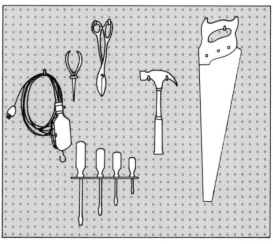

Pegboard with metal hooks is a good shop-tool storage area; hooks can be moved to conform to any shape.

133

Shelves and closets

Drawers and storage bins

In its construction, a drawer or bin is a simple box. You may want to construct drawers as part of a closet, as part of a storage unit including shelves, or for a storage cabinet. Several ways to build a drawer are illustrated above.

When building a box, remember you are dealing with wood joints that are at right angles; therefore keep a tri-square or combination square handy and use it frequently to check that your work is squared accurately.

Reinforcing the corners: The simplest drawer consists of four sides cut on the square and a bottom panel also squared; the sides are joined with butt joints, as illustrated, below left, glued, and nailed

flush at their ends; the bottom is nailed to the bottom edges on all four sides. Such a drawer is nothing more than a box with added supports to help it withstand the stress of sliding in and out of another box, its case, or cabinet. You can reinforce the interior corners of a drawer with either triangular or square wood blocks; or, the sides can be rabbeted with grooves to hold the other sides and the bottom in a rigid structure, as illustrated below.

The rabbet/dado joint, glued and nailed, is a good choice for any drawer that will see heavy use—particularly kitchen cabinet and tool storage drawers in utility cabinets.

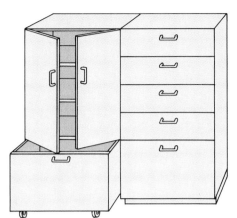

Drawers, shelves, bin are combined in one unit.

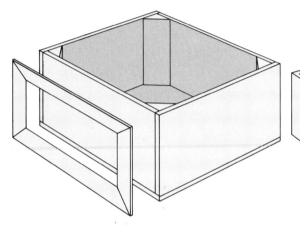

A drawer with butt joints is reinforced at the inside corners with triangular wood blocks. A frame of wood attached to front of drawer conceals edges of butt joints.

Rabbeted dado joints employ grooves cut in the sides, back, and front of the drawer. Dados are a strong form of construction that will last, and are especially suitable for plywood; plywood edges are protected by the rabbeted channels.

Drawer guides

Wood absorbs moisture from the air and swells in humid weather. Unless space is left between a drawer and the walls of its surrounding cavity, the drawer will bind and may be impossible to pull open. A

very tight fit of a drawer in its cavity would cause friction and trap air behind the open drawer, making it hard to push shut. For such reasons, drawers are made smaller than the box-like cavities

into which they are designed to fit. To keep them in line, strips of wood called guides must be attached to the drawer itself or to the inside walls of the cavity around the drawer.

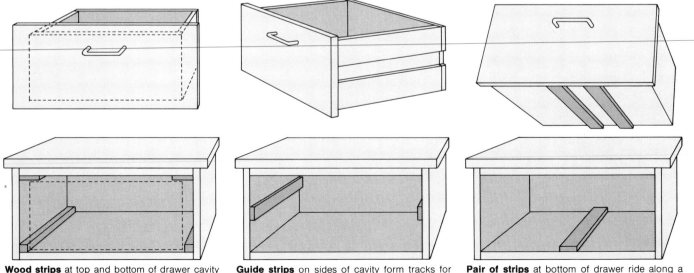

Wood strips at top and bottom of drawer cavity act as guides to keep drawer aligned. Front of drawer overlaps and covers opening.

Guide strips on sides of cavity form tracks for rabbet grooves in drawer. Bottom of drawer is not in contact with the bottom of cavity.

Pair of strips at bottom of drawer ride along a central guide in cavity, an arrangement for drawer fronts that do not overlap opening.

Manufactured guides and glides

Homemade waxed wooden drawer guides work well enough on dresser and table drawers that do not get heavy use. But for kitchen cabinet drawers and such that are opened and closed frequently, commercial grade metal or plastic guides and glides are more practical. Wood absorbs moisture and then swells. Metal and plastic do not. Metal is harder than plastic, and more resistant to wear. Commercial drawer guides often include rollers. Rollers made of plastic produce an almost frictionless slide and are designed to allow maximum extension of the drawer.

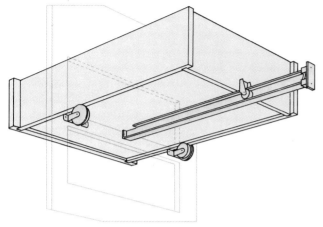

Steel guide is fastened to frame under drawer, forming track for a roller attached to drawer back. Edges of drawer ride on rollers fastened to front of frame; rollers support the extended drawer.

Metal or plastic glides fastened to either side of the drawer slide on guides that are attached to the sides of the frame cavity. Other designs employ rollers that are fastened to the sides of drawer and ride on frame cavity guides.

Understair storage

Every house with a basement or second floor has at least one set of stairs. In many homes the staircases have a triangular volume of empty space underneath. The space can be paneled in and sealed off for the sake of appearance. Not only does this waste good storage area, it may also cause dry rot to develop in the sealed compartment, eventually weakening the staircase. It is better to open up such space and make use of it for general storage.

The basic design problem of understairs storage areas derives from their wedgelike shape. You can make part of this space into a closet—the part under the higher end of the stairs. Shelves put into the space under the lower stairs become a hard-to-reach junk-collecting repository. Once filled up, they usually stay that way.

One solution is to build a series of open-fronted boxes on casters to serve as movable storage bins kept under the lower stairs. Under higher stairs, the bins can have shelves. The bins roll into understair cavities sideways, as illustrated, and have strong handles on the outside wall. Partitions separate the bins. Allow clearance between the bins and their cavity walls.

When opening a panel or cutting through a wall that seals off the space under a stairway, be sure you do not remove or weaken any of the structural members that support the stairs. Use the existing posts as studs on which to fasten partitions between shelves or bins. Do not alter existing supports; build around them.

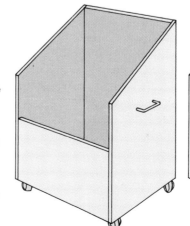
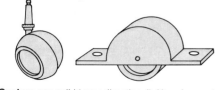

When measuring for bins on rollers (an option to the shelves shown under the stairs), allow clearance for the casters. Also allow at least ½ in. clearance all around each bin. The floor of the understair cavity may be lower than the finished floor of the room. To get your correct measure, use the height of the cavity opening between the staircase and the finished floor.

Casters can roll in any direction (left) or forward and backward (right), according to their design.

Shelves and closets

Sliding track doors

All closets and cabinets should be easily accessible. Often the size and arrangement of a room, especially a bedroom or bath, does not readily permit the use of a standard door that swings out into the room when opened. In those cases where space is limited, consider sliding doors that move sideways. Riding in grooves if they are small, or suspended by rollers on two metal tracks if they are large and heavy, they require no room space in which to open. Sliding doors overlap rather than swing out; thus, if there are no fixed panels, closet interiors are completely accessible.

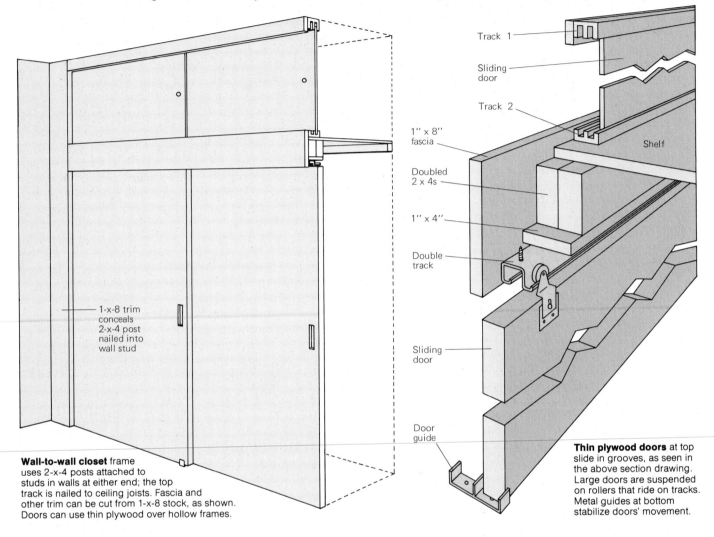

1-x-8 trim conceals 2-x-4 post nailed into wall stud

Track 1

Sliding door

Track 2

1″ x 8″ fascia

Doubled 2 x 4s

1″ x 4″

Double track

Shelf

Sliding door

Door guide

Wall-to-wall closet frame uses 2-x-4 posts attached to studs in walls at either end; the top track is nailed to ceiling joists. Fascia and other trim can be cut from 1-x-8 stock, as shown. Doors can use thin plywood over hollow frames.

Thin plywood doors at top slide in grooves, as seen in the above section drawing. Large doors are suspended on rollers that ride on tracks. Metal guides at bottom stabilize doors' movement.

Mounting wall cabinets

Homemade wall cabinets, especially those that are to be used for storing dishes and other heavy items, must be solidly built and well supported. Cabinet walls can be of thin (¼ inch) plywood but the frame and shelves must be of strong stock. Use screws and waterproof glue to fasten elements, and be sure exposed plywood edges are sanded smooth and rounded, or trimmed with molding strips.

To hang a homemade cabinet, attach a 1-x-4 ledger to wall studs with lag bolts. Screw metal right-angle brackets to the back of the cabinet near its top. These should be fastened to the cabinet with screws that go into the sturdy frame. Wood blocks are attached to the back of the cabinet to make it hang flush with the wall. The metal brackets are hooked over nails in the top of the ledger.

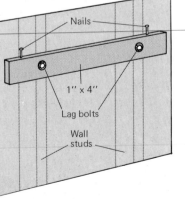

Nails

1″ x 4″

Lag bolts

Wall studs

A simple approach to mounting a homemade wall cabinet employs metal brackets and a ledger strip nailed to wall studs. The brackets, on the back of the cabinet, have holes that slip over nails in the ledger (see also pp.150–157).

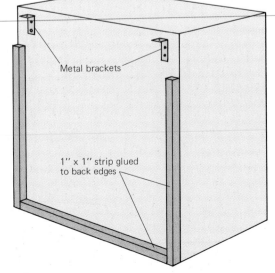

Metal brackets

1″ x 1″ strip glued to back edges

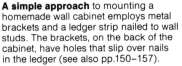

136

Fasteners

Shelf brackets are attached to walls with fasteners such as those pictured at right. The weight to be borne by the shelves, and the construction of the wall to which they are attached determine your choice of fastener. Basically, all such fasteners are bolts. All but one, the lag bolt, have some kind of specialized nut that engages the threads for tightening.

Of the three main types of walls on which fasteners are used, plasterboard walls are the easiest to work with, taking simple toggle bolts. A second type, made of plaster applied over wood or metal lath, presents more difficulties, requiring special expansion anchors. Solid masonry faced with plaster, the third type of wall, requires the use of a masonry drill to seat the bolt anchor.

After careful measurement, holes are drilled in the wall to accept the anchors; the anchors are inserted, and screws or bolts are driven into them.

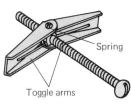
Gravity toggle bolt has swivel toggle that drops down when bolt is pushed through a hole drilled into wall cavity. It works in plasterboard and in lath and plaster walls.

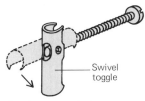
Split wing toggle has spring-loaded arms that pop out when pushed through hole drilled into wall cavity; It is best for plasterboard or lath and plaster with deep cavities.

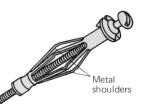
Collapsible anchor or Molly bolt is put through hole drilled into the wall cavity; its metal shoulders draw back as bolt is tightened. Does not work in masonry or plaster.

Jack nut is a small Molly bolt used on hollow doors, such as closets may have. The anchor collapses inside the door cavity. It is not designed to support heavy weights.

Lag bolt is not a true bolt, but a heavy screw, in that it has no nut. It is turned with a wrench, is used in wood or masonry in pre-drilled holes, and carries a heavy load.

Masonry bolt is used in both plaster and concrete walls; its anchor circumscribes its shaft. When tightened, it expands lead or plastic anchor to fill a pre-drilled hole.

Catches

Catches are designed to hold doors in position, usually the closed position. There are two basic types of catch. One works by friction—gripping the striker by means of either of two spring-metal arms or a special roller. The other works by magnetic action on the metal of the striker. Both types are automatic. One need not physically manipulate the catch, as with a hook and eye. A little force disengages the catch from the striker. The magnetic catch is smooth working, and in addition it has no moving parts to suffer wear. It must be kept free of dirt.

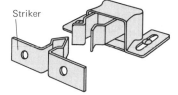
Friction catch is attached to door. When engaged, the triangular head of the striker is gripped by spring-metal arms in the catch assembly.

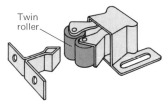
Single roller catch employs a plastic roller that is attached to the door. The type shown holds well initially, but fails as roller wears.

Double roller catch has its plastic rollers on spring arms that grip the triangular striker on door. It has several moving parts; wears well.

Magnetic catch uses magnetic force to grip the flat metal striker. Grease or dirt residues on magnet can affect the strength of its grip.

Hinges

Hinges for cabinet and closet doors come in a wide variety. They can be decorative as well as utilitarian and contribute to the general decor of a room, be it Early American, Victorian, or modern in style. Some can be used on either left or right-handed doors. Others are limited to a particular use, and must be chosen carefully. While looks are important, a hinge must also stand up to the weight of the door and the frequency of the door's opening and closing. An attractive but weak ornamental hinge has no place on a kitchen cabinet door that is opened repeatedly, or that is heavy. If a door must be removable, be sure to select hinges with pins that are easily taken out.

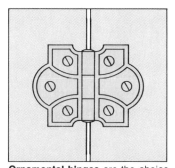
Loose-pin hinges allow the removal of a door without unscrewing the hinge from the wood. The type shown is best for cabinet doors.

Ornamental hinges are the choice when you want hardware that adds to a room's decor. Many types are sold; some are not strong.

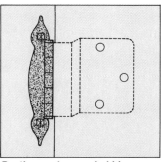
Rustic, semiconcealed hinges are also used to enhance over-all room decor. Some come in antique finishes and with antique fasteners.

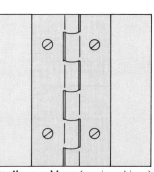
Continuous hinge (or piano hinge) is used where strength is vital. Cabinets with fronts that drop down to form a work space often use them.

Wood stoves and fireplaces

Safe installations

Logs blazing on an open hearth are a romantic sight but an inefficient source of heat. Far more practical is the iron or steel low-draft wood or coal stove. For maximum effect place it in the center of a room or against an internal wall. If a room has an existing fireplace and chimney on an outside wall, the stove can be connected to the flue for a practical unit that will be easy to install. And even if an existing chimney has no opening, it may still be simpler to tap into it rather than to run a stovepipe up through higher floors and the roof.

Flues: Each fire requires its own separate flue. Do not attach two stoves to the same flue in a chimney, or a stove to the furnace flue. Gases from two stoves, or from the furnace and a stove, produce an excess of soot buildup with dangerous levels of creosote. Chances are the flue draft will not be sufficient to handle rising gases and the sparks from two sources, posing the threat of asphyxiation and chimney fires.

In selecting a stove for an existing chimney, a good rule of thumb is to pick a stove that has an exhaust flue whose inner diameter is the same as the chimney's flue. A great disparity may result in a house full of smoke.

Stovepipes: Avoid or minimize horizontal runs of stovepipe. Creosote, a tar-like product of wood combustion, builds up rapidly in elbows and horizontal runs, requiring frequent cleaning. There is a great danger of a very hot flue fire (chimney fire) if the creosote should ignite. This kind of fire can so heat a flue that adjacent house timbers and walls can be set afire. If a fire occurs, call the fire department and wrap a wet blanket around the stovepipe and throw another over the stove; keep the blankets sopping wet until the fire goes out and the flue cools off.

Stove location: All wood- or coal-burning stoves should stand on non-combustible bases. The base can be firebrick, ceramic tile at least ½-inch thick, or a heavy slab of stone. The base must shield the floor area from the bottom of the stove. Stoves should be placed at least 3 feet away from walls, woodwork, and furniture—20 inches from a wall if the wall has a metal heat shield (set an inch out from the wall).

Routine care: Routine care keeps a wood-burning system trim and safe, as discussed on pages 140 and 141. Burn only seasoned hardwood, which produces little creosote. Build a hot, brisk fire, but don't over-fuel a fire; too big and too hot a fire is dangerous. Inspect flues regularly for creosote build-up. A simple pipe cleaning procedure is described on page 140. Have the flue cleaned professionally every year.

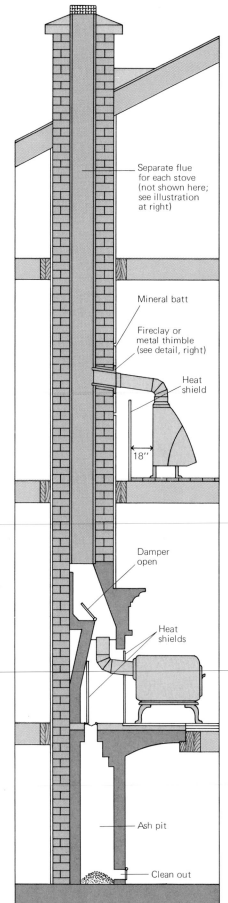

Separate flue for each stove (not shown here; see illustration at right)

Mineral batt

Fireclay or metal thimble (see detail, right)

Heat shield

18"

Damper open

Heat shields

Ash pit

Clean out

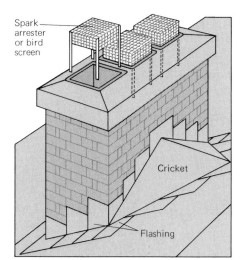

Spark arrester or bird screen

Cricket

Flashing

Whether in a fireplace, a furnace, or a stove, each fire must have its separate flue and a spark-arresting cap or screen at the top of the flue. Doubling up fires on one flue invites malfunction, asphyxiation, and chimney fires.

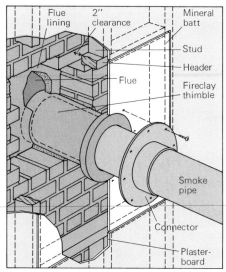

Flue lining

2" clearance

Mineral batt

Stud

Header

Flue

Fireclay thimble

Smoke pipe

Connector

Plasterboard

Stovepipe is seen in a typical hook-up. Here, the masonry was previously furred out 2 in. with studs and covered with plasterboard to hide the chimney. Part of the plasterboard is replaced with a fireproof panel, such as mineral millboard. Connections through combustible materials pose fire hazards. Many communities require a permit to install a stove, given only after approval of your plans. Follow the National Fire Protection Association (Quincy MA 02269) standards.

Stove attached to chimney should have exhaust flue whose inner diameter equals that of chimney flue used. Stoves should stand on fire and heat-proof bases to protect floors. In drawing, a stove is shown hooked up to a flue at fireplace; a second stove is seen connected through combustible wall by means of ventilated metal thimble to another flue on second floor. Fireplace face is sealed with sheet metal through which stove exhaust flue extends. For airtight stoves, this installation should be airtight; sheet must be removable to allow for cleaning chimney flue. Fireplace damper is left open, ash pit trap door kept closed. Heat shields are used to protect walls—an additional one set at back of fireplace is a plus. Soot collected in fireplace must be cleaned out. Never use fireplace ash pit as a storage place for soot, since creosote in soot could ignite.

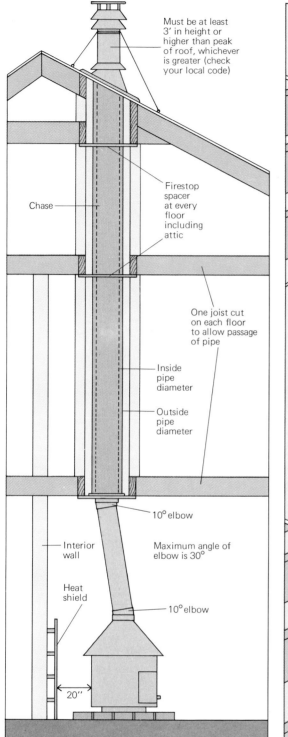

Must be at least 3′ in height or higher than peak of roof, whichever is greater (check your local code)

Chase

Firestop spacer at every floor including attic

One joist cut on each floor to allow passage of pipe

Inside pipe diameter

Outside pipe diameter

10° elbow

Maximum angle of elbow is 30°

Interior wall

Heat shield

10° elbow

20″

A stove set in central area of a room where no chimney is available can be given a chimney of double- or triple-walled, all-steel, insulated pipe. These modern chimneys can be safely passed through ceilings, walls, and roof with small clearances at joists, studs, and other combustible elements, whereas ordinary stovepipe requires clearances as great as 18 in. to 2 ft. all around. Follow manufacturer's installation instructions and National Fire Protection Association standards. Flue should be rigged vertical, right over stove smoke vent, if possible. A 30° angled pipe from stove to ceiling can be used safely. Pipe will need metal sleeve supports as it runs through upper floors. Pipe joints must be airtight. The top of flue must extend at least 3 ft. above house roof. It must be supported by a cable and it requires a storm collar cap.

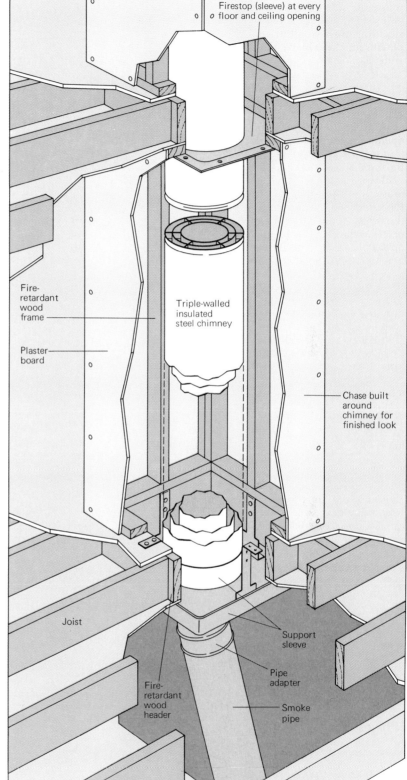

Firestop (sleeve) at every floor and ceiling opening

Fire-retardant wood frame

Plaster-board

Triple-walled insulated steel chimney

Chase built around chimney for finished look

Joist

Support sleeve

Pipe adapter

Fire-retardant wood header

Smoke pipe

Triple-walled insulated steel chimneys come from manufacturers with support sleeves that serve as guides for safe clearance of combustible floor and ceiling joists. A hole is cut into the ceiling and floor above the stove, and the opening is framed to the dimensions of the support sleeve, as seen in the drawing above. The chimney support sleeve is set from below, nailed in place between new header joists. A plumb line is used to position all floor holes over the stove in a vertical line. Be sure that all pipe joints are tight and that there is no contact with any wood members or house insulation. Follow National Fire Protection Association standards.

Wood stoves and fireplaces

Exterior metal chimney pipe

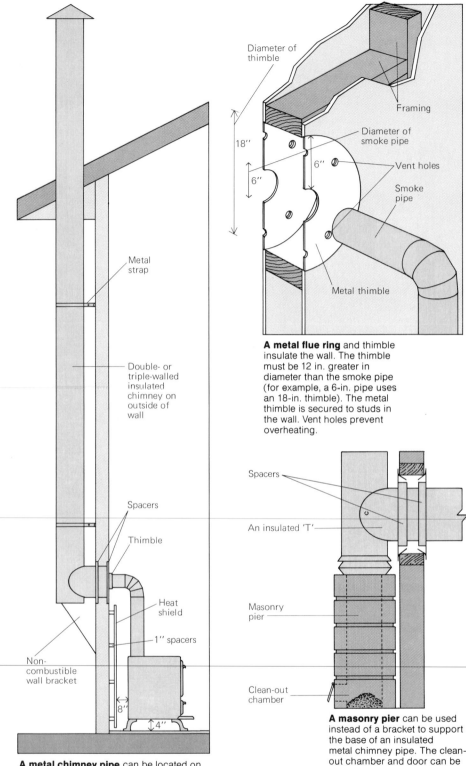

Diameter of thimble

18″

6″

6″

Framing

Diameter of smoke pipe

Vent holes

Smoke pipe

Metal thimble

A metal flue ring and thimble insulate the wall. The thimble must be 12 in. greater in diameter than the smoke pipe (for example, a 6-in. pipe uses an 18-in. thimble). The metal thimble is secured to studs in the wall. Vent holes prevent overheating.

Metal strap

Double- or triple-walled insulated chimney on outside of wall

Spacers

Thimble

Heat shield

1″ spacers

Non-combustible wall bracket

8″

4″

A metal chimney pipe can be located on an outside wall of a house, which thereby eliminates the mess of cutting through ceilings and floors to run the chimney up to the roof. An exterior metal chimney is usually supported at bottom by a metal bracket attached to the house wall. Metal straps hold the vertical run of pipe at a uniform distance of at least 12 in. from the house wall. A metal thimble insulates the pipe where it passes through the wall. The interior wall requires a heat shield behind the stove. An airtight clean-out door is located at the base of the chimney.

Spacers

An insulated 'T'

Masonry pier

Clean-out chamber

A masonry pier can be used instead of a bracket to support the base of an insulated metal chimney pipe. The clean-out chamber and door can be built into the masonry pier base. Make sure that all mortar joints are airtight.

Operating a wood stove efficiently

Low-draft wood stoves of the airtight type are efficient heaters. But, like any system they require monitoring and maintenance. The wood you cut and store may be less costly than oil, but a wood stove and its attached pipes and flues demand attention far more frequently.

Stove temperature is vital; it should be kept constantly close to 400°F. The firebox must be cleaned of ashes regularly. But the key to safe, efficient wood stove operation lies in minimizing, if not eliminating, creosote buildup.

Creosote is a gray-black, gummy tar that is distilled when wood is burned. It will condense on the insides of pipes and flues, hardening to a dense glossy substance. When reheated, it expands, choking the pipes. And if it gets really hot, it will burst into flames and burn with an intense heat. As pipes and flues grow hotter, any flammable material adjacent to them can catch fire.

The way to avoid such fire hazards is to minimize creosote buildup by the use of the right fuel and by regularly cleaning out creosote deposits. Burn only hardwoods, never pine or other conifers. Use well-seasoned wood and be sure your wood is dry. Once a week build up the fire so that it burns briskly for a short time and drives off creosote residues before they reach danger level. A stove thermometer that measures the surface temperature of your stove is useful in determining if your fires are hot enough to minimize creosote buildup in the smoke pipe and flue.

Nails

Stovepipe scraper

Horizontal sections of smoke pipes collect the most creosote. To clean them, let them cool, then take them apart, or open the clean-out door if there is one in the pipe elbow. In some cases you can reach smoke pipes through the front of the stove with a homemade tool. This can be a hoe with its blade edge hacksawed into a curved shape, or a broomstick handle nailed to a scraper—such as a half-circle of scrap wood. The scraper should be several inches smaller than the interior diameter of the stove pipe. Hammer 6- or 8-penny nails halfway into the scraper all round its circular edge to form teeth.

The best way to clean a stovepipe is to remove it and put one end in a bucket and scrub it with the scraping tool. If you can't remove the pipe, scrape out as much creosote as possible with the pipe in place (see illustration, below). The job ought to be done at least every two weeks during the heating season. The longer you wait the harder the job and the greater the danger of fire.

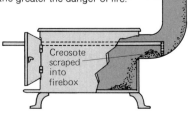

Creosote scraped into firebox

Stovepipe and chimney problems and their cures

Air leaks can retard or disturb the draft of a flue. Such leaks can let sparks escape, and sparks start fires. A partly blocked flue can cause a smokey backup in a stove and in the room where the stove is located. The blockage is also a spot at which flammable soot and creosote residues collect in dangerous quantities. Broken flue tiles or improperly joined smoke pipes are a grave fire hazard.

All such chimney problems are related to improper construction or lack of maintenance. These hazards should be eliminated.

Regular inspection: You should inspect a chimney system at least twice a year. Direct observation will reveal many of the above problems, if they exist. For less accessible parts of the system, use a mirror and a flashlight to detect difficulties. To find leaks in what should be an airtight system, set a small, smokey smudge fire in the stove—a handful of tarpaper makes a good fuel. The thick smoke from the smudge fire will find its way out through any leaks in pipes and flues. Correct problems right away by tightening connections and cleaning out creosote and soot residues.

Troubleshooting the system: Here are a number of things to look for:

(1) If your measurements show that the opening at the top of a flue is not the same cross-sectional size as the inside of the flue, enlarge that opening to match the diameter of the flue. A constriction in the flue retards its draft.

(2) Any pipe extension at the top of the flue must have the same cross-sectional area as the flue itself. If it does not, change the pipe.

(3) The pipe extension at the top of the flue must reach at least 2 feet above the peak of the roof, if within 10 feet of the roof peak or ridge; if the chimney is farther than 10 feet from the peak, it must extend at least 3 feet above the highest point on the roof within 10 feet of it. Metal chimneys require support by steel cables or braces.

(4) A chimney flue that doesn't draw as it should may be partly blocked. Birds, mice, and squirrels sometimes get into flues and build nests. A long pole or a weight on a line dropped down the flue from the roof may dislodge nests.

(5) An improperly built chimney may have a flue constriction caused by a house beam that projects into it. This dangerous situation, found in some older houses, is a violation of modern building codes; it requires correction by a professional brick or stone contractor.

(6) A break in the chimney flue lining is an escape route for sparks.

(7) Clear soot yourself from any easily reached narrow space. Use a weighted round brush on a long pole to scrape the flue, or lower a bag of rough burlap filled with gravel into the flue.

(8) If a flue has more than one opening or an unused smoke pipe leading into it, the extra openings must be closed off and the holes sealed. Each flue, no matter how large, can handle only a single fire. Aside from draft problems there is always the danger of sparks and hot noxious gases from one stove or the furnace getting into another stove if it is hooked up to the same flue.

(9) A stovepipe that projects too far into the flue is like any other flue constriction. The flue will not draw properly and the constriction collects soot and creosote. Cut back the pipe to lie flush with the flue lining.

(10) Air leaks at soot clean-out doors should be cemented up or otherwise sealed. A smudge fire (see previous paragraphs) will reveal such leaks.

(11) All partitions between flues must reach down to the chimney floor level, completely sealing each flue off from others within the same chimney.

(12) Where a smoke pipe enters the chimney, the flue lining must reach below it. If it does not, extend the lining.

(13) Where a smoke pipe enters the flue, the joint must be airtight. If leaks become evident during the smudge fire test, cement the porous joints.

(14) A smoke pipe must never enter the flue on a downward angle. It should be reset so that it goes into the flue at a 90° ascending angle, or better. Horizontal pipes are the greatest collectors of creosote. Inspect them frequently.

(15) If soot gathers at some constriction in the flue or pipe, it should be cleaned away frequently. Or better, eliminate the constriction if possible.

(16) Be sure the handle of any damper corresponds to the correct open/closed position. Where one does not, remove and replace the pipe section with a new section and damper, or otherwise correct the handle-damper relationship. This defect can lead to human error that can cause stifled fires—excessively dampered fires that produce a lot of creosote, and fire backlash when the stove door is opened.

(17) Clean-out doors on smoke pipe elbows must make airtight seals when closed. If they are not airtight, flame will be visible and may come through openings. Cement or tighten connections.

(18) The clean-out pan at the base of the chimney must be fitted tightly so no air leaks around it. The smudge fire test will disclose leaks.

Chimneys are like any other man-made device. Establish a routine of periodic checks so that minor defects do not evolve into hazards.

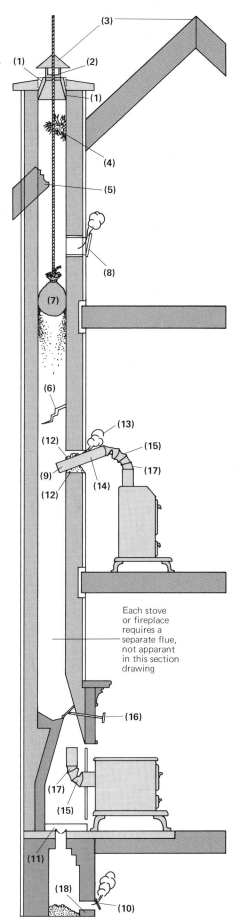

Each stove or fireplace requires a separate flue, not apparant in this section drawing

Wood stoves and fireplaces

Converting a wood stove for hot-water heat

A wood stove can heat several rooms if there is good air circulation between them. But basically, a wood stove makes heat for only one room in the immediate area of the stove unless it is linked either to an air convection system or to the hot-water heating system of the house.

Kits are available to adapt wood stoves for use as hot-water boilers. A fireplate heat exchanger is installed in the top part of the stove. Water passing through the exchanger is heated, and then moves through a pipe to the boiler of your existing furnace. The preheated water in the boiler circulates through furnace pipes to radiators throughout the house. As the radiator water cools, it is returned to the boiler and then to the heat exchanger to be heated again by the wood stove fire.

This system works in conjunction with your furnace boiler and should have the same safety features built into it. It has a pump that moves hot water from the heat exchanger to the boiler and cool water to the stove. And it has emergency drain pipes for the pressure-relief valves and an electric switch for the circulation pump.

When the wood stove is in operation, the regular furnace burner unit fired by oil or gas will not cut in. But when you allow the fire in the wood stove to die down and cool, your furnace thermostat will turn on your furnace burner, which takes over the job of heating water for circulation through radiators.

A wood stove that is converted to supplement a furnace in a hot-water heating system need not be located on the same floor as the furnace. But pipe running between the stove and boiler should be insulated. If the boiler has a domestic hot-water heating coil for producing bathing and washing water, this will not be affected by the modification. Be sure that all safety valves function.

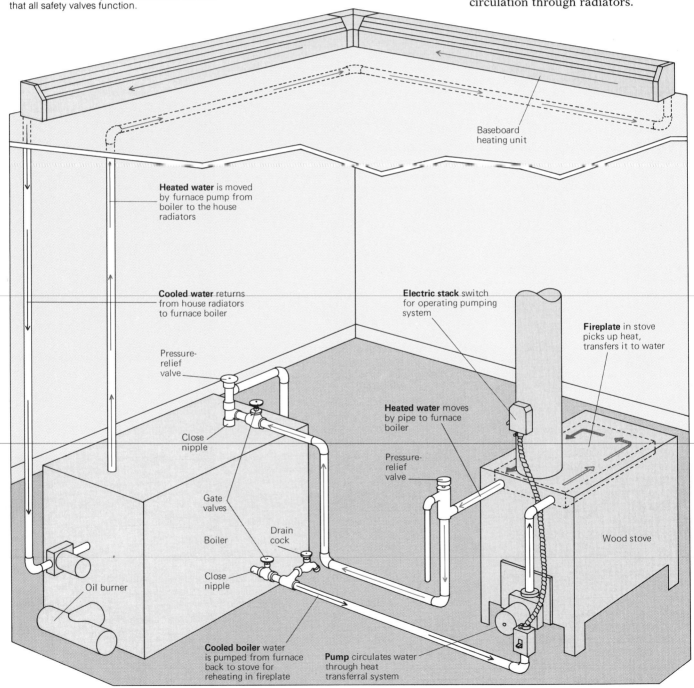

Baseboard heating unit

Heated water is moved by furnace pump from boiler to the house radiators

Cooled water returns from house radiators to furnace boiler

Electric stack switch for operating pumping system

Fireplate in stove picks up heat, transfers it to water

Pressure-relief valve

Close nipple

Heated water moves by pipe to furnace boiler

Pressure-relief valve

Gate valves

Boiler

Drain cock

Wood stove

Close nipple

Oil burner

Cooled boiler water is pumped from furnace back to stove for reheating in fireplate

Pump circulates water through heat transferral system

Energy efficient fireplaces

An ordinary fireplace is an inefficient heating system. Only about 10 percent of the heat from the fire on the hearth ever reaches the interior of the house. But if you install one of the many available heat-circulating fireplace and chimney adapter systems, you can increase efficiency up to about 40 percent. Such heat convection systems consist of a double-walled firebox, a group of air-transporting ducts, and sometimes, a blower to speed the heated air on its way.

Such systems achieve their higher efficiency because the circulating air in the firebox walls and ducts is sealed off from the combustible air entering the fireplace and going up the chimney. The heat from the firebox is transferred through the metal to the circulating air within the firebox walls.

Convection fireplace systems are usually closed off from the room by tempered, heat-proof glass doors, which are positioned across the front of the firebox. The glass prevents radiant heat from escaping directly into the room and at the same time it prevents air from being sucked into the fire and sent up the flue. Combustible air for the fire comes from a duct that pulls air down from an unheated attic or from outside the house. To assure that such ducts do not act as flues, they open into the firebox at forward, lower levels.

The warm-air heating system consists of ducts that open into the room on either side of the fireplace and firebox. House air is drawn into the double walls of the firebox where it is heated and distributed to the rooms.

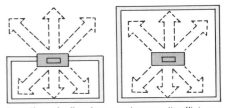

Location of a fireplace can improve its efficiency. If set in the center of the house and not on an outside wall, more heat will enter rooms.

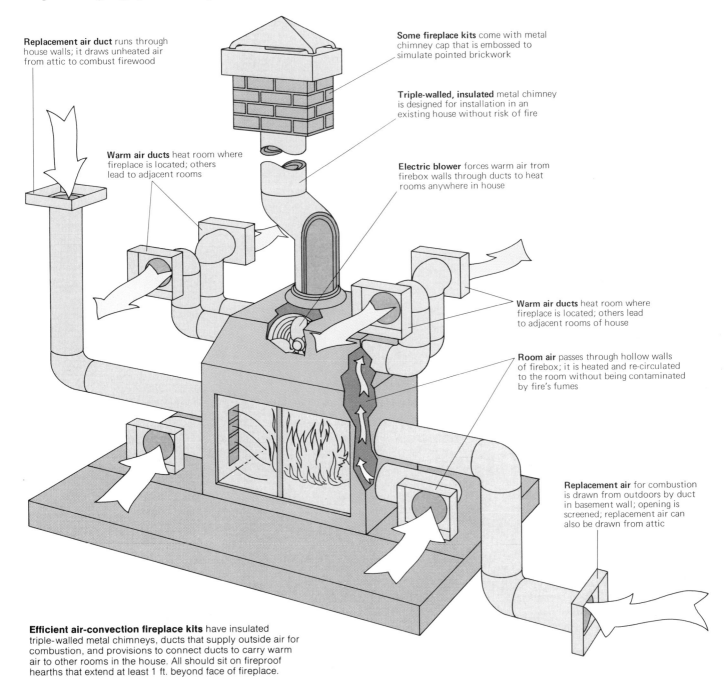

Replacement air duct runs through house walls; it draws unheated air from attic to combust firewood

Warm air ducts heat room where fireplace is located; others lead to adjacent rooms

Some fireplace kits come with metal chimney cap that is embossed to simulate pointed brickwork

Triple-walled, insulated metal chimney is designed for installation in an existing house without risk of fire

Electric blower forces warm air from firebox walls through ducts to heat rooms anywhere in house

Warm air ducts heat room where fireplace is located; others lead to adjacent rooms of house

Room air passes through hollow walls of firebox; it is heated and re-circulated to the room without being contaminated by fire's fumes

Replacement air for combustion is drawn from outdoors by duct in basement wall; opening is screened; replacement air can also be drawn from attic

Efficient air-convection fireplace kits have insulated triple-walled metal chimneys, ducts that supply outside air for combustion, and provisions to connect ducts to carry warm air to other rooms in the house. All should sit on fireproof hearths that extend at least 1 ft. beyond face of fireplace.

New and remodeled bathrooms

Planning and arranging fixtures

Adding a new bathroom where none existed is a complex project. It entails placing heavy bathroom fixtures, which may require structural reinforcement of underlying floor joists; new water supply, drain, and vent pipes must be run behind inside walls and under the floor. Remodeling an old bathroom is much simpler, especially when the existing plumbing can be used for new fixtures that fit the old rough-in positions.

Planning: Check your local building and plumbing codes and map the affected structural components of your house. Professional help or guidance is advisable for an extensive project. Plans should be completed before anything is touched or purchased (see *Drawing your own plans*, p.47).

Plumbing core: The first step in planning a new bathroom is to find the plumbing core of your house. An average residential house has one core area where most plumbing facilities are clustered (see p.202). Larger houses may have two cores (see p.221). Place the new bathroom in a core area so as to minimize the labor and cost of routing new pipes. Arrange fixtures so that pipes can be installed in a single "wet wall." You can eliminate the work of tearing up an existing floor to route drain pipes by building a shallow platform as a false floor on top of the old one (p.149) providing your existing ceiling is high enough to assure adequate head room in the new bath.

Floor plans: The drawings on this page suggest a variety of floor plans for new or remodeled bathrooms, ranging from half-baths to luxurious contemporary bathrooms where space is no problem. You need a minimum floor area of 4 x 4 feet for a half-bath or powder room, and 5 x 7 feet for a small full bath. For such small rooms, check your local code for minimum clearances (see diagram below). Remember, minimum clearances mean minimum comfort.

Minimum clearances

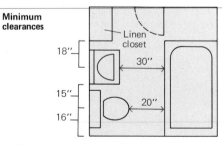

You can use the information in this chapter whether you do the work yourself or hire a contractor. For related work, see *New plumbing* (pp.202–224), *Posts, beams, and joists* (pp.70–75), *Non-bearing partitions* (pp.86–87), *Working with plasterboard* (pp.88–91), and *Installing ceramic tile* (pp.112–119).

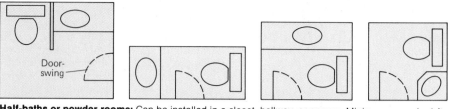

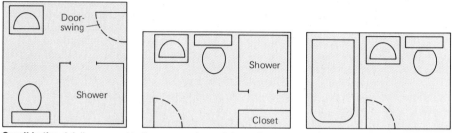

Half-baths or powder rooms: Can be installed in a closet, hallway, or garage. Minimum area, 4 x 4 ft.

Small baths: A full, compact bathroom needs a minimum 5-x-7 ft. area, including tub or shower stall.

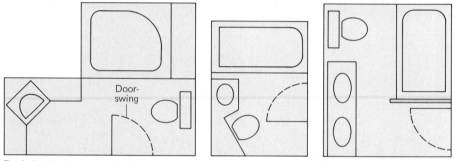

Basic baths: A standard full bath has room for a larger tub and more counter and storage space.

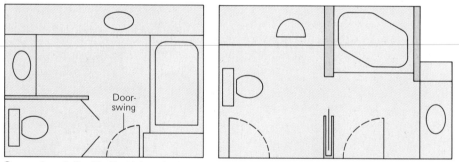

Compartmentalized baths: A large bathroom may have partitions for privacy.

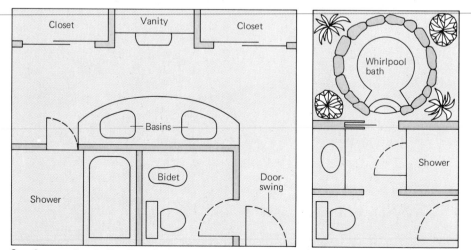

Spacious modern baths: Extra fixtures, whirlpools, saunas, and rock gardens are all possibilities.

Selecting a toilet

In adding a new bathroom or remodeling an old one, your choice of fixtures will be based on comfort, your esthetic aspirations, and your budget.

Rough-in specification: Toilets vary slightly in dimensions, the shape of the bowl (round or oval), the height of the seat, and the position of the outlet opening. The location of the toilet's outlet opening is a crucial consideration for a remodeled bathroom, for which you will want to choose a new toilet that fits the rough-in position of the existing soil pipe. The distance between the center of the bowl outlet and the back wall is usually 12 inches. A space of ¾ to 1 inch should be left between the tank and the wall. It is essential that you check the manufacturer's rough-in measurements for any model you are considering to see if it will fit your existing plumbing installations, unless you are willing and able to move the existing waste bend and soil pipe—a laborious and expensive plumbing and carpentry job.

Designs: Based on outward appearance, toilets come in about six different designs (see below). An old-fashioned floor-mounted toilet bowl gets its water from a wall-hung tank. A newer version seen in many homes today is the free-standing model. This is easy to install. A modern freestanding toilet combines the tank and the bowl in a single piece. A completely wall-hung design (both bowl and tank) makes it easy to clean the floor, but it must be supported by a large bracket secured to the studs in the wall-frame. The soil pipe for this model goes through the back wall instead of through the floor. For mini-bathrooms, where space is at a premium, a corner toilet may be the answer. The newest, most up-to-date, and most dramatic model is the low-profile toilet, which combines a low-slung bowl with a low tank. This design is enthusiastically hailed by orthopedists who have criticized the traditional toilet as a possible cause of backache.

Flushing mechanism: The flushing mechanism affects a toilet's efficiency in water consumption, its cleanliness, its quietness of operation, and its cost. When a toilet is flushed, water from the tank rushes into and scours the bowl; the water then flows down through a built-in trap, which is part of every toilet. As water rushes through the downward bend of the trapway, it creates a partial vacuum at the trap entrance, thus siphoning the waste through the trap and into the closet bend and the soil stack.

Four flushing designs: These basic flushing principles vary from model to model. But all toilets employ one of four general flushing designs (see drawings, bottom of page). The simplest is the *washdown* model. It operates by a simple washout action. Its front trapway is irregular in some places and is likely to clog. Much of the bowl is not covered by water, thus the area is easily stained and contaminated, and is difficult to clean. This model is the least efficient, and the noisiest, although it is the cheapest. Some codes now forbid the installation of the washdown toilet.

The *reverse trap* toilet has a larger and smoother trapway located at the back. Waste is siphoned into the trap in a more efficient manner. Its operation is less noisy than the washdown. Higher up on the scale is the *siphon jet*, whose siphoning action is made powerful by a much larger trapway and a built-in water jet. This model is easier to clean and quieter than the reverse trap. The *siphon vortex* (or *siphon whirlpool*) is the most efficient and most expensive model. It works with very little noise and is easy to clean. It usually has its tank and bowl in a single, low-profile piece.

In addition to the above toilet designs there are special models for special situations. One floor-mounted toilet with its outlet through the wall is designed for a bathroom with a concrete floor. Another type, the upward-flushing toilet, is designed for below-the-grade basement installation.

Toilet designs

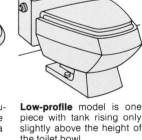

Freestanding toilet has a tank sitting on top of bowl; bowl is mounted on bathroom floor.

One-piece toilet is similar to freestanding model, except that the tank and bowl are a single piece.

Wall-hung toilet requires a strong support in the wall. It discharges through a waste pipe in the wall.

Corner toilet has a triangular tank. It takes up little space and is good for a small bathroom.

Low-profile model is one piece with tank rising only slightly above the height of the toilet bowl.

Flushing designs

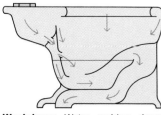
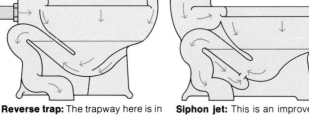

Washdown: Water rushing down from toilet tank washes out waste in bowl through trapway, which is located in front, giving toilet a characteristic bulge. A sizable area of bowl is not covered by water.

Reverse trap: The trapway here is in back. The design causes the water to siphon the waste through the trapway. It has a larger trapway and more water surface in bowl than washdown type toilets.

Siphon jet: This is an improved version of the reverse trap, with a built-in water jet that starts the siphon action. The trapway is much larger; so is the water surface of the bowl. Flushing is quieter and smoother.

Siphon vortex: Flushing is activated by a whirlpool-like action of water, typically from a low-slung tank. It has an all-water surface inside the bowl. Its flushing operation is virtually silent. Model is expensive.

New and remodeled bathrooms

Selecting a bathtub and shower

The variety of bathing equipment available to today's homeowner could be called astonishing. Models range from humble tubs to Beverly Hills-style whirlpool baths with hydro-massage jets for a small committee; functional locker room shower stalls to futuristic bathing "environments" offering a program-it-yourself climate with man-made heat, sunshine, rain, and gentle breezes. Thus you can install any kind of bathing facility in your home that suits your taste and lifestyle, limited only by your available space and pocketbook.

Bathtubs great and small: The traditional porcelain-enameled cast-iron bathtub with its massive legs and exposed plumbing is easy to install; but its weight (350 to 500 pounds) requires a strong reinforcement of floor joists. The most common bathtub in contemporary homes is the rectangular enclosed tub (typical dimensions: 60 x 30 x 16 inches) that needs no joist reinforcement; but the rim next to the wall must be braced with supports (see p.149). The tub can be placed against one wall, in a corner, or recessed in an alcove. A new version of this tub has a contoured interior and is installed half sunken into the floor. Quite popular for newer homes are square, round, or oval tubs made of fiberglass reinforced polyester. Sizes range from 3 x 3 feet for a small bathroom, through 5 x 5 feet, to a room-sized 5½ x 7 feet.

Hot tubs are now popular across the country. These tubs come in either traditional wood or molded plastic, accommodating from one to six bathers. If you are custom-building your bathroom and want to lend a Roman touch to it, a luxurious tub of tile, marble, or wood can be built to order. If space and cost are not problems, flank it with a solarium and a small garden.

Prefabricated units; saunas: Practical, easy to clean, and modern-looking, are the increasingly popular prefabricated tubs and/or showers complete with a "surround" (adjacent walls). Made of fiberglass, they come in one piece (for installation before bathroom walls are framed), or in a four-piece unassembled kit (for remodeling existing bathrooms). These tubs or shower stalls have built-in seats, soap dishes, grab bars, and skid-resistant floors. Manufacturer's installation instructions should be followed closely. Some shower stalls have steam generators, making them usable as saunas.

A traditional European fixture now gaining acceptance in this country for personal hygiene is the bidet (pronounced *be-day'*). The bidet has hot and cold water running down its rim. Some have a fountain jet.

Bathtubs

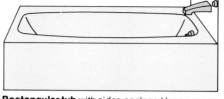

Rectangular tub with sides enclosed by an apron is the commonest type of bathtub found in homes today; it is relatively lightweight.

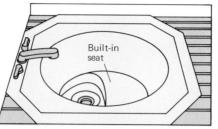

Hot tub (*furo* in Japanese) may be made of traditional wood, or fiberglass as shown above. It is mainly for soaking, used with a shower.

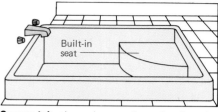

Square tub, shown here partly sunken into the floor, has a built-in seat and is molded from a single piece of plastic material.

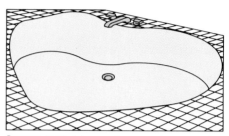

Custom-built tub can be any shape or size. Complete with shower, it is usually sunken into a tiled floor, or surrounded by a tiled platform.

Prefabricated tub and shower kits

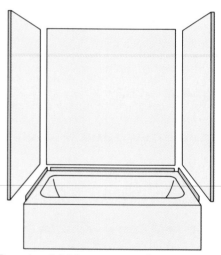

Tub/shower surround, made of lightweight fiberglass, is shown being installed. It requires specially built partitions to support the tub walls. Because of its bulk, it is generally used only in a new bathroom under construction.

Four-piece tub/shower surround can be moved through an existing bathroom door and quickly assembled in a remodeled bathroom. It has five easily caulked seams; otherwise, it is the same as the one-piece fiberglass model.

Freestanding shower stall from a prefab kit can be installed anywhere where there are plumbing pipes. Made of heavy-duty polypropylene with built-in handrail and soap dish, it comes with either a door or a shower curtain and rod.

Bidet

Europe's hygienic bidet is now becoming popular in custom-built homes in this country. Shown here is a traditional model, with hot and cold water faucets and a drain pipe with a stopper. A bidet is usually installed next to a toilet.

Selecting a basin or vanity

Bathroom basins, technically called lavatories, are a type of sink. They are called vanities when mounted on the countertop of a cabinet. In choosing a new basin for your bathroom, the first consideration is its size. For a very small bathroom, basins 1 foot square are available. A triangular basin for the corner is also a space-saver.

Materials: Basins come in many materials: porcelain-enameled cast-iron, porcelain-enameled formed steel, vitreous china, metal, marble, molded plastic, and synthetic marble. The synthetic materials are less scratch resistant than enamel or china. The shape of a basin may be round, square, oval, triangular, rectangular, trapezoid, or of some exotic contour such as the clamshell.

Mounting: From the functional viewpoint, an important consideration is the basin's method of support. Drawings on this page show how basins of various types are mounted. The usual way to mount a bathroom basin is simply to hang it on a wall. If your existing basin is not wall-hung, you will have to break open the wall to hang a new one of this design (top right). Some older wall-hung basins were reinforced with legs or pedestals. Long out of fashion, pedestaled basins are now staging a comeback.

The current mode is for large basins supported over cabinets. These vanities have considerable storage space in the cabinet under the basin and are easy to mount. Vanity basins can be mounted in at least four different ways (see drawings, this page). The recess-mounted can present a cleaning problem. The flush-mounted has two seams. Self-rimming vanity basins with their rims extending over the countertop hole are not difficult to mount or to clean, but seamless integral-top vanities are the easiest to work with in both departments.

Plumbing fittings are installed through the vanity top instead of through the basin itself, as in standard lavatories, except in the case of the self-rimming basins. Some basins and many vanities have splashbacks to protect the wall.

Accessories; installation: Some vanities come with shampoo sprayers, swivel spouts, and liquid soap or lotion dispensers. Whenever possible, faucets and spouts should be installed before the basin or vanity itself is installed. Standard height for a basin is 31 to 34 inches. For a double-basin vanity, the basin edges should be at least a foot apart to provide adequate counter area and elbow room for users. Water supply pipes and the drain pipe should be roughed-in but not connected until the basin is securely mounted on the wall or the cabinet.

Basins

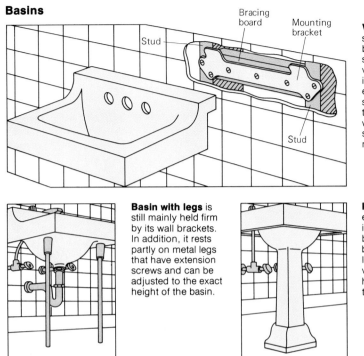

Wall-hung basin is supported by sturdy brackets secured to studs in wall. Since a vitreous china basin is heavy even when empty, the brackets should be fastened to a bracing board, which in turn is screwed onto two notched studs.

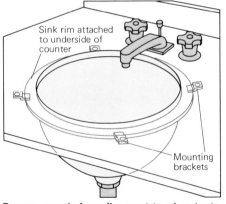

Basin with legs is still mainly held firm by its wall brackets. In addition, it rests partly on metal legs that have extension screws and can be adjusted to the exact height of the basin.

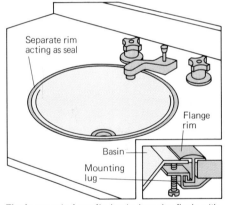

Pedestal basin can either rest entirely on its pedestal, or it can be partly supported by a wall bracket. It is usually made of vitreous china. The hollow pedestal hides the drain pipes.

Vanities

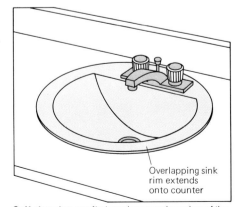

Recess-mounted vanity consists of a basin mounted under a pre-cut hole in the countertop. The basin is secured under the counter with brackets. Plumber's putty is used to seal the joint between the basin rim and the countertop.

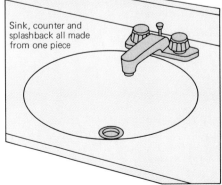

Flush-mounted vanity basin has rim flush with the countertop. A flange rim, buttered with plumber's putty, is inserted around the basin rim to act as a seal. Mounting lugs secure the basin rim to the rim of the frame (inset).

Self-rimming vanity is an improved version of the flush-mounted variety. Instead of a separate frame rim, the basin's own rim extends and overlaps the hole in the countertop. The faucets and water spout go through back of basin rim.

Integral mounted vanity has basin that is part of molded countertop. It is one seamless piece of plastic or synthetic marble, with holes for faucets and spout. The molded unit rests on and is secured easily to the vanity cabinet.

New and remodeled bathrooms

Finishing and furnishing the bathroom

The bathroom of today is no longer a purely utilitarian place equipped with austere fixtures. In many contemporary homes it is a room where one can perform hygienic functions amid lavish amenities and pleasant decor. Adding a new bathroom or remodeling an old one gives you the opportunity to create a comfortable environment by finishing the room and furnishing it with accessories to your liking.

Floor, walls, ceiling: The floor, walls, and ceiling should be moisture-proof, sound-dampening, and decorative. For easy cleaning, bathroom floor coverings are usually tile or vinyl, but rugs reduce noise and add a touch of comfort. Walls can be covered with waterproof paint, ceramic tile, vinyl wallpaper, or the increasingly popular plastic laminates. Ceiling wallboard or tile should be moisture-proof and, preferably, sound-deadening. Bathroom colors are solely a matter of preference; most people choose light pastels to create a sense of spaciousness and relaxation. Accent colors are supplied by bright or deeply shaded accessories, including towels and curtains.

Cabinets: Among the indispensable bathroom accessories is the medicine cabinet with its hinged or sliding mirror doors. A common type is the 14-inch wide unit, which can be installed recessed into the wall between two studs (see lower left). Wider recess-mounted cabinets are available, but installation involves cutting into one or more studs of a non-bearing partition (see pp.86–87). Surface-mounted cabinets (see lower middle) pose few installation problems, but protrude into the room and take up space.

Mirrors: If a medicine cabinet is not installed above a lavatory, a large, plain mirror can take its place. The upper edge of such a mirror should be at least 6 feet from the floor. Its lower edge should be about 8 inches from the top of the lavatory. If you have a vanity with a splashback, the mirror can reach all the way to its top. Mirrors can be mounted with mirror clips or J clips. Avoid using adhesive, which cannot be removed.

Lighting: Ambience can be greatly enhanced by lighting. A window takes care of ventilation and daytime lighting. A skylight lends an elegant touch to a windowless bathroom. Artificial lighting requirements are 3½–4 watts of incandescent light per square foot of floor space—or about half that wattage with fluorescent light. White incandescent bulbs show up natural skintone. Fluorescent tubes should be warm white, not cool white.

Think of your lighting in terms of both general and directed illumination. General illumination is usually from the ceiling, in the form of a single light, a row of track lights, or luminous panels (light bulbs behind light-diffusing panels). Some modern bathrooms have a completely luminous ceiling that gives soft, diffused, and shadowless lighting.

Directed illumination occurs above the basin or vanity, for shaving, combing hair, and applying make-up. The light source can be above the mirror or medicine cabinet, or on both sides of it. The lights should be aimed at the face, not the mirror. They can be in the form of individual lamps, a fluorescent tube, or a luminous panel in a soffit. Many medicine cabinets come with built-in lights. One way to perk up the bathroom is to use theatrical lights along the top and/or sides of a mirror, with a number of 15-watt naked bulbs, reminiscent of actors' dressing rooms. For a large compartmentalized bathroom, additional lights may be needed.

Water and electricity are a dangerous combination, so install light switches and outlets in spots where a person cannot reach them from the tub, shower, or basin. All circuits must have ground-fault interrupters (p.178).

Storage and accessories: Additional storage space is supplied by the vanity counter, linen closets, and drawers in a large bathroom, or open shelves for frequently used items and colorful towels. Other regular bathroom accessories include towel rods installed 36 to 41 inches above the floor, rings or hooks, toothbrush and cup holders, soap dishes (at least 24 inches above the floor, or 48 to 54 inches in shower stalls). A toilet paper holder, always within easy reach of the toilet seat, should be installed 2½ feet above the floor, either flush with or recessed into the wall.

Ventilation, heating: Most codes require a ventilating fan for a windowless bathroom. It is installed in the wall or ceiling (see drawings, this page). The fan should be capable of changing the room's air completely every five minutes. Some fans come with combined heaters or lights. If you want an additional space heater, install protective grilles, and locate it where a bather cannot touch it by accident. It should not be near towels or other flammable items. A ceiling infrared lamp is a safe, quick heater.

Other amenities you may want to install are a sun lamp, a night light, a negative-ion generator to freshen up the air, a built-in hamper, a scale, magazine racks, and ceiling-recessed stereo speakers. The drawings on the opposite page illustrate solutions to some of the structural problems that may be encountered when installing bathroom fixtures and plumbing (see also, *New plumbing*, pp.202–224).

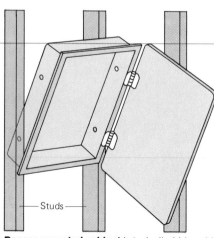

Recess-mounted cabinet is typically 14 in. wide and 3½ in. deep. Positioned 8 in. above the basin or vanity, the cabinet is secured to exposed studs with screws through the mounting holes in the cabinet's side walls.

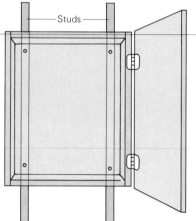

Surface-mounted cabinet is mounted on the wall with screws through its back, secured to two or more studs. Since cabinets of this type are not limited in size by any wall opening, their dimensions vary greatly.

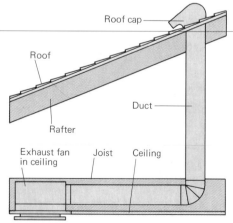

Ceiling ventilating fan is installed in the ceiling, connected to a duct that carries the fan exhaust outdoors, typically through a roof cap. The diameter of the duct varies from 3 to 8 in. depending on the size and power of the fan.

Bathroom installation tips

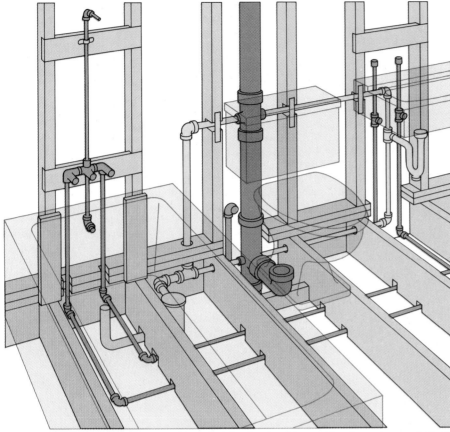

Positioning fixtures in a bathroom: After carefully planning the exact locations of every major fixture—bathtub or shower stall, toilet, and wash basin—for a new bathroom, both the water supply and DWV pipes are installed inside the wall (or walls) and the floor. The exact rough-in positions depend on your plan and fixture manufacturer's specifications.

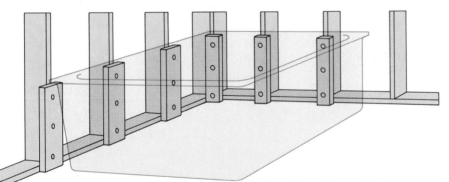

Supporting an enclosed bathtub: The tub's rim adjacent to the wall must be supported with hidden pieces of 2 x 4, or with horizontal 1-x-4 pieces, fitting the rim height exactly.

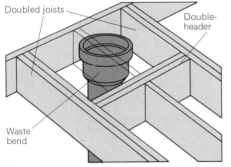

If part of a joist must be removed for a toilet waste bend, support shortened joist with a double header, and double adjacent joists.

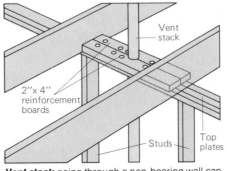

Vent stack going through a non-bearing wall can be firmly secured by nailing two 2-x-4 boards to the top plates as a reinforcement.

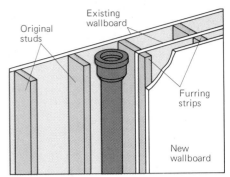

If wall built of 2-x-4 studs has no room for a full-size soil stack, wall cavity can be thickened by nailing 2-x-2 furring strips on the studs, and covering them with new wallboard.

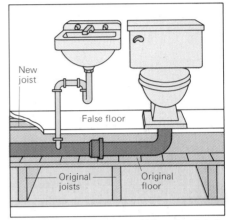

A false floor offers a way to hide soil and drain pipes over a concrete floor or without ripping up an existing wood floor. Joists for the new floor parallel direction of pipe.

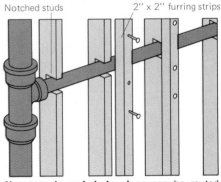

New supply and drain pipes can be routed horizontally through a non-bearing partition by notching the wall studs and adding furring strips.

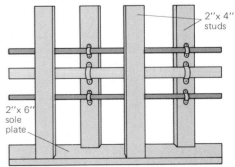

A new wet wall can be built with 2-x-6 top and sole plates, and 2-x-4 studs staggered along plate edges so as to leave room for pipes.

149

Renovating kitchens

Planning a renovation

You may want to renovate a kitchen because of its shortcomings: insufficient counter space, inefficient or outmoded appliances, inefficient layout, inadequate or inaccessible cabinet volume, dreary or deteriorating decoration, or poor lighting or ventilation. Because of today's high prices and the need for kitchen furniture to be built-in precisely, renovating a kitchen requires more careful and complete planning than any other room in the house.

Begin a renovation by listing the faults you have found in your present kitchen and your requirements for the new one. Get ideas about renovation possibilities from kitchen appliance and cabinet showrooms and manufacturer's catalogs. After you consider the principles of kitchen arrangement discussed below, and the limits on your time and budget, plan your renovation.

Kitchen areas: The kitchen should be thought of as several interrelated areas,

each with a primary function, and requiring its own space and facilities.

One kitchen area is for food storage and mixing; it is centered around the refrigerator, which is best located near the door through which groceries are carried into the kitchen. This area should have at least 15 to 18 inches of counter length, placed beside the refrigerator on the latch side of its door (many modern refrigerators can be ordered with the hinge on either side; some allow the swing to reverse). This space is used for sorting groceries, and for the preparation of dishes that require combining ingredients, such as baked goods, salads, and desserts. Cabinets in this area should have enough capacity for utensils used in mixing, such as bowls and measuring cups, and for storage wraps and containers used in the refrigerator. As with the other centers, deployment of supplies and utensils depends on the homemaker's habits.

The food preparation and cleaning center is based around the sink. This area generally requires the largest expanse of counter space, at least 30 inches, plus storage space for utensils such as small pots and pans, everyday dishes, and cleaning supplies. Dishes, utensils, and seasonings used to prepare food are also stored here. Counter space must be sufficient to stack dishes. A dishwasher is usually placed beside the sink; if no dishwasher is planned immediately, it is good to leave a base cabinet 24 inches wide beside the sink so one can be installed later. A double-bowl sink is usual if there is no dishwasher; a single-bowl will do if there is one. The kitchen garbage can is often placed in a cabinet beneath the sink.

The cooking and serving center, based at the range and oven, is usually put opposite the sink or the refrigerator. It includes at least 24 inches of counter space and storage space for pans, skil-

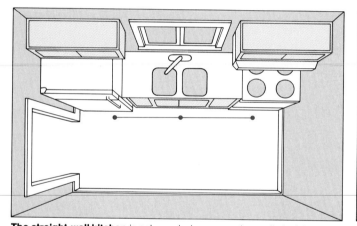

The straight-wall kitchen is only used where space is very limited, because it is the least efficient kitchen design. Counter space must be adequate, without being so large that it destroys efficiency.

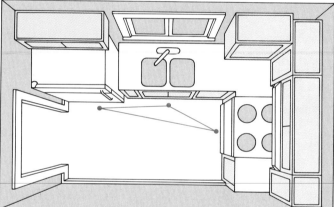

The L-shape is best for small kitchens; or it can concentrate work area in a large kitchen and set off space for dining. This arrangement allows much flexibility in the positioning of smaller appliances.

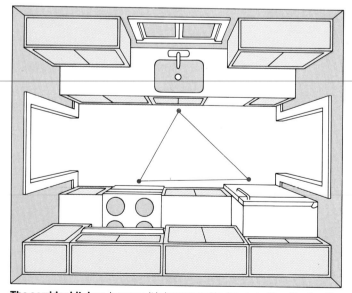

The corridor kitchen, because it is interrupted by house traffic, often has the sink and stove, the busiest area, on the same side. Appliances are staggered so they do not interfere with one another.

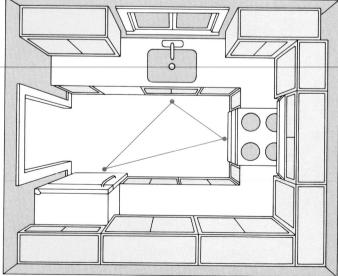

The U-shaped kitchen is the best design for isolating the kitchen work area from family traffic. If one of the arms of the U forms a peninsula (see diagrams opposite), it can be used for informal dining.

lets, stirring spoons, and other utensils and seasonings used in cooking. Serving dishes for meats and other hot food are often stored here as well.

The work triangle: The travel between these three work areas is immense—it is estimated that to prepare breakfast and dinner for a year, the family cook walks 120 miles. About 40 of these miles are unnecessary and can be eliminated by an efficient arrangement.

The most efficient arrangement is a triangle, the so-called work triangle. Because most cooking procedures require movement from the refrigerator to the sink, to the stove, the sink is usually positioned between the other two. The distance from the sink to the stove should be 4 to 6 feet, from the sink to the refrigerator 4 to 7 feet, and from the stove to the refrigerator 4 to 9 feet. The total perimeter of the work triangle should not exceed 22 feet, nor should a one-wall kitchen exceed 22 feet in length, or it will require too much walking and reduce the efficiency of the kitchen. The triangle should be designed to have little or no household traffic passing through it. Peninsulas and islands are sometimes added in larger renovations to improve the work triangle and to isolate it from traffic patterns, as well as to provide additional storage space and an eating area. Four traditional kitchen arrangements, and two incorporating an island and peninsula, are shown below.

Principles of kitchen arrangement: Your renovation should be designed to meet your needs. Do you bake often? Do you need a space in the kitchen for eating snacks and light meals? Do you do large-scale gourmet cooking? The kitchen should be arranged to accommodate what you will use it for.

Standard vertical dimensions for the placement of cabinets and appliances, shown in the diagram below, are for a homemaker of average height; if you are unusually tall or short, you may wish to adjust the dimensions of the kitchen accordingly (adjusted cabinets must be large enough to accommodate appliances; and having a manufacturer alter cabinets will add at least 50 percent to their cost).

Here are some general principles of kitchen arrangement to bear in mind: Electrical capacity may have to be upgraded if you are installing new appliances. All electrical and plumbing work must comply with local building codes.

Be sure the swings of the appliance and room doors and drawers do not interfere with each other. This is especially important in corners of the kitchen; major appliances are usually placed away from the corners. Corner cabinets containing revolving shelves work much better. Aisles should be at least 4 feet wide, if possible, to help prevent interference. Don't place a dish-

Continued next page

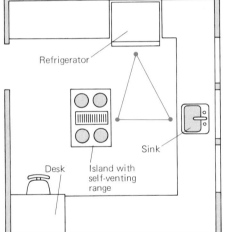

This kitchen contains an island with range that ventilates down through the floor. The desk area is used to conduct household business.

This kitchen has a peninsular countertop that functions as a serving counter. The corner range is an efficient way to use an awkward spot.

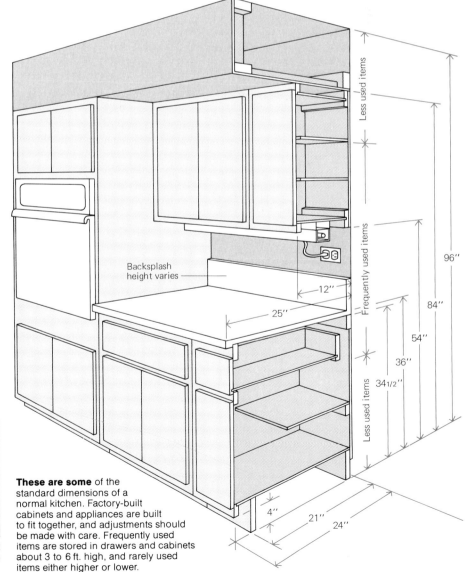

These are some of the standard dimensions of a normal kitchen. Factory-built cabinets and appliances are built to fit together, and adjustments should be made with care. Frequently used items are stored in drawers and cabinets about 3 to 6 ft. high, and rarely used items either higher or lower.

151

Renovating kitchens

Planning a renovation (continued)

washer at right angles to a sink; the dishwasher door would block access to the sink and make movement awkward.

The sink is often placed beneath a window. This provides natural light over the sink. More important, because cabinets are not usually placed over a sink, this arrangement does not sacrifice cabinet space. Stoves are not placed beneath windows; window curtains above and the need to reach across the stove to open the window are hazards.

Do not install a dishwasher next to the refrigerator; they both emit heat and will diminish each other's efficiency and operational lifetime.

Ventilation: Good ventilation is necessary to prevent the approximately 200 pounds of residues from moisture, smoke, and greasy vapor produced by a year's cooking from settling in the house. The vapors from the stove can be directed out of the house, through a passage in the wall, a project usually

part of larger renovation work. If this is impossible or too expensive, a filtering system can be installed in the hood over the stove. Though this is cheaper than exterior ventilation, it requires cleaning every few weeks, and does nothing to reduce the heat or humidity in the kitchen. Stoves built in islands away from the wall sometimes have ventilators that run straight up through the roof (see illustrations, p.156).

Ventilators, which are rated by the volume of air they pass in cubic feet per minute (cfm), must have sufficient capacity to ventilate the area they serve. As a general rule, for a kitchen with an 8 foot ceiling, the ventilator should have twice the capacity in cfm as the area of the floor in square feet. For example, an area 200 square feet requires a ventilator with a capacity of 400 cfm.

Lighting: Kitchen light should be bright enough so you can easily read the small print on food packages. It should

be distributed so that nowhere in the kitchen must you work in your own shadow. And it should help create a cheery ambiance to ease the long hours often spent there. In general, every 50 square feet of kitchen requires a total of 150-175 watts of incandescent or 60-80 watts of fluorescent lighting. Most of the lighting can usually be provided by ceiling fixtures, which are augmented by fixtures above the range, above the sink, under the wall cabinets to illuminate the counter, and anywhere else they are needed. The use of bright wallpaper and paint will, of course, reduce the need for artificial light.

Drawing your kitchen: Before you can plan exactly how your renovation will look, you must make an accurate drawing of the kitchen. First measure the floor of the room and draw it in scale on a piece of graph paper. Take all measurements because rooms are seldom exactly square. Record distances to

Cabinet and appliance dimensions

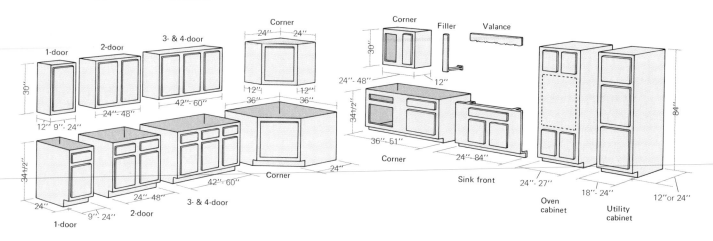

Wall cabinets: The standard height of a wall cabinet set over a countertop is 30 in. However, 18-in. cabinets are often set over a range, and 15-in. over a refrigerator (though of course this depends on the height of the refrigerator). Corners can be filled with diagonal corner cabinets or adjustable blind corner cabinets (see facing page). The decorative valance fills the space between the cabinet and the soffit or ceiling above it.

Base cabinets: Base cabinets come in a greater variety than wall cabinets. They are available with, for example, all drawers, drawers and doors, half or whole shelves, slide-out shelves, vertical tray dividers, pull-out cutting boards, and pull-out garbage containers. An enclosed sink cabinet can be used as well as the sink front shown here. The oven cabinet can accept several sizes of standard and microwave ovens.

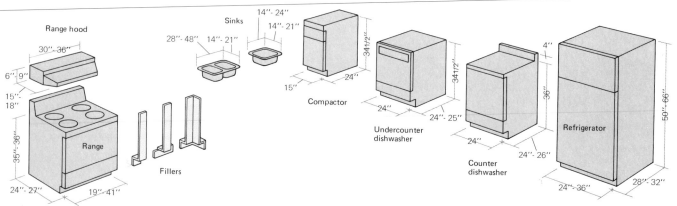

Appliances: Ranges are available with finished sides, as shown here, with unfinished sides to sit between cabinets, and as burners alone which sit upon special base cabinets. Sinks vary a great deal in size; the size to use depends on its use and whether or not there is a dishwasher to lighten the load. Of the other appliances, the refrigerator varies the most in size. Older refrigerators, unlike new ones, often need space at the back and above them for ventilation.

the fraction of an inch; fitting in kitchens must be precise. Mark doorways, including the thickness of the trim, and note which way doors swing.

After the floor plan is completed, make a drawing (elevation drawing) of each wall (see illustrations, p.154). Include the dimensions of the walls, doors, and windows, including trim. Also note the location of electrical and plumbing outlets, heating ducts, hot water heaters, and any other objects that will remain in the kitchen.

Designing your renovation: The final information you need is the exact dimensions of the cabinets and appliances that will go into the kitchen. Standard dimensions are shown on the facing page, but you should check the manufacturer's specifications of the cabinets and appliances you plan to buy. Kitchen measurements must be precise. The one area where you are allowed a little leeway is the corners, where some cabinets can adjust to fit exactly. Four treatments of corner cabinets are shown in the drawings below.

You now combine general principles of arrangement, specific needs, dimensions of the kitchen and of the cabinets and appliances that will fill it—all into an exact layout of your new kitchen. Finished floor plans and elevation drawings for the L-shaped kitchen shown on page 150 can be seen on page 154. If you have trouble beginning the plan, start with the sink—it is often under the window (a good place to leave it), and moving the water line is a task best avoided.

Cabinets: The largest component by far in most kitchens is the cabinets. They serve not only as the kitchen storage area, but also as the primary visual element of the room. High among the criteria for choosing cabinets (see below) should be how much you think you will enjoy looking at them every day for years to come.

There are two types of kitchen cabinets. Base cabinets, which sit on the floor, are generally 34½ inches high (with the countertop they come to 36 inches). Wall cabinets, which are attached to the wall, vary in height. Most factory-built cabinets are available in widths beginning at 9 inches and increasing in 3-inch increments.

Custom-made cabinets, built to fit your kitchen exactly, usually cost about twice as much as similar factory-made cabinets. There is also a wide range of prices for factory-made cabinets. You should evaluate the materials and workmanship of a cabinet before you buy it—all cabinets look good from the outside, from a distance. The cabinet box should be totally enclosed, made of sturdy wood, plywood, or particle board. Mortise or dovetail joints will last longer than butt joints. Shelves should be adjustable; movable pins set in holes in particle board cabinet walls will not

Continued next page

Fitting cabinets at corners

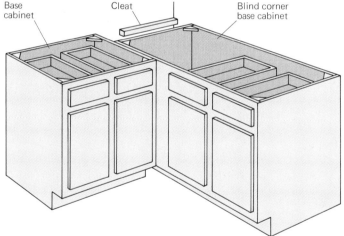

Blind corner cabinets have drawers and/or doors on one side, the other side butting into the corner. Blind wall corner cabinets can be pulled away from the corner up to 3 in.; base cabinets can have a wider gap.

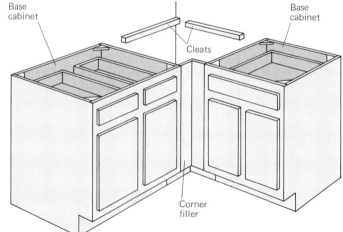

The butted base corner sacrifices corner storage area, and is usually used as an economy measure. Filler pieces, supported by cleats, are used so the drawers, or their handles, do not interfere with each other.

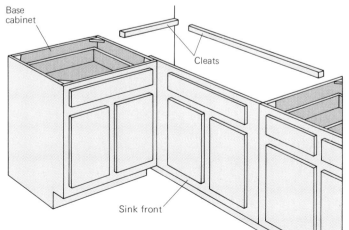

Sink front running out of a corner has a bottom that extends an extra 24 in. to provide a base for the storage area. As with other base corner cabinets, horizontal cleats attached to the wall support the end of the countertop.

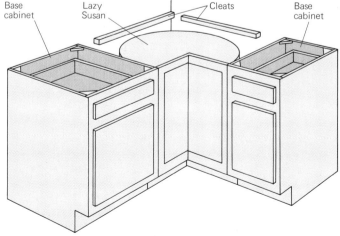

This Lazy Susan, an efficient corner cabinet (see also the diagonal corner on facing page) has attached doors; when pushed, they revolve into the cabinet and the Lazy Susan spins around. Others have doors that open out.

Renovating kitchens

Planning a renovation (continued)

last nearly as long as metal supporting clips set in metal shelf standards. Nylon or metal ball-bearing slides in cabinet drawers last longer than nylon guides, which last longer than wood sliding on wood. Hinges with magnetic catches last twice as long as springloaded hinges. The inside of a good cabinet should be finished with stain and lacquer, eliminating the need for liners.

Installing cabinets is discussed on pages 155–157. If your cabinets are to be installed by professionals, you should still choose the product carefully. An installer can often be helpful in reviewing your plans for a renovation.

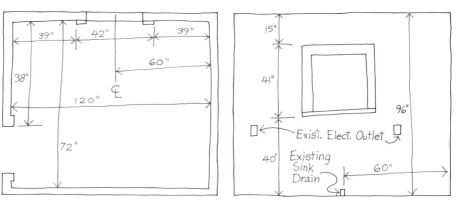

Exact measurements of the empty room are made on a rough floor plan (left) and on up to four elevation drawings (right). The floor plan is the basis of the finished drawings, below.

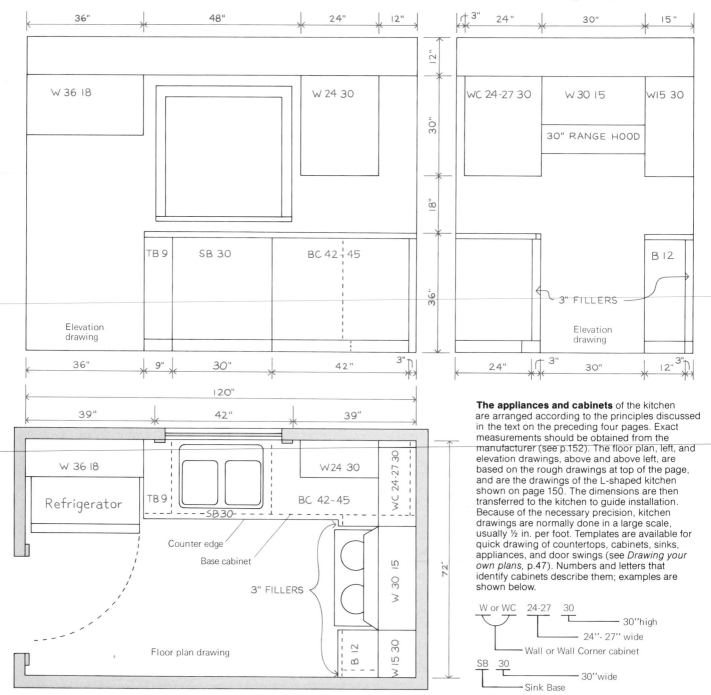

The appliances and cabinets of the kitchen are arranged according to the principles discussed in the text on the preceding four pages. Exact measurements should be obtained from the manufacturer (see p.152). The floor plan, left, and elevation drawings, above and above left, are based on the rough drawings at top of the page, and are the drawings of the L-shaped kitchen shown on page 150. The dimensions are then transferred to the kitchen to guide installation. Because of the necessary precision, kitchen drawings are normally done in a large scale, usually ½ in. per foot. Templates are available for quick drawing of countertops, cabinets, sinks, appliances, and door swings (see *Drawing your own plans*, p.47). Numbers and letters that identify cabinets describe them; examples are shown below.

Preparing the kitchen for renovation

Before you begin removing old kitchen cabinets and appliances, shut off water, gas, and electrical lines.

It is best to empty the kitchen completely, and essential if you are installing new flooring. Remove the sink, the old countertops, then the old cabinets, doing as little damage to the walls and floor as possible. Remove the baseboard and any molding that will interfere with cabinet installation. If you are installing new flooring, you may have to remove the old flooring, depending on what the old flooring is, its condition, and what you will cover it with (see pp.112–121).

Uneven areas of the floors and walls must be located before installation of the cabinets and appliances is begun. To find high spots in an uneven floor, place a straight 2 x 4 several feet long on the floor with a level atop it. Move it across the floor to detect tilting. Determine the highest spot in the floor that will lie beneath any of the installed cabinets or appliances. Using a chalk line and level, draw a level line at this height on the walls all around the room; this is the base line from which all vertical measurements in the renovation will begin.

The walls are similarly checked for unevenness with a piece of lumber and level; cabinets installed on an uneven surface can rack or twist, causing the cabinet doors and drawers to malfunction. Protruding spots in the wall can be sanded down. Recessed areas that fall where the cabinets are to be attached (which can be determined when the cabinet plan is drawn on the wall; see below) are corrected with shims made of thin pieces of wood.

Locate the studs with a magnetic stud finder, by tapping the walls, or by driving a small finishing nail through the wall where the hole will not be seen later. (After the baseboards are removed, nailheads in the bottom of the walls often indicate the position of the studs.) Because studs are normally spaced 16 inches on center, once you find one you can usually find the others by measuring. Mark the location of the studs on the wall where the marks will be visible while the cabinets are installed; the cabinets must be fastened through the wall directly into the studs.

Finally, transfer the measurements from the plans you have drawn (see facing page) to the walls and draw accurately the location of all of the cabinets. Use the level base line as the reference point for all vertical measurements.

Installing cabinets

The installation of cabinets, the essential kitchen furniture, is described on this and the following pages. Other work involved in kitchen renovation, such as electrical, plumbing, drywalling and wall and floor covering, is described in other sections of this book.

Cabinets must be installed exactly level, not only to enhance their appearance, but to ensure that cabinet doors and drawers work properly. Level installation entails a series of painstaking measurements, shimming, and adjustments. Installing cabinets should not be attempted by anyone lacking woodworking experience.

Wall cabinets: Some manufacturers recommend that base cabinets be installed before wall cabinets, and once the base cabinets are in, temporary braces placed on the countertops support the wall cabinets as they are installed. This is questionable advice because it exposes the new base cabinets and countertops to unnecessary damage, and makes work on the wall cabinets more awkward.

Wall cabinets should be installed first, held by temporary wood braces that rest on the floor. The brace, which can be built of scrap wood, is designed to hold

Continued next page

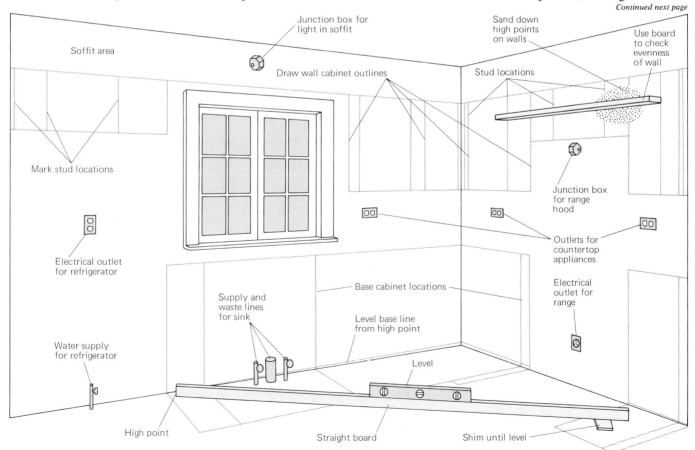

The surfaces of the kitchen must be level and square before the renovation is begun. The floor is checked with a 2 x 4 and level. A level line marked around the room at the height of the high point is the reference line for vertical measurements. Walls are sanded flat. If necessary, electrical outlets and plumbing lines are added or moved. The measurements from the plans (opposite) are drawn on the walls and floor to guide installation.

Renovating kitchens

Installing cabinets (continued)

the cabinet up at the top reference line (generally 84 inches above the base line) drawn during preparation (see p.155). Begin with a corner cabinet. When it is exactly in place, open the cabinet door and drill pilot holes through the back of the cabinet near the top (a mounting rail is usually provided). These holes are for the screws that will hold the cabinet to the wall; thus the holes must go through the wall and into the studs (following the marks made during preparation), and their diameter depends on the size of the screws. The screws are not tightened all the way until after several cabinets are installed, shimmed, and leveled.

The neighboring cabinet is raised into place and installed in the same way. The two cabinets are aligned vertically and horizontally, and held that way with C-clamps. Two ¼-inch diameter holes are drilled through the touching walls, one near the top and the other near the bottom of the cabinet. Bolts are pushed through and nuts are tightened firmly to secure the alignment; the C-clamps are removed. Some manufacturers suggest wood screws rather than bolts.

A row of cabinets is installed, each attached to its neighbors, before final installation is made. Cabinets can also be aligned and bolted together on the floor, and then attached to the wall as a unit. Either way, once the cabinets are in place, filler strips (pieces of wood with a finish identical to the cabinets), which fill the space between the end of the cabinet row and the wall, are screwed in. The cabinets are checked for level and plumb, and any necessary shims are pushed in behind them. When all adjustments and shimming are com-

pleted, and check out level, the screws in the back of the cabinets are tightened all the way to secure the cabinets permanently to the wall.

Base cabinets: Base cabinets are installed much like wall cabinets. Beginning at the corner, the cabinets are put in place. Each is shimmed to raise it level with the guide line marked on the wall. Holes are drilled between the cabinets to connect them with bolts or screws. After they are carefully checked for evenness, level, and plumb, they are

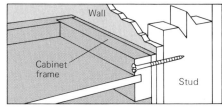

Top of frame is attached by screws to wall studs.

tightly screwed into the wall through drilled pilot holes.

If you install a corner cabinet containing a large Lazy Susan or a base cabinet with no back, you must install wood cleats to the wall. These 1 x 2s are attached at the same height as the front of the cabinet to support the back edge of the countertop (see diagrams, p.153).

Check the doors and drawers of the base cabinets to be sure they work properly. If they don't, the cabinet is probably installed off square; check the cabinets with a level and make necessary adjustments to the shims or to the mounting screws. Do this before the countertop is installed; afterwards, adjustments are very difficult.

Countertops: It is best to wait until the cabinets are installed before taking measurements and ordering a countertop. The manufacturer needs accurate dimensions in every direction. Note whether the ends of the countertop will abut an appliance or an open space; these ends are covered with a laminated end cap made of the same material as the countertop. Where the countertop will abut a wall or a wall oven, the countertop is given a stiff upper lip called an end splash (it is called a backsplash along a long wall) to prevent water from running off the counter and down the wall. Also note the exact dimensions of the sink (as well as the make and model) and its location in the counter so a hole can be cut for it. Countertops with finished edges are available for islands and peninsulas.

You can make your own countertop with a do-it-yourself kit. After you cut the surface to the proper length, you cut any necessary miters for joints, and the sink cut-out. You then apply the backsplashes, which are provided.

Most base cabinets have triangular corner blocks to anchor screws that secure the countertops. Drill pilot holes through the blocks and, if possible, into the countertop, *but not through it*. Install the screws from inside the cabinet.

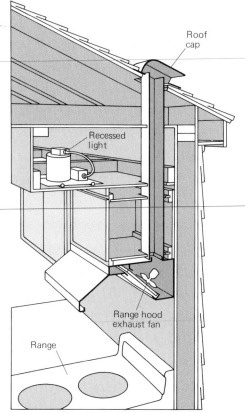

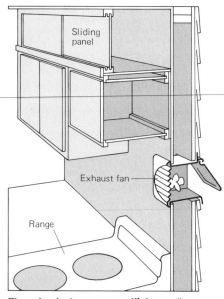

The simplest range ventilator pulls vapors straight through the wall. The soffit in this kitchen (above the cabinets) has sliding panels, allowing the soffit area to be used for storage.

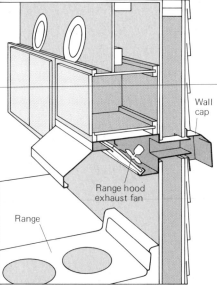

The range hood in this kitchen, and the one to the right, catch vapors and direct them toward the ventilator. This soffit is set back; the front can be used to display dishes.

This ventilator pushes vapors up through a long duct and out the roof. A similar set-up can be used for a range placed on an island away from the walls. Soffit projects, and houses a lighting fixture.

1. The first cabinet is held by a wooden brace at the height of the guideline. Pilot holes are drilled through the top of the cabinet frame. Mounting screws are attached loosely.

2. The neighboring cabinet, held up by a brace, is attached with bolts to the first. Before the screws are tightened, a level is used to check both cabinets for level and plumb.

3. More cabinets are bolted to their neighbors, leveled, and screwed into wall studs. The old flowered wallpaper was left exposed on areas that will be covered by cabinets or soffits.

4. This cabinet sits above the new location of the stove. The hood being installed will gather cooking vapors, which will then be forced out a duct in the wall by a ventilating fan.

5. Soffits often enclose the area between cabinets and the ceiling. This unusual soffit (see opposite) is installed after the cabinets, to guide boards already attached to the ceiling.

6. The base cabinets, like the wall cabinets, are carefully aligned and held firmly with C-clamps. After holes are drilled through the cabinet walls, bolts are passed through and tightened.

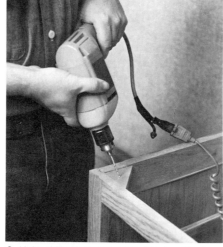

7. Shims are driven beneath each base cabinet until it is aligned with the reference mark on the wall. A level atop the cabinet is checked to make sure cabinet is perfectly level.

8. Holes drilled in the triangular blocks of the base cabinet are for screws to secure the countertop. Holes are drilled at an angle to provide clearance as the screws are tightened from underneath.

9. The countertop is put in place, and the screws are tightened. The sink is held up on blocks as watertight caulking is squeezed in. The blocks are removed and the sink is set in the caulking.

157

Finishing basements

Planning for the job

A finished basement can turn the cluttered family storage space into a pleasant area tailored for work or play.

Thorough and comprehensive planning for finishing the entire basement is essential, even though the actual work can be done in stages. What is the predominant purpose of the room or rooms you will create? For example, part or all of the area could be converted to a second living room, or a party room with casual or trendy furniture—a built-in bar, poker table, all under imaginative recessed ceiling lighting. Or the area could be remodeled into a cozy den or family room where the entire family can relax and enjoy television, stereo, and home movies. A recreation room containing ping pong, billiards, or bridge tables, and equipment for such games as archery and darts, is another possibility. Basements can also be finished and equipped to contain areas for work shops, a sewing center, a small gym with a sauna, a photographic darkroom, a home office, or even a home disco. Facilities and decor can range from the pragmatic to the offbeat. The only limitations are your own imagination and needs, your skills as a do-it-yourselfer, and your budget.

Damp-proofing: One prerequisite for finishing a basement is that the founda-

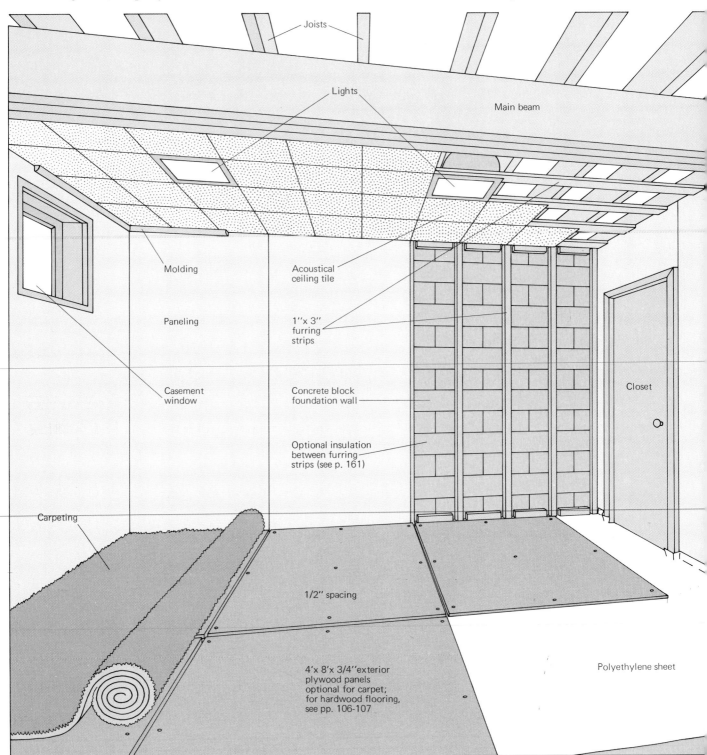

Joists

Lights

Main beam

Molding

Acoustical
ceiling tile

Paneling

1"x 3"
furring
strips

Casement
window

Concrete block
foundation wall

Closet

Optional insulation
between furring
strips (see p. 161)

Carpeting

1/2" spacing

4'x 8'x 3/4"exterior
plywood panels
optional for carpet;
for hardwood flooring,
see pp. 106-107

Polyethylene sheet

tion not leak water and that plumbing not drip condensation. Such problems can usually be cured, if they exist (see *Waterproofing basements*, pp.66–69). Once you determine that your basement is dry or can be made so, go ahead with your planning. On many features, including the floor plan, you may have to make compromises. You will want to enclose the boiler or furnace in a fireproof room and partition off the laundry facilities and any workshop or specialized spaces to separate them from recreation and living areas.

Building codes: Remember that your finished basement must meet the requirements of your local building code (pp.21–37). You will need a ceiling height of at least 7½ feet; in some cases you can "raise the ceiling" by excavating the basement floor downward. This should be done by a professional since it may require the reinforcing of foundation walls. Adequate ventilation and a fire exit are also basic considerations.

The drawing below shows a partly finished basement. The next two pages suggest alternatives for finishing, and give details for several practical projects. Chapters in this book on walls, floors, ceilings, partitions, electrical wiring, etc., show the basic techniques used in finishing basements.

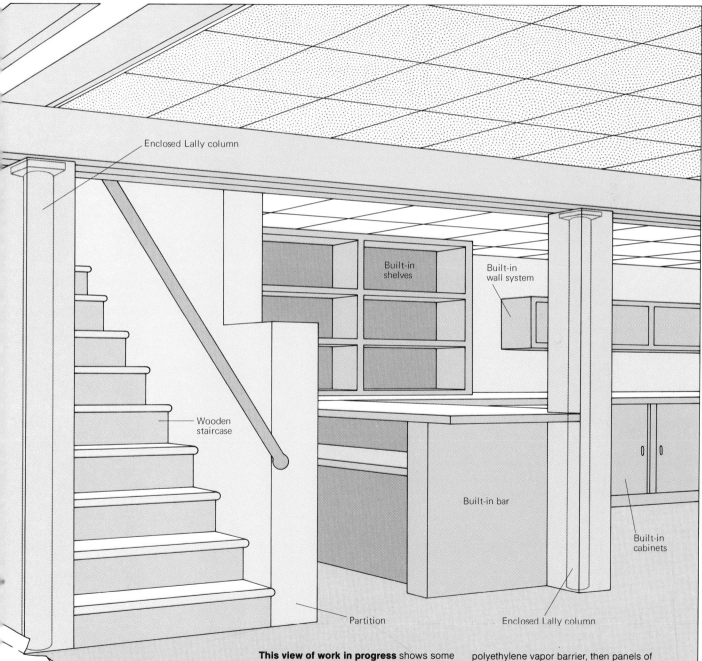

Enclosed Lally column

Built-in shelves

Built-in wall system

Wooden staircase

Built-in bar

Built-in cabinets

Partition

Enclosed Lally column

Concrete slab

This view of work in progress shows some of the common basement finishing features used by do-it-yourselfers. The ceiling is covered with acoustical tiles. The foundation walls of concrete block, are first overlaid with furring strips, then covered with paneling. The casement window is partly finished. The existing concrete slab floor is covered with a polyethylene vapor barrier, then panels of plywood as subflooring, and finally wall-to-wall carpeting. A roomy closet has been built under the stairs. On the right are built-in wall systems, shelves, and a bar. The built-up wood girder, or main beam, has been sanded and stained. Two steel Lally columns supporting the girder have been enclosed with paneling.

Finishing basements

Work steps for each area

The jobs entailed in finishing a basement are generally approached in the following convenient sequence:
1. Waterproofing,
2. Framing partitions,
3. Installing rough plumbing, heating units, and electrical wiring and boxes,
4. Opening a new window,
5. Furring out masonry walls for wallboard,
6. Installing wall covering,
7. Finishing the ceiling,
8. Finishing the floor,
9. Completing plumbing, heating, and electrical installations,
10. Installing built-in bar, wall system, shelves, and cabinets.

Depending on the dryness of your basement and the features you plan for your renovation, you may omit one or more of the above steps, and alter the sequence for others.

Most of the basic techniques used in finishing a basement are covered by other chapters of this book. Procedures that apply only to basements are described on these two pages.

General considerations: Your basement may have a dry slab and foundation walls and still get damp occasionally as the result of moisture condensing from the air. A dehumidifier may be the solution. As added protection, you may even want to seal normally dry walls and their joints at the slab floor with a waterproofing layer of cement.

Because a basement's temperature is moderated by the surrounding ground, it may not need its own separate heating system, or insulation, except in colder climates. A louvered screen in the furnace room partition can provide radiant heat and warm air to the rest of the basement. Hot-water or forced warm-air heating can be extended from the main system to the new basement rooms. However, this may affect heat distribution to the rest of the house, and the job should be analyzed by professionals. Consider electric heat.

Walls and partitions: Basement walls are relatively easy to finish. First, attach wood furring strips or studs to the wall with masonry nails or adhesive, as shown on the opposite page. Cover the furring with a polyethylene vapor barrier, and then nail plasterboard or paneling to the furring. Shim the furring strips to make a level surface if the concrete wall is uneven. Be sure to leave small breaks at the intersections of furring strips for air circulation. To conserve energy in colder regions, insulate the walls (top, facing page) before closing them with plasterboard or paneling. Partitions and room dividers are built like conventional stud walls. A window

can be opened at the top of the foundation, as illustrated on this page.

Ceilings, pipes, girders: Most basements lack enough headroom for suspended ceilings, but plasterboard or acoustical tile, fastened to a grid of furring strips nailed directly to the joists overhead, takes up little headroom and is easy to install.

In many basements plumbing pipes are attached just below the exposed joists. Small pipes can sometimes be shifted upward to be covered by the new ceiling. A big soil pipe can be boxed in with stained boards or with textured plywood disguising it as a wooden beam, as can a steel girder or main beam. Similarly, any steel Lally columns or posts that hold up the girder can be boxed with plywood or paneling.

Finishing the floor: Most basements have concrete slab floors that, if level, can be covered with vinyl floor tile, vinyl sheeting, or all-weather carpet. For better insulation and greater comfort, a plywood subfloor can be framed and installed over the concrete before tile or carpet is laid. If there is enough headroom in the basement you may want to install floor joists to create a secure base underfoot and provide greater depth for insulation over the concrete slab.

Built-ins and lighting: A basement renovation can easily accommodate built-ins. Besides a bar, an entire wall can be lined with built-in shelves and cabinets. Under-stair closets, closets that hide unsightly pipes while also providing storage space, and deep but narrow alcoves for storing odd-shaped objects, such as golf clubs, pool cues, and card tables, are other possibilities.

A convenient way to light a basement is to install recessed lights that fit into the new tiled ceiling. Mood lighting can come from strategically placed track lights, and floor and table lamps. If you are planning a planter as a decorative accent, a couple of mercury vapor lamps should be focused on the plants to supply light for growth.

Stairs: Basement stairways can be enclosed with partitions or screened to make them less obtrusive. One idea for finishing a staircase is illustrated on the facing page.

The following pages contain instructions that apply to finishing a basement:

Waterproofing, pages 66–69; electrical installations, pages 172–201; plumbing installations, pages 202–224; posts, beams, and joists, pages 70–75; ceilings, pages 92–95; non-bearing partitions, pages 86–87; wall coverings, pages 88–91, 96–97, 98–105; flooring, pages 106–110, 119–125; staircases, pages 128–129; built-ins and closets, pages 130–137; fireplaces and stoves, pages 138–143.

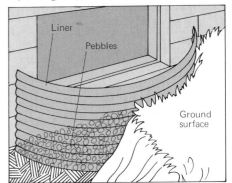

2. Chisel out blocks and install a header and jack studs. Frame window to manufacturer's rough opening (r.o.) specifications.

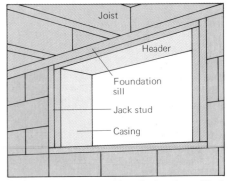

1. A well for a new basement window is excavated in ground outside foundation wall. Well is reinforced with a liner, and layered with pebbles.

3. Insert the entire window into the rough opening and secure it with screws or nails according to the manufacturer's instructions.

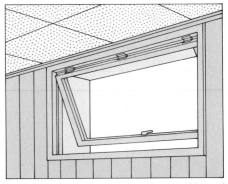

4. Caulk around the window frame inside and outside. Finish the inside wall surface with furring strips and plasterboard or paneling.

160

Insulating basement walls

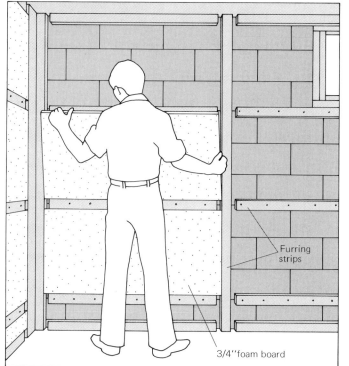

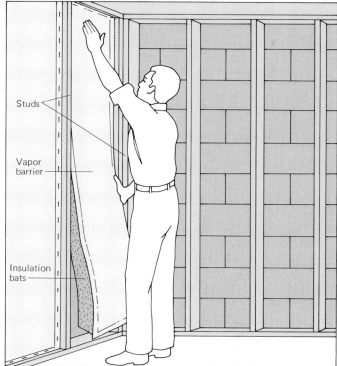

Walls are shown furred with 1 x 3s for application of paneling. Insulation being glued to walls is ¾-in.-rigid foam. Vapor barrier goes over foam.

If your climate is very cold, thicker insulation can be installed between 2-x-4 studs, using 4-in. thick fiberglass with foil side facing the room.

Dowel-pole staircase

Dowel-pole railings (left) add a decorative touch and can be removed to move bulky objects down the stairs. The 2-in. thick poles fit into holes in the ceiling and in the 2-x-6-in. base at the side of the staircase (above). The ceiling holes are 2 in. deeper than the pole tops, so that by lifting each pole, it can easily be removed.

Boxing the I-beam

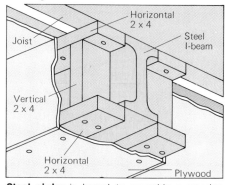

Steel girder is boxed to resemble a wooden beam by nailing a frame of 2 x 4s to ceiling joists, then covering it with plywood or Masonite.

Moving water pipes

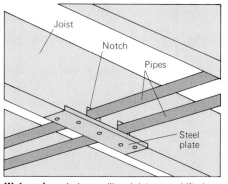

Water pipes below ceiling joists are shifted upward to notches in the bottom of the joists, which must be reinforced with steel plates.

Boxing a large pipe

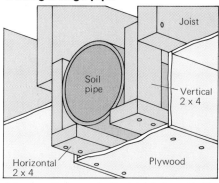

A large soil pipe under the joists is boxed in like the I-beam at far left, using a 2-x-4 frame and plywood or Masonite panels.

Finishing attics

Making the most of a unique space

A typical attic conversion involves such jobs as adding insulation; framing and installing a ceiling, partitions, and knee walls; adding dormers; installing new windows and/or skylights; running new plumbing and electrical wiring; and installing gypsum wallboard, flooring, carpeting, and wallpaper.

Step-by-step instructions for all of these jobs are carried throughout this book, as a quick glance at the table of contents will show. This chapter deals with those unique aspects of an attic renovation not covered elsewhere.

Building codes: Before you begin planning, check your local building code (see also, *Building codes/Introduction to construction*, pp.21–37). Codes typically set minimum standards for ceiling heights, emergency fire escapes, and other factors in the design of living space that do not apply when an attic is just a storeroom. You may find that to satisfy these basic require- ments you will have to add dormers, rebuild the attic staircase, or carry out other major construction jobs you do not want to take on. More than likely, though, conforming to the code will pose no great difficulty. If your renovation is so extensive as to require a building permit, obtain the permit before ordering materials (or have your contractor get the permit, if you are not doing all the work yourself). Application for permits is discussed on page 21.

Plumbing: Locate a new attic bathroom above an existing one on the floor below, if possible, so original water supply, waste and vent pipes can easily be tapped to connect the new plumbing. Enclose the existing soil stack behind a wall or with a pipe chase. Construct a raised bathroom floor directly on the existing floor to provide space for new pipes. (See also *New plumbing*, pp.202–224.)

Ceilings and ventilation: A ridge vent or vents near ridge prevent condensation in insulated cathedral ceiling; existing gable end louvers will ventilate the space above an insulated flat ceiling, installed at the level of the collar ties. Put an access panel in a flat ceiling; install a fan in either the gable or the ceiling to exhaust hot air.

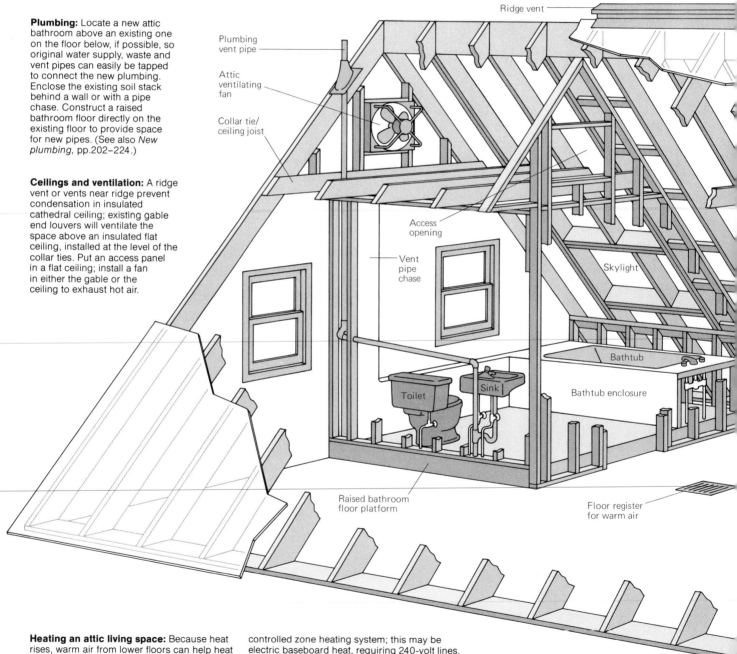

Ridge vent

Plumbing vent pipe

Attic ventilating fan

Collar tie/ceiling joist

Access opening

Vent pipe chase

Skylight

Bathtub

Toilet

Sink

Bathtub enclosure

Raised bathroom floor platform

Floor register for warm air

Heating an attic living space: Because heat rises, warm air from lower floors can help heat the attic. The drawing suggests two common approaches: a floor register is installed in an opening cut between the ceiling joists of a room below, allowing warm air to rise; the attic stairs serve as both a passage for rising warm air and as a return taking cool air down to lower floors. An attic can also be given its own individually controlled zone heating system; this may be electric baseboard heat, requiring 240-volt lines, or an extension of the present home heating system. Heat, registers, and the door at bottom of stairs are shut off when attic is unoccupied. If the attic will usually be occupied, remove any insulation that may be in the attic floor, and insulate the roof or attic ceiling and exterior walls before putting up wallboard.

Materials: Order building materials in sufficient quantity to complete the entire job. Beforehand, select a place to store your materials until you need them. If no such space exists in your house or on your property, build a shed to protect your building supplies, or simply stack them on a platform and cover them with a tarp.

Check the stairway leading to the attic to make sure building materials can be brought up to the attic. You may have to raise certain materials—such as gypsum wallboard panels—with a light block and tackle on the outside.

Conversions of totally unfinished attics begin with the installation of a subfloor over exposed ceiling joists. Sheathing grade plywood is usually specified. If the joists are smaller than 2 x 8 or in poor condition, reinforce them by nailing on new joists of the same dimensions. Older houses may have joists that are larger than today's nomi-

nal sizes; nail the reinforcement flush with the top of the existing joist. Use scraps of wood or shingles to shim them level before nailing.

Check the dimensions and spacing of existing joists and rafters. Uneven joists or rafters must be made uniform before you can install walls or flooring, as seen on ensuing pages. Before ordering new windows, remove enough of the trim from inside the attic to determine the actual size of the rough opening.

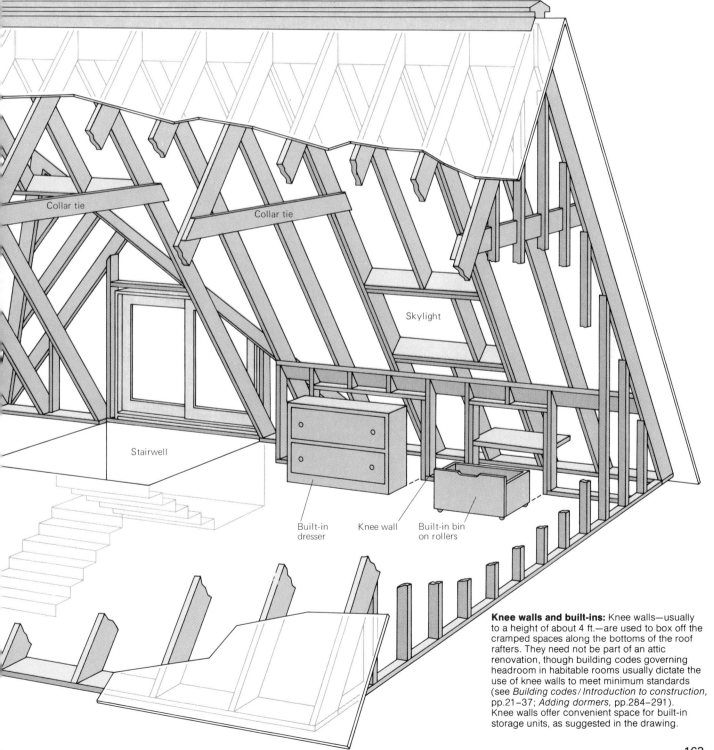

Collar tie

Collar tie

Skylight

Stairwell

Built-in dresser

Knee wall

Built-in bin on rollers

Knee walls and built-ins: Knee walls—usually to a height of about 4 ft.—are used to box off the cramped spaces along the bottoms of the roof rafters. They need not be part of an attic renovation, though building codes governing headroom in habitable rooms usually dictate the use of knee walls to meet minimum standards (see *Building codes/Introduction to construction*, pp.21–37; *Adding dormers*, pp.284–291). Knee walls offer convenient space for built-in storage units, as suggested in the drawing.

Finishing attics

Partitions and knee walls

Two factors make building partitions in attics different from building non-bearing partitions in any other part of the house (see pp.86–91). First is the difficulty of fitting a partition frame at its intersections with the sloping attic roof line. This consideration also applies to knee wall frames; the studs and/or plates are usually bevel-cut to match rafter angles and provide flush nailing surfaces for other parts of the frame as well as plasterboard wall panels. Many of the plasterboard panels must also be cut at angles to fit the sloping ceiling line, as shown on page 169.

Trimming and furring: The second consideration, peculiar particularly to the attics of older houses, relates to the lumber used for rafters. Old rafters were often rough-cut, so their dimensions may not be uniform. Moreover, their spacing may also vary. And depending on the style of the roof and the presence of dormers and gables, the rafters may enclose highly irregular volumes with roof lines of varying pitch. Aside from the obvious need for care in measuring and cutting to accurately frame partitions under such circumstances, it may also be necessary to do some preparatory carpentry just to create consistent rafter lines lest the framing and wallboard attached to the rafters not be square. This is done either by trimming back the rafters with a saw or a plane where they are too deep or by building them up with furring strips, or nailers, where they are too shallow. The result should be uniform planes throughout the attic to provide a workable base for framing. Furring of rafters may also be necessary to gain the required recesses for roof insulation.

As in any conventional partition, the framing will consist of a top plate, sole plate, and studs between the plates. When you lay the sole plate, interrupt it as you would a conventional partition wherever you want a door or an arch; install double studs at the sides of the door frame and frame out its top with cripple studs, as seen in the drawings on the opposite page.

Plumbing and wiring: Plumbing and electrical lines and boxes are installed before you put up wallboard. The position of a bathroom, darkroom, or any room requiring plumbing should be determined according to the proximity of existing water supply and waste disposal pipes on the floor below the attic. By locating attic plumbing close to or immediately above that on lower floors you will save on the labor and materials costs of connecting to existing plumbing. In cases where you have no choice but to run pipes across an attic, you can usually hide the new pipes behind your knee walls (being sure that either the pipe or the roof behind the knee wall is insulated); alternatively, you can notch the pipes into the new partition frames where they will be hidden by wallboard. Spaces behind knee walls can also be used for storage.

1. A level chalk line is snapped across the rafters at the established knee wall height (here, about 4 ft.), and the distance between the end rafters is then measured; knee wall top plate will be cut to this length.

2. At the end rafter where the knee wall joins the existing exterior wall angled under the roof, a test fit is made using scraps of the pieces meeting at this point (see large drawing, opposite page).

3. Edge of knee wall top plate—which will be built up from a pair of 2 x 4s—is bevel-cut with a circular saw. An angle gauge was used to measure the slope of the rafters, and the saw was set to this angle.

4. Studs are installed between knee wall plates. Tops of studs are bevel-cut at angle of top plate bevel to provide flush edge for plasterboard. Rafter showing white was planed back as described in text.

Typical knee wall and partition framing

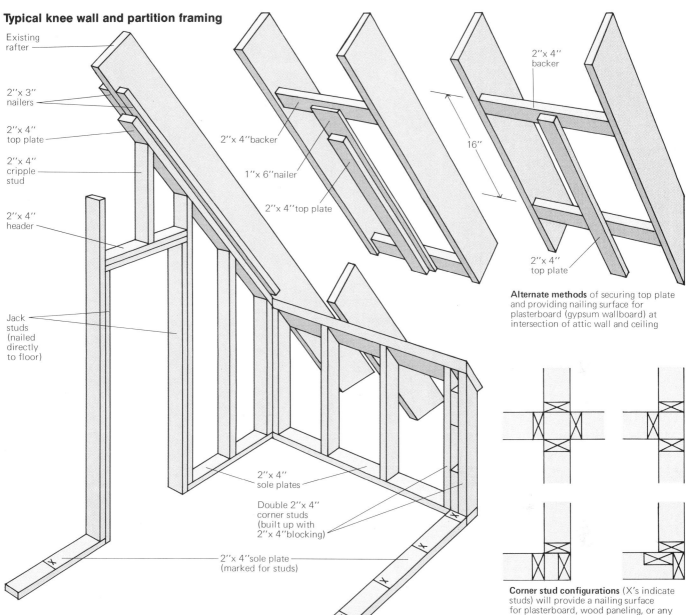

Existing rafter

2"x 3" nailers

2"x 4" top plate

2"x 4" cripple stud

2"x 4" header

Jack studs (nailed directly to floor)

2"x 4" backer

1"x 6" nailer

2"x 4" top plate

2"x 4" backer

16"

2"x 4" top plate

2"x 4" sole plates

Double 2"x 4" corner studs (built up with 2"x 4" blocking)

2"x 4" sole plate (marked for studs)

Alternate methods of securing top plate and providing nailing surface for plasterboard (gypsum wallboard) at intersection of attic wall and ceiling

Corner stud configurations (X's indicate studs) will provide a nailing surface for plasterboard, wood paneling, or any other wall surface at the junctions of two, three, or four walls

5. Built-up 2-x-4 corner studs (see illustrations above) are installed at the end of the knee wall; a partition running at right angles to the knee wall will be attached here. Note nailing block between rafters.

6. Additional nailing blocks are inserted between the rafters; the 1-x-6 nailer and the top plate of the partition wall are nailed to the blocks. Blocks provide support where frame cannot be entirely supported by a rafter.

165

Finishing attics

Partitions and knee walls (continued)

7. A 2 x 4 is nailed to 1 x 6 installed in Step 6, page 165, making the top plate for the partition wall and recesses for nailing sloping plasterboard ceiling panels at junctions with partition.

8. Partition's double top plate is secured to a nailing block under peak of roof next to chimney. A stud extends all the way up to nailing block. Note that old chimney departs from true vertical.

9. Spacing of studs is initially marked on sole plate. Before this very long stud is installed, it is aligned vertically using a carpenter's level, measured, and marked for bevel-cutting against the top plate.

10. For this shorter stud the level alone is long enough to mark a true vertical position on the top plate; afterwards, the distance from the sole plate to this mark is measured and the stud bevel-cut and installed.

11. The last stud before the double corner stud is toe nailed into place. This view, corresponding to that of the large drawing on the previous page, gives a clear picture of the knee wall and partition intersection.

12. Because the framing elements for the doorway—studs and jack studs —are slightly bowed, a helper pulls them into alignment while a header is nailed into place; header (above doorway) is then doubled.

Ceilings and ventilation

A full ceiling is not essential in a finished attic. For aesthetic reasons, you may prefer to leave part or all of the space overhead more or less as you found it. Simply putting insulation between the rafters, providing ridge vents to control humidity under the insulation, and plasterboarding over the insulation will preserve the roof lines.

Many homeowners find, however, that the addition of a ceiling makes the renovated space more congenial—particularly if its function is to be a family room or a bedroom. If you plan to partition off rooms within the attic, these rooms will certainly be more finished and offer more privacy if a ceiling is installed. The volume above the ceiling can then be insulated and given gable vents (if none are present), offering better control of interior temperatures, humidity, and condensation than insulation against the roof.

If you intend to put up a ceiling, do so before building partitions.

Collar ties: Most attics, particularly those with high peaks, are constructed with crossmembers fastened between opposing rafters. The function of these so-called collar ties (or collar beams) is to add strength to the roof, primarily by preventing the rafters from collapsing at the peak under their own weight (or placing extreme outward thrust on the walls supporting them). The collar ties can often serve as the joists for your new ceiling (see also, *Adding dormers*, pp.284–291). Add enough new collar tie/ceiling joists between opposing rafters at the proper spacing to nail plasterboard ceiling panels and accept insulation; generally, the new tie/joists should be spaced either 16 or 24 inches on center (o.c.).

Building codes often specify that the bottom of ceiling joists shall be a minimum of 7½ feet above the floor. Such requirements will determine the minimum height of the collar tie/ceiling joists you install. If your local code is not specific, the level of the existing collar ties customarily determines the distance from floor to ceiling.

You may have to raise the height of existing collar ties in a small attic with very little headroom. Similarly, you may want to raise the ties if you prefer the cathedral effect of vertical knee walls, sloping side walls inclined at the angles of the existing rafters, and a high, central ceiling. Since collar ties are major structural parts of a house, do not remove or raise them without guidance from an architect or builder.

Lightweight acoustical tiles or panels may be preferred for ceilings because of their sound-absorbing properties. A suspended ceiling (pp.96–97) may be the best solution. In any case, you will need a supporting framework like the type described. Since the specific design of the ceiling framing may be dictated by the ceiling material you choose, consult with your building supply dealer at the outset.

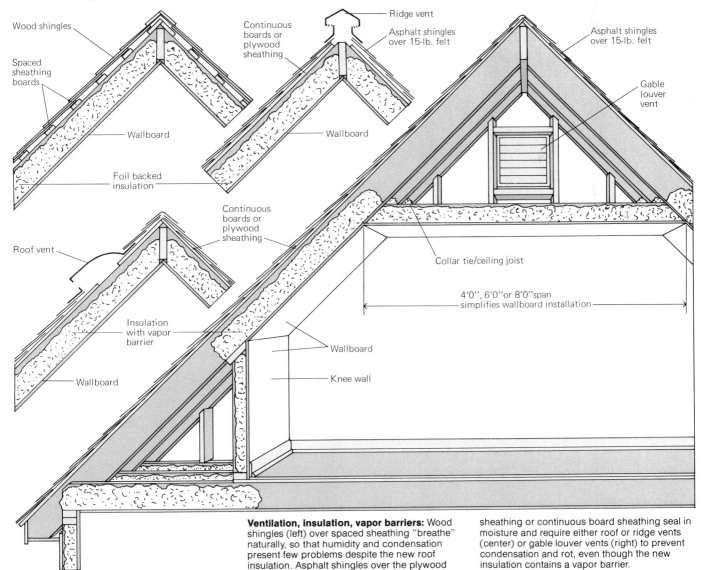

Ventilation, insulation, vapor barriers: Wood shingles (left) over spaced sheathing "breathe" naturally, so that humidity and condensation present few problems despite the new roof insulation. Asphalt shingles over the plywood sheathing or continuous board sheathing seal in moisture and require either roof or ridge vents (center) or gable louver vents (right) to prevent condensation and rot, even though the new insulation contains a vapor barrier.

167

Finishing attics

Shims, nailers, and insulation

Electrical and plumbing service should be roughed in, although not necessarily connected to power and water supplies, before insulation and wallboard are installed. You need not wait for the plumber or electrician to begin installing nailers—also called furring or shims.

Both insulating materials and finishing products such as gypsum wallboard are supplied in modular sizes that are multiples of 1 foot and/or 16 inches—24 inches, 48 inches, 96 inches, and so on. If your attic is constructed with regular surfaces and has even spacing between the rafters, you need only make sure that there are enough existing structural elements to allow you to staple the insulation and securely nail the finishing material—for example 48-x-96-inch gypsum wallboard panels. Chances are, you will find that you have to put in nailers to raise the depth of shallow rafters and to standardize the distance between the rafters. Your aim is to make the rafters uniform so they will accept

the insulation and wallboard as they are sold by the manufacturer.

Protruding rafters will have to be cut back with a jack plane or power saw. A tape measure will disclose rafters that are irregularly spaced. And a long straightedge—a long carpenter's level is excellent for this work—will indicate rafters that are too high or too shallow.

Scrap lumber is generally suitable for nailers. Nailers need not be as large as the rafters, provided the rafters are structurally sound. If a rafter is unsound, simply nail a trimmer rafter of the same dimensions to it.

While you are installing nailers check carefully for leaks or cracks in the roofing. Defects should be corrected before installing the insulation. (Roofing is discussed in several chapters of this book, including *Building codes*, pp.21–37; *Adding a wing*, pp.241–275; and *Restoring an old house*, pp.337–342.)

Types of insulation: Insulation for attic floors is generally sold in batts;

these are rigid sheets and rely on a friction fit between floor joists to remain in place. Insulation for use between rafters is generally supplied in rolls of up to 100 feet in 16 or 24 inch widths. At the edges of the roll you will find thin stapling flanges, which may have targets to indicate where the staples should be placed—generally at 6-inch intervals.

Install the thickest insulation possible, but be sure that the depth of the blanket does not interfere with the free passage of air behind it. An air space of 1 to 2 inches should be left between the blanket and the roof. Select a product containing a vapor barrier; this prevents moisture from inside the house from penetrating the insulation, condensing when it cools, and wetting it and the rafters and roof sheathing. Obviously, wet wood is subject to rotting if the condition lasts for a long time.

Installing insulation is covered in more detail on pages 359–361.

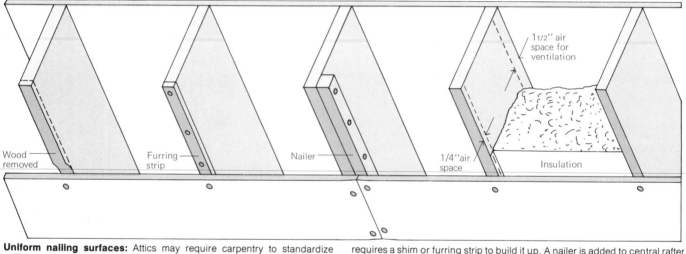

Uniform nailing surfaces: Attics may require carpentry to standardize nailing surfaces for insulation and wallboard. Oversized rafter at far left is planed to depth of other rafters, while the undersize rafter next to it requires a shim or furring strip to build it up. A nailer is added to central rafter to enlarge surface for nailing wallboard. Insulation must have air space behind it for ventilation.

A long carpenter's level is used to check shims and nailers installed to provide recesses for insulation and nailing surfaces for wallboard.

Following check with carpenter's level, a rafter shim is planed back to the depth of the nailers attached to the adjoining rafter.

An electric staple gun is employed to attach insulation blanket paper; flanges with targets for staples are fastened inside rafters.

Installing wallboard

Renovations that seek to preserve sloping attic ceiling lines may present special problems in fitting wallboard. (The application of gypsum wallboard in conventional rooms is covered by the chapter headed *Working with plasterboard*, pp.87–91). The most challenging task will be fitting panels neatly at gable ends and on partitions that follow the slope of the roof.

You can make a cardboard template, or pattern, to act as a cutting guide for these angled cuts. One simple way to do this is illustrated at right. A sheet of cardboard is held against the bottom of a rafter—or temporarily tacked to the rafter—so that it protrudes a few feet down from the ceiling at exactly the same angle as the rafter. Using a level, align a second, larger cardboard panel vertically next to the first piece and trace the rafter angle onto it. Cut the panel along this line, discarding the lower part and using the top part as your template.

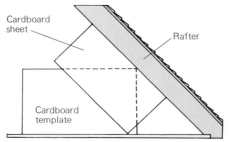
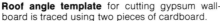

Roof angle template for cutting gypsum wallboard is traced using two pieces of cardboard.

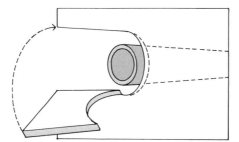

When cutting wallboard to fit around a pipe, leave a hinge of uncut paper on the exterior.

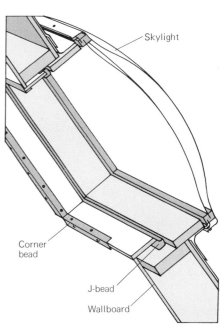

Metal corner bead and J-bead are used to finish wallboard ends and corners at a skylight.

A wallboard panel is installed across the bottom half of the skylight and then cut out with hand saws; a key hole saw is used to turn the corners. The top half of the skylight is handled the same way.

A strip of corner bead is marked for cutting along the side of the skylight. The beads are nailed in place after they are cut to size. The beads will be finished with joint compound before painting walls.

A second angle-cut gypsum wallboard panel slides into place. It is cut using a cardboard template (illustrated, above), positioned so that low side of cut falls at height of adjacent wallboard panel.

A taped wallboard seam in an attic gable is finished with joint compound. Worker uses knife in each hand, one to hold a supply of compound and to clean the blade of the application knife.

Demolition

Dismantling and salvage

Whether you are removing an entire wall or dismantling a piece of antique trim for re-use, you should work carefully and methodically.

General precautions: When demolishing plaster, wallboard, or masonry, work that creates clouds of fine dust, wear a dust mask and protective goggles. Depending on the nature of the debris, wear a cap to shield your hair or a hard-hat to protect your skull. Wear heavy gloves when handling glass or lumber filled with sharp nails. Open all windows to provide ventilation. Protect floors and furniture with drop cloths.

Walls: If you plan to remove a load-bearing wall, refer to pages 76-85. Plaster and stucco surfaces and wood lath backings are stripped as illustrated on this page. Metal lath is more difficult to remove; shears may be useful; wear heavy gloves. Check to determine whether plumbing, heating, or electrical installations are inside a wall before tearing it down. Sometimes the difficulty of rerouting such systems may argue against demolition of a wall.

Old wallpaper can be removed from plaster by slitting the paper, soaking it with a wet sponge, and scraping it off. But a rented electric wallpaper steamer makes stripping much easier. Vinyl is stripped by simply pulling it away, starting at a corner.

Floors: When linoleum is ripped up, a residue of adhesive invariably remains on the floor. Old-style linoleum paste can usually be sponged off, after first soaking it with hot water containing detergent or trisodium phosphate. Most modern adhesives for vinyl floor-covering are not water soluble; they must be scraped off, after softening with a heat lamp, hot-air gun, or wallpaper steamer. Some adhesives can be scraped away after softening with a paint remover. Wall-to-wall carpeting is removed by rolling it up and cutting it on the back side in sections with a utility knife.

Windows: First dismantle window trim around the frames, then slide out the sashes. Most molding trim is too cheap and fragile to save. (If the moldings are valuable, see next paragraph.)

Woodwork: Wood trim can be removed with a thin-bladed pry bar. If such firmly installed woodwork as wainscoting is to be removed for re-use, protect the woodwork and the wall behind it by gingerly inserting first one, then a second, putty knife between them; then lightly tap a screwdriver or cold chisel between the knives to pry away the woodwork slightly. Use a key-hole saw to cut any nails within reach, then pry off the woodwork completely.

Wood shingles: To remove a single wood shingle for replacement, first split the damaged shingle into strips with a wood chisel and hammer. Remove the strips. Next, pull off the nails, which are hidden under the butts of upper shingles, using a slate-puller (a roofer's tool). Or you can saw off the nail heads by inserting a long hacksaw blade under the shingle butts.

Siding: To take out a rotted or damaged section of clapboard siding, tap wedges under the edge of the section, then cut the section away with a hacksaw. To remove a whole piece of clapboard, tap a broad putty knife into the joint below the board to shield the lower board, then insert a crowbar from below and pry up the board a ½ inch. Tap the board back to reveal nails in the lower edge. Remove the nails. Repeat the process along the entire lower edge until the entire length of clapboard is freed.

Asphalt roof shingles: Insert a spade under a tile from below until it catches the roofing nails in the top edge; pry up the nails. Work course by course from the roof ridge downward.

Glass: To remove a broken window pane, glue two pieces of manila paper to both sides of the glass with rubber cement, and tap around the edges of the glass with a hammer. Soften putty with muriatic acid or paint remover.

Electrical wiring: Switch off the electricity to the circuit at the circuit breaker or fuse box (see p.183). Switch outlet and junction boxes can be re-used after dismantling (pp.184-195). Old cables should be discarded. If you intend to re-wire the same circuit with new wire, tie the ends of the new and old cables together tightly with metal wire before you pull out the length of old cable. As you pull out the cable, its replacement cable will snake into place. The technique is used for individual pieces of cable—between outlets and switches in the circuit, and between the main distribution panel and the first outlet box on the circuit.

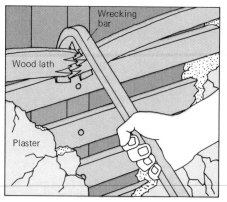

Plaster wall: First, break up plaster with crowbar or hammer. Then with a bar pull off exposed wood laths. Remove studs and plates last (p.82), using ceiling supports at a bearing wall.

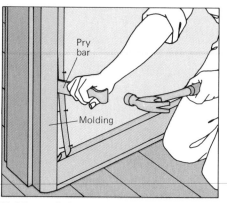

Molding and trim are removed by inserting a thin pry bar into joints, and prying strips gently. Use a pair of pliers to remove any finishing nails that may remain on the frame.

Dismantled roofing is thrown directly into a small rented truck. Heavy debris from interior demolition, such as bricks and plaster, can be dumped into the truck via a chute. Typically a chute has a sturdy frame of 2-x-4 side rails along its entire length, with 2-x-4 ribs between rails every 2 to 3 ft. under the skin. Sturdy ¾ in. plywood makes the best skin. Make the chute 1½ ft. wide with sides at least 6 in. high. The upper end of the chute is firmly hooked to the window ledge using 2 x 4s. The mid-section of a long chute should be supported by scaffolding. In urban areas the use of a chute may require a permit.

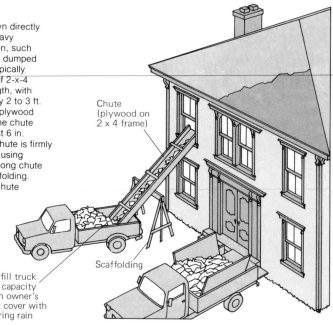

Chute (plywood on 2 x 4 frame)

Scaffolding

Do not fill truck beyond capacity stated in owner's manual; cover with tarp during rain

Electrical and plumbing systems

WARNING

Electrical voltages can shock, burn, or cause death.

Turn off power before working on any electrical circuit or component.

The electrical and plumbing systems of a house are known technically as its mechanical systems. In the past, few home-owners were willing to take on the demanding jobs of extend-ing or altering these systems. Today, given the rising cost of professional help, more people are doing such jobs themselves, if the jobs are manageable. The ensuing pages identify those tasks that usually must, by law, be done by licensed tradesmen. Even if you decide not to do any work yourself, you can use this section in both planning renovations and presenting your specifications to the professionals.

contents

How power reaches your home

High voltage, a-c transmission

The current that flows through the electrical wiring of your house, causing light bulbs to glow and the motors of appliances to turn, is made up of charged particles called electrons.

Electrons are the negatively charged parts of the tiny atoms that form all matter. Much smaller than the positively charged atomic nucleus, or center of the atom, they are in constant vibration around the nucleus. In metals and alloys that are good conductors of electricity, certain electrons surrounding the nucleus are only loosely bound to the atom; many are so lightly attached as to be called "free electrons." A short piece of narrow copper wire contains billions of such free electrons. When these electrons are subjected to the forces of changing magnetic fields—as happens in the turbines of power plants—they are set in motion. Traveling through the power company's transmission and distribution lines, these electrons form the electrical current that enters your house.

As electrons stream through power company lines and your house wiring they collide with one another and also with the atoms in the metal structure of the wire. The heat generated by these collisions is known as the heat of resistance. The larger the wire's diameter the easier it is for the electrons to pass. The resistance of an ordinary conductor is inversely proportional to its cross-section. Thus, currents of strong electron flow require thicker, or heavier gauge wire than weak currents, lest the heat of resistance destroy the conductor and cause fire.

Alternating current: The power supplied to most residences is alternating current. Alternating current flows first in one direction and then back in the opposite direction in phase with the mechanical rotation of a turbine generator's armature in a magnetic field; roughly speaking, the electrons are first forced in one direction by the magnetic north pole, and then drawn again back by the magnet's south pole as the armature turns. In the U.S., the standard frequency for alternating current is 60 such cycles per second. Direct current—as from an automobile battery—flows in one direction only; it does not oscillate. But a-c generation and transmission is generally cheaper than d-c because it makes use of the actual reciprocating current from the turbine, transmitting an oscillating current without any intervening conversion equipment. Although the transmission losses for d-c current are lower than for a-c, a line would have to be several hundred miles long before this economy offset the cost of reactive power supplies, converters,

and other controls required to convert a turbine's a-c to d-c.

Three-phase transmission: A single-phase a-c transmission line would consist of two conductors—one hot wire, bearing live current, and one neutral wire at nominal zero voltage. The addition of a third conductor makes possible three-phase transmission—that is, the transmission of three currents virtually simultaneously. The voltages and currents in the wires are one-third cycle (120°) out of step, and the result is a system capable of carrying as much power as three individual single-phase lines containing six wires. This system, the basis of modern a-c transmission, has the additional advantage of operating more smoothly than if the flow of electrons pulsated every 1/60th of a second as in single-phase transmission. The neutral conductor, where ideally no voltage should be present, is grounded, so that any current in it flows to earth.

Lines and cables: The most efficient transmission of power is achieved at high voltages; thus, at high voltages transmission lines can be thinner, less weighty, and less costly.

Aluminum is now widely used as the principal conductor in power transmission lines. For 380,000-volt lines, cables are more than 1.5 inches in diameter; they are made up of more than 50 aluminum wires around a core of about 20 steel wires. The heat of resistance is dissipated into the air around the lines. At even higher voltages—new lines exceeding 700,000 volts are becoming commonplace—smaller diameter cables, typically three, are strung parallel

to one another in a special triangular configuration called a "bundle." Bundling minimizes both heating from resistance and "corona"—the ionizing of the air around the cables, producing a hissing sound, and radio frequency radiation and interference. Relays and circuit breakers protect the power distribution system from short circuits, lightning, and other accidents by automatically disconnecting the affected line or lines from the system as a whole.

Substations and transformers: Power is delivered to residences at approximately 120 volts. Therefore very high long-line transmission voltages—hundreds of thousands of volts—must be greatly reduced before power is delivered to your home. This is done by the power company's substation transformers that step down voltage as they distribute electricity over several subtransmission circuits before it is then stepped down one final time in your neighborhood, usually by a transformer mounted on a pole, for distribution to individual customers.

Most houses built before World War II initially had only two-wire—one hot wire and one neutral—120-volt service. To accommodate such modern heating appliances as water heaters, dryers, and electric ranges, many older houses have been refitted for three-wire, 240-volt service—two 120-volt hot wires and one neutral wire. All houses built recently carry such 240-volt service.

Voltage spread: The voltage delivered by utilities varies with customer demand over the course of the day, the year, and according to the patterns of

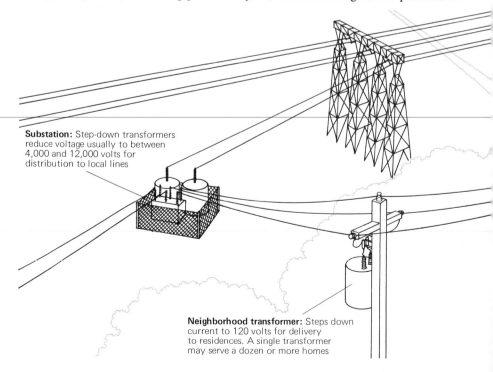

Substation: Step-down transformers reduce voltage usually to between 4,000 and 12,000 volts for distribution to local lines

Neighborhood transformer: Steps down current to 120 volts for delivery to residences. A single transformer may serve a dozen or more homes

the region. In general, voltage is highest at a residence in the off-peak hours—around midnight—and lowest during peak loads. Because the satisfactory performance of many modern appliances and machines cannot be maintained on widely fluctuating voltages, the voltage spread at the customer's premises is often controlled by government regulations; it usually must not exceed between 5 and 10 percent of standard voltage. (Remember, in an a-c system, 120 volts or 240 volts are themselves only the nominal values of a voltage that is actually oscillating.)

With the growth in electrical demand, utilities may encounter temporary problems in upgrading service to given communities or neighborhoods. Adding service to your own home may in some cases have to await the power company's upgrading of transmission substations or the addition of new lines and local transformers.

Electrical terminology

Volt:	Unit for measuring the difference in potential between points on a circuit. Residential hot wires have a nominal potential of 120 volts, while the neutral wire, and the earth, have zero potential. The neutral wire forms the return circuit for current after it has done the work of operating an appliance, a lamp, or a motor, and, depleted by resistance, has dropped to zero potential. A short circuit occurs when some defect, such as broken insulation, permits direct contact between hot and neutral wires, causing a voltage and heating in the neutral wire.
Ampere:	Unit for measuring current, or the number of electrons flowing past a given point in a conductor in a given period of time; one ampere represents the flow of more than 6 billion billion electrons in one second.
Watt:	Unit for measuring power produced by a generator and consumed by an appliance, lamp, or electric motor. Watts are equal to volts multiplied by amperes. For example, a single 20-amp, 120-volt circuit ideally can provide up to 2,400 watts of power to operate lights and equipment in your home; a 60-watt light bulb would draw ½ ampere of current from this circuit (60 watts ÷ 120 volts = ½ amp). A 1,200-watt toaster would draw another 10 amperes. An electric range, using 4,000–8,000 watts, would require its own separate 240-volt 35-ampere line to accommodate the upper limit of demand.
Ohm:	Unit for measuring electrical resistance in a conductor, such as a wire or appliance. A wire's degree of resistance depends on what it is made of (aluminum is more resistant to the flow of electricity than copper); how long the wire is; and the thickness, or gauge, of the wire (the thicker the wire the less resistance it offers). Volts, ohms, and amperes are related by the equation: amperes = volts ÷ ohms; thus a hot plate's 12-ohm heating element will draw 10 amperes of current from a 120-volt circuit.
Kilowatt hour:	Unit for measuring amounts of energy consumed; a 100-watt light bulb burning for 10 hours uses one kilowatt hour of energy.

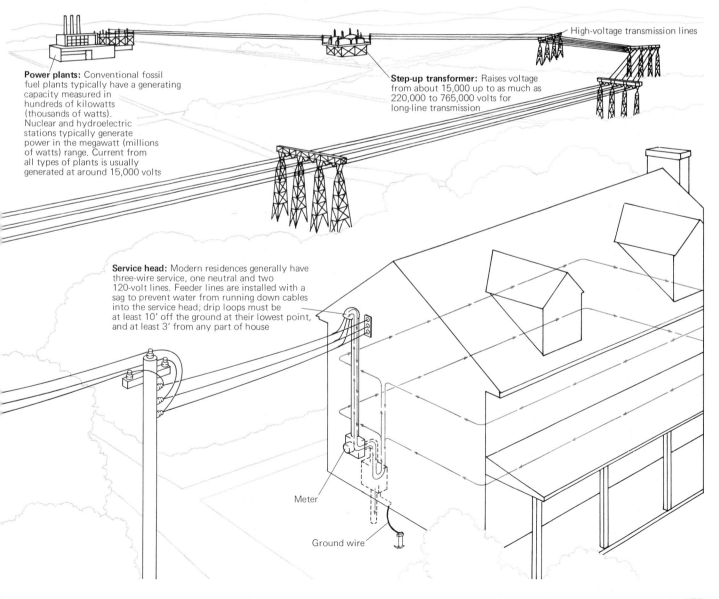

Power plants: Conventional fossil fuel plants typically have a generating capacity measured in hundreds of kilowatts (thousands of watts). Nuclear and hydroelectric stations typically generate power in the megawatt (millions of watts) range. Current from all types of plants is usually generated at around 15,000 volts

High-voltage transmission lines

Step-up transformer: Raises voltage from about 15,000 up to as much as 220,000 to 765,000 volts for long-line transmission

Service head: Modern residences generally have three-wire service, one neutral and two 120-volt lines. Feeder lines are installed with a sag to prevent water from running down cables into the service head; drip loops must be at least 10' off the ground at their lowest point, and at least 3' from any part of house

Meter

Ground wire

Distribution of electricity in your home

The distribution panel

After passing through the electric meter installed outside your house (pp.174-175), electric current enters the distribution panel. This panel is also called the circuit breaker box or fuse box. The panel has two major functions: to act as the terminal from which branch circuits that run throughout your house begin and end; to prevent the flow of a dangerously high current through your house wiring.

The electric current coming from the power company to your distribution panel is at very high amperage. If it were allowed to pass directly through the wires of your home enough heat would be generated to cause fire. With the exception of special 240-volt lines for such appliances as water heaters, dryers, and electric ranges, most house wiring is designed to handle no more than 15 or 20 amps. Too many appliances running on a single circuit can draw more amperage than is safe for that circuit. This uncontrolled amperage would quickly burn out the wire, as would a short circuit—for example, a live wire accidentally coming in touch with a neutral wire.

Fuse and breaker ratings: In a fuse-protected system, the electric current from each circuit passes through a thin, heat-sensitive strip of metal in the fuse before it enters the circuit. If the circuit wires controlled by the fuse are designed to carry no more than 20 amps, a 20-amp fuse is used. If more than 20 amps flows through the metal strip in the fuse, the heat build-up melts and breaks the strip instantly, and electricity cannot continue through the circuit.

Breakers work on a principle similar to thermostats. When amperage increases beyond a safe level, the added heat causes a metal strip to expand, permitting a spring to break the electrical connection to the circuit.

The illustrations on these pages show a typical distribution panel. (Panels made by different manufacturers vary considerably in design.) The illustration on the opposite page shows the panel as it appears with breakers and wiring attached, while the drawing on this page reveals the underlying configuration of bus bars, insulators, and other parts normally hidden from view.

Electric baseboard heat, water heaters, clothes dryers, electric ranges, oil furnaces, and other equipment drawing heavy voltages and amperes often have separate lines connected to independent subpanels.

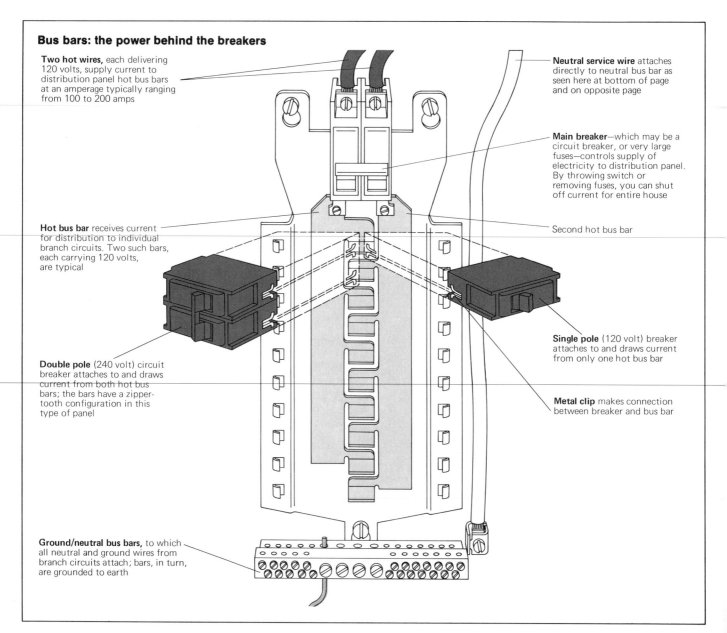

Bus bars: the power behind the breakers

Two hot wires, each delivering 120 volts, supply current to distribution panel hot bus bars at an amperage typically ranging from 100 to 200 amps

Neutral service wire attaches directly to neutral bus bar as seen here at bottom of page and on opposite page

Main breaker—which may be a circuit breaker, or very large fuses—controls supply of electricity to distribution panel. By throwing switch or removing fuses, you can shut off current for entire house

Hot bus bar receives current for distribution to individual branch circuits. Two such bars, each carrying 120 volts, are typical

Second hot bus bar

Double pole (240 volt) circuit breaker attaches to and draws current from both hot bus bars; the bars have a zipper-tooth configuration in this type of panel

Single pole (120 volt) breaker attaches to and draws current from only one hot bus bar

Metal clip makes connection between breaker and bus bar

Ground/neutral bus bars, to which all neutral and ground wires from branch circuits attach; bars, in turn, are grounded to earth

Panel with breakers and branch circuits intact

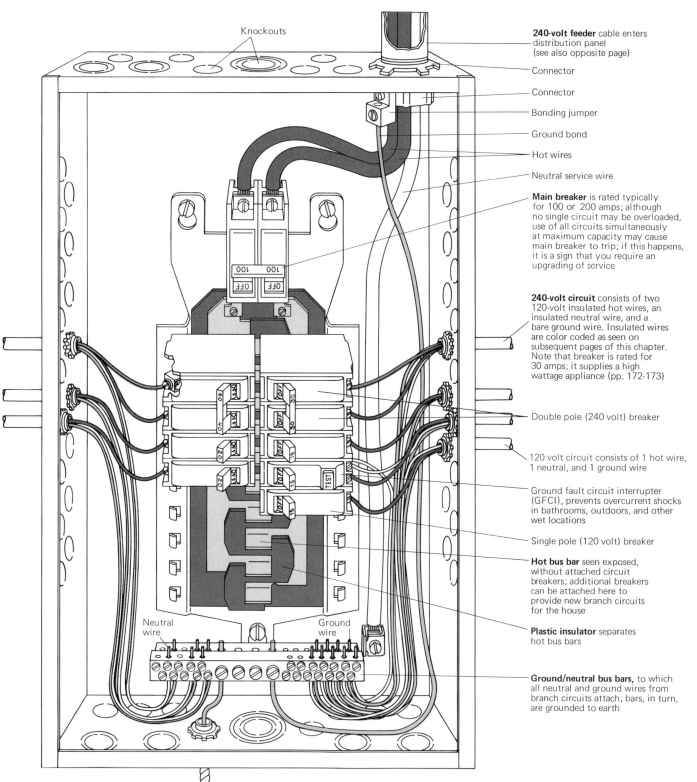

Knockouts

240-volt feeder cable enters distribution panel (see also opposite page)

Connector

Connector

Bonding jumper

Ground bond

Hot wires

Neutral service wire

Main breaker is rated typically for 100 or 200 amps; although no single circuit may be overloaded, use of all circuits simultaneously at maximum capacity may cause main breaker to trip; if this happens, it is a sign that you require an upgrading of service

240-volt circuit consists of two 120-volt insulated hot wires, an insulated neutral wire, and a bare ground wire. Insulated wires are color coded as seen on subsequent pages of this chapter. Note that breaker is rated for 30 amps; it supplies a high wattage appliance (pp. 172-173)

Double pole (240 volt) breaker

120 volt circuit consists of 1 hot wire, 1 neutral, and 1 ground wire

Ground fault circuit interrupter (GFCI), prevents overcurrent shocks in bathrooms, outdoors, and other wet locations

Single pole (120 volt) breaker

Hot bus bar seen exposed, without attached circuit breakers; additional breakers can be attached here to provide new branch circuits for the house

Plastic insulator separates hot bus bars

Ground/neutral bus bars, to which all neutral and ground wires from branch circuits attach; bars, in turn, are grounded to earth

Neutral wire

Ground wire

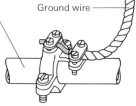

Metal water pipe   Ground wire

In properly wired homes, a ground wire is attached to every receptacle switch and junction box. Many appliance plugs have a third prong for grounding. If a fault occurs that would cause sparks, overheating, or the flow of current through an unintended conductor, the current will instead follow the path of least resistance—the ground wire. The ground wire is the bare copper wire in the circuits in your home. Ground wires terminate at the distribution panel; they are fastened to a special bolt that also grounds the panel itself. Usually the connection is made at one end of the neutral bus bar. From there, the electrical system is grounded either to the water pipes in the basement or to a copper rod driven into the earth outside the house as close as possible to the meter. The ground wire is securely fastened to it. (Many codes require grounding to a copper rod even if the system is grounded to a water main.)

Assessing your power

Circuit mapping and load ratings

Before you begin any wiring project, you should have a good idea of the electrical capacity of your home. The first step is to make a map of all the circuits in the house. If the structure is very small or old, there may be just a few. Newer homes will have many. You can produce a permanently useful circuit map by following the instructions on the opposite page.

The wattage/amperage chart: The chart below, when used with a complete circuit map can be an extremely useful and money-saving tool. It can show which circuits have a reserve of capacity so that you can safely add outlets and perhaps extend a branch circuit without running wires all the way to the distribution panel. Together, the chart and a circuit map of your house can help identify circuits that are dangerously overused, thus allowing you to move portable appliances elsewhere.

Your calculations will be approximate, and for your own personal use. First, estimate the amperage drawn through general circuits used for lighting and convenience receptacles. You may want to add every bulb, radio, and electric clock to reach this figure, or you may wish only to approximate it by multiplying 3 watts by every square foot of floor space served by the circuit. In practice, a typical room will use from 5 to 7 amps in general circuits—not in-

cluding electrical devices, such as phonographs, electric blankets, toasters, television sets, or other appliances. The amperage of these appliances must be added to the total for the circuit.

How to use the chart: Wattage is the measure of the total amount of electrical power in use, both the volts and the amperes. It is found by multiplying volts times amperes. For example, an air conditioner using 11 amps and 120 volts would have a rating of about 1,320 watts. In most cases, you won't need to determine the wattage rating, for it will be listed on the appliance nameplate. You will use that wattage rating in determining the amperage load upon the circuit containing the appliance.

The only way you can know for sure if you are overtaxing a circuit is to calculate the number of amps you are drawing through it. To find the amps for appliances not listed on the chart, simply divide the watts by the voltage of the circuit. In the above example, the appliance is on a 120-volt circuit; in consuming 1,320 watts of power, therefore, the appliance draws 11 amps.

The chart lists the amp rating for many appliances, but you may own some that are not listed. The amp rating may be given on the appliance nameplate; if not, you can calculate the amperage load from the wattage listing by the method employed in the above ex-

ample. Appliances may differ widely from one brand to another in their energy efficiency; thus you should check manufacturer's nameplates and, where wattage listings differ from those given in the chart, calculate yourself.

Risk of overload: When adding up the entire potential load for an individual circuit, you may find that it is higher than the rating of the fuse or circuit breaker protecting the circuit. In actuality, one rarely uses all the appliances on a circuit at any given time; thus you may want to modify your load calculations by counting only those appliances on a circuit that you can conceive of ever using at the same time. That will give you an idea of the probable peak amperage. Compare that with the circuit's fuse or breaker rating and you will have an idea of your risk of an overload.

Main breaker rating: Particularly in older houses that have been given new branch circuits for modern ranges, clothes dryers, etc., it is possible to overload a main breaker although the individual circuits themselves may not be overtaxed. To determine whether your service panel has the capacity to meet your total needs, add together the likely amperage demands on all the circuits in your home at a moment of maximum electrical use; include electric heat (or air conditioning, whichever has higher amperage—but not both,

Appliances: wattage and amperage ratings

Appliance		Watts number	Amperes* (120 volts)	Amperes* (240 volts)
Air conditioner (central)		5000	—	21
	(room size, small)	800	6.5	—
	(room size, medium)	1300	11	5.5
	(room size, large)	1600	13.5	6.5
Blender		Up to 1000	1–8	—
Broiler		1500	12.5	—
Can opener		150	1.2	—
Coffee maker		500–1000	4–8	—
Dishwasher		1000–1500	8.5–12.5	—
Dryer		4000–8000	—	16.5–34
Electric blanket		200	1.5	—
Fan (permanent-installation)		400	3.5	—
	(portable)	250	2	—
Freezer (frost-free)		350–500	3–4	—
	(standard)	250–400	2–3.5	—
Frying pan (electric)		1100	9	—
Furnace (oil) fan and controls		750–1600	6.5–13.5	—
Garbage disposal		400–900	3.5–7.5	—
Hair dryer		350–1400	3–11.5	—
Heat, permanent installation (medium density)		250 per linear ft.	—	1 per linear ft.
Heater, portable electric		1250 and up	10 and up	—
Heat lamp		250	2	—
Hotplate (each burner)		750	6	—

Appliance		Watts number	Amperes* (120 volts)	Amperes* (240 volts)
Iron		1050	9	—
Microwave oven		600	5	—
Mixer		150	1	—
Range (oven)		4000–8000	—	16.5–34
	(top)	4000–5000	—	16.5–21
Refrigerator (frost-free)		300–450	2.5–4	—
	(standard)	250–350	2–3	—
Rotisserie		1400	11.5	—
Sander (hand-held)		750	6	—
Saw (bench)		1300–1600	11–13.5	—
Sewing machine		100	1	—
Space heater		1250	10.5	—
Stereo phonograph		300	2.5	—
Sump pump		300	2.5	—
Sun lamp		400	3.5	—
Television (black and white)		250	2	—
	(color)	300	2.5	—
Toaster		1100	9	—
Vacuum cleaner		720–1300	6–11	—
Waffle iron		900	7.5	—
Washing machine		1500	12.5	—
Water heater		2000–5000	—	8.5–21
Well pump		460	4	—

*More accurate amperage can be calculated by dividing the wattage rating on the appliance nameplate by the average effective voltage of 120 and 240 volt service in your community—110 or 115 or 210, 220 or 230 volts. Check with your power company.

since they will not be used simultaneously), washer, dryer, water heater, range, and all general house circuits. Compare that total with the amperage rating of the main breaker. Where a large deficit exists, talk to your local power company and with a local electrical code enforcement officer to learn how you can upgrade your service.

Circuit mapping: To map the branch circuits in your home:

1. Mark every circuit breaker or fuse in your service panel with a number. You can buy numbered adhesive labels in electrical supply stores.

2. Draw a floor plan of your home similar to the one shown. Draw a separate plan for each floor of the house.

3. Using symbols like those shown in the legend, add all switches, outlets, and light fixtures to your floor plan(s).

4. Add all 240-volt circuits for heavy

appliances. Each 240-volt circuit serves a single appliance, so you can easily compare the amperage rating of the appliance with the capacity of the breaker controlling the circuit. There should be a margin of safety; for example, a range requiring 25 amps should have 30- or even 40-amp wiring and breaker capacity.

5. List separately the amperage ratings of the 240-volt appliances (including electric heat or air conditioning, whichever is higher, not both). Add them together.

6. Trace the general circuits in your home. You can save time by turning on one ceiling fixture and one lamp in every room. Then trip a single breaker or disconnect a fuse. In a typical house, the lights in one or more rooms will go out, locating the circuit. A single breaker may control only the refrigera-

tor, dishwasher, garbage disposer—or one of the kitchen's 20-amp small appliance circuits. Check such possibilities if all lights remain on.

7. Once you locate the circuit controlled by the breaker, test each outlet and switch in that room. In some cases a single circuit serves more than one room—it may extend to hallways, closets, and even lights outside the house. A circuit might extend vertically, feeding floors on one side of the house. Label each receptacle switch and light fixture on your map with the number of the breaker controlling it.

8. Map every circuit. Your map may have a few unnumbered receptacles. Usually you can decide which circuits they must belong to.

Electrical symbols

	120-volt outlet		S	Switch
R	240-volt range outlet		○	Light fixture
D	240-volt dryer outlet		- - -	Circuit from light to controlling switch
W	240-volt hot-water heater		H	Permanent baseboard heat

Electrical wiring floor plan

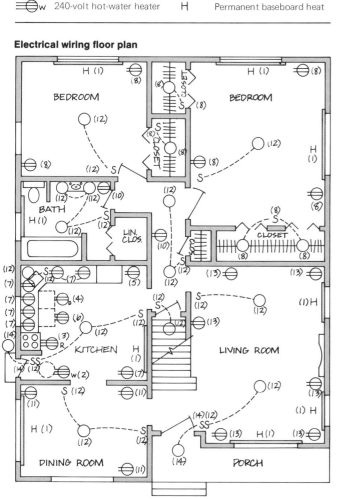

Identifying circuits: Numbered labels affixed to main service panel (right) identify numbered circuits on floor plan above.

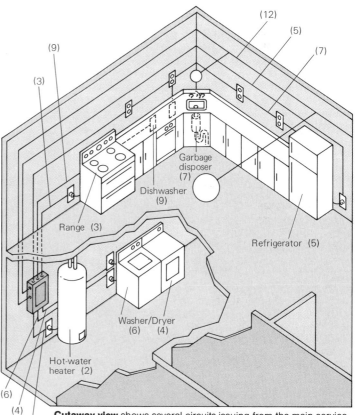

Cutaway view shows several circuits issuing from the main service panel in basement. Note that major appliances—water heater, range, washer, and dryer—are on individual 240-volt lines.

Main service panel

MAIN			
Perm. baseboard heat	1	240	240	2	Hot-water heater
Kitchen range	3	240	240	4	Dryer
Refrigerator	5	120	120	6	Washer
Garbage disposer & small appliances	7	120	120	8	Bedroom & closets
Dishwasher	9	120	120	10	Bathroom & hall
Dining room	11	120	120	12	Interior perm. ceiling fixtures
Living room	13	120	120	14	Porch & outside lights

Increasing electrical capacity

Five causes of inadequate power in your home

By most expert estimates, a majority of houses, apartments, and other dwellings in the United States have inadequate electrical capacity. This is so primarily because of the increasing number of electricity-consuming devices commonly used in today's households, including such heating and cooling equipment as frost-free refrigerators, clothes dryers, electric ranges and ovens, air conditioners, and water heaters; such devices with powerful electric motors as oil furnaces, washing machines, dishwashers, refrigerator compressors, and power tools.

Few houses—even those built in recent decades—were initially planned to accommodate such unforeseen demands for power. The following paragraphs list the five common sources of inadequate residential power, and explain how you can upgrade capacity.

Limited service panel capacity: If the main fuse or circuit breaker in your main service panel fails frequently, chances are you are using more electricity than the panel is designed to provide. This is particularly likely if the main fuse or breaker is rated at 65 amps or less—or even 100 amps or more if you have two or more major heat-producing electrical appliances. The chart on page 176 will assist you in calculating your total amperage needs.

The size of your service panel might limit your capacity in another way. If it has no space left in which to insert additional fuses or circuit breakers on the bus bars (pp.174–175), you will not be able to add more branch circuits to your home. If the panel can handle the additional amperage requirements of the new circuits but is simply too small in size, the solution is relatively easy: you can add a subpanel on which the new circuits can be run. However, if the amperage rating of the old panel cannot accommodate the added demands of new circuits, you will need a licensed electrician to install a new main panel.

Overloaded circuits: By making a circuit map, as described on pages 176–177, you can determine whether your circuits are overtaxed. A circuit is overloaded if the maximum demand you can reasonably expect to place on it at any given time exceeds the amperage rating of the breaker or fuse controlling it. In actuality, the circuit might be overloaded even when the demand does not appear to exceed the breaker rating, because many appliances with electric motors require an initial surge of power to start them running. Unless the breakers or fuses are designed to tolerate that surge (time-delayed fuses or breakers), they will blow even if the amperage exceeds the rating for only an

Main service panel and types of circuit breakers

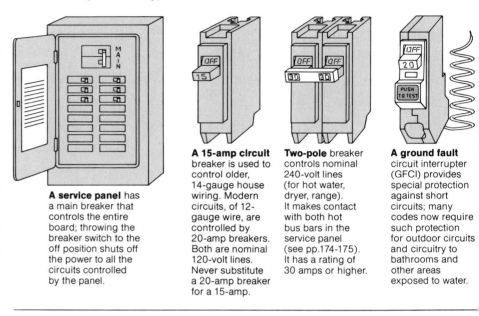

A service panel has a main breaker that controls the entire board; throwing the breaker switch to the off position shuts off the power to all the circuits controlled by the panel.

A 15-amp circuit breaker is used to control older, 14-gauge house wiring. Modern circuits, of 12-gauge wire, are controlled by 20-amp breakers. Both are nominal 120-volt lines. Never substitute a 20-amp breaker for a 15-amp.

Two-pole breaker controls nominal 240-volt lines (for hot water, dryer, range). It makes contact with both hot bus bars in the service panel (see pp.174-175). It has a rating of 30 amps or higher.

A ground fault circuit interrupter (GFCI) provides special protection against short circuits; many codes now require such protection for outdoor circuits and circuitry to bathrooms and other areas exposed to water.

instant. Allow a safety margin of a few amps between maximum demand on a circuit and the breaker or fuse rating.

Large users of current—oil furnace motors, ranges, dryers, and water heaters—should be wired in single-appliance circuits. If the surge of your furnace motor or refrigerator compressor causes lights to dim or the TV picture to shrink, either these appliances are overloading individual circuits, or the main panel requires upgrading.

If your circuits already approach or surpass their maximum safe amperage, you should not wire additional receptacles into them; nor should you simply replace the old fuses or breakers with new ones of a higher amperage rating. You must run new circuits from the panel, or you invite the risk of fire.

Insufficient number of outlets: The National Electric Code recommends at least one outlet for every 12 feet of wall space in a room. This means you should be able to stand against the wall of any room in your home and be no more than 6 feet away from an outlet.

There are two exceptions. Only one outlet is required in the bathroom; and, in the kitchen, you need one receptacle for every 4 feet of wall space. (Some local codes require a kitchen receptacle for each countertop.)

Common sense suggests that you should have more outlets if you find yourself using multi-outlet extension plugs and cords as a permanent means of bringing electricity to lamps, television sets, and other appliances. The typical extension cord is not designed to carry the heavy amperage demanded of permanent wiring. Excess loads will

overheat it, posing the risk of fire. In some cases, simply adding new receptacles to a circuit may solve the problem (see *Overloaded circuits*, this page).

Inadequate feeder lines: If your home was built before the mid-1940s, you may still have the original two-wire feeder system running from the power company's nearest utility pole to your house. One of the pair of wires in the cable is a 120-volt hot wire (effective voltage averaging about 110-115 volts in most communities) and the other is a neutral wire, as discussed previously.

Obviously, no major appliance requiring a 240-volt line can operate on this system. Your amperage may also be too low to power simultaneously more than a few of the 120-volt appliances found in the modern home. The electric company, at its own expense, may replace a two-wire system with a three-wire one, bringing two 120-volt lines to your house, if you request it. You will have to pay to install a new service panel to handle the added capacity.

Overtaxed transformer: In older, high-density neighborhoods the power company transformer serving the area may have been in place for many years. While the electrical demands of the neighborhood have increased, the transformer may not have been replaced with one of higher capacity. Your upgraded service could be the additional burden that causes the transformer to burn out.

The power company itself usually keeps a close watch on the capacity of its transformers and the demands being made on them. Still, if you live in a crowded neighborhood, ask the com-

Fuse box and types of fuses

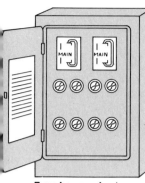

Fuse box service is controlled by pull-outs containing large fuse cartridges like those shown at far right. Power is cut off to the entire box by removing pull-outs.

A single-plug fuse controls each circuit connected to the fuse box. Fuses rated 15 and 20 amps control, respectively, nominal 120-volt 14-gauge and 12-gauge branch circuits. Ratings of 30 amps and higher are for nominal 240-volt circuits.

Time delay fuses are sold under several trade names. They are designed for special circuits serving powerful electric motors that draw a heavy surge of power briefly on starting up. The time-delay fuse will not blow because of this initial surge, even though it exceeds circuit's amp rating.

A type S (or non-tamperable fuse) is a time-delay fuse with a special adapter; the adapter is screwed into the fuse opening, and the Type S fuse is then screwed into its adapter. Only a fuse of the proper rating will fit the adapter, protecting the circuit against a sustained overload.

A screw-in breaker can be inserted into a fuse box, replacing the conventional plug screw; should the breaker trip, it is simply reset, whereas a blown fuse must be replaced with a new fuse.

15 to 60 amp.

60 to 600 amp.

Cartridge fuses, installed in pull-outs in fuse box, must conform to the rating of power company's feeder lines bringing service to your house.

---

pany to check into the matter before planning your new service.

Improper house wiring: A serious result of improper house wiring is the danger of fire. Even today when local ordinances and the National Electric Code establish standards for wiring, one out of eight home fires results from inadequate or improper wiring. The following pages give step-by-step guidance in properly and safely completing the most common rewiring jobs.

Tips and cautions for the do-it-yourselfer

The most important part of any job—planning—should be completed before you pick up a single tool. If you plan your work carefully—anticipating the problems you are likely to encounter and deciding on your solutions before you start—you will get the job done with fewer frustrations than if you plunge ahead and "take things as they come."

Plan for future needs: What new demands will you have to meet? Think the whole project through. Will one new circuit be enough, or do you require two? Will your present main service panel be adequate to handle another circuit or will you have to add a sub-panel? Will you have to replace old wires and also run new circuits?

Plan to install all the outlets, circuits, switches, and service capacity (see text, opposite page) you will need next year or the year after. If you can't make up your mind whether or not to put in an additional receptacle on a new circuit, go ahead and add it. It will cost only a few extra dollars, and you will have the outlet whether or not you ever use it. On the other hand, if you don't install the outlet and discover later that you need it, another expensive and time-consuming rewiring project lies before you.

Check local codes: Most likely your local electrical code stipulates certain regulations regarding the project you are planning; therefore, you should familiarize yourself with the code. Consult your inspector early on for safety's sake and to avoid having to tear out a project and re-do it because your inspector has decided that it does not meet the local standards.

Observe safety precautions: Properly done, electrical wiring projects are no more dangerous than using power tools or driving an automobile. Work only when rested and alert, and never when under the influence of alcohol; keep attentive, maintain a healthy respect for the forces you are controlling, and take every possible precaution.

Make sure the electric power is shut off before working on or near live wires. If working on a single circuit, identify the fuse or circuit breaker controlling that circuit (see pp.174–177) and disconnect the fuse or throw the breaker. If there is any possibility that the work involves more than one circuit, disconnect the main fuse or circuit breaker feeding the entire panel.

Work in a neat, orderly manner. Haste can produce slipshod work that could endanger your home and/or require days of painstaking labor to remedy. One example: A man spent a day and a half tracking down a break in a new circuit he had installed in his bedroom. The circuit had worked fine originally, but when he nailed the drywall to the studs, he jarred loose a poorly connected Wire Nut, causing the wires to separate. Every switch, outlet, and junction box had to be examined to locate the problem.

Use proper tools: In doing electrical wiring, there is no such thing as "good enough." There is a right way and a wrong way, and there are the correct tools and improper tools. While the home electrician need not buy the most expensive equipment, he should have the tools described on the next page.

Allow access to all connections: All codes require that you be able to reach wiring connections without tearing out the walls of the house. Access to switches and outlets is not difficult: with the circuit shut off at the main panel, you simply remove the face plate and pull out the receptacle or switch and examine its connections.

Junction boxes must be equally accessible. When located in walls, they should be covered by the removable metal plates designed for such boxes. Similar installations can be used in ceilings. Where ceilings are suspended and ceiling panels can be easily removed, junction boxes can be installed above them. Check your local code for recommendations regarding junction box accessibility. As a practical matter of convenience, you should make sure you can reach every junction box with minimal effort.

Electrical wiring tools and materials

Selecting the proper wire

The wiring that you will use in the circuitry of your home will be protected by a rubber or plastic insulating cable. The number of wires in the cable will vary from two to four, and the cable will vary in specifications, depending on the use to which you intend to put it. Some cables are water-resistant, others can withstand high temperatures.

When you buy wire, get exactly what you need. Buy moisture-resistant cable for damp basements and outdoor areas, heat-resistant cable if the wire is to be run near boilers, baseboard heaters, and such. Determine whether you will need two-wire (one hot, one neutral) or three-wire (two hot, one neutral) cable. (Don't be confused—a copper ground wire is included in most cables, but only the hot and neutral wires are counted.)

General circuits: If you are adding a new general circuit for lights, radios, and other low-wattage devices, you will probably want to use # 12 gauge wire, recommended by most codes today. The # 12 wire will handle 20 amps safely and can thus be protected by a 20-amp fuse or circuit breaker.

If you are extending an already existing circuit, however, and your house is not new, you will probably discover that the existing circuit is 14-gauge wire, once the universal standard and still permitted in some areas. A 14-gauge wire is too thin to withstand the heat generated by 20 amps, so it is always protected by no more than a 15-amp fuse or circuit breaker. Today, 12-gauge

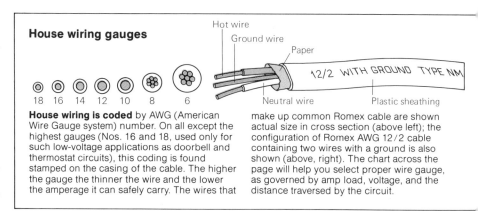

House wiring gauges

18 16 14 12 10 8 6

House wiring is coded by AWG (American Wire Gauge system) number. On all except the highest gauges (Nos. 16 and 18, used only for such low-voltage applications as doorbell and thermostat circuits), this coding is found stamped on the casing of the cable. The higher the gauge the thinner the wire and the lower the amperage it can safely carry. The wires that

12/2 WITH GROUND TYPE NM

make up common Romex cable are shown actual size in cross section (above left); the configuration of Romex AWG 12/2 cable containing two wires with a ground is also shown (above, right). The chart across the page will help you select proper wire gauge, as governed by amp load, voltage, and the distance traversed by the circuit.

wire is more widely available and often less expensive than 14-gauge. There is no danger of fire in extending a 14-gauge circuit by using 12-gauge wire as long as the rating of its circuit breaker or fuse is correct (see pp.181–182).

If you have questions concerning the gauge of wire to use for a particular project, check with your local code officer. Remember that any gauge too high—too thin—for its intended amperage is a fire hazard; never use a fuse or breaker of a higher amp rating than that of the gauge of the wire in the circuit (see chart titled *Determining wire gauge for nominal 120-volt circuits,* opposite page).

Small appliance circuits: The National Electric Code requires that small appliance circuits in the kitchen, dining room, pantry, breakfast room, and laundry use 12-gauge wire and 20-amp

fuses, since using merely a toaster and an egg poacher at the same time would overload 14-gauge, 15-amp wiring.

Single appliance circuits: The size wire needed for such high-wattage appliances as water heaters, washers and dryers, heavy duty workshop equipment, ranges, and oil burners varies according to the amount of electricity the appliance requires. Usually, major 120-volt appliances require # 10 wires; 240-volt equipment uses either # 8 or # 6. Check with your electrical supplier for the recommended wire gauge for 240-volt circuits.

Gauge, amps, distance: General circuits for lights, radios, etc., will usually be 120-volt, 20-amp, 12-gauge lines, as previously noted. In planning special 120-volt circuits, find the amperage or wattage on the nameplates of the equipment to be served by the new line

Aluminum wiring: the hazards

To save on costs, builders some years ago began using aluminum wiring, particularly in suburban tract house developments. Aluminum was then about half as expensive as copper. Today the price difference— perhaps $200 to $500 in the wiring of a single home—remains, but it is just about the only benefit proponents of aluminum wire can claim. Opponents point to a warning by the United States Consumer Product Safety Commission that many residential fires have been caused by aluminum wiring.

The heat of resistance causes aluminum wiring to loosen. And when aluminum is connected to the brass terminals on receptacles, switches, and fixtures, the contact between the two dissimilar metals causes a corrosive reaction. Additionally, wherever insulation is removed and the aluminum comes in contact with the air, it begins to oxidize. This corrosion and oxidation cause higher resistance, which can result in heat that causes fire.

Since aluminum is not as efficient a conductor as copper, it must be thicker to safely carry the same load. For example, it

would take a # 12 gauge aluminum wire to carry the same load as a # 14 gauge copper cable. Aluminum wire is also given to greater expansion and contraction under changing temperature conditions than copper, consequently, unless all connections are made very tightly, the wiring may pull loose as a result of the heat of resistance.

Special precautions: With specially designed switches and outlets and proper installation, aluminum can be used safely. After you strip the insulation, you must coat the bare wire with an oxide-inhibiting compound. Receptacles should be marked CO-ALR for 15- and 20-amp lines, which indicates they are designed to prevent the aluminum wires from corroding. (If you have aluminum wiring already installed in your house, use CO-ALR coded equipment for new work.)

A compromise alternative, copper-clad aluminum wire, is less expensive than pure copper wire and is less troublesome to install than aluminum. It is used where heavy wires must be run for significant distances, such as on ranches and farms.

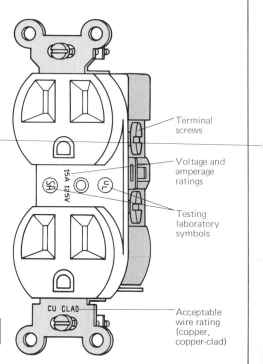

Terminal screws

Voltage and amperage ratings

Testing laboratory symbols

Acceptable wire rating (copper, copper-clad)

E7378   10/2   AL 3411 W/GND

Plastic sheathed aluminum wire

Determining wire gauge for copper wire circuits

Circuit wire gauge with maximum fuse or breaker rating	Maximum distance of circuit as determined by load in amps or watts					
	5 amps (575 watts)	10 amps (1150 watts)	15 amps (1725 watts)	20 amps (2300 watts)	25 amps (2875 watts)	35 amps (4025 watts)
#14 (15 amps)	90 feet	45 feet	30 feet			
#12 (20 amps)	140 feet	70 feet	45 feet	35 feet		
#10 (30 amps)	220 feet	110 feet	70 feet	55 feet	45 feet	
# 8 (40 amps)	360 feet	175 feet	120 feet	90 feet	70 feet	50 feet
# 6 (55 amps)	560 feet	280 feet	180 feet	140 feet	110 feet	80 feet

Wire characteristics

Type	Features	Use
NM		Indoor, dry
NMC		Indoor, damp; outdoor above ground
UF	Waterproof	Outdoor underground
RH	Heat resistant	General
RU		General
RW	Moisture-resistant	General, wet locations
RH-RW (RHW)	Moisture-and-heat-resistant	General and wet locations
T	Thermoplastic	General
TW	Moisture-resistant thermoplastic	General and wet locations
THW	Moisture-and-heat-resistant thermoplastic	General and wet locations
BX	Metal-sheathed	Where required by code

(see chart, p.176). Then, determine the required wiring for the circuit according to the table on this page titled *Determining wire gauge for nominal 120-volt circuits.*

Remember that the longer a circuit extends, the more voltage will be dissipated in overcoming the wire's resistance. When the circuit is excessively long, the voltage drop may be so great that an insufficient current reaches the appliances at the far end of the circuit. Appliances will run poorly or not at all and motors may be damaged. The solution: use a thicker, or lower gauge, wire for longer circuits, as seen in the table.

Characteristics of materials: Insulation on individual wires is color-coded. Black or red indicate the hot wires, white is usually neutral (although you cannot assume this in working with existing wiring). The copper ground wire is uninsulated because bare wire can more readily pick up and conduct any leak of electric current safely to the ground at the service panel.

The codes stamped or printed on cable disclose its characteristics. The first number is the number of wires in the cable not including the ground. For example, a cable labeled 12/2 with ground is a 12-gauge cable with two wires (one for hot, one for neutral) plus a bare ground wire. Other symbols used in wire coding are detailed in the chart at top right on this page.

How much wire to buy: A common mistake made by home electricians is to underestimate the amount of wire they will need in running new circuits. Here are some ways to avoid running short:
▷Add an extra 8 inches of wire for each box in the circuit, whether it is an outlet, switch, or junction box.

▷Be sure to calculate the additional wiring needed for routing above doors and windows and around other obstacles that might prevent taking the shortest route.
▷Remember to account for the distance from the service panel to the start of the circuit. This is part of the total length of the circuit (see p.181).
▷Add 20 percent extra footage to your wire estimate, because the cable will not follow as straight a route as your tape measure does.

Selecting your tools

All electrical tools should have insulated handles. *Linemen's pliers* perform a variety of jobs, including cutting cable, bending wire, and removing service panel knockouts; they are often used in combination with *long-nosed pliers* to manipulate wire. The *multipurpose tool* contains slots for measuring and cutting different gauges of wire; it is thus a more precise stripping tool than a penknife. The *utility knife* is excellent for cutting a cable's sheathing and separating its wires before stripping them of insulation. A *test light* provides a simple method of determining whether switches, outlets, and wires are live. A *fish tape* is used to run new wiring through existing walls, floors, and ceilings. Other tools and materials—including connectors and Wire Nuts—are shown on ensuing pages.

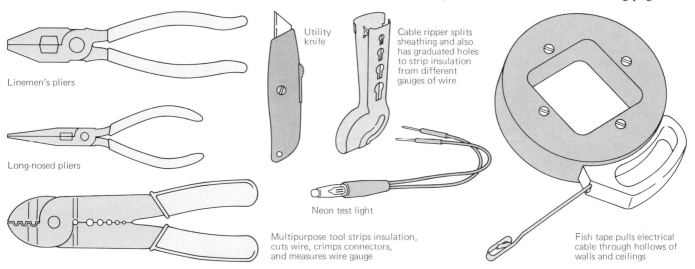

Linemen's pliers

Long-nosed pliers

Utility knife

Cable ripper splits sheathing and also has graduated holes to strip insulation from different gauges of wire

Neon test light

Multipurpose tool strips insulation, cuts wire, crimps connectors, and measures wire gauge

Fish tape pulls electrical cable through hollows of walls and ceilings

Working at the main distribution panel

Planning and preparation

The last step you will actually perform in wiring new branch circuits is connecting them at the main distribution panel, also called the main service panel. But all planning begins with the main panel: does it have the necessary capacity in amperes to service the additional circuits you plan, or must your service be upgraded to a higher amperage; if service is adequate, does the panel have the extra space for new breakers or fuses, or will you have to install a subpanel?

Another consideration is the location of the main panel. The distance a new branch circuit runs from the panel will affect the gauge of wire used (see chart, p.181, and the illustration on this page); thus you should map and measure your new circuits beforehand, determining the shortest and the most convenient routes the wires can follow from the main panel. Where new wiring is simply added as an extension to the end of an existing circuit, you may have to lower the fuse or breaker capacity for that circuit at the main panel to be sure the extra distance does not result in an overload (chart, p.181).

Because the main panel is the common denominator in any rewiring or new wiring job, the task of connecting circuits to it is covered on this and the next three pages; the techniques used in running new circuits make up most of the remainder of this chapter.

Safety precautions: After you have run your new branch circuits and connected their receptacles and switches, the final step is to hook up the circuits to the distribution panel. Until now, none of the new circuits will be live. Some locales will not permit you to do this yourself, but require that it be done by a licensed electrician. Check with your local electrical code officer.

If you are permitted to connect circuits at the main panel, you will find it is not a difficult job, but the work can be dangerous. Unless you have the power company pull the meter or shut off the electricity to your house—a procedure recommended if you are replacing the entire panel—the cables feeding your main panel will still be hot.

Always trip the main breaker or remove the main fuse box pull-out(s) before beginning work. This action cuts off the current to the hot bus bars, which feed all the branch circuits. But even after you cut off power to the distribution panel by tripping the main breaker or removing fuse box pull-outs, the feeder lines remain live; therefore, you must work carefully—particularly at fuse boxes, where the feeder line terminals may be exposed and subject to accidental contact.

Voltage test: To be certain there is no leakage current in the panel after you shut off the main supply, check it with an inexpensive neon voltage tester (see illustrations, opposite page). If the panel shows a voltage, check for another main breaker or pull-out and shut off the power there. Should the main panel continue to register a charge, call in a professional electrician. Proceed no further at the main panel yourself; to do so poses the risk of serious shock.

Continuity test: Before connecting a branch circuit's hot wire you can check for breaks or shorts in the new wiring by using a continuity tester. It is powered by batteries and contains a buzzer or bell (more expensive models may have meters). With the main breaker tripped, one of the tester's two wires is

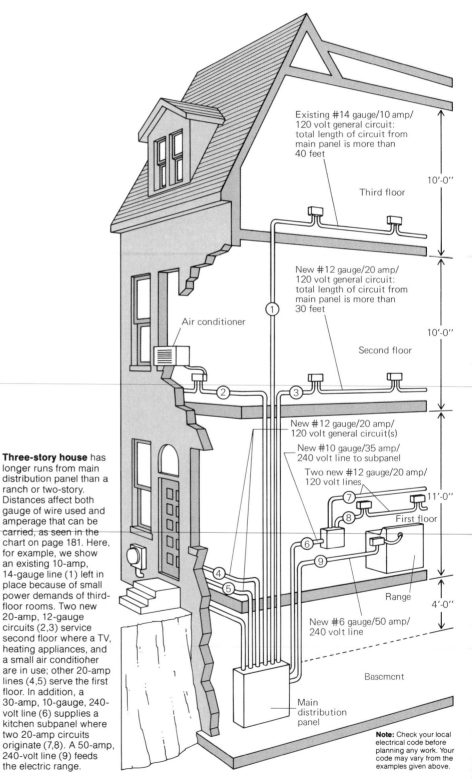

Existing #14 gauge/10 amp/ 120 volt general circuit: total length of circuit from main panel is more than 40 feet

Third floor

New #12 gauge/20 amp/ 120 volt general circuit: total length of circuit from main panel is more than 30 feet

Second floor

Air conditioner

10'-0''

10'-0''

New #12 gauge/20 amp/ 120 volt general circuit(s)

New #10 gauge/35 amp/ 240 volt line to subpanel

Two new #12 gauge/20 amp/ 120 volt lines

First floor

11'-0''

Range

New #6 gauge/50 amp/ 240 volt line

Basement

4'-0''

Main distribution panel

Three-story house has longer runs from main distribution panel than a ranch or two-story. Distances affect both gauge of wire used and amperage that can be carried, as seen in the chart on page 181. Here, for example, we show an existing 10-amp, 14-gauge line (1) left in place because of small power demands of third-floor rooms. Two new 20-amp, 12-gauge circuits (2,3) service second floor where a TV, heating appliances, and a small air conditioner are in use; other 20-amp lines (4,5) serve the first floor. In addition, a 30-amp, 10-gauge, 240-volt line (6) supplies a kitchen subpanel where two 20-amp circuits originate (7,8). A 50-amp, 240-volt line (9) feeds the electric range.

Note: Check your local electrical code before planning any work. Your code may vary from the examples given above.

placed against the unconnected hot wire; the other is clipped to the neutral bar in the de-energized panel, where the circuit's neutral wire is connected.

The continuity tester sends a small electric charge through the circuit. When all receptacles are empty and the lights are switched to the OFF position, the circuit is open and the tester will not respond unless there is a short. But when any switch in the circuit is in the ON position and a bulb is in the socket controlled by that switch, the tester will respond, indicating a complete circuit to the neutral bus bar in the panel.

Use the continuity tester to make both tests described in the above paragraph. If the new circuit fails either test—indicating either a short or an open circuit—check all your connections at switches and junction boxes and correct any defects, (see pp.194–197); then, make the tests again, and when the circuit is right, hook up the hot black wire at the fuse or breaker.

The final step is to return power to the panel by flipping the main breaker to ON, or replacing the main pull-out(s). (If the power company shut off the power, have it restored.)

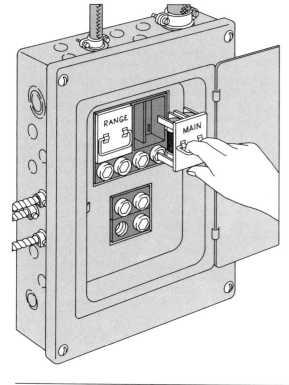

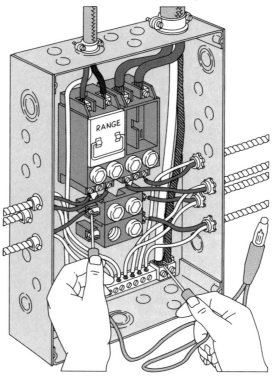

In ordinary fuse box (left), one main pull-out controls all current except for the range. Remove both pull-outs before unscrewing the front panel to work at the box. In other fuse boxes, called split bus bar boxes, you remove four pull-outs to shut off current to the box.

Voltage test: After you remove the pull-outs, test the box (right) to determine possible presence of leakage current that could cause a lethal shock. Place one probe of the neon voltage tester against the ground/neutral bus bar and the other against each set screw next to the fuses. If tester indicates voltage, look for additional pull-outs. If you search and find none, call in an electrician.

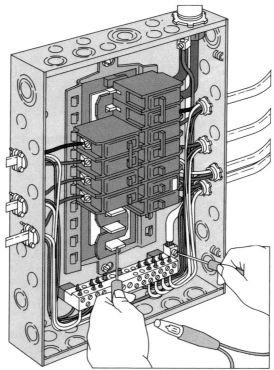

In a standard circuit breaker distribution panel, one or more main breakers (left) are tripped to shut off all current. Throw these breakers before removing the front panel in order to work inside.

Voltage test: After you trip the main breakers, test for the possible presence of leakage current that could cause a lethal shock. Place one probe of the neon voltage tester (right) against the ground/neutral bar and the other on an open space, first on one and then on the other hot bus bar. You can remove a breaker to expose the bus bars by pulling it toward you at one end and then slipping it left or right to dislodge it from the hook at the other end.

Working at the main distribution panel

Making the connections

Before running new electrical circuits in your house, check your main distribution panel for the necessary space for additional breakers or fuses. If there is none, you may have to install a sub-panel (see pp.198–201).

(**Caution:** After wiring a new branch circuit in your house you are ready to connect it at the distribution panel. First, shut off power to the panel by tripping the main breakers or removing the master pull-outs; remove the panel's face plate, and make the voltage test as shown on page 183. If the floor is damp or wet, mop up the moisture and stand on a dry board while you work.)

Remove a knockout in the panel to make an opening for connecting new wires. The procedures for removing knockouts and connecting circuits to the panel are illustrated below and on the opposite page. The tools you will need are shown in use in the drawings

here, and are described on page 181. You will need the following materials:

Cable connectors: These connectors, whose installation is illustrated below, come in different sizes to match the

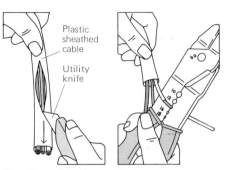

Stripping cable: Use a utility knife or cable ripper to split and cut cable sheathing (left) to length necessary to make connections inside distribution panel; use wire stripper (right) to remove insulation from ends of individual wires.

panel's knockouts. Except for a cable heavier than 10 gauge (8 or 6 gauge), you will use one of the panel's ½-inch knockouts, which take standard connectors. Buy your connectors at the same time you purchase your wiring and boxes.

Circuit breakers, fuses, adapters: If yours is a breaker panel, note its manufacturer and model number; take this information with you to your electrical supply shop. Breakers made for one panel may not fit others. If you have a fuse box, buy a fuse and a fuse adapter for each new circuit; both fuse and adapter must be of the same amperage rating, which must not exceed the capacity of the circuit (see chart, p.181).

240-volt lines: If you are connecting a nominal 240-volt line, you will need a double-pole breaker for a breaker panel or a pull-out cartridge fuse for a fuse box (see pp.174–175).

Removing distribution panel knockouts

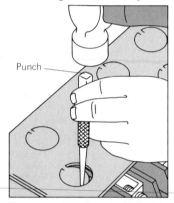

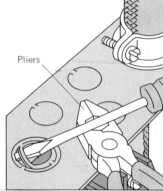

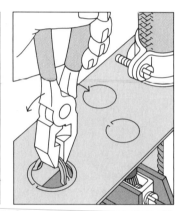

To remove ½-in knockout (for 10-, 12-, and 14-gauge cable), place nail set or punch on either side as shown and give tool a sharp rap with hammer to force edges inward.

From inside the main panel, grip bent edges of knockout with pliers and work them back and forth until knockout comes off. Cable is passed through knockout as shown below.

Multisection knockouts are also present (for 6 and 8 gauge 240-volt lines). Remove center as for ½-in. knockout, then pry up next ring using screwdriver levered on pliers.

Grip pried-up edges of ring with pliers from outside panel and pull off ring; to complete the opening, tap last ring inward and remove it with pliers from inside panel.

Connecting circuits at a breaker panel

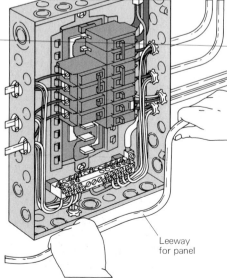

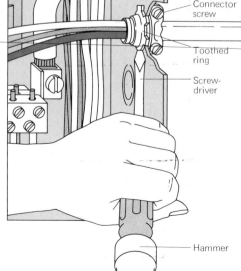

1. After removing a knockout, you can connect the circuit. Cut wire (left) allowing leeway for distribution panel. (You can easily cut away excess wire; adding on if you have cut short is prohibited by code.) Use a utility knife to split the plastic cable sheathing down the center; be careful not to nick the wire insulation inside the sheathing. Bend the sheathing and cut it off.

Slip the outer ring of the cable connector over the wires; run the wires through the knockout, with the connector outside the panel. Working in the panel, pass the inner connector ring over the wires and screw the connector together, allowing only enough cable sheathing to enter the panel to give purchase to the connector. Tighten the connector's toothed inner ring using a screwdriver and hammer (right), then tighten the screws on the connector outside the panel.

Connecting circuits at a breaker panel (continued)

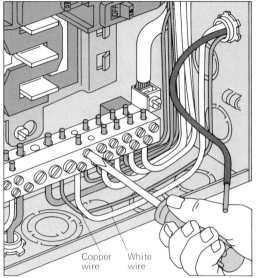

Copper wire   White wire

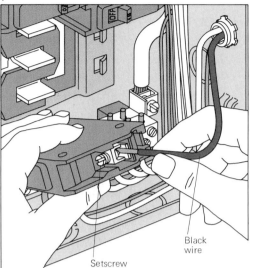

Setscrew   Black wire

2. Before proceeding with your circuit connections inside panel, permanently fasten the cable externally to a stud or a joist a foot or less away from the panel; use an electrician's staple.

Insert stripped end of white neutral wire in an available neutral location in ground/neutral bar (left); tighten setscrew. Connect the bare copper ground wire to a ground location in the bar.

Connect end of black hot wire (stripped to length indicated by gauge on breaker) to breaker (right); slip it into the terminal slot and tighten setscrew. Double-pole (240-volt) breakers have two such terminal openings. One takes the black hot wire, one the other hot wire, usually coded red.

Caution: Shut off power to panel by throwing main breaker before doing any work at panel.

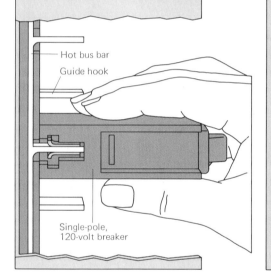

Hot bus bar

Guide hook

Single-pole, 120-volt breaker

MAIN

HOT WATER

WASHR

BATHRM

BD. RM.

LIV. RM

KIT. RANGE

KITCH.

KIT. DIN. RM.

3. Slide your circuit breaker onto the guide hook. Press it firmly on the hot bus bar until it snaps into place (left). A double-pole breaker will attach to both the panel's hot bus bars, but it is pressed into place just as a single-pole breaker is.

Punch open the appropriate knockout in the distribution panel's face plate; your new breaker will protrude from this space when you attach the plate.

Attach the face plate and restore power to the distribution panel by returning the main breaker to the ON position. Label the face plate (right) to indicate all the rooms, appliances, or equipment controlled by the new circuit breaker.

Caution: Shut off power to panel by throwing main breaker before doing any work at panel.

Connecting circuits at fuse boxes

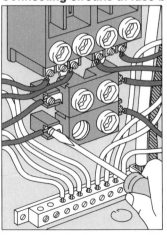

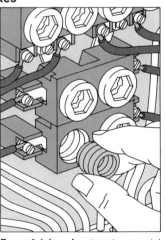

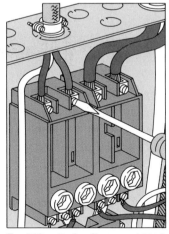

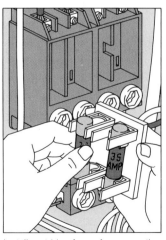

Remove knockouts; connect cable, neutral, and ground wires as for breaker panel; then, for 120-volt line, attach black hot wire using setscrew next to an empty fuse socket.

For safety's sake, insert a special Type S fuse adapter whose amp rating matches circuit (p.181). Once in place, it cannot be removed and accepts fuse only of proper rating.

For 240-volt circuit, connect black hot wire to one setscrew at an unused pull-out housing; connect the other hot wire, usually coded red, to setscrew on other side of housing.

Install cartridge fuse of proper rating in pull-out housing. Attach face plate, replace pull-out, and restore power to the box. Label new circuits on face plate.

Switches, outlets, and junctions

Choosing the right boxes

Whenever you connect the wires of a circuit to an outlet, switch, or light fixture, or make junctions to form branch circuits, the National Electrical Code (NEC) requires that connections be enclosed in protective metal or plastic boxes. Boxes are available in a variety of shapes and sizes that have different functions and accommodate greater or lesser numbers of connections.

Box shapes: For switches, wall outlets, and most wall-mounted lights, you will need rectangular boxes. Ceiling lights require octagonal or circular boxes. Junction boxes, used where several wires join, are either square or octagonal in shape.

Box sizes: Boxes for a given function vary little, if at all, in area: octagonal boxes are usually 4 inches on each of their eight faces; square boxes, either 4 or $4^{11}/_{16}$ inches on a side; rectangular wall switches and outlets, 3 x 2 inches. But within each category there are major differences in depth, or volume, as shown in the chart on this page. Increased volume permits more connections. The NEC prohibits the overcrowding of boxes. The chart indicates the maximum number of connections permitted by the NEC, according to the wire gauge size and the box depth.

chances are good that there is a box to meet your needs. Some common types are illustrated on these pages.

Box connections: To use the chart properly, you must understand what the NEC defines as a connection. All ground wires coming into the box are counted as a single connection. All built-in cable clamps are counted as another connection. Switch or outlet terminals are counted as an additional connection. And, finally, each hot or neutral wire entering the box counts as one connection.

By the above reckoning, a wall box with just a single switch has five connections, the maximum number allowed in a 2½-inch-deep box if the circuit employs standard 12-gauge wire with ground (see chart). The simplest solution to this problem is to buy boxes deeper than 2½ inches, as the chart suggests. But there are also other approaches. One is to use exterior cable connectors; they hold the wires as securely as the interior types, without cluttering, and do not count as a connection in the box.

Another alternative is to gang two boxes together, as illustrated on this page. The sides are removed from the two boxes and they are then joined to form a single large box. A protective face plate is placed over that part of the

Boxes for new construction

Single square box

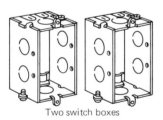

Two switch boxes

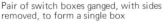

Pair of switch boxes ganged, with sides removed, to form a single box

Switch boxes can be ganged to form a box that holds as many connections as a square box.

There are also special "pancake" and "stringbean" boxes for narrow spaces, as well as large multiple outlet boxes. If you have an unusual space problem, talk to your electrical supply dealer—

Side bracket

Stud

Front bracket

Side bracket mounted: For new construction, where studs are exposed, these plastic boxes are the most frequently used and easiest to install. Before wallboard goes up, they are attached to the sides of wall studs with nails, positioned to extend out from the stud a distance equal to the thickness of the drywall or paneling you plan to install. Thus they will be flush with the finished wall when the wallboard is applied.

Front bracket mounted: This box is also mounted on the wall stud, but on the front of it. The front bracket has two advantages: in new construction, you can usually install it without measuring to allow for the protrusion required to bring the box flush with the finished wall, since the brackets are recessed to compensate for the exact thickness of common drywall; in old plaster walls, front bracketed boxes are also convenient—instead of ripping out a large part of the wall to reach the side of a stud, a space for the box is cut next to a stud and plaster is removed (and later patched) from face of stud to nail bracket.

combined box not used for a switch or an outlet. Be sure, however, that both boxes are made by the same manufacturer and are identical—otherwise you may not be able to join them.

Mounting boxes: Today's home electrician has several options when deciding how to attach electrical boxes to a wall or ceiling. The boxes shown on these two pages will meet most needs, allowing you to place an outlet, a switch, a light fixture, or a junction box virtually anywhere. Instructions for installing the boxes in older construction are on pages 188-189. Wiring new construction—open stud walls and ceiling joists—is covered on subsequent pages.

Permissible connections in boxes

Type of box	Sides	Depth	Number of connections			
			#14	#12	#10	#8
Octagonal	4"	1¼"	6	5	5	4
	4"	1½"	7	6	6	5
	4"	2½"	10	9	8	7
Square	4"	1¼"	9	8	7	6
	4"	1½"	10	9	8	7
	4"	2⅛"	15	13	12	10
	4¹¹⁄₁₆"	1¼"	12	11	10	8
	4¹¹⁄₁₆"	1½"	14	13	11	9
Switch	3" x 2"	2¼"	5	4	4	3
	3" x 2"	2½"	6	5	5	4
	3" x 2"	2¾"	7	6	5	4
	3" x 2"	3½"	9	8	7	6

Boxes for old construction

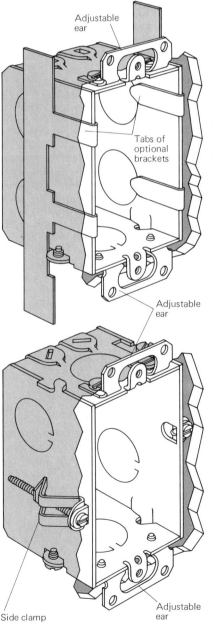

Adjustable ear

Tabs of optional brackets

Adjustable ear

Side clamp

Adjustable ear

Ear-mounted, with optional brackets: Simplest and most versatile of all to use, this box can be attached by its adjustable ears to existing wood lath or any other firm material into which screws can bite—wood paneling, for example. For gypsum wallboard or metal lath, the optional brackets, sold separately, clamp the box in place; the tabs on the brackets are folded around the edge of the box to secure it.

Ear and side-clamp mounted: The screws on either side of this box draw its side clamps against the back surface of the wall, while its adjustable ears hold the box snugly at top and bottom in front. It is a good choice when a box must be placed in a wood-paneled wall. Non-metal snap-in brackets are used on gypsum wallboard; they work on the same principle as the side clamps shown. The brackets fold against the box as it is inserted into the wallboard, then spring outward to brace the box.

Ceiling boxes

Outlet/junction boxes: Square or octagonal, these can be fastened directly to joists or studs with nails. Alternatively, hanger bars can be used to install boxes between ceiling joists. An offset hanger bar will position the box so that it will be flush with a finished ceiling. These boxes are used for both ceiling fixtures and circuit junctions. The boxes are installed—and wired—before gypsum wallboard is applied to cover the exposed joists.

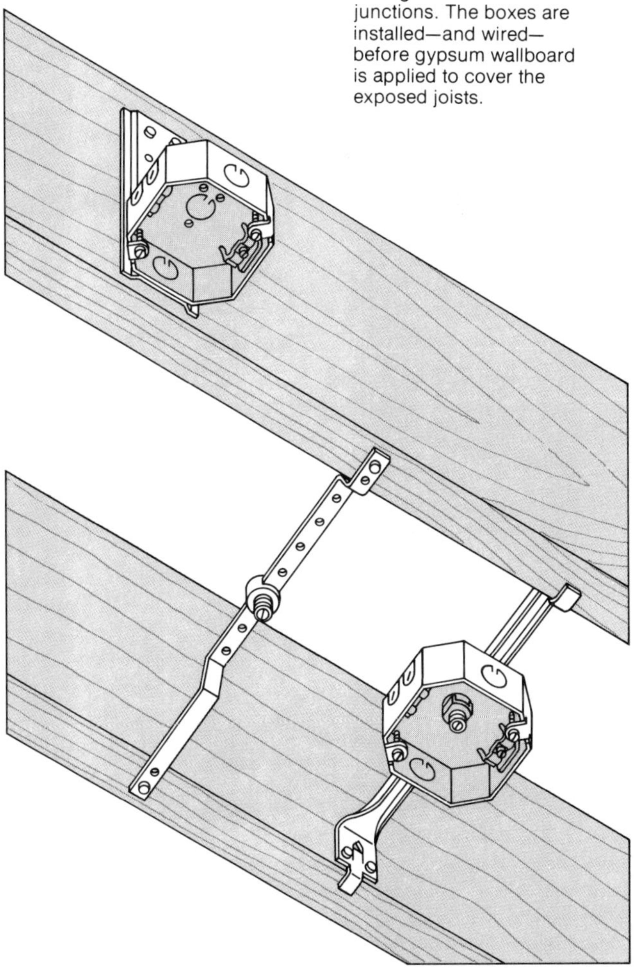

Running new circuits in an existing house

Mounting boxes for outlets and switches

New outlets and switches are installed using the boxes described on the preceding page. The cable is passed through the knockouts on the boxes as illustrated on page 194, and the wiring connections are made inside the boxes as seen on pages 194–197.

These two pages illustrate the techniques used to mount the boxes in existing walls. They are installed in the spaces between studs, as shown in the drawings below. The box design and mounting hardware vary with the material of which the wall is made—plaster on wood lath, plaster on metal lath, wood panel, or drywall (gypsum wallboard, or plasterboard).

In the case of plaster walls and ceilings, you may have to use spackling plaster to touch up around the opening you make for the box.

The National Electrical Code stipulates the placement of switches and outlets. A new wall switch must be positioned at a height of 4 ft. from the floor on the side of a doorway on which the door opens into a room; thus the door, when opened into the room, will not block access to the switch. Outlets are raised 12 to 18 in. from the floor, with an outlet located every 12 ft. along the walls of the room, except in the case of the kitchen, where more outlets are required (p.177).

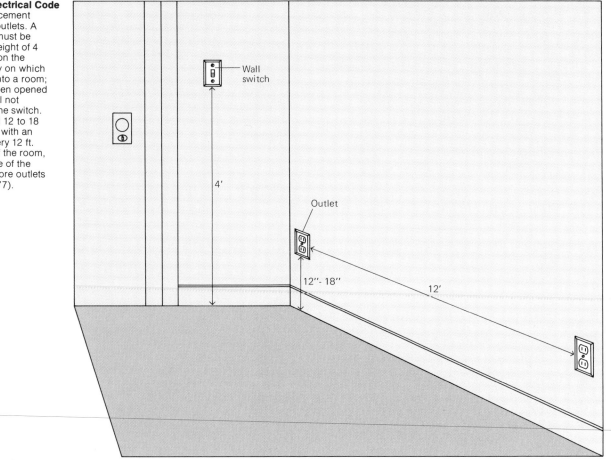

Plaster and lath

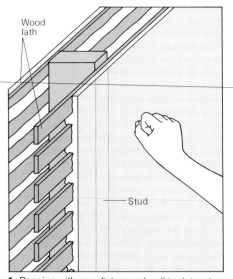

1. Rapping with your fist, sound wall to determine solid spots indicating studs. In existing plaster walls, new switch and outlet boxes are installed in hollows between studs.

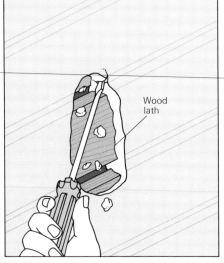

2. When you determine where to install box, chip away enough plaster to expose a full strip of underlying wood lath. (If metal or gypsum lath is present, see Step 3, opposite page.)

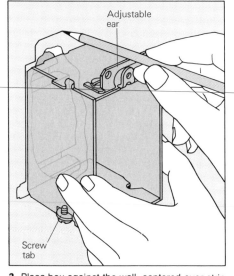

3. Place box against the wall, centered over strip of exposed wood lath. Trace outline of box, including adjustable ears at top and bottom. Drill ⅜-in. holes at corners of outline for screw tabs.

Plaster and lath (continued)

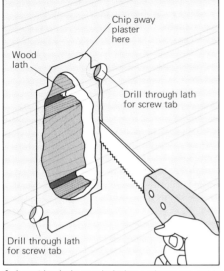

Chip away plaster here

Wood lath

Drill through lath for screw tab

Drill through lath for screw tab

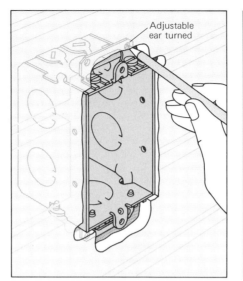

Adjustable ear turned

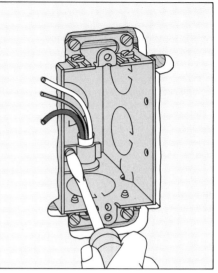

4. Insert keyhole saw in holes and saw smoothly all around outline of box, except areas for adjustable ears. Chip away plaster from spaces for ears, exposing lath behind.

5. Adjust ears. Place box in opening; mark positions of screw holes on wood lath strips to mount adjustable ears. Remove box and drill pilot holes in lath with fine twist bit.

6. With ears adjusted so box sits flush with wall surface, feed cable into box, position and mount box on lath with screws, and secure cable connector. (To connect wires, see pp.194–197.)

Drywall and wood panel

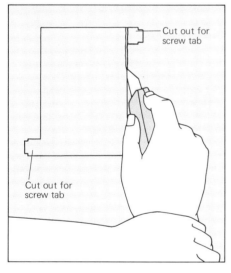

Cut out for screw tab

Cut out for screw tab

1. Begin by locating studs as shown in Step 1 on opposite page. Trace outline of box on plasterboard, then cut along edge of outline, using utility knife. Begin at the top; steady your wrist with your free hand. Go back over rectangle, being sure you have cut all the way through paper covering on wallboard. Push cutout into hollow behind wall; cut out holes for screw tabs last. Trim ragged edges with knife blade.

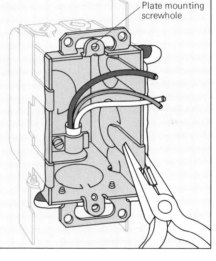

Plate mounting screwhole

3. Compress all the bracket tabs with pliers to hold box firmly in wall. (Ears will be covered when plate is attached to box.) Switch and outlet terminals are wired as seen on pages 194–197.

Boxes are installed in plaster on gypsum or metal lath walls as shown, using optional side brackets; opening is made in metal, not with utility knife, but by chipping off plaster and cutting lath with saber saw.

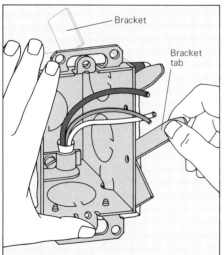

Bracket

Bracket tab

2. Feed cable into box, strip sheathing, strip the wires, and secure the cable clamp (see pp.184, 194). Put box in opening. You will use optional side brackets to mount box in plasterboard (see pp.186–187). Holding box in wall with one hand, insert a bracket with the other. Grip bracket firmly; if it drops into hollow behind wall, you have lost it. Push bracket up alongside box until its top arm catches in corner of opening in wall, then slip bottom of bracket into opening. Bend tabs around box edge.

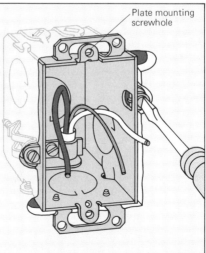

Plate mounting screwhole

For a wood panel wall, use box with side-mounted clamps (pp.186–187). Sound for studs and trace outline of box on wall, as for other boxes described. Bore holes for side clamps on either side of box, and another pair of holes at top and bottom for switch or outlet plate mounting screws. Saw opening as shown in Step 4, above. If necessary, adjust the ears so box is flush with wall. Attach cable, holding box in place; tighten clamp screws until ears on box are drawn against the wall.

189

Running new circuits in an existing house

Fishing cable

Installing electrical circuits in new construction is not difficult: studs, plates, and joists are exposed, simplifying the mounting of electrical boxes and running of cable. But unless surface wiring is used (pp.192–193), an existing house is much harder to rewire; walls and ceilings must be opened to mount boxes (pp.188–189), and most cable must be threaded through hidden spaces behind wall and ceiling coverings, and through holes drilled or cut in plates and firestopping. The work may be time consuming, requiring trial-and-error procedures, and you should have a helper.

The large drawing here shows a composite of a number of common wiring jobs as they might most typically and efficiently be performed in an ordinary frame house. A new subpanel is added in the attic, on a new line run up from the main distribution panel in the basement; this subpanel will provide power for room air conditioners in second-floor bedrooms on new circuits run down from the attic—and will also preposition the necessary service for a finished attic room planned for the future.

New lines are also being run on the first floor of the house where a partition subdividing a large living-dining area has occasioned the need for new outlets. The first-floor rewiring is done directly from the basement below, as described by the labels accompanying the large drawing at right.

An unusually useful tool in rewiring old houses is the fish tape, shown on page 181 and in the illustrations at bottom, here. The fish tape is inserted through holes cut in walls and ceilings in order to pull, or fish, new cable through the hollows between studs and joists. The drawings at bottom show how to attach cable to the tape.

Line for air conditioner in 2nd-floor bedroom is run down from attic subpanel through wall cavity between studs. By sounding wall with fist, studs are located and hole for outlet box is cut midway between two of the studs.

By measuring from corners of room and attic a point directly above outlet is located on top plate of bedroom wall (accessible from attic); a 1'' hole is drilled through plate to wall cavity at this point.

Here, firestopping was discovered between studs during sounding of the wall; a hole is opened (and later patched), and a notch for passage of cable chiseled in firestopping

Electric meter belongs to power company; if you are planning to replace your main distribution panel to upgrade service (raise the amperage available for your house circuits), the power company should be called to "pull" —disconnect—the meter before the old panel is removed, shutting off all power to panel. Power is restored only when new panel is installed and all circuits are attached to it. (See pp. 200-201)

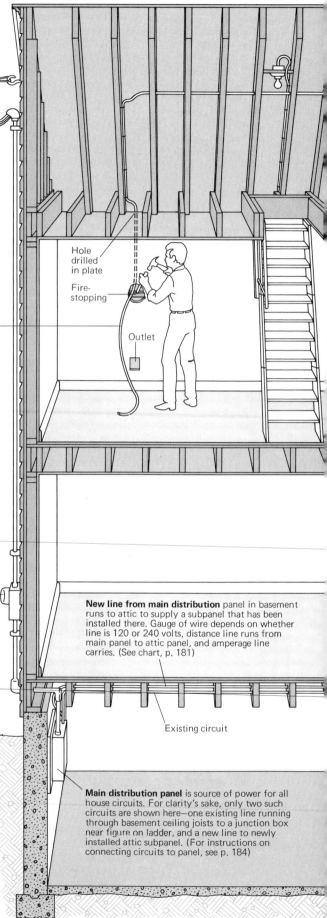

Hole drilled in plate

Fire-stopping

Outlet

New line from main distribution panel in basement runs to attic to supply a subpanel that has been installed there. Gauge of wire depends on whether line is 120 or 240 volts, distance line runs from main panel to attic panel, and amperage line carries. (See chart, p. 181)

Existing circuit

Main distribution panel is source of power for all house circuits. For clarity's sake, only two such circuits are shown here—one existing line running through basement ceiling joists to a junction box near figure on ladder, and a new line to newly installed attic subpanel. (For instructions on connecting circuits to panel, see p. 184)

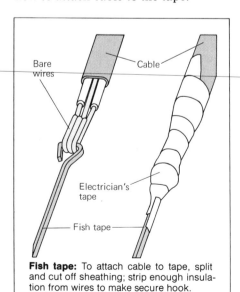

Bare wires

Cable

Electrician's tape

Fish tape

Fish tape: To attach cable to tape, split and cut off sheathing; strip enough insulation from wires to make secure hook.

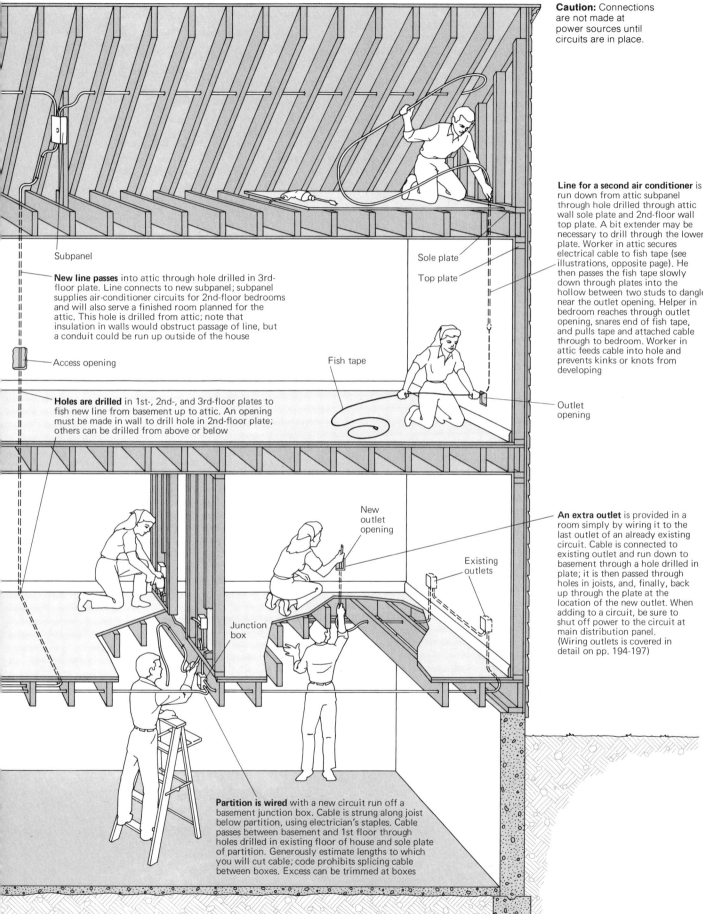

Caution: Connections are not made at power sources until circuits are in place.

Subpanel

New line passes into attic through hole drilled in 3rd-floor plate. Line connects to new subpanel; subpanel supplies air-conditioner circuits for 2nd-floor bedrooms and will also serve a finished room planned for the attic. This hole is drilled from attic; note that insulation in walls would obstruct passage of line, but a conduit could be run up outside of the house

Access opening

Holes are drilled in 1st-, 2nd-, and 3rd-floor plates to fish new line from basement up to attic. An opening must be made in wall to drill hole in 2nd-floor plate; others can be drilled from above or below

Sole plate

Top plate

Line for a second air conditioner is run down from attic subpanel through hole drilled through attic wall sole plate and 2nd-floor wall top plate. A bit extender may be necessary to drill through the lower plate. Worker in attic secures electrical cable to fish tape (see illustrations, opposite page). He then passes the fish tape slowly down through plates into the hollow between two studs to dangle near the outlet opening. Helper in bedroom reaches through outlet opening, snares end of fish tape, and pulls tape and attached cable through to bedroom. Worker in attic feeds cable into hole and prevents kinks or knots from developing

Fish tape

Outlet opening

New outlet opening

Junction box

Existing outlets

An extra outlet is provided in a room simply by wiring it to the last outlet of an already existing circuit. Cable is connected to existing outlet and run down to basement through a hole drilled in plate; it is then passed through holes in joists, and, finally, back up through the plate at the location of the new outlet. When adding to a circuit, be sure to shut off power to the circuit at main distribution panel. (Wiring outlets is covered in detail on pp. 194-197)

Partition is wired with a new circuit run off a basement junction box. Cable is strung along joist below partition, using electrician's staples. Cable passes between basement and 1st floor through holes drilled in existing floor of house and sole plate of partition. Generously estimate lengths to which you will cut cable; code prohibits splicing cable between boxes. Excess can be trimmed at boxes

Running new circuits in an existing house

Cable fishing techniques

A new circuit may originate at the main distribution panel (pp.184–185); at a subpanel (p.198); or at a branch circuit from a junction box (pp.194–197).

Whatever a circuit's origin, a pathway must be provided for it. This can be done with surface metal raceways, as seen on the opposite page. More commonly, the cable is passed behind the walls, as detailed in the illustration at right. A snake, commonly called a fish tape, is then used to pull, or fish the cable through wall hollows.

Run new cable along the straightest possible paths. These will usually be in one of the hollows between a pair of studs in the wood frame (see pp.190–191). You will have to drill holes in the plates of the wood frame—the horizontal members at floor and ceiling.

Cable fishing requires the cutting of openings in the walls—and in some cases, the ceilings—of one or more rooms. The illustrations below show how to patch these openings once you have finished your electrical work.

Fishing insulated walls: If your house is insulated, you may have to cut more openings in your walls than the drawings here indicate. Insulation fills the hollows between the studs and blocks the passage of fish tapes and cable. Cutting several openings a few feet apart allows you to reach into the wall hollow to take hold of the cable by hand; you can then force it up to the next higher or down to a lower opening.

Conduit: Alternatively, you can run new cable on the outside of the house wall—drilling holes for the cable to come out from the main panel in the basement and to re-enter the house on a higher floor. Exterior lines employ one of the types of the metal conduit discussed at bottom, on the opposite page.

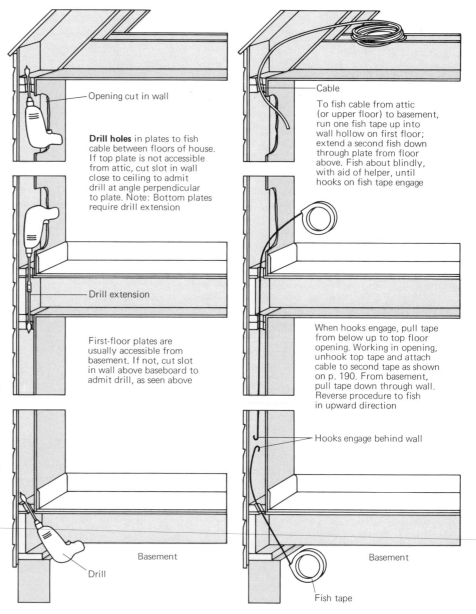

Opening cut in wall

Drill holes in plates to fish cable between floors of house. If top plate is not accessible from attic, cut slot in wall close to ceiling to admit drill at angle perpendicular to plate. Note: Bottom plates require drill extension

Drill extension

First-floor plates are usually accessible from basement. If not, cut slot in wall above baseboard to admit drill, as seen above

Drill

Basement

Cable

To fish cable from attic (or upper floor) to basement, run one fish tape up into wall hollow on first floor; extend a second fish down through plate from floor above. Fish about blindly, with aid of helper, until hooks on fish tape engage

When hooks engage, pull tape from below up to top floor opening. Working in opening, unhook top tape and attach cable to second tape as shown on p. 190. From basement, pull tape down through wall. Reverse procedure to fish in upward direction

Hooks engage behind wall

Basement

Fish tape

Patching plaster walls

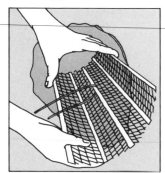

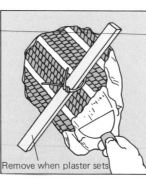

Remove when plaster sets

To fish cable behind walls, cut openings no larger than necessary—just big enough to admit a drill and to permit you to work with your hands in wall hollow. Cut the openings with tools and techniques similar to those employed in installing boxes (pp.188–189). Patch a plaster wall by inserting a backing of metal lath or factory cloth cut to size and held in place with string and scrap wood. After the patching plaster sets, remove string and wood and touch up the area.

Patching plasterboard walls

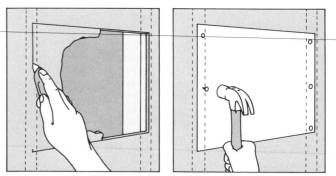

Patch gypsum wallboard by cutting away a panel around the opening. Use a utility knife with a sharp blade. Cut through the tape and joint compound over the seams (here, at the studs shown in dotted lines). Carefully remove the panel and tape to leave a neat opening; then, cut a patching panel to size and nail it to the studs. Apply tape and joint compound (see p.91), prime the panel with sealer, and—as with a plaster wall—repaint or repair the affected part of the wall.

Surface metal raceway and Plugmold

Metal raceway wiring is exposed on the surfaces of walls and ceilings. It avoids the messy and time-consuming opening of walls and ceilings described on previous pages. But raceway is unsightly, and its use is restricted by some local codes for safety reasons. A form of surface wiring called Wiremold or Plugmold is convenient for installation along countertops and as baseboard trim. Again, check your local code before planning its installation.

One advantage of raceway (and of conduit, described below) is its suitability for masonry walls. It is fastened to the wall using a masonry drill and lead or plastic anchors; drill the holes, insert the anchors, and drive the screws of the raceway base plates and clips into the anchors.

All these forms of surface wiring come with manufacturer's installation instructions and drawings. Plugmold is available as pre-assembled, pre-wired units; they require little more work than laying out and mounting the parts and attaching simple pressure connectors between the wires of neighboring units.

Tools and procedures: Raceway is more difficult to work with. You will need special tools, including shears to cut the length to size and a fish tape to draw the wires through the raceway. You may need a helper to assist you if the layout is complex. Plan and mark on walls and ceilings the paths of your circuits and the locations of outlets and switches. Mount the baseplates for boxes first, then cut straight lengths of raceway to fit between the plates. Mount the raceway using the clips provided, (In plaster and wallboard, plates and clips are screwed into studs.) Snap tee and elbow fittings in place after you fish the wires through the raceway.

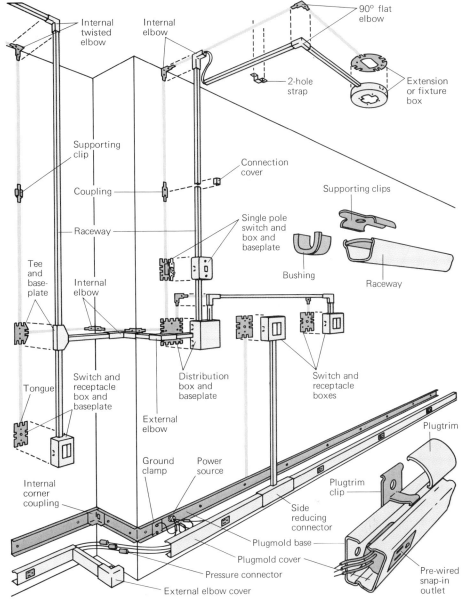

Thinwall conduit (metal or plastic)

Thinwall conduit (electrical metallic tubing or PVC) is of two types—exterior and interior conduit. Metal can be bent with a special tool that makes curves without producing kinks. The lines are run using the connectors, couplings, brackets, and other hardware shown in the illustrations. Most local codes specify the use of interior conduit in workshops, garages, and other places where lines require extra strong sheathing to prevent accidental damage. Exterior conduit is used to run lines on the outside of the house or underground. Rigid conduit—the type used for feeder service from the weatherhead to the meter and panel—may be required under a driveway.

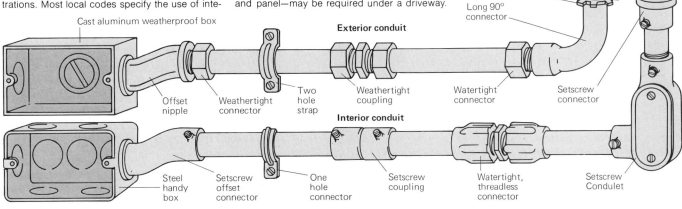

Connecting switches, outlets, and junction boxes

Wiring procedures

The illustrations on this and the following three pages show how to wire the most common house circuits. Variations are made by adding or subtracting switches and outlets from the configurations we have illustrated.

Once you have decided where to put the switch and outlet boxes, and have run the appropriate cables to them (pp.190–193), install the cables in the boxes in the manner shown below. Pull enough cable (about 8 inches) into the box to allow adequate length with which to work, then split and cut the cable sheathing as illustrated on page 184.

Caution: Always shut off power to a circuit before handling wires (see pp. 182-183) or working with boxes.

The proper methods to strip and connect wires are shown below. Some switches and receptacles come with screw terminals as well as easy-to-use terminals of the push-in, self-clamping type. Today, many licensed professionals consider the push-in connectors

unreliable. Such connectors should not be used with aluminum wires.

Color coding wire: Wherever possible, connect wires according to the color rules given at right. In some cases a white wire must serve as a black wire. To avoid confusion should this occur, wrap black tape around the end of the white wire the rules say should be black.

Rules for grounding the non-current-carrying metal in electrical devices are becoming more stringent. Metal boxes, for example, at one time could depend on the BX cable to which they were joined to act as a link to ground. Now you may be required to ground a metal box with a separate ground wire connected to a screw in the back of the box or to a ground clip on the lip of the box.

Our illustrations show the most extensive ground wire arrangements you will encounter. Older switches might not have green-colored grounding screws, so you have no way to ground them. Plastic boxes are not grounded.

Color rules

Connect wires to the screw terminals according to colors shown. Red and black wires are "hot"; white are neutral; green or bare copper are ground.

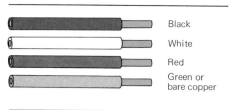

Black	Brass screw
White	Chrome screw
Red	Brass or chrome screw
Green or bare copper	Green screw

Color key

Wires on the following three pages are colored according to the color key shown here.

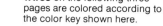

	Black
	White
	Red
	Green or bare copper

Installing cable in boxes

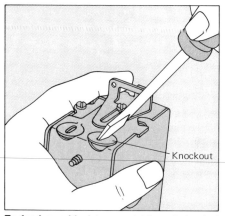
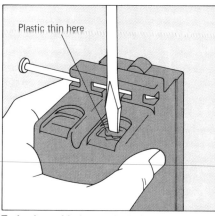
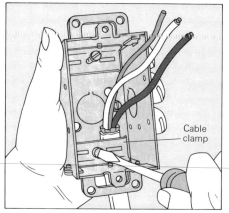

To feed a cable into a metal box, first select knockout adjacent to a cable clamp inside the box, then pry the knockout up and twist it off with a screwdriver. Insert the cable.

To feed a cable into a plastic box, first break a feed hole through the plastic by pressing down hard with a screwdriver where the box wall is thin. Feed the cable through the hole.

Tighten cable clamp inside metal box after pulling cable through the feed hole. Since plastic boxes do not have clamps, staple the cable to the stud next to the box.

Connecting the wires

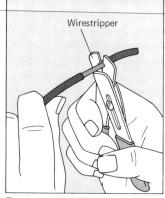
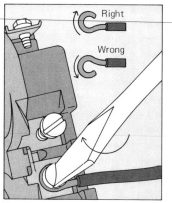
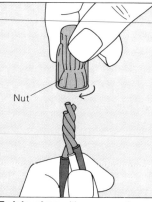
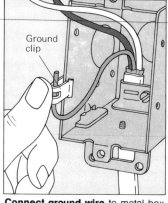

To connect a wire, first remove a ¾-in. segment of insulation from wire end with a wirestripper such as the one shown here or the tool illustrated on page 184.

To attach wire to a screw terminal, bend a hook in its end with long nose pliers; hook end around screw, and tighten. Attached wire should hook clockwise around screw as shown.

To join wires with a connecting nut, insert wire ends into nut and tighten clockwise. Some nut manufacturers specify that wire ends be twisted with pliers before being inserted.

Connect ground wire to metal box using ground screw in back of box or a ground clip as shown here. Insert ground wire under clip and force clip onto rim of the box.

Wall switches

Of the four types of wall mounted toggle switches, the single-pole and three-way switches, illustrated below, are the most common. The double-pole, which works like the single-pole but breaks both black and white wires instead of just the black when open, is rarely used in residential wiring. The fourth type, the four-way switch, is added to three-way circuits when more than two switches are desired to control a single fixture.

Switches are marked with a voltage and current rating, and are also marked with the letter "T" if the switch is deemed safe for use with tungsten filament lamps (light bulbs). Tungsten lamps draw high currents the instant they are turned on, and the switch must be able to handle such currents.

A switch, for example, may be marked 10A-125V T, 5A-250V. This means the switch can be used to control resistive devices that draw up to 10 amperes at a nominal 120 volts (up to 125 volts), or 5 amperes at a nominal 240 volts (up to 250 volts, see p.173). Resistive devices are those that do not include an electric motor, such as lights, radios, and toasters. For motors, the switch is rated at half the marked amperages—5 amperes and 2½ amperes in the example. The "T" means the switch can be used with 120-volt light bulbs.

Single-pole switch

Ceiling lamp is controlled by single-pole or simple on-off wall switch. Power feeds into switch box. See wiring details below.

Three-way switch

Ceiling lamp is controlled by 2 three-way switches and is turned on or off by either one. Power feeds into lamp box. See wiring details.

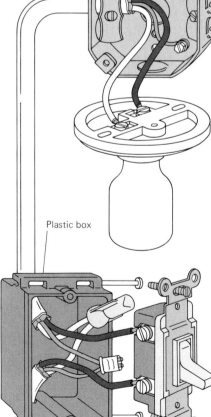

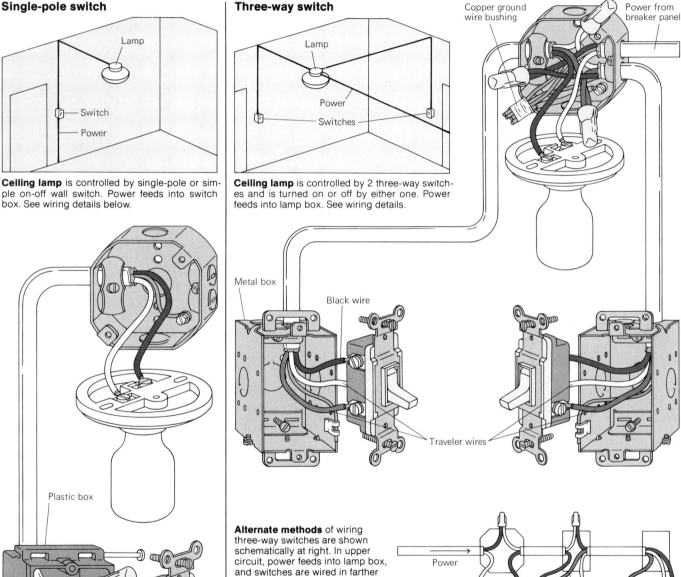

Alternate methods of wiring three-way switches are shown schematically at right. In upper circuit, power feeds into lamp box, and switches are wired in farther down the line. In lower circuit, power feeds into switches that precede the lamp. Ground wires in diagrams are omitted for clarity. In all three-way switch circuits, a black wire from the lamp is attached to the black screw terminal on one of the switches; another black wire, running from the power feed, is attached to the black screw terminal on the other switch. The other two screw terminals of the switches are colored brass and are connected in any order by a pair of any colored wires called traveler wires.

Connecting switches, outlets, and junction boxes

Wall outlets

Wall outlets can be conventional or split. Split receptacles allow you to turn a table or floor lamp on and off by flipping a wall switch (usually wired to the lower half of the receptacle; the upper half remains hot continuously).

The illustrations here are for wall receptacles designed to receive three-pronged plugs. A two-prong plug receptacle does not have a ground terminal, so the ground wire to the receptacle is omitted when wiring this type.

Receptacles are marked with voltage and current capacities as are switches (see preceding page), and these limits must be observed.

For convenience, electrical supply stores stock 6-inch lengths of green insulated wire with a ground screw attached to one end. These are called pigtails. Pigtails make it easier to ground metal outlets and switch boxes. In our drawings, both insulated and bare grounds are shown in the same color.

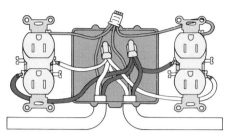

Wire dual receptacles like separate receptacles whose boxes have been ganged as shown in drawings on page 186.

Conventional outlet

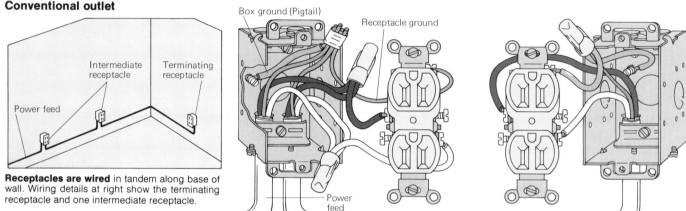

Receptacles are wired in tandem along base of wall. Wiring details at right show the terminating receptacle and one intermediate receptacle.

Split circuit outlet

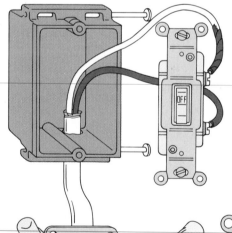

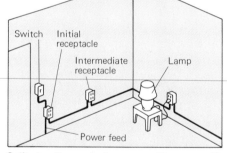

Split circuit receptacles are used in rooms without ceiling lamps. Details show initial receptacle with power feed and intermediate receptacle.

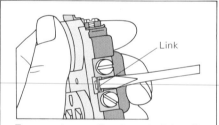

To convert conventional receptacle to split circuit receptacle, break electrical link joining brass screw terminals. Pry up with screwdriver and use pliers if necessary to snap the link.

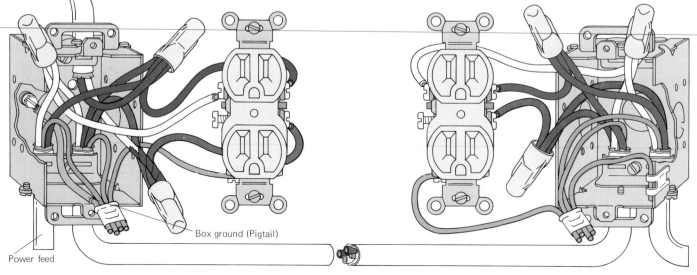

Ground fault circuit interrupters

Most codes now require ground fault circuit interrupters (GFCIs) in bathrooms and for outdoor receptacles. Fuses and conventional circuit breakers do not protect you from electric shocks. In potentially wet areas, such as bathrooms, garages, outdoors, and next to swimming pools, the ground fault shock hazard is dangerous enough to require circuit interrupters that guard against it. Such devices offer no protection against shorts such as a child could create by poking metal objects into both sides of a receptacle. Rather, they protect someone who while standing in a puddle or sitting in a bathtub touches an appliance that is electrically live because of some defect.

A GFCI can be installed at any site that requires it, or in the circuit breaker panel (see p.178). An on-site GFCI can include a protected receptacle such as the one shown here. All GFCIs have test and reset buttons that should be operated once a month.

You can install GFCIs all over the house if you want to, but they are expensive. A GFCI protects all circuits and devices wired down line from it. So you could, in theory, install just a few of them at the breaker panel to encompass all the house circuits, but this fails in practice. A GFCI is hair-trigger sensitive and will trip falsely if installed to protect more than one or two devices or circuits.

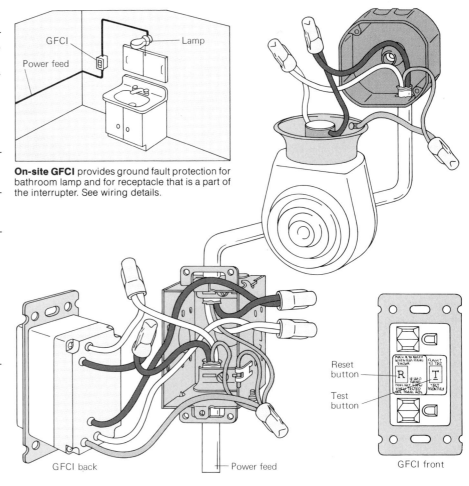

On-site GFCI provides ground fault protection for bathroom lamp and for receptacle that is a part of the interrupter. See wiring details.

GFCI back — Power feed — GFCI front

Reset button — Test button

Heavy duty outlets

An appliance that draws exceptional amounts of current or operates at 240 volts must have its own specially wired circuit. Electric ovens, for example, usually require a separate circuit with a 50-ampere capacity. Shown here is an electric dryer circuit that includes a receptacle and a power cord rated for 30 amperes. The power cord can be purchased separately, with the receptacle, but is often supplied by the appliance manufacturer. Appliances can also be wired directly to a cable in the wall, but are then difficult to move or replace.

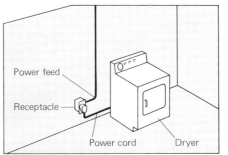

Power feed — Receptacle — Power cord — Dryer

Electrically heated dryer that operates on 240 volts has heavy-duty power cord plugged into heavy-duty wall outlet. See wiring details.

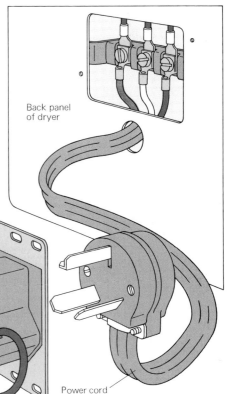

Back panel of dryer

Power feed — WHITE — Power cord

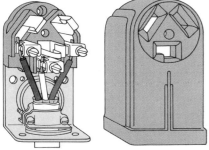

An alternate to a heavy-duty wall-mounted outlet is this freestanding outlet that is secured to the floor or against a wall. Power cable is fed up to it through the flooring.

Adding a subpanel

Providing for distant branch circuits

Installing a new subpanel is often the best solution to a common wiring problem—adding new branch circuits in a remote place in your house or on your property. If, for example, you decide to install branch circuits in a newly finished attic, a detached garage, or in a shed you have converted to a workshop, you will find it easier to connect these new circuits to a subpanel at the site than to run each separate line all the way back to the main distribution panel in your basement or utility room. For the subpanel, only one heavy-duty feeder cable need run to the main panel, where it is connected with its own main circuit breaker.

In older houses with fuse boxes, subpanels were sometimes installed near the main box to provide for additional house circuits for which the main box had no room. Today, it is considered better practice to replace an old fuse box with a larger circuit breaker panel, which has more room for circuits. Certainly, if you are having the power company upgrade your service (pp.178–179) to meet the demand of such new appliances as an electric range, clothes dryer, or air conditioner, you should remove your old fuse box and replace it with a breaker panel. (Breaker panels are more convenient than fuse boxes.)

In many parts of the country, codes require that a subpanel in a detached building contain its own main breaker, acting as an on-site switch to cut off power. Power to the subpanel is also controlled at the main distribution panel by turning on the breaker controlling the feeder cable.

Planning a subpanel: In the most common situation, a subpanel is fed from a double-pole breaker on the main panel, supplying 240 volts at 20 to 60 amps. The feeder is a three-wire cable with ground—two hot, one neutral, and one ground wire. Determine the sub-panel's breaker rating and the wire gauge for its feeder cable by first calculating how much capacity you require for the subpanel; this will depend on the number of branch circuits and the total load in amps (or watts) of the appliances, lights, etc., you will power from the subpanel (see pp.176–178). Once you know your required capacity, add the margin of safety described below. Then consult the chart on this page and the one on page 181. These two charts will help you select the right wire gauge for your feeder cable on the basis of its load in amps and the distance it travels from the main panel to the subpanel.

Margin of safety: Good electrical practice holds that the total amperage load on a subpanel be no greater than 80 percent of its main breaker size. Thus, if you calculate a total demand on the subpanel of 40 amps, you will need 50 amps breaker and feeder cable capacity for your new subpanel.

Connecting subpanel feeder cable at main panel

Shut off power to main distribution panel (see Safety tests, p.183). Find an open space for an extra double-pole breaker—commonly this will be at bottom of the bus bars. (If there is no room, install ½-in. replacement breakers for enough existing circuits to gain the needed space.) Strip away enough sheathing from your cable to allow ample lengths for making your connections inside main panel. Remove a knockout at a convenient location to pass cable through wall of box. Clamp cable at knockout with cable connector, as shown on page 184. Cut individual wires to make graceful loops to their respective terminals in ground/neutral bars and new circuit breaker. Strip insulation from wires and make connections, as shown on page 185. After work at subpanel is completed clip breaker to bus bars and remove a knockout for it in panel face plate.

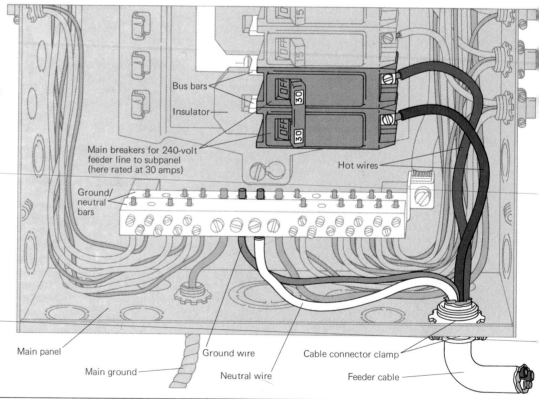

Bus bars
Insulator
Main breakers for 240-volt feeder line to subpanel (here rated at 30 amps)
Hot wires
Ground/neutral bars
Main panel
Main ground
Ground wire
Neutral wire
Cable connector clamp
Feeder cable

Determining subpanel rating and feeder cable gauge

Amperage	Wire size (AWG)
20	No. 12
30	No. 10
40	No. 8
55	No. 6
70	No. 4

Main panel breaker rating for a subpanel, and the required wire gauge for its feed cable, are usually determined as follows: Calculate the peak load planned for the subpanel—the total demand of all lights, appliances, power tools, etc., to be operated on the panel's branch circuits. Refer to the text and table on page 176 in making your calculations. Suppose your anticipated peak load comes to 9,600 watts or 40 amps for nominal 240-volt service. You must add to this a margin of safety, as described in text above, in determining the main breaker rating. In this example, the margin of safety—25%—would be 10 amps; thus your breaker should be rated at at least 50 amps. The table, left, indicates maximum amperage that can be carried safely by a given gauge of wire; in addition, the chart on page 181 shows how these requirements rise if your feeder line runs a long distance. All specifications are for copper; aluminum requires gauges up to two times as heavy as those given here.

Connecting feeder cable at the subpanel

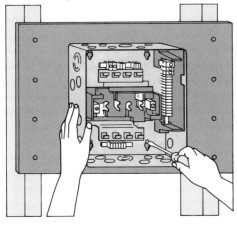

1. Mounting subpanel:
In a shed, garage, or unfinished attic, nail plywood to the exposed studs. In basement, drive masonry nails into foundation wall. Hold subpanel against plywood while helper marks screw locations. Drive roundhead screws into plywood, letting heads extend; slip panel screwholes over heads. After tightening top screws, install bottom pair. (To mount flush in wallboard, cut hole, fasten panel through its sides to studs.)

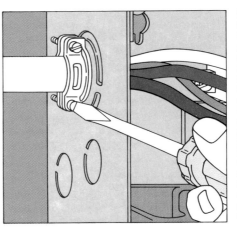

2. Installing feeder cable: Leave cable unconnected at main panel while working at subpanel box. Pull cable into box through convenient knockout and secure with cable connector clamp. To remove knockout and attach connector clamp, see pages 184–185. Note that just enough insulation is cut from wires fo allow for lengths of bare wire needed to make the terminal connections. Lug screws are tightened with a screwdriver.

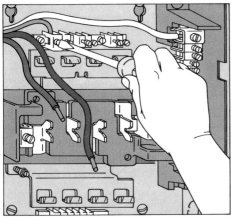

3. Making terminal connections: If installing subpanel in detached garage or outbuilding, it must have its own shut-off. Connect feeder cable as shown for main panel (pp.200–201). Within house, connect as shown here: stripped end of white neutral wire into lug at end of neutral bus bar; bare copper or green ground wire into ground bar; red and black wires into power terminals of the hot bus bars.

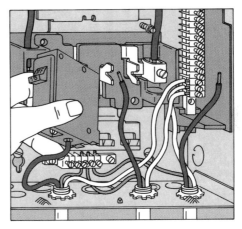

4. Wiring branch circuits: Subpanel's branch circuits are connected as are those of main panel; refer to detailed information on pages 184–185. Like main panel, subpanel accepts single-pole breakers, for nominal 120-volt service, and double-pole breakers, for nominal 240-v. Gauge on breakers is used as a guide in stripping insulation from wires. Turn on the power to subpanel only after all branch circuits are in.

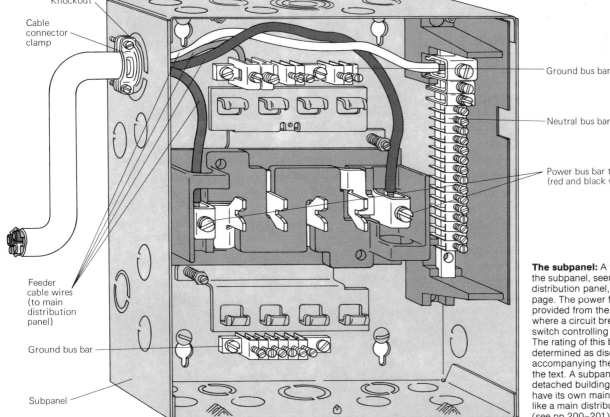

Knockout

Cable connector clamp

Ground bus bar

Neutral bus bar

Power bus bar terminals (red and black wires)

Feeder cable wires (to main distribution panel)

Ground bus bar

Subpanel

The subpanel: A feeder cable connects the subpanel, seen here, to the main distribution panel, shown on opposite page. The power for the subpanel is thus provided from the main service panel, where a circuit breaker acts as an on-off switch controlling power to the subpanel. The rating of this breaker, in amps, is determined as discussed in the caption accompanying the table opposite, and in the text. A subpanel installed in a detached building is required by code to have its own main shut-off breaker, just like a main distribution panel (see pp.200–201).

Replacing the service entrance and main panel

Planning the job

If you are rewiring an old house, you might want to replace a main fuse box with a modern breaker panel just for convenience. But the usual reason for replacing an old main panel is to upgrade service to 200 amps. Homes built prior to World War II were rarely equipped with more than 60 amps of power—not enough to run a modern electric household.

Local codes: The large drawing on this page illustrates a typical service entrance arrangement, including weatherhead and meter socket. However, local codes and your situation may call for a different arrangement (see below). Thus your first step must always be to consult your local electrical inspector. He will tell you what equipment you will need and how it must be laid out, specifying, for example, the maximum allowable distance between the meter base and the location of the main panel, the location of your grounding device, and whether or not rigid conduit must be used to connect the meter base and weatherhead.

Make your measurements and draw your plan on the basis of your electrical inspector's advice and what you find in your local code. Purchase your materials according to your plan, making sure you allow excess cable for your drip loop, bends, and connections inside the main panel.

Inspection: Coordinate your planned work schedule with your inspector and your power company. You must depend on the power company to remove the meter before you take out your old distribution panel, and to restore power after your new panel is installed and has been inspected. You will need an approval from your inspector to have the power turned back on.

By locating the new panel in the same place as the old one, you may spare yourself the job of rewiring the ends of all your existing house circuits to reach the connections on the new panel. (Remember that you cannot splice cable to lengthen circuits, except in a junction box.) If you are upgrading your existing circuits—and adding new ones—locate your new panel anywhere near the old one. You can then continue using electricity on your existing lines up until the time you hook up the new panel, when all power must be shut off by your electric company, as described above.

For 200-amp service entrance cable, the NEC requires 2/O gauge copper wire or 4/O aluminum wire. Copper is easier to shape than aluminum, and code requires that a coating of an oxide-inhibiting compound be applied to the exposed aluminum wires and terminal connections.

Installing service entrance

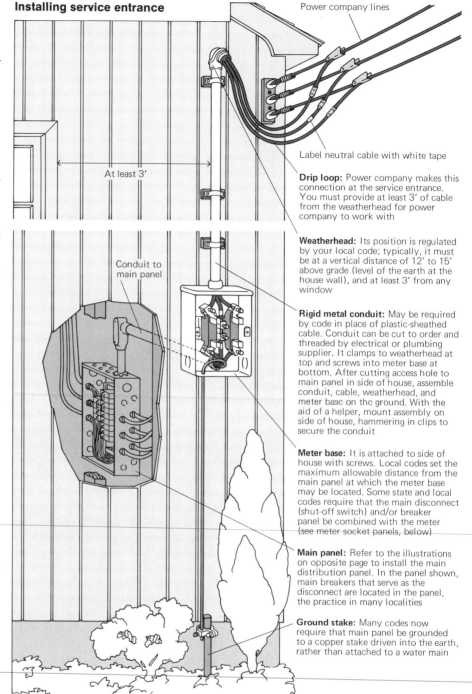

Power company lines

Label neutral cable with white tape

At least 3'

Conduit to main panel

Drip loop: Power company makes this connection at the service entrance. You must provide at least 3' of cable from the weatherhead for power company to work with

Weatherhead: Its position is regulated by your local code; typically, it must be at a vertical distance of 12' to 15' above grade (level of the earth at the house wall), and at least 3' from any window

Rigid metal conduit: May be required by code in place of plastic-sheathed cable. Conduit can be cut to order and threaded by electrical or plumbing supplier. It clamps to weatherhead at top and screws into meter base at bottom. After cutting access hole to main panel in side of house, assemble conduit, cable, weatherhead, and meter base on the ground. With the aid of a helper, mount assembly on side of house, hammering in clips to secure the conduit

Meter base: It is attached to side of house with screws. Local codes set the maximum allowable distance from the main panel at which the meter base may be located. Some state and local codes require that the main disconnect (shut-off switch) and/or breaker panel be combined with the meter (see meter socket panels, below)

Main panel: Refer to the illustrations on opposite page to install the main distribution panel. In the panel shown, main breakers that serve as the disconnect are located in the panel, the practice in many localities

Ground stake: Many codes now require that main panel be grounded to a copper stake driven into the earth, rather than attached to a water main

In the large drawing above, the service entrance arrangement has main disconnect (shut-off switch) in the breaker panel; the breaker panel is located inside the house within a specified distance of the meter on an outside wall. Some local codes may require the main disconnect with the meter outside the house, using a panel like the one shown, at left. Yet other codes require meter, main disconnect, and breakers all in the same outside unit, like panel shown at right.

Installing main distribution panel

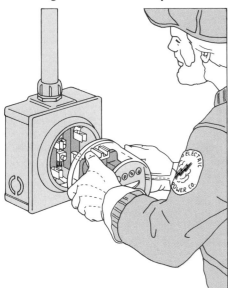

1. After you install the new service entrance (opposite page), have the power company remove your present meter, shutting off all power to your existing main distribution panel.

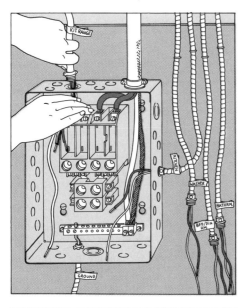

2. With your service disconnected by the power company, it should be safe to work on your main panel; but to be sure the panel is dead, conduct the test described on page 183. Then, disconnect all circuits from panel, labeling each cable as shown. Disconnect old service entrance cable; unscrew panel from wall.

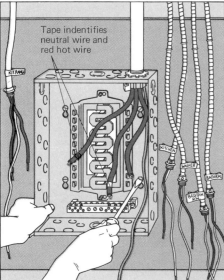

Tape indentifies neutral wire and red hot wire

3. To install panel, first connect service entrance cable from new meter base, using conduit if required by local code. Refer to pages 184–185 to attach couplings at knockouts. Screw panel to backing (see pp.198–199). Plywood backing must extend at least 8 in. out from box on all sides.

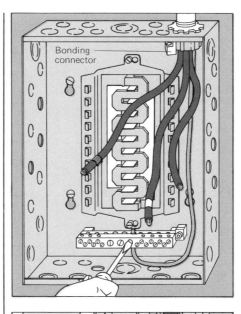

Bonding connector

4. Attach ground wire from service entrance to ground bus bar, as shown, if ground originates outside house. If ground originates inside, make connections using hardware specified by your local code.

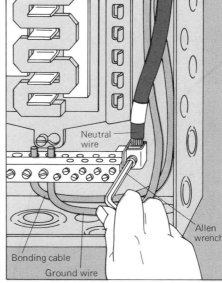

Neutral wire

Bonding cable

Ground wire

Allen wrench

5. Connect neutral wire from service entrance cable to neutral bus bar as shown. If your code requires, attach the bonding cable between neutral bus bar and the bonding jumper connector, as shown. Tighten the terminal lugs securely. Note that an oxide-inhibiting compound must be applied to wires and connections if service entrance cable is aluminum.

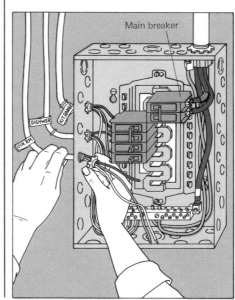

Main breaker

6. Install main breaker using its hold-down screw. Then strip and attach the two service entrance power cables to the main breaker. Finally, attach your house circuits, old and new, to the new panel (see pp.184–185). If you must rewire ends of old circuits to reach new panel, you can employ junction boxes (see pp.194–197). Have your work inspected and get inspector's approval for restoration of power.

Plumbing systems

A home plumbing system

Modernizing or adding to your home plumbing system involves much more than simply running new pipes. Although plumbing projects are no more difficult than other home improvement projects, they require careful planning. For example, in a new bathroom, what size water supply, waste, and soil pipes should you install? At what angles should they be pitched? Should fixtures be individually or collectively vented? Planning also allows you to anticipate and avoid structural obstacles you can encounter in running pipes. Careful planning before installation results in a properly functioning system.

This chapter opens with an overview of a typical home plumbing system (illustration, right) and three heating systems—hot water, hot air, and steam (illustrations on pp.204–205). The typical plumbing system is made up of four components: (1) fixtures such as faucets, sinks, tubs, and appliances; (2) water supply lines, including the main to the house, and the hot and cold lines throughout the house; (3) drainage lines, waste lines, and the soil stack; (4) and vents, which are tied into the drainage and waste system (DWV system) to allow the escape of organic gases and the entry of air to equalize pressures within the system.

Plumbing fixtures: According to the National Standard Plumbing Code, a fixture is a "receptacle or device which is either permanently or temporarily connected to the water distribution system of the premises." This definition encompasses all the sinks in bathrooms (where they are frequently called lavatories), kitchens, and utility rooms; bathtubs and showers; toilet tanks and bowls; water heaters; boilers for hot water and steam heating systems; and appliances that use water, such as washers and garbage disposers.

Water supply system: This consists of all the pipes, fittings, faucets, valves, pumps, and tanks that supply, distribute, regulate, and hold drinkable water.

The home gets its water, under pressure, usually from a high reservoir or water tower of the municipal waterworks or, in rural areas, from the tank-and-pump system of a private well. Water pressure in the supply lines in a private residence should range from 30 to 45 *psi* (pounds per square inch). Pressures lower than this range may result in insufficient flow at some faucets or fixtures. Those higher than 60 *psi* may cause pipes to hammer or even burst. As a safeguard, a pressure-reducing valve on the water-service pipe near the main shut-off valve can be installed by the homeowner. (See *Air chambers*, text, opposite page.)

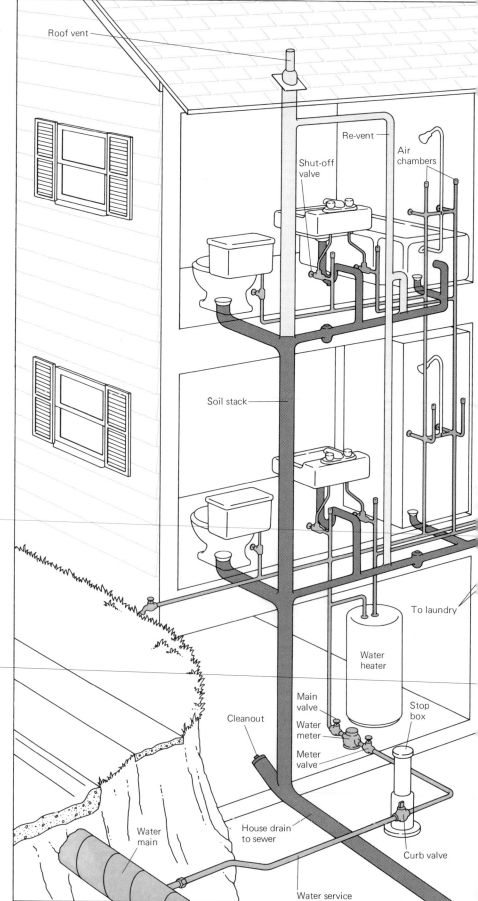

Roof vent

Re-vent

Air chambers

Shut-off valve

Soil stack

To laundry

Water heater

Main valve

Cleanout

Water meter

Meter valve

Stop box

Water main

House drain to sewer

Curb valve

Water service

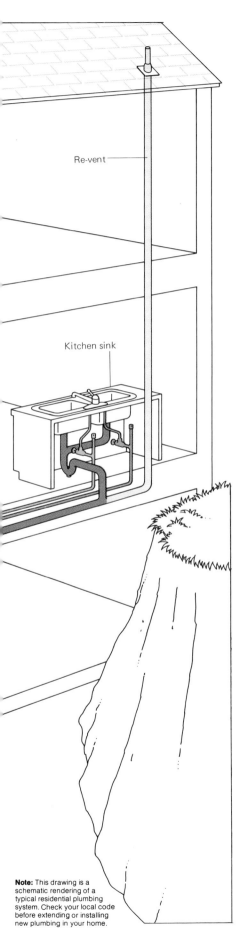

Re-vent

Kitchen sink

With a municipal water supply system, the water service pipe branches off the water main and carries water into the home, usually through a curb valve, then a meter valve, a water meter, and finally a main shut-off valve. The water service pipe, curb valve, meter valve, and water meter are the property of the water supplier. The main shut-off valve and what is beyond belong to the homeowner. The curb valve is buried in the ground inside a stop (or valve) box that is outside the house. It allows the water company to turn off the supply in an emergency, or if the homeowner fails to pay water bills. A water meter, either inside or outside the house, records the amount of water that is consumed. The meter valve, if there is one, is located on the water service pipe on the intake side of the water meter. It is used to turn water off when the meter is removed by the water company. The main shut-off valve is located on the output side of the water meter. In houses where the meter is located inside the house its valve may also serve as the main shut-off. The main shut-off valve is always inside the house. It allows you to turn off water throughout the house in an emergency.

A private water system normally uses an above-ground pump if the well is less than 25 feet deep, and an in-the-ground pump if the well is deeper. Usually, water and air are pumped into a holding tank inside the house, where the air is compressed, so that the water enters the system under pressure.

The hot-water circuit is a part of the water supply system. Generally, soon after the water service pipe enters a house it branches into the cold-water circuit and a pipe to the water heater or boiler; from here a system of pipes runs to all fixtures that require hot water.

Air chambers: Turning off a faucet abruptly causes a shock wave in the water rushing through the pipes, which may "hammer"—bang loudly, or vibrate, often with a force great enough to damage the system. Air chambers provide cushions of compressible air that act as shock absorbers to diminish hammering. They are generally 1-to-1½-foot, capped extensions of the water supply pipes; they are located in the walls near faucets. Pipes bringing cold and hot water to sinks, showers, and bathtubs should all have air chambers.

If your plumbing has air chambers, water hammering can be cured simply by draining the pipes and allowing more air to enter the system. If the air chambers were not installed in the original plumbing, add-on units that can be tapped into the water distribution pipes are available.

Fixtures other than tubs and showers should be equipped with individual shut-off valves on both the cold and the hot water supply lines. They enable you to turn off the water to make repairs. If you do not have these valves, you will lose time getting to the main shut-off valve elsewhere in the house—time during which a room could be flooded.

Drainage system: This consists of pipes that carry liquid and solid wastes, by gravity, to the house drain and then into a public sewer or private septic tank. The system is made up of:
▷ Waste pipes, which carry water from sinks, tubs, and appliances. They are pitched toward the soil stack.
▷ Soil pipes, which carry waste from toilet bowls. They are also pitched toward the soil stack.
▷ The soil stack, a large (usually 4-inch) vertical pipe that accepts the discharge from all the waste and soil pipes and carries it to the main drain.
▷ Traps, which are installed with almost all fixtures. They are usually curved pipes filled with water, which acts as a seal to keep sewage gases from entering the house from waste and soil pipes. Toilet bowls have built-in traps.

Venting system: This is tied into the drainage and waste systems, which together are called the DWV (drain-waste-vent) system, as was previously noted. A venting unit consists of a pipe that provides air circulation to the drainage system. This equalizes pressures to prevent water in drain traps from being siphoned away by the partial vacuum that would otherwise result when water rushes down a drain pipe. If this should happen, sewage gases would enter the house through the empty trap. The venting unit leads sewage gases away to escape into the atmosphere, and the air entering drains checks the build up of corrosion and slime. As long as the water level in traps is maintained, gases from waste and soil pipes cannot enter the home.

The venting system operates on a principle called wet venting, which allows fixtures within certain distances of the soil stack to be vented by direct connection to the soil stack. When fixture locations exceed these distances, the drains are usually provided with separate vent pipes that are extended to the outside directly through the roof. Alternatively, a so-called re-vent can be installed; this entails venting the new drain by installing a horizontal connecting pipe to the existing soil stack. But the connection must be made at a point higher than that of any other fixture draining into the stack, so that re-venting is generally applicable only to new fixtures installed in upper stories.

Heating systems

Hot water, steam, and warm air

A centrally heated house usually employs one of three heating systems, in which hot water, steam, or warm air is the heating medium.

Hot water: The hot-water systems installed before World War II normally did not use pumps to deliver hot water to radiators. Instead, these systems relied on convection and gravity and were relatively inefficient. Most systems installed in the past 35 years use pumps. They are called forced hot-water or hydronic systems. The delivery of hot water to radiators is rapid, making the systems highly efficient; however, they possess more parts than steam or warm air systems, and are therefore more expensive to install and repair.

Forced hot-water systems may use either a single pipe or two pipes to transfer the heating medium. In a single-pipe system, one main pipe makes a complete circuit from the boiler to the radiators and back to the boiler. Hot water enters a radiator from this main pipe, transfers heat, re-enters the same pipe, and flows to the next radiator. The disadvantage of a one-pipe system is that the radiators last in line get cooler water than radiators at the beginning of the circuit. When water leaves a boiler and enters the first radiator, it is approximately 180°F. Water entering the last radiator can be 50 degrees cooler.

With a two-pipe system, heat is more evenly distributed, because there are two mains. One carries hot water to radiators; the other takes cooled water back to the boiler. With this system, the routing of the pipes determines the heating balance throughout the house.

Steam systems: Generally found in homes built before World War II, steam systems are similar to hot-water systems. Since hot steam rises vigorously, and condensate water naturally flows downward, most home systems are of the convection-gravity type, without need of a pump.

Steam systems also use one or two pipes. In a one-pipe system—called a one-pipe reverse flow system—water is brought to a boil in the boiler and steam rises through the main to the radiators. As it gives off heat, the steam condenses, and the condensate flows back through the same main to the boiler. In a two-pipe system, one pipe transmits steam, the other returns condensate.

There are drawbacks to either type of steam system. First, radiators have a tendency to get waterlogged with condensate, which leads to noise and reduced heat output. Second, steam systems are slow to respond to temperature changes in the house.

Warm-air system: A warm-air heating system may also operate by convection and gravity; however, modern forced warm-air systems, using fans or blowers, are more efficient. Such systems are less expensive to install originally and to extend to a new addition, compared to hot water and steam systems. A great advantage of forced warm air is its easy adaptability for central air conditioning; you simply add an air cooling device near the furnace, using the same ducts and registers for cool air in summer as for heated air in winter. You can remedy the dryness of heated air by adding a central humidifier.

A warm-air system ceases sending out heat soon after the furnace quits, when heated air stops coming out of registers. Thus the temperature of the house tends to fluctuate more widely with hot-air heat than steam and hot-water systems, which continue to emit heat from pipes and radiators long after the furnace shuts off. Hot air also circulates dust, especially if the ducts and registers are not cleaned periodically.

All of these systems are controlled with thermostats. As an energy-conservation measure, a house can be divided into two or more heating zones. Each zone has its own thermostat, so that only occupied parts of the house are heated; or the thermostats can be set with timers so heating levels rise and fall according to the time of day.

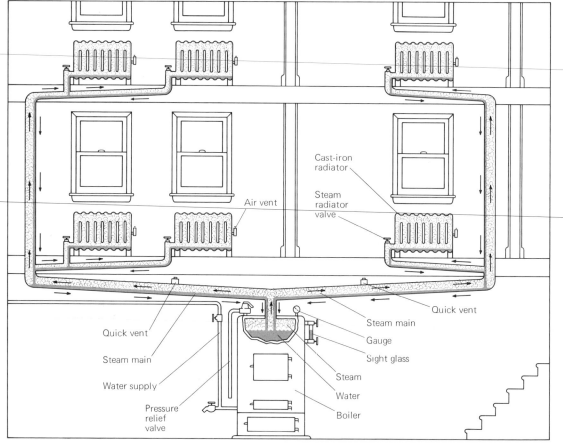

Cast-iron radiator

Air vent

Steam radiator valve

Quick vent

Quick vent

Steam main

Steam main

Gauge

Water supply

Sight glass

Pressure relief valve

Steam

Water

Boiler

In this one-pipe reverse flow system (the simplest and least expensive to install), steam rises from the boiler into mains, and enters the radiators through branch pipes. As steam displaces air in a radiator, the air is ejected through a vent. When air has been purged, the vent closes so steam is contained. Condensation that forms in the radiator flows back in the reverse direction to the boiler through the same pipes and mains that carry the steam. The radiator and pipes are pitched toward the boiler, allowing condensate water to flow by gravity. An important part of a boiler is the water gauge that lets you check the water level. If the automatic water feed system malfunctions, the water level drops and pressure rises. A safety valve will open to release excessive pressure, but sometimes the valve corrodes and sticks. Check the sight glass often and add water to the boiler if the level is low. But let the boiler cool first. Adding cold water to a hot boiler can damage the boiler.

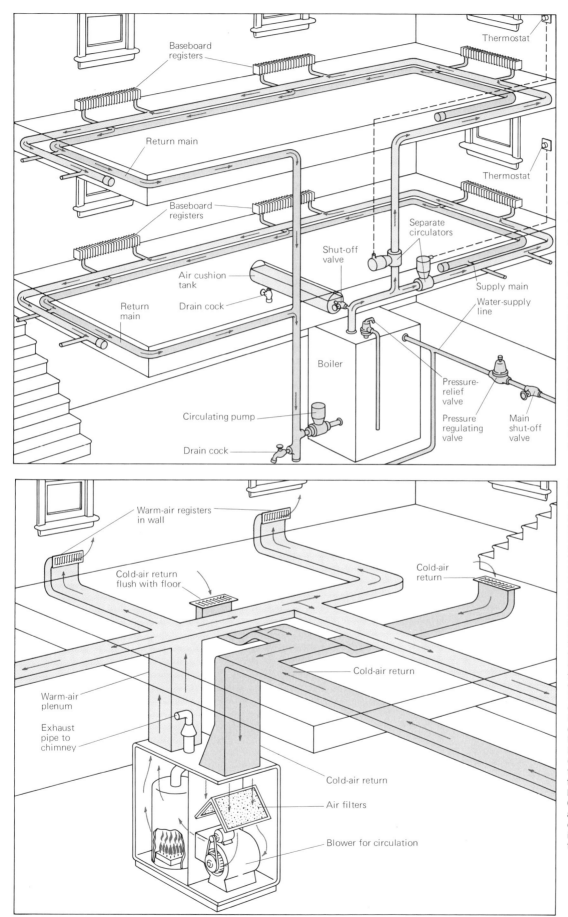

Hot-water (hydronic) heating: The system shown is a two-pipe direct return, a popular version for private dwellings. Hot water is pumped through feed mains and pipes into baseboard radiators, which are mounted along the walls. After circulating, water flows directly back from each radiator to the boiler for reheating by way of return pipes and mains. Many hydronic systems supply hot water, as well as heat, to the house. A copper coil, or heat exchanger, in the boiler transfers heat from the boiler to cold water circulating through the coil, producing hot water almost instantaneously. Hot water then flows to faucets through the hot-water supply pipes. This requires that the boiler run continually, even in warm seasons. Whether this system is more economical than a conventional hot-water tank depends on the climate in your area. If you run a boiler most of the year for heat, a heat exchanger for hot water may be advantageous. But in much of this country a hot-water tank is the more economical choice.

Forced warm-air heating: Warm air is blown from the furnace to room registers—grilles with dampers that can be closed to block the heat. Each register is served by a branch duct that taps warm air from a main duct, or plenum. Registers are placed low on walls or in floors. If possible, they should be located near outside walls, since perimeter heating provides more uniform temperatures throughout the rooms of the house. Cool air goes back to the furnace for reheating by way of cold-air returns. Ideally, there should be a cold-air return in every room, except in small enclosures such as bathrooms. A multilevel home can also have cold-air returns in areas that form natural cold air traps; for example, at bottoms of stairways. Generally, cold-air returns are placed in the bottoms of walls or in floors near interior walls, as far from the registers as possible.

Labels in upper diagram: Baseboard registers, Thermostat, Return main, Baseboard registers, Thermostat, Separate circulators, Shut-off valve, Supply main, Air cushion tank, Water-supply line, Return main, Drain cock, Boiler, Pressure-relief valve, Circulating pump, Pressure regulating valve, Main shut-off valve, Drain cock

Labels in lower diagram: Warm-air registers in wall, Cold-air return flush with floor, Cold-air return, Cold-air return, Warm-air plenum, Exhaust pipe to chimney, Cold-air return, Air filters, Blower for circulation

Plumbing tools and measurements

Plumbing tools

Flaring tool makes watertight joints between flexible copper tubing and fitting or valve. End of the tubing is slipped into a hole in the die block, and a compressor screw is tightened, forming a bell-shaped tube end.

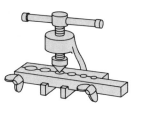

Hacksaw cuts plastic and metal pipe. Use blades with 16 teeth per in. for sawing ½- to 1-in. pipe, blades with 24 teeth per in. for sawing ⅛- to ¼-in. tubing and thin-walled pipe. Apply only slight pressure on the saw as you make your cuts.

Tube cutter is used to cut copper or brass tubing. Attach the cutter to the tubing and tighten the handle, but only enough to secure the tool to the tubing. Rotate the tool, applying a few drops of oil frequently to the work area as the cut is made.

Tube bender curves flexible copper tubing without distortion. Select a bender that closely fits the diameter of the tubing. If clearance between tubing and tool is excessive, tubing may kink as it is bent to shape.

Pipe reamer removes interior burrs from cuts before pipe or tubing is installed. Insert reamer and turn until it revolves freely. Exterior burrs are removed with file.

Propane-torch is used primarily for soldering fittings to tubing. Different nozzles are available to give flames of various shapes and sizes and, therefore, of different heat intensities.

Strap wrench grips and turns plated and thin-walled pipe that may be scratched or crushed by a wrench with serrated jaws. It is also used for working in tight spaces where other wrenches cannot fit.

Chain wrench has a heavy sprocket chain that is slipped around a pipe and then attached to the wrench handle. It is used to work on large pipes and to reach into tight places, as is the strap wrench shown above.

Pipe wrench is used for holding or turning iron pipe, and for removing damaged nuts and fittings. Serrated jaws bite into metal; it is not for use on soft or plated pipe, or on unmarred nuts and fittings.

Monkey wrench resembles a pipe wrench, except for its smooth jaws. It is used to hold or turn hardware having flat surfaces, such as nuts and drain fittings. An open-end or adjustable wrench may be substituted.

Valve-seat tool is used to remove square- and octagonal-shaped threaded faucet seats. It is a right angle bar, with one end for square nuts and the other, octagonal. A similar tool consists of a straight bar that is turned with a wrench.

Basin wrench has swiveling jaws that enable you to reach into places not easily managed with conventional wrenches. One of its major uses is to loosen and tighten nuts that hold faucets, but the tool may be adapted to other close-fit applications.

Adjustable spud wrench has unserrated jaws. It is used to turn fittings of minimum strength, such as copper and brass valves, and drain trap fittings on sinks and lavatories.

Dies are used for cutting threads outside pipe ends. Insert and turn the die. The cutting edges of the die score themselves into the softer pipe metal to form threads. Taps (not shown) are used to cut threads around the inside of pipes.

Channel-type pliers have an exceptionally wide jaw opening. They can be used to hold or turn fittings that do not require excessive force; be aware that the jaw serrations may mar metal.

Vise-grip, or locking pliers, lock securely to nuts and fittings. They are useful for holding worn hardware, leaving both hands of the plumber free for manipulations.

Making accurate measurements

Plumbing codes require an installation that is not only watertight, but also airtight. Errors in measurement will result in lost time and wasted material.

In measuring, use a flexible steel tape or folding ruler marked off in 1/16-inch increments. Planning an entire new system or a sizable extension could require calculations employing algebra, geometry, and trigonometry, but for most work dry-run measurements with simple computations are sufficient.

The drawing below illustrates several basic measurements commonly made by plumbers in installing new pipes, tubing, and fittings: center-to-center (C-C); face-to-face (F-F); end-to-end (E-E); and the screw-in allowance (S.I.A.). The last-named is the depth a pipe penetrates into a fitting; the term applies not only to threaded pipe but also to tubing. Other measurements, such as end-to-face (E-F) and end-to-center (E-C) might be required.

Technically, the most precise way to determine the actual length a pipe should be cut for installation between two fittings is to measure center to center, then deduct the distances between the pipe centers and the faces of the fittings; finally, add the screw-in allowances. To put this in a formula:

$$(E\text{-}E) = (C\text{-}C) - 2(C\text{-}F) + 2 (S.I.A.)$$

Here E-E is the actual pipe length.

Simplified calculations: In most instances, however, you can take shortcuts that greatly simplify matters. Use the dry-run method by measuring face to face between the fittings, then add the screw-in-allowance for each end.

For more elaborate installations, it is advisable to sketch the details to scale on paper, and then measure and make the computations. Double-check all figures before cutting or placing an order—cast-iron and similar pipes are best cut and threaded to order at plumbing supply stores.

At right is a table listing standard screw-in allowances. Choose the right allowances and add them to the face-to-face distances between fittings.

Screw-in allowances of metal pipes

Pipe size	Screw-in allowance (standard fittings)	Screw-in allowance (drainage fittings)
1/2"	1/2"	—
3/4"	1/2"	—
1"	5/8"	5/8"
1 1/4"	5/8"	5/8"
1 1/2"	5/8"	5/8"
2"	3/4"	7/8"
3"	—	1"
4"	—	1 1/2"

Pipe connections require one or more of these basic measurements: center-to-center, the distance between the centers of two pipes; face-to-face, the distance between two fittings; and end-to-end (actual pipe length), the face-to-face distance plus the screw-in allowance at both ends.

Plumbing codes and safety tips

The National Standard Plumbing Code (NSPC) and your municipal plumbing code are the authoritative guides that you should observe closely.

Your local plumbing code is available from your municipal or town Building Department. Call, find the hours when the department is open, go by and ask to read a copy of the code. To obtain a copy of the national code, write to the Code Secretary, National Standard Plumbing Code, 1016 20th Street NW, Washington, D.C. 20036. When your local code differs from the NSPC, follow your local stipulations.

Always observe the following safety practices:
▷ Keep your back straight and use leg muscles to lift. Get assistance if a fixture or length of pipe is heavy.
▷ Wipe up spills on the floor as soon as possible to prevent falls.
▷ Use only properly grounded electric tools. If you disconnect a home electric ground from a cold-water pipe, be sure to re-connect it after finishing work.
▷ Use a sturdy ladder that is securely positioned.

Face-to-face
Screw-in allowance
End-to-end (actual pipe length)
Center-to-center (calculated pipe length)

Computing offsets

In pipe fitting, it is often necessary to offset the position—but not the direction—of a pipe, either to bypass an obstruction or to direct the pipe into an opening on a different level.

For the purpose of computing offsets, an imaginary right triangle is constructed, as seen in the illustration below. The vertical distance between the two pipe centerlines is called the *offset*. The diagonal is called the *travel*. The horizontal distance between the pipe ends is called the *run*.

Most offset problems involve determining the travel (the calculated length of the pipe) when: either the offset and the run are known, or the offset and the angle opposite it (45° in the drawing) are known. Offset pipes are linked by pairs of standard threaded elbows of the angles listed in the table at bottom.

Technically, a master plumber can calculate any offset using geometry or trigonometry. But for most simple offsets, it is possible to use our table to obtain the travel. For example, if the offset is 10 inches and the offset angle is 45°, use 1.414 from the table and multiply it by 10 inches: the travel is 14.14 inches in actual length.

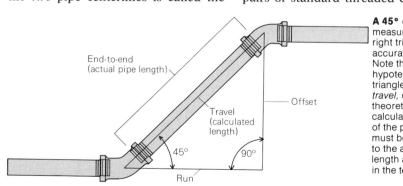

End-to-end (actual pipe length)
Travel (calculated length)
Offset
45°
90°
Run

A 45° offset is measured with a right triangle for accurate calculations. Note that the hypotenuse of this triangle, labeled *travel*, denotes the theoretical or calculated length of the pipe. It must be converted to the actual length as noted in the text at top.

Ratios in offset measurements

Offset angle	Ratio of travel to offset	Ratio of run to offset
60°	1.155	0.577
45°	1.414	1.000
30°	2.000	1.732
22 1/2°	2.613	2.414
11 1/4°	5.126	5.027
5 5/8°	10.217	10.168

Fittings, pipes, and tubing

Common fittings

Pipes do not always run straight. They curve, branch off, and may have to be connected to other pipes of different diameters. There is a fitting for virtually every plumbing need. If none of the fittings illustrated below meet your requirements, check with a plumbing parts supply store.

To prevent the galvanic action that causes corrosion when two dissimilar metals meet, select fittings of the same material as the pipe. Use a transitional adapter (see below) when joining pipes of dissimilar metals.

Most fittings and pipes for drainage are cast iron, copper, or plastic. Most fittings and pipes for water supply are galvanized steel, copper, or plastic. Fittings and pipes of black (ungalvanized) steel are intended for use only in gas distribution systems.

Fittings are joined to pipes in a number of ways, depending on the make-up of the connecting ends. Some fittings have female threads—pipes are screwed into them. Other fittings have male threads—they are screwed into pipes. Fittings also have ends that are soldered, glued, clamped, compressed, or caulked to pipes, as shown here and on subsequent pages.

When connecting fittings to pipes, make sure the joining points are continuous and free of impediments, so the delivery of water or the flow of sewage is not hampered.

Elbows (or Ls) allow pipe runs to turn. Elbows bent to form a 45° or 90° angle are standard; elbows of other angles are available. An elbow has a short, long, or extra long expanse to bridge the gap between pipes that are being joined.

Drop-ear elbows are used to fasten water supply pipes to studs at points where pipes break through walls for attachment to fixtures. The standard drop-ear elbow is a 90° fitting.

Return bends are 180° elbows, threaded at each end. They are used in drainage systems. Some have a third opening on the side or bottom of fitting. Return bends are also used as heat exchangers in steam and hot water heating systems.

Y-branches (or wyes) connect branch pipes to main pipes when they lie 45° to each other. Single wyes connect one branch; double wyes connect two, one coming from each side of the main. Wyes accommodate branches of the same diameter as the main, or smaller.

T-fittings (or tees) connect branch pipes to main pipes when they lie 90° to each other. Reducing tees have openings for smaller size branch pipes. For example, a ¾ x ½ reducing tee has ¾-in. openings for the main and a ½-in. opening for the branch.

Traps are installed in drains to retain water that prevents sewer gases from entering the home. The one illustrated here is a U-trap. Other common types are S- and P-traps. Names are based on shapes of traps.

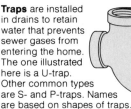

Reducers connect two pipes of different diameters. They have female threads at both ends. Order by referring to the diameters of both openings. For example, a ¾- x ½-in. reducer has one ¾-in. opening and one ½-in. opening.

Offsets divert drain and vent pipes around obstacles. Offsets come in a range of spans—from 2 to 18 in., in 2-in. increments.

Unions join lengths of pipe threaded in the same direction. When the union nut is loosened, it breaks apart the two sections of the union, disengaging one pipe from the other. Otherwise, pipes would have to be cut apart.

Nipples are pieces of pipe, 12 in. or less in length, that are externally threaded. They are used to join two fittings that lie close together. They are also used when short lengths of pipe are needed to complete runs.

Transitional adapters (couplings) allow pipes and fittings of dissimilar materials to be connected to each other without giving rise to galvanic action, which causes corrosion. Another type of coupling not shown here is the standard coupling. It is used to connect pipes of the same material and diameter.

Copper to steel

Plastic to steel

Plastic to copper

Bushings, like reducers, connect pipes of different sizes. However, they take up less room. The external threads of a bushing are screwed into the larger pipe. The smaller pipe is then screwed into bushing's internal threads.

Caps are used to seal pipes. But they have female threads for use on male-threaded pipes. Some caps must be tightened by hand; others are made to be tightened with a wrench.

Plugs are short, solid fittings inserted into the ends of female threaded pipes and fittings to seal them. They have raised or recessed hexagonal or square-shaped heads to permit tightening with a conventional or recess plug wrench.

Vent increasers are connected to the tops of soil stacks above the roof line to provide larger openings through which sewer gases can escape. Because they are wider, vents expanded by vent increasers stand less chance of being blocked by snow and ice. The added width permits more rapid dissemination of sewer gases to the atmosphere. A vent increaser assembly consists of hub and spigot fittings. Narrower hub is attached to the soil stack; the spigot accepts the vent.

Vent increaser

Vent

Pipes for the job

Four types of pipes are common to modern plumbing systems: cast iron, galvanized steel, plastic, and copper.

Cast-iron pipe: Cast-iron pipe is used only for drainage, waste, and venting (DWV). It comes in service (SV) and extra heavy (XH) grades, which refer to the metal's thickness. SV is intended for use in homes. XH is designed for underground installation. Cast-iron pipe weighs more per foot than comparable grades of other pipe. This makes the pipe difficult to handle. Consider using it if a pipe must be buried in a place where vehicles might run over it.

Galvanized-steel pipe: This is used primarily for water supply and in steam and hot water heating systems. Size for size, it is about three times more costly than plastic pipe, but about 40 percent less costly than copper tubing. It is difficult to work with because of its rigidity; and cutting and threading are also difficult tasks.

The value of galvanized-steel pipe lies in its imperviousness to physical damage. Consider using it only if parts of an installation are exposed and in areas where objects can impact against the pipe. Plastic and some grades of copper are not strong enough to withstand heavy blows.

Plastic pipe: Plastic is inexpensive, lightweight, does not corrode or rust, and is easy to handle. An insulator, it reduces the amount of heat loss from hot-water pipes. It minimizes pipe sweating, since it moderates the temperature difference between water flowing through cold-water pipes and room temperature.

Plastic pipe is used for both DWV and water supply: 40-grade ABS (acrylonitrile-butadiene-styrene) and 40-grade PVC (polyvinyl chloride) are DWV pipes: PVC pressure pipe rated at 73 degrees F. and 100 pounds per square inch (psi), or greater, is used for cold water supply; and CPVC (chlorinated polyvinyl chloride) and PB (poly-butylene) rated at 180 degrees F. and 100 psi, or greater, are used for hot water lines. Methods of joining plastic are described on ensuing pages.

If plastic is allowed by your local plumbing code for water supply lines (many codes still restrict the use of plastic to drain and waste lines), you may want to profit from its advantages over galvanized steel and copper—its lower cost and ease of installation.

Later pages of this chapter illustrate the techniques used to join pipe and fittings of various design and materials. Remember that it is necessary to employ transitional adapters when the situation involves joining pipes made of dissimilar materials.

Working with copper tubing

Copper tubing is used extensively in both water supply and DWV systems. It is lightweight, strong and easily manipulated, easy to handle, to bend, and to join. Copper tubing compares favorably with plastic in providing resistance to corrosion and scale. In this respect, either copper or plastic is preferable to galvanized-steel pipe. The main disadvantage of copper tubing is its cost.

Like plastic, copper tubing presents a smooth surface to water, offering little resistance. Therefore, you may be able to use a smaller size copper tubing than if you were installing galvanized-steel water supply pipe.

Grades and uses: Copper tubing is available in four grades: K, L, M, and DWV (Grade ACR is used in air conditioning and in refrigeration—not in plumbing.) K-grade is the heaviest and can be buried without adverse results. L-grade is a medium-weight tubing designed for indoor plumbing. M-grade is lighter-weight, and DWV-grade is even thinner than M-grade. Generally, either M- or DWV-grade are suitable for most indoor plumbing. However, many plumbing codes require the use of K or L grades only.

Copper tubing is made in soft (annealed) and hard (drawn) tempers. Soft tubing is so flexible that smaller diameter sizes come in coils, as well as in straight lengths. The coiled tubing, available in diameters up to 2 inches, is used only as water supply pipe. Straight lengths, in diameters up to 12 inches, find use both as water supply and DWV pipes. Use soft copper tubing in protected areas where pipes are not subject to impact.

Hard tubing is available in a variety of diameters and in straight lengths of 10 to 20 feet. Use hard tubing for DWV lines and for water supply in areas where impact damage is possible.

Copper pipe and copper tubing are two terms that are used interchangeably. The term "plumbing tubing" is also used in referring to copper tubing.

Methods of cutting tubing are illustrated here. Joining tubing is covered on the next two pages.

Copper tubing sizes

Type	Diameter	Thickness	Lengths
Rigid K	½"-12"	Heavy	10', 20'
Rigid L	⅛"-12"	Medium	10', 20'
Rigid M	⅛"-12"	Light	10', 20'
Soft K	¼"-12"	Heavy	30', 60', 100' coils
Soft L	¼"-12"	Medium	30', 60', 100' coils
Rigid DWV	Various	Light/ Medium	20'

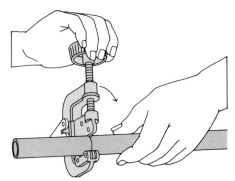

Use a tube cutter if diameter is less than 1 in. Rotate the tool slowly to assure a proper cut. Tighten handle after each turn; do not overtighten, you will kink the tube.

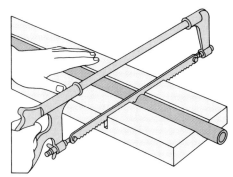

Use a hacksaw to cut tubing larger than 1 in. in diameter. Make certain pieces are measured accurately. Then place tubing in a miter box and cut slowly to assure a straight cut.

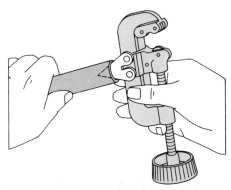

If the tube cutter has an attached reamer, use it to remove burrs inside tube. After reaming, withdraw the tool and feel for remaining burrs; file any external burrs from the tube.

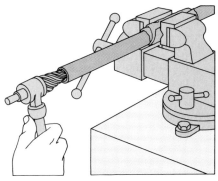

Ratchet reamer is more effective than a reamer attached to a tube cutter, especially if the tubing has rough burrs. Hold the tubing firmly with a vise, but cushion it with rags.

Copper pipe and tubing

Rigid copper tubing/soldering a joint

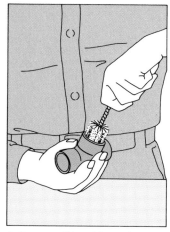

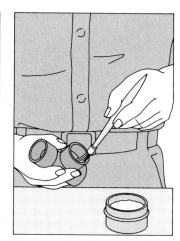

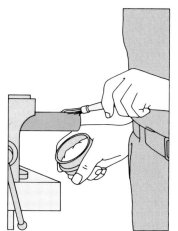

1. Remove dirt, oxide, and grease from inside the fitting with No.00 (fine) cloth-backed sandpaper or wire brush. Use light pressure. Rubbing too hard scratches metal and can weaken the joint.

2. Clean tubing for a distance just slightly more than is needed to accommodate the fitting socket. Make sure you wipe particles from the fitting and tubing to have perfect mating surfaces for the flux.

3. Apply a thin film of flux to the inside of the fitting immediately after cleaning. Use a rosin-type flux or one that is mildly corrosive and has ammonium and zinc chlorides. Same flux is used outside.

4. Apply flux to the outside of the tubing. The mating surfaces of both the fitting and tubing should have thin, even films of flux. Use a small brush or clean, lintless rags to spread the flux.

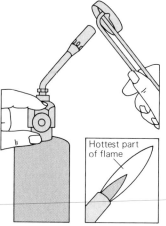

Hottest part of flame

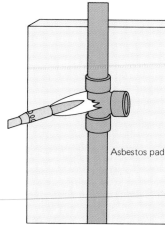

Asbestos pad

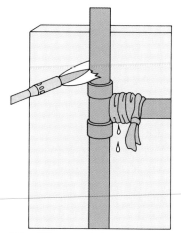

5. Insert tubing into fitting so it is firmly against fitting shoulder. Give the fitting a quarter- or half-turn to spread flux evenly over the mating surfaces. Wipe off flux that oozes from the joint.

6. Place a propane torch with a large round-shaped nozzle upright. Open the propane valve just a crack. Light the flame with a match or a sparker. Turn on more gas to adjust the flame before you begin work.

7. With an asbestos pad protecting the wall, play flame over the fitting, but not directly on the joint. The lower tubing here is inserted in position, but it has not yet been soldered to the pipe fitting.

If the fitting already has an adjacent soldered joint (right), heating it may melt the existing solder. To prevent this, wrap wet rags on the soldered joint to protect it from the heat of the flame and keep it cool.

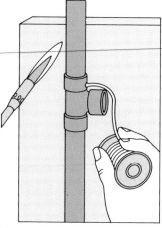

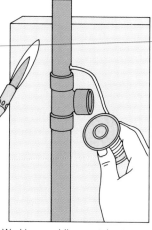

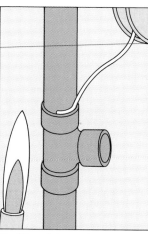

Soldered joint showing bead

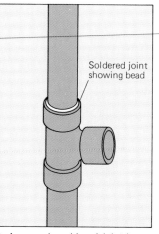

8. Use solid wire solder of half lead and half tin, not rosin- or acid-core solder. Test the hot fitting by touching it with the wire solder. If the solder melts, shift the flame to the tubing, as described in Step 9.

9. Working rapidly, next heat one side of the tubing, then test the temperature by touching the solder on the opposite side. If solder melts, the assembly is ready for soldering; if not, continue heating the tubing.

10. When fitting and tubing are hot enough, draw the flame away. Melted solder will be drawn into the joint by capillary action. If solder stops melting, re-heat the tube and fitting. Do not apply flame to the solder.

11. A properly soldered joint has a continuous bead of solder all around the joint. When all joints are soldered, cool and turn on water. If a joint leaks, drain the tubing. Re-heat the area and re-solder.

Joining rigid copper drain (DWV) pipes

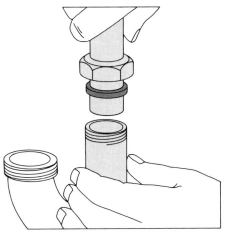

1. Cut end of the pipe as straight as possible and remove burrs. Slip the flange nut onto the pipe, then the flexible compression ring.

2. Firmly push the pipe into the opening of the drain fitting. To avoid leaks, a minimum of ½ in. of pipe should be inside the fitting.

3. Screw the flange nut onto the fitting fingertight. Be careful not to cross threads. The flexible compression ring seals the joint.

Bending and joining flexible copper tubing

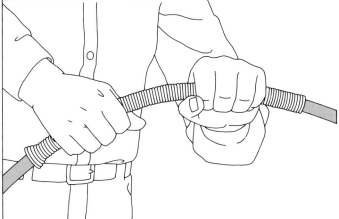

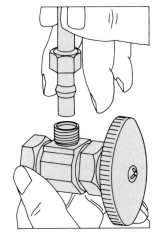

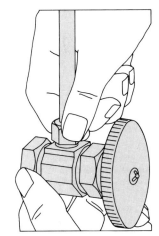

Make certain the tube bender is the correct diameter for the tubing size. A loose fit will cause tubing to kink. Insert tubing into the bender and slowly bend the tubing to the necessary configuration. Since the tube bender, seen here, is a spiral tube of flexible wire, you can slide the tool off the copper tubing without trouble. Take care not to exert too much hand pressure against the tubing's thin wall.

A faucet or toilet tank is connected to a shut-off valve by flexible tubing with a metal-ring compression joint. Slip flange nut, followed by the metal ring, onto the tubing. Nut and ring will make watertight seal.

Push the copper tubing into the fitting. Hand-tighten the flange nut. Do not use a wrench. It can distort the flexible tubing or metal ring. The metal ring will seat squarely in the fitting and seal the joint.

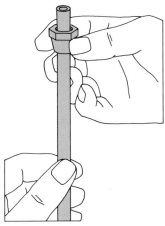

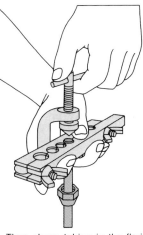

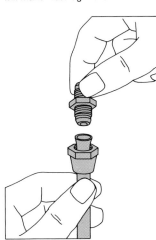

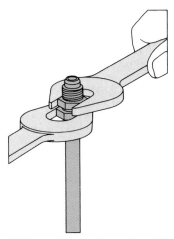

1. Flare joints make tighter seals than metal-ring compression joints and are easier than soldering. But making tight joints takes some practice. First slip a coupling nut onto the copper tubing, as shown.

2. Then clamp tubing in the flaring block without flattening it. Have the tube end stick up slightly above the block face. Attach the compressor cone and turn down the screw to form the flare for the fitting.

3. Place the fitting squarely against the flare to form the joint. Keep in mind that any foreign matter—metal slivers, burr, sand, or dirt—will disrupt metal-to-metal contact and allow water to leak.

4. Engage the coupling nut and fitting. Hand-tighten one to the other. Use two wrenches, one on the nut and the other on the fitting, as shown. Tighten the joint securely, without using excessive force.

211

Plastic pipe

Selecting and working with plastic pipe

If you want to employ plastic pipe for a project and your local code allows the use of plastic (see p.209), the first step is to determine which type to use.

Types of plastic: For drain-waste-vent (DWV) systems, polyvinyl-chloride (PVC) pipe or acrylonitrile-butadiene-styrene (ABS) pipe can be used. PVC has better resistance to detergents and household chemicals, is less likely to smolder and give off toxic fumes during a fire, and is cheaper than ABS.

For cold- and hot-water supply pipes chlorinated polyvinyl chloride (CPVC) or polybutylene (PB) can be used. CPVC is rigid and easily joined with solvent-cement. PB is flexible and easier to cut, but must be joined by means of flaring, insert, or compression fittings. It comes in coils and cannot be made perfectly straight. It is used for long pipe runs, where pipe must be threaded through difficult spaces, and in concealed areas where appearance is not important.

CPVC is good for runs of pipe interrupted frequently by fittings. In an ideal situation, CPVC can be installed from the supply source to the shut-off valves, where PB then takes over to reach the faucets or toilet ballcocks. Transition adapters are used to join pipes and fittings of different types of plastic.

When you buy plastic pipe, see that it bears the NSF (National Sanitation Foundation) seal. The NSF, which is to plastic pipe what the Underwriters Laboratories (UL) is to electrical equipment, determines whether pipe meets established standards.

Working with plastic pipes: When cutting plastic pipe, calculate lengths by measuring the face-to-face distance (p.207) and adding the amount of insertion. Cut rigid pipe with a hacksaw or tube-cutter, and flexible pipe with a sharp, sturdy knife.

Before permanently joining a rigid pipe to a fitting, always dry-assemble the parts to make sure they fit snugly. As you insert pipe into a fitting, the pipe should reach a point about halfway in, where it tightens and cannot be pushed farther into the fitting. This is the desired "interference fit", caused by the taper inside the fitting. If you find no such resistance point, try a different piece of pipe or a different fitting. Pipe and fittings from different manufacturers may not fit tightly; loose fits result in leaks. Always use pipe and fittings from one manufacturer.

If you plan on using the solvent-cement method of joining, make sure you buy either an all-purpose solvent or one that is compatible with the type of plastic in your pipes and fittings. After applying the solvent, hold the joint steady for at least 20 seconds; wait an-other three minutes before starting on the next joint. When the work is finished wait at least two hours—overnight, in cold temperatures—before running water to pressure-test supply pipes. (DWV pipes can be tested with running water immediately; simply flush toilets or run water into drains.) For supply lines, open the main supply valve just enough to get the water moving. When water starts flowing from the lowest faucet in the house, adjust pressure at the faucet to get a steady trickle. Do the same for every faucet and toilet. Let them trickle for 10 minutes as you check joints for leaks. Then shut off the main valve for 30 minutes. Repeat the process twice. Finally, run the system normally and check again for leaks.

Allowing for expansion: Plastic pipe is attached to wall studs and joists with hangers that are available at most plumbing supply houses; space the hangers 3 feet apart for supply pipe and every 4 feet for DWV pipe. Make sure the metal hangers do not cut into or abrade the softer plastic. Plastic pipe expands more than metal with temperature changes. A 10-foot length of CPVC pipe expands half an inch at 180°F. It is important that enough play be left between hangers to allow for such an expansion and that joints are not butted against any obstruction.

Plastic pipes: types for different uses

Type of plastic pipe	Available forms	Main uses	Rated temperature and pressure	Type of joints
ABS, 40-grade (acrylonitrile-butadiene-styrene)	Rigid (black) 1½", 2", 3", 4" in 10' and 20' lengths	DWV, sewers	100°F. (under pressure) 180°F. (without pressure)	Solvent Transition Threading
PVC (polyvinyl chloride)	Rigid (white, beige) ½", ¾", 1", 1¼", 1½", 2", 4" in 10' lengths or longer	DWV, cold water service and mains, sewers, gas	100°F. (under pressure) 180°F. (without pressure)	Solvent Transition Compression Flared
CPVC (chlorinated polyvinyl chloride)	Rigid (beige) ½", ¾" in 10' or longer lengths	Domestic cold and hot water service, chemical	180°F. (under 100 PSI pressure)	Solvent Transition Compression Flared
PP (polypropylene)	Rigid 1½", and as molded traps	Sink drain pipes, traps	100°F. (with pressure) 180°F. (without pressure)	Compression Threading Heat fusion
SR (styrene rubber plastic)	Rigid plastic impregnated with rubber particles	Storm drains, septic field pipes, underground de-watering drains	150°F. (without pressure)	Solvent Transition Compression
PE (polyethylene)	Flexible (black) in several grades and densities. ½", ¾", 1", 2". By foot or in 100' coils	Cold water service (esp. outdoor), irrigation, gas, chemical	100°F. (under pressure)	Insert Transition Compression Flared Heat fusion
PB (polybutylene)	Flexible (beige, black) ⅜", ½", ¾", 1", 1½", 2", by foot or in 25', 100' and 500' coils	Cold and hot water service	180°F. (under 100 PSI pressure) 200°F. (without pressure)	Insert Transition Compression Flared Heat fusion

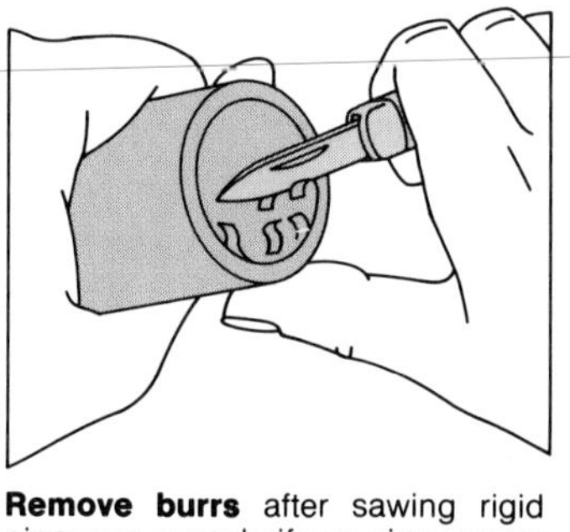

Remove burrs after sawing rigid pipe; use a penknife or pipe reamer. Apply only light pressure, to avoid slicing into plastic.

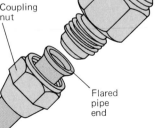

Coupling nut

Flared pipe end

Flared joints are made with plastic as is done with copper pipe (see p.211). First, heat end of plastic pipe in very warm water.

Joining rigid plastic pipe

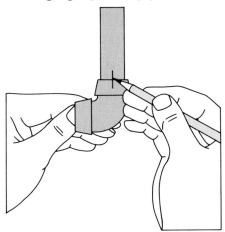

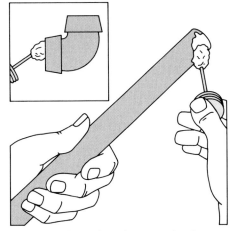

1. Mark for proper alignment before applying solvent-cement. Dry-assemble all pipes and fittings and make alignment marks, as seen here. This step is important; the solvent-cementing method leaves little time for making adjustments once the adhesive is applied.

2. Using a plastic pipe primer or a cleaning compound, clean end of pipe and fitting socket to prevent dirt and grease from spoiling solvent joint. Keep components dry before applying the adhesive. Water will disrupt uncured solvent and weaken the joint.

3. Employing the proper solvent-cement for your type of pipe, rapidly brush solvent on the primed area of the pipe. Make sure entire surface to be inserted in socket is coated with solvent. To speed application use a brush as wide as the depth to which the pipe will be inserted.

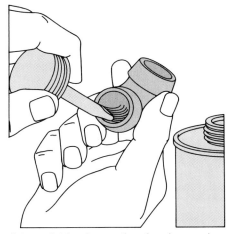

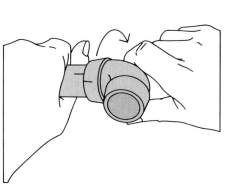

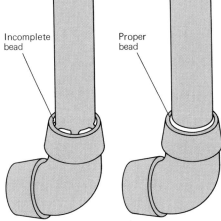

4. Immediately after coating the pipe, apply a liberal layer of solvent inside the fitting. Work rapidly because once this quick-drying cement begins to set components will not adhere. Finally apply a second coating of the solvent-cement to the end of the pipe.

5. Insert pipe into fitting, twist it to bring parts into alignment, and push pipe into the socket. You have about 30 seconds to attain alignment from the time you first begin coating the pipe. After that, the mated plastic components become permanently immovable.

6. A properly solvent-cemented joint should show a continuous bead all around. If the bead has gaps, testing (text, p.212) will determine if the joint leaks. If it does, cut away the section and do the job again with new parts and fresh applications of solvent-cement.

Joining flexible plastic pipe

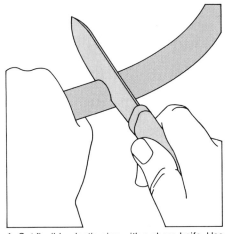

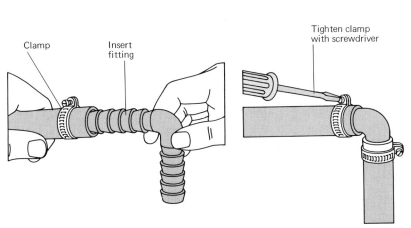

1. Cut flexible plastic pipe with a sharp knife. Use pipes a size larger than required to counteract retardation of flow by insert fittings. Put pipe in a miter box to assure a square end.

2. Insert fittings, made from either metal or rigid plastic, are used to couple lengths of flexible plastic pipe. Push each end of the fitting into the pipe as far as it will go.

3. Automotive hose clamps are used to secure joints at insert fittings. Tightening screws on clamps locks the flexible plastic to ridges on the fittings (see previous illustration).

Cast-iron drain pipe

Working with cast-iron DWV pipe

The great strength and durability of cast-iron pipe have made it the most extensively used drain-waste-vent pipe. However, it is extremely heavy and difficult to join. The average homeowner should leave this work to professional plumbers, unless he has do-it-yourself plumbing experience or guidance from an experienced friend.

Pipe types: Cast-iron pipe is of four types (illustrations, right): modern pipe evolved from the traditional hub-and-spigot type, through the single- and double-hub types, to today's widely manufactured no-hub variety. All are still made and used today.

Hub-and-spigot varieties are manufactured in standard 5- and 10-foot lengths; no-hub pipe is made in 10-foot lengths. A 10-foot length of 4 inch diameter hub-and-spigot pipe weighs about 82 pounds; a no-hub piece of the same size weighs 74 pounds. Pieces should be lifted with slings, by at least two persons. During installation, each joint is supported with strap-iron hangers for horizontal runs, or a pipe bracket on vertical sections. Cast-iron pipe can be cut with either a hacksaw or a cold chisel and a hammer. If a soil-pipe snapper is available from a tool rental shop, the job will be faster, but still difficult. The cutting chain of the snapper is wrapped around the pipe and locked; the chain is rotated, scoring the pipe. The snapper is then moved to one side of the score line. By pushing the handle down, you break off your length.

Standard hub-and-spigot pipe is joined and caulked with oakum (tar-impregnated hemp or jute) and molten lead. Such joints are strong, but difficult and even risky for non-professionals. The more modern single-hub pipe can be joined with a neoprene gasket placed inside the hub. The end of the next length is then lubricated and rammed into the gasket with a special tool. Double-hub pipe is designed to be cut into short lengths: when cut, both pieces have usable hub and plain ends. The most modern no-hub variety is joined with a neoprene sleeve, stainless-steel shield, and pipe clamps, as seen in the illustrations. Although hub-and-spigot pipe is still in use, the no-hub variety is gaining favor because of its lighter weight and ease in handling.

Spigot — Hub — Hub — Hub — Hub

| Standard pipe | Double-hub pipe | Single-hub pipe | No-hub pipe |

Cutting pipe

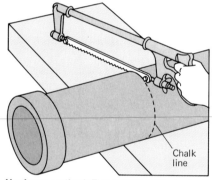

Chalk line

Hacksaw method: The desired cut is marked on the pipe with chalk. A coarse-toothed hacksaw is used to score a 1/16-in. groove all around the pipe. The shorter section of the pipe is then extended from a supporting board and broken off with a hammer.

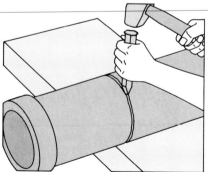

Cold chisel and hammer method: A dull-edged cold chisel and a hammer are used to tap a deep groove around the pipe. Then, the shorter section of the pipe is extended from the board and broken off with blows of the hammer. This method is best for heavy pipe.

Joining standard pipes

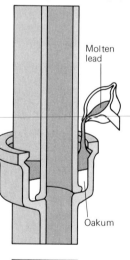

Molten lead

Oakum

1. Spigot of one pipe is centered in hub of another. Oakum is wrapped around pipe and packed tightly into joint with a tool called a yarning iron, leaving a space of 1 in. Molten lead is ladled into space from a plumber's furnace. The joint must be completely dry; any moisture will result in a dangerous explosion.

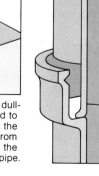

Outside caulking iron

2. Pouring stops when lead is about 1/8-in. above top. After lead cools, it is packed tightly against hub with hammer and tool called an outside caulking iron. Next, an inside caulking iron is used to pack lead against spigot pipe. Horizontal joints are made with a special tool that is called an asbestos joint-runner; it keeps lead from leaking out of hub during pouring.

Joining no-hub pipe

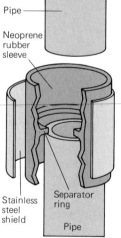

Pipe

Neoprene rubber sleeve

Stainless steel shield

Separator ring

Pipe

1. Equipment for joining hubless pipes are neoprene rubber sleeve, stainless steel shield, and two pipe clamps. Slide the neoprene sleeve onto one of the pipes until pipe end butts against the separator ring inside sleeve. Then slide the stainless steel shield over the sleeve.

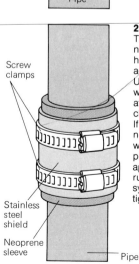

Screw clamps

Stainless steel shield

Neoprene sleeve

Pipe

2. Attach pipe clamps. Then insert end of next pipe into empty half of sleeve, butting it against separator ring. Use a torque wrench with screwdriver attachment to tighten clamps to 60-in.-lb. If torque wrench is not available, tighten with screwdriver until pipes cannot be moved apart. Test joints by running water through system. If a joint leaks, tighten clamps farther.

Joining pipes of different materials

Transition techniques

Whether you intend only to replace a part of your existing plumbing or to extend it for a new installation, plastic is your best choice, if allowed by your local code. The new plastic pipes can easily be joined to existing metal pipe, by using transition adapters.

Adapter types: Water supply pipe adapters generally have screw threads on the end that is to be joined to metal, and solvent cement on the other end, which is joined to the plastic; some designs provide for compression or sweat-soldered joints. Adapters for joining flexible plastic employ inserts (p.213). DWV plastic pipe is joined to hub-and-spigot with male or female threaded adapters, or lead and oakum, or compression gaskets (p.214). Plastic is joined to hubless cast-iron using a neoprene sleeve (below).

In using threaded adapters apply Teflon tape or pipe dope over the male threads before coupling. After hand-tightening, turn the nut up to one full turn with a wrench.

Several examples of how to tap into existing plumbing systems are illustrated. They consist of branching a metal water supply line using plastic pipe; installing a shut-off valve and faucet on new or existing plastic pipe; tapping into a cast-iron soil stack with PVC soil pipe; and installing a new sink, basin, or wet bar. Other ways can be inferred from these examples.

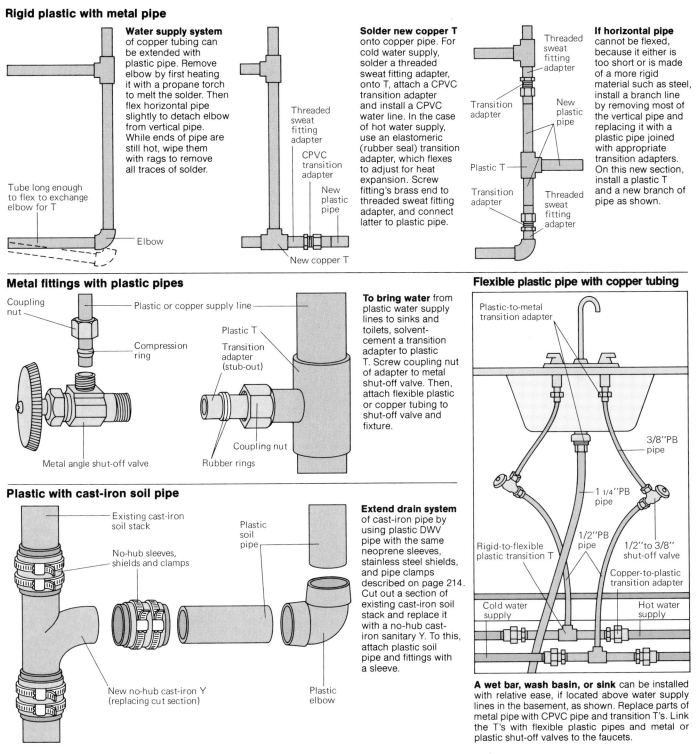

Rigid plastic with metal pipe

Water supply system of copper tubing can be extended with plastic pipe. Remove elbow by first heating it with a propane torch to melt the solder. Then flex horizontal pipe slightly to detach elbow from vertical pipe. While ends of pipe are still hot, wipe them with rags to remove all traces of solder.

Tube long enough to flex to exchange elbow for T

Elbow

Threaded sweat fitting adapter

CPVC transition adapter

New plastic pipe

New copper T

Solder new copper T onto copper pipe. For cold water supply, solder a threaded sweat fitting adapter, onto T, attach a CPVC transition adapter and install a CPVC water line. In the case of hot water supply, use an elastomeric (rubber seal) transition adapter, which flexes to adjust for heat expansion. Screw fitting's brass end to threaded sweat fitting adapter, and connect latter to plastic pipe.

Threaded sweat fitting adapter

Transition adapter

New plastic pipe

Plastic T

Transition adapter

Threaded sweat fitting adapter

If horizontal pipe cannot be flexed, because it either is too short or is made of a more rigid material such as steel, install a branch line by removing most of the vertical pipe and replacing it with a plastic pipe joined with appropriate transition adapters. On this new section, install a plastic T and a new branch of pipe as shown.

Metal fittings with plastic pipes

Coupling nut

Plastic or copper supply line

Compression ring

Metal angle shut-off valve

Plastic T

Transition adapter (stub-out)

Coupling nut

Rubber rings

To bring water from plastic water supply lines to sinks and toilets, solvent-cement a transition adapter to plastic T. Screw coupling nut of adapter to metal shut-off valve. Then, attach flexible plastic or copper tubing to shut-off valve and fixture.

Flexible plastic pipe with copper tubing

Plastic-to-metal transition adapter

3/8" PB pipe

1 1/4" PB pipe

1/2" PB pipe

Rigid-to-flexible plastic transition T

1/2" to 3/8" shut-off valve

Copper-to-plastic transition adapter

Cold water supply

Hot water supply

Plastic with cast-iron soil pipe

Existing cast-iron soil stack

No-hub sleeves, shields and clamps

Plastic soil pipe

New no-hub cast-iron Y (replacing cut section)

Plastic elbow

Extend drain system of cast-iron pipe by using plastic DWV pipe with the same neoprene sleeves, stainless steel shields, and pipe clamps described on page 214. Cut out a section of existing cast-iron soil stack and replace it with a no-hub cast-iron sanitary Y. To this, attach plastic soil pipe and fittings with a sleeve.

A wet bar, wash basin, or sink can be installed with relative ease, if located above water supply lines in the basement, as shown. Replace parts of metal pipe with CPVC pipe and transition T's. Link the T's with flexible plastic pipes and metal or plastic shut-off valves to the faucets.

Bathroom fixtures

Installing a toilet

Replacing an old toilet with a new one is simpler than installing a unit in a newly constructed bathroom because you can make use of the existing water supply and soil pipes. In a new bathroom, you must also install and connect the supply and soil pipes leading to the fixtures—an operation called "roughing-in".

These two pages show the key plumbing connections made to install a toilet. The toilet depicted is a common floor-mounted, tank-on-bowl type. For a general discussion of bathroom planning, selection of fixtures, and roughing-in, see the chapter on remodeling and adding bathrooms (pp.144–149).

Removing the existing toilet: To remove an old toilet, first shut off the water supply pipe to the tank. Then loosen the pipe coupling nuts (illustrations this page) and remove the pipe. Take off the tank cover and flush the toilet. Use a sponge or towel to sop up the water remaining in the tank. Then remove the water from the bowl. Next, disconnect the bolts holding the tank to the bowl and remove the tank. (To take off the tank and bowl as a single unit, it weighs 80 to 100 pounds, would require the help of another person to carry the assembly.) Remove the bowl from the floor by prying off (or unscrewing, in the case of very old units) the porcelain caps on either side of the base; then remove the exposed nuts holding the base. Rock the bowl from side to side and back to front, breaking free the wax ring seal between the toilet horn and the flange. Scrape old wax from the flange.

Installation procedure: For a floor-mounted toilet, install the bowl first and then the tank, as follows:

▷ Slide the heads of the hold-down bolts into their slots in the flange, and place the bowl on the flange.

▷ Use a carpenter's level to make sure the bowl is level. If it is not, place metal shims beneath the bowl to make it level.

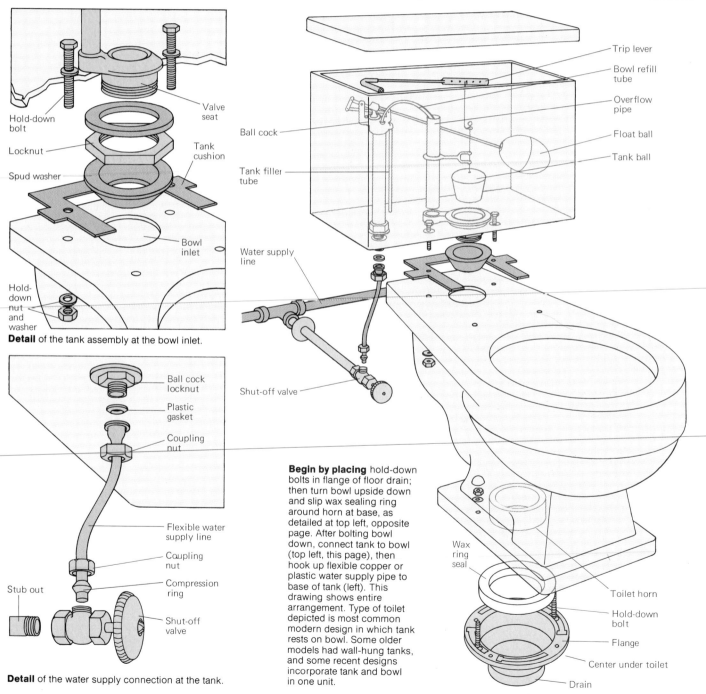

Valve seat

Hold-down bolt

Locknut

Spud washer

Tank cushion

Bowl inlet

Hold-down nut and washer

Detail of the tank assembly at the bowl inlet.

Ball cock locknut

Plastic gasket

Coupling nut

Flexible water supply line

Coupling nut

Compression ring

Stub out

Shut-off valve

Detail of the water supply connection at the tank.

Trip lever

Bowl refill tube

Overflow pipe

Float ball

Tank ball

Ball cock

Tank filler tube

Water supply line

Shut-off valve

Begin by placing hold-down bolts in flange of floor drain; then turn bowl upside down and slip wax sealing ring around horn at base, as detailed at top left, opposite page. After bolting bowl down, connect tank to bowl (top left, this page), then hook up flexible copper or plastic water supply pipe to base of tank (left). This drawing shows entire arrangement. Type of toilet depicted is most common modern design in which tank rests on bowl. Some older models had wall-hung tanks, and some recent designs incorporate tank and bowl in one unit.

Wax ring seal

Toilet horn

Hold-down bolt

Flange

Center under toilet

Drain

▷ Remove the bowl. Secure any shims used to the floor with an adhesive that will bond with the flooring (adhesives are available for ceramic tile, vinyl tile, sheet vinyl, hardwood, and concrete).

▷ Turn the bowl upside down and press a new wax ring seal around the horn (illustration at bottom right, p.216, and top left, here).

▷ Position the bowl on the flange so that the horn fits squarely in the discharge opening of the drain. Hold-down bolts should protrude through the holes in the base of the toilet bowl, as seen in the large drawing on this page. If necessary, gently twist the bowl back and forth to get it in position. Then apply firm downward pressure to get the wax ring seal and flange into contact.

▷ Tighten the nuts on the hold-down bolts securely. But do not overtighten or you may crack the rim.

▷ Fill the porcelain caps with plaster and press them down onto the bolts.

Secure the valve seat (illustrations, p.216) with a seal and a locknut; put a spud washer into the bowl's water inlet. Place the tank on the bowl so its valve seat fits in the spud washer. Bolt the tank to the bowl, install the float assembly, and connect the water supply pipe, making the toilet operational.

Special treatment: If a floor-mounted toilet is to be replaced with a more expensive wall-mounted type, you must repair the floor and re-route the soil stack with a tee through the wall. If you are installing a toilet in a basement below the level of the main waste pipe, consider buying an upward-flushing toilet. It utilizes water pressure to push waste into an overhead drain, which connects to the main sewer line.

Venting toilet soil pipe: Your location of a new toilet, with a newly installed soil pipe, will be affected by venting considerations. Refer to the illustration on page 224.

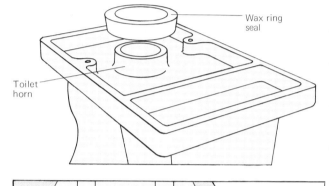

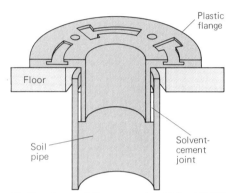

Wax ring seal slips over the horn in toilet bowl base in order to make a watertight connection with soil pipe. Turn bowl upside down onto a pad of old newspapers or bath towels. Press wax ring over horn firmly so it stays in place. Lift bowl right-side-up and put it on flange of floor drain. The base of the bowl is anchored by hold-down bolts in the flange (see the drawing below and on the opposite page).

Plastic pipe and flange are joined by solvent cement; flange fits inside soil pipe. Toilet horn (not shown) fits inside flange from above.

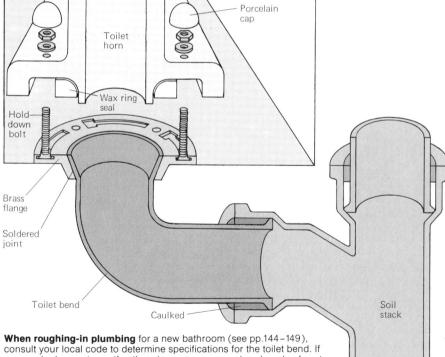

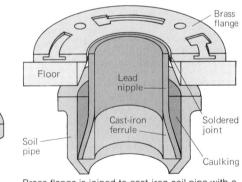

Brass flange is joined to cast-iron soil pipe with a lead nipple; joint is caulked and a cast-iron ferrule is driven in to tighten seal.

When roughing-in plumbing for a new bathroom (see pp.144–149), consult your local code to determine specifications for the toilet bend. If your code does not specify otherwise, you can use a bend made of cast iron, plastic, copper, or lead. The bend should be the same size as the existing soil stack. A cast-iron bend is joined to a cast-iron soil pipe by employing a Y, as shown on page 214; a plastic bend is joined to cast iron as on page 215. Plastic is joined to a plastic soil pipe using a plastic Y and solvent-cementing procedures shown on page 213. In the case of a copper bend and a copper soil pipe, connections are made at the Y by soldering. (Do-it-yourselfers should avoid the use of lead bends, which require professional experience.) Small drawings at right on this page show several common methods of connecting bends to toilet flanges. When roughing-in plumbing, the bend must be supported underneath; usually, this is done with a brace of 2 x 3 or 2 x 4 scrap wood that is nailed to the floor joists.

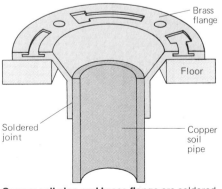

Copper soil pipe and brass flange are soldered. For such a joint, choose a funnel-shaped flange that fits the pipe snugly.

Bathroom fixtures

Installing a tub with shower

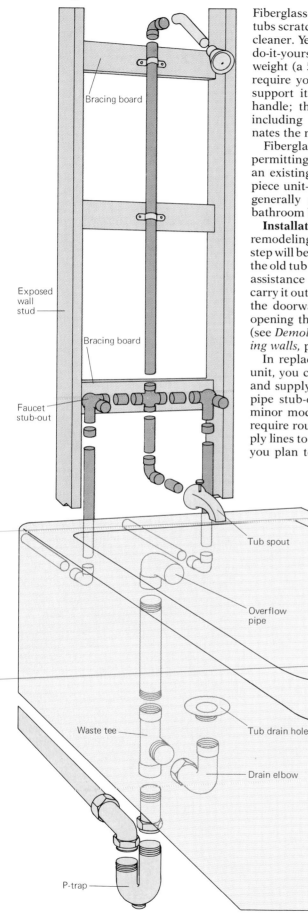

Bracing board

Exposed
wall
stud

Bracing board

Faucet
stub-out

Tub spout

Overflow
pipe

Waste tee

Tub drain hole

Drain elbow

P-trap

Fiberglass-reinforced polyester bathtubs scratch if scoured with an abrasive cleaner. Yet they are the choice of most do-it-yourselfers; they are light in weight (a 500-pound cast-iron tub may require you to shore up floor joists to support its weight); they are easy to handle; they come as complete units including stall showers, which eliminates the need for tiling walls.

Fiberglass units come unassembled, permitting you to take the parts through an existing bathroom doorway. A one-piece unit—or a cast-iron or steel tub—generally should be moved into the bathroom before the doorframe is built.

Installation procedures: If you are remodeling an existing bath, your first step will be to remove the old tub. Where the old tub is cast-iron, you will need the assistance of at least three helpers to carry it out. If the tub cannot fit through the doorway, you will have to cut an opening through the wall to remove it (see *Demolition*, p.171, and *Interior bearing walls*, pp.76–85).

In replacing an old tub with a new unit, you can usually make both drain and supply connections to the existing pipe stub-outs (ends), with just some minor modifications. (New bathrooms require roughing-in new drain and supply lines to the specifications of the unit you plan to install; see pp.146–151.) In-

stall the drain elbow and overflow pipe to the drain opening in the floor or wall (illustrations this page). Move the tub into position and assemble the crosspiece, attaching a large flat washer to the drain elbow's slip nut. Then connect the overflow pipe to the tub's overflow hole, and install the stopper linkage. Cover the overflow hole with a large beveled washer and attach the overflow plate (illustrations, below, and next page).

Supply pipes: The faucet and shower assembly are installed in the wall above the tub head. The showerhead and faucets are supported by 2-x-4 bracing nailed between wall studs (which means opening up the wall in an existing bath). The bracing is set back far enough so that the stub-out connections with the showerhead, faucets, and spout will be flush with the finished wall surface.

Pitching the tub: Manufacturer's instructions tell whether the tub must be pitched toward the drain. If pitching is required, the slope is usually ⅛-inch per foot. Use ⅜-inch rubber padding under the tub. Plumbing codes prohibit shimming, which can cause a tub to crack.

Access panel: If you are building a new bathroom, provide an access door in the tub plumbing wall, if feasible; it will let you get at the pipes and the tub drum trap for repairs. Install the access panel in the wall of a closet, hallway, or room that is behind the plumbing wall.

Use plumber's dope, putty, or tape to seal screw-thread pipe connections. For cast-iron drain pipe, oakum and lead may be required (see p.214).

Water supply system

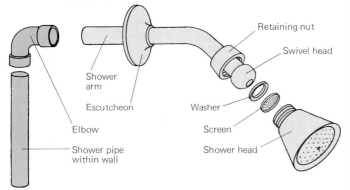

Shower arm
Retaining nut
Swivel head
Escutcheon
Washer
Elbow
Screen
Shower pipe within wall
Shower head

Install the shower assembly so the showerhead is at the desired height. Showerheads are generally positioned 5 to 6 ft. from the base of the tub. Nail a piece of 2-x-4 bracing across exposed studs of the wall at a point slightly below the elbow and secure the water supply pipe to the brace.

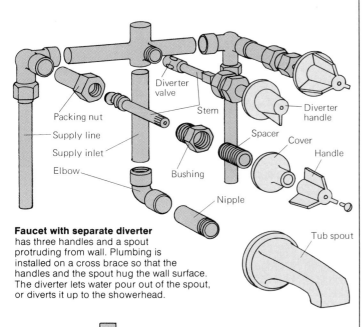

Diverter valve
Stem
Packing nut
Diverter handle
Supply line
Spacer
Supply inlet
Cover
Elbow
Handle
Bushing
Nipple
Tub spout

Faucet with separate diverter
has three handles and a spout protruding from wall. Plumbing is installed on a cross brace so that the handles and the spout hug the wall surface. The diverter lets water pour out of the spout, or diverts it up to the showerhead.

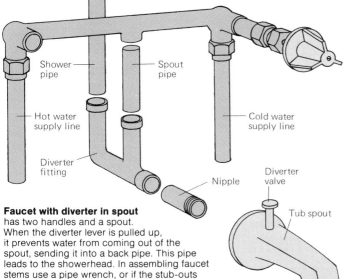

Shower pipe
Spout pipe
Hot water supply line
Cold water supply line
Diverter fitting
Nipple
Diverter valve
Tub spout

Faucet with diverter in spout
has two handles and a spout. When the diverter lever is pulled up, it prevents water from coming out of the spout, sending it into a back pipe. This pipe leads to the showerhead. In assembling faucet stems use a pipe wrench, or if the stub-outs are deep in the wall, a socket-wrench.

Drain system

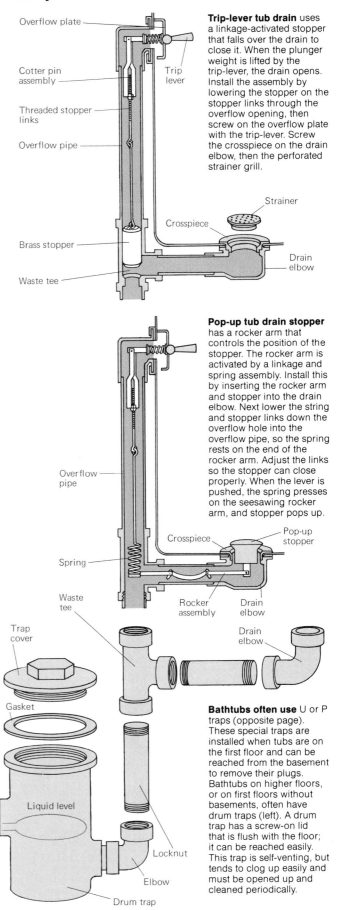

Overflow plate
Cotter pin assembly
Threaded stopper links
Overflow pipe
Brass stopper
Waste tee
Trip lever
Strainer
Crosspiece
Drain elbow

Trip-lever tub drain uses a linkage-activated stopper that falls over the drain to close it. When the plunger weight is lifted by the trip-lever, the drain opens. Install the assembly by lowering the stopper on the stopper links through the overflow opening, then screw on the overflow plate with the trip-lever. Screw the crosspiece on the drain elbow, then the perforated strainer grill.

Pop-up tub drain stopper has a rocker arm that controls the position of the stopper. The rocker arm is activated by a linkage and spring assembly. Install this by inserting the rocker arm and stopper into the drain elbow. Next lower the string and stopper links down the overflow hole into the overflow pipe, so the spring rests on the end of the rocker arm. Adjust the links so the stopper can close properly. When the lever is pushed, the spring presses on the seesawing rocker arm, and stopper pops up.

Overflow pipe
Spring
Waste tee
Crosspiece
Pop-up stopper
Rocker assembly
Drain elbow
Trap cover
Drain elbow
Gasket
Liquid level
Locknut
Elbow
Drum trap

Bathtubs often use U or P traps (opposite page). These special traps are installed when tubs are on the first floor and can be reached from the basement to remove their plugs. Bathtubs on higher floors, or on first floors without basements, often have drum traps (left). A drum trap has a screw-on lid that is flush with the floor; it can be reached easily. This trap is self-venting, but tends to clog up easily and must be opened up and cleaned periodically.

Basins and sinks

Installing basins, sinks, and garbage disposers

Bathroom basins (lavatories), kitchen sinks, and laundry sinks all have faucets supplying hot and cold water. Basins have drains with either pop-up stoppers, or old-fashioned crosspieces and rubber plugs. Sinks have larger drain pipes, with strainers at their enlarged drain holes. In localities with adequate sewer systems, a garbage disposer may be connected to a kitchen sink. However, disposers should not be used in homes with septic tanks or narrow sewer lines.

These two pages discuss the key plumbing connections for a common wash basin, a kitchen sink with a spray hose, and a garbage disposer.

Installation procedures: If you are replacing an old fixture with a new one, you can simply make your connections to the existing stub-outs. But for new installations, you will have to open up the walls and install tees and stub-outs in the existing plumbing to connect drain, vent, and water supply lines. Take accurate measurements, lay out the job on paper, and take your plan along to your plumbing supplier when you buy pipe, tubing, and fittings. Tees and stub-outs must be of the same material—copper, stainless steel, etc.—as the existing pipes to avoid galvanic corrosion between dissimilar metals. Transition adapters can be used to make connections of unlike materials between the stub-outs, shut-off valves, and faucet tailpieces. To facilitate these connections, the stub-outs should be located at least 1½ feet below the tailpieces.

To prevent galvanic corrosion, secure metal stub-outs to studs with straps of the same metal. If a stub-out is not near enough to a stud for attachment to it, nail a 2-x-4-bracing board across a pair of studs to anchor the stub-out. If a shut-off valve must be removed in the future, a braced stub-out will not twist when force is applied with a wrench.

Install faucets before putting the basin in place. It is easier to turn the fixture upside down and tighten the faucet holding nuts than to crawl under the basin to do the job later. Apply silicone sealant or plumber's putty around the threaded faucet tailpieces, put on the washers and holding nuts, and tighten the nuts.

Position the basin but do not immediately secure it. Install the trap and drop a plumb line down the basin drain opening to make sure the opening and trap are aligned. Adjust the basin, if necessary, then secure it.

Connect the flexible water supply tubing, and bend it into alignment with the faucet tailpieces. Water tubing of ⅜-inch diameter is recommended for most basins. Test for leaks before installing the stopper assembly.

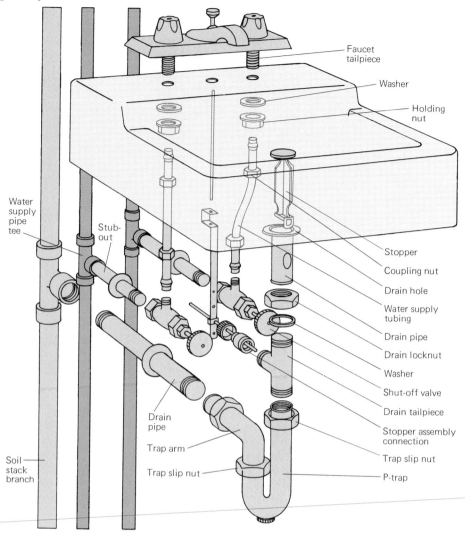

Faucet tailpiece

Washer

Holding nut

Stopper

Coupling nut

Drain hole

Water supply tubing

Drain pipe

Drain locknut

Washer

Shut-off valve

Drain tailpiece

Stopper assembly connection

Trap slip nut

P-trap

Water supply pipe tee

Stub-out

Drain pipe

Trap arm

Soil stack branch

Trap slip nut

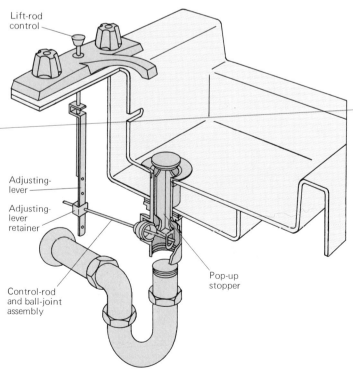

Lift-rod control

Adjusting-lever

Adjusting-lever retainer

Control-rod and ball-joint assembly

Pop-up stopper

To install a basin, first assemble the faucets with the basin upside down on the floor. Then set the basin upright. (Standard basin height is 32 in. from floor to rim.) Install the trap and drain pipe. Connect the water supply tubing. Finally, install the pop-up stopper (left) by first linking the lift rod, and the adjusting lever, and control rod with the ball assembly. Then insert the stopper in the drain hole and engage it to the control rod. Adjust the elevation of the stopper by selecting the appropriate hole in the adjusting lever.

Sink and garbage disposers

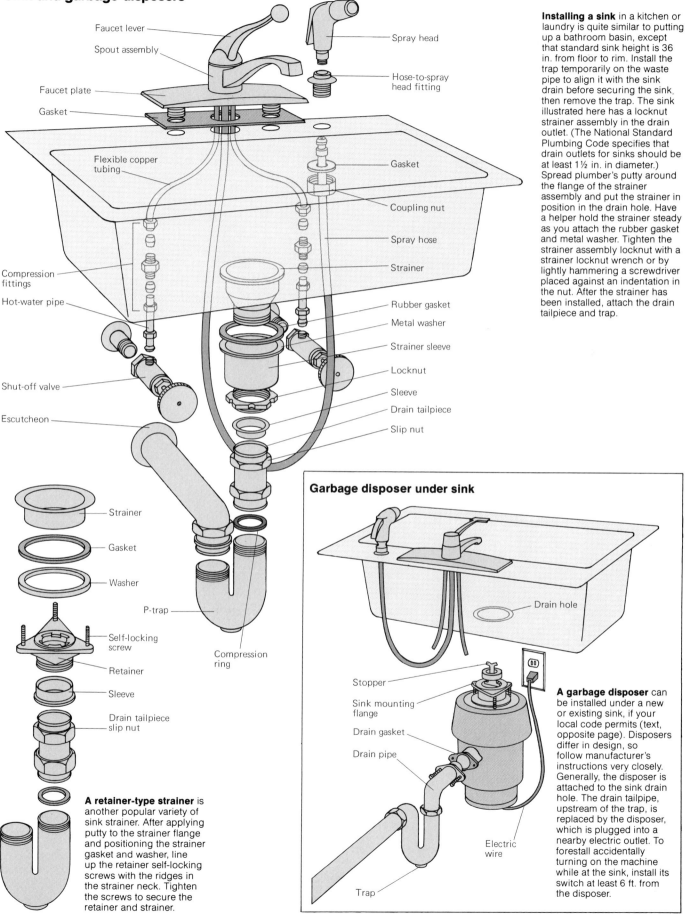

Faucet lever
Spout assembly
Faucet plate
Gasket
Spray head
Hose-to-spray head fitting
Flexible copper tubing
Gasket
Coupling nut
Spray hose
Strainer
Compression fittings
Hot-water pipe
Rubber gasket
Metal washer
Strainer sleeve
Locknut
Sleeve
Drain tailpiece
Slip nut
Shut-off valve
Escutcheon
Strainer
Gasket
Washer
Self-locking screw
Retainer
Sleeve
Drain tailpiece slip nut
P-trap
Compression ring

A retainer-type strainer is another popular variety of sink strainer. After applying putty to the strainer flange and positioning the strainer gasket and washer, line up the retainer self-locking screws with the ridges in the strainer neck. Tighten the screws to secure the retainer and strainer.

Installing a sink in a kitchen or laundry is quite similar to putting up a bathroom basin, except that standard sink height is 36 in. from floor to rim. Install the trap temporarily on the waste pipe to align it with the sink drain before securing the sink, then remove the trap. The sink illustrated here has a locknut strainer assembly in the drain outlet. (The National Standard Plumbing Code specifies that drain outlets for sinks should be at least 1½ in. in diameter.) Spread plumber's putty around the flange of the strainer assembly and put the strainer in position in the drain hole. Have a helper hold the strainer steady as you attach the rubber gasket and metal washer. Tighten the strainer assembly locknut with a strainer locknut wrench or by lightly hammering a screwdriver placed against an indentation in the nut. After the strainer has been installed, attach the drain tailpiece and trap.

Garbage disposer under sink

Drain hole
Stopper
Sink mounting flange
Drain gasket
Drain pipe
Electric wire
Trap

A garbage disposer can be installed under a new or existing sink, if your local code permits (text, opposite page). Disposers differ in design, so follow manufacturer's instructions very closely. Generally, the disposer is attached to the sink drain hole. The drain tailpipe, upstream of the trap, is replaced by the disposer, which is plugged into a nearby electric outlet. To forestall accidentally turning on the machine while at the sink, install its switch at least 6 ft. from the disposer.

Installing appliances

Dishwashers and washing machines

Before the installation of a dishwasher or a washing machine, always check your local plumbing code and read the manufacturer's instructions. A dishwasher requires no cold water, but it should be placed close to a hot-water pipe and a sink. Hot water can be tapped from the sink's existing hot water supply pipe by installing a tee (upper illustration, this page) and connecting a new length of permanent pipe to the dishwasher water supply inlet.

Saddle tee: If the existing hot-water pipe is rigid—or is at least a ⅝-inch flexible copper tubing—you can save the work of cutting it by using a saddle tee. The tee is clamped to the hot-water pipe, a drill bit is inserted through the valve hole of the tee, and a hole is drilled in the existing pipe—after shutting off and draining the water. The National Plumbing Code specifies that the pipe leading from the tee must have a minimum diameter of ½ inch. The pipe is connected to the dishwasher inlet pipe with a compression fitting. It is advisable to install a shut-off valve on the line.

Drain connections: Generally, the dishwasher drain pipe can be connected directly to a waste tee installed in the sink drain pipe, or into the side of a garbage disposer. Some local codes require an air gap between the appliance drain hose and the sink drain pipe to guard against back-siphoning. If such is the case, an air gap fitting can be installed between the two drain pipes. These new extensions can be made with plastic pipe and joined to the existing plumbing lines with special transition adapters (see discussion, p.215).

Washing machine: This appliance is much easier to install than a dishwasher because it comes with three flexible hoses—the hot-water inlet, cold-water inlet, and the drain for quick connections. The inlet hoses are equipped with female-screw-thread connectors that can be screwed to the existing laundry sink faucets. However, it will then be necessary to disconnect the hoses when you want to use the sink. A better solution is to install faucets for the hoses (bottom illustration, this page). Since the washing cycle results in the frequent and abrupt shutting off of water, air chambers are essential to protect the pipes, which should have a minimum diameter of half an inch.

The drain hose can be led into the laundry sink, or a standpipe can be connected to a trap and a drain pipe. Standpipes should extend no less than 18 inches and no more than 30 inches above the trap. Insert the drain hose into the standpipe at a point above the machine's water level to prevent back-siphoning of water from the machine.

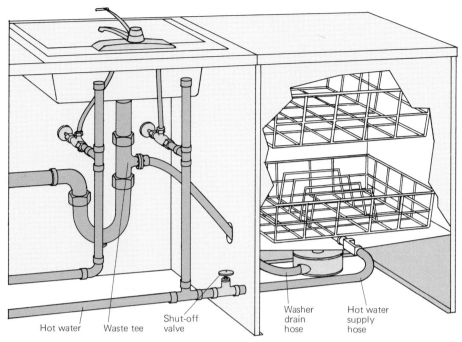

Hot water   Waste tee   Shut-off valve   Washer drain hose   Hot water supply hose

Dishwashers require two connections. The hot-water inlet pipe is tapped into the hot-water supply pipe with a tee and a shut-off valve. The drain hose can be connected either to a waste tee installed on the sink drain pipe just above the trap or, if the sink has a garbage disposer, to the inlet hole present on most garbage disposers.

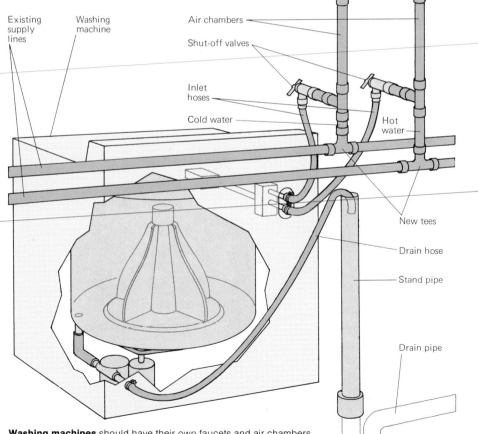

Existing supply lines   Washing machine   Air chambers   Shut-off valves   Inlet hoses   Cold water   Hot water   New tees   Drain hose   Stand pipe   Drain pipe

Washing machines should have their own faucets and air chambers. If a machine is near existing supply pipes, the faucets and air chambers can easily be installed by connecting tees on the existing pipes as shown. The drain hose is inserted into a standpipe whose diameter should be ½ in. larger than that of the hose.

Electric water heaters

In many homes the domestic hot-water unit runs off the boiler that heats the house (see *Heating systems*, pp.204–205). In others, the house may be heated by a warm-air furnace or electric baseboard units, leaving the hot water to a water heater. Most codes require that the installation of an oil- or gas-fired water heater be done by professionals, but a homeowner may be allowed to install an electric water heater himself.

Valves and unions: Once the pipe runs are in, installing an electric water heater is just a matter of connecting the cold-water pipe to the cold-water inlet, which has a shut-off valve, and connecting the hot-water outlet to the hot-water outlet pipe, which does not have a shut-off valve. To eliminate stress on pipes, the tank should rest firmly on the floor.

To save a lot of work later on, connect the heater to both cold- and hot-water pipes with unions. The unions can be joined and taken apart easily (see *Pipe fittings*, p.208). If the heater comes with two short-threaded pipes protruding from it, attach them to water pipes with unions. If the heater comes with only two threaded holes, screw nipples into them, and then attach the nipples to the pipes with unions.

Safety precautions: A water heater can explode if it overheats as the result of a failed automatic heating element or thermostat. Each heater must have safeguards in the form of temperature and pressure relief valves. Most modern heaters use a combination temperature-pressure relief valve (see below). If your local code does not specify the type of relief valve to use, follow the National Plumbing Code, which notes the specific valve temperature and pressure settings. In addition, a high-temperature, electrical shut-off, which is mounted in tandem with the upper heating element, shuts off the electricity whenever the water in the tank overheats.

Filling the water heater: After the heater is connected to the pipes, connect it to the proper power source, but do not switch on the electricity. First, fill the water heater with cold water. Do this by opening a hot-water faucet in a nearby sink, then the cold water shut-off valve at the heater. When water flows from the open faucet, the water heater is full. Set the heater thermostat at a moderate, energy-saving 120°–140°F., and turn on the electricity.

If the existing water heater in your house does not produce enough hot water quickly, you can install an additional heater in series (right, below). If your house has a boiler that heats both the house and the hot water, you can save on fuel costs by installing an additional heater in series. In warmer seasons, switch off the boiler.

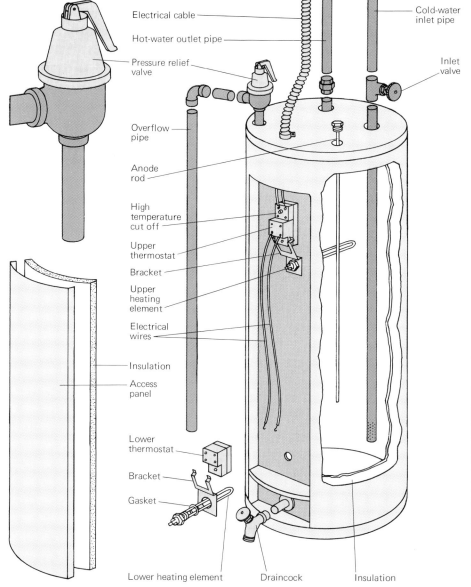

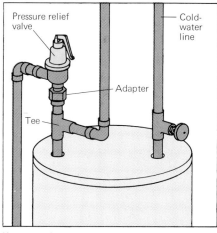

If a water heater has no opening for a temperature pressure relief valve, this valve is installed on the hot-water pipe immediately after it comes out of the heater. Install a discharge pipe at the outlet of the pressure relief valve.

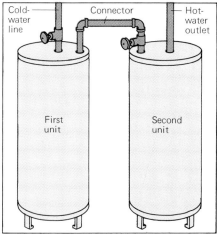

Connect two tanks in series for more hot water. The tank accepting cold water wears out faster because of temperature variations. To equalize the wear, use unions to make connections so tanks can be disconnected and switched.

223

Venting the plumbing system

A basic plan for the DWV network

The part of the DWV (drain-waste-vent) system that is least visible happens to be the one that is most closely regulated by plumbing codes, because it is designed to deal with health hazards (see p.203). Whether you are adding a new fixture, remodeling a bathroom, or building a completely new bath, a basic knowledge of the venting system is essential to your planning. Although the information given here is standard, it is, of course, superseded by your local code, which may require that a professional plan or check your venting system.

Soil stacks and core areas: Whenever possible, cluster the plumbing fixtures around the soil stack, since this saves on the cost of material and labor. If you have more fixtures in the house than can be conveniently grouped into a single core area, you may need a second vent stack (refer to the schematic drawing below). A stack has two components:

the soil stack, which carries waste and drain water; and the vent stack, which draws air from the roof, but carries no waste or water.

Dry and wet venting: All fixtures—bathtubs, shower stalls, toilets, and sinks—drain into the soil stack, which leads to the house drain. There are two possible arrangements for this: dry venting and wet venting. In dry venting, the drain is vented with a pipe that leads directly to the roof with no intervening fixtures, and thus carries no waste. In wet venting, the venting is also used as a drain for a higher fixture on the same pipe run. However, a wet vent can become clogged by waste from an upper-floor fixture—especially in older two- or three-story houses where all the toilets may back up at the same time. Because of this, some codes do not allow wet venting at all, while others permit only wet-vented toilets.

Minimum distances: The distance permitted between a fixture and a soil stack is complicated by the size of the drain pipe. Although codes can differ in details, the following table gives some fairly standard maximum allowable distances based on pipe sizes.

Waste pipe size (inner diameter)	Maximum allowable distance to soil stack
1½ in.	3½ ft.
2 in.	5 ft.
3 in.	6 ft.

Not all fixtures can be vented directly through the soil stack (stack venting), but must employ branch vents (re-vent or back venting). A branch vent usually rises vertically for at least 42 inches before it goes horizontal, when it is pitched at ⅛ inch per foot. The vent stack must rise 18 to 24 inches above the roof. Codes may require vent increasers above the roof to prevent clogging.

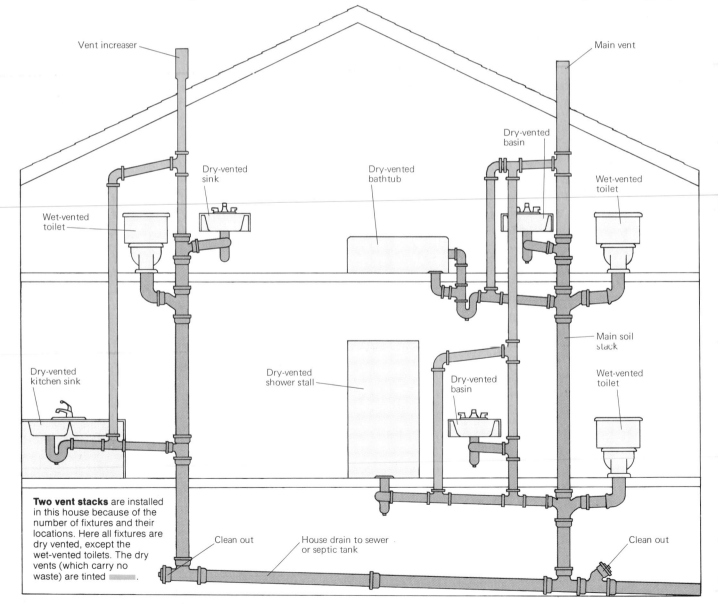

Vent increaser

Main vent

Dry-vented basin

Dry-vented sink

Dry-vented bathtub

Wet-vented toilet

Wet-vented toilet

Main soil stack

Dry-vented kitchen sink

Dry-vented shower stall

Dry-vented basin

Wet-vented toilet

Two vent stacks are installed in this house because of the number of fixtures and their locations. Here all fixtures are dry vented, except the wet-vented toilets. The dry vents (which carry no waste) are tinted ▨▨▨.

Clean out

House drain to sewer or septic tank

Clean out

Exterior improvements

This section begins with color photographs showing exterior improvements in contemporary styles, materials, and methods of construction. There are new wings and landscaped gardens, decks and patios, enclosed porches, new sidings, converted garages—a host of projects by Americans in a nationwide effort to make existing homes more spacious, more attractive, and more livable. In a time of costly new construction and high mortgage rates, improving the homes they live in seems to be the choice of more and more families. Ideas portrayed in color are followed by planning and building instructions.

contents

Siding

An ingredient that adds character

Siding is available in many colors, textures, and materials. If you are building an addition, you can choose a siding that matches what is presently on your house, or come very close to it.

When buying siding, you will want to select material that harmonizes with the style of your house as well as with its surroundings. Rough textures, wood or synthetic, look best in a rustic site, while aluminum or vinyl siding is more formal. Another important consideration is the cost, not only of the siding itself but also its installation and maintenance over the years.

Plywood siding, available in a wide variety of patterns and textures, combines the beauty of wood with the toughness of plywood. In the house pictured at the right, the same cedar plywood siding used on the house was used on the fence (in the foreground of the photograph).

Plywood siding comes in fir, cedar, redwood, and pine, and can be finished with a semi-transparent stain to emphasize the grain, an opaque stain for a uniformity of color, or with an acrylic latex paint applied over a stain-resistant prime coat.

Courtesy of Georgia-Pacific Corporation

James Brett / Designed by Walter A. Fair

Because the designer of this Connecticut saltbox wanted the look of old, weathered clapboards seen so often in New England, he used red cedar boards turned with the inside facing out. He secured them with broadheaded nails that resemble old, handmade Colonial nails. The house now looks as sturdy and warm as do its 200-year-old counterparts.

Red Cedar Shingle & Shake Bureau

Red cedar shakes, an appropriate choice for a modern house (above) in a rugged setting, are hand-cut shingles that are 16 to 18 in. long, of random widths, and tapered at one end.

Red cedar shakes are applied in their natural, unprotected state, which is a light reddish-brown color. They are allowed to weather to a soft gray.

Z-BRICK® Company

A mineral-filled stucco that has an acrylic base can be applied to any one of a variety of clean, structurally sound surfaces such as exterior grade plywood, cement block, concrete, polystyrene foam board, or brick.

This stucco comes pre-mixed and can be used as siding (see the photograph above), or as a means of making a foundation of cement or concrete block more attractive.

226

Vinyl siding, durable and easy to maintain, comes in 4- and 8-in. widths, and in a 10-in. vertical style. It is available in a variety of colors in addition to the white shown here. Because the color is part of the material, vinyl siding does not show scratches, and does not need periodic painting.

Hardboard siding, made of wood cellulose fibers that have been bonded together, is available in a variety of colors and styles, such as the rustic siding shown at left with its embossed rough cedar texture.

Hardboard siding, a good thermal insulator, can be stained or painted, and is also available prefinished.

Brick facing, which creates the look of brick without the weight of traditional masonry, can be applied to any flat exterior surface, such as plywood or cement block. Brick facing is applied with an adhesive mortar, and is protected after installation with a weatherproofing sealer. It is available in a variety of colors and patterns.

Aluminum siding, the most popular in the U.S., is available in both 4- and 8-in. widths and in a 16-in. vertical style, and comes in a variety of colors and textures. Shown here are a century-old house (above, right) restored with 4-in. siding used horizontally and vertically, and a turn-of-the-century house (above, left) covered with fish scales, hand cut from .20 gauge aluminum coil stock, on top of 4-in. siding.

Roofing

Overhead protection in a variety of styles

Most homeowners pay little attention to the roof; it is simply there to keep out water and to afford protection from heat and cold. But if you need to replace your roof or if you are building a new house or addition, you will want to consider the various materials, and the variety of styles and colors available.

Roofs can be made from, among other things, galvanized steel, slate, wood shakes, tile, asphalt shingle, or fiberglass shingle. The choice you make will depend as much on the style of your house and the climate in your area as it will on your taste.

Tile roofs, whether traditional clay (above) or concrete (right), last for the life of the house and need no maintenance. Both kinds of tile come in a variety of styles and colors. Concrete tiles are less expensive than clay tiles.

The S-shape clay tiles (above) are a natural red color caused by iron oxide in the shale and clay used to make the tiles. But any of a dozen other colors can be added to the clay before it is fired in a kiln.

Other styles include half round, sculptured, shingle, and flat interlocking. Clay tiles, frost-proofed to be durable in any climate, are installed on top of plywood and a vapor barrier.

Slate roofs are very durable and usually last for the life of the house. Slate can crack, however, and cannot withstand heavy weight. Never walk on a slate roof or allow ice to collect on an unheated house for a long period.

The non-fading mottled green and purple slates on this roof were quarried in Eureka Quarry, Vermont. The slates are 3/16 to 1/4-in. thick, 18 in. long, and come in random widths.

Fiberglass shingles are asphalt shingles with a base of inorganic fiberglass mat. This mat has replaced the organic felt base (made from wood pulp and waste-paper products) of conventional asphalt shingles. Fiberglass shingles are resistant to rot and fire and are extremely durable. Shingles made with fiberglass mat have a heavier coating of weatherproofing asphalt.

Fiberglass shingles are available in a variety of colors from traditional dark brown and green to more contemporary gold, gray, and white, and in a variety of styles from a rustic, random-cut look to a more sleek, modern style.

Vincent Brass & Aluminum Company / Colorklad® Roofing Material / Designed by Carl A. Strauss & Associates, Cincinnati, Ohio

The roof at left is pre-painted metal, 24-gauge galvanized steel that is primed and finished on one side with a polymer coating. The sheet metal is available in 36 and 48 in. widths and lengths up to 144 in., and can be cut, formed, nailed, or riveted with hand or power tools.

The metal roof is available in three styles: batten seam (left), standing seam, and mansard; in two textured finishes: dull matte, and medium gloss; and in a range of colors to suit any style.

A galvanized steel roof costs approximately half that of copper and is appropriate for houses in any climate from extremely cold to blazing hot.

Koppers Company, Inc.

Red Cedar Shingle & Handsplit Shake Bureau

Red cedar shingles are applied in their natural state, a soft reddish-brown color, and allowed to weather to a light gray.

A traditional use of red cedar shingles (left) creates a rustic look with shingles that are 16 to 18 in. long and of random widths. Fancy-butt red cedar shingles (above) in round, arrow, and ocean-wave designs were used on the turret of a Tudor-style house. Some red cedar shingles are chemically treated with a fire retardant.

Bird & Son, inc.

Celotex Roofing Products Division / Dimensional™ Shake Shingles

Asphalt shingles, a popular roofing material, are made of an asphalt-saturated felt that is coated on top and bottom with a layer of weatherproofing asphalt. The top surface is covered with mineral granules that act as armor against the elements. Asphalt shingles are available in many colors and styles, including those with a rustic appearance (above) that simulates wood shakes and a smoother texture (left) appropriate for any style house.

Greenhouses

For horticulture or passive solar heating

A greenhouse is a boon to gardeners because it extends the growing season by capturing and retaining solar heat, requiring little back-up heating.

Greenhouses are also used as solar collectors, and if the installation meets certain requirements, such as being used as an alternate source of energy and not as a place for growing plants, the owner may be eligible for a tax credit consisting of a percentage of the cost of materials. If you plan to install such a greenhouse, refer to *Energy-saving renovations,* pages 364–369. Kits are available through most home centers.

This 12-x-5½-ft. greenhouse, made of double-insulated panels of fiberglass reinforced with acrylic, comes in a kit that includes a combination storm-screen door. No foundation is necessary because the unit has a built-in elasticity due to the use of special PVC gaskets between the aluminum beams. This greenhouse was added to grow plants; if it had been added to the southern side as a passive solar collector, the homeowner would then have qualified for a tax credit.

A lean-to greenhouse built onto the side of a garage has a floor of pebbles that aids drainage and retains heat. The greenhouse comes in a kit with 2-ft. panels; the minimum order is four panels. The greenhouse shown above is 16 ft. long by 8 ft. 7¾ in. deep and is designed to be built on an 8-in. curbing. Standard items in the kit are a door for one end, a vent for the other, and vents in every other roof panel. This greenhouse can be adapted for use as a passive solar collector.

A greenhouse was attached onto the back of a wood-frame townhouse (left) to provide a new eating area for the newly renovated kitchen (above). The wall between kitchen and eating area was removed.

The wall-mounted greenhouse is designed to be supported by a base; the owner built this base to fit one of the manufacturer's standard-size units. This one is 12 ft. long by 8 ft. deep.

The greenhouse, which is passive solar and faces south, heats the eat-in kitchen and a nearby dining room by natural convection. To control the temperature inside, a vent opens automatically to release heat when the temperature reaches a certain degree. To prevent heat build-up, manually controlled aluminum sun-shade blinds were installed on the outside of the unit. Exterior blinds are much more effective than interior ones in controlling heat because they prevent passage of light through the glass. According to California law, a tax credit was allowed for part of the cost of materials.

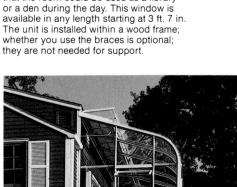

This double-glazed window greenhouse comes in a kit and is completely assembled. It has side vents for proper air circulation and painted steel rod shelves for plants. The kit is available in a variety of sizes, from 3 to 6 ft. wide, from 3 to 4 ft. high, and either 12 or 16 in. deep, to fit almost any size window. It can be installed directly into a window frame or onto furring strips nailed into the exterior wall.

This 18-in.-deep greenhouse window replaced the master bedroom window so that the room could be used as a library or a den during the day. This window is available in any length starting at 3 ft. 7 in. The unit is installed within a wood frame; whether you use the braces is optional; they are not needed for support.

An 8-x-10-ft. greenhouse, custom designed for a 1905 Victorian house, is made of standard double-insulated glass door panels, which are as effective as but less expensive than greenhouse panels. Built with a rock floor for heat storage, the greenhouse maintains a temperature of 80°F. A circular arch (barely visible through the glass panels) was built so the room inside, a bedroom, could be warmed by the greenhouse.

A passive solar greenhouse was built on a deck that protrudes from the second-story living room of a house facing the ocean. The 25-ft.-long unit is made of standard sections that include a roof vent that opens automatically at 85°F. in summer, and manually-operated, awning-style side vents. A custom feature is a set of three fans that turn on automatically in winter when the temperature reaches 85°F. and blow the heated air through insulated ducts to other rooms on the floor.

Decks

Outdoor living in city and country

A deck, a wooden platform on a support, is an outdoor area with many uses.

Decks can be built from kits, be designed by architects, or they can be owner-designed do-it-yourself projects.

The wood should be treated or naturally resistant to moisture—redwood, cedar, or cypress. Douglas fir, hemlock, spruce, and pine require treating.

For best results, decks should have supports with concrete footings, and should slope slightly away from the house for drainage. Otherwise, a deck is limited only by the amount of space you have and the type of terrain.

This redwood deck, made of 2 x 4s, is supported by a system of doubled 2 x 6 stringers attached to the sides of wooden posts. The steps and benches are made of butcher block 2 x 4s nailed together. The steps in the foreground were cut at an angle so they are flush with the wall. The deck, off the dining room, was designed to be built in stages; the lower deck was added at a later date.

A 15-x-20-ft. redwood deck, built at a 30° angle from the house with 2 x 6s laid diagonally, is two steps down from 8-x-11-ft. platform that is next to the house. A ramp (to the left of the photograph) connects the new deck with an existing patio and barbecue. The redwood benches at the sides of the deck are made of 2 x 4s on edge. Both deck and the supporting structure are made of a rustic, knot-textured garden grade redwood.

Two-level deck serves as outdoor living space for two different areas of this house; upper wedge-shaped deck is an extension of kitchen and living room while the lower octagonal deck is just outside a greenhouse that is used as a den. The L-shaped house, on a corner property, provides privacy for the decks.

The decks, made of fir 2 x 6s treated with clear creosote stain, are supported by concrete piers. The connecting stairway, the rectangular planters that are used in place of railings on the steps, and the bench are also made of fir.

A quarry-tile terrace and a redwood deck are both accessible from the kitchen and breakfast room on the parlor floor of a Brooklyn, N.Y., townhouse. Deck and terrace are atop two garages.

The terrace is flush with the kitchen floor; the deck sits three steps above the terrace and ends in a picnic table for use at the terrace level. The deck rests on the roof's original tar covering and is designed to be removed in sections to facilitate cleaning beneath it. The trellis can support hanging plants, and, eventually, a grapevine. The rear walls of neighboring houses provide privacy.

The deck at left extends from one end of a prefabricated barn and was designed by the owner to take advantage of the view (left, top) and to conform to the land (left, bottom). Made of salvaged lumber, it is supported by posts set in concrete. The design of this deck is irregular: a square is next to the house and several triangles that echo the house's triangular gable and diamond-shaped window project from the square. The deck was built on several levels so railings that could obscure the view would not be necessary. In order to accommodate the child's pool, a 28-in.-deep hole was dug in the ground and a circle was made in the deck. The step down to the level of the chaise lounge can also be used for seating. The bench at right of deck has a removable top and storage space below. Construction details appear in the chapter on decks.

Deborah Agrest / Designed by Fred Ward

Karl H. Riek, Photography / Charles Lester, ASID, and Associates

Rather than attempt to move a huge, indigenous boulder the owner incorporated it into the design of the deck. To lay the ends of the boards beneath the rock, he had to lift the rock temporarily with a car jack.

A redwood veranda and deck (at left in the photograph) were built onto this 1950s ranch house in the hills near San Francisco. They define the front entrance and provide outdoor living space. The 6-ft.-wide veranda, made of 2 x 6s, runs the length of the house and can be reached through French doors from the dining room or from the main entrance of the house, which is the set-back beyond the dining room doors. The veranda is several steps up from the driveway which is just beyond view in the foreground of the photograph.

The 12-ft.-square main deck, two steps down from the veranda and separated from it by a long redwood planter, projects out over a wooded ravine. This deck provides an outside living area in what is otherwise an inaccessible spot. To take advantage of the view and to integrate the new outdoor area with the house, a large picture window was installed in the dining room.

233

Patios

Simple outdoor living

A patio used for outdoor cooking, eating, playing, and entertaining can add to your enjoyment of your backyard.

When planning a patio, make sure you have privacy by building a fence or planting shrubbery in strategic places. Situate the patio so it has areas of sunlight and shade. Consider the accessibility of the patio from the house, and from the rest of the backyard. If you plan to eat and entertain outdoors, keep the patio close to the kitchen to make serving and cleaning up easier. And use materials that are easy to maintain so your patio will be a joy.

Ken Agle / Designed by Robert W. Miller, ASID / Courtesy of HOME

Because the owner of this house entertains frequently for business reasons, he wanted to make the backyard an extension of the living area. To accomplish this, he cleared away much of the grass and installed a large, free-form pebbled concrete patio that is easily accessible from the dining room.

The border between patio and surrounding shrubbery is outlined with a row of rocks. Flowering plants and herbs are grown in pots that can be moved around if necessary.

Gottscho-Schleisner, Inc. / Designed by Alice Dustan Kollar

Linda Hammer

This circular patio made of broken flagstone (above) is at the far end of the yard and is connected to the house by a curving walkway made of the same stones. The patio has a round grindstone in the center with the flagstones radiating out from it. The stones were installed level with the lawn so that a mower could be used to trim the grass between the stones, thus eliminating the need for hand trimming.

The free-form patio (left) is made of bluestones set in a bed of crushed white rock. To prevent weeds and grass from growing between the slates, the owner first dug up 6 in. of dirt, which he replaced with a layer of crushed rock followed by a layer of sand. He positioned the slates on top of this, poured on crushed rock and brushed it into place. The layers of crushed rock and sand allow water to drain through the patio. Proper drainage is essential in a yard so full of shrubbery.

Hedrich-Blessing

Kent Oppenheimer / Designed by John Haase

Here, both patios, making good use of narrow lots, are paved with brick to the edge of the property and end with high fences built for privacy.

The patio above, left, has a patterned floor that combines red brick and gray cut stone. The shrubbery creates a lush atmosphere, while providing privacy.

The patio above, right, was converted from a large driveway. Most of the work—building a grapestake fence and laying bricks in modules of 50 with redwood strip borders—was done by the owners. For variety, some of the modules are covered with wood grating while others are filled with redwood bark and potted plants.

Courtesy Creative Homeowner Press / Philip Graham, Landscape Architect

© 1980 James Brett / Designed by Arthur Klonsky

A deck with a trellis was extended on two sides by a brick patio. Because drainage was necessary in a yard so full of trees, the bricks could not be set in mortar but had to be set in sand. To do this, the area was dug to a depth of 4 in. and outlined with 2 × 4s. The area was then filled with 1½ in. of builder's sand, which has only a small clay content. The bricks were laid; more sand was poured on top and swept into place with a broom. In yards with fewer plants, part of the patio could be set in mortar and part set in sand.

An artful combination of a brick terrace and a brick patio creates an unusual two-level outdoor living area for this home. The terrace, built at the floor level of the house, is a rectangle, while the patio, two steps down, is free form in shape. The low walls, constructed of brick and topped with flagstone, separate different areas of activity and help to direct traffic. The patio was designed to take advantage of the nearby trees for shade.

Backyard landscaping

Working with nature

The most beautifully landscaped back-yards are done by those who recognize the potential of the land and enhance it.

When planning new landscaping, it makes sense to work with the flowers, shrubs, and trees that will thrive in your part of the country, and to arrange them so they each have optimum conditions for growth. Landscaping plans should allow for adequate privacy and, if needed, for separate areas for growing plants, children's play, and quiet contemplation.

Backyard improvements can be done slowly and in stages, but to keep these individual improvements harmonious plans should be developed for the entire property and then finished section by section as time and budget allow.

The path shown (right) leads from an enclosed patio to a garden and is made of 4-in.-square redwood posts crosscut into 4-in.-deep pieces. Redwood was used because it is resistant to rot. To build the path, a 6-in. channel was dug and filled with 2 in. of sand. The wood pieces were placed loosely so when the ground swells after a rain, the wood pieces would not pop out.

The pathway (above) of wood planks leads from the house to a pool area. It was placed on top of a layer of pebbles to keep weeds from growing under it.

The bricks set in sand (left) create a pathway through an herb garden and also serve as dividers between the beds. In making such a path, place the top of the bricks even with or slightly below grade level to help maintain a smooth surface when the ground swells from frost or from rain.

Old railroad ties are ideal for re-cycling in the garden since they are quite large (usually 7 x 9 x 86 in.), sturdy, and rustic. And they come already treated with creosote, a preservative. The large planter (left), made of railroad ties and filled with good topsoil, was built because the sandy soil native to the area did not support the flowering plants favored by the owner. Not all plants and shrubs tolerate creosote, so if you build such a planter, check with a local nursery before you begin planting.

The vegetable garden (above) is separated from the rest of the yard by a border of railroad ties.

To assure easy maintenance, this garden is covered with pea gravel (which absorbs rain and snow), and is bordered with a fence made of cedar posts. The plants chosen for the garden are mostly those that do not lose their leaves, such as rhododendron, Oregon grape holly, and ferns. This eliminates any raking of leaves.

A path made of stepping stones leads from a concrete patio (not visible in the foreground of the photograph), around a large rock, and to the Japanese stone lantern at the back of the garden.

A change of grade between two patios in this garden was bridged with a wooden walkway, which was placed between existing trees to maintain the woodsy charm. The heavy slabs of cast concrete used for the steps have the same pebbled surface as the patios, and require less intricate form work than steps cast in place. The walkway simply rests on the top step.

Several stairways like this one of heavy bluestone lead from a driveway at the bottom of the hill to the house at the top. Risers and treads were cut to size by a stonecutter and assembled at the site. Seaside plants and areas of cedar chips prevent erosion on the hill since there is no grass or other ground cover on the sandy soil—the ocean is opposite the driveway.

Additions

Contrast and harmony in designs

Many families need more space than they have, but they may not want to uproot themselves to find it. "Adding on" is one solution to the dilemma, and a practical one in view of the increasing costs of building or buying a house.

Also, many families find their lives are so entrenched in their community—because of the schools, the proximity of shopping, their amiable neighbors, and a real fondness for their houses—that remodeling is preferable to moving.

As shown on these pages, an addition can resemble the existing house or it can be radically different in style.

The dramatic change in appearance of this house, from a traditional 1950s Cape Cod to a modern eclectic, was accomplished by erecting a new facade. The new front ties together a two-car garage remodeled into a family room and the additions of a foyer, a mud room, and tool shed.

The facade, a freestanding wall with an opening for entry, conceals the original Cape Cod from the street and also helps reflect the morning sun into the house. The new wall has a frame of 2 x 4s with a stucco finish on wire lath applied to the frame.

The new entrance foyer has a 12-ft. ceiling and a wooden front door (visible through the opening in the new wall) that is perpendicular to the original facade of the house. A view of the mud room is shielded from the foyer by a latticework wall. The tool shed behind the mud room can be entered through the mud room or through its own door on the far side of the original house.

This small, 12-ft.-square addition created a family room that is twice as large as the original den. The ceiling-high windows allow in so much sunlight the owners call the room a solarium. Sliding glass doors on the far side of the addition lead to the patio and backyard. The aluminum siding and asphalt roof shingles on the addition are identical to those on the house. The addition's shallow hip roof, in contrast to the pitched roof of the house, was specifically designed so its peak would fall below the bottom sill of the double window on the second floor.

One family's need for an informal room where members could indulge in a favorite pastime, playing chamber music, was the impetus behind this one-room addition. In order to provide the 12-ft. ceiling the owners wanted, the architect put the floor of the new room at ground level; a stairway leads down to the music room from the living room. The large window that wraps around the side and back was custom designed from stock parts; the door at the back leads to the patio. Although more modern in style than the house, the addition is integrated by using the same materials: weathered gray shingles and painted white woodwork.

This large, rambling Victorian house, built around 1900 in rural Connecticut, had a small living room with no view of the expansive lawn. In building the two-story addition to the living room, the architect selected a design and materials that contrast greatly with the original house rather than attempt a modern re-creation of the Victorian style of nearly a century ago. To heighten the contrast between old and new parts of the house, the red cedar siding, applied diagonally, was left natural. The new living room is built at an angle to the house and the huge picture window provides a view of the surroundings.

A new family room with large windows overlooking a brook was added to a small cottage that was built around 1845. Because the house is protected by an historic preservation law, the architect was limited in the changes he could make. The addition, in the back of the house and not visible from the road, was designed to look like structures that had once been part of the house but were moved to another location—a clapboard shed and outhouse. To make it look like part of the original house, the new addition is sheathed in the same wood clapboard siding and asphalt roof shingles used on the house. A door leads from the new family room to the deck, which is private because it is shielded by the L-shaped addition.

For a new family room, the owners of this ranch house chose to build a second-floor addition to take advantage of a view.

The addition is a 25-ft.-square loft room and a sun deck that sit atop the garage. The new room can be entered through a stairway built in a corner of the garage.

The new room, which is supported by added structural braces, has large windows on three sides. The deck at the back is 6 ft. above the second story, accessible through a sliding glass door and an exterior redwood stairway.

The addition and the front of the house are covered in a rough textured hardboard siding. Both the new siding and original redwood siding on the back and far side of the house are finished with a deep red stain.

Additions

Moving an exterior bearing wall

The kitchen of the suburban house shown below was too small to meet the needs of a growing family. The home-owner's solution was to expand the kitchen by moving an exterior house wall outward. The new kitchen wall, built over a new foundation, assumed part of the roof load that formerly rested on the old wall, which was removed. A new side wall was also built, a new area of roof was extended from the old roof, and an enclosed porch was constructed beside the kitchen. This do-it-yourself project is illustrated in detail in *Expanding a room outward*, pages 276–283.

The wall of the existing house (above) was moved out to expand the kitchen (right). A new porch was built beside it. The load supported by the old wall was assumed by the new wall and by a new beam installed beneath the roof in the new kitchen (below). Skylights and a large bay window make the new kitchen lighter and airier than the old.

The views above and left are from the interior of the new kitchen. The new hardwood ceiling extends into the wells of the skylights. Incandescent and fluorescent lighting fixtures were also added. Finished cabinets were installed by the owner. The sink base cabinet, sitting in the middle of the new kitchen, is on the same site as the sink that was against old kitchen wall, making new plumbing lines unnecessary. (See also *Renovating kitchens*, beginning on p.150.)

Photographs on this page by Joe D. Barnell / Armstrong World Industries (Woodstock Plank Flooring) / Therma-Tru Division of LST Corporation (Therma-Tru entry door system) / Whirlpool Corporation (Refrigerator) / Wood Mode Cabinetry (A Division of Wood Metal Industries, Inc.)

Adding a wing

The homeowner as contractor

Short of building an entire house, adding a wing or an addition is the most complex building project you can undertake. In a residential neighborhood in northern New Jersey, a homeowner undertook to add a separate two-story living space to his two-family ninety-year-old brick house. We observed and photographed the work from the initial planning stage to the finished addition—the entire project is illustrated on pages 242–275.

Even if you never intend to pick up a hammer and saw, you will find this entire chapter on *Adding a wing* extremely useful. The chapter describes from start to finish all the jobs, in sequence, that must be performed—and performed correctly—if any construction project is to be successful. Thus these pages can serve as an authoritative reference in any dealings you may have with tradesmen and contractors. They will help you recognize when something is not being done that should be done, or when it is being done poorly.

Learning from new experience: The owner of the house, though experienced in carpentry and cabinetmaking, had no experience in large construction or in construction contracting. Nevertheless, he took his architect's plans and served as his own general contractor for the job. He did much of the work himself, especially the finishing.

He subcontracted a mason to do the site layout, excavation, grading, foundation, and concrete slab work. He hired a framing crew to do the wood framing (though because of weather delays and other obligations of the crew, he ended up doing part of the framing himself). He also subcontracted the plumbing and electrical work, and the taping and spackling of the wallboard. Through bitter experience, he learned many things that, he says, he wishes he had known before he started.

Scheduling delays: The important lesson is that things take longer than you expect, sometimes far longer. Delays are inevitable; and when subcontracting jobs follow in sequence, one early delay can destroy the scheduling that follows. Flexibility is necessary, and should be built into the schedule.

Architect vs. subcontractors: As intermediary between the architect and the subcontractors, our homeowner now wishes he could have gathered them all together before work started, to resolve differences between them and to rectify omissions in the plans. For example, the plumber arrived to find no provision for hiding the bathroom pipes—an oversight that could easily have been corrected by the architect and the framer had it been detected earlier. Our man built false chase walls to hide the pipes, an improvisation typical of problem-solving often required.

Subcontractors may perform their tasks with no heed to the tasks that follow, he says. This is another reason to have them meet—to prevent their working at cross-purposes. For example, the framer installed two of the long roof rafters 1½ inches lower than the others, though this made it impossible to install a level gypsum wallboard ceiling. Long sections of the two rafters had to be sawed away before doing the ceiling.

Check regularly with subcontractors as they work, for the good of everyone. It is better to resolve misunderstandings on the job than to fight them out in court later. On this job, the mason omitted an interior footing called for in the plans and the framer changed the direction of some roof framing members. When you challenge a subcontractor, you may find that he is quite capable of convincing you that he alone knows what is best; at such times, confer with your architect.

Our man selected his subcontractors by their reputations as attested to by his architect and local contractors. Yet the quality of their work varied quite a bit. He took one to court and had his fee reduced because of poor workmanship.

The work on the addition often disrupted life in the existing house, especially when the addition was filled with workers. When the wall between the house and the addition was removed after the addition was almost finished, dirt and dust made its way into the house. Yet, despite all the headaches, the work resulted in a dramatic new living space, and our man's personal contribution saved him thousands of dollars.

The existing house before construction began.

Materials for the addition covered in this chapter were provided by:

Alenco, div. of Redman Building Products (window greenhouse kit)
American Olean Tile Co., div. of National Gypsum Co.
American-Standard, Inc. (toilet and sink)
Benjamin Moore & Co. (exterior stain and paint; urethane wood finish)
Big Timber Wood Stove (wood stove)
Bird & Son (roofing)
Bruce Hardwood Floors, div. of Triangle Pacific Co.
Fireline, Inc. (hot water transfer system)
Georgia-Pacific Corp. (exterior wood siding)
Halo Lighting
Import Specialist, New York, N.Y. (ceiling fans)
Moen, div. of Stanadyne (faucet, sink)
Nutone, div. of Scovill (mirror, range exhaust system)
Oriental Antiques, Chris Sisson, Madison, N.J. (cabinet, wall hanging)
Owens Corning Fiberglas Corp. (fiberglass insulation)
Reynolds Metal Co. (sliding doors)
United States Mineral Products Co. (rigid foam insulation)
Velux-America, Inc. (roof windows)
Vulcan-Hart Corp. (range)

Same view of house, showing completed addition. See also pages 274–275.

Adding a wing

A slab and masonry foundation

This and the following nine pages illustrate the first stage in the construction of an addition—the excavation and foundation work.

The cutaway diagram below shows a perimeter foundation with a slab floor; this was laid in the addition created as a special project for this book (p.241). Also shown are some of the devices that guided this foundation's layout and construction. (For a discussion of other foundations, see *Building Codes/Introduction to construction*, pp.22–23.) Because soil conditions were normal, the construction specifications are typical. However, the two levels of the slab and the step footing add to the foundation for our project a degree of complexity missing in most small additions.

About this section: The large drawing below provides an overview for the pages that follow, where the specific jobs entailed in building the foundation are illustrated. The lines for construc-

tion are precisely marked, and the site is readied for excavation as seen on pages 244–245; the excavation is then dug. Though the concrete footings in this addition were poured by a subcontractor (p.247), concrete for small foundations can readily be mixed by the homeowner in a rented power mixer. Mixing concrete is discussed on page 246. The foundation walls are made of mortar and concrete block (rather than poured, a more difficult process, as shown on pp.248–249). Finally, the slab is poured, as seen on pages 250–251.

Alternative techniques: Several alternatives to the techniques used in this addition are discussed in later pages. Others are shown at the top of the opposite page: foundation walls can be insulated on the outside, rather than the inside; passages can be made through the foundation wall for pipes and conduits; foundation walls can be attached to bedrock; piers, which are sometimes

used to support buildings without basements, are formed as shown.

Visual orientation: The small diagram immediately below shows the existing house with the foundation for the addition completed. The orientation is the same as in the large drawing. This same view is used throughout.

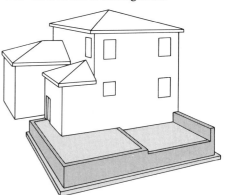

Diagram of house and foundation for addition.

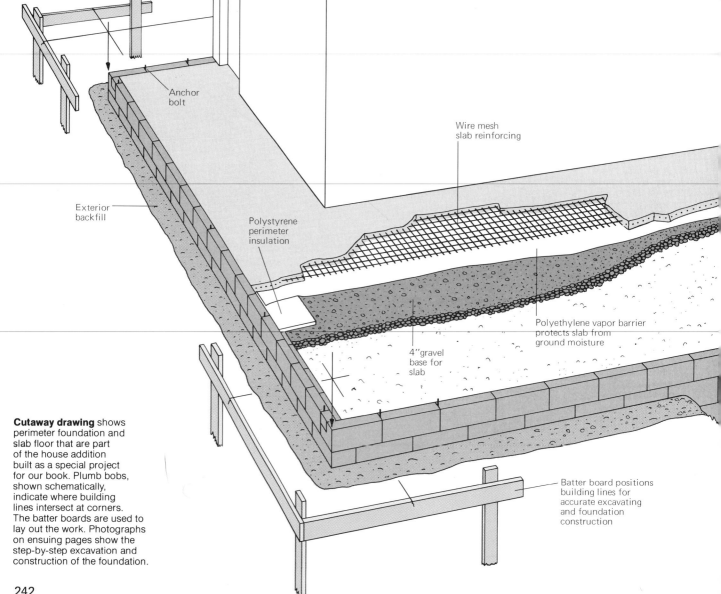

Anchor bolt

Wire mesh slab reinforcing

Exterior backfill

Polystyrene perimeter insulation

Polyethylene vapor barrier protects slab from ground moisture

4" gravel base for slab

Batter board positions building lines for accurate excavating and foundation construction

Cutaway drawing shows perimeter foundation and slab floor that are part of the house addition built as a special project for our book. Plumb bobs, shown schematically, indicate where building lines intersect at corners. The batter boards are used to lay out the work. Photographs on ensuing pages show the step-by-step excavation and construction of the foundation.

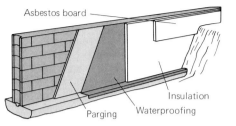

Insulation can be attached over the waterproofing on the outside of the foundation wall. The concrete board protects the insulation.

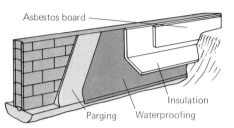

By sloping insulation out into the surrounding soil, ground temperature can be drawn upon to moderate the temperature of the house.

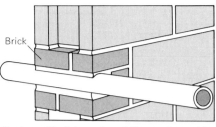

Block omitted from foundation wall provides opening for pipe or conduit to pass through. Space around pipe is filled with brick and mortar.

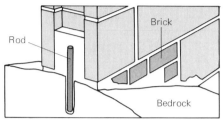

A foundation can be anchored to bedrock by means of reinforcing rods embedded in the rock. Mortar holds the rods on both ends.

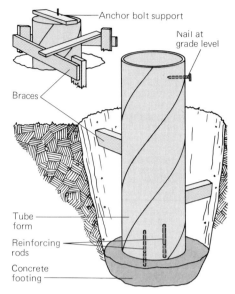

Piers (pp.22–23) are poured into supported cardboard forms. Reinforcing rods and anchor bolts connect piers to footing and wood frame.

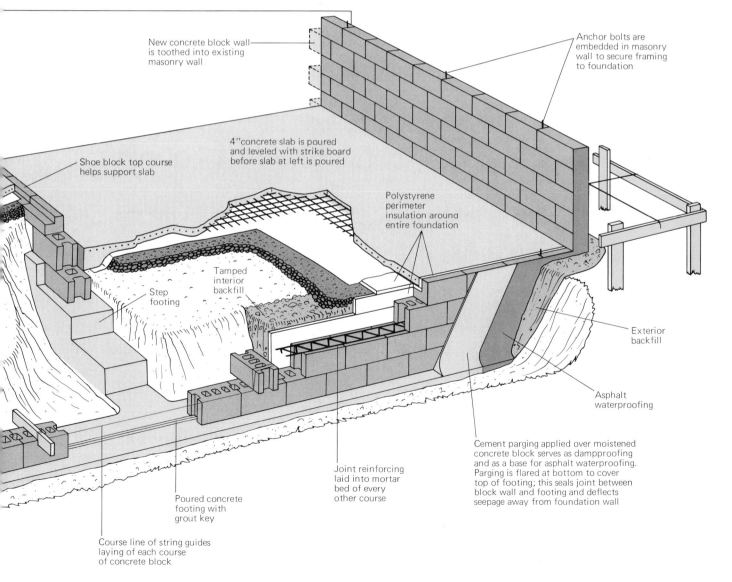

New concrete block wall is toothed into existing masonry wall

Anchor bolts are embedded in masonry wall to secure framing to foundation

4" concrete slab is poured and leveled with strike board before slab at left is poured

Shoe block top course helps support slab

Polystyrene perimeter insulation around entire foundation

Tamped interior backfill

Step footing

Exterior backfill

Asphalt waterproofing

Joint reinforcing laid into mortar bed of every other course

Poured concrete footing with grout key

Course line of string guides laying of each course of concrete block

Cement parging applied over moistened concrete block serves as dampproofing and as a base for asphalt waterproofing. Parging is flared at bottom to cover top of footing; this seals joint between block wall and footing and deflects seepage away from foundation wall

Adding a wing

Site preparation

Before building is begun, the site must be cleared and the lines of the excavation and construction must be established and marked with great care.

The first step is the elimination of such obstructions at the site as trees and manmade structures. For this particular project a small shed and a row of bushes standing within the boundaries of the new addition were removed. There should be room to store building materials clear of the work area, as there must be adequate access for any necessary heavy machinery.

Building lines: The lines establishing the perimeter of the excavation and the foundation must be marked precisely.

For our addition, these lines were determined with a builder's level, a small telescope mounted on a tripod. It can turn 360° on the horizontal (level) plane, and is so calibrated that angles can be measured or laid out using it. Another, more sophisticated instrument, the transit-level (or transit), is also available. It pivots in the vertical as well as the horizontal direction. Though this capability can make some work easier, a transit-level is not usually needed for such small projects as typical home additions.

If you are having a surveyor mark your property lines, have him mark the construction lines as well. In our project, the mason set these lines; he was not as skilled as a surveyor, and took a long while. If you have the time, you

can borrow or rent a builder's level and mark the lines yourself. The level and a calibrated pole are also used to measure elevations (see opposite page, bottom).

It can be handy to have the builder's level on the site throughout foundation work, but it isn't necessary once the batter boards have been set (see below). Accidents occur, however; in our project, one batter board was run over during the excavation. A builder's level was needed to re-establish the corner.

For small projects, building lines can be established by triangulation as described elsewhere on this page, or simply by sight ("eyeballing"). Simpler carpenter's or line levels can be used to level the batter boards.

Stakes and batter boards: Building lines are usually established by using stakes and batter boards.

Stakes are driven into the ground at the corners; the stakes are removed during excavation.

Batter boards are staked into the ground at right angles outside the actual corners of the excavation. Saw kerfs (notches) are cut in these boards and strings are stretched between them; the strings precisely mark the excavation and foundation lines.

Batter boards must be far enough outside the excavation that they are not disturbed by the excavation process. They must be made of solid lumber, sturdily assembled, and staked. The ledgers (cross pieces) should all be the same height; the boards then form a vertical as well as a horizontal point of reference for the excavation and foundation work. The strings are attached to and removed from the boards as required during the different stages.

Once the batter boards are set, they should be checked. Plumb lines hung from the intersections of the strings should hang precisely over the foundation corner stakes.

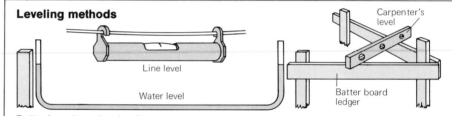

Leveling methods

Batter boards and string lines establish a reference for foundation height. Carpenter's level levels individual pairs of batter board ledgers; either a line level or water level insures uniform height of all lines. Water level is fashioned from clear plastic tubing.

Building layout methods

Sighting along the wall of the existing building, a line extending the wall is run to the first batter board as shown in the diagram at right. A saw kerf (small notch) is made in the batter board and the string is set between the corner of the building and the kerf.

A tape is used to measure and mark on the string the distance to the first corner of the planned addition. A stake is set in the ground at this point, and a finishing nail is driven into the stake to mark the exact corner. The builder's level is set up directly over the finishing nail and rotated 90° (or whatever the angle is); the next line is marked, measured, and staked for the next corner.

Triangulation: You can measure accurate right angles using a 3:4:5 triangle. For example, starting at the corner (A) in the diagram, make a 6 foot measurement along the existing wall to point B. Attach a string 8 feet long at point A, and a second string 10 feet long at point B. Where the ends of these two meet (point C), drive a nail into the ground. A line from this nail to the corner (A) will create a right angle (D). A

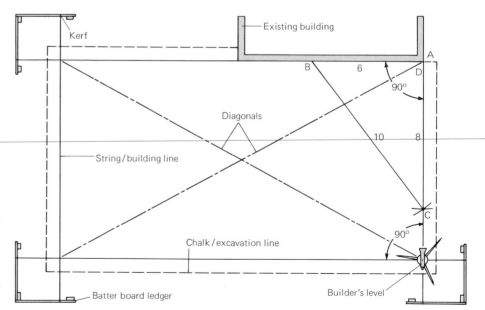

more precise triangulation can be made using a steel tape measure, which will not stretch as string tends to do; arcs are scratched in the dirt at a radius of 10 feet from B and 8 feet from A, and the

nail is driven where the arcs intersect.

Diagonals: The diagonals of any square or rectangle are equal. Adjust the corners in your site until the diagonals measure equal lengths.

Laying out building lines

Sighting along a string, a workman establishes a line continuous with an existing wall; point is marked on batter board by his helper.

Transit-level is set over the first corner stake. It is rotated 90° to establish a line perpendicular to the line set in the above step.

A line is laid slightly outside the building lines. Powdered chalk is poured over the line; this is the guide for the excavation.

Elevation of the first-floor subfloor is marked on the wall. This is used as a reference point for all other vertical measurements.

Excavating

Certain soil conditions warrant professional consultation before excavation, and ordinarily a professional contractor to do the digging: for example, if the soil is fill, rather than virgin soil (this can be difficult to determine); if the excavation will run below the normal groundwater level of the soil; if the soil is unstable or expansive.

If the soil conditions are stable, consider the quality of the soil, the number of rocks, and the size of the job. It would be grueling to excavate for a large project by hand.

If you decide to hire an excavator, call several for estimates. The excavating machine called a backhoe is ordinarily rented by the day, though sometimes backhoes are available by the half day for very small jobs. You must show or describe the plot to the excavator so that he can select a backhoe of appropriate size; if it is too large it can seriously damage your site.

Before any digging starts make sure that no pipes, wires, or septic systems will be dug up inadvertently.

The excavation shown in the photographs on this page acted as the mold or formwork for the footing; in poorer soils, or for heavier loads, wooden formwork is sometimes constructed, as seen on page 246. The excavation must be square and the bottom flat (usually done with a hand shovel) so the footing can properly distribute weight.

Pier foundations and basements are illustrated on pages 22–23. If an excavation hits bedrock, the foundation can be anchored to the rock (p.243).

Guided by the chalk lines that were laid during the site preparation, the backhoe is used to dig the excavation. Here it excavates the ground to be occupied by the slab.

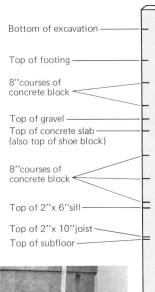

Bottom of excavation
Top of footing
8″ courses of concrete block
Top of gravel
Top of concrete slab (also top of shoe block)
8″ courses of concrete block
Top of 2″ x 6″ sill
Top of 2″ x 10″ joist
Top of subfloor

Checking the footing depth: Here the vertical measurements are determined by using a builder's level in combination with a story pole. The story pole has marks indicating the planned heights of different levels of construction, as seen in drawing, above right. Using the level, a fixed point, such as the floor level on the existing house, is sighted and established as the vertical reference point, or bench mark, from which all measurements are made with the story pole. Thereafter, the story pole can be positioned with the builder's level to determine the exact height for any part of the construction. In photo at left, depth of the excavation is being checked (builder's level is in the background). In photo at right, stakes are driven at height to which footing will be poured. The story pole is used to check the height of each stake.

Adding a wing

Determining your concrete needs

If the total volume of your planned concrete work is less than 1 cubic yard you can mix the concrete yourself with a rental power mixer. To calculate cubic yards, multiply the length x height x width of the foundation or slab in feet and divide by 27. For example a 4-inch-thick concrete floor 25 x 15 feet would require 4.63 cubic yards of concrete: 25 x 15 x ⅓ (4 inches is ⅓ foot) equals 125 cubic feet; this divided by 27 equals 4.63 yards. Allow 10% for waste.

You have the choice of bags of dry ready-mixed concrete, which is convenient, or the separate components, which can be more economical. Concrete is a mixture of Portland cement, fine aggregate (sand), coarse aggregate (gravel or crushed stone), and water. Its qualities depend on the proportions.

For most additions, it will be necessary to order concrete from a truck (transit mixer). A footing or slab must be poured at once in its entirety; you cannot pour in small batches.

The concrete is mixed by the contractor according to certain specifications, including: the maximum size of the aggregate (not more than ¼ the thickness of a slab, when it is for a slab); the minimum cement content (usually 5 bags per cubic yard for footings and foundation walls, 6 bags for slabs); the maximum slump (a rough measure of consistency, normally not to exceed 4 inches); the load-bearing capacity (at least 3,500 psi at 28 days; see opposite page); the entrained air content (6%).

Concrete for footings and slabs is mixed with an agent that entraps air, making the concrete more durable. If only because it is not possible to mix concrete vigorously enough by hand to entrain sufficient air, hand-mixed concrete is never used in footings or slabs.

Mixing: If you decide to rent a power mixer and prepare the concrete yourself, use only components that are clean, and, if possible, intended for use only in concrete. Foreign matter in the aggregate can destroy the cohesion of the concrete. The water should be clean enough to be drinkable.

Store the aggregates separately on a clean, hard surface. Cover them with plastic if they are stored outdoors. Cement must be kept dry; enclose cement bags in plastic bags.

For a footing, 1 cubic yard of concrete typically consists of 5 bags of cement, 15 cubic feet of fine aggregate (sand), 20 cubic feet of coarse aggregate (gravel or crushed stone), and 24 to 31 gallons of water, depending on the wetness of the sand. (After mixing the combined ingredients have about ⅔ of the original bulk.) For a slab the mix contains 1 extra bag of cement and 1 extra cubic foot of coarse aggregate. The air-entraining element either comes mixed in with the cement, or must be added. Check with your concrete supplier.

Additives: Your supplier might also be able to advise you about additives. Additives to concrete mixes can, for example, speed or retard the setting time of the concrete; make it watertight or dampproof; make the surface non-dusting or non-slip; change its color; reduce the water needed in the mix, etc.

Using the mixer: With the mixer stopped add all the coarse aggregate and half the water (with the air-entraining agent, if it is separate). Start the mixer, add the sand, cement, and the rest of the water. Because of the moisture in the sand, you will have to gauge the amount of water to add by observing the mix. The goal is a mushy, but not soupy, concrete that will stick together without crumbling. Continue mixing for 3 minutes, or until the concrete appears uniform in texture.

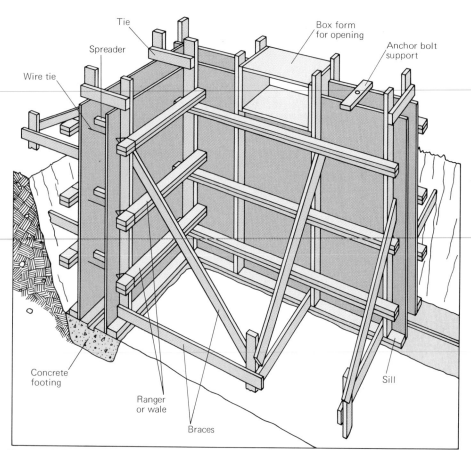

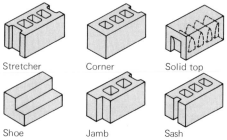

A power mixer can be rented to mix concrete for small foundations. The mixer can also be used to mix mortar for concrete block construction.

Stretcher   Corner   Solid top

Shoe   Jamb   Sash

Concrete blocks: Some of the most common types of blocks are shown. Block construction (pp. 248-249) is cheaper than poured concrete work, and was used in the addition illustrated in this chapter. When you order block, specify the required number of each type of block.

Formwork: Plywood formwork is used to build a mold for poured concrete footings and foundation walls. It is used only when the soil cannot adequately support wet concrete, or when extra strength or a particular shape is desired. You can build formwork with heavy reinforcement, or you can rent it.

Tie

Box form for opening

Anchor bolt support

Spreader

Wire tie

Concrete footing

Ranger or wale

Braces

Sill

Contracting for a poured footing

Most work involving footings and slabs requires a concrete contractor, as noted on the opposite page. The contractor mixes and delivers the concrete in a truck. Architects' specifications usually call for concrete able to withstand a certain pressure, measured in pounds per square inch (psi). The contractor knows the mixture that will satisfy the strength requirement and meet any special demands of your climate. For footings and slabs in ordinary dwellings, 3,500 psi usually suffices (4,000 psi for slabs in garages and driveways).

Concrete trucks: If you decide to have the concrete mixed and delivered in a truck, get estimates from several contractors. They will need to know the volume (the footing shown here used 5.7 cubic yards) and strength you need.

Before the truck arrives, prepare the site. If the truck remains at the site more than 45 minutes to an hour you are charged extra. A loaded truck is very heavy, and can damage driveways, curbs, sidewalks, and lawns. It is wise to place wooden planks 2 inches thick to make a path for the truck. Make absolutely certain that the truck does not pass close to or over the cesspool, septic tanks, drainage tiles, or oil tanks.

Trucks are usually equipped with a chute 10–15 feet in length, and an extension. You can also erect your own wooden extension chutes to reach remote areas. It is easier to build and move chutes than to move wet concrete that weighs about 150 pounds per cubic foot. The limit for a pour on level ground is 25 to 30 feet. If you cannot move the truck within that range, use wheelbarrows to take the concrete from the truck to the site. Place plywood sheets in the path of the wheelbarrows.

Pouring the concrete: Concrete is best poured on a day when the temperature is from 50 to 75°F. Below 50°F the chemical reaction proceeds too slowly; above 75°F water may evaporate before it can be chemically bonded. If the pouring must be on a hot or a cold day, retardants or accelerants can be added.

The truck driver should arrive on schedule, set up, and control the flow of concrete from the truck. The ingredients are mixed while the truck is enroute; more water can be added.

For the footing seen in the photographs below, a normal consistency of concrete was mixed and poured into the section of the footing nearest the truck. For areas farther away more water was added to make the mix flow more freely through the chute and extensions.

The concrete is pushed off the chute into the excavation. It should never be dropped more than a few feet because its components may separate. Pouring continues until concrete reaches the top of the stakes. The stakes are then pulled out, and the concrete is leveled.

A stick or shovel is repeatedly pushed into the concrete to break up air bubbles; however, this process should not be overdone because it can destroy the homogeneity of the concrete. The surface can then be tamped and floated (smoothed).

A grout key form is inserted into the concrete. The form is made of 2 x 3 or 2 x 4 lumber, usually tapered for easy removal. It is pushed in until its top is level with the top of the footing. When the form is removed it leaves a continuous groove that anchors the mortar bed for the foundation wall.

Remove concrete from all tools and clothing before it sets. Beware of its corrosive effect on leather and skin. It is best to wear rubber boots and gloves.

The concrete should be sprinkled with water each day for a week, and covered with plastic after wetting.

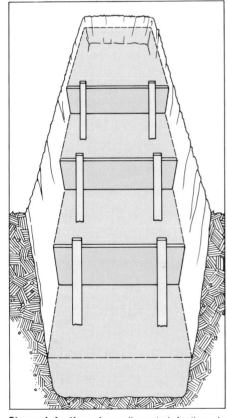

Stepped footing: A small central footing descends in three steps from the existing wall to the outside footing of the addition, which is 24 in. lower. Stepped footings save extra excavation work and concrete. Boards are erected to dam steps at proper heights.

Concrete flows into an extension chute, which is supported by wooden horses. Concrete is pulled off with rakes. Stakes mark final footing height.

For far recesses, concrete mix is made thinner to flow easier. Concrete is raked to fill excavation completely. Workmen wear high rubber boots.

After pouring is complete, stakes are removed. Tamper pushes down aggregate, and gives tooth to the footing, helping to anchor foundation wall.

247

Adding a wing

Building a concrete block foundation wall

As in most modern houses and additions, the foundation wall in our project was constructed of concrete block.

Concrete block: The most common types of concrete block are shown on page 246. The stretcher, the type of block most often used, weighs about 30 pounds. It measures 7⅝ x 7⅝ x 15⅝ inches; when assembled with ⅜-inch mortar beds, construction proceeds in 8- and 16-inch increments.

Tools: Most of the tools necessary for concrete block construction are seen in use in the photographs below.

If you want to mix mortar by machine, you can rent the necessary equipment from your supplier. A power mixer (p.246) is the best choice for large jobs, but you can also rent a simple hand-held machine that is used to stir small batches eggbeater fashion in buckets or drums. Small batches can also be mixed by hand, using a trough or wheelbarrow and a shovel or hoe.

To apply the mortar get a trowel with a durable handle, because it is used to tap the blocks into place. A long mason's or carpenter's level is needed to check the line of the blocks. A bricklayer's hammer and chisel are used to break blocks. A mason's jointer is used

to finish the mortar joints; a ⅝-inch metal rod or pipe will do just as well. A mortar board holds the mortar at the immediate place of work.

A course string, which extends down each course from the corner blocks to guide the block placement, sits on a holder that can be purchased or made from wood. Wrapping the string around

a spare block will do as well. A story pole (p.245) marked in 8-inch increments is used to check the height of each successive course of blocks.

Mortar: Mortar is a mixture of masonry cement (premixed Portland cement and hydrated lime), sand and water. It is mixed in small batches either by machine or by hand.

After the footing sets: 1. Elevation of first course of concrete block is checked with story pole and builder's level (see pp.242–245). Adjustments in height can be made by altering the standard ⅜-in. thickness of the mortar bed on top of the footing and in each succeeding course of blocks.

2. First course has been laid on footing and filled with concrete. Here end of a stretcher block is buttered with mortar to start second course.

3. Guided by line extended from the corner, each block is pressed into the mortar bed. Mortar joints should all be ⅜-in. thick.

4. Each block is checked with a level to ensure it is exactly horizontal. Adjustments are made by tapping block with handle of trowel.

5. The level is also used to check the plane of the wall. Notice that corners are built up several courses above the rest of the wall.

6. Metal reinforcement is laid into every other course of mortar. Here it is cut (with bolt cutters) and bent around a corner.

7. The level is used to check the height of the course across a corner. The two blocks in foreground are sash blocks (see p.246).

248

The dry ingredients are mixed carefully; then water is added. The water must be clean enough to be drinkable. The consistency of the mortar is very important. Add only enough water to make it workable. The mortar should spread smoothly, but retain its shape; it should cling to vertical and horizontal surfaces, but not flow out of the joints.

Mix only as much mortar as you will use within the subsequent 2½ hours. After that the mortar will begin to set and cannot be used.

You will need about one 70-pound bag of masonry cement and 3 cubic feet of sand per 100 concrete blocks. To make each batch of mortar, mix 1 part masonry cement (which already contains the correct amount of lime) to 3 parts sand. Mix the dry ingredients until every grain of sand is completely covered; then, adding a little water at a time, mix until the mortar takes on a uniform color and texture.

Laying the blocks: The top of the footing is swept and rinsed off. The lines from the batter boards (pp. 242–247) are re-strung; their intersections mark the positions of the corner blocks.

Using the mortar board and trowel, a bed of mortar ½ inch thick is laid on the footing, a bit thicker on the edges than in the middle. The first corner block is pressed firmly into place, compressing the mortar bed to ⅜ inch. A block is then positioned and laid at the opposite corner. A string is stretched between the corner blocks and used as a guide to lay the rest of the blocks working from the corners in. The web of concrete blocks has a thick and a thin side; the thin side should always face down.

Each block is "buttered" at the ends with mortar, and laid in place. Stretcher blocks are ordinarily used between the corners, but as is shown in the photos, extra corner or sash blocks will do as well. After the first course is completed, the corners are built up several courses above the rest of the wall.

The ends of the foundation wall that abut the existing building are toothed into the building. If the existing wall is very hard, the new wall can be connected using reinforcing rods (see the drawing of the foundation on p. 243).

After the first two courses are laid, they are filled with concrete (here 2,000 psi) to help solidify the wall.

The top course of the wall is made of solid shoe blocks, which help support the slab to be poured above. Anchor bolts, which connect the foundation to the wooden frame, are laid into the top course. In this project, the anchor bolts are 12 inches long and ⅜ inch in diameter, spaced every 8 feet along the wall (but not in doorways). They must be set at the proper depth to accomplish the thickness of the sill, because only about the top 1½ inches are threaded.

If pipes or conduits must pass through the foundation wall (none do in this project), it is far easier to make provision for a passage than to knock a hole in a finished wall (see the detail drawing, p. 243).

Parging: A parging is a coating of cement applied by trowel to a wall to help waterproof it. The second of the two ¼-inch layers of cement should also extend over the top of the footing, to protect the juncture between the footing and foundation wall.

In wet soil, or soil with poor drainage, the parging can be covered with a layer of asphalt as a waterproofing agent, and then with building paper while the asphalt is still sticky. This is especially important if the wall will enclose a living area. After the final covering is applied to the foundation and has set, the excavation is backfilled.

8. Holes are chiseled in the existing wall so that every other course of the new wall can penetrate. This procedure is called toothing.

9. Blocks are cut by scoring the line of the break with a mason's hammer or chisel. One sound blow will then break the block.

10. The cut pieces are fit in, near the middle of the wall, not at the corners. The small pieces should be staggered between the courses.

11. Before mortar hardens, it is trimmed back at the joints with the jointer. Excess mortar is removed. This helps to waterproof wall.

12. A parging, or layer of cement, is applied with a trowel. The parging should consist of two ¼ in. coatings, applied 24 hours apart.

13. Anchor bolts are laid in the joints of the top course (here made of shoe blocks). They extend into course below, and are anchored with mortar.

249

Adding a wing

Pouring a slab floor

Before the slab is poured, the soil bed beneath the slab is leveled and compacted. Unless the soil is firm and especially dry, sandy, and gravelly, a layer of gravel or crushed stone is spread over it. The soil beneath our addition was known to bear weight well; and a 4-inch layer of gravel was approved by the architect and mason.

Gravel is laid, graded, and compacted as evenly as possible to ensure that the slab is of even thickness. The elevation of the gravel is checked with the story pole and the builder's level (if it is still at the site), or with the batter board lines (pp.242–245).

Gravel is ordered from a building supply yard, by volume (in cubic yards). For purposes of billing and transportation, it is transposed by the yard into weight, in tons. This project required about 5 cubic yards of gravel.

Insulation: Insulation is attached to the foundation wall to minimize heat loss through the slab. A stiff insulating material, such as styrofoam, is generally used. It is attached to the wall by a special adhesive that will adhere to both the insulator and the concrete.

In our addition, the 2-inch-thick insulation was cut and glued to the L-shaped inside surfaces of the shoe block that forms the top course of the foundation wall (pp.242–243). Sheets of insulation also extend 2 feet down the inside of the foundation wall. Such insulation is applied before the gravel is laid, and should reach to below the frost line in northern parts of the country.

After the gravel was spread at our site, a 2-foot width of insulation was laid around the perimeter of the slab, atop the gravel. This insulation was depressed into the gravel so that the top of the insulation lies flush with the top of the gravel in the uncovered section. Some builders favor placing a complete layer of insulation over the entire gravel bed. Others maintain that the temperature of the earth is a favorable moderating influence in all seasons and that blanket insulation under the slab interferes with this beneficial influence. In any case, the air trapped between the pieces of gravel provides some insulation beneath the slab.

Vapor barrier: A polyethylene vapor barrier is laid over the gravel and perimeter insulation, overlapping itself at least 6 inches at the seams. It is temporarily held in place with pieces of wood until the reinforcement is laid.

Reinforcement: Metal reinforcement is placed so that it will be embedded in slab when the concrete is poured. The reinforcement here is an 8/8 gauge wire mesh. It should be rolled out, then cut to measurement with bolt cutters. It is

treacherous stuff and requires care, and a helper. In a thick slab, small rocks or special wire devices called bridges are used to elevate the reinforcement so it will sit in the middle of the slab. None was used in our thin (4 inches) slab.

All mechanical installations, such as heating ducts and water pipes that are situated in or pass through the slab must be set in place before the slab is poured. We had none in our addition.

Two-in.-thick polystyrene is applied with adhesive to L-shaped recess of shoe block course and 2 ft. down the inside of foundation wall.

Pouring the concrete: The volume of the slab is calculated and the concrete is ordered, just as for a footing (see pp.246–247). Extension chutes are set up to reach from the concrete truck to various points of the slab, from which the concrete is then tamped and evenly distributed by hand. Our concrete was poured separately from the truck via extension chutes into each of the four sections of the slab.

A 4-in. gravel bed is being laid and graduated. Insulation extends 2 ft. in from perimeter and is set flush with top of gravel.

The gravel has been graded and tamped, and perimeter insulation is in place. The elevation of the gravel bed is being spot-checked with the builder's level and story pole. This is important; if the bed is not flat, the slab, when poured, will be of uneven thickness.

Polyethylene vapor barrier is laid and temporarily held down by boards around perimeter. Barrier should overlap at least 6 in. at the seams.

Metal reinforcement is rolled out and flattened, then cut with bolt cutters. Be careful; it is springy and dangerous to work with.

It is wise to keep an extra wheelbarrow full of concrete when the truck leaves; it may be needed to fill gaps after striking off (below).

Finishing the concrete: The concrete is tamped, to push any jutting coarse aggregate into the slab, and to burst any air bubbles. A striking board, a long 2 x 4, is drawn across the surface, guided by the top of the foundation wall and the fiber board nailed to the existing wall. This levels the surface. Any gaps are filled with the excess concrete.

After the concrete sets for a while, wooden boards can be placed on the slab to support the weight of a worker. Walking and kneeling on these boards, a person can then work the concrete with a steel trowel and give the slab a smooth finish with a wooden float; the slab for a patio is given a rougher finish with a broom for greater traction.

Fiber board is nailed to existing building. It serves as an expansion joint for the slab, and guides striking board when wet concrete is leveled.

Chutes are set up to pour the concrete from the truck. Here extension chutes are used to transport the concrete in as far as possible.

Concrete is moved down chute with a hoe, rake, or shovel. The concrete is poured separately into each section of the slab and leveled.

Tamper and rake are used to pull away and distribute the wet concrete from the chute. Tamper is also used to push down coarse aggregate that juts up through the surface (next photograph).

After concrete is tamped (man standing), a long 2 x 4 is used to smooth, or strike off, slab; 2 x 4 is guided by shoe blocks and fiber board against existing wall. Man at rear must smooth out his footprints.

A scaffolding distributes workman's weight to prevent impressions in the setting concrete as he smooths concrete with a steel trowel.

This float with a long handle is used to give a smooth finish to that part of slab that will serve as the floor inside the addition.

Broom gives a textured finish, improving traction on patio slab. An edging tool makes clean outside lines along sections.

Adding a wing
Building the wood frame

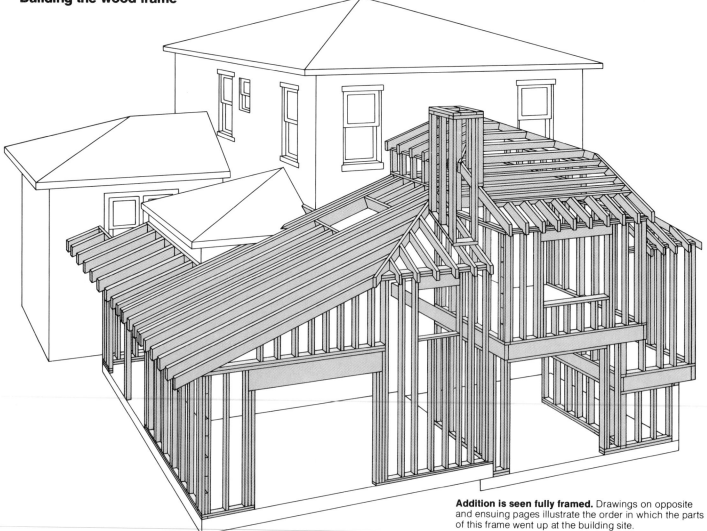

Addition is seen fully framed. Drawings on opposite and ensuing pages illustrate the order in which the parts of this frame went up at the building site.

The process of framing an addition varies according to the demands of the structure and the preferences of the carpenter. On this and the following six pages are drawings and photographs of the major steps in the framing of our addition, as our carpenter chose to do it. Carpenters have their own techniques and shortcuts; don't be alarmed if what you see here differs in some respects from what you, or someone you hire, plan to do with your house. What matters is that the frame is sturdy and safe. The illustrations at the top of each page illustrate first the finished frame and then the sequence of the procedure.

The framing process: The sill, made of wood treated to resist moisture and termites (because it rests on the slab, and is therefore near to the earth), is installed over fiberglass insulation. The first-story walls—plates, studs, and other elements—are assembled flat, and then raised into place, as seen in the photographs on the opposite page. Temporary cross bracing prevents walls from twisting or falling. Because this

particular wood-frame addition has a slab floor, there are no first-floor joists.

Nooks to hold girder ends are cut into the adjoining wall of the house and the first girders are installed. Girders are usually made of two or three boards fastened together instead of one heavy timber. They can be preassembled and installed as completed units; or the parts can be installed separately and fastened in place. Metal shims are placed in the nooks beneath the girders for the final leveling. Small adjustments are required throughout the process.

Upper floors: The second-floor joists and subflooring are installed, then the second-story walls go up. Framing for the windows is often built in as the walls are assembled (flat, upon the second-floor subflooring). In our addition, this was done after the walls were up.

The ceiling joists are put in, then the small attic walls, and the bathroom wall. The roof rafters are installed. Our roof is far more complex than most, but the techniques and sequence of construction are similar to those used in

simpler designs. The walls and roof are covered with plywood sheathing. Finally the chimney chase is constructed. The studs, joists, and rafters in this addition are, for the most part, spaced at the standard residential construction interval, 16 inches, on center.

Most wood members are measured and cut before they are installed. Others, particularly rafters and joists that extend to the outside of the frame, are installed rough; they are then measured and cut in place, making the line of the finish more accurate.

Framing invariably provides surprises. You may have to redo some parts, improvising to fit others; don't be deterred. But do be sure that changes and improvizations do not compromise the integrity of the structure.

Building codes: For a general discussion about framing and the function of the elements of the frame, see *Building Codes*, pages 24–29. The frame must be fastened in a manner consistent with your local code. For typical requirements, see the nailing schedule (p.36).

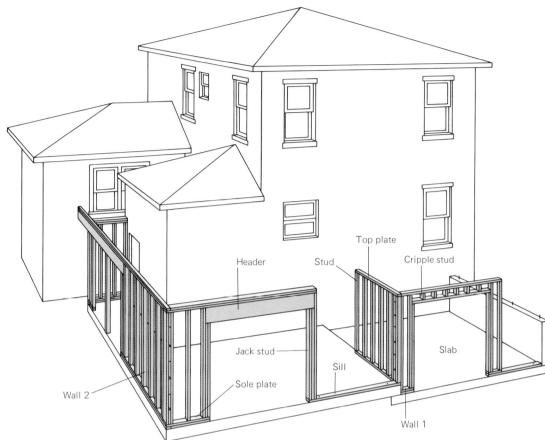

First framing stage:
First-floor walls—
including 2 x 4 sole
plates, top plates,
studs, and all other
elements—are
laid out on the slab
foundation at the
places where they will
be erected. They are
assembled, fastened,
raised into place, and
nailed to the sills.

Top plate

Header

Stud

Cripple stud

Jack stud

Sill

Slab

Sole plate

Wall 2

Wall 1

1. Fiberglass insulation cut to fit around the perimeter of the slab also helps stop termite infiltration. It is pressed into place; the anchor bolts pass through it (see next step).

2. The sill, made of treated 2 x 4s, is measured to fit perimeter. Anchor bolt locations are marked, then drilled in sill. The sill is placed over sill-seal insulation and bolted down.

3. The studs and plate of wall #1 (see drawing above) are laid on the slab and end-nailed together. This wall is open because it holds a large door; side wall is more typical.

4. The assembled wall is raised into place and nailed to the sill. Like many steps in framing, this procedure is difficult to accomplish without the aid of an assistant.

5. A temporary cross bracing on each wall prevents it from twisting or falling. The cross bracing remains in place until the frame is finished and plywood sheathing is applied.

6. Additional bracing is put in place perpendicular to the wall. As in Step 5, a level is used to determine the exact vertical before these props are nailed in. *(continued)*

Adding a wing

Building the wood frame (continued)

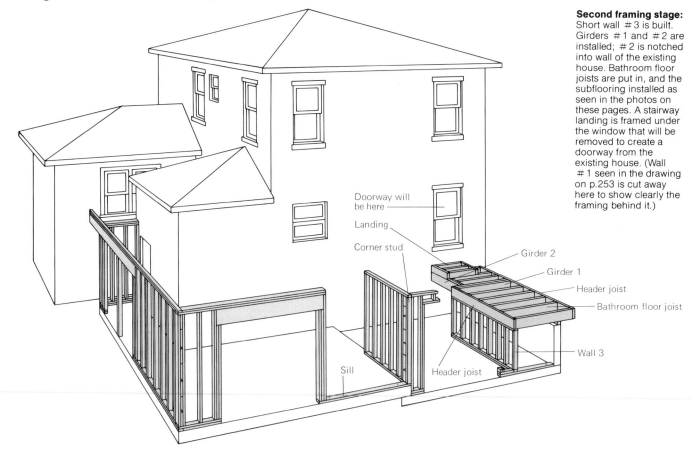

Second framing stage:
Short wall #3 is built. Girders #1 and #2 are installed; #2 is notched into wall of the existing house. Bathroom floor joists are put in, and the subflooring installed as seen in the photos on these pages. A stairway landing is framed under the window that will be removed to create a doorway from the existing house. (Wall #1 seen in the drawing on p.253 is cut away here to show clearly the framing behind it.)

Doorway will be here

Landing

Corner stud

Girder 2

Girder 1

Header joist

Bathroom floor joist

Wall 3

Sill

Header joist

7. For strength and nailing area, corner stud is built up from 2 x 4s and scrap. Stud is built into a wall and raised with it; adjoining wall is nailed to it.

8. Notches are drilled and chiseled to hold ends of girders. Notches must be deep enough so girder bearing is at least 3 in. This notch is cut for girder #2.

9. Here all the walls shown in the drawing on page 253 are erected. Atop the short wall (#3, this page) that will support the bathroom floor joists, a 2-x-10 header-joist is toenailed into place. Cross-bracing at rear is temporary.

10. Intervals of 16 in. are marked on inside of a header-joist, and bathroom floor joists are then set in place and end-nailed to it. Floor joists are 2 x 10s because of the weight imposed by bathroom fixtures and shower stall.

11. The other ends of the joists extend over the masonry wall. Each joist is toenailed to the sill. The joist ends are then trimmed off with a saw (Step 12).

12. A chalk line marks the joists for trimming. In general, it is more accurate to install members on the frame and then saw them than to cut them beforehand.

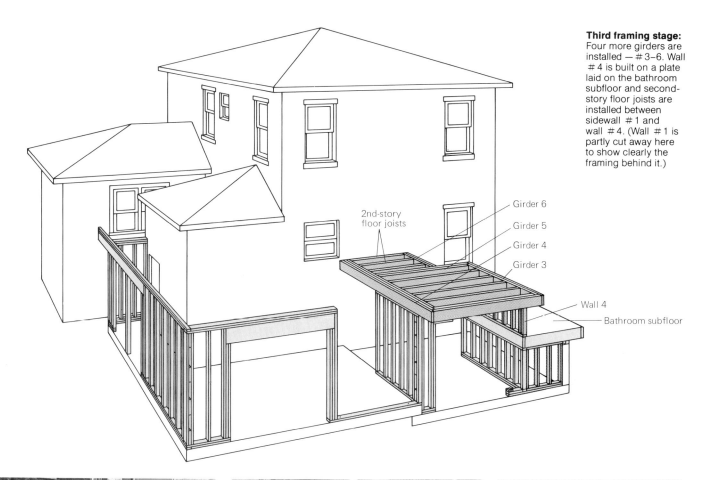

Third framing stage:
Four more girders are installed — #3–6. Wall #4 is built on a plate laid on the bathroom subfloor and second-story floor joists are installed between sidewall #1 and wall #4. (Wall #1 is partly cut away here to show clearly the framing behind it.)

2nd-story floor joists

Girder 6
Girder 5
Girder 4
Girder 3

Wall 4

Bathroom subfloor

13. The second of the 2 x 10s that form girder #2 is pushed into its notch and nailed to the first 2 x 10. Girders are sometimes assembled before they are installed (Step 17).

14. The girder is attached to the last joist with a joist hanger, which strengthens corner joint. Building codes often require that connections between perpendicular beams and joists be made with joist hangers.

15. Here the hanger is inserted between a floor joist and a header joist. Holes in the hanger make it possible for the nails to pass through into the wood.

16. When all the floor joists and headers are in place, plywood subflooring (here ½ in. thick) is cut to fit, laid down on the joists, and nailed in position.

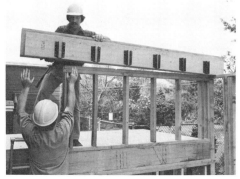

17. Girder #3 is hoisted into place atop wall #4. Note that this girder was assembled before installation. Joist hangers are attached every 16 in.; the header is then toenailed to top plate of wall.

18. As in Step 5, wall is braced while level is used to determine vertical. Here, end of brace is nailed to a piece of scrap wood, which is in turn nailed to subfloor. *(continued)*

Adding a wing

Building the wood frame (continued)

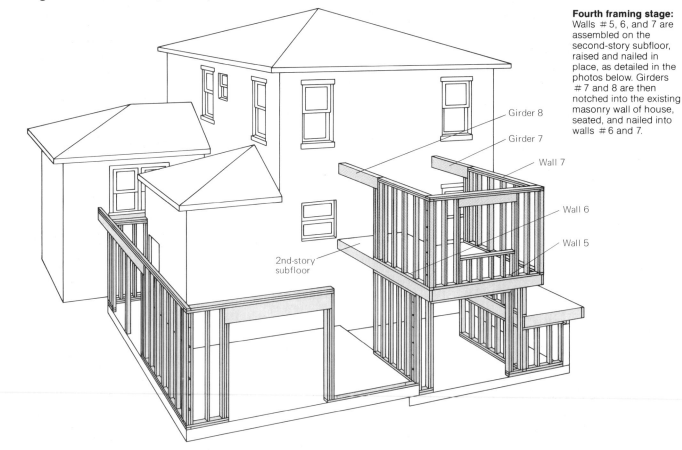

Fourth framing stage:
Walls #5, 6, and 7 are assembled on the second-story subfloor, raised and nailed in place, as detailed in the photos below. Girders #7 and 8 are then notched into the existing masonry wall of house, seated, and nailed into walls #6 and 7.

Girder 8

Girder 7

Wall 7

Wall 6

Wall 5

2nd-story subfloor

19. The interior corners of the built-up girders are formed of staggered boards. This creates an interlocking corner joint, which provides extra strength.

20. Girder #4 (p.255) is in place. It consists of doubled 2 x 12s with a 2 x 10 nailed inside to create a 2-in. recess flush with the floor joists for nailing subflooring. Here, joists are set in place and nailed through the joist hanger.

21. The second-story subflooring is cut to fit. Here a lone workman pulls a sheet of plywood into place with his boot. He will nail the panel to the joists.

22. Bedroom side wall (#7) is assembled atop the second-floor subfloor, and then raised and nailed in. Notice built-up corner post (Step 7, p.254). Wall will be temporarily cross-braced.

23. Bedroom front wall (#5) is assembled on the subfloor and raised into position. The end studs are nailed permanently into the doubled corner posts of walls #6 and #7.

24. The rough framing for the bedroom window is nailed into wall #5. Often window and door framing is built into the frame when it is lying flat, before it is raised into place.

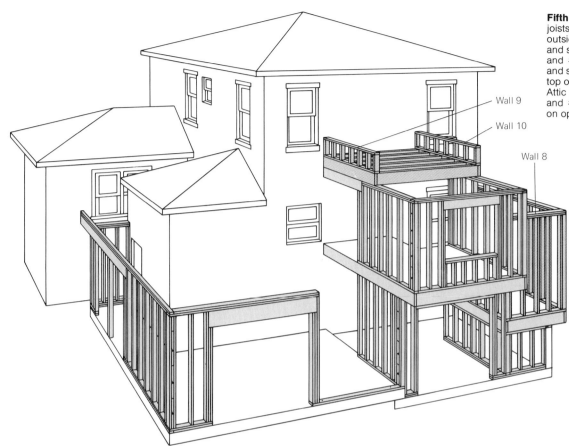

Fifth framing stage: Ceiling joists are installed. The outside bathroom wall (#8) and short attic walls (#9 and #10) are constructed and set in place on top of header joists. Attic rests on girders #7 and #8. (See drawing on opposite page.)

Wall 9

Wall 10

Wall 8

25. Bricks were cleared to create notches to hold girders #7 and #8 (see Step 8, p.254), which are seen installed. The first ceiling joists are being toenailed to the girders.

26. Wall #9 is nailed to the ceiling joists. Uninstalled wall #10 lies beside it. A central 2-x-4 brace prevents joists from twisting. Workmen kneels on board as temporary scaffolding.

27. A hole is drilled into the brick. A lead anchor is installed. Lag bolt here attaches wall #10 to the anchor. This technique is used wherever studs and rafters abut the brick wall.

28. The pitch of the roof is set using this tool, called a rafter square. It indicates the line on which the top and bottom rafter ends should be cut with the saw.

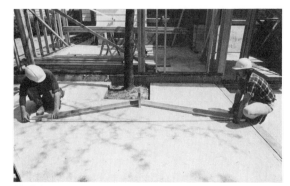

29. When the first two rafters' ends are cut, they are laid flat, with a temporary ridge board in place, to see whether they are exactly square. The first two boards are then used as templates for cutting other rafters.

30. The first two rafters are bolted to the brick wall. Notice the way the small cut, or "bird's mouth," is sawed so the rafter will sit flush on the plate. *(continued)*

257

Adding a wing

Building the wood frame (continued)

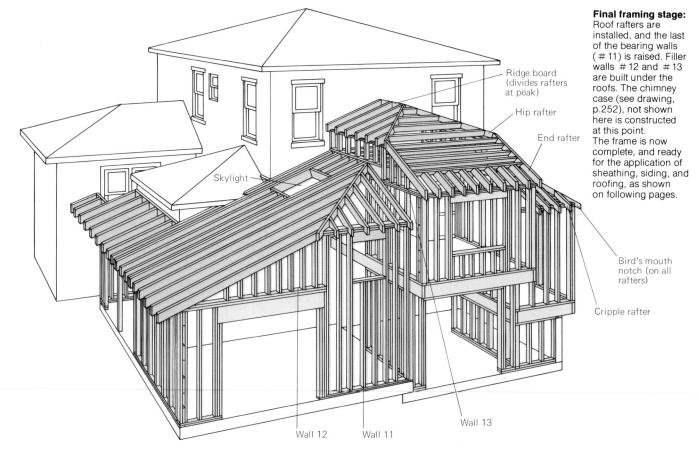

Ridge board (divides rafters at peak)

Hip rafter

End rafter

Skylight

Bird's mouth notch (on all rafters)

Cripple rafter

Wall 12   Wall 11   Wall 13

Final framing stage: Roof rafters are installed, and the last of the bearing walls (#11) is raised. Filler walls #12 and #13 are built under the roofs. The chimney case (see drawing, p.252), not shown here is constructed at this point.
The frame is now complete, and ready for the application of sheathing, siding, and roofing, as shown on following pages.

31. Ridge board is set in place, held up by two pairs of opposing rafters. The remaining rafters are end-nailed to the ridge board, spaced 16 inches o.c. These rafters are 2 x 8s.

32. A 2 x 4 bracing the ridge board rests on the brace shown in Step 26, page 257. The rafter is nailed in, as shown. Then the hip rafters and cripple rafters are installed.

33. The first long rafter is held in place. The lines for the ridge cut and bird's mouth are marked. After this rafter is cut, it serves as a template for cutting the other long rafters.

34. Framing for a skylight, or roof window, is installed between the long roof rafter. A skylight on the far roof (not shown) is framed in a similar fashion.

35. Chalk line is snapped across rafters. A level is used to mark rafter faces with cutting lines perpendicular to chalk lines. A power saw trims rafters evenly.

36. Metal cross bridging was installed between the rafters to prevent twisting. Here, solid wood blocking is driven into the narrower rafter gaps. When reinforcement is complete, plywood sheathing is installed over the entire frame, walls, and roof.

Laying the roofing

After framing and sheathing are complete, roofing and siding are normally applied before any interior work is done—to protect the interior from inclement weather.

Fascia: Fascia and trim are installed along the eaves. They help support the shingles, and weatherproof the eaves.

Roof edge: A strip of metal is nailed to the roof so it extends 1½ inches over the edge. This roof edge causes water coming off the roof to drip clear of rather than down the wall. It also provides additional support for the first course of shingles.

Building paper: Fifteen-pound building paper (paper that weighs 15 pounds per roofing square, or 100 square feet) is tacked over the entire roof. When the shingles are in place, the weight of the shingles secures the paper. The paper overlaps several inches at the seams. The uproof course must always overlap the downroof course, thus enabling the water to run off the roof.

Shingles: Our addition is roofed with asphalt shingles in standard 3-foot-long strips. Asphalt shingle strips frequently have tabs every foot; when applied to the roof, the tabs have the look of individual shingles. On this house, however, the architect selected shingles without tabs, so the line of the shingles across the roof is unbroken.

The first, or starter, course of shingles is attached along the eave and consists of two layers. The bottom layer is a course of inverted shingles; that is, the normal downroof side—the tabs—faces uproof. A starter course of wood shingles is sometimes used instead. Atop this bottom layer is the first course of shingles, laid normally. Each succeeding course overlaps the course below it, leaving an exposure of 5 inches. A chalk line is snapped across the roof every few courses. This is done in order to make sure that the lines of the shingles are straight and the spacing even.

The second course begins with a shingle strip cut 6 inches shorter in length than the first course. This staggers the joints between courses, making water penetration more difficult. Every other course is staggered in this way. Shingles can be broken by repeated bending along the intended line of the break; cut with a mat knife guided by a building square, or cut with shears. Cutting should be done on the downward face, the face without granules. The ridge caps are installed on the peak of the roof after the other shingling is complete. Tapered segments of shingles about 1 foot long are cut from the standard lengths to form the ridge caps. They are installed so each piece overlaps the one below by 5 or 6 inches.

Continued next page.

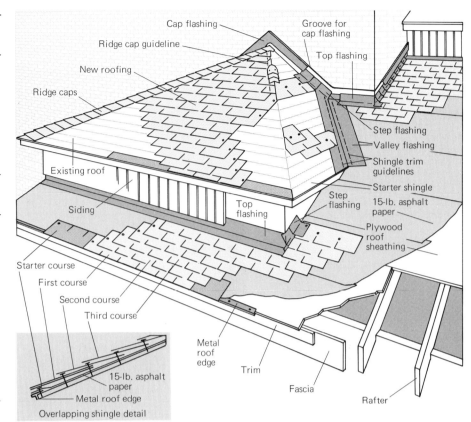

Drawing shows position of roofing elements: building paper over plywood sheathing; shingles over building paper on addition and over old shingles on existing roof; flashings and trim. Shingling proceeds from eaves upward; here, shingles are omitted in some areas to show flashing.

1. The fascia (here already installed) and molding (being installed) are attached to the eave before the roof covering is applied.

2. Metal roof edge extends over edge of sheathing so water will drip clear of wall. It also provides support for the first course of shingles.

3. Fifteen-pound building paper is tacked to the sheathing. Each row of paper overlaps the one downroof of it by several inches.

4. First piece of aluminum step flashing is nailed in place. First shingle is stapled over it. One piece is used beneath each course. *(continued)*

Adding a wing

Laying the roofing (continued)

Application of shingles: Shingles are attached to the new roof with a staple hammer, a device that when swung drives a special roofing staple into the roof and automatically reloads; it requires the use of only one hand. Shingle strips are attached at the ends and at least two intermediate points.

Re-roofing: In our project, the roof adjoining the addition is re-shingled to match the addition. The first course of a re-roofing fits exactly over the exposed first course of the old roof; this smooths the surface so the new shingles lie flat over the old. The new shingles are fastened with roofing nails because staples will not penetrate deep enough to hold them securely. You cannot pile up new roofings indefinitely; three layers are normally the limit.

Flashing: Where the side of a roof abuts a wall, step flashing is installed to prevent leaks. Step flashing is made of small square pieces of aluminum, which can be bought pre-cut or cut from the roll. One piece of step flashing is nailed beneath the end of each course of shingles. Each piece of flashing must be longer than the exposure of the shingles. In this addition, each overlaps the one below it by 5 inches.

After the shingles are all applied, a top layer of flashing is often applied over the step flashing. It is attached to the wall in a groove sawed for that purpose, or, if possible, laid into the mortar joints of a brick wall (see Step 20, p.261). If the step flashing can be tacked under the existing siding, this second flashing is not necessary. You then caulk the flashing to prevent leaks.

Flashing is laid in all valleys—where adjacent roof slopes meet—and carefully caulked. Shingles are cut so that only the center 4 inches of the flashing are left exposed in the valley. Nailing should be spare, because nail holes defeat the purpose of the flashing.

5. A staple hammer is used to install the starter course of shingles (see text). Wood shingles are sometimes used for the starter course.

6. A regular 3-ft. length of shingle is installed with staple hammer. Note step flashing and staggered lengths of shingle at wall.

7. A chalk line is snapped across the roof every several courses to ensure that the courses of shingles are straight and evenly spaced.

8. Flashing is cut with metal shears to fit beneath the existing roof. The siding is removed and replaced after flashing is installed.

9. The side flashing is nailed in. A front piece of flashing is installed, over the top course of shingles. Shingling now proceeds.

10. The existing roof is re-shingled to match the new roof. First the ridge cap of the existing roof is removed with the claw of a hammer.

11. Valley between the new and existing roof is measured for flashing. Building paper is down; shingles are installed after flashing is in.

12. After the flashing is cut from the roll the valley is formed using a form made of 2 x 4s and a hammer to produce a straight bend.

13. A coating of tar is placed in the valley and flashing is nailed over old roof. Flashing is nailed along roof perimeter only.

14. Another layer of tar is troweled over the edge of the flashing. Wherever a roof abuts a wall, heavy caulking is necessary to prevent leaks.

15. The next course of shingles is now laid with the staple hammer, as shingling continues up the roof over the flashing.

16. A shingle is cut for the starter course on the existing roof. Shingles can be scored on the smooth side and broken with the hands.

17. Starter course fits exactly over the exposed portion of first course of old roof. New fascia and siding have been installed.

18. A 2-in. exposure is marked on each side of valley flashing. When shingles are applied over flashing, they will be cut to fit these lines.

19. The second course of shingles is being attached to the existing roof. The first course has been cut along the line drawn in Step 18.

20. Cap flashing is applied over the step flashing. It is laid into a groove sawed into the wall (as shown) or laid into the mortar joints.

21. Shingles are trimmed along the ridge over a hip rafter. Here a chalk line is snapped over the shingles for placement of the ridge cap.

22. A mat knife cuts pieces of shingle for the ridge cap. The uproof side of the 1-ft. lengths are tapered like the piece to the right.

23. Ridge cap shingles are nailed along the lines drawn in Step 21. Note that the first shingle is precisely trimmed to fit corner.

24. At the apex of the roof the ridge caps over the hip rafters meet; one shingle overlays the other. Here the last piece is nailed in.

25. This typical roofing scene shows work on a flashing. Shingles in valley reveal flashing below. A 2 x 4 prevents tar pail from toppling.

261

Adding a wing

Installing skylights in a new roof

Skylights are installed in three places in the new roof of our addition to improve lighting and ventilation. (For existing attic roofs, see pp.162–169.)

The design of the skylights and the mounting accessories supplied with them vary with the manufacturer. Our skylights are triple-glazed—they have three layers of glass. They come with mounting brackets; removable aluminum cladding that fits over and weatherproofs the skylight's wood frame; and a complete set of flashings—head and sill sections, and step flashing for the sides—to weatherproof joints between the skylight and the roof.

Installation: An opening in the roof is framed for the skylight (as seen on previous pages) according to the manufacturer's specifications for the rough opening (r.o.). The skylight, with the mounting brackets attached, is set in place and its operation tested; the brackets are then screwed into the roof sheathing, either over or under a layer of building paper.

The sill flashing section is attached to the skylight overlaying the course of shingles below it. Step flashing is run up the sides of the skylight. Each piece of step flashing overlays the course of shingles and the step flashing below it, and underlays the course of shingles and flashing above it to form an interlocking edge. The step flashing is installed as the shingle courses are laid.

The head flashing section is waterproofed with roofing tar. The next course of shingles overlays it; shingling then proceeds up the roof.

Installing doors and windows

Once the roofing is installed, the next operation is to further weatherproof our new addition by installing doors and windows.

Doors: The metal frames (jambs, sills, and heads) for sliding doors must first be assembled. Caulking is inserted over the screws, and at the joints. The frame is then put in place and nails are driven through slots in the frame into the surrounding wood frame. At first the nails are not driven in all the way, permitting their easy removal if the frame requires greater adjustment than the slots allow. The holes in the sill are marked on the concrete slab below. The sill is then removed, holes are drilled in the concrete to hold lead anchors, and the sill is replaced, checked with a level, and lag-bolted down. (Ordinary wood screws would be used to secure the frame to a wood plate.)

The sill is again checked with a level and the diagonals are measured to check squareness. This is especially important for doors, because the slightest obliqueness will prevent them from opening and closing smoothly. Adjustments are made. The nails are repositioned, if necessary, then driven in all the way. Galvanized nails are used, about one per foot of frame. Round head screws can also be used.

Shimming the frame: Wood shims are cut to fit the gaps between the door frame and the wooden frame. The shims act as spacers, so the frame is not bent out of shape when it is screwed or nailed in. Shims can also be made of two wedge-shaped pieces of cedar shingle, pushed into the space from opposite directions.

One panel of each sliding door remains fixed, while the other is left free to open and close. The perimeter of the frame is carefully caulked to prevent air and water leaks. A threshold is placed over the trafficked part of the track.

Windows: Like doors, metal-frame windows are installed in rough openings, checked for level and squareness, secured, and weathersealed. A window frame does not have to be assembled as does a door. A window can be installed with the glass in place, which helps hold the frame square. For a heavy window, remove the glass; install it later.

The installation of doors and windows in existing houses differs from the procedures shown here, where the frame of the addition was planned with these units in mind. Cutting and framing existing walls to take new doors and windows may involve the special steps of post and lintel construction (see pp.76–85) and other procedures (see *Adding entrance doors* and *Adding and replacing windows*, pp.293–297).

Skylight sections

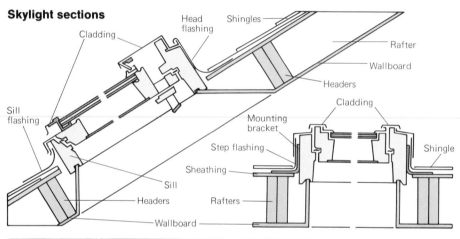

Cladding · Head flashing · Shingles · Rafter · Wallboard · Headers · Sill flashing · Cladding · Mounting bracket · Step flashing · Shingle · Sheathing · Sill · Headers · Rafters · Wallboard

1. The skylight, with the mounting brackets attached to the frame, is lowered into the roof opening. The brackets are screwed into the roof sheathing, through the building paper.

2. The sill is checked with a level. Diagonals are measured to ensure the corners are square. A second layer of building paper is laid. The sill flashing section is attached.

3. One piece of the skylight step flashing is laid under each course of shingles on the surrounding roof. This procedure is like the one shown on pages 259–260, Steps 4–6.

4. Aluminum cladding is attached to the frame. The head flashing section is attached and heavily caulked with roofing tar. Successive shingle courses will cover the head flashing.

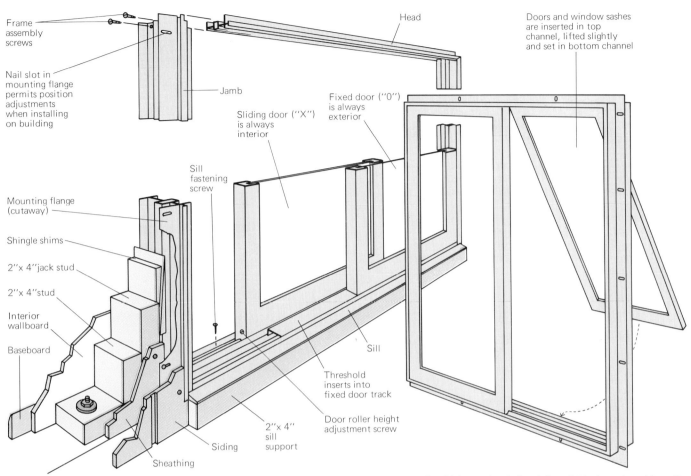

Frame assembly screws

Nail slot in mounting flange permits position adjustments when installing on building

Jamb

Head

Doors and window sashes are inserted in top channel, lifted slightly and set in bottom channel

Sill fastening screw

Sliding door ("X") is always interior

Fixed door ("O") is always exterior

Mounting flange (cutaway)

Shingle shims

2"x 4"jack stud

2"x 4"stud

Interior wallboard

Baseboard

Sill

Threshold inserts into fixed door track

Door roller height adjustment screw

2"x 4" sill support

Siding

Sheathing

Sliding doors and windows are installed after sheathing is in place but before siding is attached. Sliding units have one stationary ("O") and one operating ("X") panel. When ordering wooden sliding doors and windows, you must specify which panel—whether left or right when viewed from the outside—is operable and which stationary. With metal units, you can arrange the panels to your specifications at the site.

1. The frame of the sliding door is assembled on a level surface according to manufacturer's directions. Caulking is placed over the screws and in the joints of the frame.

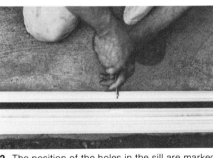

2. The position of the holes in the sill are marked on the concrete slab. The sill is removed, holes are drilled, and lead anchors are installed. The sill is replaced and bolted in.

3. The metal frame is nailed loosely into the rough opening. Diagonals are measured in order to check squareness. After adjustments are made, the frame is nailed in permanently.

4. Wood shims are cut to fit the gaps between the door frame and the studs and headers. They are used as spacers so that the door frame is not bent when it is nailed in permanently.

5. A threshold is installed over the trafficked section of track. The assembled metal frame is now securely in place, and the sliding doors are installed on the tracks.

6. Windows are installed in rough openings much like doors. Small sliding windows and windows with fixed panels are installed with glass in place, which helps keep frame square.

Adding a wing

Applying the siding

Once the siding is installed, the addition is finally enclosed and weatherproofed. Electrical, plumbing, and interior finish work can proceed without risk of damage by the elements.

The siding used on our addition is 4-x-8-foot plywood paneling, with an attractive, weather-resistant exterior surface. Plywood paneling is one of the easiest and least expensive exterior wall coverings you can install. Other types of siding are covered on ensuing pages.

Building paper: Fifteen-pound building paper is stapled over the sheathing. Each course overlaps the one below it by several inches.

Furring strips: Furring strips made of 1-x-3 lumber are attached with masonry nails over the masonry and concrete surfaces that will be covered with siding. They are spaced 16 inches o.c. (the same as the studs), so they can be located easily when siding is installed.

Applying the panels: The 4-x-8-foot siding panels are nailed through the sheathing into the studs. Aluminum nails are spaced about every 6 inches around the perimeters of the panels, whose edges should fall on the studs. Nails are also driven at 12-inch intervals through the panels into the intermediate studs. Ideally, the nailheads will be hidden by the grooves in the siding.

Each panel has one side edge with the top surface recessed and one side edge with the bottom surface recessed; when applied, the panels lap along these edges. If a panel must be cut between the vertical grooves, which are spaced every 8 inches on these panels, a router is used to re-establish a recessed edge on the cut line.

On wall faces higher than 8 feet, panels also meet along their short edges. In our addition, the architect had a decorative board laid into these joints, surrounded by flashing to prevent water infiltration. Simpler alternatives are illustrated at right.

When fitting siding around doors and windows, it was found that cutting the panels into small sections and reassembling them in place was easier and more accurate than trying to cut one large hole into the junction of two panels.

Soffits: Boards (generally made of plywood) placed under overhangs are called soffits. The soffits under the eaves include central vents, which allow ventilation under the roof. Where soffits cover the only available access spaces for roof insulation, insulation is tucked in before the soffit is installed.

Finish: The siding and trim is given a coat of stain and preservative. Its function is largely decorative, because the panels are themselves weatherproof. Exposed nailheads can be painted over.

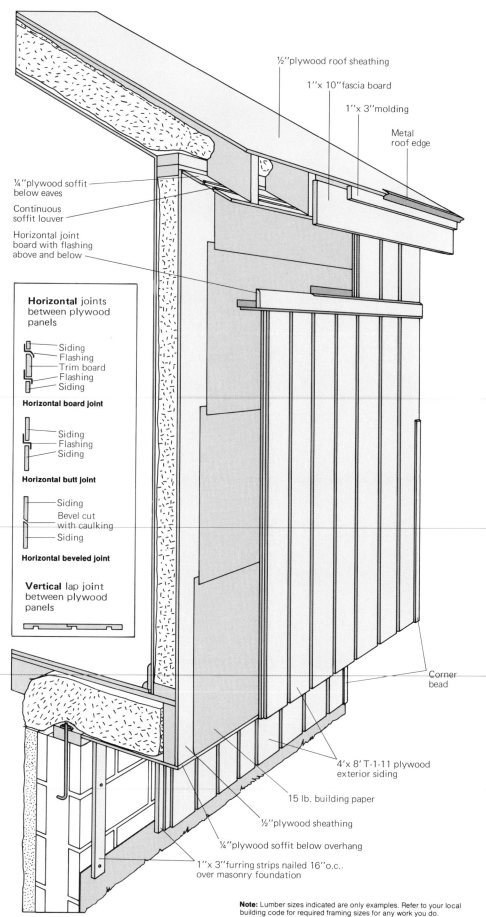

½"plywood roof sheathing

1"x 10"fascia board

1"x 3"molding

Metal roof edge

¼"plywood soffit below eaves

Continuous soffit louver

Horizontal joint board with flashing above and below

Horizontal joints between plywood panels

Siding
Flashing
Trim board
Flashing
Siding

Horizontal board joint

Siding
Flashing
Siding

Horizontal butt joint

Siding
Bevel cut with caulking
Siding

Horizontal beveled joint

Vertical lap joint between plywood panels

Corner bead

4'x 8' T-1-11 plywood exterior siding

15 lb. building paper

½"plywood sheathing

¼"plywood soffit below overhang

1"x 3"furring strips nailed 16"o.c.. over masonry foundation

Note: Lumber sizes indicated are only examples. Refer to your local building code for required framing sizes for any work you do.

1. Working from bottom of wall upward, building paper is rolled out and stapled to sheathing. Each course overlays the one below it about 2 in.

2. Where necessary, the plywood siding panels are cut with a circular saw before they are installed. A sawing guide is clamped to the panel.

3. Siding panels are nailed to furring strips, which are nailed to the concrete block wall of the addition. Plywood soffit has been installed.

4. Panels are nailed over the sheathing, as many nails going into the studs as possible. The side edge of each board laps the edge of its neighbor.

5. A decorative board lies in the horizontal joint between two panels (see illustration, left). Flashing above and below prevents water infiltration.

6. Caulking is applied to the small gap between the existing house wall and the siding on the roof of the addition. Note flashing on roof above.

7. The soffit is installed under the end rafter, where the trim is already in place. Note that this soffit does not have a vent.

8. The soffit under the eaves has a central vent permitting air to circulate beneath the roof; it is installed in two pieces.

9. A soffit panel is nailed in place under an insulated overhang. Note that joints of panels rest on nailers holding insulation.

10. The chimney chase is paneled and the chimney cap is in place. The corner guard molding being applied is used on every corner of addition.

11. When a cut does not fall on a panel groove, a router is used on the edge of the panel; the cut panels will then overlap at their edges.

12. All of the siding and trim is brushed over with a coat of wood stain and preservative. The function of the coat is mostly decorative.

Adding a wing

Alternative sidings: aluminum and vinyl

Though it was not used on our addition, aluminum siding is now the most commonly employed siding in the United States. It is long-lasting, durable, easy to clean, and light (thus easy to work with). The maintenance is minimal. It is available in many colors and textures; finishes on the siding are generally guaranteed for between 20 and 40 years.

Materials and equipment: When installed with backing, aluminum siding contributes to the thermal insulation of the house. Corner posts, backer tabs, flashings, and other accessories used to install aluminum siding are shown on the opposite page.

The installation involves the use of sturdy ladders and scaffolding. A pump jack, which travels up and down 4-x-4-inch wooden columns, is frequently used to support a working platform. A cut-off table or trim table holds a movable power saw. The saw is used to make accurate cuts, miters, and bevels in the siding panels. A portable brake is used to bend pieces of aluminum stock to fit—for example, window casing and sill trim. Because all of the above equipment is necessary, aluminum siding is usually installed by professionals. Nonetheless, the drawings presented on these pages can help you decide on whether aluminum siding is right for you, and whether your contractor is observing proper procedures.

Surface preparation: Aluminum siding must be installed over a sound surface. If the aluminum is to be the first siding on a new house, no special preparation is required. If it is applied over old siding, furring or shimming must be installed where needed to make the wall straight and flat. Loose pieces of existing siding must be fixed, and rotting ones replaced. Old caulking and putty must be removed, and new caulking applied. Downspouts and other objects that would interfere with installation are removed. Some contractors will give you a better price if you do the job of surface preparation.

Furring and installing foil: Furring, most often of ⅜-inch lath strips, may be used to provide a smooth, level nailing base for the siding; 1 x 3s are used over masonry and brick. The furring is installed in parallel rows spaced 16 inches apart. If the siding is horizontal the furring runs vertically (see illustration, below), and vice versa. Furring an entire wall improves its insulating value.

If the wall is furred, the trim at doors and windows might have to be built out to maintain the original appearance. Furring must often be applied above and below windows, above doors, and under eaves to serve as spacers and supports for the siding.

Underlayment board, which comes in large sheets or accordion-fold panels, is sometimes used instead of furring. It provides additional insulation value. Aluminum reflector foil, which also aids insulation, is stapled to the existing wall, or over the furring strips. It is applied over the entire surface, overlapping at joints by 1 or 2 inches.

Installing aluminum siding: The first course of horizontal siding is aligned along the bottom of the house using chalk lines, as illustrated at top right on this page. Inside and outside corner posts are nailed in before the siding is put up. Then, following the chalk lines, the starter strip is nailed all the way around the house. If insulated siding is being used, the starter strip is furred out to the thickness of the insulation.

All-purpose trim is installed along the bottom of the eaves to receive the siding. Windowsills and casings can be covered with aluminum stock, which must be bent to fit on the site with a portable brake.

Aluminum siding can be cut with a power saw, as previously noted, with tin-snips, or by scoring with a utility knife and bending the siding back and forth along the score. This last method is good for cutting along the length of the panel or for a section notched to fit over a door or window.

The first course is put in place, its bottom edge locking over the edge of the starter strip. First, slide the panel into the corner post recess, then press it upward so its bottom edge locks in place along the starter strip.

The siding is installed from the back of the house toward the front, each

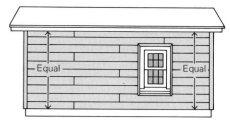

Aligning the starter strip: Horizontal panels are applied from the bottom of the house up. To align the starter strip for the first course of siding, snap chalk lines between points measured an equal distance down from the eaves; one such line is snapped on each wall of the building. The lines, parallel with the eaves, must meet exactly at the corners of the house. Starter strip is nailed along these lines.

panel overlapping the one behind it by about ½ inch. Aluminum nails are centered in the nailing slots; the slots allow the siding to expand and contract.

Succeeding courses are installed the same way, each interlocking with the course below. The seams are made in a regular, evenly-spaced pattern. (Backer tabs, used at overlaps and corners of uninsulated 8-inch panels only, are put in as each course goes up; 8-inch siding is sometimes covered at the corners with individual corner caps, one applied over each course. This preserves the lap appearance at the corners.)

Vertical siding: The installation of vertical siding is much the same as for horizontal siding, except that the starter strip is applied vertically. The courses interlock vertically, and can proceed in both directions from the starter strip.

Vinyl siding: Vinyl siding is made from stiff polyvinyl chloride. It cannot be bent as aluminum can; otherwise its installation is virtually the same.

Insulation methods

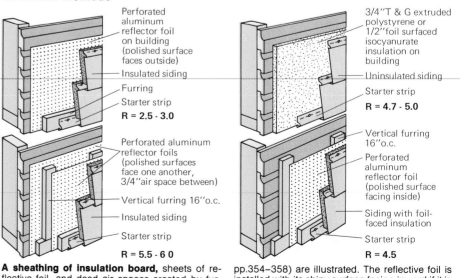

Perforated aluminum reflector foil on building (polished surface faces outside)
Insulated siding
Furring
Starter strip
R = 2.5 - 3.0

Perforated aluminum reflector foils (polished surfaces face one another, 3/4" air space between)
Vertical furring 16" o.c.
Insulated siding
Starter strip
R = 5.5 - 6 0

3/4" T & G extruded polystyrene or 1/2" foil surfaced isocyanurate insulation on building
Uninsulated siding
Starter strip
R = 4.7 - 5.0

Vertical furring 16" o.c.
Perforated aluminum reflector foil (polished surface facing inside)
Siding with foil-faced insulation
Starter strip
R = 4.5

A sheathing of insulation board, sheets of reflective foil, and dead air spaces created by furring, all add significantly to aluminum's negligible insulating properties. Four common installation methods that raise aluminum's R-value (see pp.354–358) are illustrated. The reflective foil is installed with its shiny surface facing inward if it is applied over furring. If the foil is applied over existing siding, the perforated ("breather") type will prevent condensation inside the wall.

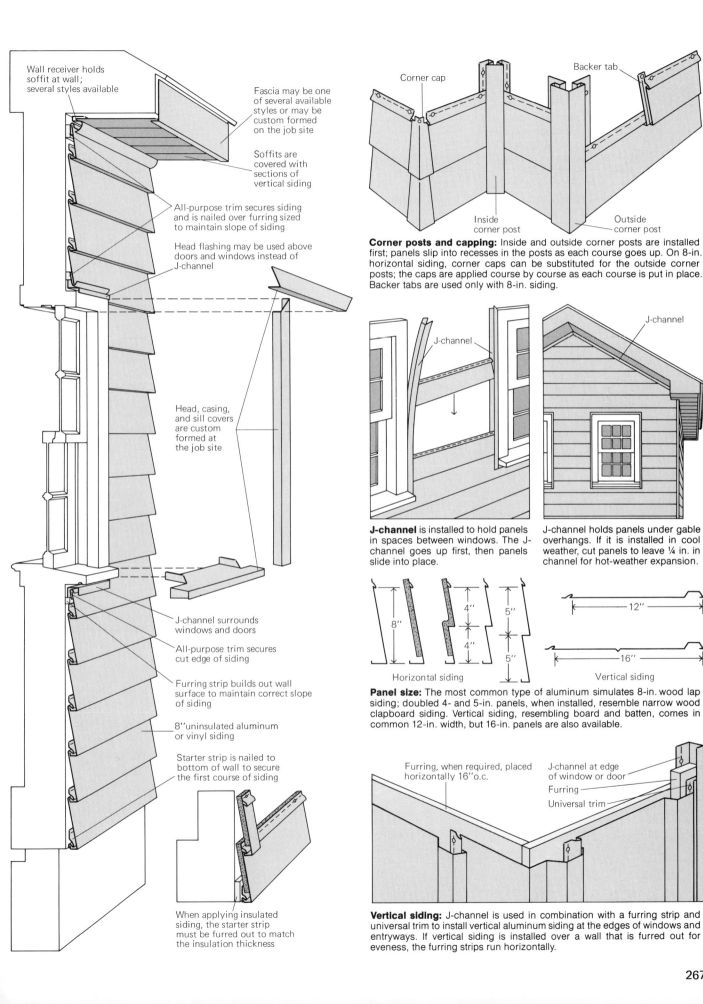

Wall receiver holds
soffit at wall;
several styles available

Fascia may be one
of several available
styles or may be
custom formed
on the job site

Soffits are
covered with
sections of
vertical siding

All-purpose trim secures siding
and is nailed over furring sized
to maintain slope of siding

Head flashing may be used above
doors and windows instead of
J-channel

Head, casing,
and sill covers
are custom
formed at
the job site

J-channel surrounds
windows and doors

All-purpose trim secures
cut edge of siding

Furring strip builds out wall
surface to maintain correct slope
of siding

8"uninsulated aluminum
or vinyl siding

Starter strip is nailed to
bottom of wall to secure
the first course of siding

When applying insulated
siding, the starter strip
must be furred out to match
the insulation thickness

Corner cap

Backer tab

Inside
corner post

Outside
corner post

Corner posts and capping: Inside and outside corner posts are installed first; panels slip into recesses in the posts as each course goes up. On 8-in. horizontal siding, corner caps can be substituted for the outside corner posts; the caps are applied course by course as each course is put in place. Backer tabs are used only with 8-in. siding.

J-channel

J-channel

J-channel is installed to hold panels in spaces between windows. The J-channel goes up first, then panels slide into place.

J-channel holds panels under gable overhangs. If it is installed in cool weather, cut panels to leave ¼ in. in channel for hot-weather expansion.

8"

4"

4"

5"

5"

Horizontal siding

12"

16"

Vertical siding

Panel size: The most common type of aluminum simulates 8-in. wood lap siding; doubled 4- and 5-in. panels, when installed, resemble narrow wood clapboard siding. Vertical siding, resembling board and batten, comes in common 12-in. width, but 16-in. panels are also available.

Furring, when required, placed
horizontally 16"o.c.

J-channel at edge
of window or door

Furring

Universal trim

Vertical siding: J-channel is used in combination with a furring strip and universal trim to install vertical aluminum siding at the edges of windows and entryways. If vertical siding is installed over a wall that is furred out for evenness, the furring strips run horizontally.

Adding a wing

A siding alternative: stucco

Stucco is a mixture of Portland cement and sand that can give a building a hard, strong, weather-resistant covering that is a fairly good insulator. If mixed and applied properly, its density and strength increase with age.

Preparing the building: Stucco can be applied directly over masonry or cast concrete if it has a rough, firm surface. Over wood or inadequate masonry surfaces, metal lath, (a backing made of expanded metal or wire fabric) is attached. Applied over the lath, the stucco forms a slab of reinforced cement. Surfaces that receive a coating of stucco—old siding or sheathing—must be rigid and strong. Stucco can be applied over open wood-frame construction (without sheathing) if a backing for it is made of parallel columns of heavy wire nailed tightly between the outside faces of the studs at 6-inch intervals. The walls are then covered with building paper before the lath is installed.

The lath must be furred out at least ¼ inch from the backing surface so that the wet stucco can get behind it. Self-furring lath is available. Wooden furring strips nailed over building paper are sometimes used. Some builders maintain that the furring strips should only run vertically, so that moisture behind the stucco can escape from the top or bottom of the wall. Others are opposed to the use of continuous furring, because it creates lines of weakness along which the stucco can crack. The lath is nailed firmly into the furring and wall. Flashing is installed to prevent water infiltration.

Mixing stucco: Stucco is usually applied in three layers (only two layers are required over masonry). The mixture for the first, or scratch, coat consists of one part cement to three parts sand (for example, one 70-pound bag of cement to 3 cubic feet of sand). If the sand is well graded, with a high proportion of coarse particles, the mixture can contain 3½ or 4 parts sand. The second, or brown, coat contains slightly more sand than the scratch coat. The last, or finish coat, often contains marble dust in place of sand; it is usually purchased premixed. A plasticizer, usually lime, is included to make the mixture more workable when it is applied. Lime is often premixed into bags of stucco cement, and thus does not have to be added separately. Mineral pigments can be added to color the stucco.

The dry materials are mixed thoroughly, then clean water is added,

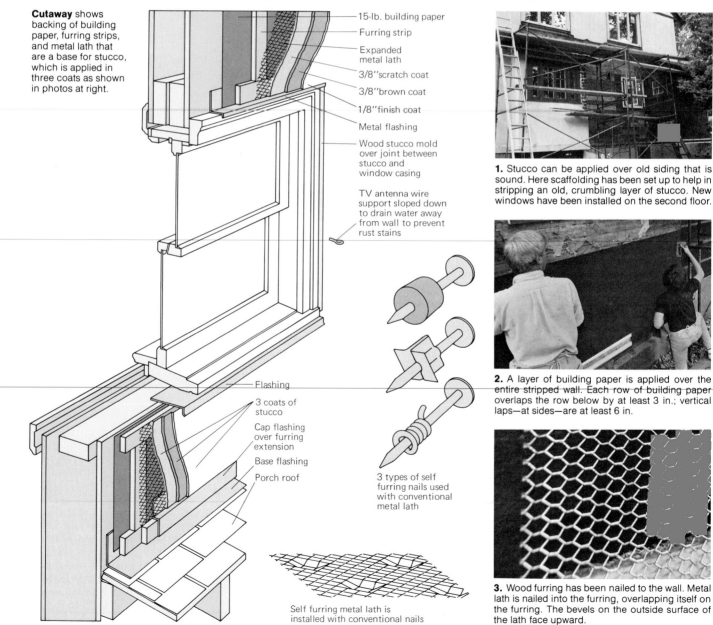

Cutaway shows backing of building paper, furring strips, and metal lath that are a base for stucco, which is applied in three coats as shown in photos at right.

- 15-lb. building paper
- Furring strip
- Expanded metal lath
- 3/8"scratch coat
- 3/8"brown coat
- 1/8"finish coat
- Metal flashing
- Wood stucco mold over joint between stucco and window casing
- TV antenna wire support sloped down to drain water away from wall to prevent rust stains

- Flashing
- 3 coats of stucco
- Cap flashing over furring extension
- Base flashing
- Porch roof

3 types of self furring nails used with conventional metal lath

Self furring metal lath is installed with conventional nails

1. Stucco can be applied over old siding that is sound. Here scaffolding has been set up to help in stripping an old, crumbling layer of stucco. New windows have been installed on the second floor.

2. A layer of building paper is applied over the entire stripped wall. Each row of building paper overlaps the row below by at least 3 in.; vertical laps—at sides—are at least 6 in.

3. Wood furring has been nailed to the wall. Metal lath is nailed into the furring, overlapping itself on the furring. The bevels on the outside surface of the lath face upward.

enough to make the mixture workable. A large power mixer or a hand-held rotary mixer can be used. Stirring with a hoe produces less uniform results.

Applying the stucco: The first, or scratch, coat of wet stucco is pushed into the lath with a trowel, working from the top of the wall downward. After a uniform ⅜-inch layer has been applied, the surface is scratched with a tool to promote the adhesion of the next layer. The stucco is allowed to set for two days. The surface is kept wet by spraying (moist curing) so the mixture sets completely. The ⅜ inch brown coat is then applied in much the same way. Its surface is roughened with a wooden float. It is moist cured for two days.

The finish coat is not applied for at least five more days. The finish coat can be textured with tools or painted.

4. The cement, sand, water, and any additives are mixed together, here by a hand-held rotary mixer. A power mixer should be used for at least 5 minutes; hand mixing should last 10-15 minutes.

5. The thick cement stucco mix is pressed into the metal lath by hand with a trowel. This first, or scratch coat, and the second, or brown coat, should each be about ⅜ in. thick.

6. A tool is used to scratch the surface of the first coat while it is still wet. After two days the brown coat is applied over it. Seven days later the final, ready-mix coat is applied.

Gutters and downspouts

Gutters collect the water runoff from a roof and direct it into downspouts or leaders, which bring it to the ground. Most gutters and downspouts are now made of aluminum or vinyl.

The pieces of the gutter system, shown below, are purchased and laid out on the ground beneath the wall where they will be installed. They assemble by sliding together, creating a 1½- to 2-inch overlap, which should always step down toward the downspouts. Gutter-sealant mastic and pop rivets, and sometimes slip joint connectors, are used to connect the sections. A chalk line is snapped on the wall to guide installation. Though many gutters are installed level, it is best to slope them 1/16 inch per foot to aid drainage.

The gutter is held in place by brackets or hangers. They are attached with aluminum nails or screws to the fascia or to the rafter ends every 32 inches (the spacing of the rafters). New free-floating systems allow gutters held by brackets to slide as they expand and contract with changes in temperature. The gutter should be attached beneath the line of the roof, so that ice sliding off can clear the gutter. Basket strainers are placed over the outlets to prevent leaves and debris from clogging the downspouts, or the entire length of the gutter can be covered with a screen.

Downspouts are assembled and then attached to the gutter. They should lie flush against the wall, to which they are strapped. The downspouts must be large enough to accommodate the runoff of the roof. In general, 1 square inch of downspout suffices for each 100 square feet of roof area.

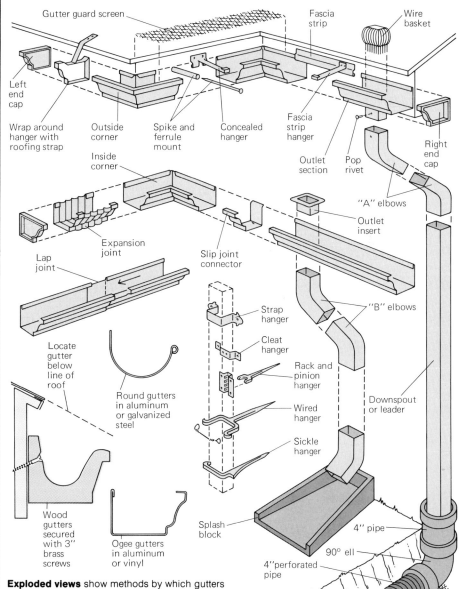

Exploded views show methods by which gutters and downspouts are typically installed. Note the different types of connectors for expansion, lap, and slip joints, and the variety of special hangers.

Adding a wing

Electrical, heating, and plumbing systems

With the application of the roofing and siding, the addition is weatherproofed. Work now begins on the interior. The first task is the installation of mechanical systems that lie within the walls, floors, and ceilings—the electrical, heating, and plumbing systems. The open studs and joists can then be insulated and covered with wallboard or paneled.

Electrical system: The electrical system for our addition is supplied through the main panel in the existing house. Wires running through the addition to supply the new outlets and appliances pass via the most direct and convenient paths—around windows and doors, through studs, and through the floor where necessary. Electrical boxes for outlets, appliances, and switches are nailed to wall studs and ceiling joists so that the outlets and switches will lie flush with the gypsum wallboard when it is installed. All switches and all outlets are placed at standard heights. This looks good and makes them easier to find.

Boxes for outdoor outlets and switches are installed in holes cut in the exterior siding and sheathing, and are mounted on the siding with screws.

Wiring follows the electrical plan provided by the architect. Aside from the light fixtures and outlets, receptacles are installed for the two ceiling fans. A nominal 240-volt line is installed for an air conditioner. Following the local building code, special ground-fault circuit-interrupter (GFCI) outlets, which contain their own circuit breakers, are installed in the bathroom. Part of the electrical plan for this addition is shown on page 46. Electrical wiring is discussed in detail on pages 172–201.

Heating system: The hot-water heating system for our addition was designed to include a wood-burning stove in its plumbing loop. While wood is burning, the stove provides direct radi-

1. Recessed (ceiling) lights are held by hangers nailed to the joists. They will be flush with the gypsum board applied to the ceiling.

2. Holes for wires, ½ to 1 in. in diameter, are drilled in plates subfloor, and studs. Here the worker uses heavy-duty electrician's right-angle drill.

3. An outlet box is nailed to a stud and wired. Outlet will lie flush with wallboard. All outlets will be about 1 ft. from floor.

4. A hole is cut in the exterior siding for an outdoor outlet. The mounting flange of the box is screwed directly into the wood panel.

5. A hole for an outlet box is chiseled into the concrete wall of the existing house. Box is nailed to a furring strip.

6. Metal plates on the furring strips protect the electrical cables from being damaged by gypsum wallboard installation nails.

ant heat. At the same time, water is pumped through internal passages in the stove and is piped to a 120-gallon stone-lined storage tank. When the heating system is activated by the thermostat, the hot water is pumped from the tank through a circuit of baseboard heating elements throughout the addition. Even when no wood is burning, stored heat from the stove is still available. The system is also connected to the existing oil burner, which provides back-up capacity in case of severe prolonged cold. Two large ceiling fans circulate the air to keep the temperature uniform throughout the addition. Con-

verting wood stoves to this system is described on pages 140–145.

Plumbing system: New plumbing was necessary only for the bathroom in our addition; the bathroom contains a stall shower, sink, and toilet. Copper supply pipes were run from the existing house through the walls and floor to the location of the fixtures. Temporary caps were soldered to the ends of the pipes. After the wallboard and bathroom fixtures were installed, the caps were removed and the pipes were connected.

The waste (DWV) pipes are made of white plastic, a material that is cheaper and easier to work with than copper.

The individual waste pipes merge as they descend, and are attached to the main soil waste pipe of the existing house. Plastic vent pipes are run up from the new bathroom; one large stack vent passes through the roof. Plumbing systems are discussed in detail on pages 202–224.

Whenever possible, run long lengths of pipe or cable parallel to joists or studs. The pipe or cable can then be fastened to the sides of these structural elements. Notching or drilling holes to pass pipe and cable weakens structural members, and the practice is closely governed by code (see pp.21–37).

7. The large tank being installed stores hot water from the wood-burning stove; pump circulates water through the baseboard heating elements.

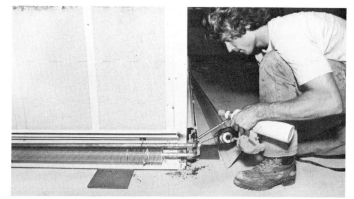

8. Baseboard heating elements are installed. Note that wallboard is in place. Scrap wood temporarily props elements at proper height.

9. Copper supply lines lead to the shower valve, shown being installed. Scrap wallboard determines precise placement of valve.

10. Temporary caps are soldered on supply lines for the sink. White pipes are plastic waste lines. Pipe at far right is a vent.

11. Edge of lead pan is turned up using hammer and wood blocks. Pan makes waterproof subfloor for shower tiles.

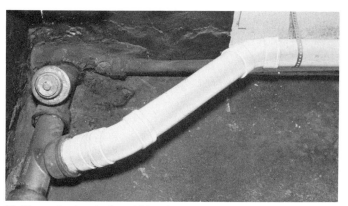

12. The waste pipes for the addition all empty into one large pipe, which here joins the cast-iron soil pipe of the existing house.

271

Adding a wing

Finishing the interior

After all the structural work, illustrated on previous pages, was completed, the interior of our addition was given a final finish. Finishing the interior is a deceptively simple phrase, as the work involved in making an interior habitable is usually estimated to take as long as all the structural work combined. In our addition, for example, finishing took over a year of part-time do-it-yourself work to complete down to the last detail, including tiling and finish flooring.

The illustrations on this and the facing page show only a small sample of typical finishing jobs (refer to pp.274–275 to see final results). Finishing our addition included the insulation of exterior walls, wallboarding, installing subfloors and floors, installing electrical and plumbing fixtures to connect with the outlets and lines already in place in the walls, installing cabinets and other kitchen work, tiling the bathroom and installing its fixtures, building stairs, installing and connecting the wood-burning stove, and innumerable other trim and surface details that only became apparent when the need for them was immediate.

Sequence of work: Each of the tasks shown here is dealt with in greater detail elsewhere in this book. Refer to the table of contents under the appropriate chapter headings (for example, *Working with plasterboard*, p.88; *Hardwood floors*, p.106 *Ceramic tile*, p.112; *Wood stoves*, p.138; *Plumbing fixtures*, p.216). The photographs here suggest the sequence in which the jobs are normally done: the insulation goes into the walls before plasterboard is put up; subflooring is installed early on, whereas the finish floor is not applied until all the potentially messy tasks, including interior painting and tiling, are completed.

Pages 50 to 64 contain color photographs showing finished interiors of newly remodeled and expanded homes completed recently in various parts of the country. These photographs can be a source of ideas for your own planning. In addition, the chapter titled *Expanding a room outward*, pages 276–283, shows in step-by-step photos all the work that went into a do-it-yourselfer's kitchen expansion, the attractive results of which appear in color on page 240.

But there are no hard and fast rules that hold for every fine detail of interior finishing. In general you will want to get the new interior into roughly livable condition as soon as possible, installing ceilings and wall coverings, subflooring, kitchen and bathroom fixtures, lights, etc. Leave until later the finer finishing details, such as tiling, hardwood finish flooring, baseboards, and trim.

Wallboard: After Owens-Corning foil-backed insulation is stapled inside the open studs, gypsum wallboard (plasterboard) is nailed to the studs to form the interior walls, and over the rafters and second-story joists to make the ceilings. Here tape and joint compound are applied over the seams between the 4-x-8-ft. gypsum panels already in place.

Wall paneling: Though most of the interior wall area of the addition is covered with gypsum board, this wall in the bathroom is paneled with 1 x 4 tongue-and-groove mahogany boards over the gypsum board. This paneling matches the shower stall and the front of the vanity, in a motif patterned after wooden Japanese baths admired by the owner.

Finishing the brick: Part of the weathered brick wall that was the exterior surface of the existing house is now an interior wall of the addition. The old brick is brushed vigorously with a wire brush, washed with a mild solution of muriatic acid, to emphasize its soft antique look, and then sealed with a coat of concrete sealant to preserve the surface.

Subflooring: Over the concrete slab, 1 x 2s called sleepers or screeds are laid to raise the subfloor off the concrete and prevent rotting of the wood. The subfloor, which is made of 4- to 8-ft. sheets of plywood, is nailed to the sleepers. Elsewhere in the addition the subfloor is attached with nails to the floor joists in the wood frame.

Hardwood flooring: This flooring, manufactured by Bruce Hardwood Flooring, is made of varying lengths and widths of tongue-and-groove hardwood. The first course is ordinarily face-nailed into the subfloor. Because of a pipe passing beneath the subfloor at this point, a construction adhesive (left) was used instead of nails to fasten the flooring. After the first two courses, normal installation resumed, using a floor-nailer (right), a device that, when hit with a hammer, drives a nail between the tongue and front edge of the strip—blind nailing so that nailheads will not be visible in the finished floor (see *Hardwood floors*, p.106). The last course of the floor is face-nailed directly through the top of the plank and set with a nail punch.

Tile floor: Large primitive ceramic tiles are pressed into a mortar bed applied over the concrete slab; they form the living-room floor. A rubber mallet helps set them into mortar. Spacer sticks maintain uniform spacing between the tiles. Smaller ceramic tiles are used in the bathroom and on the kitchen counter (as seen on pp.274–275).

Fluorescent lighting: These two fixtures recessed into the suspended ceiling of the kitchen illuminate area near the sink and stove (see *New ceilings*, p.92). Incandescent track lighting provides additional artificial light in the room, and natural light comes through a window greenhouse not seen here. (See also photos on pp.274–275.)

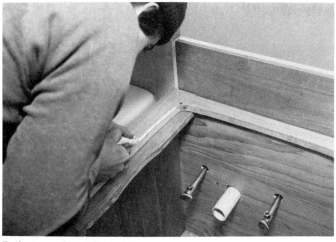

Bathroom cabinet: Back of bathroom cabinet, or vanity, is cut to fit around plumbing lines already in place. Caulking is applied (shown here); the sink is laid in; and plumbing lines are connected to the sink. Other interior finishing must also be done to accommodate the built-in mechanical systems—the plumbing, electrical, and heating systems.

Kitchen counter: The kitchen counter and the plywood backsplash behind it are covered with ceramic tile. When the tile adhesive sets, the sink (now seen lying beneath the counter) will then be installed and connected to the plumbing lines. The new electrical outlets and greenhouse window are already installed and in place.

Adding a wing

The finished addition

Exterior of addition is seen from a driveway at rear of house. The concrete slab patio was poured around the locust tree, which endured the trauma of construction to continue thriving. Barbecue to the right of the patio is fueled by natural gas through a pipe extending from the addition. Exterior lights can illuminate the entire patio. See photograph on page 241.

An alcove and air well was left open between the addition and a part of the existing house that is itself a former addition covered with lap siding. The alcove, used to store trash cans, is attractively screened by a swinging door.

At side opposite the air well, the new addition butts directly against brick wall of existing house. A window, recessed in a well, provides cross-ventilation in the addition. The addition's downspout feeds into existing spout.

This view of our addition's interior shows the living room and a loft bedroom (through the open wall behind the fans). The wood-burning stove is hooked up through a hot-water storage tank in the cellar of the existing house to baseboard heating elements; it sits atop a platform made of flagstone and brick, and the combustible wall behind it is shielded by a brick wall. A 2½-in. gap is left between the brick and the fire-resistant gypsum wallboard to enhance the insulating effect. The black metal flue is connected to an insulated stainless steel chimney before it enters the ceiling and the exterior chimney chase. Ceiling fans can be used to vent hot air up through the skylight in the summer, and by reversing direction of rotation, to direct warmer air down into the living room during winter.

View from work area shows brick wall of existing house, incorporated as an interior wall of addition. Note step-down from living room to office area. The living room has a ceramic tile floor (left), and the office a hardwood floor. High-hat lights are set into ceiling below loft bedroom. The brick of existing house wall has been cleaned and sealed. Behind stairway to right is an opening that allows access to mechanical systems and a storage area below bathroom.

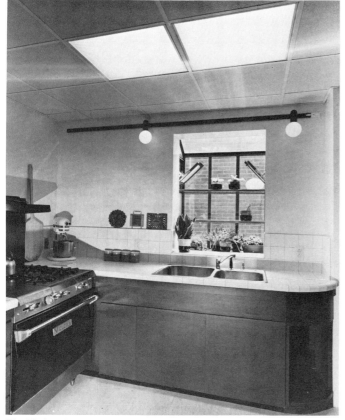

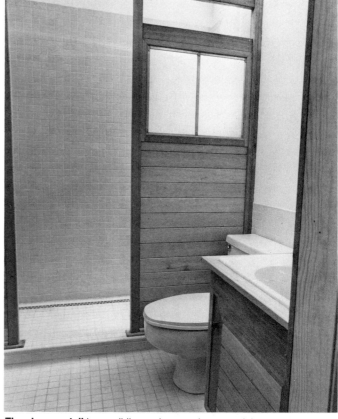

The kitchen features a protruding greenhouse window with panels that open from the sides to promote cross-ventilation. Incandescent track lighting and fluorescent fixtures recessed in the suspended ceiling provide the artificial light. Ceramic tile covers the countertop and the backsplash. The long counter and frequent outlets accommodate the use of small appliances. A large refrigerator and more cabinets and counter space lie outside this photographed area. The gas range and oven unit visible at left is restaurant-sized—for a family that loves to cook.

The shower stall has a sliding mahogany door containing two translucent panels. The bathroom floor and the floor and wall of the shower stall are covered with glazed ceramic tile. Our do-it-yourselfer's use of wood in the bath reflects a fascination with Japanese decor—an interest he developed while serving with the armed forces in the Far East. A light, airy "Japanese house" look is evident in the design of the entire addition. A pair of skylights, not visible in this photo, provide natural light and ventilation, allowing the use of windowless wall space for installations.

This corridor runs along one side of the addition—toward the backyard. The decorative black kimono strikes a vivid contrast against the long white wall. Incandescent track lights are directed at the walls along this side of the addition, creating a diffuse, reflected light. The sliding doors on the side wall open onto the driveway; those at back, onto the patio.

The finished bathroom features a vanity with horizontal mahogany panels that match the panels in the shower stall (to the left) and on the opposite wall (out of the photograph). The outlet above the sink contains a ground-fault interrupter to prevent shocks. (The lines of the small room are square; the close-up wide-angle photography creates some distortion.)

Expanding a room outward

Relocating an exterior bearing wall

The floor area of a house can be expanded by the construction of an entire new wing or freestanding addition, as shown on pages 240–275, but a single room can be made larger by the extension outward of an existing floor, construction of new walls, and marrying a new roof to the existing one. In the project shown on this and the following seven pages, a homeowner expanded his kitchen in just this way.

This expansion, a one-story extension of a one-story house, sits atop a new continuous-poured concrete footing and concrete block foundation wall. The footing was poured in two stages: the first for the footing beneath the expanded kitchen; and the second for the footing and slab for the new porch that stands beside the expansion. The porch, which has a slab floor, is enclosed with posts and screens. The expansion has a wood-frame floor, several feet higher than the porch floor; a crawl space is left beneath this floor. The new kitchen includes both the old kitchen space and the area of the expansion.

The two wood-frame walls for the expansion were assembled lying flat, according to standard construction procedure, raised, and attached to the new floor and to the existing walls. Gaps were left for the rough framing of the door and window. These were framed to the rough opening (r.o.) specifications provided by the manufacturers of pre-assembled units ordered to fill the spaces. The long rafters for the new roof ran from the top plate of the new wall to partway up the existing roof, where they were nailed in. Gaps were left between the rafters for the skylights. The weight of both the new and old roofs was supported by a new beam that replaced the old kitchen wall as described below.

The existing kitchen wall was a load-bearing wall, supporting the ceiling joists and roof rafters above it. The central problem of this project was to support this load, so the kitchen wall could be removed. The solution, shown below and on page 282, was to insert a large beam, supported on one end by the new wall next to the porch, and at the other end by the existing family room wall. The beam sits just outside the original kitchen wall. The interior of the new kitchen was then wired, insulated, and finished. Foundation work and wood-frame construction are shown in greater detail in *Adding a wing*, pages 240–275.

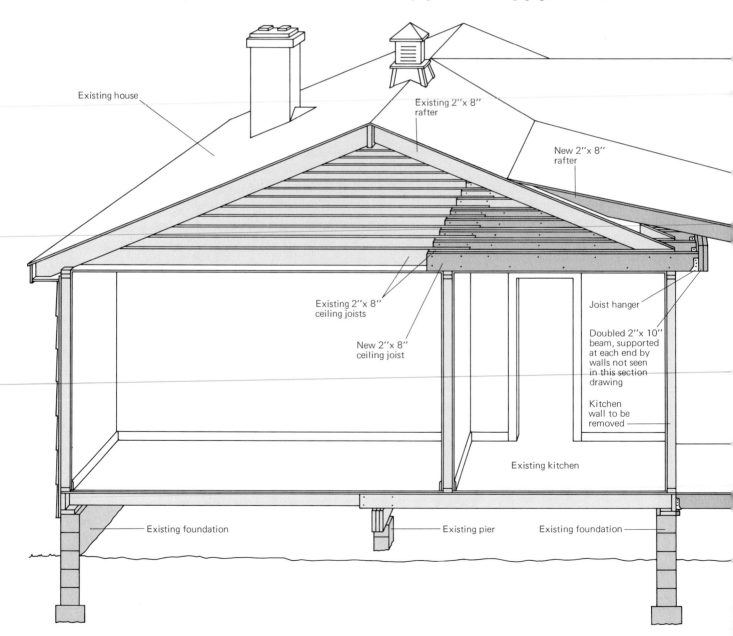

Existing house

Existing 2"x 8" rafter

New 2"x 8" rafter

Existing 2"x 8" ceiling joists

New 2"x 8" ceiling joist

Joist hanger

Doubled 2"x 10" beam, supported at each end by walls not seen in this section drawing

Kitchen wall to be removed

Existing kitchen

Existing foundation

Existing pier

Existing foundation

The owner of this home, an experienced builder and handyman, did much of the work on this project himself. In places he exceeded common practice, or guidelines established by building codes, to make his home that much more permanent and solid.

The work was done evenings and on weekends; it was planned to proceed in steps, and could halt for days without endangering the new work or the existing house, or inconveniencing its occupants. The existing kitchen remained operable; the old wall remained until the expansion was completely enclosed.

Though done during spare time, this was a large undertaking. The owner figures that even with the help he received from friends and relatives, he himself devoted several hundred hours to the project.

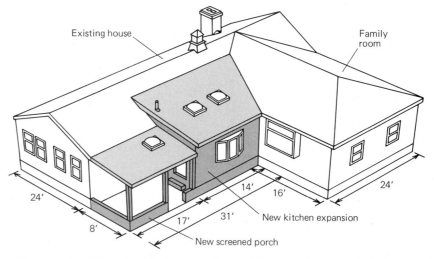

This is an overhead view of original house with completed expansion. New porch, foreground, is enclosed only with screens. The new kitchen area is completely enclosed with weatherproofed, insulated walls. Existing family room, right, is an older expansion of original house.

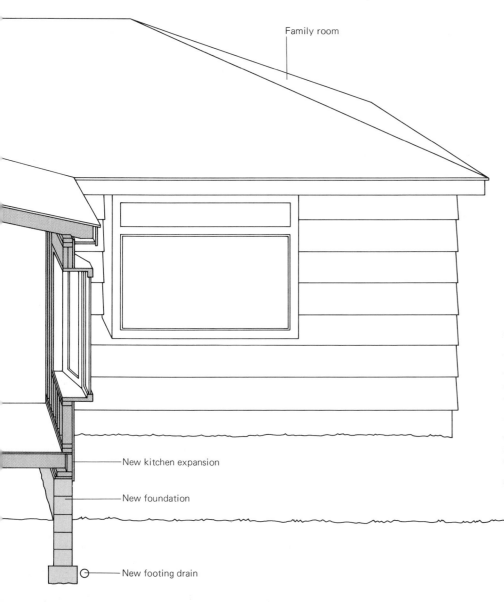

Major structural problem of this project is to support roof load originally borne by existing kitchen wall; wall will be removed to open kitchen for expansion. This homeowner's solution was to construct a new beam outside top plate of old kitchen wall; this new beam, in combination with a new bearing wall located 8 ft. outside old line of kitchen, carries load of both old and new roofs. The beam, of doubled 2 x 10s, is supported on one end by top plate of existing family room wall, and on other end by new kitchen wall next to porch (see diagram above). The beam supports new joists installed alongside each of the existing ceiling joists. Each new joist is fastened to the beam with a joist hanger, and also nailed to the adjacent existing joist.

The illustration at left is a general section drawing (see pp.42–43) of the house and the expansion. The foundation of the expansion is built to support the new floor at the exact height of the existing kitchen floor (see p.279).

The structural solution used here requires more lumber than would some alternatives. But it has advantages: (1) It projects the new beam out several inches from the existing kitchen wall, which provides working space beneath the existing roof eave to nail new joists to new beam; this allows the beam to be installed before the existing kitchen wall is removed. (2) It eliminates the need for temporary supports, allowing the existing wall to remain undisturbed until the extension has been enclosed, wired, and insulated—thereby keeping construction mess out, and heat within the existing kitchen, which was in full-time use while the work proceeded. (3) Once the beam is installed, the kitchen wall is no longer load-bearing, and can be removed.

Expanding a room outward

A foundation for the extension

1. Excavation is dug for a continuous footing for the expanded kitchen and new porch. The excavation must be wide enough to contain the formwork and the footing drain.

2. Steps leading to an existing family room are broken up with a crowbar and removed. Slabs of slate surrounding the steps are lifted and removed from the site with a hand truck.

3. A piece of siding is pried off bottom of existing wall. A measurement is made to ensure distance from existing kitchen floor to bottom of footing of new foundation is correct.

4. Strings strung between batter boards set at corners of excavation ensure that footings will be square (see p.242). A story pole measures from string to bottom of excavation (p.244).

5. Wooden formwork will contain the poured continuous concrete footing, which is 8 in. wide and 35 in. deep. Cross braces provide extra support at the corners.

6. A pipe that serves both as a footing drain and as a conduit for water from roof downspouts is laid in the excavation. The inside edge of the formwork has been backfilled with earth.

7. All backfill is tamped down. Wooden spacers inside form will be pulled out as concrete is poured. Formwork is covered with oil so it can be pulled from the dry concrete.

8. Footing is poured in two sections—one for kitchen, one for porch. Here, after first section sets, the starter course of concrete blocks for the foundation wall is laid.

9. Anchor bolts are cemented in every 4 ft. along the top course of the foundation wall. Small rocks partially fill cavities of blocks in top course to form a base for mortar.

10. Panels of 1-in.-thick styrofoam are glued inside foundation wall from top of footing to top of wall. A vapor barrier of polyethylene sheeting covers outside of foundation wall.

11. Continuous pourings from wheelbarrows create both the footing and the 4-in. slab for the new porch. Here, the layer of gravel and steel reinforcement mesh for the slab are in place.

12. Wet concrete slab is covered with plastic. During first week, plastic is raised once a day to hose down concrete. It is watered a final time one week later. Total setting time: three weeks.

Framing the floor

After the foundation is completed, the expansion is framed. The new floor, which sits above a crawl space, is constructed exactly level with the existing kitchen floor (see diagram, right). The frame walls are assembled flat, raised, and nailed to the existing house where siding has been stripped to accept them. The eaves of the existing roof are cut back to expose the top plates. Rafters for the expansion run from the new exterior wall partway up the existing roof; the rafters are beveled so that they can be nailed to the existing rafters (through the shingles) and form a smooth transition where the two roofs meet. The roof is sheathed, the skylights are put in, and building paper and shingles are applied. A beam that assumes the load held by the existing kitchen wall, is installed (see diagrams, pp.276–277, 282). The expansion is then completely enclosed by installing the remaining sheathing, and the window, door, and siding.

New wiring and insulation are installed. The kitchen wall, no longer needed for load-bearing or weather protection, is removed. Plumbing and gas lines are altered to accommodate the new floor plan. Then new cabinets, wall and ceiling coverings, and other interior finishes are installed, using methods described elsewhere.

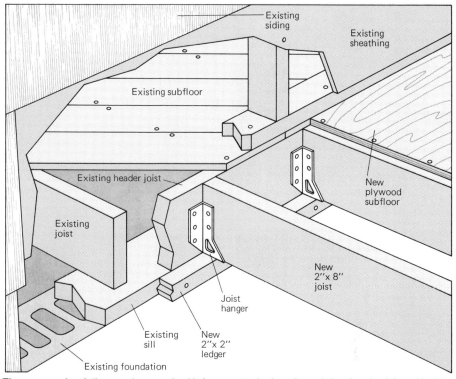

The new and existing portions of the kitchen floor must align exactly. A piece of the existing siding is stripped away. A 2-x-2 ledger strip is nailed into the sill, and becomes, in effect, the sill for the new floor joists (the ledger strip positions the joists, but does not support them). The new floor joists, 2 x 8s like the existing joists, are attached to the existing header joist with joist hangers, atop the ledger strip. Plywood subflooring is then installed. Because the combined height of the new ledger strip, joists, and subfloor is the same as that of the existing sill, joists, and subfloor, the new and existing kitchen floors meet at the same level.

1. Strip of roof edge is seen being installed to serve as termite stop. Small scraps of wood atop foundation are shims to level 1-x-10 base plate and 2-x-8 sill, propped at left.

2. Nuts on anchor bolts secure base plate and sill (through drilled holes) to foundation wall. Base plate and sill are treated with preservative. Drain for downspout is in foreground.

3. Siding on existing house is cut away to reveal sill, joists, and subfloor of present kitchen (see diagram, above). This allows extended kitchen floor to be aligned exactly with old floor.

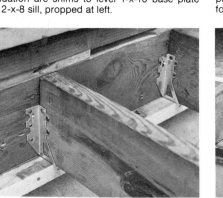

4. A 2 x 2 is nailed to existing sill (bottom). This serves as a ledger to guide placement of new joists. The new 2-x-8 joists are attached with joist hangers to existing header joist.

5. A building square is used to measure 16-in. intervals at which new joists are end nailed to new header joist. The joists and header joist are supported by sill attached in Step 2.

6. Frame for floor is being completed. The end joist, next to covered slab (which will become the porch floor), is made of a doubled 2 x 8 bolted together at center and both ends. *(continued)*

279

Expanding a room outward

Framing, sheathing, and a dry well

7. Cross-bracing is installed between floor joists for firmness. Bracing is made of scrap; 2 x 4s were used here, but 1 x 2s would suffice.

8. Footing drain runs downhill into a dry well, a hole 6 ft. deep containing two stacked 5-gallon cans with holes in their sides and bottoms.

9. Cans are surrounded and covered with rock. Layer of plastic covers rock 2 ft. below grade. Soil, over plastic, fills well to grade.

10. Part of eave of kitchen roof is cut away to expose top plate of existing wall. It is a load-bearing wall (see diagram, pp.276–277).

11. Once top plate is exposed, all protruding rafters will be sawed off flush with the plate, as can be seen here and in Step 18.

12. The first wall is framed lying flat, and is lifted into place. Large header in center of this wall supports roof over new kitchen window.

13. First wall is checked for level and nailed to house; a strip of siding has been removed to seat it flush on sheathing.

14. Second wall is assembled and installed. A second top plate interlocks both walls at the corner. Temporary braces are in place.

15. Plywood sheathing is nailed to outside of second wall facing the porch. Sheathing on the other wall is attached later (Step 32).

16. The porch wall, made of several built-up posts spaced far apart, is raised and attached to the foundation wall and to the kitchen wall.

17. The rafters for the porch and kitchen expansion (Step 20) are installed. The porch sheathing and skylight area are put in (Step 26).

18. A heavy-duty reciprocating saw whose blade can be rotated to cut at any angle is used to cut away the rafters and sheathing in the valley.

280

Roofing and a new beam

19. Top plate of wall perpendicular to existing kitchen has been cleared of roofing. It will hold new beam to support roof.

20. Rafters for expansion are bevel-cut and nailed flush with existing roof through the shingles. Wide spaces between rafters are for skylights.

21. Joist hangers support wood cross members (headers) that will support skylights. The rafters on either side of the skylight are doubled.

22. Ends of each of the short rafters traversing the valley must be cut at different angles. Plywood sheets in the valley serve as nailers.

23. Roof sheathing slides under a course of shingles and is nailed to rafters. Extended plumbing vent now passes through the new roof.

24. Old metal flashing in valley is lifted; new roll roofing is slipped beneath it and existing roofing to form new valley flashing.

25. Top sheet of building paper that will cover the entire new roof slides beneath the last course of shingles on the existing roof.

26. Two kitchen skylights here being installed in roof sheathing are waterproofed with two coatings of asphalt—under and over their flashings.

27. Building paper overlaps edges of skylights. Pieces of building paper will fill the gaps between them to completely cover the roof.

28. The new roof is shingled to match the existing roof. The new shingles extend across the valley and under the existing shingles.

29. New joists with joist hangers slide in beside existing kitchen ceiling joists. Their far ends are nailed to existing joists from attic.

30. First board of built-up beam is installed. At one end it rests on exposed top plate of an existing wall, at other, on porch wall. *(continued)*

Expanding a room outward

Finishing the expansion

31. After first half of new beam is nailed to joist hangers, second board is nailed to it. Beam now bears the load of the roof.

32. Framing for rough opening of new window is completed to specifications for a pre-assembled unit. Plywood sheathing is applied.

33. Building paper is attached around opening for new kitchen window. The pre-assembled window is installed in one piece and leveled.

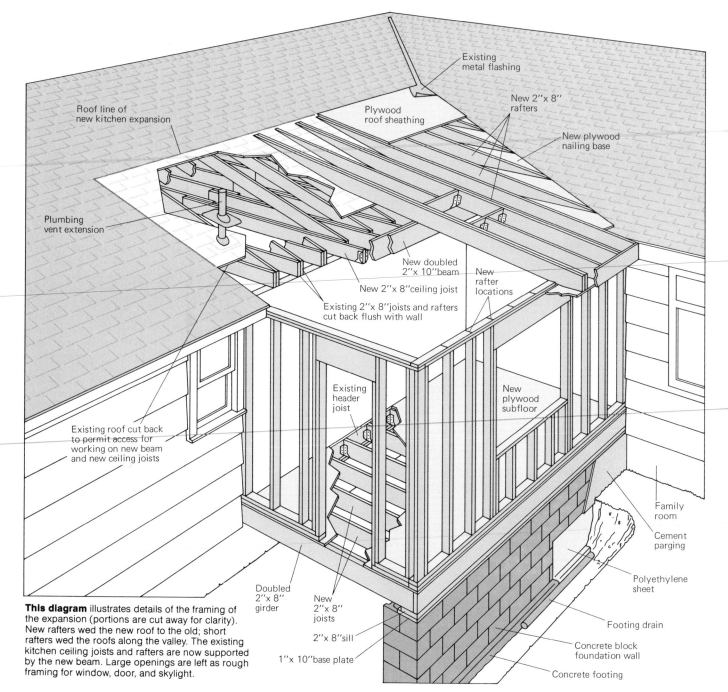

Existing metal flashing

New 2"x 8" rafters

Plywood roof sheathing

New plywood nailing base

Roof line of new kitchen expansion

Plumbing vent extension

New doubled 2"x 10"beam

New 2"x 8"ceiling joist

New rafter locations

Existing 2"x 8"joists and rafters cut back flush with wall

Existing header joist

New plywood subfloor

Existing roof cut back to permit access for working on new beam and new ceiling joists

Family room

Cement parging

Polyethylene sheet

Footing drain

Doubled 2"x 8" girder

New 2"x 8" joists

2"x 8"sill

1"x 10"base plate

Concrete block foundation wall

Concrete footing

This diagram illustrates details of the framing of the expansion (portions are cut away for clarity). New rafters wed the new roof to the old; short rafters wed the roofs along the valley. The existing kitchen ceiling joists and rafters are now supported by the new beam. Large openings are left as rough framing for window, door, and skylight.

34. Pre-hung door leading from new kitchen to porch is installed in rough opening (framed to size) and exactly positioned with shims.

35. Wall sheathing of expansion is covered with building paper. Siding, made of vertical rustic cedar boards, is seen being installed.

36. The expansion is wired for electricity. Here a wire travels through holes bored in the studs to supply a box for an outlet beneath the window.

37. A layer of foil-backed insulation is stapled between studs and between ceiling rafters. Wiring is completed before insulation is begun.

38. With expansion totally enclosed, old kitchen exterior siding is removed. Here, the old kitchen window is taken out in one piece.

39. Studs are first removed from wall. With top plate, here, comes a piece of interior gypsum wallboard. Rest of gypsum board is then removed.

40. Ceiling finish is made of matching 1-x-8 cedar boards. Here, pieces of cedar board are installed around the recessed skylight.

41. Vent of old kitchen sink is cut off. It is given a temporary copper cap, which is removed when the new sink is hooked up (Step 45).

42. Plywood subfloor is installed in the expansion. The stove, for which the gas line has already been extended, is moved into position.

43. With old sink removed, T-joint (see Step 41) on waste pipe is removed; it will be replaced by an elbow facing the other direction.

44. Plumbing protrudes from subfloor where old sink has been removed. A new base cabinet is brought in and set in place on the floor.

45. New sink is hooked up to existing drain pipe and supply lines (which cross because sink now faces opposite way). Shut-off valves are installed.

Adding a dormer

General planning and preparation

The living space of an attic can be expanded through the addition of one or more dormers. Besides the extra space dormers provide, their windows admit daylight, offer added ventilation, and afford a means of escape in case of fire.

All are important considerations if the attic is being converted into a habitable room, such as a den, family room, studio, or a bedroom. Most building codes establish certain minimum standards of light and ventilation, as well as requiring a window to serve as a fire escape for habitable rooms on upper floors. In many attic conversions, these code specifications can most easily be met by the incorporation of dormers.

While the construction of a dormer requires at least some familiarity with carpentry, any competent do-it-yourselfer with experience need not fear tackling the job, providing he works carefully. If the span of the roof opening for the dormer is to be 8 feet or less in width, the framing can probably be done over a long weekend with some occasional assistance. The framing lumber will consist of pieces no heavier than long 2 x 6s or 2 x 8s for joists and rafters. Aside from a hammer, electric drill, saber saw, circular saw, tape measure, chalk line, and a spirit level, you need 16-penny nails for general framing, 10-penny nails for toenailing, and 8-penny common nails for attaching the exterior plywood sheathing. The framing can be done with hand tools but then the work will take much longer and it will be much more tiring.

Dormer designs: There are basically two types of dormers—gable and shed roof. Drawings showing the design and structural elements of each type appear on these two pages; the dormer seen in the construction photographs on pages 289–291 is a shed roof design, which provides the most additional interior space within the attic. The stages in the construction of both types are similar.

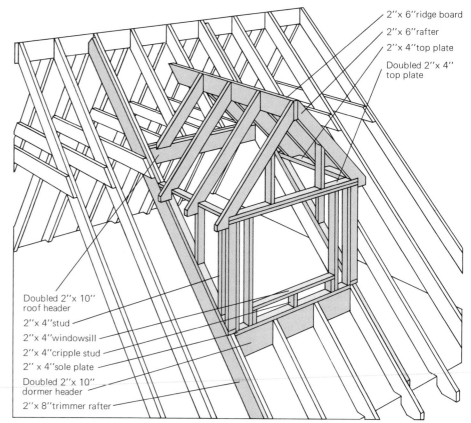

Doubled 2"x 10" roof header
2"x 4"stud
2"x 4"windowsill
2"x 4"cripple stud
2" x 4"sole plate
Doubled 2"x 10" dormer header
2"x 8"trimmer rafter

2"x 6"ridge board
2"x 6"rafter
2"x 4"top plate
Doubled 2"x 4" top plate

Gable roof dormer: Framing elements of dormer (tinted brown) are seen tied into the existing roof frame of a house. Usually a gabled dormer is built to admit light and provide ventilation and a means of emergency fire exit, rather than to enlarge a converted attic's living space.

The dimensions given in the drawings for the framing lumber meet most building code standards for a dormer of the size described in following paragraphs; however, check your own local code. You may have to acquire a building permit to construct a dormer. (See p.21 for more detailed imformation.)

Framing the window opening: If you are planning to install a prefabricated window in the dormer, you must size the dormer frame you build to the rough opening (r.o.) specified in the window manufacturer's catalog. The rough opening allows a small margin (about ½ inch extra space all around the window), which permits the window to be squared up and then shimmed into place. The installation of windows is illustrated on pages 294–297 of this book, and building code regulation of wood-frame construction is discussed on pages 21–37. The window used in the dormer photographed for these pages was an Andersen Thermopane Perma-Shield Casement Window, 4 x 3½ feet.

Opening the roof: The roof can be opened either by working inside the

Roof pitch: the basic consideration

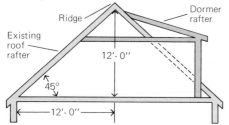
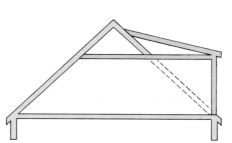
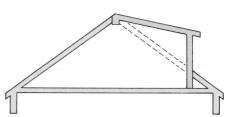

Load stresses in traditional gabled roofs are more easily balanced and contained when the pitch of the roof is steep. The shallower the pitch, the more the rafters tend to collapse at the ridge line under their own weight.

Builders measure the pitch of a roof in terms of its slope ratio. For example, if over a horizontal distance of 12 ft. the roof rises at a 45° angle to a ridge height of 12 ft., this would

be a one to one (1:1) pitch (see also pages 38–41). The critical pitch for a dormer is usually considered to be no less than 3:1; if its rafters rise less than 1 ft. for every 3 ft. of horizontal distance, special framing may be needed to support the dormer roof. You can calculate the pitch of your roof using a tape measure.

In the first two diagrams, dormer roof pitch is 3:1 or steeper; the differences in construction

relate to the creation of added living space, greater in the second diagram than the first. But in Diagram 3, the 3:1 pitch could not be obtained and still provide adequate headroom, because of the lower ridge (shallower pitch) of the existing roof; hence the dormer rafters were taken all the way to the existing roof ridge, where they will require the support of a lintel or bearing wall inside the attic to prevent their collapse.

attic or by working on the roof, as discussed on page 288. All the framing can be done on the attic floor and can then be lifted into place, as shown on pages 290–291. Cover the roof opening with a tarpaulin or plastic sheeting if the work is stopped overnight or if inclement weather develops while you are working. Because speed is essential in closing the roof opening, have tools and materials at hand before starting to work. The materials used to frame and finish a dormer are detailed on page 287.

Key planning considerations: In building a shed roof dormer, with the object of enlarging the living space of an attic room, there are important interrelated factors to consider. The first is the *headroom*—the vertical distance from floor to ceiling—within the dormer and the attic as a whole. In most designs, the ceiling joists of the dormer will be at the same height and run parallel to the existing collar ties be-

tween the attic roof rafters—establishing the ceiling height within the entire attic. Building codes govern minimum headroom (see *Building codes*, pp.21–37), generally requiring that the ceiling height average some 7½ feet over most of the floor area of any habitable room. Thus it will usually be necessary to plan the dormer so that its ceiling joists allow at least 7½ feet of headroom (except in the case of a small gable or shed dormer whose function is simply to provide ventilation and let daylight in).

The question of headroom, in turn, relates to the height of the existing attic ridge (the peak of the rafters). The height of the existing ridge will affect the location of the opening in the roof and the slope of the dormer's rafters, as discussed on the opposite page.

The large illustration on this page shows all the elements in a shed dormer frame, and the way the dormer frame ties into the existing roof frame of the

house. If you intend to use the instructions in this section to add a dormer to your house, be sure to read the entire chapter to develop a full understanding of the materials and carpentry procedures. Then, make the necessary calculations regarding the location of the roof opening, and draw your own plans for the frame, like those shown in this section. Our drawings are for a dormer opening 8 feet in width, with a roof pitch of approximately three to one (3:1). Your own drawings are likely to vary from these dimensions.

As a general precaution, you should not remove more than three existing roof rafters when adding a dormer, unless you have some professional guidance. This will give you the distance between five rafters as the width of your dormer. Most rafters are spaced 16 inches on center (o.c.), permitting a dormer width of up to 64 inches by removing three rafters.

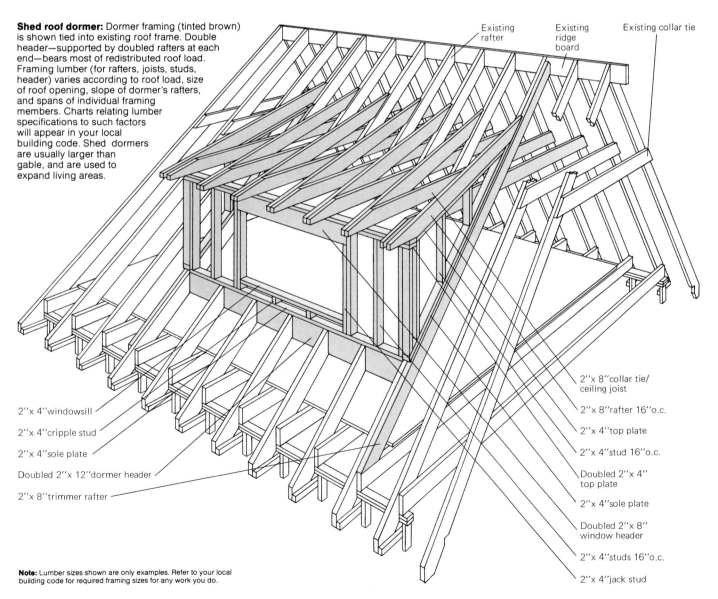

Shed roof dormer: Dormer framing (tinted brown) is shown tied into existing roof frame. Double header—supported by doubled rafters at each end—bears most of redistributed roof load. Framing lumber (for rafters, joists, studs, header) varies according to roof load, size of roof opening, slope of dormer's rafters, and spans of individual framing members. Charts relating lumber specifications to such factors will appear in your local building code. Shed dormers are usually larger than gable, and are used to expand living areas.

Existing rafter
Existing ridge board
Existing collar tie

2"x 8"collar tie/ ceiling joist
2"x 8"rafter 16"o.c.
2"x 4"top plate
2"x 4"stud 16"o.c.
Doubled 2"x 4" top plate
2"x 4"sole plate
Doubled 2"x 8" window header
2"x 4"studs 16"o.c.
2"x 4"jack stud

2"x 4"windowsill
2"x 4"cripple stud
2"x 4"sole plate
Doubled 2"x 12"dormer header
2"x 8"trimmer rafter

Note: Lumber sizes shown are only examples. Refer to your local building code for required framing sizes for any work you do.

Adding a dormer

Finishing the dormer

The illustrations on this page show, in cutaway view, a typical shed dormer frame integrated into an attic interior. The cutaway view on the opposite page details the various materials used to finish the dormer.

Joists and collar ties: As noted on preceding pages, headroom within the dormer and finished attic is a key consideration in planning a dormer. In the interior cutaway shown below, the new dormer ceiling joists are aligned with the existing collar ties running between the existing rafters; thus the original collar ties double in service as ceiling joists in the finished attic.

It may not be possible or desirable, however, to employ the existing collar ties as attic ceiling joists. A steep roof might be so high at the peak, for ex-

ample, that the collar ties are too high off the floor for a desirable ceiling height. In such cases, new ceiling joists might be installed throughout the attic at the level of the dormer joists, as planned for headroom of, say, 7½ or 8 feet. Insulation and wallboard would then be applied to these joists to make a ceiling of uniform height within both attic and dormer. The structurally necessary old collar ties would all be left untouched, of course, remaining in place in the space between the newly built attic ceiling and the roof ridge.

In cases where the dormer ceiling joists can be aligned with the existing collar ties, as in the cutaway drawing below, the framing, if possible, should be planned so that none of the existing ties need be removed; this can often be done by running the joists on the side of the rafters opposite the ties.

Redistributing load: Note that the roof load originally carried by rafters

removed for the dormer opening is now borne by the dormer rafters and ceiling joists, which, in turn, transfer the load down onto the dormer's front wall and window frame, and, finally, to the dormer header, supported at either end by doubled rafters—a trimmer rafter added to the original rafter. In other words, a load larger than that originally distributed over a number of rafters is now mainly carried by the two doubled rafters at the sides of the dormer. The greater the width of the dormer opening and the more rafters removed, the larger becomes the load borne by this critical pair of doubled rafters. In extremely large dormers (not recommended for the non-professional), these rafters might be tripled, not simply doubled—with counterbalancing doubling or tripling of the opposing rafters on the other side of the ridge board.

Finishing: The finished contours of the attic interior are a matter of per-

Cutaway view of dormer and attic interior

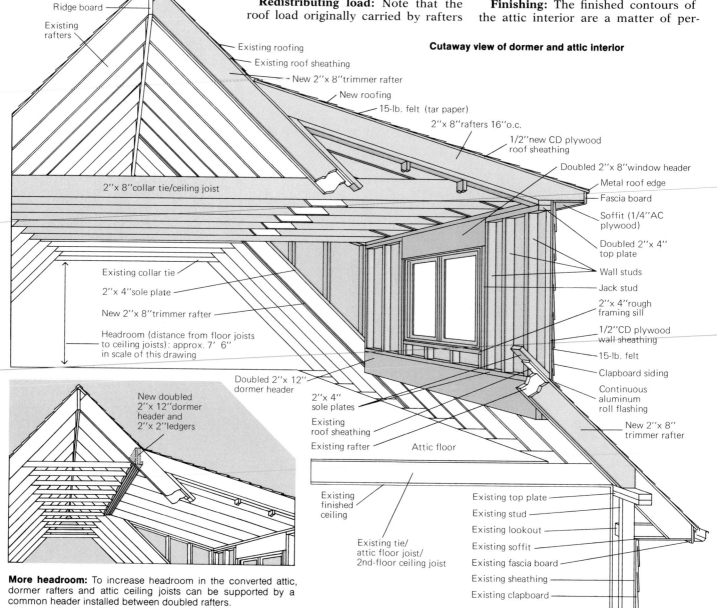

More headroom: To increase headroom in the converted attic, dormer rafters and attic ceiling joists can be supported by a common header installed between doubled rafters.

sonal taste. Most commonly, someone finishing the attic shown below would build a knee wall (see section on finishing attics, pp.163–170) along one side or around the entire perimeter of the room, and under the dormer header. The wall could include built-in shelves, cupboards, or cabinetry to provide storage space in the triangular volume between it and the base of the rafters, and would offer a vertical wall against which to locate a bed, desk, or other furniture or equipment. If the knee wall were built to a height of, say, 4 feet, the resulting interior—combining the contours of dormer, the original roof slope and knee wall—could well become one of the most interesting rooms in the house, retaining much of the rustic charm of garret architecture. Information on installing insulation, building partitions, Sheetrocking, paneling, wiring, ordering materials, as well as the other jobs entailed in finishing an attic

can be found in several other chapters of this book.

Materials: The order of the work of building a dormer is covered in detailed illustrations on the next four pages. The cutaway drawing on this page shows the placement of materials in the dormer. As would be expected, the general order of the work will be from the inside out, beginning with the frame.

Exceptions to this work order are the frieze board, soffit, and rake along the overhanging dormer roof edges, which go on before the exterior siding of wood shingles or clapboard. The window is put in place after the front has been sheathed in plywood and felted. The window trim is attached before the siding goes on, except in the case of vertical cedar boards and various other forms of paneling.

The most commonly used sheathing is ½-inch CD plywood; plywood imparts rigidity to the frame, keeping it from

twisting. Strips of 15-pound felt building paper, overlapping at their seams, top piece over bottom piece, are applied to the sheathed roof, and felt is also tacked to the dormer's side and front walls. At this stage, flashing is put in place all around the bottom of the dormer to make a watertight barrier where the dormer frame meets the existing house roof. Continuous aluminum roll flashing is laid along the bottom of the dormer's front wall, step flashing along the side walls (as shown in the small inset drawing at bottom right on this page). The corner seam where the two types of flashing meet is waterproofed with asphalt caulking. The final step is roofing and siding.

Dormer roofs with a slope much shallower than 3:1 are normally covered with roll roofing rather than shingles because water tends to back up under shingles on flat surfaces, causing leaks and rot.

Materials used in dormer construction

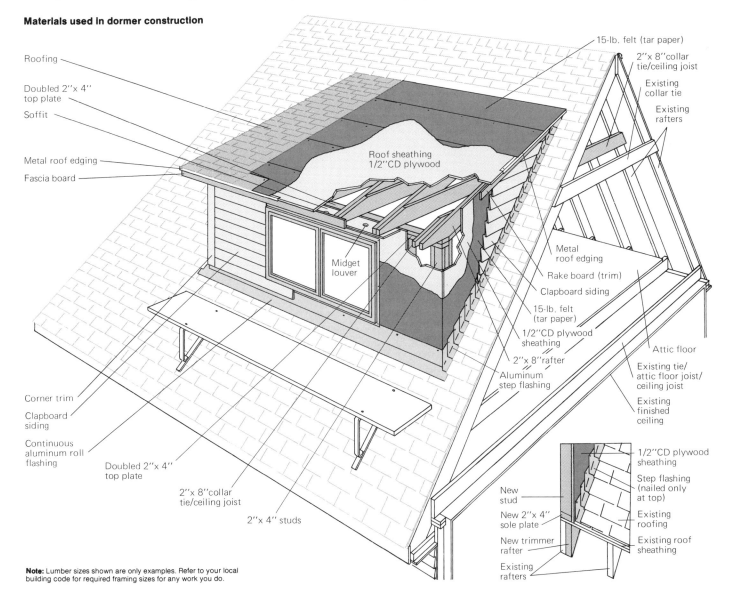

Roofing
Doubled 2"x 4" top plate
Soffit
Metal roof edging
Fascia board
Corner trim
Clapboard siding
Continuous aluminum roll flashing
Doubled 2"x 4" top plate
2"x 8"collar tie/ceiling joist
2"x 4" studs

Roof sheathing 1/2"CD plywood
Midget louver

15-lb. felt (tar paper)
2"x 8"collar tie/ceiling joist
Existing collar tie
Existing rafters
Metal roof edging
Rake board (trim)
Clapboard siding
15-lb. felt (tar paper)
1/2"CD plywood sheathing
2"x 8"rafter
Aluminum step flashing
Attic floor
Existing tie/ attic floor joist/ ceiling joist
Existing finished ceiling

New stud
New 2"x 4" sole plate
New trimmer rafter
Existing rafters
1/2"CD plywood sheathing
Step flashing (nailed only at top)
Existing roofing
Existing roof sheathing

Note: Lumber sizes shown are only examples. Refer to your local building code for required framing sizes for any work you do.

Adding a dormer

Opening the roof from outside

The dormer opening can be cut either from inside the attic or from the rooftop outside. The drawings on this page illustrate the completed dormer opening, together with the key steps in cutting it from outside. The illustrations on the opposite page show how to go about the same job, but working inside the attic. The building of the dormer is highlighted in pictures on pages 290–291.

A number of factors will influence your decision on how to cut the roof opening—whether from inside the attic or outside. If the slope of your house roof is extremely steep, you may wish to do as much of the work as possible from inside the attic, thus minimizing the chances of an accident by a fall or the dropping of tools on passersby below.

By working outside, however, you gain certain advantages. It is possible, as seen in the illustrations, to remove all the roof shingles down to the bare sheathing before cutting. This not only saves wear and tear on your saw, but produces neater and more orderly work. When cutting from inside, the saw must pass through both sheathing and shingles; moreover, the removal of additional shingles along the sides and top of the opening—to expose a margin of bare sheathing for proper nailing of dormer rafters and sole plates, and the attaching of step flashing—will require working on a ladder set up inside the attic, which can be awkward. In addition, when cutting the opening from outside, you can carefully remove the existing plywood roof sheathing with panels intact. These panels can be salvaged and they can then be used as sheathing on the dormer.

Measuring and marking: Whether opening the roof from inside or outside, the initial laying out is done from inside the attic. First, mark the top, sides, and front of the dormer opening on the sheathing between the attic roof rafters. Remember that construction will be simplified if the sides of the dormer are located flush with existing roof rafters, as seen on pages 285 and 286. Unless your dormer is going to extend to the existing roof ridge, mark the top of the opening at a vertical distance 8 to 9 feet off the attic floor to accommodate joists and allow adequate headroom.

If you are opening the roof from outside, drive a nail from the attic through the roof sheathing at each of the four corners of the layout. The protruding nails will be visible when you go outside to work on the roof, as described in captions accompanying drawings on this page.

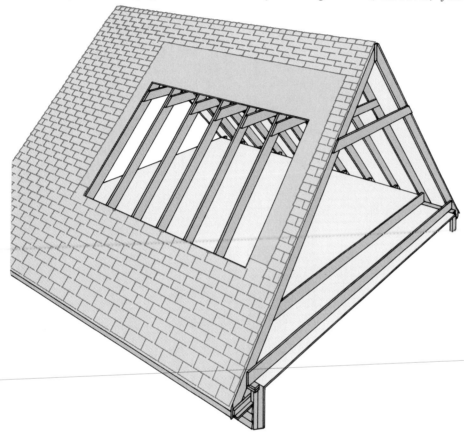

Scaffolding or platform (not shown) facilitates removal of shingles and sheathing on steep roof, but you can work from inside attic. Temporary supports are put up in attic before cutting rafters.

Marking roof opening: Nails driven through roof from attic mark location of dormer. Snap chalk line between bottom nails to determine dormer's front edge, between top nails to establish where dormer joists will pass. At sides, mark lines 5½ inches outside nails.

Exposing sheathing: Use heavy shears to cut along chalk lines at sides and bottom. Remove all the shingles and building paper within this area; a flat shovel makes a convenient tool. Depending on planned pitch of dormer rafters, remove another 1 to 3 ft. of shingles above top line.

Cutting: Snap new chalk lines between nails on exposed sheathing. Cut along these lines with circular saw set at thickness of plywood (probably ½ or ⅝ in.), or roofing boards (probably ¾ in.). You can determine setting by cutting a small test section between rafters. Remove sheathing.

Opening the roof from inside

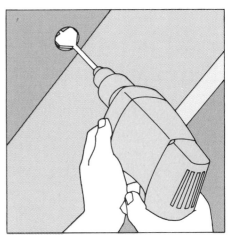

1. After laying out dormer opening on roof boards or sheathing, erect a temporary frame on the attic floor to support the rafters. Framework will bear weight of roof while you build the dormer. Place the support above line where rafters are to be cut—probably 8 to 9 ft. straight up from the floor.

2. Position a second temporary support where the rafters are to be cut for the dormer's front wall. Situate the support a foot or so below the cut line to allow space for installing the dormer header (see pp. 285 and 286). The supports are temporarily nailed to the floor and rafters.

3. Drill a hole an inch in diameter as close as possible to the inside face of the rafter marking the right side of the dormer opening, then drill another hole at the rafter marking the left side. A reciprocating saw will be inserted through these holes to make the cuts described in Step 4.

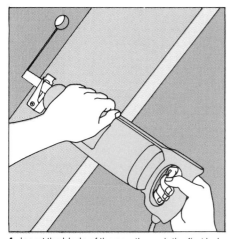

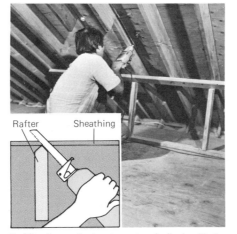

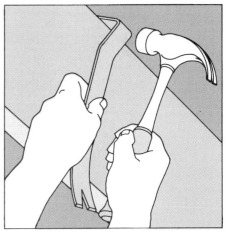

4. Insert the blade of the saw through the first hole drilled in Step 3. Make a clean, straight cut flush with the inside face of the rafter. Cut through both the sheathing and its attached roofing, from the top to the bottom of the dormer opening. Repeat procedure on the second rafter.

5. After the vertical cuts are made flush with the rafters at the sides of the dormer opening, the first horizontal cut is made along the dormer opening's bottom line. Cut and remove the sheathing with its attached roofing in manageable sections. Inset shows saw angled to cut behind rafter.

Rafter   Sheathing

6. A bar and a hammer are used to pry up a free section of sheathing and roofing where it is nailed to a rafter. The entire section is loosened from the rafters in this way and then brought into the attic for disposal, as seen in the next step. Rafters are left intact, to be cut away later.

7. Section by section, the sheathing and roofing are cut out with the saw, pried loose from the rafters, and brought into the attic. If you are working alone, take out the roof in many small sections that are easily handled. Slide them inside between the rafters and onto the attic floor.

8. Again, the reciprocating saw is employed to cut through the sheathing and shingles, freeing a patch of roof for removal. Note that the work began at the bottom of the dormer, moving progressively higher on the roof. This working order facilitates the handling of roofing pieces.

9. The last large section of roofing is pried loose from the rafters. The final cutting and trimming, and key steps in building the dormer, are shown in the photos and illustrations on the following two pages. Although carpentry practices do vary, those shown will result in sound workmanship.

Adding a dormer

Framing the dormer

1. To prepare for framing the dormer, the last of the existing roof rafters is cut out. All rafter sections are trimmed to uniform length just below the temporary support. The dormer-attic ceiling joists eventually will be put in at approximately the level of the rafter ends.

2. Trimming is also done at the bottom front of the dormer. The roofing is cut through to the rafters; next, the roofing is pried loose and is removed. The rafter sections are then trimmed to a flush vertical line to act as a nailing surface for the dormer header.

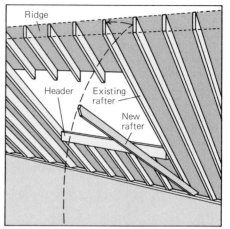

3. Dormer double header is nailed to end rafters and to rafter sections under opening at front. New trimmer rafters are first bevel-cut to lie flush against sole plate and ridge board, then raised into position. Trimmers are then nailed tightly to existing rafters.

4. With the new trimmer rafters and dormer header in place, the front wall frame is constructed on the attic floor. The window opening is laid out to the rough opening (r.o.) that has been specified for your window in the window manufacturer's catalog.

5. Once the front wall frame is complete, it is nailed into place on the header, plumbed for vertical, and secured with braces. Here, the left side temporary brace is seen being nailed into place. Braces at both sides temporarily anchor the front wall frame.

6. The lumber for the dormer rafters must be checked for any distortions caused by warping. Normally, long lengths of wood will warp into a slight crown, or high spot, along one of the long edges. Rafters and joists should be positioned with the crown facing up.

7. The dormer rafters are notched so that they will lie flush on the dormer wall top plate and provide an overhang of several inches above the dormer front wall; the rafters are bevel-cut at the opposite end to lie flush with the existing roof. Inset drawing shows "birdsmouth" notch.

8. After the first rafter has been measured, cut, and test-fit, it is used as a template to mark all the remaining rafters. Here, the first rafter is seen in use to mark the location of the "birdsmouth" notch, the eave end, and the angular upper end of the rafter on a fresh piece of lumber.

9. A circular saw can be used to make the simple pair of cuts for the "birdsmouth" notch, as seen here. The same saw can be employed to make the angular cuts that allow the upper ends of the dormer rafters to lie flush with the existing roofing or exposed sheathing.

10. The dormer rafters are toenailed (nailed through both pieces of wood at an angle) to the front wall top plate, as shown here. Note that roofing has not yet been trimmed away from the end rafter; this will be done before the side wall studs are nailed to the rafter.

11. Plywood sheathing is nailed to the dormer rafters. Normally, the dormer would have been completely framed in, including ceiling joists, before the roof sheathing was attached. This project's order of work was changed in reaction to the approach of a summer storm.

12. By the time the rains came, the opening in the roof had been fully covered with a tarp. The exposed wood along the bottom of the dormer was also carefully protected with plastic wrap. Work on the dormer was resumed the next day, when the roof was again dry.

13. Once the dormer's side wall studs are in place, the plywood wall sheathing is cut and attached. Here, the dormer studs were nailed to the inner faces of the reinforced roof rafters; more common practice is to locate the studs on top of a plate that is supported by the rafters.

14. The dormer sheathing is now all in place. Next, flashing should be installed around the dormer, where its walls meet the existing roof. Given the procedures used to build this particular dormer, it will be necessary to remove some shingles to install the step flashing (see p.287).

15. Building paper is tacked to the inside of rough opening, then folded around frame and tacked to the exterior sheathing. Window is then set in place, anchored with a few nails, and tested before final nailing. Trim, felt, roofing, and siding are attached as shown on page 287.

16. Dormer-attic ceiling joists are positioned and nailed to the existing house roof rafters. The joists are also nailed to the dormer rafters in front, where both rest side by side on the top plate. After this work is secure, the large temporary support inside the attic can be removed.

17. Insulation is now installed between the dormer-attic ceiling joists, and between the existing roof rafters. The vapor barrier and/or reflective foil on insulation faces inward. Here, staple gun is used to attach insulation. Recesses are deep enough to provide proper air spaces.

18. The dormer is seen with roofing, metal roof edge, trim, and siding in place. Hexagonal side-wall windows are a special feature of this dormer; homeowner had acquired the windows as salvage and incorporated them into his design later to provide additional light for the attic.

Converting a garage to living space

Planning the job

Converting an attached garage can be the easiest and most economical way to add new living space to a house. And because the building already exists, problems with zoning ordinances and building departments are minimal.

If the frame of the garage and its foundation, slab, and roofing are in good condition, the cost will always be less than attaching a wing to the house, where foundation, framing, roofing, and siding must all be built from scratch. An attached garage generally poses few heat, plumbing, or electrical problems. The existing systems in the house proper can often be extended to serve the converted garage.

You will, however, have the problem of sheltering your family car or cars. Since a garage generally does not re- quire heat or plumbing, and needs only minimal electrical service, a new garage or carport can be constructed farther from the house. The money saved on the conversion can still be considerable. For these reasons, garage conversions are becoming a popular form of home extension in many parts of the country.

Basic considerations: First evaluate the soundness of your garage. If its slab

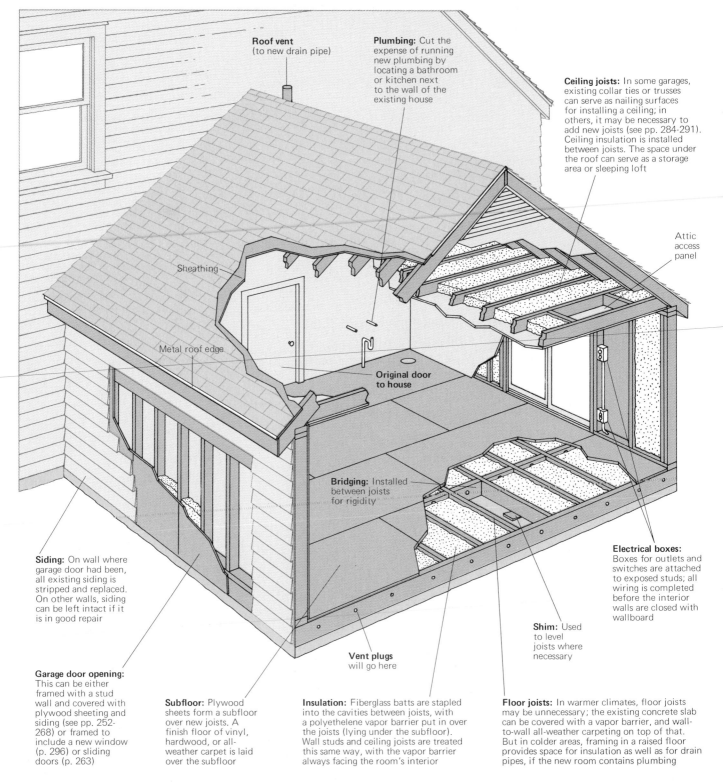

Roof vent (to new drain pipe)

Plumbing: Cut the expense of running new plumbing by locating a bathroom or kitchen next to the wall of the existing house

Ceiling joists: In some garages, existing collar ties or trusses can serve as nailing surfaces for installing a ceiling; in others, it may be necessary to add new joists (see pp. 284-291). Ceiling insulation is installed between joists. The space under the roof can serve as a storage area or sleeping loft

Attic access panel

Sheathing

Metal roof edge

Original door to house

Bridging: Installed between joists for rigidity

Electrical boxes: Boxes for outlets and switches are attached to exposed studs; all wiring is completed before the interior walls are closed with wallboard

Siding: On wall where garage door had been, all existing siding is stripped and replaced. On other walls, siding can be left intact if it is in good repair

Shim: Used to level joists where necessary

Vent plugs will go here

Garage door opening: This can be either framed with a stud wall and covered with plywood sheeting and siding (see pp. 252-268) or framed to include a new window (p. 296) or sliding doors (p. 263)

Subfloor: Plywood sheets form a subfloor over new joists. A finish floor of vinyl, hardwood, or all-weather carpet is laid over the subfloor

Insulation: Fiberglass batts are stapled into the cavities between joists, with a polyethelene vapor barrier put in over the joists (lying under the subfloor). Wall studs and ceiling joists are treated this same way, with the vapor barrier always facing the room's interior

Floor joists: In warmer climates, floor joists may be unnecessary; the existing concrete slab can be covered with a vapor barrier, and wall-to-wall all-weather carpeting on top of that. But in colder areas, framing in a raised floor provides space for insulation as well as for drain pipes, if the new room contains plumbing

or foundation are cracked, its roof leaks, and its siding is rotting and falling off, you may do better to seek your new living space elsewhere—in a converted attic or a new addition. If the garage is in good condition, you must decide whether it can provide enough new space to meet your need—be that a new dining room, den, or bedrooms.

Draw your own rough plans (see pp.38–41), showing all details right down to the lumber sizes you will use for new joists and studs, insulation, plumbing, electrical hook-ups, new windows, and so forth. Follow your local building codes (pp.21–37) in drawing up your plans, and then have them approved by your building department officials before estimating costs, ordering materials (pp.42–48), and setting to work.

Contracting or doing it yourself: You may prefer to do all the work, part of it, or none of it yourself. Converting a garage can be a major project. (One advantage of a garage conversion is that the project can remain ongoing without disturbing normal living patterns in the rest of the house, whereas an addition, which may involve opening up the existing house structure, is bound to disturb the household.)

Many do-it-yourselfers might prefer to hire a plumber to extend water supply, drain-waste-vent (DWV) lines, and heating ducts or pipes, unless electric baseboard heat is planned. Some might find it convenient to hire an electrician to do the electrical work.

Floors and ceilings: Except for framing in the old garage door opening with new studs, the framing and siding for the walls will be mostly if not totally intact. Insulation is installed between the studs, covered with a vapor barrier, and the interior is then finished, typically with plaster or paneling.

The floor and ceiling may require more work than the walls, however. In warmer climates, a vapor barrier can be laid over the concrete slab and then covered with wall-to-wall all-weather carpeting. But in colder areas, where floor insulation is advisable, you will want to frame in joists over the slab and build a subfloor, as shown in the drawing on the opposite page, and in greater detail on pages 106–110. If possible, lay floor joists in the direction that will make it easier for the plumber to run new pipes through the floor. Insulate and close up the floor only after the plumbing is installed. To install the ceiling you may have to add new ceiling joists, as shown opposite, and described in greater detail on pages 284–291. The original door between house and garage can usually serve as the doorway to the finished conversion.

Two ideas for converting an attached garage

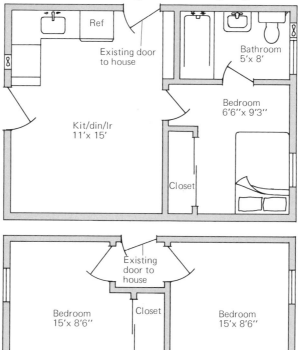

Ref

Existing door to house

Kit/din/lr 11' x 15'

Bathroom 5' x 8'

Bedroom 6'6" x 9'3"

Closet

Floor plan shows an attached garage that has been converted to provide an efficiency apartment for a relative. Note that the bath area, including toilet and tub, is adjacent to a small bedroom, which is isolated by partitions and a closet. The kitchen sink is located on the same side of the garage as the bath to cluster all the plumbing, a factor affecting cost. The main room is a combined kitchen, dining, and living room. Careful design provides for many functions in a small space, plus privacy for the bedroom.

Existing door to house

Bedroom 15' x 8'6"

Closet

Bedroom 15' x 8'6"

Closet

In this floor plan, an attached garage is converted to provide two new bedrooms for a growing family. The two rooms are divided by a studwall partition covered with panels of plasterboard, and the ample side-by-side closets along the partition also help dampen sound. The old doorway from the house still gives access to the renovated garage, and each bedroom has its own door opening onto a small hallway. The bedrooms can have as many windows or skylights as you desire. Building codes set minimum standards for fire exits and ventilation.

Bunk bed partition creates two separate children's bedrooms

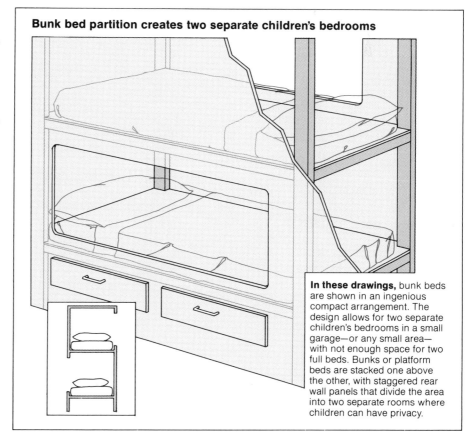

In these drawings, bunk beds are shown in an ingenious compact arrangement. The design allows for two separate children's bedrooms in a small area—or any small area—with not enough space for two full beds. Bunks or platform beds are stacked one above the other, with staggered rear wall panels that divide the area into two separate rooms where children can have privacy.

Entrance doors

Pre-hung door assemblies

Manufactured pre-hung entrance doors are available at most home centers and lumberyards. The most popular models have steel or aluminum skins over an insulating core of a material such as polyurethane. They have insulating properties greater than a solid wood door together with its traditional storm door. A continuous weatherstripping blocks cold drafts around the top and sides of the door. Adjustable thresholds mate with bottom sweeps to make an airtight barrier at the bottom. Vinyl "thermal breaks" separate the outer and inner skins to prevent heat loss by conduction through the metal.

Metal doors come from the factory pre-primed; you apply the finish coat of paint yourself, in whatever color and shade you desire to harmonize with the exterior of your house. Door-stops and exterior trim come pre-assembled with the unit, but you supply your own interior trim—again, to suit your own decor. Most manufacturers provide double or triple glazing with their glass doors, and large units are available with pre-assembled fan and sidelights.

Installation: Modern pre-assembled doors are a boon to do-it-yourselfers. They come already mounted on their hinges, eliminating the time-consuming work associated with leveling and hanging older doors. The doors are hung plumb in wood/vinyl shell frames. The shell frames are simply nailed or screwed through their jambs and exterior trim (brick mold) directly into the jack studs of the rough doorway frame. The nails or screws are not visible when the door is closed. Doors can be purchased with lock-sets and strikeplates in place, or with pre-cut openings for standard equipment. Some manufacturers offer all-steel frames that make entrances virtually burglar proof.

Look over several manufacturers' brochures before selecting your door. If you are installing a door in new construction—say, a converted garage or new wing—or cutting open a wall where no door had existed, first select your door and then frame the rough opening (r.o.) to fit the specifications in your manufacturer's catalog. If you are buying a replacement door—a new unit to replace an old existing door—carefully pry off interior trim around the door frame, measure the rough opening and buy a door to fit it. (The r.o. is usually 3 inches taller than the door itself, and 2½ inches wider; see p.128.)

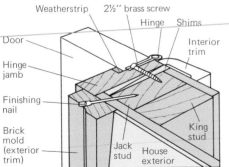

Cutaway shows installation details at jamb.

Door sizes: Standard door height is 6 feet 8 inches. Most manufacturers also produce 7-foot doors. Standard single door widths are 2 feet 8 inches, and 3 feet; standard double door widths are 5 feet 4 inches, and 6 feet.

Opening and framing the doorway

1. If enlarging a window opening for a doorway, remove interior trim, sashes, and wallboard first, then saw out exterior siding and sheathing down to foundation sill, as shown; finally, knock out window sill and cripple studs.

2. Rough-in header and jack studs (illustrations, opposite; p.128). These elements—together with rough sill (next step)—define the rough opening (r.o.); it must be squared and of right size to match door manufacturers' specifications.

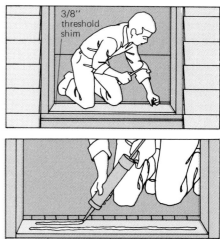

3. A wood shim (top) may be needed on sill to raise threshold of new door to level of interior finish floor (illustrations, opposite). Measure finish floor; shim by amount the thickness exceeds ⅜ in. Caulk sill with mastic (below); install door.

Installing a pre-hung door

1. From outside house, center pre-assembled entrance door unit in rough opening (r.o.) of doorway, with sill/threshold resting on the caulked rough sill or sill shim. A helper standing inside will make the following steps easier.

2. Do not open door. Using a carpenter's level to plumb hinge side of unit, tack through exterior trim (called brick mold) into jack stud. Use 16-penny galvanized finish nails. Start nails; then drive them home while plumbing jamb.

3. From inside the house, tap solid wood shims cut from scrap wood into the space between the hinge jamb and the jack stud. Insert a shim directly behind each hinge, adding shims at both the top and the bottom of the jamb.

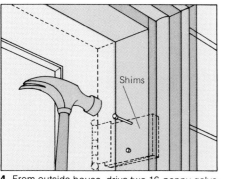

4. From outside house, drive two 16-penny galvanized finish nails through the hinge jamb into the jack stud at the location of each hinge. These nails pass through the wood shims inserted from inside house in previous step.

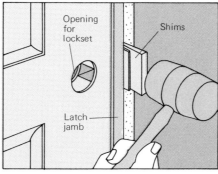

5. Working outside, weatherstrip lock jamb if no stripping is in place. Adjust jamb to get a seal between door and weatherstrip. Tack brick mold in place. Inside, shim behind strike plate, as shown, and at top and bottom of the jamb.

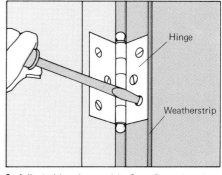

6. Adjust shims inserted in Step 5 to give clearance of ³⁄₃₂-in. between door and lock jamb. Nail through lock jamb and shims into jack stud. Complete nailing of brick mold. Finally, open door; drive long screws through empty holes in hinges.

Windows

General features

You can buy manufactured windows from window suppliers for almost any application. Traditional double-hung windows may be best suited to your budget and the style of your house, but fixed picture windows, as well as sliding, casement, and awning windows are available, as either single units (shown below) or in various combinations.

Window designs, materials: Manufactured windows with wooden frames are the least expensive and are good insulators. But they are prone to insect attack and rot, and they require periodic painting. Vinyl-clad windows—vinyl over a wood or aluminum core or frame—are more expensive, but never need repainting. Better-quality metal frames have vinyl or epoxy "thermal breaks" sandwiched between their inner and outer halves to reduce heat loss and sweating. Any metal frame—steel or aluminum—should have a plastic or baked-enamel coating to prevent corrosion. Double glazing is expensive, but it can eliminate the need for storm windows.

Metal channels in wood-frame double-hung windows prevent the sticking often caused by wood swelling and paint buildup over the years. Cleaning is the most frequent window maintenance chore. If the windows cannot be reached from the ground, look for designs that can be cleaned easily from inside.

The practical work: It is easier to replace a window if the new window is the same size as the old one. Measure the old window's rough opening (r.o.) and buy a replacement window that fits it. Since fitting a modern, standard-size window into the rough opening of an old, odd-sized window can be both costly and difficult, some firms offer custom-size windows.

If you are putting in windows in a new structure (see *Dormers*, pp.284–291; *Adding a Wing*, p.262), first select your windows, then frame the rough openings to the window manufacturer's specifications. Similarly, you can replace a small existing window with a larger window, including a bay window, by enlarging the rough opening. This may entail reinforcing the header and jack studs to support the greater load.

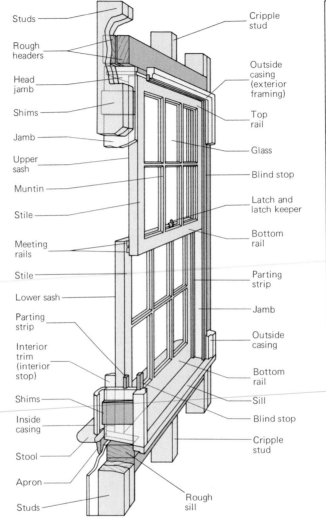

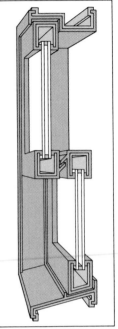

Thermal break aluminum windows are clad in vinyl. The vinyl provides snug weatherstripping, and insulates the metal to retard the loss of heat by conduction.

Window elements (left) are shown for a typical double-hung window. Manufacturers specify rough openings (r.o.) for their windows—the space defined by the rough sill, rough header, and studs at sides of opening.

Types of windows

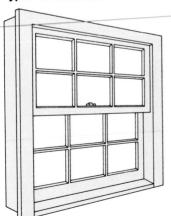

Double-hung window is an excellent ventilator. Raised lower sash admits cool air; lowered upper sash lets out hot air. If upper sash cannot move, unit is called single-hung.

Sliding window is like double-hung window turned on its side. For ease of cleaning, most models have removable sashes. You lift sash up and tilt bottom rail out of channel.

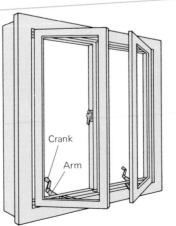

Casement window swings outward on hinges at top and bottom. Older versions are opened by hand, modern versions by a crank coupled to an extension arm.

Awning window swings out at bottom and keeps out rain when left open. If window swings out at top rather than at bottom, it is called a hopper window.

Installing a pre-assembled window

1. To install a same-size or larger window in place of an existing double-hung window, first pry off inside trim and remove the lower sash. Then pry off the parting strip and remove the upper sash. As you work, be careful that the sashes do not slip free and fall out. (Window parts are labeled on the large drawing on opposite page.)

2. After removing sashes from the inside, pry off the outside casing, jambs, and sill. At the same time, remove old caulking, paint, and nails. If new window is taller than the opening you have made, remove rough sill and cut cripple studs shorter. Level new rough sill with wood-scrap shims and nail it to cripple studs.

3. As helper holds and steadies new window, drive in nails part way, starting at the bottom corners and working upward. At the same time, block bottom of window and shim its sides. Drive in more nails, check window level, readjust blocks and shims. Do this until all nails are in, unit is square, and easily opens and closes. Nail permanently.

4. Attach trim board (outside casing) to cover gaps at sides. The trim board is shown being nailed in place at one side of the window. Prefabricated units often provide casing of a given width. If it does not fit, cut it to the proper width or carefully trim back your siding to make a neat fit. Trim interior as necessary. Caulk all joints.

Bay windows

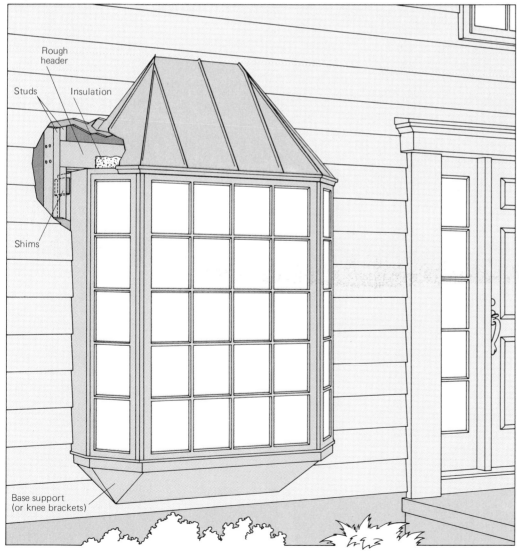

A bay window makes an attractive and sunny addition to any house. It contributes a sense of added space to a small room, and can provide a window seat or shelf for growing house plants. It offers a wide-angle view of your grounds.

A bay window can be bought as a single-piece prefabricated unit that is ready for installation. Various sizes are available, in widths ranging from 5 to 10 ft. The center window is usually fixed, while side windows open for cross ventilation. You can choose either 30° or 45° for the angle the side windows make with the house wall. Another variation, called a bow window, graduates the window segments to form an easy continuous curve. A prefabricated unit often does not include the decorative roof or knee brackets. If these brackets are structurally necessary, you will have to add them to the unit yourself.

A bay window is installed in much the same way as an ordinary one, as illustrated above, though the job is on a larger scale. You will have to enlarge the rough opening by first cutting away adjacent siding, sheathing, and studs, and then constructing a strong header to carry the load of the house above the window. The construction procedures are similar to those shown on pages 76–85, and may require a temporary support for the ceiling joists until the new header is in. Observe your local building code in all work you do.

A bay window is heavy. You will need two or three helpers to support it as you install it. Temporary props such as sawhorses help support the window during installation.

297

Enclosing a porch

A convenient way to gain added living space

Porches are always popular targets for renovation. Whether at the front, the side, or the back of the house, a porch can be enclosed to provide additional living space—a new bedroom, an expanded kitchen-dining area—or converted to a screened porch or a solarium for enjoying the insect-free out-of-doors or the healthful winter sunshine. These two pages illustrate the key steps involved in enclosing a porch to create a new room; page 300 describes solarium and screening construction.

Enclosing a porch is a particularly good beginner's project for a do-it-your-

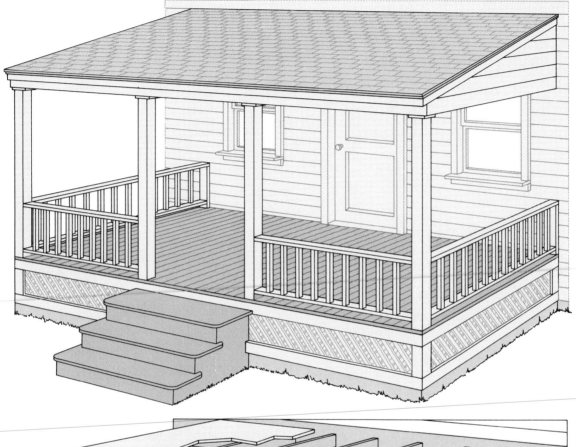

If the foundation, floor, and porch roof are sound, enclosing a porch to make a new room is comparatively easy. You can insulate the floor from the crawl space beneath the porch, as shown on page 361; the vapor barrier on the insulation should be face up. Support the roof while framing in new stud walls, as shown on the opposite page. After applying the siding of your choice, insulate between the wall studs and ceiling joists—if you erect a ceiling—or between the porch roof rafters. Lay all-weather carpeting on the floor, or apply a new finish floor of hardwood or vinyl. Finish the interior walls with plasterboard or paneling. These techniques are covered in appropriate chapters of this book. What you do with any windows in the house wall is up to you—cover them for privacy, or leave them for a sense of air and communication.

Joist
Bridging
4" x 4" pier
Girder
2 x 4s
Perimeter foundation

If a perimeter foundation has crumbled or settled, you may have to replace all or part of it. A new perimeter foundation can be excavated and poured under the porch, as suggested here and shown in step-by-step detail on pages 338–340. Note footing and pier in center of porch; piers may be needed to support a central girder. A pier can be a wood post on a concrete footing, or formed entirely of concrete.

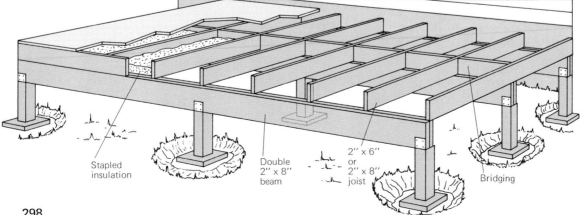

Stapled insulation
Double 2" x 8" beam
2" x 6" or 2" x 8" joist
Bridging

A pier foundation can be replaced completely or in part with concrete piers; you can make the forms yourself, or buy cylindrical paper forms at a lumberyard. As with the perimeter foundation shown above, footings must extend to below the local frost line in colder regions. A rotted sill, girder, or floor joists can be reinforced or replaced individually, or the whole floor can be ripped up and reframed.

selfer. Because a porch is attached to the house, no changes in building lines are necessary—meaning little or no trouble with zoning ordinances. (All new construction must meet standards estab-lished by your local building code, how-ever; see pp.21–37.) If the foundation and underfloor framing of the porch are sound, and if the roof does not leak, you will begin the project with the most costly and difficult work of a completely new addition already in place. You need only support the roof while framing in and finishing new walls, as shown in the two illustrations below.

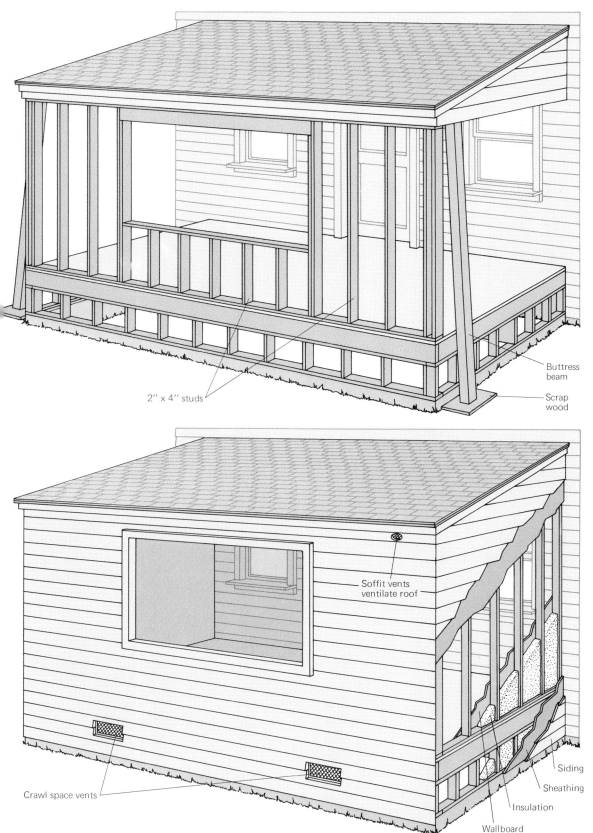

2″ x 4″ studs

Buttress beam

Scrap wood

Soffit vents ventilate roof

Crawl space vents

Wallboard

Insulation

Sheathing

Siding

Support the porch roof with a pair of 4-x-4 posts at either outside corner, using scrap wood to give the posts a firm base. With the roof thus braced, remove the existing porch rails and columns. Build stud walls to frame in the porch as described on pages 86–87, including any doors or windows, as described on pages 294–297.

Conventional frames use 2-x-4 studs spaced 16-in. on center (o.c.). If your local building code allows it, and you live in a cold climate, consider framing the walls with 2 x 6s 24-in. o.c. The 2 x 6s provide a deeper cavity for insulation. Floor joists should also be insulated, as shown on the opposite page and on page 361.

When you are ready to lift the walls into place, re-position the temporary roof braces to raise the porch roof about ½-in.; this facilitates slipping the frames into position.

Plywood sheathing and siding are applied to the walls as seen here and described in detail on pages 264–268. Gutters and downspouts (p.269) are attached, if they are not already on the roof. Drainage for downspouts can be provided by dry wells (p.320), which you dig yourself. Here, the wall insulation is shown in cutaway; in practice, the insulation is put in only after the walls have been closed on the outside with sheathing and siding. Fiberglass blankets or batts are stapled between the studs, the vapor barrier facing inward. Other chapters of this book describe the window, wallboard, floor, ceiling, electrical, and plumbing work required to finish the porch.

Enclosing a porch

Screening a porch

A screened-in porch offers all the pleasures of being outside in shade in warm weather, with the same protection against rain and insects you enjoy inside your home. Screening a porch is a relatively simple and inexpensive project to undertake.

Permanent screens are available in such materials as aluminum, fiberglass, and vinyl. Weather does not affect them at all, even if they are left up all year round. A framework, typically of 2-x-3- or 2-x-4-inch lumber, is installed in all the openings of the porch. The lumber should be cedar, redwood, or a good stock that you treat with a preservative.

Working procedure: Screens are stapled to their own individual frames, generally made of 1-x-4 stock, and finally the framed screens are fastened to the porch framework. If you prefer you can make removable screen frames, installing moldings around the inside edges of the porch frame. The moldings are set back a distance equal to the screen frame width from the edges of the porch frame. Metal turn buttons hold the screens in place. This arrangement lets you replace screens with lightweight acrylic windows in winter.

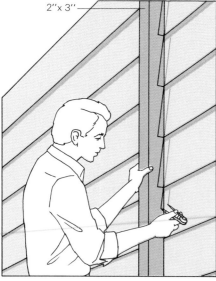

Porch frame of 2-x-3 lumber follows contours of siding and ornamental columns to which it will be attached. Hold stud to siding or column. Set a compass for the widest gap between the stud and existing surfaces. Follow contour so pencil scribes same line on stud. Saw stud along line.

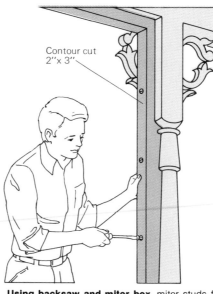

Using backsaw and miter box, miter studs for the porch frame to match sole and top plates of frame. (Or join studs to plates at right angles without mitering.) Screw contour-cut studs to the clapboards and columns. Screen can be stapled directly to frame, or to individual screen frames.

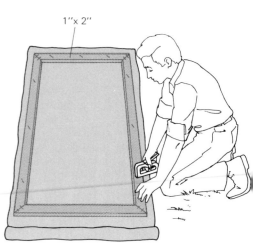

For removable screen frames use 1 x 3s or 1 x 4s. Miter cut ends of each piece, then join with waterproof glue, end nails, and corrugated fasteners. Staple on screen. Cover staples with lattice or molding. Add molding stops to porch frame, with turn buttons to hold screen frames.

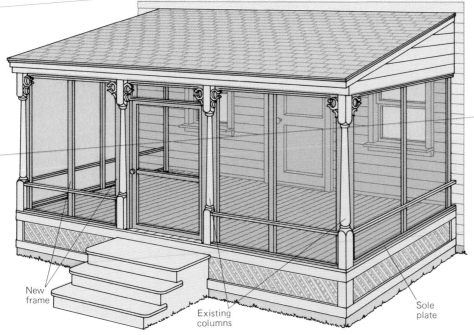

Elements of the porch frame: Sole plate, the bottom member of the frame, should have small weepholes to allow water to drain off porch floor. Porch doorway is typically framed with 2-x-3 lumber with the door itself of the same size lumber. Feathered or splined miter joints (see right) are best for a door that undergoes regular stress; the door should have at least one interior cross brace. Molding is used to form a doorstop on the doorframe (see pp.126–127). Loose-pin hinges are good if the door is to be replaced in winter by an insulating acrylic storm door.

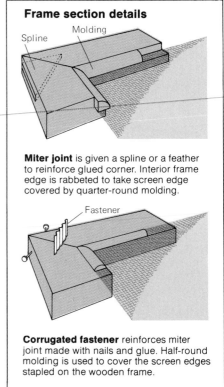

Frame section details

Miter joint is given a spline or a feather to reinforce glued corner. Interior frame edge is rabbeted to take screen edge covered by quarter-round molding.

Corrugated fastener reinforces miter joint made with nails and glue. Half-round molding is used to cover the screen edges stapled on the wooden frame.

Building an A-frame cabin

Basic problems and solutions

An A-frame cabin is a basic structure that someone with carpentry experience can build with the timely assistance of helpers. The compact model illustrated here stresses the full use of limited space. The living area has built-in sofas that double as beds, book shelves, a closet, and a storage loft over the bathroom and kitchen. In larger A-frames the loft becomes a sleeping area.

The wood-burning stove's location on the center line assures full distribution of heat. The insulated metal stovepipe and triple-walled metal chimney, plus a heat shield, provide fire protection.

Other chapters cover all construction details, including framing, shingling, dormer construction, installing tile and plumbing, and the building of chimneys, decks, and piers. Typically, the two pairs of end rafters are put together flat, with scrap-wood spacers in place of a ridge board. The ends are then raised, held in place with temporary supports, and nailed; next, the ridge board is nailed in, and the intermediate rafters are installed in pairs.

Vertical section: The A-frame rests on poured-concrete piers that must extend below frost line. Pouring of the piers is easier with aid of prefabricated cylindrical forms. Headroom is obtained by placing all plumbing on outside walls and adding a dormer.

Floor plan: A-frame's exterior is 20 x 20 ft; cabin's interior is 19 x 12 ft. Even so compact a cabin offers adequate space in which several vacationers can live, sleep, eat, and cook, with some activity centered on the deck.

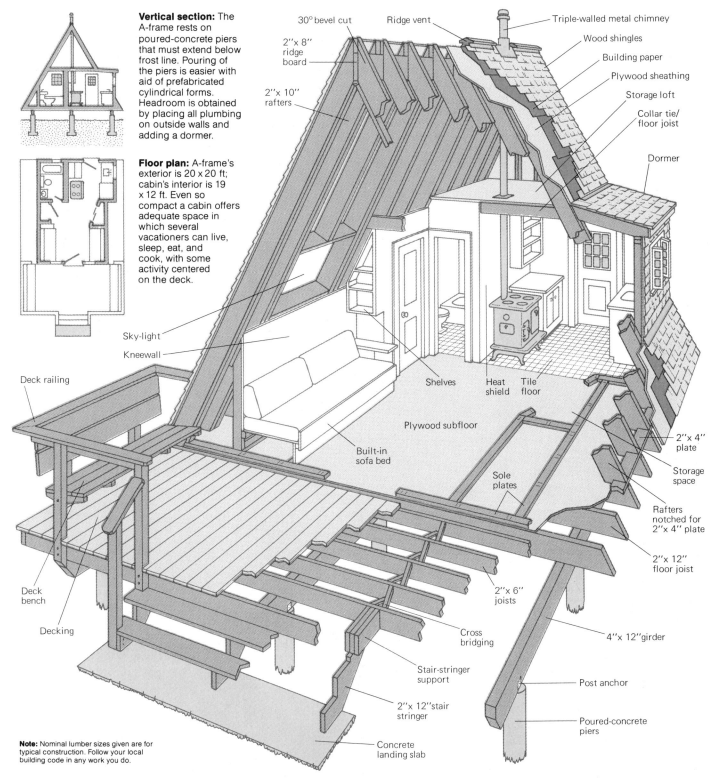

30° bevel cut

Ridge vent

Triple-walled metal chimney

2'' x 8'' ridge board

Wood shingles

Building paper

2'' x 10'' rafters

Plywood sheathing

Storage loft

Collar tie/ floor joist

Dormer

Sky-light

Kneewall

Deck railing

Shelves

Heat shield

Tile floor

Built-in sofa bed

Plywood subfloor

2'' x 4'' plate

Storage space

Sole plates

Rafters notched for 2'' x 4'' plate

2'' x 12'' floor joist

Deck bench

Decking

2'' x 6'' joists

Cross bridging

Stair-stringer support

4'' x 12'' girder

Post anchor

2'' x 12'' stair stringer

Poured-concrete piers

Concrete landing slab

Note: Nominal lumber sizes given are for typical construction. Follow your local building code in any work you do.

301

Wood decks

Planning a deck

A carefully designed deck can substantially increase the living space of your house and make the outdoors more accessible for relaxation, dining, and recreation. Begin planning by making a list of how you will use your deck, such as an outdoor dining space, a pool or fountain, a children's play area, or a barbecue. Consider all the possible sites, keeping in mind how much space you need, privacy desired, sun and shade patterns, and access. It is easiest to build on a flat area, but a deck, unlike a patio, can be designed to accommodate even the hilliest sites. For some ideas, look at the color photographs on pages 232–233. Once you have a rough idea of what you want, draw your plans to scale on graph paper (see p.304).

Building codes: Many construction and materials details for decks are specified in local codes, and permits are often required, so it is essential that you consult your local building department before you begin (see *Building codes/An introduction to construction*, pp.21–37). Because code specifications include such diverse items as allowable sites, depth of footings, height of railings, lumber dimensions, joist spans, and much more, the information given throughout this chapter is for typical construction. You must be sure that your plans satisfy your local code.

Wood and hardware: When you have final detailed plans, including a framing diagram (right), estimate what materials you will need (see *Ordering materials and estimating costs*, p.48). For a deck, choosing the wood will be your most important decision. Only woods designated for outdoor use will adequately resist rot. Some woods, such as redwood, western red cedar, and cypress, are naturally rot resistant and very attractive, but they are expensive. Softwoods can be rendered extremely rot resistant by forcing preservative chemicals deep into the wood under high pressure. Such pressure-treated wood is relatively inexpensive, but it has a distinctive green color. Your lumberyard can tell you what outdoor woods are suitable for your area. Hardware for a deck must be rustproof. Use stainless steel, hot-dipped galvanized steel, or aluminum alloy fasteners.

Once you have plans, permits, and materials, start to work. Whether you are planning a simple deck at ground level or a multilevel deck with many built-in features, the basic elements are illustrated on the next six pages.

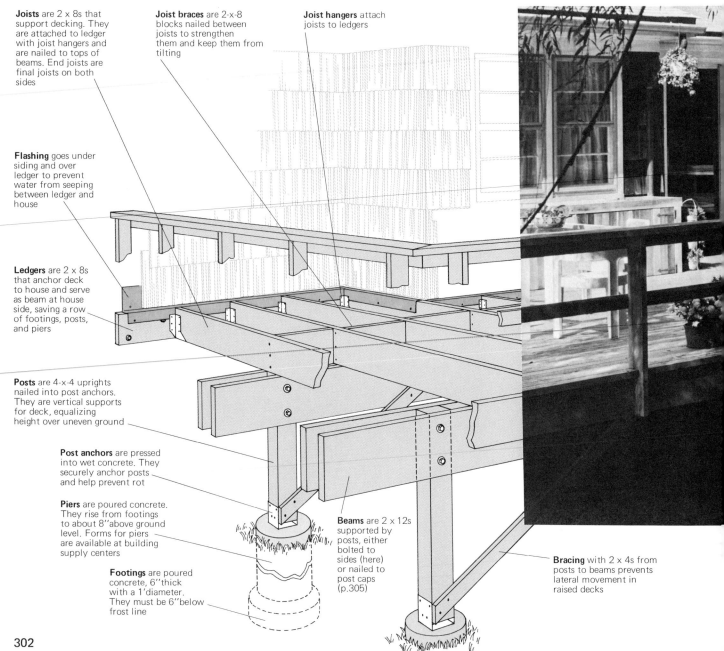

Joists are 2 x 8s that support decking. They are attached to ledger with joist hangers and are nailed to tops of beams. End joists are final joists on both sides

Joist braces are 2-x-8 blocks nailed between joists to strengthen them and keep them from tilting

Joist hangers attach joists to ledgers

Flashing goes under siding and over ledger to prevent water from seeping between ledger and house

Ledgers are 2 x 8s that anchor deck to house and serve as beam at house side, saving a row of footings, posts, and piers

Posts are 4-x-4 uprights nailed into post anchors. They are vertical supports for deck, equalizing height over uneven ground

Post anchors are pressed into wet concrete. They securely anchor posts and help prevent rot

Piers are poured concrete. They rise from footings to about 8"above ground level. Forms for piers are available at building supply centers

Footings are poured concrete, 6"thick with a 1'diameter. They must be 6"below frost line

Beams are 2 x 12s supported by posts, either bolted to sides (here) or nailed to post caps (p.305)

Bracing with 2 x 4s from posts to beams prevents lateral movement in raised decks

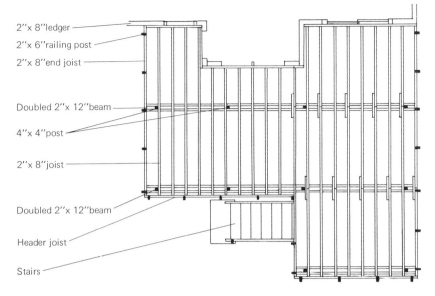

2″x 8″ ledger
2″x 6″ railing post
2″x 8″ end joist

Doubled 2″x 12″ beam

4″x 4″ post

2″x 8″ joist

Doubled 2″x 12″ beam

Header joist

Stairs

A framing diagram shows all the supporting members of the deck in correct proportion to each other. The lumber dimensions are all labeled, as are distances between posts, beams, and joists. With a proper framing diagram, you can determine whether the support system for your deck will meet building code specifications.

This diagram is for the deck illustrated below. For other construction techniques, see page 305. Here, the 4-x-4 posts are set 7–10 ft. apart. They support doubled 2-x-12 beams, which are bolted to the sides of the posts. The beams are 8 ft. (o.c.). The house side is supported by 2-x-8 ledgers instead of posts and beams. The joists, 16 in. (o.c.), are 2 x 8s; they attach to the ledgers with joist hangers and are toenailed to the tops of the beams. Where the joists must run more than 20 ft. (the longest standard-dimension lumber), they are spliced together with wood gussets made of 2 x 8s. The header joists, also 2 x 8s, are nailed to the ends of the joists and the 2-x-6 railing posts are bolted to the end joists and header joists.

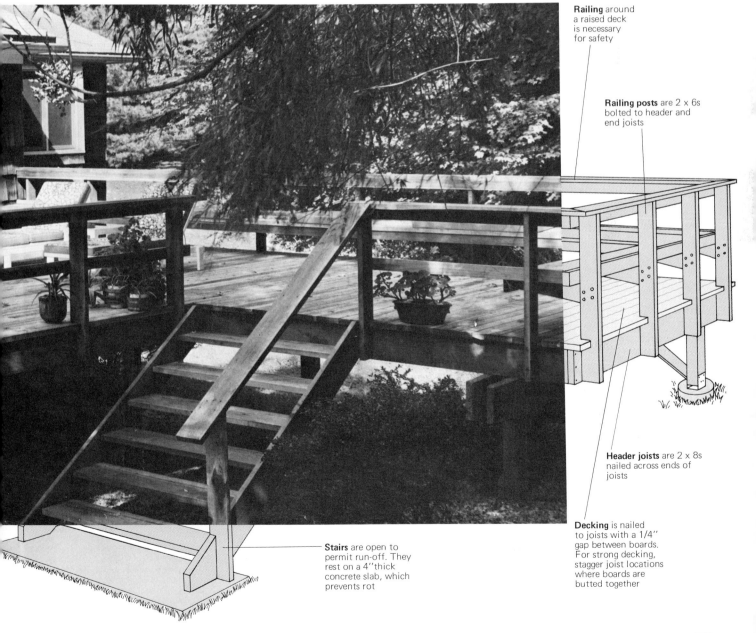

Railing around a raised deck is necessary for safety

Railing posts are 2 x 6s bolted to header and end joists

Header joists are 2 x 8s nailed across ends of joists

Decking is nailed to joists with a 1/4″ gap between boards. For strong decking, stagger joist locations where boards are butted together

Stairs are open to permit run-off. They rest on a 4″ thick concrete slab, which prevents rot

Wood decks

Basic steps in building a deck

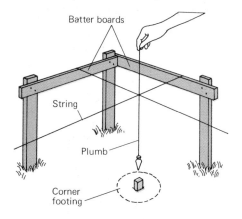

Batter boards
String
Plumb
Corner footing

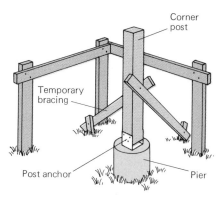

Corner post
Temporary bracing
Post anchor
Pier

1. Lay out lines indicating the centers of the corner posts as shown in *Site preparation*, page 244. Mark the locations of any underground septic, water, gas, or electric pipe or conduit. Mark the position of each footing along your guide lines, making sure the footings line up perfectly and will not interfere with utility pipes.

2. Remove the strings but leave the batter boards in place. With a post-hole digger, dig the holes for the concrete footings and piers to the depth and size specified in your code (p.22). If the earth is fill, compact it to provide a firm base. Mix the concrete (see *Determining your concrete needs*, p.246) and pour the footings.

3. Replace strings on batter boards to center the piers and post anchors precisely. Pour the piers into forms set on the footings, and press post anchors into the piers. The piers should rise 8 in. above ground. When the concrete has set, fit the posts into the anchors, plumb the posts with a level, nail them in place, and brace them.

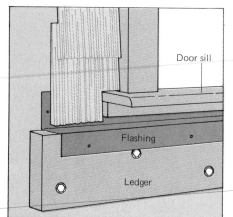

Door sill
Flashing
Ledger

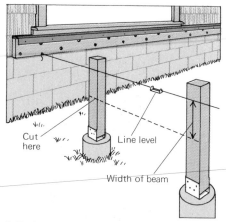

Cut here
Line level
Width of beam

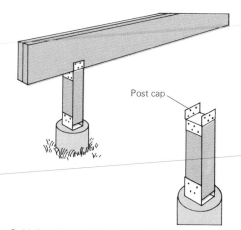

Post cap

4. To position the ledger, measure down 1 in. plus the thickness of the decking from the bottom of the door sill. Level ledger and bolt it to the house (use lag screws for wood or stucco, expansion bolts for brick). The ledger must extend 2 in. beyond the last joist, to allow for the joist hangers. Flash ledger to prevent rot.

5. To determine the heights of the posts, set nails in the bottom of the ledger in line with each row of posts. Run string from the nails to the last post and level the string with a line level (see p.244). Mark the posts where they meet the string, then subtract the width of the beams. Mark and cut the posts at these points.

6. Nail post caps to the tops of the posts so that the beams fit into the caps parallel to the ledger. Set the beams in place and nail them to the upper section of the post caps. The tops of the beams will be at the same height as the bottom of the ledger. (Note: A different method of attaching beams is shown on pp.302–303.)

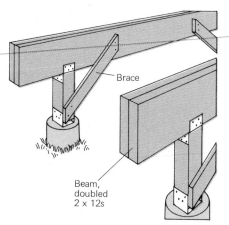

Brace
Beam, doubled 2 x 12s

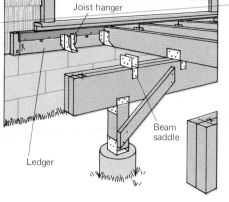

Joist hanger
Ledger
Beam saddle

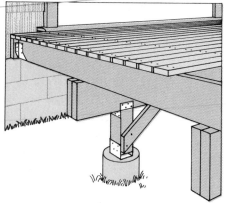

7. If the deck is raised more than 2 ft. off the ground, brace the posts and beams to prevent lateral movement. The most solid type of brace forms a 45° right triangle with the post and beam. Use 2 x 4s for the braces, nailing one end to the side of the post and the other end to the side of its respective beam all along the deck.

8. Carefully measure and mark the points where the joist will cross the beams and butt the ledger (see *Allowable spans for floor joists*, p.37). Set beam saddles on the beams where they will support the joists. Fit the joists into the beam saddles and joist hangers. When all the hardware and joists are in place, nail everything.

9. Nail header joists to the joist ends. Lay the decking, leaving a ¼-in. gap between boards for runoff. Use two nails at each joist. Measure as you work so that any necessary adjustments can be made gradually. To make straight edges, snap a chalk line (see p.288) along ends of the boards and cut along the lines with a power saw.

Designing a custom deck

This barn-style kit house, built with timbers, was positioned to take maximum advantage of a lovely view, and the deck was designed to augment these features. The local building code required that any section more than 2 feet off the ground have a 3-foot railing. This would have interfered with the view, so a multilevel deck close to the ground was chosen (only one short section has a railing). Reclaimed rafters from an old mill were used as planking, in keeping with the wood used for the house. Varying the angle of the planking in different areas creates interesting visual effects; these patterns, along with the level changes, give the deck its custom-designed flavor. A children's pool built into the far corner keeps the play area separated yet visible from the main deck.

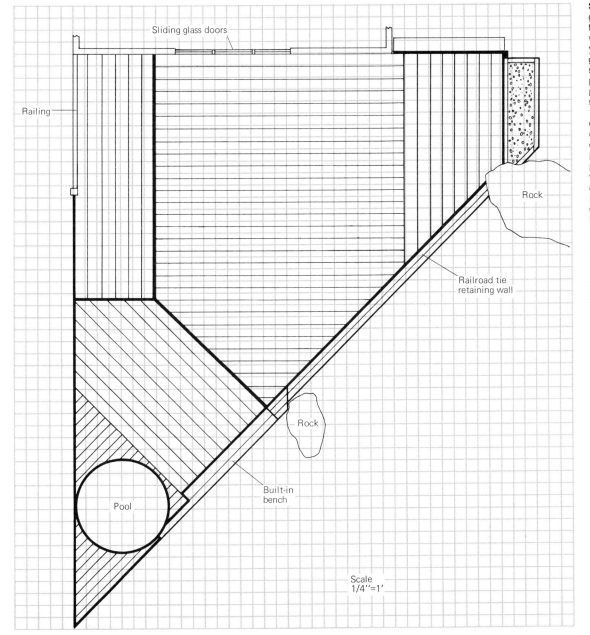

Sliding glass doors

Railing

Rock

Railroad tie retaining wall

Rock

Built-in bench

Pool

Scale
1/4"=1'

Scale drawings on graph paper allow you to see how your plans will actually fit in with your house and grounds, sometimes suggesting changes or pointing up unforeseen problems. A good scale to use is ¼ in. = 1 ft., which is large enough to show details clearly but is small enough to fit the whole plan on one sheet of paper. If you have a variety of ideas, try all of them out on graph paper until you are completely satisfied. Be sure to include any large trees that might shade the deck, rocks too big to move that must be built around, and any other special features of your site. When determining the final dimensions of the deck, adjust your plans to utilize standard-size lumber; this will save materials, labor, and time during actual construction.

Wood decks

Modular decking

Modules offer a simple method of building a flexible deck that can be moved, altered, or stored away whenever necessary. Each module is a self-contained 3-foot-square platform. These are laid out in any desired pattern with the edges butted together; their weight keeps them in place. A modular deck can be set in a bed of gravel and sand (2 inches of gravel covered with 2 inches of sand) or on top of an existing concrete patio you want to cover. The modules can be positioned around a tree to provide shade, or one square can be removed to accommodate a small garden or pool.

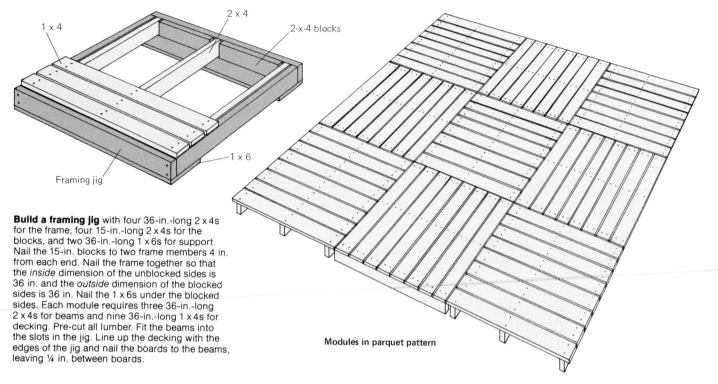

Build a framing jig with four 36-in.-long 2 x 4s for the frame, four 15-in.-long 2 x 4s for the blocks, and two 36-in.-long 1 x 6s for support. Nail the 15-in. blocks to two frame members 4 in. from each end. Nail the frame together so that the *inside* dimension of the unblocked sides is 36 in. and the *outside* dimension of the blocked sides is 36 in. Nail the 1 x 6s under the blocked sides. Each module requires three 36-in.-long 2 x 4s for beams and nine 36-in.-long 1 x 4s for decking. Pre-cut all lumber. Fit the beams into the slots in the jig. Line up the decking with the edges of the jig and nail the boards to the beams, leaving ¼ in. between boards.

Modules in parquet pattern

Finishing details

A variety of built-in features can be added to a basic deck, either to meet building code requirements or to add special touches, or both. Two of the constructions shown, the extended-post railing and the tree cutout, must be included in the original plans because they require changes in the deck's structure. The others can all be added later, including the stairs (if, for example, you want to add ground-level access to a second-story deck). If you want to cover your deck or screen it in, calculate how much extra weight the deck can support before building.

Railings

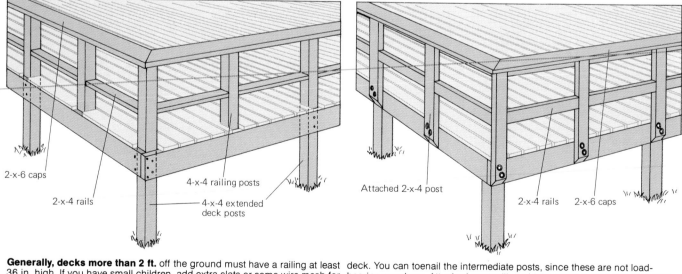

Generally, decks more than 2 ft. off the ground must have a railing at least 36 in. high. If you have small children, add extra slats or some wire mesh for safety. There are two ways of supporting a railing so that it has adequate structural strength. Extended-post railings (left) use the same posts that support the deck to support the railing. If you plan this kind of railing, omit Step 5 shown on page 304. Instead, bolt the beams to the sides of the posts as shown on page 302 and use posts long enough to rise 36 in. above the deck. You can toenail the intermediate posts, since these are not load-bearing members. Attached-post railings (right) can be added to any deck. Bolt the posts to the header joists and outside joists with carriage bolts, using two offset bolts per post. In both railings, toenail the intermediate rails to the posts, nail the top rail to the inside of and flush with the tops of the posts, and nail the cap to the tops of the posts. All work must conform to local building codes.

Benches

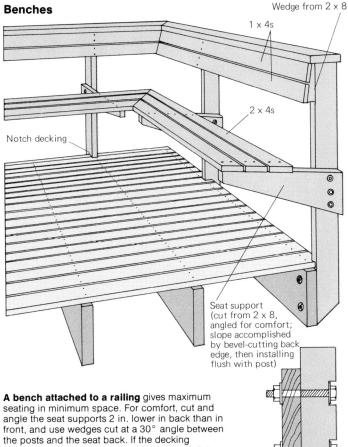

Wedge from 2 x 8

1 x 4s

2 x 4s

Notch decking

Seat support
(cut from 2 x 8,
angled for comfort;
slope accomplished
by bevel-cutting back
edge, then installing
flush with post)

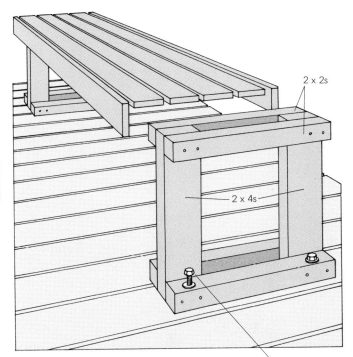

2 x 2s

2 x 4s

Carriage bolts
through decking

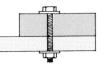

A bench attached to a railing gives maximum seating in minimum space. For comfort, cut and angle the seat supports 2 in. lower in back than in front, and use wedges cut at a 30° angle between the posts and the seat back. If the decking overhangs the header and end joists, notch it to accommodate the posts. For added strength, bolt the posts to the joists with hex-head bolts and use washers under nuts and bolts. Drill recesses to prevent the bolts from protruding.

This simple, sturdy bench can also be used as a plant stand or low table. The benches are bolted to the decking with only four carriage bolts each, so they can easily be rearranged. Use long, heavy-duty nails with large heads to hold the bases together. Nail the seat and edging boards to the bases. If you do not want to bolt the benches to the decking, brace the bases with diagonal 2 x 4s from the bottom of one base to the top of the other to prevent lateral movement.

Stairs

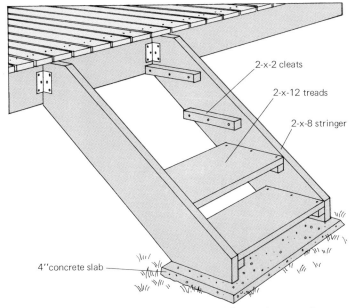

2-x-2 cleats

2-x-12 treads

2-x-8 stringer

4"concrete slab

Width of treads (not less than 9 in.) and vertical distance between risers (not more than 8 in.) must be exactly the same for every step, or someone might trip. Attach the stringers to the deck with framing anchors. Set the bottoms of the stringers on a concrete slab to prevent rot. Very carefully measure the positions for the cleats, level them, and nail them to the stringers. Nail the treads to the cleats. If you have more than a few steps, continue the deck railing on the stairs.

Tree cutouts

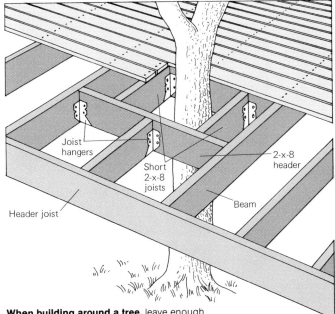

Joist
hangers

Short
2-x-8
joists

2-x-8
header

Beam

Header joist

When building around a tree, leave enough room for the tree to grow and to move when the wind blows. Attach headers with joist hangers to the full-length joists on both sides of the tree; then fit short joists from the beams to the headers with joist hangers. Nail the decking to the full and short joists.

Paths, patios, barbecues

Construction alternatives for paths and patios

A patio or garden path enhances any backyard, making it more conducive to outdoor living. Brick or natural stone can be set in mortar for a smooth, durable surface, or set in sand for a casual patio or a winding path where a smooth surface is not required. In cold climates where frost causes the ground to swell, bricks or stones should be set with mortar on a base that includes a layer of wire-mesh reinforced concrete and a layer of grout (see bottom drawing).

Lay out the patio area with string and stakes, and dig out the dirt. The depth of the excavation, ranging from 4½ to 10 inches, will depend on whether mortar is used and on how thick the base is. If the ground slopes or is exceptionally

uneven, you should stake 1-x-10 edge boards around the perimeter of the excavation for added support.

For bricks set in sand: Excavate to a depth of about 4½ inches. To aid drainage, slope a patio away from the house about ⅛ to ¼ inch per foot; if the patio does not adjoin the house or garage, make the highest point in the center and create a slope out to the sides. On level lawns, slope paths slightly to one side.

For a patio, pour in a layer of sand to a depth of about 2 inches. Tamp it down. You can put down under the sand a layer of heavy building paper impregnated with weed killer to discourage weeds. Lay the bricks in the sand in the desired pattern, starting at one edge and work-

ing to the opposite edge. (For brick and flagstone patterns, see p.310.) Spread sand and sweep it over the bricks until all the joints are filled.

For a path, excavate 5½ inches of dirt. To form the border, set bricks on edge along each side of the trench. Fill the center of the trench with sand to a depth of 2 inches, and lay the bricks. Fill the joints between bricks with sand.

For brick or stone set in mortar: The construction alternatives are shown below, and step-by-step procedure is illustrated opposite. In cold climates, the area must be excavated to a depth below the frost line, and a layer of reinforced concrete must be placed between the crushed stone and grout.

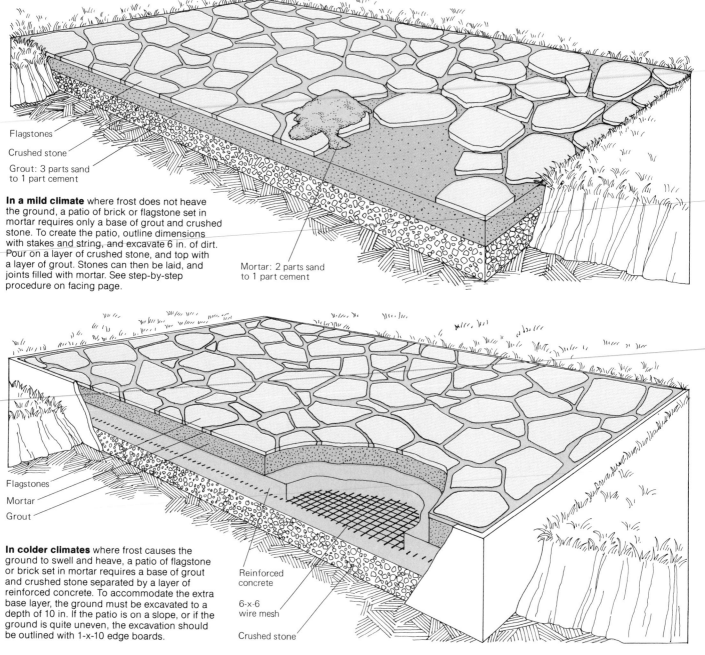

Flagstones
Crushed stone
Grout: 3 parts sand to 1 part cement

In a mild climate where frost does not heave the ground, a patio of brick or flagstone set in mortar requires only a base of grout and crushed stone. To create the patio, outline dimensions with stakes and string, and excavate 6 in. of dirt. Pour on a layer of crushed stone, and top with a layer of grout. Stones can then be laid, and joints filled with mortar. See step-by-step procedure on facing page.

Mortar: 2 parts sand to 1 part cement

Flagstones
Mortar
Grout

In colder climates where frost causes the ground to swell and heave, a patio of flagstone or brick set in mortar requires a base of grout and crushed stone separated by a layer of reinforced concrete. To accommodate the extra base layer, the ground must be excavated to a depth of 10 in. If the patio is on a slope, or if the ground is quite uneven, the excavation should be outlined with 1-x-10 edge boards.

Reinforced concrete
6-x-6 wire mesh
Crushed stone

Brick or flagstone set in mortar

1. When you have decided on the dimensions of your patio, outline its perimeter by driving stakes into the ground and connecting them with string. Excavate about 6 in. of dirt. To excavate for a patio in a colder climate, see text and bottom drawing opposite. If the patio is on a slope or if the ground is especially uneven, you can use a permanent edging of treated 1-x-10 boards to help support the layers of gravel and sand. For a more detailed discussion on the subject of working with crushed stone, cement, and concrete, see pages 246–247.

2. Cover the area with crushed stone to a depth of 3½ in. (p.48). Level with a board and pack down firmly. In cold climates, pour 4 in. of concrete on top of crushed stone, and sink in a 6-x-6 wire mesh reinforcement (pp.250–251). Roughen the surface with a rake.

3. On top of the crushed stone, add a layer of sand or damp grout composed of three parts sand to one part cement. You will have to mix the grout yourself—to the consistency of damp sand. Smooth it off to a level that leaves enough space for the thickness of the stones you will lay.

4. Beginning in one corner of the patio, lay the stones in the pattern you have chosen (see p.310 for a selection of patterns). Work from one edge to the opposite edge, leaving ½-in. joint spaces between the stones. Stagger the stones to avoid any long lines of continuous joints.

5. Tamp each stone into place with a heavy piece of wood such as an old 4 x 4 or ax handle. Use a level to make sure that each stone is level. If some stones are not level, you can put additional grout or sand under the thinner stones and remove grout from under the thicker ones.

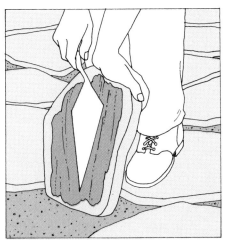

6. After leveling the stones, turn up each one individually and coat the underside with a mixture of Portland cement and water. This mixture should have the consistency of heavy cream. It acts as an adhesive, bonding with the materials that compose the underlying grout.

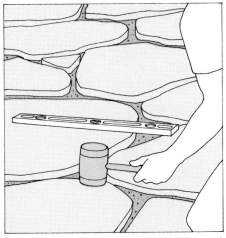

7. Lay down each stone, tamp it again lightly, and check to make sure it is level. Continue this procedure until all the stones have had cement applied and are tamped into place. Allow the cement to set overnight before mortaring the joints between the stones.

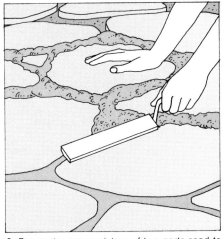

8. For mortar use a mixture of two parts sand to one part cement. Trowel this into joints with a jointing tool (pp.314–315), pressing the mortar down firmly. When mortar hardens, rub off any excess with a dry cloth. Use a wet sponge to clean each stone; do not touch mortar with sponge.

Paths, patios, barbecues

Patterns of brick and flagstone

The drawings below show some traditional paving patterns for brick or flagstone patios and garden paths. Which pattern you use will depend on the arrangement that appeals to you, on how experienced you are in laying bricks or flagstones, and on the amount of time you want to spend on the project. To help you determine which pattern to choose, you can use old bricks, or purchase enough new bricks to lay out several repeats of a design. If the work seems too time-consuming, choose one of the simpler patterns below, or create a pattern of your own.

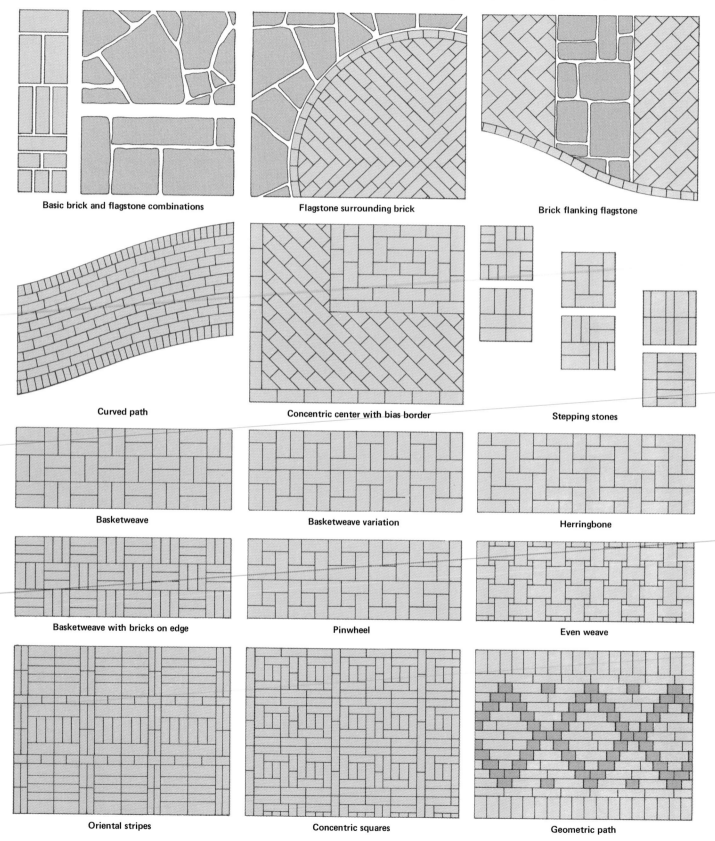

Basic brick and flagstone combinations

Flagstone surrounding brick

Brick flanking flagstone

Curved path

Concentric center with bias border

Stepping stones

Basketweave

Basketweave variation

Herringbone

Basketweave with bricks on edge

Pinwheel

Even weave

Oriental stripes

Concentric squares

Geometric path

A brick barbecue

To build this brick barbecue, purchase a cooking grill and a fire grate and use these to determine the dimensions of the barbecue. (A fire grate is similar to a cooking grill, but the rods are closer together.) The barbecue is built with fire brick for the cavity and SW grade brick for the exterior. The storage bin shown has both a top and base of poured concrete. For the door and doorframe, cedar is the most weather-resistant, but pine and fir are also durable. There are three separate levels for the cooking grill. The fire grate is removable so a fire can be built directly on the bricks.

If your patio has a sturdy base, you can use it as the foundation for the barbecue, otherwise you will need a slab. To make the slab, remove sod and soil to a depth of 4 inches. Level the ground, and then cover it with crushed stone. Build a form with 2 x 4s set on edge. Use 1:2½:3½ concrete (see p.246).

Storage bin: Cast the top for the storage bin at the same time that you make the base slab, using the same concrete mix. Make a form of scrap wood. Cut an extra piece of scrap the same size as the top of the doorframe and set it in the front edge of the form to make the doorframe indentation. Place the form on a flat surface, and fill it with concrete. Allow concrete to cure.

Cut the doorframe sides; then drive nails through them (see drawing, bottom left). When the base slab has cured, begin the bricklaying (see pp.312–315). After the first course of bricks are laid, fill the base of the storage bin with the same concrete mix used for the slab.

Bent rod supports: Supports for the cooking grill and the fire grate use lengths of ⅜- or ½-inch steel rods. Bend one end of the rod; the short end will be anchored in the side of the cavity and the long end in the back wall. Set the bent rod supports for the fire grate into the mortar joints between bricks after the third course of bricks are laid. Set the supports for the cooking grill into the mortar after the fifth, sixth, and seventh courses. Set the doorframe sides in place, pushing the nails into the wet mortar.

Doorframe: Nail the doorframe top to the sides as seen below, left. Place the concrete storage bin top in the mortar bed on the sixth course. Spread mortar and lay bricks over it. To make the door, cross strips are clinch-nailed to hold the door panels; nail from the outside with 2-inch galvanized nails. Attach a door pull, then secure the door to the frame, as shown below, right. Many people like to prepare the food right where it is cooked. If you prefer a butcher block work surface next to the grill, build the bin's top of heavy planking. Lay the wood on the mortar bed after the seventh course; lay the eighth course around the grill only, and make a higher storage bin door for the larger opening.

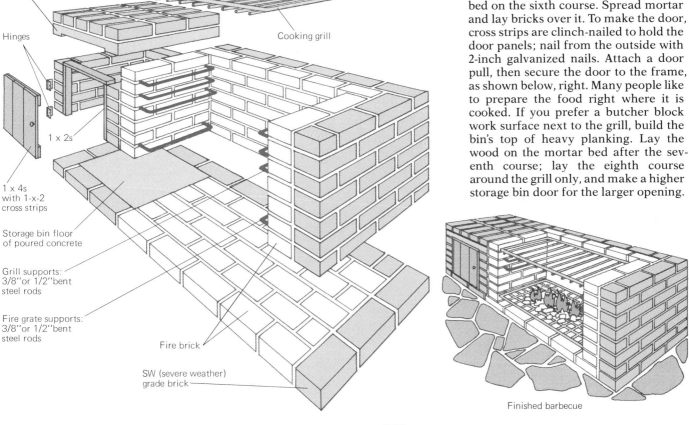

Concrete slab for top of storage bin

Hinges

Cooking grill

1 x 2s

1 x 4s with 1-x-2 cross strips

Storage bin floor of poured concrete

Grill supports: 3/8"or 1/2"bent steel rods

Fire grate supports: 3/8"or 1/2"bent steel rods

Fire brick

SW (severe weather) grade brick

Finished barbecue

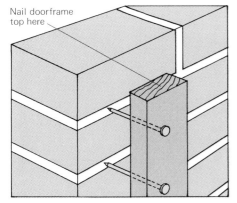

Nail doorframe top here

For doorframe sides, cut 1 x 4s to the desired length. Drill holes through wood and use screws and lead anchors or masonry nails to fasten the wood to the wall, if the mortar is dry. Or space galvanized nails as shown, and after the sixth course of bricks are laid, set the doorframe sides in place, pushing the nails into the still-wet mortar.

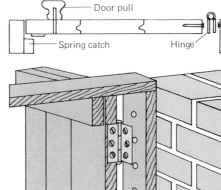

Door pull

Spring catch

Hinge

To attach the door to the doorframe use two butt hinges. Screw one side of each hinge to the edge of the door. Then place the door in position and screw the opposite face of the hinges to the doorframe sides. Attach a spring catch inside the door.

Brick garden walls

Design for utility, build for durability

Your choice of design for a garden wall should reflect the use you plan for the wall. A garden wall designed to keep an auto out of your flowers would need far more strength than one planned to keep rabbits out of your lettuce. The greater the wall's strength, the greater its cost.

Running and open bond walls have only one thickness of brick. American and English bond are of double thickness. All the stronger walls use more bricks per linear yard, and require a sound foundation—reaching below the frost line in cold climates. If set on a slope, the foundation must be stepped

with mortar rising 3 inches in height; this assures that the bricks at the base of the wall have no direct contact with moisture in the soil (see p.242).

Bricks and mortar mixtures: Use either SW (severe weathering) or MW

Course alignment line at built-up corner

(medium weathering) bricks, depending on the extremes of your climate. You can set your courses of brick with prepared dry mix mortar. Or, if the wall is large, you can save money by mixing your own mortar to either of the following formulas: 1 part masonry cement, 3 parts sand; or, 1 part Portland cement, 1 part hydrated lime, 6 parts sand. Mix the dry ingredients with water, added a little at a time, until the mortar takes on a uniform texture (see pp.248–249).

If you are going to build a wall that will last, your best insurance is to use the best quality materials, correctly.

Brick garden walls

Lay out, excavate, and pour concrete footing for wall as discussed on pages 242–245. Wet bricks thoroughly with spray from garden hose, and lay ½-in. bed of mortar for first course. With first course in place, build up two leads, or levels of brick, at each corner, the top lead shorter. Insert course alignment pins and line to guide laying of second course.

All mortar joints are ½-in. thick. Use a 4-ft.-long bubble level as a straightedge to check each brick. Bubble level assures that the entire course is level; keep it clean, since the smallest chunk of mortar stuck to the edge can affect your alignment. The same is true of bits of hardened mortar on brick; clean bricks as you work.

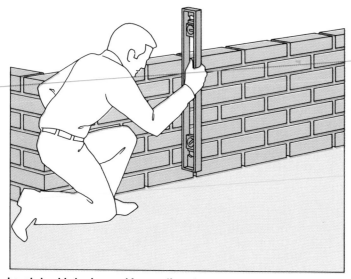

Level should also be used frequently on face of wall to insure that courses of brick are in true vertical. The level's straightedge will tell you if bricks are in transverse alignment, or must be tapped flush with face of wall. If a brick isn't even with others, creating a depression, hold level against wall face, then tap brick into place from opposite side.

Each brick at top of wall should be especially well seated in mortar; tap bricks down with trowel handle. Top bricks are exposed to weather on three sides and have no weight to snug them down into the mortar. For best protection, top course of wall should be capped with mortar or tile. If water seeps between bricks, and freezes, the wall will crack.

Types of bond

Running bond

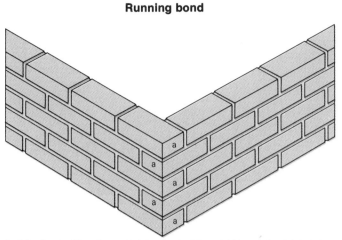

In this simplest bond, most bricks are stretchers laid to overlap joints below. Bricks extending at corners are headers (a) of interlocking courses. (Wall end closers are bats, half-bricks.) Running bond is weak, being only a brick wide. Do not use for long, high walls.

American bond

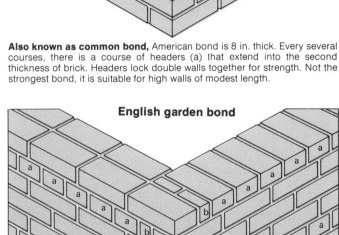

Also known as common bond, American bond is 8 in. thick. Every several courses, there is a course of headers (a) that extend into the second thickness of brick. Headers lock double walls together for strength. Not the strongest bond, it is suitable for high walls of modest length.

English bond

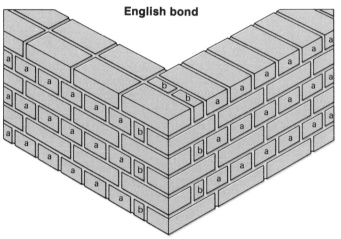

Good for a solid, 8-in.-thick (two widths of brick) wall, English bond's strength is owed to alternating courses of headers (a) with courses of stretchers. Joints are staggered by inserting half-bats (b), quarter sections of brick. English bond is ideal for a high, long wall.

English garden bond

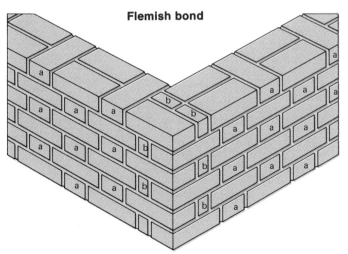

Not as complicated to lay as English bond because it contains fewer header courses (a)—one for every three stretcher courses—English garden bond also uses half-bats (b) to stagger joints. It is weaker transversely, but suitable for most higher walls of long courses.

Flemish bond

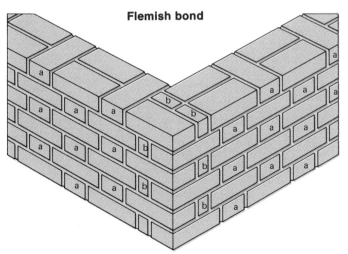

This bond has identical, if complex, courses. Each course is formed by alternating one header (a) with two, side-by-side stretchers. Overlapping joints are staggered by using half-bats (b). Flemish bond produces a wall of great transverse and longitudinal strength.

Open bond

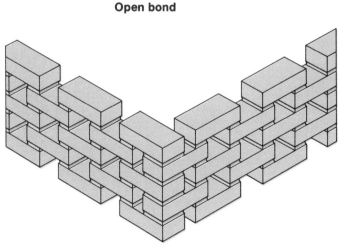

A running bond opened up with spaces between bricks, this design is a good screening or vine trellis wall that will let air circulate. It is a weak bond best used only for short courses and low decorative walls, unless it is given some additional support.

Pointing and re-pointing brick

Bringing old brick walls back to life

Under constant attack from moisture and weather, both the brick and the mortar in a brick wall will deteriorate. The exposed edges of a mortar joint are its most vulnerable points. For a wall to endure, these edges must be properly sealed through pointing. And if, with time, the mortar of those edges starts to deteriorate, re-pointing is the only way to re-establish the security of the bond and the wall's attractive look.

Pointing and re-pointing are much the same, except that in re-pointing the worn edge mortar is first chiseled out to a depth of one-half inch, using first a plugging chisel and then a cape chisel. The resulting cavity is then filled with new mortar. (This can be a specially mixed resilient mortar not often used in original construction.) Afterwards, as in pointing, the edges of the mortar are smoothed and shaped, using a brick jointer or slicker.

Tools: For removing old mortar, you will need a 2½-pound hammer to tap your chisels. It is possible to use a power

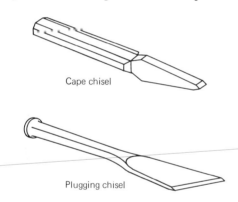

Cape chisel

Plugging chisel

grinder to remove old mortar from a wall, but the tool requires careful and skillful handling. On the whole, power grinders are best left to professional bricklayers. One wrong move and you could destroy a good brick.

You will need a long, thin brush to remove loose bits of old mortar and dust from joints after chipping. Other necessary or useful tools are a trowel to hold mortar while working, a tuck pointer to fill joints with mortar, and a brick jointer for special finishes. Also useful are some polyethylene plastic drop cloth sheets or burlap to keep the mortar drippings off grass and shrubbery.

Mortar mixes: When you point a new-built brick wall you will use the basic mortar you have employed as a bond in laying the wall. But when you re-point an old wall you have choices. If you know the composition of the old mortar, you can match it. If you do not know it, you can either use one of the standard mixes (see p.312), or mix up a special mortar containing a much

higher percentage of hydrated lime. One widely used traditional mix contains 2 parts of lime, 1 part of Portland cement, and 8 parts of sand. The added lime makes a mortar that will seal old cracks, cushion the bricks, work easily, and bond well. It is better than a mortar that

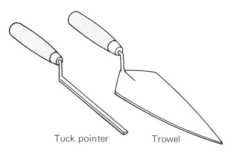

Tuck pointer   Trowel

has a higher percentage of Portland cement, which cures harder than brick. Under pressure, such a mortar can cause bricks to chip or crack.

With all re-pointing mortars, add enough coloring to make the mixture appear darker when wet than the older mortar; then when the mortar dries it will match the shade of existing mortar.

Mortar for re-pointing, especially if it contains a large amount of lime, is mixed slightly dryer than that used in general bricklaying. But heavily limed mortar may need prehydrating—that is, it is mixed, allowed to sit for a time, and then a little more water is added just prior to use. In every case, the best consistency for re-pointing mortar is a slightly stiff, paste-like mixture that is easy to press into the joints.

When to work: As in laying a new wall, re-pointing should be undertaken only in months of moderate, mid-range temperatures, day or night. The optimum range is about 50° to 75°F., since freezing cold and dry heat can cause serious problems. If the moisture in a mortar freezes, it will expand, forcing mortar

out of the joints. Mortar will also dry brittle. And if the temperature climbs into the high 80s and the humidity is low, the mortar will dry out too quickly from evaporation. It will then become weak and powdery.

Freezing in cold weather can be retarded by using plastic sheeting or burlap coverings that help the wall retain residual heat. In hot weather, wet mortar with a fine spray mist from a garden hose or a portable sprayer, then cover the wall with plastic or damp burlap. More spraying may be required.

Working procedures: Begin re-pointing by chiseling out old mortar in chunks about 1 inch in length. Work slowly and wear safety goggles or glasses. Use a scaffolding, never a ladder, to reach high wall sections.

Remove old mortar from a section of wall 1 square yard in area; then thoroughly wet both the brick faces and joint cavities. (Dry brick and old, dry mortar will draw moisture from your new mortar and dry it out.) Force the new mortar into the vertical joints first, then do the horizontal joints. Finish the edges of the mortar joints before you go on to another wall section.

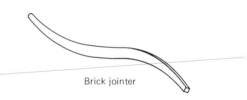

Brick jointer

When re-pointing is finished and mortar has hardened, go back over the wall and remove any unsightly mortar burrs. For this task use a wood spatula, a flat stick, or a chisel. Use the chisel gently to avoid doing any damage to the bricks. Finally, scrub the wall with a stiff bristle fiber brush, then hose it down and scrub it again.

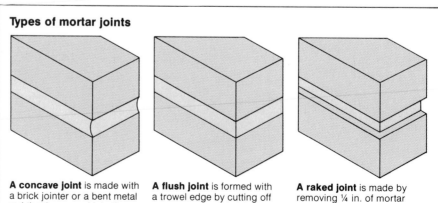

Types of mortar joints

A concave joint is made with a brick jointer or a bent metal rod that is pressed into the mortar and drawn along the center. Easy to form, concave joints resist water and they look attractive.

A flush joint is formed with a trowel edge by cutting off excess mortar at brick face. It produces a smooth, even wall face surface that is easy to clean, but not very moisture-resistant.

A raked joint is made by removing ¼ in. of mortar from joint with a scraper, then running striking tool along mortar edge, making it flat, smooth, and parallel with brick face; it resists water.

How to re-point an old brick wall

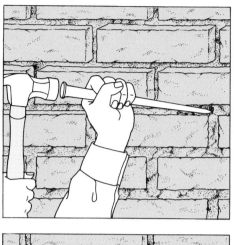

1. Break up old mortar with the point of a plugging chisel, then use a cape chisel to clean out the joint thoroughly. Do not use hard blows but tap on chisels with the hammer. Cut mortar in sections 1 in. at a time to a ½ in. depth. Wear safety glasses or goggles. Use scaffold to reach high areas. Work on a single area of 1 sq. yd. at a time. Work slowly and carefully.

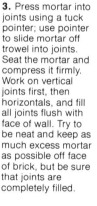

2. Brush away dust and loose mortar from joints and wall face. Brush vertical joints first, then brush the horizontals. You need a brush with ⅜-in.-thick semi-stiff fiber bristles long enough to reach deep into the joint.

3. Press mortar into joints using a tuck pointer; use pointer to slide mortar off trowel into joints. Seat the mortar and compress it firmly. Work on vertical joints first, then horizontals, and fill all joints flush with face of wall. Try to be neat and keep as much excess mortar as possible off face of brick, but be sure that joints are completely filled.

Tuck pointer

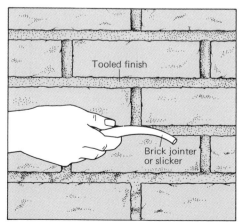

Tooled finish

Brick jointer or slicker

4. Finish pointing all joints in a section with a brick jointer, a striking tool, or a curved rod. For a V-edged joint use the point of the trowel. Always keep pressure on the mortar with your tool as you form edge of joint, and check often to be sure you haven't left voids. Some excess wet mortar can be cleaned from bricks' faces with trowel, but be sure not to deform joint. Entire wall is cleaned when dry.

5. To replace a broken brick, chisel away mortar around it, then use a wide, straight-bladed chisel to remove brick itself. Brick may have to be further broken up to get it out of wall. Work very carefully, tapping the chisel lightly to avoid damaging the adjacent bricks.

6. Use a chisel to clean all chunks of mortar from the cavity, then brush the cavity completely free of dust, as shown. Before you begin the actual replacement, make sure that you give the cavity a liberal spray so old bricks do not suck moisture from your mortar.

Mortar in wall cavity

Mortar on brick

7. Butter top, sides, and back of brick with mortar. Also spread mortar in the cavity. Do not skimp on mortar; remember, too much on the back of the brick can make it hard to seat brick flush with face of wall. Before you insert brick, be sure there are no voids in the mortar.

8. Force brick into wall cavity as far as you can, then use the trowel handle to tap it flush with the other bricks. Now finish up by pointing mortar with brick jointer or other tool and clean off the excess mortar.

Retaining walls and terraces

Solutions to a problem slope

Retaining walls are built to restrain the earth on sloping land. These pages show four different types. Although the principles shown here apply to walls of greater height, we recommend that a homeowner building a wall without consulting an engineer build no higher than 4 feet. For all walls the base of the footing—in cold climates, placed below frost line to prevent heaving—should be built on a 4 to 7-inch layer of well-compacted sand or gravel to assure firm support. Weepholes to facilitate drainage are necessary in concrete so the wall does not become a dam that holds back water. Install 4-inch-diameter pipes every 5 to 10 feet, and place heavy screening or lath over the openings. Put a 12-inch layer of coarse gravel or crushed stone around each weephole.

Concrete-block gravity wall: The cavities in the blocks are filled with grout. The wall depends on its weight for stability; it must have a base thickness equal to one half to three quarters of its height. This type of wall is not recommended for heights over 4 feet. To construct the wall, refer to pages 248–249.

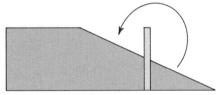

Position a retaining wall so the amount of soil removed can later be placed behind the wall.

Place weepholes in the third or fourth course so the openings will be several inches above the finished grade. To chop out the block to install the weepholes, refer to page 243. Allow the mortar to harden for 24 hours before filling with grout, a mixture of sand or gravel, cement, and water (p.308). Wait at least seven days after grouting before replacing the backfill. To add a decorative stucco-like parge coat of cement to the front, refer to pages 243 and 268.

Reinforced concrete-block masonry wall: Made of stretchers and bond beams in alternate courses, this wall sits on a poured concrete base. Excavate for the size base you need. Make a form for the concrete; arrange the horizontal and longitudinal reinforcing rods, referring to the drawing and chart on the facing page; attach the bent rods to the horizontal rods with wire. Pour in the concrete and allow it to set for 24 hours before beginning the masonry (pp.248–249). Position two ½-inch horizontal reinforcing rods in every other course—the bond beam courses—and fill the blocks with grout to support the rods. For added support for the wall, fill the cavities in the top three courses of block

with grout. To prevent grout from filling the other courses, place a piece of metal lath on top of the blocks that are not to be filled, and secure it with mortar. Make sure the metal lath does not protrude beyond the mortar on the outside of the wall. Insert vertical reinforcing rods, referring to the chart. Finish the top course with a coping, and seal the vertical joints with a caulking compound. For a parge coat, refer to pages 243 and 268. Although this is a complex

wall to construct, it can be extended to greater heights than 4 feet.

Poured concrete gravity wall: This wall requires no reinforcements. Construct forms for the concrete or rent them from a local builder or concrete company. For weepholes, cut 4-inch-diameter pipe to fit, and wedge the pipes in the form, or cut holes in the form and insert the pipes through the holes. To estimate and order the concrete you will need, see pages 246–247.

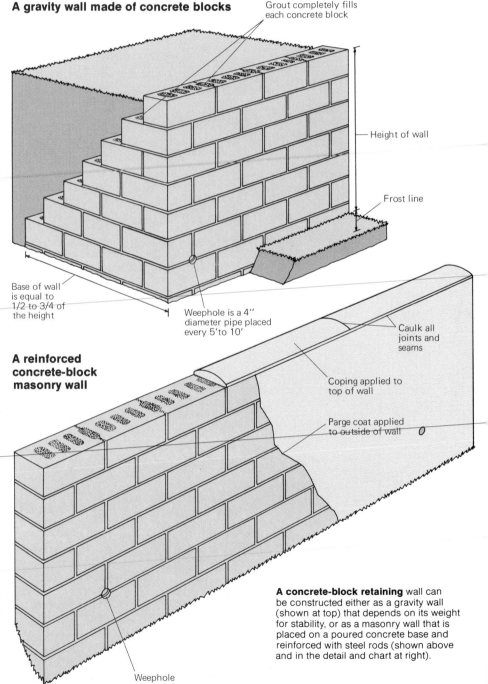

A gravity wall made of concrete blocks

Grout completely fills each concrete block

Height of wall

Frost line

Base of wall is equal to 1/2 to 3/4 of the height

Weephole is a 4'' diameter pipe placed every 5' to 10'

A reinforced concrete-block masonry wall

Caulk all joints and seams

Coping applied to top of wall

Parge coat applied to outside of wall

Weephole

A concrete-block retaining wall can be constructed either as a gravity wall (shown at top) that depends on its weight for stability, or as a masonry wall that is placed on a poured concrete base and reinforced with steel rods (shown above and in the detail and chart at right).

Retaining wall of railroad ties: The wall is supported by a T-shaped anchor made of half ties; the anchor will be buried in the backfill. One course of ties must be placed below grade level. To reinforce joints along the face of the wall, at the ends of the ties, and at the anchor, drill a hole through each tie and into the one below. Drill at an angle from the back to front and drive a galvanized spike or length of reinforcing rod through the hole.

A terraced slope of railroad ties

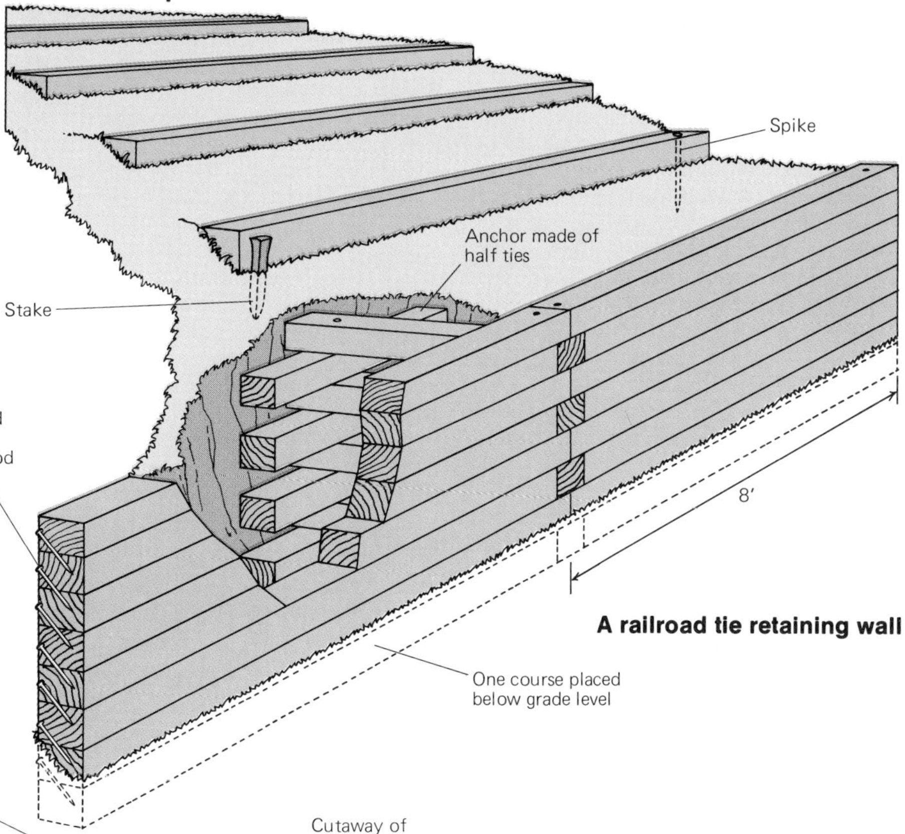

Spike

Anchor made of half ties

Stake

Large galvanized spike or length of reinforcing rod

8'

A railroad tie retaining wall

One course placed below grade level

A poured concrete gravity wall

Cutaway of poured concrete gravity wall

Porous backfill

10''

Height of wall

Weephole is a 4''diameter pipe placed every 5' to 10'

Frost line

Width of base is equal to half the height

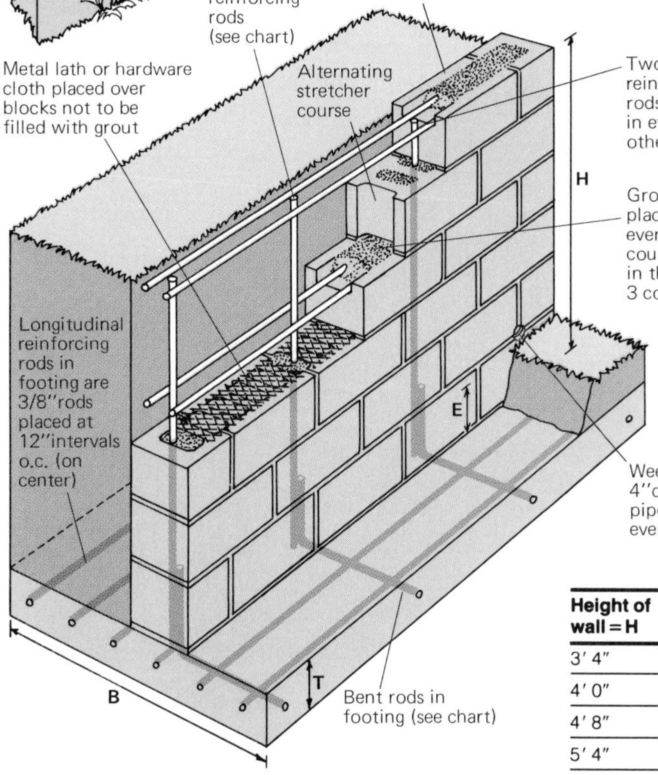

Vertical reinforcing rods (see chart)

Alternating lintel block bond beam course

Alternating stretcher course

Metal lath or hardware cloth placed over blocks not to be filled with grout

Two 1/2'' reinforcing rods placed in every other course

Grout is placed in every other course and in the top 3 courses

H

Longitudinal reinforcing rods in footing are 3/8''rods placed at 12''intervals o.c. (on center)

E

Weephole is a 4''diameter pipe placed every 5'to 10'

B

T

Bent rods in footing (see chart)

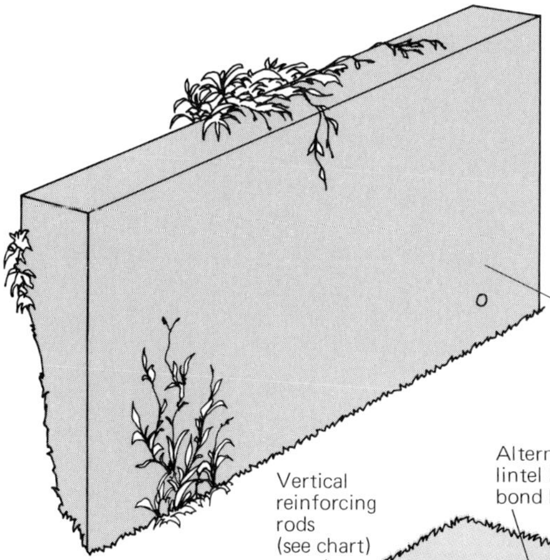

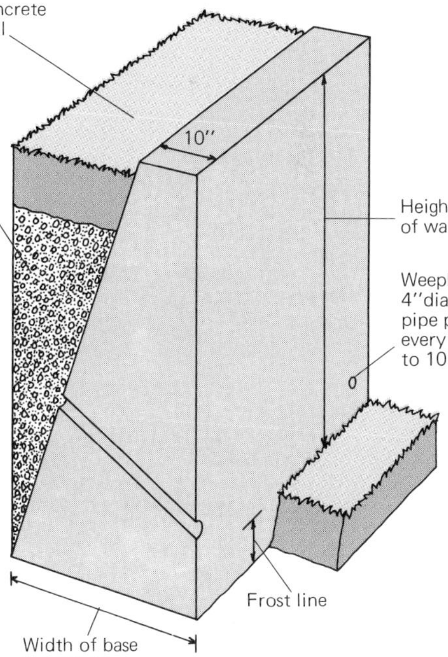

Height of wall = H	Width of base = B	Thickness of base = T	Distance to exposed face of wall = E	Vertical rods and bent rods	Horizontal rods in footing
3' 4"	2' 4"	9"	8"	3/8" at 32"	3/8" at 27"
4' 0"	2' 9"	9"	10"	1/2" at 32"	3/8" at 27"
4' 8"	3' 3"	10"	12"	5/8" at 32"	3/8" at 27"
5' 4"	3' 8"	10"	14"	1/2" at 16"	1/2" at 30"

Home security systems

Electronic alarms alert you and deter burglars

There are two ways to defeat a burglar. You can bar his entry with locks. And you can make it impossible for him to get inside your home without triggering an alarm. But if you use the two together they can present the housebreaker with a powerful psychological and physical obstacle to overcome.

Dead bolts: For periods when you are away from home, dead bolt locks that open only with keys from outside and inside are more effective than ordinary locks. The burglar knows he must leave by the same window he broke to enter—making it difficult to remove large objects from the house, or to escape if he is surprised. The sight of such locks alone can become a deterrent to a thief. And if your home also has an alarm system, the thief may be scared off at the outset.

Perimeter alarms: In planning a perimeter alarm system for your home,

keep in mind that it is like a wall, and a wall with a hole in it is not much of a barrier. All ground-floor doors and windows should be tied into the system. Basement windows and upper floor windows easily reached from trees, sun decks, the roof, or a strong vine trellis should also be rigged with detectors.

A perimeter alarm system is made up of a network of detectors around the exterior of the house. All the detectors are tied in by wire or radio to a central control panel, and to remote master control panels or consoles. Such systems generally work on 12-volt electric current. Wired systems have a central master panel connected to a transformer that is in turn plugged into a standard 110–120 volt house current socket. Wired systems include a 12-volt storage battery for backup use if house power fails. In radio systems, the master

control panel also runs off house current, with backup battery. But each detector contains a radio transmitter that is battery-powered. A radio system is easier to install, but requires regular checking of batteries.

Switches: When you install an electronic alarm system, you must be prepared to live with a series of buttons and switches and to remember when and how to use them. Besides those on master and remote control panels you will need shunt switches to cut off the power to frequently opened windows and doors. Shunt switches must be reset to put a detector back on line. Timed switches shut off power to a detector for a brief period to allow exit or entry through a door; the switch automatically resets the detector. Failure to use shunt or timed switches properly is a common cause of false alarms. In addi-

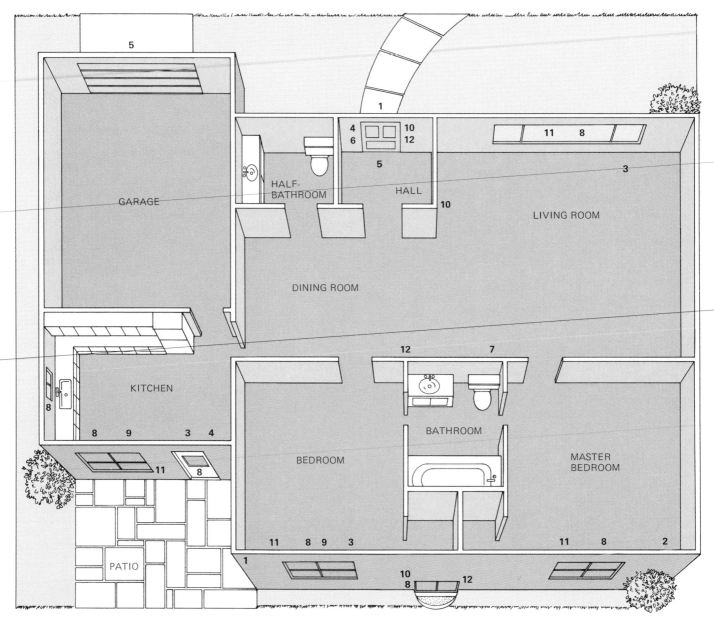

tion, panic and reset buttons allow you to set off the alarm manually and then reset the system manually. And there are key-operated switches for disarming the entire system, or arming it; these are often located outside the house.

Detectors: Magnetic detectors are used on windows and doors. They consist of a magnet that is fastened to the door or window, and an electrically powered switch. Opening the window or door breaks the magnetic field, triggering the alarm; moreover, if the wires running to the switch are cut the alarm goes off. Magnetic detectors can be installed in the open or hidden by recessing in a door jamb or window frame. Recessing prevents the intruder from studying a detector's workings.

Burglars often carry glass cutters to avoid smashing glass and making noise. A window can be taped with strips of metallic foil so that if the glass is cut an alarm will sound. A special detector can also be installed directly against the glass. If a burglar working on the glass breaks it, the alarm will sound. Such detectors are good for large picture windows or sliding doors.

Advanced designs: The most sophisticated detectors employ ultrasonic, infrared, or microwave sensors. Ultrasonic detectors cover broad areas, setting off an alarm if their sound patterns are disturbed. Infrared sensors react to an intruder's body heat. Infrared beams are used together with photoelectric cells in another type of sensor, in which breaking the beam sets off the alarm. Microwave sensors that emit high-frequency radio waves also work on the broken-beam principle.

Defense-in-depth: In combination with floor mat detectors, ultrasonic sensors create defense-in-depth within a home. Sonic detectors that respond to the sound of breaking glass anywhere in the house can be made part of this defense. (Remember that floor mat detectors can be set off by pets and children, as well as by burglars.)

Alarm signals: A system can be rigged to turn on or flash house lights, sound a bell or a horn (85 decibels for inside, 105 decibels outside). The signal can be a recorded telephone message to your local police, or an alert automatically telephoned to a private security firm or a neighbor. Before you decide on your alarm signal, check out all the options. Some local police forces prohibit recorded telephone alarm messages. Private security firms are often costly. Loud alarms, especially if they are false alarms as some will be, will not make you popular with your neighbors.

1.

Outdoor horn or bell alarm should be coupled with indoor horn or bell in case former is deactivated by a burglar. Alarms used with relays that turn on the lights discourage potential housebreakers.

2.
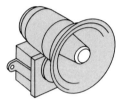
Master control panel ties in all parts of alarm system and has a battery for emergency power. It is usually installed in master bedroom or hidden in master bedroom closet.

3.
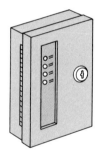
Remote master control console serves same function as master panel but looks more attractive. It has its own panic button, reset switch, horn, and other control switches.

4.
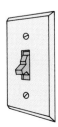
A shunt switch cuts off a particular sensor so that a door or window can be opened. It must be reset to reactivate sensor. Forgetting to use shunts is one of most typical causes of false alarms.

5.

Pressure-sensitive mat may be put under rug at doorways, by vulnerable windows, or in halls. A pressure-sensitive sensor cable tied into alarm system can also be used at entrance of driveways to signal approach of a car at nighttime.

6.

Remote key-operated switches are for turning system off or on. If the weatherproofed type, it can be installed outside.

7.
Ultrasonic detector will cover a large interior area, a defense-in-depth inside house. Movement into area disturbs pattern of ultrasonic waves, setting off alarm.

8.

Glass detector reacts to the vibration of shattering glass but not to usual house vibrations. Danger is that careful burglar with glass cutter may be able to remove part of pane without triggering alarm. Foil tape on window provides better security. If tape is cut, alarm sounds.

9.
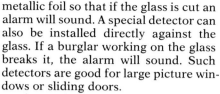
Panic buttons are used for emergency sounding of the alarm. Reset buttons are used to reactivate the alarm system. Both are manually operated and are best installed in pairs in key locations.

10.
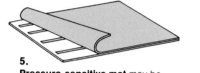
Detectors can be hidden by recessing them into the woodwork. More secure and neater in appearance, they are also more trouble to install. When the magnet moves, breaking magnetic field, alarm goes off.

11.

Magnetic detectors are two-part units. Magnet goes on door or window; switch goes on the frame. Components do not touch; a magnetic field exists in the slight separation between them. Breaking field sets off alarm.

12.
A system hooked up to a relay unit will turn on or flash house lights when sensor sets off an alarm. A sudden lighting up of a home often scares off night burglars.

Drainage and septic systems

Dry wells

A home roof collects a lot of rainwater. If gutter downspouts pour this water out near the foundation wall, the basement will become damp or flooded (see *Waterproofing basements*, pp.66–69). A splash block placed under the end of a downspout will divert some water away from the wall, but a better solution is to connect a downspout to a storm sewer or dry well to carry off the excess water.

The opening for a dry well is simply a hole in the ground dug a distance of at least 10 feet from the basement wall. The opening should measure a minimum of 9 square feet (3 × 3 feet) in area, and be dug to a depth of 5 to 10 feet. You can dig your holes with a pick and shovel or a small rented backhoe. For a deep well with a small surface opening, you may have to excavate a larger volume and then fill in around the well liner with the excess earth.

Put into each well an old 55-gallon drum with the top removed (or a commercially available cast concrete dry well unit); puncture the sides and bottom of the drum with many small holes. If a concrete block lining is used, the well opening should be 16 to 36 square feet in area (4 to 6 feet on a side). The well bottom is bare earth. An unlined hole is also workable. All wells are filled to within 18 inches of grade (ground level) with broken rocks and rubble.

A tile drain or plastic drain pipe is run in a trench from downspout to the upper edge of the well. This pipe should slope toward the well a half-inch for every foot of its length. Pour crushed stone down around the walls of the liner to fill the well cavity. Place treated planks over top of the liner. Fill the remaining 18 inches to grade with crushed stones, then earth topped with sod, as seen in the illustrations below.

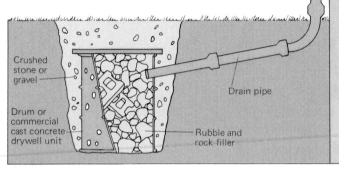

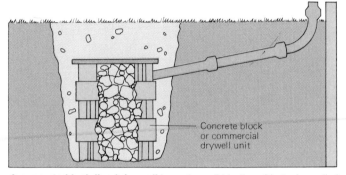

A 55-gallon metal drum with top removed and perforated bottom and sides makes a good liner for a dry well. The holes should be ½ to 1 in. diameter, and treated boards form the well cap. Drain tile or plastic pipe runs in a trench originating at downspout. Drum is filled with rocks and rubble. Cap is buried.

A concrete-block-lined dry well has a bare dirt bottom. Mortar is applied sparingly or not at all to allow water to seep out into earth. A block-lined well, with a large cross section, is ideal for large quantities of water. Do not locate dry wells near trees. Roots may die or eventually clog the well.

Maintaining septic systems

Hire professional help to clean and rejuvenate a septic system. But as the owner, you can monitor your system to watch for signs of correctable problems.
▷ Bubbles welling up from drains indicate detergent problems. Switch to low-suds types or use laundry soap.
▷ Liquids backing up in drains may mean tree roots are plugging your drain field lines. Have the roots removed by professional septic system workers.
▷ Fast-growing grass and bushes along drain field lines indicate sewage is flowing from the lines. Pump the septic tank.

▷ Back-up due to cooking grease can be eliminated by a grease trap or by using caustic soda to dissolve residues.
▷ Try speeding up sluggish drains by using lime or sulphate of alumina to precipitate solid waste.
▷ Brewer's yeast mixed with warm water, if flushed down the toilet can speed up tank bacterial action.
▷ Seepage pits added to a drain field can increase the liquid dispersal.
▷ Blockages can also be caused by rags, coffee grounds, or other insoluble material getting into the house drains.

Distance from bottom of tank outlet to top of sludge

Tank capacity (gallons)	Liquid depth (feet)		
	3	4	5
	Sludge depth		
500	11"	16"	21"
750	6"	10"	13"
900	4"	7"	10"
1,000	4"	6"	8"

Remove tank cover and push stick wrapped with a light cloth down through liquid to tank bottom. Table indicates when tanks of different size require pumping out. Stain on cloth will show sludge level on bottom. Check tank at least once a year.

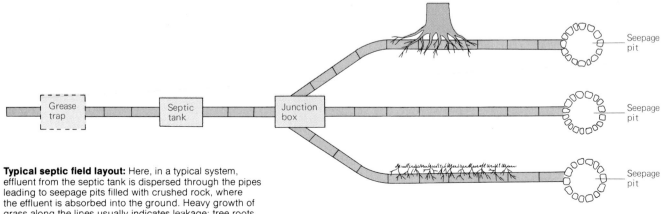

Typical septic field layout: Here, in a typical system, effluent from the septic tank is dispersed through the pipes leading to seepage pits filled with crushed rock, where the effluent is absorbed into the ground. Heavy growth of grass along the lines usually indicates leakage; tree roots may grow into the lines and clog them. Such problems should be handled by professionals.

Town and country alternatives

Today's do-it-yourselfers are adapting their talents to fit many unique opportunities in both town and country. As the ensuing color photographs show, some Americans are restoring old frame houses in rural settings, while others are tackling urban rowhouse rehabilitations. They are building vacation homes from kits, and are working with prefabricated materials.

contents

Urban rehabilitation

Revitalizing our cities

Rehabilitation (see pp.343–347) is defined as fixing up or making habitable, usually with modern conveniences, a building that has fallen into disrepair. In many older cities, the practice of bulldozing blighted areas has given way, through the efforts of urban architects and interested citizens, to a recognition of the value of the buildings as well as the existing neighborhoods. Much rehabilitation is being done by owners who plan to live in the houses—a trend aided by government-sponsored homesteading programs. Many of the owners are doing the work themselves.

A Baltimore carriage house built in the early 1800s was in total disrepair (near right) when an architect transformed it into his home (far right). The barn door on the 10-ft.-wide building was replaced with a new front door and window. The mortar-covered bricks were stripped clean and supplemented with bricks from nearby old houses. There are two stories; the roof was built at a 45° angle visible from the front to keep the house in scale with neighboring buildings. At the back, the house is 3½ stories high with a large glass wall that provides passive solar heat to the entire house.

The living room occupies the back half of the house and has a ceiling that peaks to 38 ft. Each of the upper floors has a balcony overlooking this space. A wood-burning stove augments the passive solar heat in the winter.

Phil Lambdin

Phil Lambdin / Designed by Edwin Stretch

Steve Grubman / Designed by Douglas Schroeder, FAIA / Courtesy of HOME

A Chicago couple with three young children wanted to remain city dwellers but needed space for their growing family. They saw great potential in an 1888 townhouse (left) that had been divided into three apartments. With the help of an architect who specializes in rehabilitations, the couple chose an open, contemporary look (above), which was achieved by tearing down existing partitions. The open-plan living room, dining room, and entry hall shown above were once four small Victorian rooms. A new oak strip floor was laid but the woodwork is original. The brickwork on the outside of the house was in good condition. For added strength and to enhance its look, it was re-pointed, a process whereby the deteriorated mortar is cleaned out and new mortar put in.

A block in San Francisco that was demolished remained zoned for the same 3-story townhouses with narrow backyards that had been there for nearly a century. Each backyard was designed by a landscape architect, and has high wooden walls for privacy and two entrances, one through a door at garden level, the other up a flight of stairs.

One backyard (far left) has two seating areas separated by a flagstone walkway; the stairs are railroad ties.

Another yard (near left) has a large center area covered with gravel and surrounded with built-in benches. The rest of the garden is planted with ivy.

To revitalize neglected older blocks such as Hanover Street (right), the city of Baltimore offers to lease the houses at moderate rates to individuals who agree to restore and live in them (below). A deed to the house is turned over to the individual only after the completion of renovations that meet the city building codes.

A neighborhood association organized to oversee the rehabilitations stipulated that the exteriors be restored to their original historical style while the owners were free to renovate interiors as they chose—from an historical re-creation to a sleek modern renovation. Hanover Street has three-story Greek Revival and Victorian townhouses build from 1840 to 1890 and one smaller, two-story Federal house.

Lofts

Renovating commercial space for living

In many of our cities, former commercial buildings that have been vacated by businesses are increasingly a source of unique residential housing. Such old manufacturing sites offer large spaces (usually with high ceilings and tall windows) that can be rehabilitated to suit the needs and lifestyle of the new owner-tenant.

The photographs on these pages show various loft renovations. Each renovation, although employing different materials and designs, has succeeded in retaining the loft's most appealing characteristic—spaciousness.

Lilo Raymond, Photography / Designed by Felix Arbeo

To take advantage of natural light coming through the wall of windows at the right, the living area of this turn-of-the-century loft was stripped almost free of partitions. The kitchen is open to the living room (see p.53); the enclosure in the center of the loft contains the bathroom, which has a translucent ceiling to permit the penetration of light inside the windowless walls. A wall at the far end of the loft screens the bedroom. Note that all of the lighting is overhead, suspended from pipes under the ceiling. Oak floor and window moldings are restored originals.

Lilo Raymond, Photography

Lilo Raymond, Photography / Designed by Michael Kwart

This 25-x-60-ft. loft projected a feeling of immense space just by maintaining its original structural elements—exposed ceiling beams, maple floors, brick walls, and large windows. The archway at right leads into a separate room that the owner, a painter, uses as a studio. Most of the renovation of this loft entailed cleaning and restoring: removing tar from the floors, painting the brick walls white, and removing decades of dirt from the ceiling beams. This loft is on the top floor, and because of the shape of the building, the ceiling slopes gradually from a height of 13 ft. at the rear to 10 ft. at the front.

To bring natural light into the windowless living area of this loft, skylights were installed in the ceiling of the den and hall at the rear, and the den was enclosed with glass walls. The stairway, which leads to the bedrooms on the second floor, is made of solid birch 1⅛ in. thick. Shelves along the stairway wall and along the glass wall in the den are made of birch veneer plywood. Before any building started, lightweight concrete was poured over the floor to level it. Concrete also makes the room soundproof.

Lilo Raymond, Photography / Designed by Michael A. Rubenstein AIA

The apartment shown in the two views above was built in a New York business-district loft by erecting wallboard partitions to separate the rooms. The floors are original hard maple, but the mahogany window molding is new, as are the windows of Lexan plastic—stronger than glass and selected for purposes of security. The corner of a bedroom juts out dramatically to isolate the dining area, which is further defined by the use of the hanging lamp over the circular table. Carpet lies in path of main traffic.

Lilo Raymond, Photography

The voluminousness of this loft was not diminished even though separate rooms were carved from it. A bedroom and a study that doubles as a guest room are at the far end. Dining room, living room, kitchen, and den are in main area, communicating among the large pillars (created by boxing in the old posts). Note the broad expanse of maple floor and tin ceiling.

Lilo Raymond, Photography / Designed by Robert Bayley

The owner designed this loft as a large axial space with a separate bedroom, bath, kitchen, and studio built along one side. This takes advantage of the natural light coming in through the tall windows at the front and back. In the large room, the living area is separated from the dining area by a custom-built aviary—the owner raises birds. Beyond the dining area is a home office. The supporting column in the center is boxed in and forms one wall of the kitchen. The walls are Sheetrock; the maple floor and 13-ft. ceiling are original.

Town and country alternatives

Solar houses

Solar energy heating systems collect, store, and distribute the direct energy of the sun. Basically, all solar systems fall into two categories, active and passive. Active solar systems include mechanical components, such as fans and pumps, which circulate the solar-heated air or water through the house. This allows the heat collectors and storage components to be located anywhere—even outside the house itself. Passive solar systems are incorporated into the house and use no mechanical systems; the sun warms massive masonry or large containers of water,

That solar roof collectors need not be bizarre eyesores is proved by this traditional Spanish-style house near San Diego, California. The white stucco walls and red tile roofs have been repeated in the housings for the collectors. In this area, where sunlight is abundant and cold days are rare, the active solar system can provide all heat and hot water. A passive system would be inappropriate here, because energy-efficient design dictates that there be virtually no south windows, in order to keep the house cool.

A trombe wall passive system utilizes both convection currents and direct radiant heat to warm a house day and night. The outside southern exposure of this house in Durham, Connecticut, consists of double-glazed sliding glass doors that collect solar heat. Set 6 in. behind the glass is the trombe wall itself—a massive, 8-in.-thick concrete-block wall painted black for maximum heat absorption, with vents to the house along the top and bottom. On sunny days the vents are opened and cool air from the house flows through the bottom vents into the space between the glass and the wall. As the air heats up, it rises, returning warm air to the house through the top vents. At night and on cloudy days the vents are closed, an insulated shade is drawn between the wall and the glass, and stored heat is radiated from the wall into the house.

Retrofitting an older home for solar energy while retaining its essential character was the challenge presented by this house in a National Historic Preservation District in Asheville, North Carolina. The most important alteration was to enclose two south-facing porches, turning them into sunrooms with large expanses of double-glazed windows, which serve as solar collectors. To store the heat, huge plastic cylinders filled with dyed water (dark colors absorb and retain heat best) were installed behind the windows and brick floors were laid to provide thermal mass (above). Quilted shades keep the heat in at night. An active hot-air system with a collector set in the south wall heats north rooms by blowing warm air through ducts with a fan.

which hold heat much longer than the air. At night or on cloudy days the stored heat is radiated into the house for as long as the storage system is warmer than the air. Natural convection currents (hot air rises, cold air falls) carry the warm air through the house.

When retrofitting an older home for solar energy, you should carefully calculate which energy-saving renovations are appropriate and cost-effective (see pp.354–357). Solar energy systems can be expensive, but the costs are partially offset by federal, state, and local tax incentives, which have been increasing.

An expensive combination of active and passive components have been integrated into this state-of-the-art solar home, a demonstration project built by the Copper Development Association in Greenwich, Connecticut. The southern exposure is dominated by a two-story solar greenhouse backed up by a heat storage system of water-filled copper tubes and flagstone floors set in concrete. Collectors for the active hot water and heating systems flank the greenhouse. A photovoltaic array (left) converts sunlight to electricity. A home computer monitors and activates all energy systems, depending on heat and light conditions.

Robert Perron / Courtesy Copper Development Association, Inc.

Tim Snider

Solar greenhouses are ideal additions to existing homes because they can be built onto any south-facing wall and require no structural changes in the house. The large greenhouse attached to this small Cape Cod in Topsham, Maine, provides extra living space and a pleasant indoor garden as well as the advantages of solar heat. Doors between the greenhouse and the main house are closed at night to prevent warm house air from being drawn into the greenhouse.

John Johnson / Greenhouse by Levi Ross

The south wall on this single-story ranch house near Seattle, Washington, was made to order for a long sunroom. The glass wall and skylight collect solar energy during the day. At night quilted thermal shades are pulled down to insulate the wall, and reflective panels slide over the large skylight, preventing heat loss (interior, right). A homemade solar collector is set into the other end of the south wall (above, right). Aluminum beverage cans, opened top and bottom and painted flat black for maximum heat absorption, are stacked behind glass. Air in the cans heats up, rises, and enters the room through the vent at the top of the collector, while cool room air is drawn into the collector through the bottom vent; the process forms an endless convective energy loop for as long as the sun shines.

327

Kit houses

Prefabricated cottages, bungalows, or suburban units

If you dream of building your own home but shy away from such an enormous enterprise, a kit house may provide the answer. With a kit you can build a house that fits your abilities and your budget; you can do as much of the work as you are able to; and you can select a house to fit your lifestyle.

Manufacturers produce kit houses that include the framework only, the framework and outer sheathing, or the complete interior and exterior of the house. Many kit manufacturers offer a choice of additional features so each kit house can be made to fit the homeowner's needs. As shown in these photographs, kits range from a 12-foot-square shelter to a five-bedroom house.

Building a log cabin is for those who desire the rustic life with an emphasis on the natural beauty of wood. Log cabin kits include the logs and log posts as well as doors, windows, frames, sills, insulation strips, all interior partitions, roof framing materials, asphalt roof shingles, and all the necessary hardware.

Log cabins have an excellent R-rating (see *Energy-saving renovations*), and range in style from the modest one-bedroom house shown at left to a spacious five-bedroom model.

A geodesic dome is not only an unusual house but also an economical one. Its unique shape minimizes building materials and heat exchange with the environment. The dome kit consists of pre-assembled triangles; all the interior and exterior finishing materials are supplied by the buyer so each dome can fulfill individual needs. Dormers, skylights, and additional windows can be added to the basic structure.

This simple shelter is a 12-ft.-square weathertight shell made of post and beam framing with a shed room and open porch. The kit includes pre-cut and pre-drilled lumber, and all necessary tools (no power tools are needed). The walls are non-load bearing; the floor and roof are supported by six beams, which are secured in poured concrete piers. This shelter is designed to have a variety of modules added to it.

Old Yankee ingenuity created the original barn and now some modern ingenuity has helped create a barn kit that uses antique yellow pine posts and beams (6 x 6s and 6 x 10s) with modern finishing materials. Walls and floors come in sandwich panels consisting of the exterior and interior siding with solid foam insulation between. The exterior siding is ⅝-in. grooved, rough sawed plywood to give the look of an old plank barn. The interior siding is cedar. All windows, doors, and trim are included. Although the supporting posts cannot be changed, interior partitions can be eliminated or moved to create rooms that fulfill any homeowner's needs.

This pine-sheathed, two-story house utilizes passive solar heat that enters by windows that face south, east, and west. The heated air is distributed through the house by fans, and any excess is stored in the special insulated concrete slab developed by the company for use as the foundation. The kit includes well-insulated walls and roof, and window shutters.

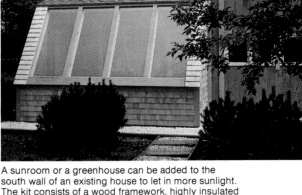

A sunroom or a greenhouse can be added to the south wall of an existing house to let in more sunlight. The kit consists of a wood framework, highly insulated walls, and cedar shingle siding, and is designed to be placed on a special insulated concrete slab foundation. Used as a greenhouse, the shed will add weeks to the growing season.

Not all houses available as kits are meant to be vacation retreats. The saltbox model at left is a four-bedroom house with a two-car garage. It was designed for year-round living. The basic kit includes all the materials necessary for completely finishing the exterior. For more money a kit is available that includes both interior and exterior. The house can be built by especially adept do-it-yourselfers or the work can be done by a contractor.
The styles available range from a starter model, a modest two-bedroom, to a luxurious five-bedroom house.

Unique living places

Out-of-the-ordinary vacation retreats

A vacation house in the country, at the shore, or in the mountains may offer a chance to combine expressive design and relaxed living in one architectural setting. The houses shown on these pages reflect their owners' personal views of what makes a good place to relax in, work in, or play in, whether a cabin in the woods, a restored railroad station, or a sumptuous converted barn. Often the most important satisfaction is the thrill of making real one's own plans and designs, or success in the quest for just the right old house in just the right pastoral, woodsy, or seaside setting.

This prefabricated vacation cabin has plastic window panes and plywood walls. The ⅜-in.-thick plywood panels come in 4-x-8-ft. sheets. The wood trim under the eaves is modeled on the Victorian style known as Carpenter Gothic. This small, 10-ft.-sq. cabin can accommodate four people in the second-story sleeping loft.

Large fiberglass-reinforced plastic window at rear corner of this cabin in the woods admits sunlight to warm a black-painted concrete block wall inside the house. This is a trombe wall, a passive solar heating innovation described in detail on page 326. It works well in cabins and small houses.

An A-frame house, designed as a ski chalet, has a roof built at a steep angle to avoid a snow build-up. Large double-glazed windows face south for added warmth; the lower left and right window panels are louvered for ventilation. Most of the flue of the freestanding, wood-burning fireplace is on the inside to retain as much heat as possible.

Built by an architect enamored of Victorian gingerbread houses, this modern three-bedroom house is a tribute to the 1890s originals. The builder installed board-and-batten style plywood siding vertically, and used an aluminum roof to simulate the original tin roof. The decorative plywood gingerbread trim is cut by hand.

The upper two floors of an old, 40 x 80 ft. stone barn were converted into a vacation house, leaving intact the stable walls on the first floor. The enormous beams and wood floors are original, and the exterior walls are covered with new barn siding. On the upper level the ceiling is open to the peak of the roof so the huge structural beams are visible. All the windows are original except for one that was added during the renovation. The barn is lived in only in the summer so heating such a large space is not a problem.

A 100-year-old railroad station was converted into a country retreat despite its neglected appearance. The original wood floors and walls were sandblasted to remove years of dirt, and most of the details such as the ticket window were left intact. The living room occupies the original waiting room; a new kitchen was installed in the former Railway Express Office at the back (visible through the archway). The stairway next to the kitchen was added to provide access to a second-level bedroom and bath. Both the first and second floors have high, 13-ft. ceilings, and there is an attic above the bedroom.

When this 1875 carriage house was converted, the only exterior change was to pull aside the sliding door and fill the open space with a multi-paned window. On the main floor, the original horse stalls became bedrooms without making any changes in floor plan; a kitchen and bath were added. On the second floor, the coachman's room remains intact.

Old house restorations

Preserving the past

Restoring an old house, returning it to its former, historically authentic condition, is becoming more popular as new construction costs steadily rise. Older homes are also bought for their character and quality of workmanship.

Some old houses are restored by people who respect the workmanship of an earlier era and try to re-create the details as authentically as possible. Other homeowners temper the historical details with modern conveniences, and add central heating, to make old-house living more comfortable. Whichever style of restoration is used, the houses, examples of which are shown on these and the next two pages, offer us a real glimpse of the past.

Photographs on this page © 1973 Robert Perron

This saltbox house built in 1710 in rural Connecticut remained in the same family until the 1930s. It was probably built in one piece. If the lean-to at the back had been added later, the roofline would not be continuous, but would show a break—and the clapboards would be broken. The present owners were extremely fortunate to find the original hearths, beams, floorboards, and other smaller details intact. The clapboards had deteriorated and were replaced with beaded boards that duplicate the originals. The entry and stairway (above), with its original woodwork, is typical of the narrow, compact stairways built in saltbox houses. The cooking hearth (left) had at one point been filled in to make a smaller fireplace. It is now opened up and restored to its original size.

332

This 1750 garrison-style house (right) was in dilapidated condition when a couple with an interest in history bought it. They chose to remove additions and any changes made to it after 1800; they opened up its six fireplaces, which had been boarded over, replaced the old sash windows, removed the Victorian shingles, and repaired the original clapboard. In a concession to modern living, they installed new wiring and baseboard heating. The floors were painted but not sanded, since sanding would have destroyed the character of the worn surface. In the bedroom (above), the owners continue to use the fireplace for heat.

A Cape Cod house built in 1730 (above) has been lovingly restored by its owner, who did most of the work herself. The new handsplit cedar shingles and cedar shakes were applied in their natural state and allowed to weather. The double-hung windows with 12 over 12 panes, custom-made because each opening was slightly different in size, were copied from the one original window left in the house. To make the house more livable, insulation was installed and the walls plastered. Yet a bedroom under the eaves (right, top) retains its 18th-century charm because the original beams were left exposed. To make the large kitchen that also serves as a family room (right, bottom), one wall was removed and two rooms combined. The wood used to panel the kitchen walls and to make storage shelves was salvaged from the house as well as from neighboring houses of the same historical period. The wide-plank floor in the kitchen was part of the original kitchen.

Old house restorations

Preserving the past

© 1980 Karen Bussolini / Designed by Kenneth Kraus

A pair of semidetached brick townhouses (left) in New Haven, Connecticut, were rehabilitated by an architect who specializes in urban work. He combined restoration of historical details with renovating the houses into rental apartments (see pp.343–347).

The exterior of the house was in excellent condition; the wood trim required only paint; and the original oak doors were stripped. In the parlor (below, left), old plaster walls were replaced with Sheetrock but the window and door moldings and ornate fireplace mantel are original, as is the wide-plank fir floor. To transform the lower level into a family room (below, right), a greenhouse was added at the back with access through a door that originally led to the outside. A new tile floor was laid, the stairs were carpeted, the back door replaced with a French door, and new windows installed in the original openings.

Van Jones Martin / Designed by Mrs. Reuben Clark

A Savannah, Georgia home (above) looks almost exactly the same as it did when it was built in 1793. Although repaired extensively over the years, the house has its original clapboards and front porch, and the chimney is reputed to be the oldest in Savannah. In the upstairs bedroom (right), the fireplace was closed off to provide more room. Insulation, central heating, and air conditioning were added. The wide-plank floors are original.

These townhouses in Philadelphia's Society Hill area have been restored after years of neglect. The 2½-story Georgian houses (left) built around 1780 have a pronounced wooden pediment over the door, a brick belt course at each level, and windows of 9 over 9 panes. The 3½-story Federal houses (center) built in 1810 have high marble steps and wrought-iron railings, both copies of the originals. The doors have leaded-glass fanlights; the door on the left has its sidelights still intact. The Federal houses (right) built in 1825 have a high foundation, curved steps, both paneled and louvered shutters, and windows of 6 over 6 panes.

Victorian houses built between 1880 and 1910 have become ripe targets for restoration by owners who love the intricate details characteristic of this style. The small San Francisco Victorian (left) had its shell-shaped wooden shingles and moldings intact except for the arch in front of the entrance. The arch had been replaced with a style of wood trim popular in Victorian times. A larger Victorian house (detail, above) was in a state of total disrepair and had entirely new siding installed. The wooden ornament at the roof peak and the wrought-iron balustrade are new. Many manufacturers are now making historically accurate ornamentation for both interior and exterior use on houses dating as far back as the early 1700s. Homeowners choosing to restore can match decorative pieces from a range of styles offered.

Restoring an old house

Before and after

The Snider house in Port Townsend, following its restoration by its owner.

The condition of Snider house at the time of purchase.

Photographs on this page by John Johnson.
Materials courtesy of: Eccles Nursery and Garden Center (Landscaping); J & P Sales, The Garden Store (miscellaneous);
Kelly-Moore Paint Company (paint); Port Townsend Lumber Company (lumber).

More than a bargain

As would-be homeowners face high mortgage rates and inflated prices for new housing, many are turning to this country's pool of older housing as a way of fulfilling their dreams. An older house often needs considerable improvement, which is why the selling price is well within reach of people with ordinary incomes. But a fixer-upper may be more than just a bargain. When tastefully restored, an old house has all the charm of an earlier era when houses were built with an individuality lacking in much modern construction.

The more restoration work you do yourself, the greater your bargain will be, of course—and the more satisfaction you will find in living in your house. The subject of this chapter is an old Victorian house in Port Townsend, Washington, not far from Seattle. It was restored by Tim Snider, a consultant for our book, who had previously fixed up a number of houses. Anyone with less do-it-yourself know-how should be cautious about a house in such a serious state of disrepair (see drawing, opposite page). Because he had the skill and experience, Snider was able to jack the house level and pour new foundations, and to put on an entire new wood-shingle roof. Both of these major structural jobs are illustrated in detail on the following five pages. In addition, he did all the rewiring, wallpapering, and many of the other tasks necessary to restore his house. We believe the general information on Snider's decisions and methods will be useful to anyone less experienced who may be thinking of taking on a similar project.

Choosing a house to restore: If you are thinking of buying a fixer-upper, it is best to find an expert—an architect, a building contractor, or an experienced friend—to determine the condition of the house and to estimate the magnitude and difficulty of the restoration.

If you make the evaluation yourself, here are some things to look for:

▷ Where an old house touches or is close to the ground, rot and termite damage can occur. Push the point of a penknife into beams in the basement or crawl spaces; if the knife penetrates more than ¼ inch, the beam might have to be replaced, a difficult process (see pp.338–340). Look for small piles of dust and signs of boring in the beams, symptoms of termites or other insects. Sills, roof rafters, and siding must also be checked for rot.

▷ Look for signs of structural weaknesses. Floors pulling away from exterior walls, walls off vertical (plumb), broken lintels, large cracks in the walls or in the basement floor, floors that shake, sag, or feel as if they might give way are all signs of big problems. Run a string across the first-floor beams and joists; if they sag more than 1 inch per 12 feet, they will need additional support. Look for light-colored mortar and cement (signs of patching) and crumbling mortar in masonry walls. Check the squareness and plumb of the doors and windows.

▷ Look at the ridge of the roof, from either the attic or atop the roof. A straight ridge is a good indication that the house is basically sound.

▷ Check the condition of the roofing from inside the attic and on the roof itself, if possible. Look at spots vulnerable to water infiltration, such as in valleys and around chimneys. See if the flashing is uncorroded and still tightly in place. Deterioration in the roof indicates not only that the roofing must be replaced, but also that water may have already caused damage to framing, insulation, wiring, and interior finish. Check gutters and downspouts for corrosion and tightness.

▷ Turn on the taps. Rust in the water is a sign of deteriorating plumbing. Look for leaks in the pipe fittings in the basement. Look for water spots around the plumbing and on the ceilings below bathrooms. If the pipes are not copper, they will have to be replaced eventually. Check the basement for signs of leaks.

▷ Electrical systems must be checked carefully. A house as old as this one (almost 100 years) probably will have to be rewired completely.

Choosing the jobs to do yourself: Restoration work is usually done by the homeowner and hired subcontractors. Minor carpentry and painting, for example, can be done by almost anyone. Tasks such as tiling and putting up partition walls can be learned on the job (with the aid of the technical chapters in this book); you can attain professional results if you have patience and are willing to devote the time. More complex jobs or those that pose hazards, including completely new plumbing, heating, and electrical wiring, require great expertise; if you do not have it, hire a professional.

Planning and scheduling: Scheduling the work, and doing it in the proper order, are often the most difficult tasks for the first-time restorer. Snider suggests that do-it-yourselfers plan to spend twice as long on their restoration as they expect. He did the foundation work and roofing in the balmy days of spring and summer, then moved indoors to do the wiring, plastering, painting, and wallpapering in the wintertime. He built the new walls and roof for the kitchen in the off-season, when carpenters were available to help; dur-

ing the summer they would not have taken such a small job. He paced his work so that he knew there would be sufficient cash for each project at hand. Although it is cheaper to buy materials all at one time it may not always be possible or practial to do so.

Snider hired a plumber to do all the plumbing work. This saved time, and he did not have to buy or rent tools. He did the electrical work himself.

The new electrical wiring: The old bathroom and kitchen were housed in a dilapidated lean-to addition to the original house. When Snider demolished the lean-to (which he later rebuilt), all of the plumbing and much of the wiring were exposed. They were worn and outdated, and they were replaced.

The power was completely shut off before demolition began. The old meter was pulled out and the main lines to the pole were disconnected. New service and breaker panels, upgraded to 200 amps, were installed and a work circuit was added. The system was then inspected by building officials and power was restored, providing light and allowing the use of power tools.

Wiring the new kitchen and bathroom, when they were built, was easy. Rewiring the existing part of the house was more difficult. The upper story wires had to be pushed into the wall cavities from the attic through holes drilled in the top plates. Often wires would not go straight through to the far holes through which the circuits were connected, and a helper had to fish for them with a coat hanger, cord, or fish tape. Occasionally a hole had to be made in a wall to notch a piece of framing to allow the wiring to pass.

Once the second floor was wired, a shopcord on the first floor supplied all the necessary power, enabling Snider to put off the messy first-floor wiring. Later he got around to it, pushing wires up into the wall cavities from the crawl space beneath the house. He built the outlets into the high baseboards, with extreme care.

The restoration spirit: Tim Snider describes a strong emotional involvement in renovation work. His first sight of the house, and the anticipation of restoring it, were exhilarating. After the purchase, the size of the task often seemed overwhelming. Certain stages of the work were too risky, such as when the house was jacked off its foundation, and when rainclouds appeared with only a tarp covering part of the unshingled roof. Other stages were satisfying—when the first bedroom was finished, when the kitchen became functional. Completion was at first a relief, later a source of satisfaction.

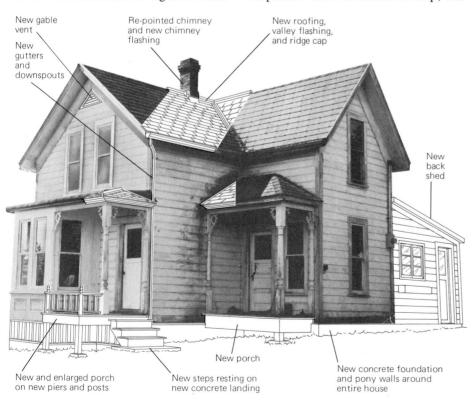

New gable vent

New gutters and downspouts

Re-pointed chimney and new chimney flashing

New roofing, valley flashing, and ridge cap

New back shed

New and enlarged porch on new piers and posts

New steps resting on new concrete landing

New porch

New concrete foundation and pony walls around entire house

In this photo of the Snider house, the parts shown as line drawing indicate some of the major repairs and renovations performed by the owner, mostly working alone, but with the help of professional tradesmen for the most difficult jobs. These included pouring new footings and foundations, applying a new wood shingle roof, and framing a new lean-to shed.

Restoring an old house

Building a new foundation beneath an existing house

The original foundation of the old house in Port Townsend consisted of cedar footings and posts. Direct contact with or proximity to the soil had caused some of the footings, posts, and beams beneath the house to rot. The front and back of the house had settled at different rates, leaving the house somewhat off level after several score years.

The first step of this restoration was to replace the foundation. The house was jacked up one section at a time. The old footings and posts under that section were removed. Then, a continuous concrete footing and foundation wall were excavated and poured for the entire house. Finally, concrete pier footings and wood posts, carefully adjusted to provide a level base were set beneath the interior beams, and the house was lowered onto its new underpinnings. Only when the house was level and solidly supported could further work proceed inside and outside the house.

1. A hydraulic jack is placed beneath a beam to lift a section of the perimeter off its foundation so old decaying cedar footings and posts can be removed. The house is raised one section at a time, and never lifted more than 1 in. off its foundation.

2. A post that has been cut to the required height is placed beneath the raised beam, freeing the jack to raise the next segment of the beam.

3. The foundation wall, which will be 6 in. wide, and the footing, which will be 18 in. wide, must be centered below the sill. Using a plumb line as a guide, the outside edge of the footing is located with a tape measure and staked for excavation.

4. To keep the trench for the new foundation straight, boards are laid to mark the lines of the excavation. Once the soil has been dug along the guide boards, they are removed and the excavation is completed.

5. The depth of the trench, here 16 in., is checked with a tape measure. When it is correct for the entire length, the bottom is checked with a level. It is then dug further or filled in as necessary to make it flat.

6. A wooden mold, or form, is built to hold concrete for the foundation wall. The footing will fill the trench, but the foundation wall must be contained by the form from ground level up. First, stakes are driven in around the perimeter of the foundation. Each stake is checked with a level.

7. Next, the cross pieces, or forming boards, are tacked to the stakes. Each is checked with a level before it is finally nailed in position.

8. The position of the forming board is checked with a plumb line to ensure that the corner of the foundation will be directly below the corner of the house. Stakes are nailed to house to help position form. A supporting log is behind the trench.

9. Before the second forming board is set on top of the first, metal straps are laid in. The straps hold the boards rigidly in place, preventing the wet concrete from bowing the form outward, and thereby maintaining the correct foundation thickness. The straps remain in the concrete after the concrete sets.

10. The first forming board on the other side of the foundation wall is tacked in place and is checked with a level. An iron reinforcing rod that will run through the length of the footing is set in place. Later it will be tied to the straps so that it will be embedded in the center of the concrete.

11. The metal straps are held in place by wedges driven into slots in the straps on the outside of the forming boards. The straps have two sets of slots, so they can be used with lumber 2-in. thick, as here, or 1-in. thick. With 1-in. lumber, the straps are placed closer together for extra reinforcement.

12. The top of the form is checked with a level to be sure that both sides are exactly the same height. The top of the form corresponds exactly with what will be the top of the foundation wall, so the form must be straight and even if foundation is to be flat.

13. Similarly, a level is used to check across a corner of the form. This ensures different segments of the foundation will be the same height.

14. The forms for the foundation beneath an extension of the house and the main building behind it have been completed. The boards across the top also reinforce the forms by holding the sides together. This type of bracing is needed where a single forming board comprises one side of the form, making it impossible to use straps. It is also used for additional bracing wherever necessary.

15. An opening is cut in the form where the foundation walls for the extension and for the main building will intersect. This allows the concrete of the two walls to bond, creating greater strength. The reinforcing rods are tied with wire to the straps so that the rods will be embedded in the middle of the foundation wall, not at the bottom.

16. The forms for the foundation on the sides of the house follow the incline of the grade in steps. The boards at the end of each step will dam the wet concrete.

17. Wherever two forms of different heights meet, as under this corner, an end board is needed to complete the higher form, or the wet concrete would flow out the end.

18. Concrete is poured into the top of the forms and flows out the bottom, filling the trench up to the bottom of the forms to create the footing. More concrete is poured, until the forms are also filled; thus, footing and foundation wall are one piece. The cement is shoveled to distribute it evenly, then the shovel is used to agitate the cement so that any air pockets are filled.

19. A screed board is pulled across the top of a form to level the concrete, so that the top surface of the foundation wall will be flat.

20. The anchor bolts that will secure the wood framing to the foundation are embedded in the wet concrete. Each bolt is inserted at an angle, then rotated straight up as it is pushed to the proper depth. The bolt must protrude from the concrete a distance equal to the thickness of the sill, plus the thickness of the washer and nut used to fasten the bolt.

21. A hammer is used to tap the bolt to its final depth. Hammer blows agitate the concrete, helping to form a good bond between the bolt and the concrete and filling any air pockets in the concrete.

22. After the concrete is leveled with the screed board, it is troweled smooth. Applying water to the concrete while troweling produces a smooth, polished surface for the pony walls. (Pony walls are small wood-frame walls that sit directly on top of the foundation wall and support the house proper above them.)

23. When the concrete has set for 24 hours the forms are removed. First, the stakes are pulled off the house and cut flush with the footing. The wedges and the boards across the tops of the forms are removed. The forming boards are pulled away from the concrete and cut flush with the footing. The ends of the straps are hammered flat against the foundation wall. Finally, the concrete footing is backfilled with earth.

24. A pony wall is an open structure of 2 x 4s that allows air to circulate below the house. Its bottom sill rests directly on the foundation, and its top sill supports the first-floor joists of the house. Pony walls are assembled before they are installed. These were built to different heights to accommodate a stepped foundation, thereby saving excavation effort, formwork, and concrete.

Restoring an old house

Building a new foundation beneath an existing house (continued)

25. The positions of the anchor bolts are marked on the mud sills and the holes are drilled before the pony walls are assembled. The mud sills are notched so that the pony walls will slide easily into position on the bolts. This section of the house has not yet been lowered onto the pony wall; it is still jacked up and supported by logs.

26. Where the distance between the foundation and the house is small, as in this part of the stepped foundation, doubled 2-x-4 blocks are used as the intermediate members of the pony wall. When the height of the foundation walls was being planned, the dimensions of standard framing lumber were kept in mind so that this pony wall would fit correctly without planing the 2 x 4s.

27. The stepped sections of the pony wall are in place. The double post at the corner will become a triple post when the adjoining pony wall is installed, giving the corner of the foundation added strength and rigidity. The nuts are tightened down permanently only after all pony walls are installed and house is lowered.

28. The crawl space under the house is only a few inches deep in places, and some beams actually contact the ground. The cedar pier footings and posts, as well as some beams, have rotted badly, and there is insect damage. In order to excavate the crawl space to a minimum depth of 2 ft., the floor boards on the first floor of the house are lifted.

29. After the crawl space has been excavated, it must be leveled and packed down hard so as to provide a firm footing on undisturbed soil for the new concrete footings. The interior beams of the house are then jacked up and carefully leveled so that when the old pier footings and posts are replaced, the house will be perfectly level. Again, logs are placed under the raised members so that the jack can be moved.

30. Do-it-yourselfers usually buy pre-cast concrete pier footings, but our man procured forms for the pier footings. When the concrete truck came to pour the foundation, he cast the pier footings himself.

31. All of the concrete pier footings are placed in their permanent positions under the house, and the distance between each footing and the leveled beam above is measured with a tape measure. These measurements determine the height of each wood pier. The final position of the house was actually about 1½ in. below its original position.

32. Each wood pier is cut to fit precisely between its footing and beam so that when the house rests on its new foundation and piers, it will be absolutely level. The wood piers are treated with pentachlorophenol before being installed to make them rot and termite resistant.

33. As soon as the structurally sound beams have been leveled and are sitting solidly on the new pier footings and posts, the rotted sections are chain-sawed away.

34. A new beam is spliced into the existing beams to replace each segment that was cut away. The newly excavated crawl space ensures that no beams will contact the ground. A concrete footing and wood post can be seen supporting the old beam just where it joins the new beam, minimizing the load on the joint.

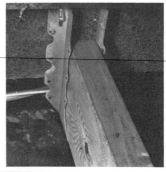

35. Where the end of a new beam abuts a crossing beam, it is secured with a joist hanger that is solidly nailed to both beams. Such a joint can support heavy loads.

36. This view shows a finished section of the crawl space from above before the floor is replaced. The new concrete pier footings and wood posts support the beams, two new segments have been spliced into the old beams, and the crawl space has been excavated. Only concrete contacts the ground; air circulates freely, effectively preventing rot and insect damage to the house frame.

Re-roofing with wood shingles

The existing roof on the house consisted of a worn layer of asphalt shingles over the original covering of wood shingles. Although it had not yet begun to leak, signs of deterioration indicated that the entire roof needed to be replaced, as is shown below and on the next page.

The owner decided that a roof covering of cedar shingles was most in keeping with the Victorian character of the house. He chose red cedar shingles, which turn an attractive silver shade after they have been exposed to the elements and sea air for a few years.

While the roof was being recovered, new flashing was installed in the valleys and around the chimney, and the chimney was re-pointed at the same time.

1. The existing roof of asphalt shingles was applied about 30 years ago over the original wood shingles, which were put on when the house was built in 1891. The steep pitch of the roof has helped prevent leaks, but signs of deterioration—rust stains from the nails, granules on the asphalt worn smooth, the growth of moss—indicate that a new roof is needed. (The unattractive appearance of the asphalt shingle roof also figured strongly in the decision to put on a new roof.) Since the owner planned to renovate the interior of the house, it made sense to replace the roof first and thus protect the walls, ceilings, and floors from potential leaks.

2. A crowbar is used to pry up the old layers of roofing, starting from the top of the roof and working downward. Only as much of the roof as can be replaced in one day is stripped, so that the house is not exposed to weather damage. If part of the roof must be left without roofing, secure a tarp over it.

3. While the old shingles are being stripped off, the nailers underneath are examined for structural soundness. These long 1 x 6 fir boards were still completely sound, and so do not have to be replaced. Protruding nails are either pulled or hammered back into the nailers so that the new shingles will lie flat. The new shingles will be attached directly to the nailers; sheathing is not used on this roof. The spacing of the nailers depends on the spacing, or exposure, of the shingles. The gaps between the nailers allow air to circulate beneath the shingles, so that warm, moisture-laden air from inside the house can escape without condensing on the underside of the shingles, which could rot and ruin the ceiling beneath the roof.

4. A board is installed along the rake to serve as a guide for the shingle overlap at the rake. If the shingles stopped exactly at the edge of the roof, water might seep under them and cause leaks. The shingles are irregularly sized, ranging from about 3 in. to 10 in. wide and about 14 in. long. Four bundles of cedar shingles cover a roofing square (100 sq. ft.).

5. Shingles are applied randomly as they are pulled from the bundles. When they do not fit properly, they are trimmed with a utility knife. The butt end of the shingle (the fat end) always faces downroof. Here the first, or starter, course is installed, overhanging the roof by a bit so that runoff will fall freely into the gutter. The starter course is made of two layers of shingles, one directly atop the other. The joints between shingles are staggered between layers so that water cannot penetrate.

6. A roofing hatchet with a guide measures the distance between courses as they are installed to ensure that the exposed part of each shingle (the exposure) is the same thoughout the roof. Each shingle is attached with two galvanized shingle nails placed ¼ in. from each edge and ½ in. above the butt line of the next course. Thus all nails are protected by shingles laid over them.

7. A ¼-in. gap is left between neighboring shingles to allow them to expand when they get wet. (If this were not done, the roof would buckle and crack in time.) The joints between the shingles are staggered in successive courses to help prevent water infiltration. Every area of the roof is covered by at least three layers of shingles; this triple overlap is what ensures that the house will be adequately protected from the rain, wind, ice, and snow.

8. Ideally, all courses of shingles should be parallel and have identical exposures if the roof is to have a neat appearance when finished. This requires regular checking and adjustment as the work proceeds. Every several courses, a tape measure is run up to the ridge of the roof, from two or more points along the butt of the last course of shingles laid. If it becomes apparent that the spacing of the shingles will result in a last narrow course along the ridge, the remaining courses can be adjusted (by about ¼ in. each course) so they will all come out even. Here a chalk line (see p.288) is snapped to guide the adjusted placement of the next course of shingles.

Restoring an old house

9. To install courses that cannot be reached from a ladder, toe boards are nailed across the roof to support the roofer and prevent him from slipping. To make a toe board, the butt edge of a shingle is nailed to each end of a 2 x 4; the board is flipped over and positioned on the roof so its top is aligned with what will be the bottom of the next course of shingles (see next photo).

10. The shingles are nailed down to the nailer, using extra nails for added support. The remainder of the shingles for that course are nailed in place with their butt ends on the chalk line. When the toe board is no longer needed, the end shingles are cut off with a utility knife flush with the top of the board, so that they are properly aligned with other shingles in the course.

11. A sheet of galvanized steel flashing about 22 in. wide is tacked into the valley. It comes with a preformed ridge (splash deflector) in the center of the valley to prevent water from running off one face of the roof and up the other. The factory-formed flashing is bent to the proper angle and tacked to the nailers.

12. A chalk line is snapped to each side of the center of the flashing, establishing the several inches of flashing that will be left exposed once the shingles are laid. One shingle for each side is measured and marked at the correct angle, using the chalk lines as guides. The shingles are then cut along the lines marked with a utility knife or power saw. Each shingle will serve as a template for all shingles on the same side of the valley.

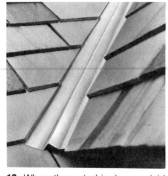

13. When the cut shingles are laid over the flashing they overlap each other so that they have the same exposure as the rest of the shingles. Each course is started at the flashing to be sure that the angled shingles fit properly and that the gaps between shingles are staggered from course to course on the roof.

14. The vent pipe protruding up through the roof is flashed with a rubber pad and collar. The pad and collar are installed and the shingles are cut to fit around them when the shingling process reaches that particular section of the roof.

15. Step flashing is installed around the chimney to prevent water from infiltrating between the chimney and the roof. The squares are cut from a roll of flashing aluminum. The first piece of step flashing is folded to fit exactly into the valley. It extends to the downroof edge of the chimney and is tucked beneath the old flashing, which is still attached to the brick of the chimney.

16. The first piece of step flashing is nailed to the shingle below it. The next piece overlaps the first. Step flashing is installed in layers just as the shingles are; both serve to direct water down over the roof. The installation of step flashing is illustrated in detail on pages 259–260.

17. The chimney is re-pointed to improve its appearance and structural integrity. First all of the loose mortar is removed with a cold chisel and mason's hammer. Fresh mortar is pushed off a trowel into the cleared joints with a jointer. Where the chimney widens, the mortar is beveled so that water will run down the chimney and not into the joints.

18. Another layer of flashing, called counter flashing, is laid into the mortar joints of the chimney while the mortar is still wet. The pieces of counter flashing are laid in successive horizontal joints, following the slope of the roof. Once in place, the counter flashing is folded over the step flashing. This adds one more layer of protection against water and ice and snow infiltration.

19. The shingles at the top of each face are sawed off flush with the ridge. The ridge cap, which comes in 10-ft. lengths of preformed galvanized steel, is nailed in place over the shingles. A finial at the open end of the ridge cap closes the end of the ridge vent and provides a neat and attractive decorative touch.

20. The other end of the ridge cap overlaps the counter flashing laid into the mortar joints of the chimney. After the mortar in the re-pointed chimney has set for a day, it is brushed with muriatic acid.

Rehabilitating urban houses

Developing and homesteading

As in many older cities, an urban metamorphosis is flourishing in New Haven, Connecticut. The old policy of bulldozing areas considered to be obsolete or blighted is changing. Preservationists, ecologists, architects, historians, and citizens are forcing redevelopment agencies to recognize the value of preserving both the physical structures and the social fabric in existing city neighborhoods.

A New Haven architect, Kenneth Kraus, is among those who have begun to rehabilitate urban properties. Based on Kraus' experiences, this chapter illustrates the rehabbing of two houses at 144-146 Bradley Street in New Haven. Hopefully, this general account will serve as a source of ideas and information for those—including do-it-yourselfers—who are considering an urban rehabilitation project. Specific instructions for each job required can be found elsewhere in this book.

Some general terms: A "home improvement" is work done to make a basically livable home attractive, more functional, more modern, etc. The improvements are made for their own sake, not necessarily as an investment. This reflects a basic fact of the real estate business: a $30,000 house in a neighborhood where that is the market value of most houses probably will not sell for $50,000 because of $20,000 in improvements. Its market value reflects its surroundings.

"Restoration" refers to returning a building to its former, historically authentic condition. "Renovation" and "rehabilitation" refer to fixing up—making habitable, with modern conveniences—a building fallen into disrepair. These terms can also mean converting an old nonresidential building—barn, church, railroad station, industrial loft—to residential use, commercial use, or a combination of both. A rehabilitation is often done by owners intending to make a home for themselves and perhaps an income-producing rental apartment or two in addition. Or a building can be rehabilitated by a developer (an individual or a company) strictly as an investment; this kind of rehabilitation is called recycling.

Why rehabilitate?: Why rehabilitate a city building, why not tear it down and start anew?

Attitudes about rehabilitation are changing as prices for new construction soar. Would-be city homeowners, as well as developers, are beginning to realize that the savings in energy and materials often make rehabilitation cheaper. Old city homes are now sought-after because their graceful scale and careful detail are not generally attainable in new housing. Older buildings need not and often do not conform to modern zoning and setback regulations; in many places only a much smaller building could be built on the lot if the old one were razed. To build with the same character and quality of workmanship that exists in many old houses is nearly impossible today because of increased costs, inferior materials, and a shortage of artisans skilled in the old crafts. People love ceilings higher than the standard 8 feet, windows larger than 2 x 3 feet, marble fireplaces, decorative plaster ceilings, all of the wonderful and unexpected things that give an old house character. Such architectural details give real esthetic and economic value to the older building. They are, in terms of the mass market, irreplaceable.

Rehabilitation offers a unique opportunity to own a desirable home that yields current income and is a good investment. Kraus says, "an owner-occupied urban home with an income-producing rental unit is one of the few ways a young family is going to survive the fuel and financial crises of the '80's". With the help of federal and local homesteading programs and neighborhood planning and assistance agencies, home ownership is becoming possible for larger numbers of ordinary city dwellers, often in the same buildings in which they formerly rented apartments. For many urban homesteaders, planning and doing the work themselves is a large part of the satisfaction, but they must enjoy the work. While it can be profitable, there are too many challenges to do it just for the money.

Choosing a house to rehabilitate: The location of a house is as crucial as the actual renovations. A house can be rented or sold only in a neighborhood where people (including *you*) want to live. If others are already renovating houses on a block, then the value of surrounding properties will probably increase in value or at least remain stable. Few people will want to live in a bombed-out block, no matter how much of a masterpiece the one renovated house is. Also, the total costs of a house should be in keeping with the neighborhood's average housing prices.

Locating the right neighborhood and house requires study, legwork, and time. Read the real estate section of the local paper to learn about trends, and read the ads to compare selling prices in many areas over a period of time. Go to open houses sponsored by real estate agencies, and find an agent who understands what you are looking for. Don't discount the value of word-of-mouth or of walking and driving around just looking. Look for features that will increase the value of a home, such as nearby parks, good transportation, the presence nearby of a big company, a university, a hospital, or some other employer whose personnel form a large rental market; waterfront property; a stable tax base; or location in a vacation community with high seasonal rents.

Kenneth Kraus's aim was not just to buy into a neighborhood, but to help re-create it. "When a single house is restored on any block, no matter how beautiful it is, its impact can be diminished and it can be swallowed up by its surroundings. I wanted to make an im-

These rehabilitated townhouses are part of an urban renaissance in New Haven, Connecticut.

Continued, next page.

Rehabilitating urban houses

Developing and homesteading (continued)

pact on a city neighborhood and start a positive chain reaction." Kraus saw an ad in the paper, for two old frame houses built before 1850, at 131 and 133 Bradley Street, a block away from a recently rehabilitated historical square. The houses were divided into overcrowded rooming house apartments, but they were structurally sound, easily rehabilitated, and lovely; he bought both houses. Kraus also noticed a pair of vacant semi-detached brick townhouses across the street. He tracked down the owner and bought 144 and 146 Bradley Street as well. Few individual home-buyers could afford Kraus's approach. But a group of like-minded individuals and families, acting in concert, can achieve the same impact—working in unison to change the character of an urban environment.

Buyer beware: Don't get carried away with a real estate agent's enthusiastic talk about "potential." The agent wants to sell the house; you need hard facts. If you are not experienced, ask a friend who is a contractor, a carpenter, or an experienced do-it-yourselfer to examine and evaluate the property; or hire a professional. Many architects, builders, and structural engineers will advise you on an hourly basis. Have the building carefully checked from top to bottom, and be there yourself—you will learn a lot. Your adviser will check for structural soundness and termites; tell you what must be replaced, what can be repaired, and what is acceptable as is; and tell you what must be done to conform to building, housing, and fire codes. Such services are well worth the expense—they can save you from costly, time-consuming mistakes.

Always be sure that you know what you are buying, and have it in writing. It is illegal for the agent or seller to misrepresent the property, but only a written contract can protect you. You will need an experienced real estate lawyer for this. The lawyer should be representing *your* interests alone; do not share an attorney with the seller because you think it will save you money. Regulations as to what is included with the purchase of a house vary from state to state; specifically, the terms "fixed" and "removable" are defined differently in different localities. What about refrigerators, washing machines, sinks, light fixtures, stair railings? If you think that you are buying these or any other items, have it in writing. If the owner claims that all mechanical systems are in good working order, have it in writing. Some cities have ordinances requiring that a house be brought up to code *before* it is sold. In this case, who will be responsible for making repairs? Your purchase agreement can be written so that the sale is contingent upon such work being done by the owner or by you. It can also be contingent upon your receiving a mortgage commitment or a zoning variance, or on any number of conditions.

Should you be your own contractor?: According to Jan C. K. Anderson of Restore, a New York training program that teaches restoration skills to members of the building trades, "Rehabilitation is more labor-intensive and cost effective than new construction. For every dollar spent on new construction, 70 cents is spent on materials and 30 cents on labor. The ratio is reversed on restoration work." If 70 per-

cent of your cost is for hired labor, you lose money every time the work stops or slows down. On the other hand, you save a great deal when you do a job yourself. But remember, time is money when you are financing a home that cannot be occupied until completion.

If you are inexperienced, a contractor will run the job more efficiently than you can. He knows the building codes and has a working relationship with building officials. Subcontractors are more likely to do a good job and to be there on schedule for a contractor than for a homeowner, because they depend upon the contractor for repeat business. A contractor knows how things should be done. When he needs information, it is his business to know where to get it. It is the contractor's job to be on site to coordinate and inspect work. He will save you time, materials, and the possible frustration of finding out after a building inspection that something was done wrong in the beginning and must be torn out.

However, if you are knowledgeable about the work to be done, supervising it yourself may be the most effective way to achieve the kind of quality you want. You must weigh the value of your own time against the cost of hiring a professional.

Some rehabilitation projects are small enough to be done part time. You may opt to do most of the planning yourself, then hire a carpenter to double-check the plans and to do some of the more skilled jobs. Many types of working relationships can be negotiated between the extremes of doing all of the work yourself and having it all done for you.

A new wall and door were built in the entryway to shield the first-floor apartment from the common stairway. The old plaster wall on the right was basically in good condition and so was patched, but the plaster wall visible through the door was

so badly crumbled that it had to be removed. Old trim in keeping with the architectural detail of the house was recycled to frame the new door. The original carved wooden newel post and balustrade were stripped of old paint and refinished.

Because the entryway and stairs were to be carpeted, only the hall floor was refinished. Paneled double doors, a salvaged chandelier, a delicate antique table, and plush carpeting lend the finished entryway an elegant air.

The high ceilings, tall windows, and ornate carved mantelpiece give the parlor floor a graceful, spacious character that was developed in the new plan. The plaster walls were in bad condition and had to be replaced, but all of the original window and door trim was saved. Although some floor boards had to be replaced, the original wide-board floors were rescued by sanding them down and sealing them with polyurethane varnish, a protective finish virtually impervious to wear. Period furniture and a portrait over the mantel added the perfect finishing touches.

Urban homesteading: Balancing the value of your time against the cost of a general contractor may not be the question at all; you may not be able to afford to rehabilitate a building *unless* you do it yourself. If your goal is a home of reasonable value and comfort for a minimum cash outlay, your costs will be restricted to materials and those subcontractors you must hire. An urban homesteader increases the value of his property with his labor, building with "sweat equity" rather than hard cash. This self-help approach has always been the hallmark of homesteaders.

Recognizing their responsibility for providing decent and affordable housing for all citizens, many cities have established programs to help low-income people obtain property for homesteading. The cities then benefit from the stability generated by rehabilitated owner-occupied properties. Various government and private agencies provide technical assistance, information, mortgage counseling, financing, and grants for rehabilitation or energy conservation. As the need for these services increases, more programs are being developed and funded in cities across the nation. If yours is a young family, such programs may be your best opportunity to become a homeowner.

Planning the work: Of course, the ideal building to rehabilitate is one that is sound structurally and requires only cosmetic changes. Almost any part of a building can be replaced if necessary, but the replacement costs for structural members can be prohibitive. No matter how much or how little work is involved, the key to success is always the same—planning.

Measure each room and draw floor plans of the building as is. Then, develop a new, functional design as close to the existing floor plan as possible. It

is more economical to save existing walls, floors, moldings, etc., than to tear them out and replace them, and the esthetic advantages are often great, since many features of older buildings cannot be duplicated with modern materials. Kraus tries to include as many bedrooms and baths as he can, as these increase the market value of the property. When you have decided what you will save and what will be changed, make working drawings of the new plan; at that point you are ready to ask subcontractors to submit bids on each phase of the work (see pp.38–48). Try to get at least three bids in order to compare prices. The following extremes were received as estimates by a colleague of Kraus's; they illustrate the necessity of getting several estimates: interior painting $450-$3,600; sanding floors $900-$2,500; taping plasterboard and spraying ceilings $1,700-$4,000.

Mechanical systems: Professional advice is crucial in evaluating existing electrical, plumbing, and heating systems. Make use of as much of the existing systems as possible. If you are doing the work yourself, the cost of replacement materials may be more critical than time. But if a subcontractor does the work, it is often more economical to replace the whole system than to pay for the time it takes to find and replace defective sections.

Quite often the plumbing in an old house is adequate and can be lived with, particularly if your budget is slim. But you run the risk of eventual leaks that can ruin new plasterboard and carpets if you miscalculate the condition of the existing system.

In some cases, the existing electrical service can be retained intact and new panel boxes added for additional branch circuits (see pp.173–179). Plan the use of existing circuits—probably

old 14-gauge, 15-amp lines—so that they are undertaxed. Old kitchens almost always need to be completely rewired, as modern demands far exceed the capacity of most old systems. Check the wiring by removing several outlets; if you see frayed wires or cable with rotten or broken insulation, chances are that the existing circuits are in bad condition in other places as well, and the house should be completely rewired.

Radiators and pipes in steam and hot-water heating systems can last in-

Continued, next page.

Finding programs and agencies in your area

▷ Call your state government's central information line.
▷ Check with your City Redevelopment Agency, Urban Rehabilitation Department, Housing Authority, and City Planning Department.
▷ Call your state's departments of energy and housing.
▷ Call the central number for city offices and ask for listings of all housing rehabilitation departments and programs.
▷ Ask city or state agencies to refer you to private nonprofit neighborhood groups. Some of these groups are dedicated to helping people locate, redesign, and rehabilitate quality homes without relying on government funding. Some groups specialize in energy conservation and weatherization; some in financial counseling; some in do-it-yourself advice. Resident groups have a big stake in preserving neighborhoods.
▷ Ask local bank officials if you qualify for low-interest loans. Some city banks have formed coalitions with businesses to encourage rehabilitation in certain urban neighborhoods. By helping these neighborhoods the banks protect existing mortgage and loan investments.
▷ If your house is in an historic district or is of architectural significance, call your chapter of the National Trust for Historic Preservation. Financial aid and tax incentives may be available if your home qualifies for listing with the trust.

Rehabilitating urban houses

Developing and homesteading (continued)

definitely unless they have frozen. Large cast-iron radiators are efficient and retain heat longer than others, but they are not usually adaptable to zone heating. Some people find them too unattractive to keep, or changes in the floor plan make them too difficult to work around. It is possible to retain the plumbing for a steam or hot-water system when the boiler must be replaced, by properly adapting the new boiler to the old system. Because it is difficult to balance the pressure in a two-pipe system and to make connections with different size pipes, this job should be done by professionals. Steam systems run at higher temperatures than water systems, which means they are more expensive to run, but a one-pipe steam system is easy to add to. Warm-air systems add humidity to the air (beneficial to the health of old houses and their occupants), heat the space faster, are vented easily, are readily adapted to air conditioning, and are cheaper to run, than hot-water systems. The disadvantages are that the ducts take up a great deal of space and it is very difficult to weave large ducts around the existing structure of a house.

A hot-water system is the easiest to install in an existing building because the pliable ½-inch or 1-inch pipes are easier to weave in and out through the building's structure. The disadvantages are that the system is expensive to install and to run.

Chimneys are an important part of the heating system and should be checked for structural integrity, condition of the lining, creosote buildup, and blockage. Also check the mortar for deterioration, which can be caused by acid released by burning coal or by freezing. Old chimneys are often unlined and therefore do not meet modern fire codes. Cleaning and working on chimneys is very messy, so finish it before starting interior work.

Demolition: When removing walls, it is absolutely crucial that you not damage load-bearing walls. Consult an expert before you begin, especially if the building is complex or has been changed often. Carefully remove doors, trim, hardware, lighting fixtures, and other finish materials from walls before demolition begins; label everything and store it where it will be out of the way. Organized storage will save time and effort; you will only have to move the materials once, and when the time comes to refinish or reuse them, you will know where they are.

Turn off all electric power, gas, and water before you begin to demolish any walls. Remove demolished plaster, lath, brick, etc., from the site immediately; that way you only have to handle it once, and it won't be in the way of the work. Old framing, sometimes oak or chestnut, is hard and strong and can often be reused, but it can be difficult to work with. The dimensions will be different from those of modern lumber. Old and new sizes cannot be mixed, so if you want to use old framing, be sure that you have enough to complete a whole wall. Save old flooring for patching; the sizes, colors, and patina of old wood and tile are virtually impossible to match with modern materials.

Construction: You may have to install new windows, but a surprising amount of repair is possible. Check with an ice pick to see if the frames are rotted. If you can easily insert the point more than an eighth of an inch, that part is rotted. Areas where water collects are most likely to rot—sills, bottom rails, corner joints. Despite the labor involved, replacing parts of a window is frequently cheaper than replacing the entire window with a prefabricated unit; and it will probably be more in keeping with the character of the house.

When building new interior walls, the framing must be tied into the existing structure, and bearing loads must be carefully analyzed. Coordinate framing with plans for the plumbing, electrical, and heating systems. If a 5-inch plumbing stack is to go through a new wall, you will be in trouble if you have already framed the entire wall with 2 x 4s.

Before covering the frame with plasterboard, be sure that everything that goes behind the walls is in place, including electrical circuits and plumbing. Install blocks where fixtures will be screwed in and box in structures for built-ins.

Interior finishing: New walls and ceilings are most often plasterboard rather than plaster, which is far more expensive. Finish a wall entirely in one or the other. Many existing plaster walls in the Bradley Street houses were successfully patched. New partition walls were plasterboard.

After the walls are complete, it is time to hang interior doors and install trim and built-in cabinets. Salvaged materials must be coordinated with new ones. On Bradley Street, for example, there was not enough salvageable molding for baseboards. Kraus installed all new baseboard moldings in some rooms and all old ones in others.

Ceiling and wall surfaces should be painted or papered before the floors are refinished. When the walls and floors are done, install prefabricated cabinet and vanity units and set sinks into them. Install hardware, plumbing fix-

To install plumbing for the new hot water heating system, the floorboards were raised, an easier method than breaking through from the ceiling below. Pliable piping was routed to the new baseboard radiators through holes drilled in the joists.

(Careful calculations had ensured that the drilling would not damage the structural integrity of the joists.) In the finished room, baseboard radiators of the same color as the walls and molding blend in and take up little space.

tures, light fixtures, switchplates, and appliances. Finally, lay the carpeting. After a last thorough cleaning, your new home is ready for you.

Decisions: An old house is a living record of the tastes and traditions of the generations who have lived in it. Tastes may change, but an authentic old house will always endure fickle fashions.

Owners are generally constrained by budgets. Compromises must be made between preserving authenticity and modifying an old house to 20th-century standards of comfort and efficiency while keeping costs reasonable. Much research may be required before making a decision on how to spend your money. Make sure that the building is structurally sound, well protected, and functional. Remember, structural work must all be done at once, but improvements can be made at any time.

Note: The Secretary of the Interior of the U.S. has published standards governing tax incentives for architectural rehabilitations; they tell how the original character of a building must be respected if a rehabilitation is to qualify for a tax break. To obtain a copy of the Secretary of the Interior's Standards for Rehabilitation, write or call your state historic preservation office in your state capital.

To convert the third floor into an apartment, new kitchen plumbing had to be installed and new walls built. Exposed lines of bare lath on the long, windowless plaster wall indicate where old walls were demolished. The skylight in the hall was retained in the new design. The long plaster wall was in good enough condition to patch, but the plaster ceiling and other walls had to be replaced with plasterboard. The new wall in the center of the room is part of a three-sided closet that will house the refrigerator so that it cannot be seen from the living room. Prefabricated wood cabinets appropriate for both kitchen and casual living room decor were installed in the open-style kitchen. The wood floors were basically in good condition, so they were sanded and sealed with polyurethane. The old glass in the skylight was replaced with double-glazed insulated glass to conserve heat and to prevent condensation. The skylight was then boxed in with plasterboard to give it greater depth, and lights were installed to extend its dramatic effect into the night.

Only a trained eye could visualize this as potential living space. Originally, the basement had dirt floors, damp stone walls, bare pipes, hanging wires, and a large accumulation of trash. First it was thoroughly cleaned. Old pipes and wires were removed. Salvageable and potentially useful material was labeled and stored, and junk was discarded. Concrete floors were poured, new walls and ceilings were constructed, and electrical, heating, and plumbing systems were in-stalled. White tile floors were laid, and a small greenhouse, visible through a new glass door, was built into the old basement stairwell. These features brightened and expanded a dark, con-stricted space, giving it an open, airy feel.

Vacation kit houses

Making practical choices

If a custom-built vacation home is out of your price range, and you do not feel prepared to build a house from scratch, a kit house might be the perfect alternative. A kit house is the ultimate model-building project. Prefabricated components of the house are delivered to the building site along with detailed blueprints and assembly instructions, and the owner, his friends, and/or a contractor fit the pieces together.

When planning a kit house, you know exactly what the house will look like and how much the kit itself will cost. Compared to building from scratch, the shell of the house goes up very quickly. However, a kit cannot be erected everywhere, and much preparatory work must be done before the kit arrives. Your land and road must be able to accommodate large, heavy trucks; the foundation must be ready and accurate; you must have enough people on hand to unload and catalog the materials; and you must have dry storage or tarps.

Selecting a kit: Kits are available in virtually any design, and most manufacturers will make custom alterations if necessary. Basically, all kits fall into the four categories described and illustrated on the next two pages and shown in the photos on pages 330–331: panel, post-and-beam, log, and geodesic dome construction. First consider the type of design you prefer; generally, only the smaller, simpler designs can be completely built by do-it-yourselfers.

Write to a number of the manufacturers listed for their brochures so that you can get a good idea of what is available at what price. When comparing prices, keep in mind that no two kits contain exactly the same materials, so you must check one against the other item for item. Differing prices for seemingly similar kits reflect the degree of prefabrication, the quality of the materials, and the number of components included. For example, virtually no kits include foundations; some include roofs and some do not; some have double-glazed windows as standard equipment, some offer these as optional extras, while others require you to purchase your own windows; and some post-and-beam and geodesic dome kits contain only the frame.

The buyer usually pays the shipping cost, which is figured by the mile; a kit that comes more than 350 miles is rarely economical. Because kit houses must meet the requirements of many states and localities, they are usually built to the highest specifications, but be sure that a kit meets all local zoning and building codes and that you can obtain all necessary permits before ordering (see *Building codes/An introduction to construction*, pp. 21–37). If you are planning to do some or all of the work yourself, consider only manufacturers who encourage do-it-yourselfers and who offer technical assistance throughout the project. If the manufacturer is some distance away, check to see if there is a local dealer. Ask for the names of people who have built the kit you are interested in, look at a finished house, and ask its owner if the kit turned out to be as represented, what kind of help was available, whether the instructions were good, whether precision of materials or fit was a problem, and anything else you can think of.

Erecting the kit: Different kits require different degrees of building expertise. Evaluate your skills and experience honestly, then, with the advice of the manufacturer, choose a kit that matches your abilities. If you do not plan to do the construction yourself, you can hire a contractor to do the entire job. Many people have the shell erected by professionals and finish the interior themselves as time and budget permit. Some local codes demand that work be done only by licensed plumbers and electricians, while others have inspection laws that would preclude closed-wall panel kits, so check your local codes before starting. If you do decide to hire professional builders, find a contractor and crew who have built this kit before (the manufacturer or dealer can usually recommend someone).

Determining cost: When looking at brochures it is hard to remember that the price of the kit represents only a fraction of the cost of the finished house. Besides the kit itself, you will have to pay for the land, site development, foundation, shipping costs, possibly a contractor, subcontractors, materials not included in the kit, water and electrical hookups, heating, plumbing, and electrical systems, permit fees, and insurance for workmen. Adding these expenses to the price of the kit will give you a good idea of its actual cost.

The manufacturer or dealer will help you determine costs, and people who have built the same kit are an excellent source of dependable information. As a rule of thumb, a kit house will probably cost about the same as an ordinary house if you have a contractor do the entire job. You can save roughly 10 to 15 percent by acting as your own contractor, and you can save substantially more by doing part or all of the work yourself. But whether you decide to do major structural work, fine finishing details, or only the planning and overseeing, building a kit house can provide both a satisfying experience and your dream vacation home.

For additional information

Many of the manufacturers listed have dealers in other parts of the country; most charge a fee for their catalogs.

Post-and-beam kits
The Barn People, PO Box 4, South Woodstock, VT 05071

Birch Hill Builders, PO Box 416, York, ME 03909

David Howard, PO Box 295, Alstead, NH 03602

Deck House, 930 Main St., Acton, MA 01720

Dwellings, PO Box 138, Cape Porpoise ME 04014

Pre-Cut Timber Homes, PO Box 97, Woodinville, WA 98072

Shelter-Kit, PO Box 1, Tilton, NH 03276

Timber Kit, PO Box 704, Amherst, MA 01002

Timberpeg, PO Box 1358, Claremont, NH

Yankee Barn Homes, Grantham, NH 03753

Panel kits
Affordable Luxury Homes, PO Box 368, Markle, IN 46770

Continental Homes, PO Box 13106, Roanoke, VA 24031

Continental Homes of New England, Daniel Webster Hgwy. South, Nashua, NH 03060

Green Mountain Homes, Royalton, VT 05068

Heritage Homes, 4850 Boxelder St., Murray, UT 84107

Heritage Homes of New England, 456 Southampton Rd., Westfield, MA 01085

Manufactured Homes, 29269 Lexington Park Dr., Elkhart, IN 46514

Northern Homes, 10 LaCrosse St., Hudson Falls, NY 12839

Pacific Buildings, Drawer C, Marks, MS 39646

Pease Homes, 900 Laurel Ave., Hamilton, OH 45023

Precision-Bilt Homes, 2525 North Hgwy. 89-91, Ogden, UT 84404

Standard Homes, PO Box 1900, Olathe, KS 66061

Universal Homes, Camden, OH 45311

Log kits
Air-Lock Logs, PO Box 2506, Las Vegas, NM 87701

Alta Industries, PO Box 88, Halcottsville, NY 12438

Authentic Homes, PO Box 1288, Laramie, WY 82070

Beaver Log Homes, Route 2, Plymouth, WI 53073

Cabin Log Co., 2809 Hgwy. 167 N., Lafayette, LA 70507

Heritage Log Homes, PO Box 610, Gatlinburg, TN 37738

Justus Homes, PO Box 98300, Tacoma, WA 98499

Model Log Homes, 75777 Gallatin Rd., Bozeman, MT 59715

New England Log Homes, 2301 State St., PO Box 5056, Hamden, CT 06518

Northeastern Log Homes, Groton, VT 05046

Northern Products Log Homes, PO Box 616, Bomarc Rd., Bangor, ME 04401

Real Log Homes, PO Box 202, Hartland, VT 05048

Rocky Mountain Log Homes, 3353 Hgwy. 93 South, Hamilton, MT 59840

Rustics of Lindbergh Lake, Condon, MT 59826

Ward Cabin Co., PO Box 72, Houlton, ME 04730

Wilderness Log Homes, Route 2, Plymouth, WI 53073

Dome Kits
The Big Outdoors People, 26600 Fallbrook Ave., Wyoming, MN 55092

Cathedralite Domes, PO Box 880, Aptos, CA 95003

Dyna-Dome, 22226 N. 23rd Ave., Phoenix, AZ 85027

Geodesic Domes, 10290 Davison Rd., Davison, MI 48423

Hexadome of America, PO Box 2351, La Mesa, CA 92014

Monterey Domes, 1855 Iowa Ave., Riverside, CA 92517

Space Structures International, 325 Duffy Ave., Hicksville, NY 11801

Western Hemisphere, 8113 Rush St., Fort Worth, TX 76116

Post-and-beam kits

The interior walls of a post-and-beam house are applied to the outside of the frame, leaving the heavy timber posts and beams exposed throughout the house. This dramatic construction technique has been used effectively in many types of kits, ranging from ultra-modern houses with soaring cathedral ceilings to traditional barn-style houses (below), some of which actually use original timbers from old barns.

Both the advantages and disadvantages of post-and-beam houses involve the massive timbers required for the frame. Such houses are solid enough to stand for generations. Because large load-bearing members mean that fewer supports are needed, the frame can be erected quickly. Fewer posts also allow uninterrupted open spaces wherever desired. On the other hand, all but the smallest kits require professional framing crews with special equipment to wrestle the posts and beams into position and to accurately finish the finely crafted mortise-and-tenon, lap, and notch joints used to fit the posts and beams together. Once the frame is up, interior and exterior finishing can be done by even a novice do-it-yourselfer.

Panel kits

Panel kits feature wall, roof, and floor systems prefabricated in large sections that go together quickly to make up the shell of a house. There are two types of panel construction—open wall and closed wall. Open-wall panels are assembled at the factory with studs, top and bottom plates, insulation, siding, and door and window frames in place. Closed panels include electrical wiring, plumbing, and finished interior walls. Construction details are the same as for an ordinary frame house (see p.264); the only difference is that one is built in a factory, the other on the site.

Post-and-beam barn-style frame

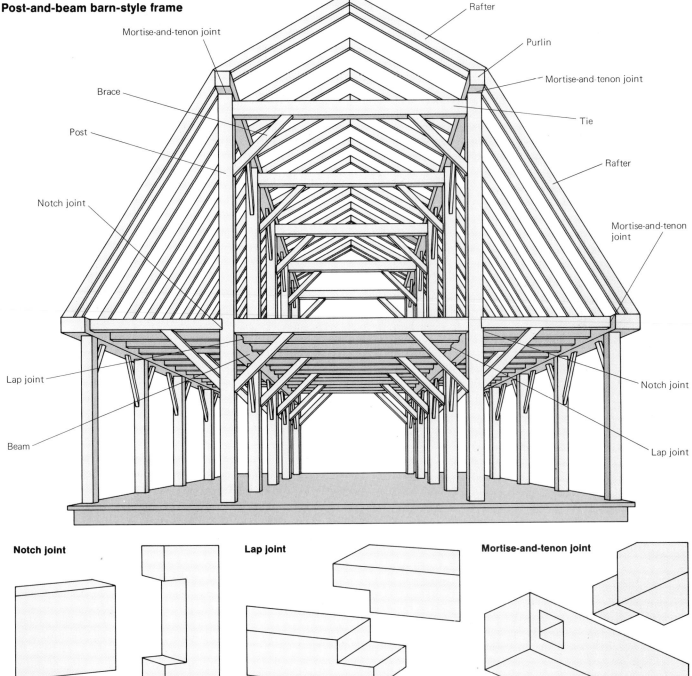

349

Vacation kit houses

Log kits

Building a kit log house is a simple process—as the walls go up, so do the frame, exterior siding, insulation, and interior walls. The biggest problem with log houses has always been keeping them weathertight. The log cabins of our ancestors were chinked with moss and mud, but modern log kit designers have developed unique sealing methods. First the logs are trimmed round, half round, or square. Some manufacturers then plane the top and bottom surfaces of the logs flat, some cut tongue-and-groove joints to lock the logs together, some hollow out the bottom of each log to fit the log beneath it. Corners may be simply planed flat, saddle-notched, or even dovetailed. Splines, sealants, gaskets, spikes, and dowels are added in various combinations to ensure a lasting weathertight seal.

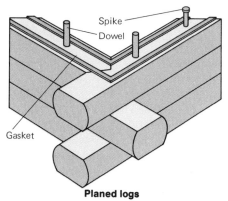

Planed logs

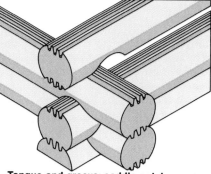

Tongue-and-groove; saddle-notch corner

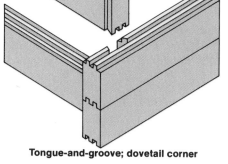

Tongue-and-groove; dovetail corner

Geodesic dome kits

Geodesic domes are based on two geometric shapes; the triangle, which is the only structurally rigid polygon, and the sphere, the three-dimensional shape that encloses the greatest space within the least surface area. The elegant efficiency of domes derives from these features. Because the frame is inherently rigid, no internal supports are needed, allowing great flexibility. Because the surface area is minimized, less construction materials are needed. Exposure to the elements is also minimized, so it is cheaper to heat a dome than a conventional structure of equal size.

Dome kits come as either preassembled triangles with the sheathing in place or with hubs, connectors, struts, and sheathing separate. Do-it-yourselfers can easily erect small domes, which can be clustered for more space.

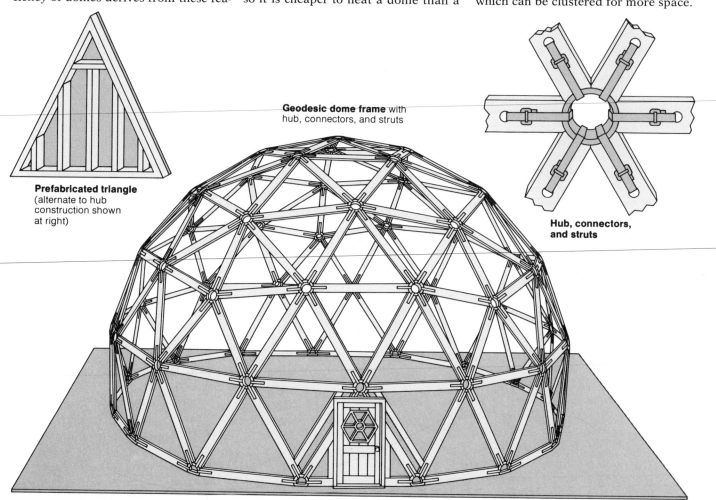

Prefabricated triangle
(alternate to hub construction shown at right)

Geodesic dome frame with hub, connectors, and struts

Hub, connectors, and struts

Energy-saving renovations

In recent years, the drive to attain energy-efficient lifestyles has become a real movement. This chapter is based on the timely experience of do-it-yourselfers and professionals who have found better approaches to insulating a house; they have solved problems related to fresh air exchange, and condensation endemic to houses that are too well insulated. In the vanguard of today's energy-conscious do-it-yourselfers are those involved in active and passive solar design. These pages survey the latest work in this field, describing projects that you can adapt to your needs.

contents

Understanding heat loss and gain

How heat flows

Any form of matter whose atoms and molecules are in motion contains heat. Heat is the jostling of the molecules of hot gas in a candle flame, the billions of collisions per second of moving electrons in a light bulb filament, the incessant movement of the molecules in warm air.

As matter becomes warmer the motion of its atoms and molecules increases. Heat is being added. Upon cooling, this motion declines, but it never stops completely except at the extreme temperature of approximately –460° F—or Absolute Zero.

In warm air the constituent molecules of oxygen, nitrogen, carbon dioxide, water vapor, and other gases, are in rapid motion—and experiencing frequent and violent collisions. This rapid activity causes warm air to expand, making it less dense than cold air; in cold air the molecules are comparatively quiet and closely packed. Being relatively dense and heavy, cold air sinks under the pull of gravity; in so doing, it displaces warmer air and forces it upward. It is the movement of cold air into your house through various openings—gaps around doors and windows, cracks in floors and walls (see illustration opposite page)—that forces heated air up to the ceilings, the attic, and out through open flues, leaks at windows, cracks and other small openings in the walls and roof. Insulation, caulking, and weatherstripping work to prevent the infiltration of cold air into your house and the escape of warm air.

Air moving as described above causes heat loss by a mechanism known as convection. But your house also loses heat by processes known as conduction and radiation, which insulation also helps retard. In general, heat always flows from warmer to cooler locations. This flow does not stop until the temperature in the two locations is equal.

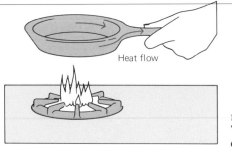

Conduction

Conduction: If you place a flame under one end of a metal bar and hold the bar at its other end, your hand will feel a rise in temperature. The bar conducts heat to your hand.

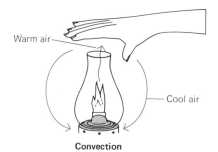

Convection

Convection: If you put your hand directly over a flame, it will feel hot because the air heated by the flame rises. The only media that can convect heat are those that flow like liquids, such as air and water.

Radiation: If you place your hand near the end of a metal bar being heated by a flame, it will soon feel warm even though your hand is not touching

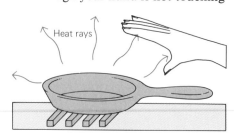

Radiation

the bar, and air currents are not convecting heat to it. The bar radiates heat to your hand. The jostling molecules in the bar behave like billions of microscopic transmitters randomly sending radio-like waves to receivers in your hand, causing the receiver molecules to jostle more rapidly. These waves are named according to their frequency (rate of oscillation). They are (in order of increasing frequency or energy) far-infrared, infrared, and light.

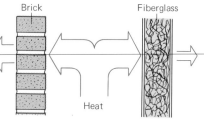

Brick vs. fiberglass insulation

Heat insulators: Materials vary enormously in their ability to conduct heat. Those at the low end of the scale are called insulators. By experimenting with different materials, natural and manufactured, heating specialists select the most effective insulators for roofs and walls to inhibit heat loss from a house. For example, 4 inches of brick conduct heat about 18 times more rapidly than 4 inches of fiberglass.

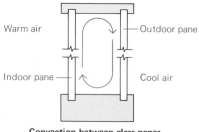

Convection between glass panes

Double-glazed windows rely on the "dead air space" between the panes to insulate, since quiet air is a very good insulator. The windows are manufactured with a spacing between panes of about one-half inch. Since insulation value generally increases with thickness, why not make the air space bigger? The reason is convection. With a wider spacing, the warmed air next to the indoor pane convects quite easily over to the cooler, outdoor pane, negating almost all the added insulating value of making the space wider.

Other considerations: Convection principles can be tricky to apply. It can take years to find and plug all the gaps in a house through which cold air enters and warm air leaks out. And you may be baffled when the air loop—the planned paths of rising warm air and returning cold air—you set up to distribute heat to a part of the house won't loop.

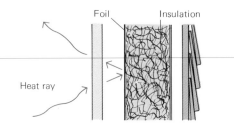

Foil reflector in wall

Thermal (heat) radiation is easier to direct. The rays do not bend around corners and they can be almost completely stopped and reflected by a thin sheet of aluminum foil. For this reason foil is often used as a vapor barrier.

Passive solar effects: If a material does not reflect radiation at its surface, the radiation passes into the material and is either absorbed by it or is released at the other side. If it is released, the material is said to be transparent to radiation. Glass, for example, is transparent to high-energy radiation given off as light by very hot bodies such as the sun; it is not, however, transparent to lower-energy radiation from lower temperature surfaces such as the heat waves from a wood stove (infrared waves). Solar collectors take advantage of this heat-trapping property of glass, known as the greenhouse effect.

How a house loses heat

For a modest sum you can retard the loss of heat from your house and save on fuel bills, particularly if your house is very old and drafty or if it was built during recent decades of cheap and plentiful fuel. The shell of your house may have cracks, gaps, uninsulated roofing, and uninsulated floors above crawl spaces, as well as hollows in walls that invite plugging and insulating, as shown in the schematic illustration of a typical old house below.

Note too that whatever steps you take to reduce heat loss will also serve to slow the entry of heat during summer. If the house is air conditioned in summer, you may save as much on your electrical bills as on your fuel.

Besides insulating, you can reduce heat loss by adding storm windows and doors, shutters, and thermal drapery, and by weatherstripping, caulking, and using other techniques for blocking air infiltration in walls and ceilings. This last may take the most time because of the difficulty of finding all the sources and paths of infiltration.

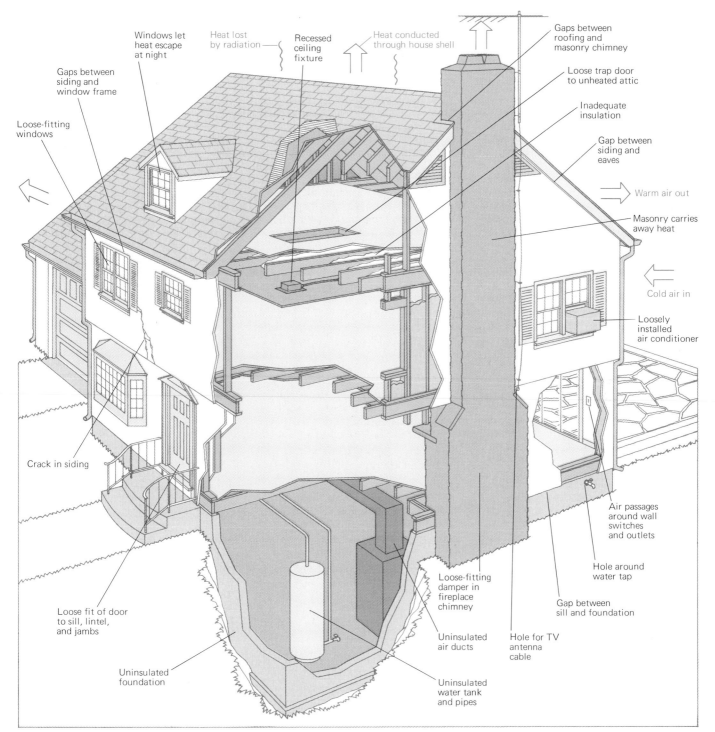

Convection is a major culprit in the loss of heat from many houses. Impelled by wind outdoors and drafts indoors, cold air seeps in through house cracks and openings and forces the warm air to leak out through similar openings in other parts of the house. In houses with an updraft the leaks will flow inward at the base and outward at the roof. The replacement, or turnover, of air in this way can vary from one-third to 10 turnovers per hour. Beside air leaks, heat can be conducted through the house shell and can radiate off the surface of the house.

Your energy-saving dollars

Insulation/Estimating costs and savings

Some heat-saving improvements, such as plugging the holes that allow air to infiltrate a house, are cheap in relation to the dollars they save. Others, such as insulation, cost proportionately more. If you want to start with the steps that pay back the most in proportion to their cost, you must first determine which they are. You can make your calculations using the chart on these pages.

Payback chart: The chart shows step by step how to calculate in months or years the payback time for investments in a typical group of heat-saving improvements. Most of the data for the chart are acquired by going about the house and measuring or estimating dimensions, insulation, and air turnover (see pp.356–358). The rest of the chart is filled in by simple arithmetic based on your data. You may round off large numbers to the nearest ten—substituting the figure 170 for 167, for example.

To use the chart for your house, draw an outline of the chart on blank paper and fill it in; or copy the chart on a copying machine and write over the sample numbers given.

Interpreting the calculations: Some of the data to be entered in the chart are necessarily crude, in a few instances little more than guesses. Also, certain effects are ignored, such as the increase in heat loss due to wind, so the calculations that follow are simply approximations. The dollars-saved figures, therefore, may easily be in error by a factor of two or more.

You are not likely to increase the accuracy by making the chart more complicated, however. Even when similar heat studies are conducted by professionals, unmeasured effects and lack of predictability stand stubbornly in the way of precise accuracy.

The chart will be most useful if used to compare savings from different improvements, particularly via the payback figures. Much chart error derives from the difficulty of estimating annual fuel bills in a time of rising energy prices. But if the payback time for one improvement is substantially shorter than that for another, you can assume the former to be more cost-effective.

The chart is flexible. By updating it

after installing an improvement, you can re-assess the payback for additional improvements. You can add or substitute improvements—more insulation in the ceiling, triple-glazed windows instead of double-glazed etc.,—and compare what savings if any these changes would bring.

For instance, consider the potential effect of doubling the new floor insulation in the examples in the chart; it would increase from 3 inches to 6 inches. As a result, the new R-value for the floor becomes 26 (4 + 11 + 11), and the new heat loss for the improvement is 660 ÷ 26 = (rounded off) 25; the difference is then 170−25 = 145; and the dollars saved annually come to $1000 × 145 ÷ 1260 = $115. Since $115 is not much more than the $100 that the initial layer of R-11 insulation was calculated to save, this demonstrates that doubling existing insulation may produce marginal rather than significant payback.

Other uses of the chart: When planning such steps as solar heating, upgrading the efficiency of your furnace, or turning down the thermostat, insert

Payback chart

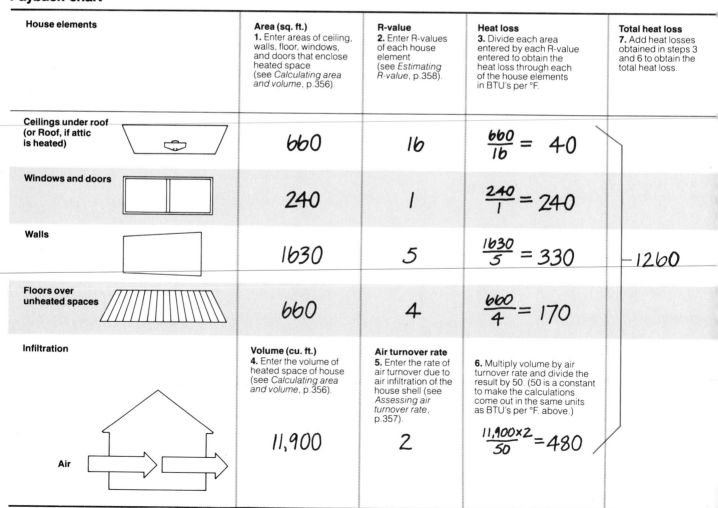

House elements	Area (sq. ft.) **1.** Enter areas of ceiling, walls, floor, windows, and doors that enclose heated space (see *Calculating area and volume*, p.356).	R-value **2.** Enter R-values of each house element (see *Estimating R-value*, p.358).	Heat loss **3.** Divide each area entered by each R-value entered to obtain the heat loss through each of the house elements in BTU's per °F.	Total heat loss **7.** Add heat losses obtained in steps 3 and 6 to obtain the total heat loss.
Ceilings under roof (or Roof, if attic is heated)	660	16	$\frac{660}{16} = 40$	
Windows and doors	240	1	$\frac{240}{1} = 240$	
Walls	1630	5	$\frac{1630}{5} = 330$	1260
Floors over unheated spaces	660	4	$\frac{660}{4} = 170$	

Infiltration	Volume (cu. ft.) **4.** Enter the volume of heated space of house (see *Calculating area and volume*, p.356).	Air turnover rate **5.** Enter the rate of air turnover due to air infiltration of the house shell (see *Assessing air turnover rate*, p.357).	**6.** Multiply volume by air turnover rate and divide the result by 50. (50 is a constant to make the calculations come out in the same units as BTU's per °F. above.)	
Air	11,900	2	$\frac{11,900 \times 2}{50} = 480$	

the fuel-bill savings you estimate they will provide into the dollars-saved-annually column. Also, deduct these savings from the prior fuel cost estimate wherever it appears in the chart ($1,000 in the example below). Then enter the cost of the new improvement and re-evaluate payback for all of the improvements. You will discover that fuel savings at the heat source affect payback times of improvements elsewhere.

For example, if you lower the thermostat in winter your new insulation will not have as great a single effect on fuel bills (longer payback time). It will continue to do as much for you, however, if instead of lowering the thermostat you weatherstrip or add storm windows. This is because any improvement to the shell of the house, such as weatherstripping, lowers the total heat loss figure (1,260 in the chart) as well as the yearly fuel cost ($1,000 in the chart), so the reductions cancel one another.

Over-investing: In planning energy-saving investments, stay away from percentages. Calculate fuel savings in dollars and then decide whether the

investment is worthwhile. Assertions by contractors of percent of fuel dollars saved should be viewed skeptically. Percentages can be raised to almost any level. A contractor may recommend many improvements, only some of which may be truly economical.

For example, if you do the weather stripping suggested in the chart, you save $190 a year, which reduces the annual fuel bill from $1000–$190 = $810.

Now, if you re-evaluate the chart, you will find that the saving to be expected from adding storm windows and doors, say, remains at $100. Nothing has changed, but in percent the saving comes to $100 ÷ $810 = .12, or 12 percent, wheras initially these additions indicated a savings of $100 ÷ $1000 = .10, or only 10 percent. Similar considerations apply to raising the R-values of your existing insulation (see p.358).

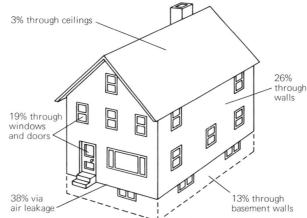

3% through ceilings
26% through walls
19% through windows and doors
38% via air leakage
13% through basement walls

Typical heat loss from a lightly insulated, loosely constructed house is shown in percentages. They are intended to give you a first impression of where house heat passes to the outdoors. The figures are from the chart below (facing page) and are calculated assuming a house whose R-values and air turnover rate are as given there. Your house is likely to differ from these figures. Still, you can see that losses via air leakage and the windows are likely to play a prominent part in your heat budget.

Improvements **8.** Select the insulating and weatherproofing improvements whose performance you wish to evaluate.	New R-values **9.** Enter the R-values that result after the improvements in each house element are made.	New heat loss **11.** Calculate new heat loss the same way as in steps 3 and 6. Use same areas and volume, but new R-values and air turnover rate.	Difference **12.** Subtract new heat loss from old heat loss through house elements and by infiltration.	Dollars saved annually **13.** Estimate annual fuel bill ($1,000 is used here; see p.357), multiply bill by heat loss difference, and divide it by total heat loss calculated in Step 7.	Cost of improvements **14.** Determine cost of each improvement. This can be a contractor's installation estimate or the materials cost if you install.	Payback in years **15.** Divide cost of improvement by dollars saved annually. This is time it takes for cost of fuel saved to equal cost of improvement.
Ceilings Add 3" more fiberglass insulation to ceiling (add R-11; see p.358).	27	$\frac{660}{27} = 20$	20	$1000 \times \frac{20}{1260} = \$20$	$450	$\frac{450}{20} = 23$ yrs.
Windows and doors Add storm windows and doors to the house (add R-1, see p. 358).	2	$\frac{240}{2} = 120$	120	$1000 \times \frac{120}{1260} = \$100$	$1000	$\frac{1000}{100} = 10$ yrs.
Walls Install 4" urethane foam insulation in the walls (add R-22; see p.358).	27	$\frac{1630}{27} = 60$	270	$1000 \times \frac{270}{1260} = \$210$	$1420	$\frac{1420}{210} = 7$ yrs.
Floors Install 3"-thick fiberglass batts under floor (add R-11; see p.358).	15	$\frac{660}{15} = 40$	130	$1000 \times \frac{130}{1260} = \$100$	$340	$\frac{340}{100} = 3\frac{1}{2}$ yrs.
Infiltration Weatherstrip around windows and doors and caulk gaps in siding (reduce estimated turnover rate from two air turnovers per hour to one per hour, see p.357).	**New turnover rate 10.** Enter new air turnover rate that is achieved after infiltration of air into house has been reduced. 1	$\frac{11,900 \times 1}{50} = 240$	240	$1000 \times \frac{240}{1260} = 190$	$210	$\frac{210}{190} = 1$ yr.

Your energy-saving dollars

Calculating area and volume

The *Payback chart* on pages 354–355 requires that you determine the areas of ceiling under the roof, the roof if your attic is heated, floors over unheated spaces, and of walls and windows in your house. The chart also requires the calculation of the volume of the heated portion of your house.

A sketch like the one below will help. Your house probably has a more complicated shape than the house illustrated. You can adjust for this by thinking of it as a number of independent box-like parts and making separate calculations for each part. The results are then added to produce the required figures for total area and volume.

If a part of the house is not box-like (as, for example, a heated attic with a sloping roof), compare it to a box. A triangular wall at an attic end, for example, can be thought equivalent to a rectangular wall of one-half the height of the triangular one. A rough estimate will do for more complicated shapes.

The numbers can be approximate. Horizontal dimensions, for example, can be obtained by pacing and multiplying the counted paces by the length of your stride. For the vertical dimension of each floor stand someone of known height against a wall and estimate the distance from the top of the person's head to the ceiling, then add that distance to his height. Use a tape measure or ruler, however, to measure the doors and windows, and add up how many of each there are.

Areas: Using the formula, length times width, calculate the areas of the ceilings, walls, and floors that enclose the heated part of the house and get a total for these areas. If you have divided the house into separate box-like parts,

do not include in the total area the area of the surfaces where the parts join. If a part of the house encloses an unheated area such as a garage, think of the walls and ceiling that adjoin the garage as part of the house floor for the purpose of these calculations.

Calculate the areas of windows and doors and total them. Also, subtract this sum from the total calculated wall area to give the net wall area.

Volume: Using the formula, length times width times height, calculate the volume of the heated part of the house. If you have divided the house into separate box-like parts, calculate the volume of each part separately, then add the results to obtain the total volume.

The areas and volume used in the payback analysis chart on pages 354–355 are from the house in the sketch. They are calculated as shown below.

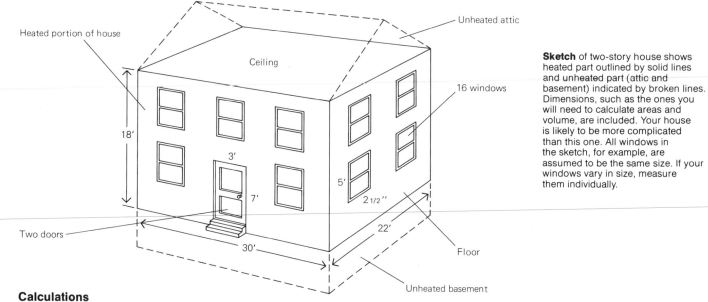

Sketch of two-story house shows heated part outlined by solid lines and unheated part (attic and basement) indicated by broken lines. Dimensions, such as the ones you will need to calculate areas and volume, are included. Your house is likely to be more complicated than this one. All windows in the sketch, for example, are assumed to be the same size. If your windows vary in size, measure them individually.

Calculations

Area	Ceiling	30' × 22'	=	660 sq. ft.
	Walls	2 walls × 30' × 18'	=	1080
		2 walls × 22' × 18'	=	790
				1870
		(windows and doors)		−240
				1630 sq. ft.
	Floor	30' × 22'	=	660 sq. ft.
	Windows/	16 windows × 2½' × 5'	=	200
	Doors	2 doors × 3' × 7'	=	40
				240 sq. ft.
Volume		18' × 30' × 22'	=	11 900 cu. ft.

Assessing air turnover in your home

The table at right provides a rough means of estimating the air turnover rate to be entered in the payback analysis chart on pages 354–355. To use the table, read through the *Condition of house* list and find the category that best describes your house. Then select the air change per hour figure for that category or a number in between, as you feel suitable.

The rate, or air change per hour, is the number of times each hour that an amount of air equal to the house's volume infiltrates (or exfiltrates) the house. For example, if the amount that enters (and exits) in one hour equals the total volume of the heated part of the house, the house is said to undergo one air change per hour.

The rate is very difficult to pin down because it depends significantly on how the house is used and what kind of winds and temperature differentials the house is exposed to during the year. Even if you have determined the rate with some precision and averaged it over several months of testing, you cannot be absolutely sure it applies to succeeding periods. For this reason we use a rough table estimate.

In addition to the table's descriptive categories, take into account the quality of workmanship. A house that is well carpentered leaks less heat; greater care was probably taken to plug holes cut into sills, joists, and studs to pass pipes and wiring through and to close openings in the frame, siding, and roof.

Incidentally, the national average of hourly house air turnover rates probably lies between one and two, and closer to one. To supply a figure for the payback analysis chart, it was assumed that the house had a turnover rate of two.

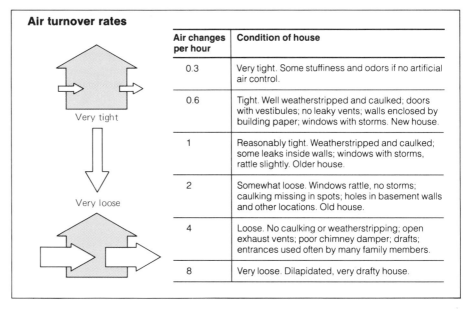

Air turnover rates

Air changes per hour	Condition of house
0.3	Very tight. Some stuffiness and odors if no artificial air control.
0.6	Tight. Well weatherstripped and caulked; doors with vestibules; no leaky vents; walls enclosed by building paper; windows with storms. New house.
1	Reasonably tight. Weatherstripped and caulked; some leaks inside walls; windows with storms, rattle slightly. Older house.
2	Somewhat loose. Windows rattle, no storms; caulking missing in spots; holes in basement walls and other locations. Old house.
4	Loose. No caulking or weatherstripping; open exhaust vents; poor chimney damper; drafts; entrances used often by many family members.
8	Very loose. Dilapidated, very drafty house.

Very tight

Very loose

Estimating your annual fuel bill

To determine the fuel bill you enter in the payback analysis chart on pages 354–355, add the amounts you paid to the oil, gas, or electric company over any recent 12-month period and add an inflation factor to cover probable price increases over the next several years. Probably, energy prices will keep pace with the general rate of inflation, reported regularly in the news media.

Often the cost of fuel includes the cost of heating hot water. If your bills reflect this, you will have to deduct the hot water cost from the total. One way to do this is to average the monthly fuel costs during the summer period when the heating system is off, then multiply the average by 12 and subtract it from the total annual bill. Assuming that hot water use has been fairly constant throughout the year, you will then have a cost figure for house heating alone (see illustration, below).

If your house has electric heat, you can use your electric bills in the same way. The year-round, non-heating part of the bill will include the cost of operating lights and appliances. Lights and some appliances help heat the house when they are on, so some error will occur when subtracting their year-round cost from total fuel cost to obtain house heating cost, but not much.

If you have air conditioning in an electrically heated house, determine from your bills the non-heating cost for a month when neither heat nor air conditioning are on, such as a month in the spring or the fall. In this way you will include air conditioning cost in the net heating cost when calculating the latter. The inclusion is appropriate and useful for determining payback, because whatever steps you take to reduce heat loss from the house inevitably lower your air conditioning bill as well.

To supply a round figure for the payback analysis chart on pages 354–355, it was assumed that the annual fuel bill for the house was $1,000. Inflation was not factored in.

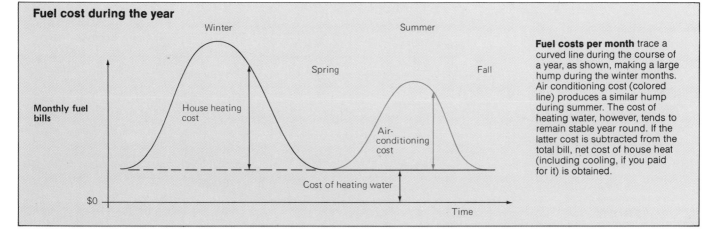

Fuel cost during the year

Winter
Summer
Spring
Fall
Monthly fuel bills
House heating cost
Air-conditioning cost
Cost of heating water
$0
Time

Fuel costs per month trace a curved line during the course of a year, as shown, making a large hump during the winter months. Air conditioning cost (colored line) produces a similar hump during summer. The cost of heating water, however, tends to remain stable year round. If the latter cost is subtracted from the total bill, net cost of house heat (including cooling, if you paid for it) is obtained.

Your energy-saving dollars

Estimating R-value

The tables on this page supply you with the R-values to use in the payback analysis chart on pages 354–355.

Uninsulated surfaces: For elements not in this table, an R-value will have to be inferred from the figures given. A wall faced with flagstone, for example, should have about the same R-value as a wall of brick or concrete.

The R-values given for the ceiling include the contribution that roofing and an air space between ceiling and roof would make. The air space can be an entire unheated attic. The R-values for the floor are estimated similarly and take into account the insulation value of the earth below, a masonry foundation, and an unheated air space (a crawl space or unheated cellar).

The R-values given for the ceiling, walls, and floor assume no insulation. If there is insulation, and you want to calculate the effect of adding some, add the R-value of the insulation to the R-value determined from the table.

R-values of insulation: Insulation R-values are given in a separate table and are stated in R-units per inch. The higher the R-value, the better the insulating effect of the material. Two inches of rock wool added to a wall, for example, will increase the R-value of the wall by 2 x 3.5 = 7.0 R-units; two inches of urethane foam, R-5.5, will provide greater insulation, R-11.

Existing insulation: Existing insulation in attic and basement areas is often visible to inspection. Check what type it is and measure its thickness with a ruler. If a likely site for insulation, such as inside a wall, is blocked from view, try to inspect it via some existing opening such as those around wall outlets, switches, and air ducts that pierce the wall. Remove flanges and cover plates to get at these openings. You may have to drill a hole through a surface to discover what lies behind it. In an attic with flooring, pry up a floor board.

To supply sample figures for the payback analysis chart, it was assumed that the walls were uninsulated wooden studs with wood siding (R = 5); the ceiling was drywall with plaster, including 3 inches of glass fiber insulation (R = 5 + 3 x 3.5 = 16); the floor was wood (R = 4), and the windows and doors were without storms (all R = 1).

Aluminum siding: If your house has uninsulated aluminum siding, the R-value is negligible, since aluminum is a conductor of heat. Newer forms of aluminum come with insulating backings of various R-values.

R-value of insulation

R-value per inch	Type of insulation
3.5	Rock wool
3.5	Glass fiber
3.5	Polystyrene
3.6	Cellulose
4.0	Urea-formaldehyde foam
5.5	Urethane foam

R-values of uninsulated surfaces

Ceiling	
R-4	Drywall
R-5	Drywall with plaster
R-6	Drywall with acoustical tile
R-8	Drywall with attic floor above
Walls	
R-5	Wooden stud wall, wood siding
R-4	8″ brick wall
R-5	12″ brick wall
R-5	Concrete block wall
add 2	Insulating sheathing
Floor	
R-4	Wood floor
R-6	Wood floor with plaster ceiling below
R-7	Wood floor with plaster and confined air space.
add 2	Carpet
Windows and doors	
R-1	Window
R-1	Door
R-2	Double-glazed window
R-2	Storm door

Looking for insulation

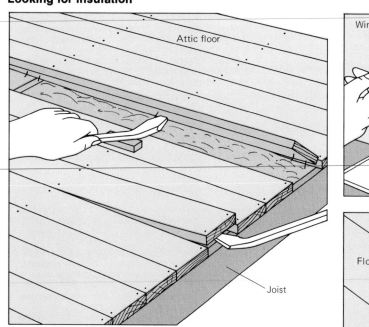

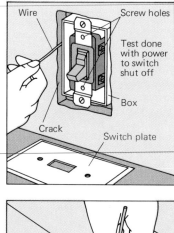

To check for hidden insulation under an attic floor, pry up a floorboard with a bar. Pry first at the end of the board, then step by step at each of the joists to which the board is nailed. After you have identified and measured the thickness of the insulation, if any, nail the board back in place. If boards are the tongue-and-groove type, you cannot pry them. Instead, use the hole-with-wire method (right).

To check for insulation in a wall, take out mounting screws and remove the face plate from a wall light switch. Look into crack along the outer edge of the switch's box. If the crack is narrow, turn off power to circuit, and probe with a stiff wire; use the wire, as shown below, to measure the depth of your insulation. To identify the type of insulation, put a hook into the end of the wire, snag a piece of insulation, and draw it out into the open.

An alternate way to check for insulation under an attic floor is to drill between joists a hole ½-in. (or larger) in diameter and look through it with a flashlight. To measure insulation thickness, insert a stiff wire until it touches the insulation, then scratch the wire. Push the wire through the insulation and scratch it again. Then measure the separation between scratches to determine the thickness.

Installing insulation

Varieties of insulation

Modern manufactured insulations are made of a number of lightweight materials that trap air in myriads of tiny, closed pockets. The insulation works because air is an insulator when rendered motionless in small spaces.

Insulation comes in different forms, as shown at right; in different types, as described below; and with different insulation capacities (R-values), as explained and tabulated on the facing page. The one you choose will depend on several factors, most importantly, the space in which you want to install the insulation. Choice of R-value, for example, is less significant where the space provides ample volume.

Glass fiber: This material is the most common commercial insulation and is standard for new wood-frame houses. It is most widely known by one of its trade names, Fiberglas, and is relatively inexpensive and easy to install. It resists damage by water and is relatively non-flammable. In blanket or batt form, it will not settle and create gaps after installation. Some people react allergically when handling fiber. Breathing masks, gloves, and other apparel will protect you from an allergic reaction.

Mineral wool: This insulation, also called by the trade name Rock Wool, has properties similar to those of glass fiber. It does not provoke an allergic reaction on contact.

Cellulose: Made of recycled paper, this material is organic and therefore susceptible to prolonged moisture retention, rot, and insect infestation. Cellulose will permanently lose much of its insulation value once it has become saturated with water, even after it dries. The material is also highly flammable and should be used only if treated by the manufacturer with a fire-retardant chemical such as boric acid. Its advantages are its low cost and the ease with which it is blown into otherwise inaccessible areas.

Polystyrene: This molded synthetic is an excellent insulator, somewhat expensive, and flammable. It is manufactured either as beadboard—many beads glued together—or as solidified boards.

Urea formaldehyde: This foam-type insulator is not damaged by water and is fire-resistant. It is injected into wall cavities as a two-part liquid that later expands and hardens. If not properly installed, the material shrinks, disintegrates, and emits toxic formaldehyde fumes. Because of this, its use has been banned by the U.S. Consumer Product Safety Commission.

Urethane: This is the most effective insulator, but flammable. It emits cyanide gas when it burns, and because of this it has been banned in some locales.

Forms of insulation

Blankets and batts

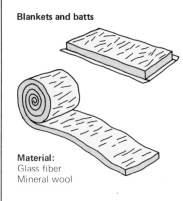

Material:
Glass fiber
Mineral wool

These products are used mostly in new construction and in unconfined areas, such as unfinished attic floors and roofs. Blankets come in rolls of up to 64 ft. Batts are simply blankets cut into 4-ft. or 8-ft. lengths. Widths are standard 16 in. or 24 in., which makes these forms of insulation best suited for wood framing that employs the same dimensions for spacing between members. Thicknesses, give or take a fraction of an inch, are usually 3 in., 6 in., and 9 in., though a 1-in. variety can also be found for special applications, such as to fill the narrow spaces inside masonry walls and around sills. The choice between blankets and batts balances convenience against cost. Blankets are clumsy to install, but where many batts must be trimmed to fit, greater waste results. Either can be found with or without a backing of aluminum foil or paper. Foil works well as a vapor barrier, paper less well unless it is treated to reduce its moisture permeability.

Rigid boards

Material:
Polystyrene
Urethane
Glass fiber

Boards come in widths of 16 in., 24 in., and 48 in. They can be as thin as ¾ in. or as thick as 7 in. The polystyrene and urethane versions have superior insulating qualities, and would for this reason be a better choice than blankets or batts were it not for their flammability. When installed inside a house, the boards require an additional covering of a minimum of ½-in.-thick fireproof material such as gypsum wallboard. A vapor barrier too must be installed with polystyrene beadboards and urethane boards, otherwise moisture penetration can cause them to lose up to half their R-value. Polystyrene foam boards and glass foam boards are impermeable to moisture. Rigid boards are commonly used as exterior sheathing for basement walls, both above and below ground. Their use as sheathing beneath aluminum and vinyl siding is increasing, though the need to ventilate behind such siding to permit moisture to escape reduces the insulation value of the boards.

Loose fill

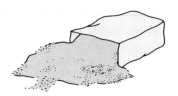

Material:
Cellulose
Glass fiber
Mineral wool

This form of insulation is marketed in bags and is the easiest to install. For unfinished attics, for example, you just pour the fill between joists and spread it with a rake or similar tool. Loose fill pours easily into cavities that are difficult for more rigid forms of insulation to enter. With professional equipment, the job of insulating a house with loose fill can be done rapidly. Just a sufficient number of openings through which the fill can be blown are needed, which may require drilling holes or removing some siding. Unfortunately, loose fill settles with time, particularly in vertical cavities such as those in walls, so care must be taken to install it at the proper density. A separate vapor barrier must be included with the fill to protect against prolonged moisture condensation. Wet cellulose shrinks and loses insulation value, and may also become a fire hazard if the water dissolves the fire-retardant chemicals used to treat the cellulose.

Foam

Material:
Urea formaldehyde
Urethane

Foam is an alternative to loose fill for insulating closed cavities that are difficult to reach, and it does not settle like loose fill. Foam, in liquid form, is pumped from tanks and injected into the cavity where it expands and sets in less than one minute. The work must be done by a competent contractor and during some part of the year when the temperatures are moderate, optimally between 50°F. and 80°F. Foam shrinks slowly for several weeks after it sets and thus loses some of its insulating effectiveness. If the installation is done correctly, the shrinkage should be less than 5%. Should it be much more than 5%, the homeowner may be stuck with a poor job or be forced to pay considerably more to have the house walls opened in order to fill in the gaps caused by the shrinkage. The insulation qualities of foam remain unaffected by water. (Urea formaldehyde foam requires a vapor barrier to protect adjacent wood.)

Installing insulation

Installation methods

However the insulation is installed, it should fill the space snugly (see also p.362). Unfilled gaps become channels for air flow and convective heat loss.

When installing insulation in attic floors, first measure the joist depth and spacing. If the spacing is uniform and near the 16- or 24-inch standard, install batts or blankets. If spacing is not uniform, use loose fill. As a general rule, for a snug fit cut the batts or blankets ½-inch wider than the joist spacing.

Before drilling holes in order to blow loose fill into walls, check to see if the wall cavity in the attic is open. If it is, you can carry the fill up to the attic and pour it into the opening (but be aware of possible obstructions farther down inside the wall).

Another method of insulating heated basements or crawl spaces, not illustrated here, is to fasten foam board to the exterior foundation. This way, the walls absorb and release heat, moderating temperature in the basement. The foam board should start two or more feet below ground level; therefore, the foundation must be excavated to that depth. Cover exposed foam with asbestos or vinyl panels.

Caution: If you reside in a frigid climate, such as northern Minnesota, Alaska, or Maine, you may not want to insulate your basement or crawl space. This is because heat leaking from the basement prevents frost heaves close to the foundation. Particularly if your ground drains poorly, such heaves can do great damage.

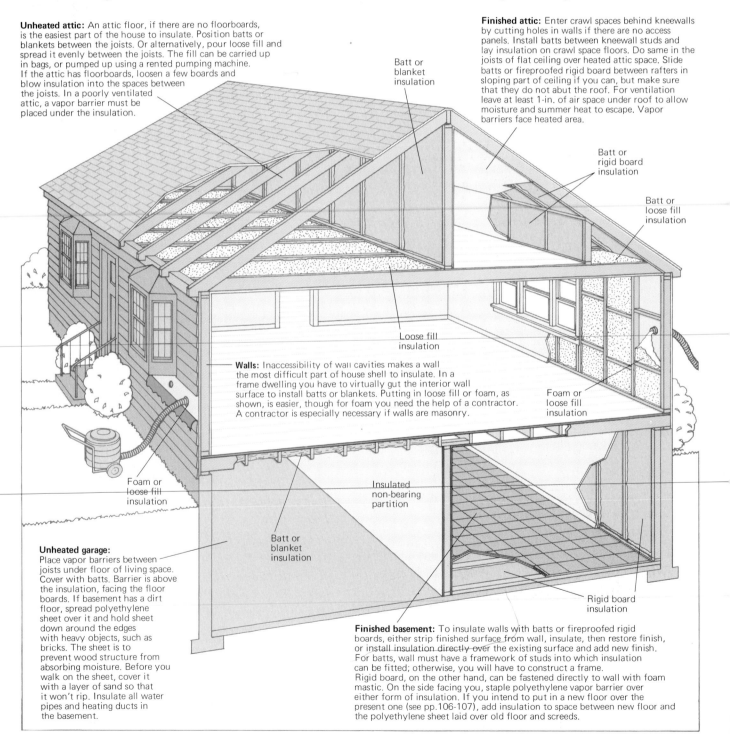

Unheated attic: An attic floor, if there are no floorboards, is the easiest part of the house to insulate. Position batts or blankets between the joists. Or alternatively, pour loose fill and spread it evenly between the joists. The fill can be carried up in bags, or pumped up using a rented pumping machine. If the attic has floorboards, loosen a few boards and blow insulation into the spaces between the joists. In a poorly ventilated attic, a vapor barrier must be placed under the insulation.

Batt or blanket insulation

Finished attic: Enter crawl spaces behind kneewalls by cutting holes in walls if there are no access panels. Install batts between kneewall studs and lay insulation on crawl space floors. Do same in the joists of flat ceiling over heated attic space. Slide batts or fireproofed rigid board between rafters in sloping part of ceiling if you can, but make sure that they do not abut the roof. For ventilation leave at least 1-in. of air space under roof to allow moisture and summer heat to escape. Vapor barriers face heated area.

Batt or rigid board insulation

Batt or loose fill insulation

Loose fill insulation

Walls: Inaccessibility of wall cavities makes a wall the most difficult part of house shell to insulate. In a frame dwelling you have to virtually gut the interior wall surface to install batts or blankets. Putting in loose fill or foam, as shown, is easier, though for foam you need the help of a contractor. A contractor is especially necessary if walls are masonry.

Foam or loose fill insulation

Foam or loose fill insulation

Insulated non-bearing partition

Unheated garage: Place vapor barriers between joists under floor of living space. Cover with batts. Barrier is above the insulation, facing the floor boards. If basement has a dirt floor, spread polyethylene sheet over it and hold sheet down around the edges with heavy objects, such as bricks. The sheet is to prevent wood structure from absorbing moisture. Before you walk on the sheet, cover it with a layer of sand so that it won't rip. Insulate all water pipes and heating ducts in the basement.

Batt or blanket insulation

Rigid board insulation

Finished basement: To insulate walls with batts or fireproofed rigid boards, either strip finished surface from wall, insulate, then restore finish, or install insulation directly over the existing surface and add new finish. For batts, wall must have a framework of studs into which insulation can be fitted; otherwise, you will have to construct a frame. Rigid board, on the other hand, can be fastened directly to wall with foam mastic. On the side facing you, staple polyethylene vapor barrier over either form of insulation. If you intend to put in a new floor over the present one (see pp.106-107), add insulation to space between new floor and the polyethylene sheet laid over old floor and screeds.

Reducing heat loss through windows

In the winter, windows lose a lot of heat to the outdoors after the sun goes down. The loss becomes serious for houses with large picture windows and glass doors. This is also a problem for passive-solar designed houses, which depend on large south-facing windows for their operations.

Storm vs. double glazing: Glass is "opaque" to radiant heat at room temperatures (the so called "greenhouse effect"), but still transmits heat by conduction and convection. To offset these effects, homeowners have traditionally installed storm windows for the winter season, or permanently installed double- or triple-glazed windows. These work better than storms because they do not leak air around the edges. Triple glazing is not much more cost effective than double glazing. This is because less benefit derives from insulation that is added to existing insulation (see pp.354–355 for more information).

Window coverings: An alternate and often cheaper way to reduce heat loss through windows is to cover them with drapes, shades, or shutters each evening or before going to bed. This works well for south-facing windows, but is less effective for north-facing ones.

On average, south-facing windows, which are natural solar-collectors, gain heat during the day. North-facing windows do not. The latter actually lose heat round the clock during the winter. So you will have to keep them covered or shuttered all winter long, or use double glazing. East- and west-facing windows fall in between.

Window coverings work more effectively when they include built-in insulation and are made as airtight as practicable. They should also include a vapor barrier, otherwise condensation will collect on the cold window behind them (see facing page). When insulated coverings such as those illustrated on this page are used in conjunction with single-glazed windows, they lose as little heat as triple-glazed windows.

Shades, blinds, and drapes: Conventional shades, blinds, and drapes are almost negligible as insulators. They are also too loose to prevent large convective losses via drafts that pass unimpeded through the spaces between them and the windows. Nevertheless, it is worth noting that they can save heat, by affecting our behavior. Standing near a window on a cold night, we feel cold because heat radiates directly from our bodies to the cold surface of the glass. If we cover the glass, the effect is diminished. This simple fact may offset the natural urge to raise the thermostat because of exaggerated perceptions of low air temperatures in the house. Heat savings produced in this way—psychological rather than physical in origin—may be hard to measure. But such savings can be substantial.

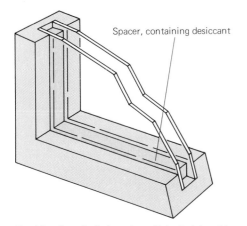

Double-glazed windows have ¼-in. to 1-in. wide air space that is factory sealed. The space may contain a desiccant (drying agent). Such windows when cracked or if improperly manufactured pass moisture that cannot be removed. Windows must be replaced when this happens.

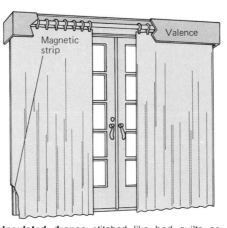

Insulated drapes stitched like bed quilts or pleated panels save more heat than conventional drapes. Valence at top retards air flow up space behind drapes. To further reduce flow, bottom of drapes should rest on floor and side edges press snugly against wall.

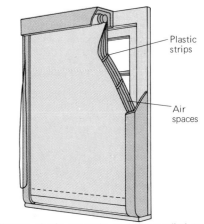

Pulldown shade expands as it is unrolled to create dead air spaces between its partitions. As shade is lowered, plastic strips bow out to separate partitions, which may be metallized to act as heat reflectors. Some shades are a quilted sandwich of partitions and fiberfill.

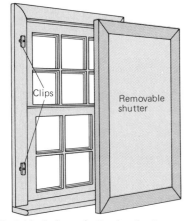

Portable indoor shutter is of a type you can make yourself at little expense; use lightweight ¾-in.-thick foam board overlaid with fiberboard, preferably fireproofed. Shutter pops into place over window and is held there by clips. Store shutters in a closet in daytime.

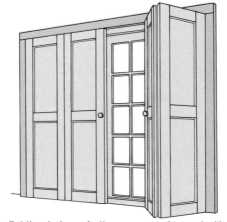

Folding indoor shutters are manufactured with solid wood frames and include a layer of foam insulation sandwiched between panels. Though costly, the shutters, in conjunction with single-glazed windows and weatherstripping installed along top and bottom, achieve an R-value of 8.

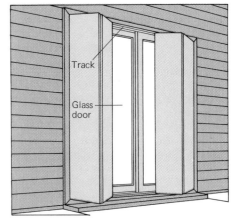

Folding outdoor shutters for glass doors can be opened with a crank from inside. They are manufactured with urethane insulation between hardwood panels. Panels slide in tracks along top and bottom to make them secure in high winds. Outdoor units cost more than indoor ones.

Weatherproofing a house

Caulking and weatherstripping

The cost of materials for weatherproofing is not great and you can do most of the work yourself. In theory, sealing your house with weatherproofing (plus heavy insulation) should save you almost all of your heat and cooling costs. In reality, however, you are restricted from carrying out such a program because your house also needs vapor control and ventilation (see p.362).

Caulking: The procedure for putting caulk into a crack with a caulking gun is shown below. Work on cracks on the outside of the house—around window and door frames, and gaps in siding. Because of the ventilation requirement—the need for some fresh air entering the house—do not overdo it. Restrict your exterior caulking to cracks that rain can penetrate. Also seal such gaps inside the house as those between the sill and the foundation, observable from the basement.

Many commercial caulk compounds are available. Least costly are butyl rubber, oil, and latex caulks. Latex is the only caulk that can be cleaned up with water. Because latex is water soluble, you must paint the caulk after you apply it outdoors. These caulks are good for comparatively fixed joints in the house shell only, such as the foundation sill or around window frames.

Many house joints are not fixed, but move readily in response to weather changes and door slams. To such joints, more expensive caulks—such as neoprene rubber, polyurethane, silicone, and polysulfide—must be applied. These caulks expand and contract with changing conditions. Of the four, polysulfide and silicone do not accept paint, so you cannot alter their color if at some later date you repaint the house.

Weatherstripping: Of the various materials on the market, the most durable weatherstripping is spring metal strip. It comes in straight lengths, or rolls of up to 100 feet. It can be of bronze, copper, stainless steel, or aluminum. Aluminum is the cheapest and is adequate for ordinary use. Common methods of applying metal strip and other weatherstripping materials are shown on the facing page.

Since it is difficult to permanently weatherstrip parts that move, you might want to try temporary seasonal weatherstripping. Windows that face north and some that face east and west and are kept closed as a rule during winter, or windows kept shut for summer air conditioning are candidates for removable, seasonal weatherstripping.

Insulating outlets and switches

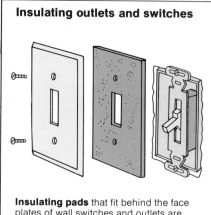

Insulating pads that fit behind the face plates of wall switches and outlets are commercially available to help reduce infiltration at these common weak points in the house weather barrier.

Caulking and weatherstripping

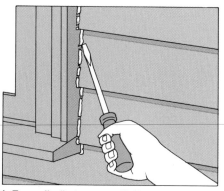

1. To caulk, first scrape all dirt, old caulk, and paint from crack with a tool, such as a screwdriver or putty knife. Make sure that crack is dry if your new caulk is not latex. Remove grease with paint thinner or similar solvent.

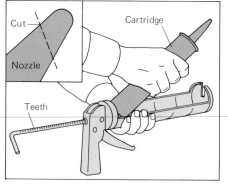

2. Pull plunger of caulking gun back and drop in disposable cartridge. Then, turn plunger so teeth point down; push it forward into cartridge until teeth engage. Snip end of cartridge nozzle to make angled opening of same width as crack.

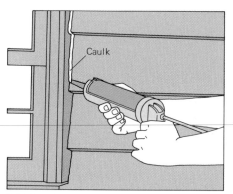

3. Hold gun at angle and apply caulk uniformly along crack. To control flow, pump gun trigger at steady rate (you will learn from practice). Make sure caulk overlaps crack edges and fills crack to several times its width.

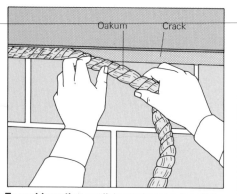

To avoid wasting caulk in cracks more than ½ in. wide or ½ in. deep, first insert filler, such as oakum (a treated hemp rope), or strips of glass fiber insulation or sponge rubber, or thin strips of wood. Then, caulk crack.

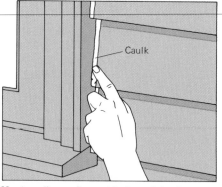

Most caulks can be molded snugly in place with a tool or a wet finger (see label that accompanies caulk). Remove excess latex or acrylic caulk immediately with a wet cloth, other caulks with a cloth dipped in recommended solvent.

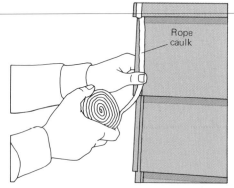

Temporary rope caulk is an alternate caulk appropriate for seasonal applications, such as around storm windows. It does not bond permanently, and lasts only a year or two. You press it into place, and peel it off whenever you desire.

Weatherstripping windows

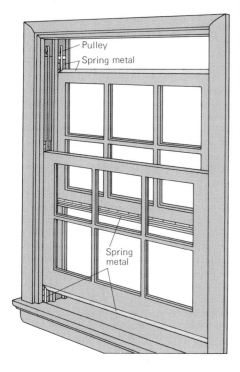

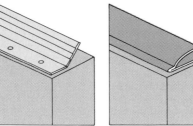

Weatherstripping for window jambs can be spring metal (left, and immediately above), vinyl, or foam rubber gasket (right). Spring metal is the more durable and it looks better—at least when the window is closed. Buy the weatherstripping in outsize lengths and cut it to fit the window, starting with the side jambs. Cut the strips so that they will reach 2 in. higher than the lower sash when window is closed. Raise the sash and slide the metal strips up the channels behind it and nail them in place. Follow the same procedure in reverse for the side jambs of the upper sash, cutting a space for the sash pulleys if the window has them. Nail strips also to the top of the upper sash, the bottom of the lower sash, and to the inside of the bottom rail of the top sash as shown, left. Wherever a sash on being raised or lowered might catch a strip edge, such as an edge next to the sash pulley, drive an extra nail into the springy side of the metal to hold down the edge that catches.

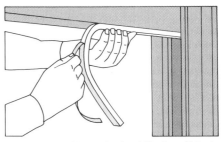

Tubular gasket of vinyl or rubber is nailed to window sash rails at top and bottom, and to window frame along sides, through nailing flange. On exterior, gasket is less noticeable.

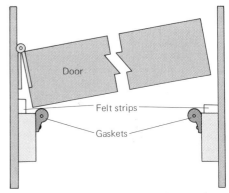

Felt or foam rubber strips in widths from ⅜ in. to 1¼ in. can be nailed or glued to bottom of sash where there is no friction. Some strips are adhesive, applied after peeling away paper.

Weatherstripping doors

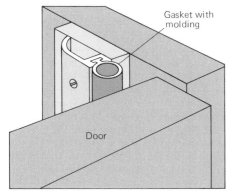

Tubular gasket, pre-attached to aluminum molding, is secured to door jamb at side and top. Cut strips to length with hack saw, fit them to abut closed door snugly, then nail or screw them every 8 to 12 in. along entire length.

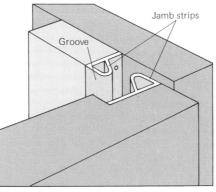

Interlocking, recessed metal jamb strips make an unobtrusive weatherseal that may be difficult to adjust should door later settle unevenly or warp. Installation requires cutting grooves along side and top of door and jamb.

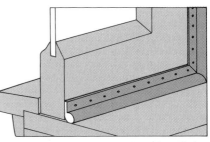

Felt strips, tubular gaskets, or spring metal can be used separately or in combination. Glue or nail correct type in locations illustrated. Foam rubber strips are not recommended for doors because they wear too quickly.

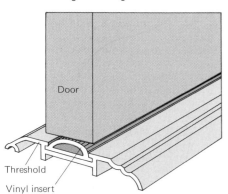

Vinyl insert in metal threshold that is screwed into floor presses snugly against closed door bottom. Insert wears with use but is replaceable. Installation requires that you first take door off hinges and saw off portion of door bottom.

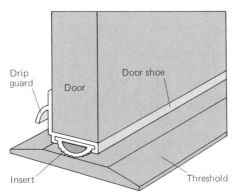

Door shoe consists of a vinyl insert in a metal retainer. It is installed in same way as threshold at left. Since vinyl in shoe is not stepped on, it wears less. The model shown includes a drip guard to protect against rain.

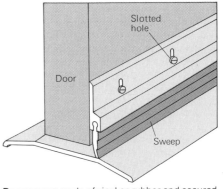

Door sweep made of vinyl or rubber and secured by a metal strip is attached inside on inward swinging door or outside on outward swinging door. Purchase one with slotted screw holes so that height of sweep can be adjusted with wear.

Getting more heat from electricity

Heat pumps

A heat pump takes heat from the outdoor air, working like an air conditioner in reverse (see below). For each kilowatt of electricity consumed, it produces from one and a half to two and a half times as much heat as conventional electric baseboard units.

Heat pumps cost about the same as central air conditioning systems, though you must add the cost of ductwork if it is not already present in your house. How efficiently heat pumps operate depends on outdoor temperature. Below freezing, they work poorly, and require an auxiliary heating system to back them up. But they can be added to an existing electric heating system to help reduce costs, or, since they are made to work as air conditioners too, they can be used as a sole heat source in areas with mild to hot climates such as in the southern states, where air conditioning is in heavy demand and heating requirements are moderate. An approximate break-even point is an average winter temperature of 38°F. In areas of the country with warmer winters than that mean figure, heat pumps at their present level of development are an economical alternative to conventional systems.

Types of units: Heat pumps are available in two configurations: a single, through-the-wall unit, as illustrated here; and a two-unit system, as illustrated below. The indoor unit of the two-unit system can be merged with the blower portion of the conventional, forced-air heating plant already existing in your home.

Most heat pumps include a back-up system consisting of electric resistance heaters in the exit duct of the internal air blower. This is a worthwhile and often a necessary addition where the heat pump system is the sole heating source for an entire house. It is unnecessary if the heat pump is being incorporated into an existing warm-air system.

Automatic defrost: Like refrigerators, which basically work the same way as air conditioners, all heat pumps have to be defrosted. In most units defrosting occurs automatically between pre-set time intervals. Though this relieves you of the burden of having to defrost the unit yourself, it works against the efficiency of the unit because it will switch into the defrost mode even when it is not

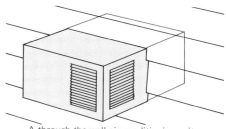

A through-the-wall air conditioning unit

necessary and waste heating and cooling capacity. A few companies now install solid state controls to solve this problem, and at least one is attempting to incorporate computer microprocessor controls. These advances can be expected to evolve a more effective product in the future.

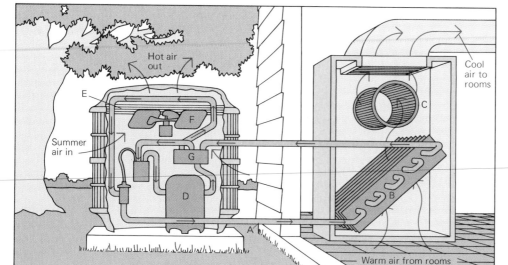

In summer, the heat pump works like a conventional air conditioner. Refrigerant (A), as it is piped through the indoor coils (B), absorbs heat from the room air and vaporizes. The cooled room air is then re-circulated in the house by a blower (C). The vaporized refrigerant flows into the compressor (D), which is a pump that both moves the refrigerant through the system and compresses it back into a liquid. The liquified refrigerant flows into the outdoor coils (E), where it releases its heat to outdoor air that is drawn through the outside unit. Air is circulated through the outside unit by a fan (F). The cooled refrigerant then flows back to the indoor coils, where the heat transfer cycle begins anew. When summer is over and winter has begun, the reversing valve (G) is switched. The refrigerant then flows in the opposite direction and serves to heat the house as described below.

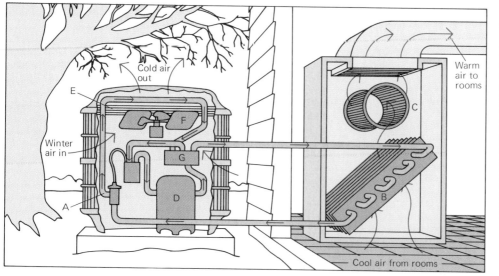

In winter, the heat pump works like a conventional air conditioner in reverse. Cold refrigerant (A) is piped through the outdoor coils (E), and absorbs heat from the outside air circulated through the outdoor coils by a fan (F). The refrigerant vaporizes and flows into the compressor (D), which compresses it into a liquid and pumps it through the system. The hot liquid refrigerant flows into the indoor coils (B), where the heat it absorbed is transferred to room air circulated through the coils by a blower (C). The refrigerant then flows back to the outdoor coils, where the heat transfer cycle starts again. When winter is over and summer has begun, the reversing valve (G) is switched. The refrigerant then flows in the opposite direction and serves to cool the house as described above.

Improving your existing heating system

Timed thermostats

By setting your thermostat back from 65°F. to 55°F. at night during the heating season, you can save from 10 to 15 percent of whatever fuel you use. Still more can be saved by setting back during the day if the house is empty.

To automate the morning and evening re-setting routine, replace your present unit with a timed thermostat. Timed units include a clock, and can be a simple one-period thermostat to control a night setback only, or a two-period unit to include a day setback. With the latter, you must manually override the setback on days when you are at home, such as on weekends and holidays.

Before purchasing a replacement thermostat, determine how your furnace (or boiler) is wired. Furnaces commonly use either 24-volt, two-wire or three-wire systems, or 750-millivolt systems. The replacement must match these specifications. Whether your furnace is two- or three-wire can be seen when you remove the old thermostat. The one shown below, for example, connects to a two-wire system. Check voltage with a voltmeter.

You can purchase a unit with a battery-operated clock, or a clock that can be wired to run off either a 24-volt, three-wire system, or off the house wiring. With a house-wired clock you must buy a 24-volt transformer that connects via a pair of wires fed through the wall to the new thermostat.

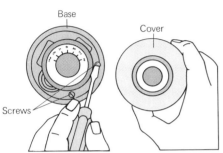

1. To replace the old thermostat with a new timed thermostat, first pry cover from old unit and remove mounting screws that secure thermostat base to wall plate.

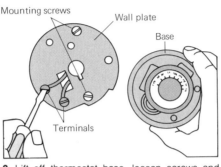

2. Lift off thermostat base, loosen screws and disconnect wires from terminals on wall plate. Then loosen wall plate mounting screws and remove the plate from the wall.

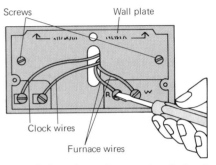

3. Put wall plate of new thermostat against wall, feed furnace wires and clock wires (if any) through plate hole, and connect them. Install plate mounting screws, but do not tighten.

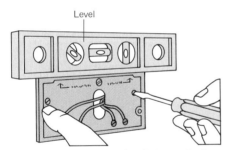

4. Place spirit level on top of wall plate and adjust the plate until the level indicates plate is horizontal. Tighten the wall plate mounting screws with a screwdriver.

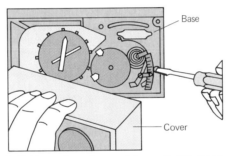

5. Put base of new thermostat on wall plate, insert mounting screws, and tighten them with screwdriver. Then snap on thermostat cover, and timed thermostat is ready to use.

For complex timing, programmable thermostat incorporating digital clock is available. Different schedules for each day can be set, altered, and skipped by pressing appropriate buttons.

Heating unit improvements

Chances are your house heating system is oversized, either because the contractor who installed the system wanted to make doubly sure that the system would heat your house on the coldest days, or because you have, in effect, oversized it by the addition of insulation.

Furnaces and boilers cycle on and off in response to the need for heat. An oversized unit wastes fuel because it goes on and off more frequently. This results in a lot of heat lost up the chimney during the off periods because the unit continues to give off heat though the house refuses it.

Changing oil burner nozzle: With a smaller nozzle combustion proceeds more slowly, so the oversized burner cycles on and off at a slower rate. This step is easy, inexpensive, and can be done during the annual checkup when nozzles are often changed anyway.

Adding automatic vent damper: This works on both oil and gas burners and is probably worth doing even when the heating unit is not oversized. A damper costs from $250 to $500 installed and, depending on how inefficient the heating system is to start with, can save from 10 to 20 percent of your fuel bill (less, if used with the flame-retention burner that is described below).

Replacing an existing oil burner with a flame-retention oil burner: Flame-retention units have smaller air intakes so that they burn hotter and more efficiently. The smaller intakes also reduce the draft through the burner, so that less heat is lost up the chimney during the off cycle. The units cost from $250 to $500 and may save 15 to 20 percent of your fuel bill. All these units qualify for Federal income tax credits as energy-conserving home improvements.

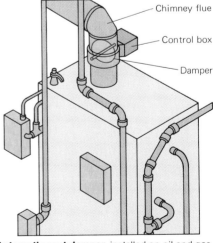

Automatic vent damper, installed on oil and gas furnaces, closes off chimney when heat is not being produced. Damper is operated by an electric motor or a solenoid. For safety reasons, unit should be installed by qualified mechanic only.

Solar heating

Introduction

Today the wide availability of economical multiple-glazed window glass makes practical a new technology based on the greenhouse effect: the transparency of glass to light but not heat waves. The amount of the sun's energy striking the earth far exceeds our energy needs. The problem has always lain in effectively collecting and storing it. Solutions are now forthcoming, though many of the methods being tried on houses today remain in the exploratory stage and still cannot compete in cost with fossil fuels.

Whether or not it is economical, energy from the sun has both political and ecological significance because it will always remain available. Government recognizes this by offering tax credits to those who install a solar energy system in their homes.

Much of the public identifies solar energy only with collector panels on the roof. Such panels are part of an active solar heating system. If a system has moving or working parts, such as valves, blowers, or thermostat controls, it is called an active system, otherwise it is called passive. Photovoltaic cells, which convert radiation directly to electricity, represent still a third category.

Active systems: Collector panels on the roof or some other part of a house take in as much solar energy as any like-sized window. Some people wonder why they cannot use a window instead of the panels. This is the strategy of the passive systems.

A collector panel's purpose is to serve as a point from which heat can be transported by some medium, such as water or air, to a storage structure in the house from which the heat can later be tapped. Such systems are complicated. They will become more competitive when they are as standardized and fault-free as the conventional heating systems that have been in our houses for decades.

Today's most effective application of active solar methods is to provide domestic hot water. The design is simpler, and a hot water supply requires a water tank for storage, in any case. In some regions, heating domestic water accounts for much of household fuel consumption, so the savings in this direction can be major.

Passive systems: Passive solar collection may require an extremely wide range of architectural alterations, including large south-facing windows, thermal mass, and convective ducts whose purpose is to maximize the use of the sun for house heat. For this reason, passive ideas work well in new house construction, but are not always readily adapted to existing houses.

With passive systems, it may be difficult to compare the energy gains of different designs. A successful mix of good architecture with solar gain, however, may create esthetic as well as fuel-economy benefits, as suggested by the photographs on pages 326–327.

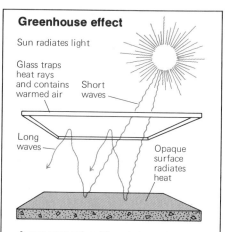

Greenhouse effect

Sun radiates light

Glass traps heat rays and contains warmed air

Short waves

Long waves

Opaque surface radiates heat

A one-way valve: Glass is transparent to the light emitted by the sun. Opaque surfaces behind glass absorb this radiant energy and re-radiate it as infrared (heat) waves. These heat waves have less energy and therefore longer wavelengths than light; the long waves cannot pass through the glass, and are trapped within, warming the greenhouse.

Passive solar methods

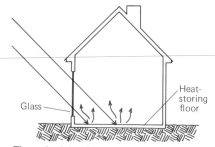

Glass

Heat-storing floor

The principle: Sun's rays pass through south-facing windows and are absorbed by floor or back wall made of heat-holding materials, such as masonry, concrete, or containers that hold water.

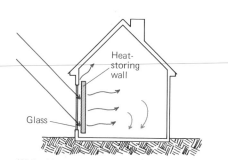

Heat-storing wall

Glass

Wall of heat-storing material (see left) is placed directly behind south-facing window to maximize storage. Sometimes called a trombe wall, it radiates heat slowly into house at right.

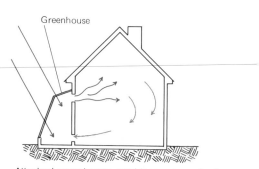

Greenhouse

Attached greenhouse combines solar collection with cultivation or solarium use, and may include heat-storage materials. Collected heat is circulated as warm air through adjacent rooms.

Active solar systems

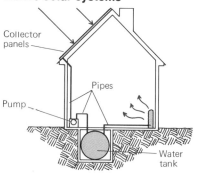

Collector panels

Pipes

Pump

Water tank

Liquid system pumps water through collector panels on roof. Solar heated water then passes to storage tank. Heat from tank is distributed via house radiators, or hot air system (facing page).

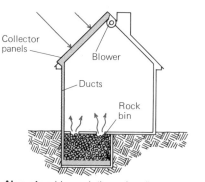

Collector panels

Blower

Ducts

Rock bin

Air system blows air through collector panels on roof. Solar heated air is ducted to storage bin or rock or water containers interleaved by air spaces, then circulated via heating system.

Photovoltaic systems

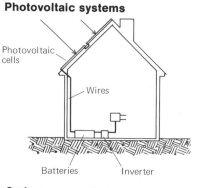

Photovoltaic cells

Wires

Batteries

Inverter

Sun's rays cause electric current to flow in photovoltaic cells on roof. Current is used directly by house or stored in batteries. If AC is desired, inverter is needed to convert from DC.

How an active solar heating system works

Water is used as the medium of heat transfer in the system illustrated in the drawings below. The water is pumped separately in two loops, a primary loop that includes the solar collector panel, or panels, and a secondary loop that includes the water storage tank. The loops meet in the heat exchanger.

The system has four modes of operation, as shown. For each of the modes, the loop pumps have to be turned on or off, and valves that direct water flow in the loops have to be opened or closed. These are tedious operations to tend to manually, so electric switches controlled by thermostats in the collector,

storage tank, and heated spaces of the house are wired into the system to make it automatic. In freezing climates, the water in the primary loop should be augmented by antifreeze. If this is not done, you will have to drain the collectors every night in winter or whenever the danger of freezing threatens.

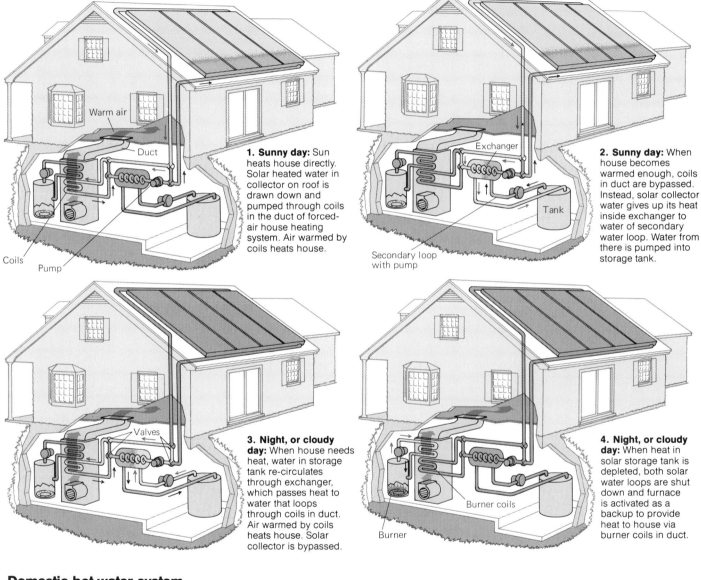

Warm air

Duct

Coils

Pump

1. Sunny day: Sun heats house directly. Solar heated water in collector on roof is drawn down and pumped through coils in the duct of forced-air house heating system. Air warmed by coils heats house.

Exchanger

Tank

Secondary loop with pump

2. Sunny day: When house becomes warmed enough, coils in duct are bypassed. Instead, solar collector water gives up its heat inside exchanger to water of secondary water loop. Water from there is pumped into storage tank.

Valves

3. Night, or cloudy day: When house needs heat, water in storage tank re-circulates through exchanger, which passes heat to water that loops through coils in duct. Air warmed by coils heats house. Solar collector is bypassed.

Burner coils

Burner

4. Night, or cloudy day: When heat in solar storage tank is depleted, both solar water loops are shut down and furnace is activated as a backup to provide heat to house via burner coils in duct.

Domestic hot water system

The sun will heat the water in a solar hot water system to about 130°F. This may be enough to support most of your hot water needs. For higher temperatures you must have a conventional backup water heater. A backup heater will be required in any case to heat your water on days when there is no sun. It may be a second water tank, to which the tank in the illustration would then be connected. If the solar water tank is placed under the ridge of your roof, the pump can be omitted because hot water from the collector rises to it by convection.

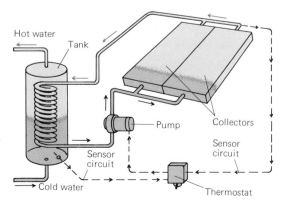

Hot water

Tank

Pump

Sensor circuit

Cold water

Collectors

Sensor circuit

Thermostat

Typical system for using sun's rays to heat water for house works like active solar heating system, above. Water in solar collector panel, after it is heated, is pumped down to coils inside water tank. The coils heat the water that you use. System includes a thermostat that senses the difference in temperature between collector and tank and turns on the pump whenever the difference is more than 5 degrees or so in favor of the collector. This is done to keep stored hot water from flowing back up to collector during cold periods and re-radiating heat back into the atmosphere. In northern climates, collector water should include antifreeze to prevent freezing.

Passive solar heating

Solar greenhouses

Traditional greenhouses provide light to grow plants. Much of the solar heat they collect must be vented outdoors to maintain the ideal greenhouse temperatures for plant cultivation. But a solar greenhouse is designed to store the excess solar heat for use in warming a house to which it is attached.

In a solar greenhouse the heat is collected and stored by means of south-facing windows, insulated walls and roof, double-glazing, window shutters, and the use of heat-absorbing materials inside the greenhouse. The greenhouse is directly attached to or built into the south wall of the house. The stored heat is then available both to keep plants above frost level on all but the coldest

nights and to circulate through the house. Unfortunately, these changes in design are limited because most house plants cannot endure constant temperatures above 90 degrees, so some of the heat that could be stored even on sunny winter days must still be vented outdoors and therefore is lost.

One common approach to this problem is not to put house plants into a solar greenhouse, but to employ it only to assist in warming the house. If you wish, you can eliminate plants altogether and let the greenhouse temperature rise to 130 degrees or more on sunny fall, late winter, and early spring days. You can then convert the greenhouse into an efficient solar collector. At night, the

solar greenhouse is shut off from the rest of the house and allowed to drop in temperature. A comparison of the differences between solar and conventional plant greenhouses is illustrated in greater detail below. You will have to decide on one or the other, or on some compromise between the two. An attached greenhouse can also serve as a solarium—but again, excess heat will have to be vented to maintain comfort.

A solar greenhouse can be installed by a contractor, or you can build it from a kit. If you want to build it from scratch, follow commercially available blueprints. Greenhouses are vulnerable to snow loads and high winds if they are not built and braced properly.

Two ways to use a solar greenhouse

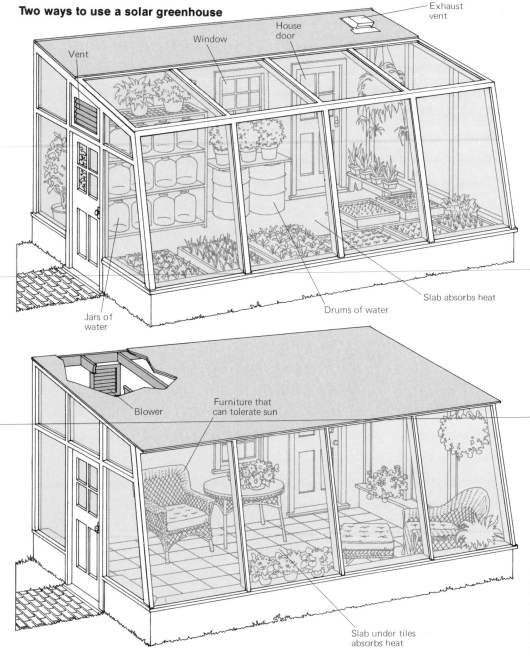

To grow plants: Include heat storing objects, such as used oil drums and plastic jars filled with water (see facing page for other storage media). Water in jars should be tinted a dark color to increase absorption of solar rays, and jars should be shelved or stacked with space left around them for air circulation. To work well, the heat storing objects have to be well positioned to catch and absorb the sun's rays, so they will not be competing with plants for sunlight. In winter, open house windows and door to vent excess heat into house. If natural convective drafts are not sufficient to move the heat, put a fan in the window or doorway to assist circulation. In summer, particularly in hot areas of the country, excess heat becomes a problem. Install shutters to block out sunlight, and vent heat either through open roof windows or doors built into the greenhouse or, more effectively, install exhaust fan.

To heat house: To achieve efficient transfer of heat from greenhouse to house, you may want to install a blower system—especially to move heat to remote parts of the house. If the greenhouse is not well insulated or does not have shutters to close, you should close off the entire greenhouse from the house at night; otherwise, the greenhouse may radiate away as much or more heat than it provides the house during daylight. (If the greenhouse has plants, heat will have to be circulated back to them at night by leaving house doors and windows partially open.) Heat stored in the greenhouse floor can provide early evening radiant heat if you use the assemblage correctly. The warm greenhouse is left open to the house during early evening to permit stored heat to enter the house; the crossover point comes during the night when you must close off the greenhouse; otherwise, you will find heat escaping from the house to the greenhouse.

Prefab and modular units

Companies now sell prefabricated solar greenhouse kits and installations in modular sizes. Some firms still offer greenhouses in the traditional plant cultivation mold—models that pay little heed to the conservation of solar heat. Glazing, for example, may often be available in only the single-pane variety.

Some greenhouses are glazed on all sides and the roof. This permits greater leeway in siting. Models with glass facing in just one direction can only be situated on the south wall of the house. Large areas of glass, on the other hand, let a great deal of heat escape at night. Such structures should be double- or triple-glazed, be provided with thermal shades, or be closable from the house at night and on overcast winter days. On sunny days, large glass areas collect and trap so much heat as to require an exhaust fan for dissipation of the heat and circulation of warm air through the rooms of the house.

Whether the greenhouse glass slants or is vertical in front is a matter of economy. Glass is slanted to provide for maximum collection of the sun's rays over a given area. Tilted vertically, up to 20 percent more glazing will be required, and you will have to pay for the additional glass that is necessary.

Prefabricated solar greenhouses are sold by many firms. Kits include wood-frame members, glazing, siding, roofing, and such options as water, concrete or rock thermal storage, window insulation, fans, and blowers. You put in the foundation at your expense. The greenhouses are generally available in sizes starting from a 12 x 12 ft. base, with add-on modules in 4-ft. segments.

Seasonal greenhouse is comparatively inexpensive and can be erected or taken down in one hour. Two layers of polyethylene are mounted over a rigid metal frame bolted to house wall. A small air blower supplied by the maker pumps air into a space between the two polyethylene layers, keeping the layers in tension and filled with a layer of air for night insulation. The polyethylene sheets wear out but are replaceable.

All-glass greenhouse installed by the manufacturer offers double or triple glazing mounted on and insulated from an aluminum frame. It has a sliding patio door, casement style windows, sliding roof curtain, and exhaust fan thermostatically operated. Many designs are available in both vertical-walled and slant-walled shapes. Greenhouse modules come in 4-ft. lengths.

Heat storage

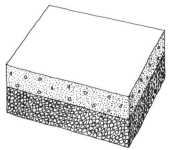

Concrete slab floor over a bed of rocks absorbs heat from sun's rays; slab radiates its heat to greenhouse after sun has gone down.

Brick wall absorbs heat like slab. It complements slab's thermal effects, particularly in a cluttered greenhouse where slab is shaded.

Metal or plastic heat-storage columns are filled with water. Water stores twice as much heat as same volume of brick or concrete.

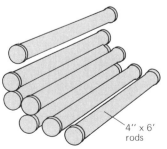

4'' x 6' rods

Rods filled with phase-change crystals employ complex chemical property of crystals to store twice as much heat as water does.

Passive solar heating

Building an attached solar greenhouse

The construction of an attached solar greenhouse differs from that of an ordinary addition in several ways. One difference is that all wood members should be treated with copper naphthenate preservative. Another difference is in the principal glazed wall; it is erected on a slant, so that it cannot stand by itself during construction. It must be temporarily propped up in some fashion with nailed pieces of scrap lumber. The supports can be angled to rest against your house wall.

The slant also creates an outward push on the foundation at the sill; therefore, the footing, foundation, and anchor bolts must be properly installed (see pp.22 and 242). In addition the greenhouse can be braced between the rafters and the studs in the glazed wall with several angled 2x4 crosspieces (not shown in the drawing).

The glazing must withstand wind pressure and rain leaks. The glazing joints tend to be the most vulnerable part of the structure, and at least one supplier of solar greenhouse blueprints offers neoprene window gaskets to take care of the problem.

A doorway in the house wall to the greenhouse is essential. If one does not already exist where you plan to locate the structure, break through the house wall and install one.

The floor of the greenhouse shown is near ground level. If the floor level of your house is several feet above ground level, stairs will have to be built from the doorway to the greenhouse floor to accommodate the difference. Or, you can build a wood, slate, or tile floor in the greenhouse at the house floor level. The space under the raised floor can be used for thermal storage by putting in crushed rock, water drums, or masonry.

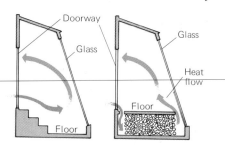

Alternate floor levels

With a raised floor glazing can still be installed to the foundation level, since that portion of the glass reaching below floor level will then serve as a type of thermosiphoning solar collector from which heat rises to the greenhouse and the house proper. The glazing below floor level should be backed by a dark, heat-absorbing material as in a solar collector panel.

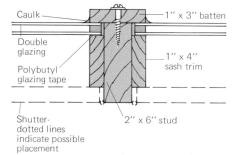

Secure double-glazing to sloping window studs as shown here in cross-section. Nail sash trim to sides of studs and mount windows stud to stud, securing windows with glazing tape. Apply caulk in gap between each pane and stud, and on window edge where batten is to be placed, then screw down batten so that it overlaps window edge firmly from top to bottom. Dotted lines indicate where to install shutters, either the folding or the roll-down type (see p.363).

Attached greenhouse is constructed of treated wood-frame members bolted to a poured foundation. The floor is reinforced concrete and the windows are double-glazed. The greenhouse doorway and the window serve to ventilate the greenhouse in summer. In the cooler months, these are kept shut and the window in the house wall is opened top and bottom to supply heat to the house, with the help of a portable fan. When it is complete, greenhouse will resemble the one shown in the center of page 327. Several firms supply blueprints for the construction of a unit of this type.

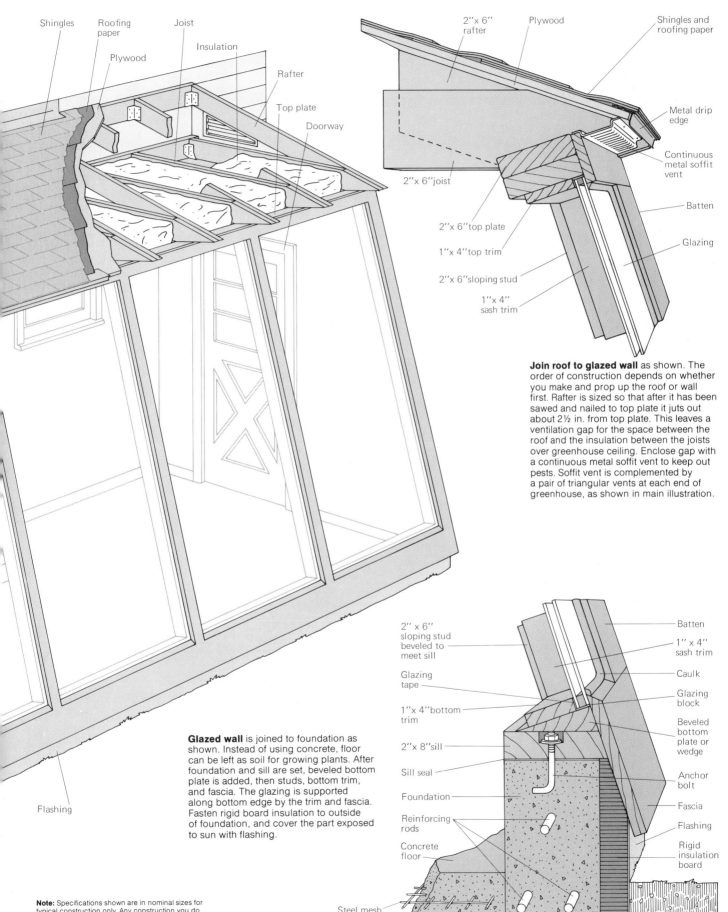

Shingles

Roofing paper

Plywood

Joist

Insulation

Rafter

Top plate

Doorway

2"x 6" rafter

Plywood

Shingles and roofing paper

Metal drip edge

Continuous metal soffit vent

Batten

Glazing

2"x 6"joist

2"x 6"top plate

1"x 4"top trim

2"x 6"sloping stud

1"x 4" sash trim

Join roof to glazed wall as shown. The order of construction depends on whether you make and prop up the roof or wall first. Rafter is sized so that after it has been sawed and nailed to top plate it juts out about 2½ in. from top plate. This leaves a ventilation gap for the space between the roof and the insulation between the joists over greenhouse ceiling. Enclose gap with a continuous metal soffit vent to keep out pests. Soffit vent is complemented by a pair of triangular vents at each end of greenhouse, as shown in main illustration.

Flashing

Glazed wall is joined to foundation as shown. Instead of using concrete, floor can be left as soil for growing plants. After foundation and sill are set, beveled bottom plate is added, then studs, bottom trim, and fascia. The glazing is supported along bottom edge by the trim and fascia. Fasten rigid board insulation to outside of foundation, and cover the part exposed to sun with flashing.

2" x 6" sloping stud beveled to meet sill

Glazing tape

1"x 4"bottom trim

2"x 8"sill

Sill seal

Foundation

Reinforcing rods

Concrete floor

Steel mesh

Batten

1" x 4" sash trim

Caulk

Glazing block

Beveled bottom plate or wedge

Anchor bolt

Fascia

Flashing

Rigid insulation board

Note: Specifications shown are in nominal sizes for typical construction only. Any construction you do must conform to your local building code.

Passive solar heating

Trends in sun-conscious architecture

Passive solar design is partly based on a very simple idea—redistributing the ordinary window area of a house so that larger windows appear on the south side of the house and smaller ones or none at all occur on the north side. Thermally massive elements for storing the sun's heat are incorporated into the design, such as the brick wall and concrete slab shown in our illustration. Window glazing is doubled or tripled; shutters may be added to keep heat from leaking out through the windows at night.

Assisting natural convection: The heat that a passive system collects becomes a liability during the summer, particularly in southern regions. Natural convection, whereby heated air rises of its own accord, can ventilate passive houses, but often the architect or homeowner has to fall back on a system involving a blower and ductwork. As compensation, the blower may also serve (as does the one illustrated) to redistribute heated air to the lower areas of the house in winter.

Striking a balance: Passive solar features make parts of the house overly bright and other parts very dark. The heat storage wall illustrated at left on this page, for example, lets too little light penetrate into the house, creating a dark interior. The large greenhouse area shown next to it lets too much light indoors. A present trend is to achieve a balance by incorporating both features as suggested by our drawing.

Clerestory windows: Another way to cope with the entry of too much light is to let it fall through clerestory windows as shown on the facing page. Shining mostly overhead, the light will not bother occupants or bleach furniture. Thermal mass placed to intercept clerestory sunlight can help the arrangement work better. But such mass has to be supported. An alternative is to make the entire rear wall of the house of masonry, to absorb clerestory light, but then the lower part of the wall will remain untouched by direct sunlight, so much of the wall's potential heat storage capacity will go unused. This can be offset by embedding steel rods vertically in the masonry to conduct heat from the upper sun-warmed portions of the wall down to parts that remain in shade.

Some passive designs require active solar features to work well—particularly blowers and ducts to transport air from hot areas of the house to cool areas, or to heat storage reservoirs. The duct seen taking air down to the first floor in our illustration, for example, could be extended to arrays of ducts embedded under the concrete slab. The slab would then serve as a floor heat radiator in daytime and as storage at night.

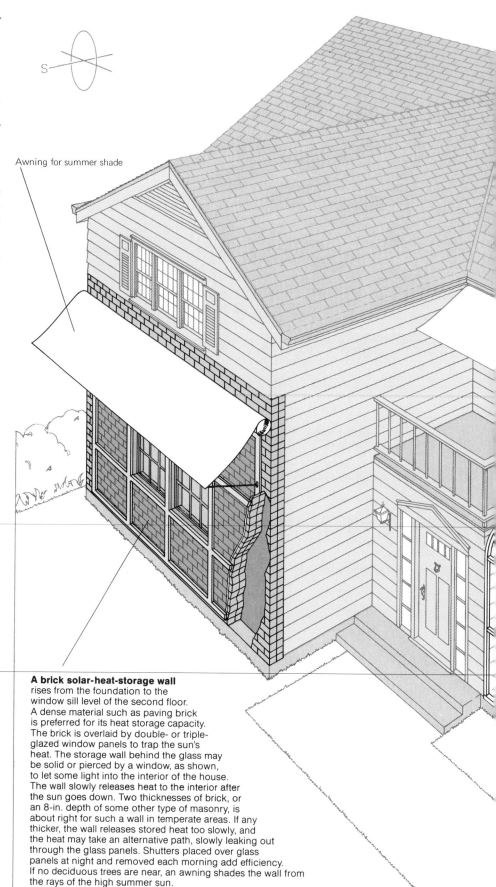

Awning for summer shade

A brick solar-heat-storage wall rises from the foundation to the window sill level of the second floor. A dense material such as paving brick is preferred for its heat storage capacity. The brick is overlaid by double- or triple-glazed window panels to trap the sun's heat. The storage wall behind the glass may be solid or pierced by a window, as shown, to let some light into the interior of the house. The wall slowly releases heat to the interior after the sun goes down. Two thicknesses of brick, or an 8-in. depth of some other type of masonry, is about right for such a wall in temperate areas. If any thicker, the wall releases stored heat too slowly, and the heat may take an alternative path, slowly leaking out through the glass panels. Shutters placed over glass panels at night and removed each morning add efficiency. If no deciduous trees are near, an awning shades the wall from the rays of the high summer sun.

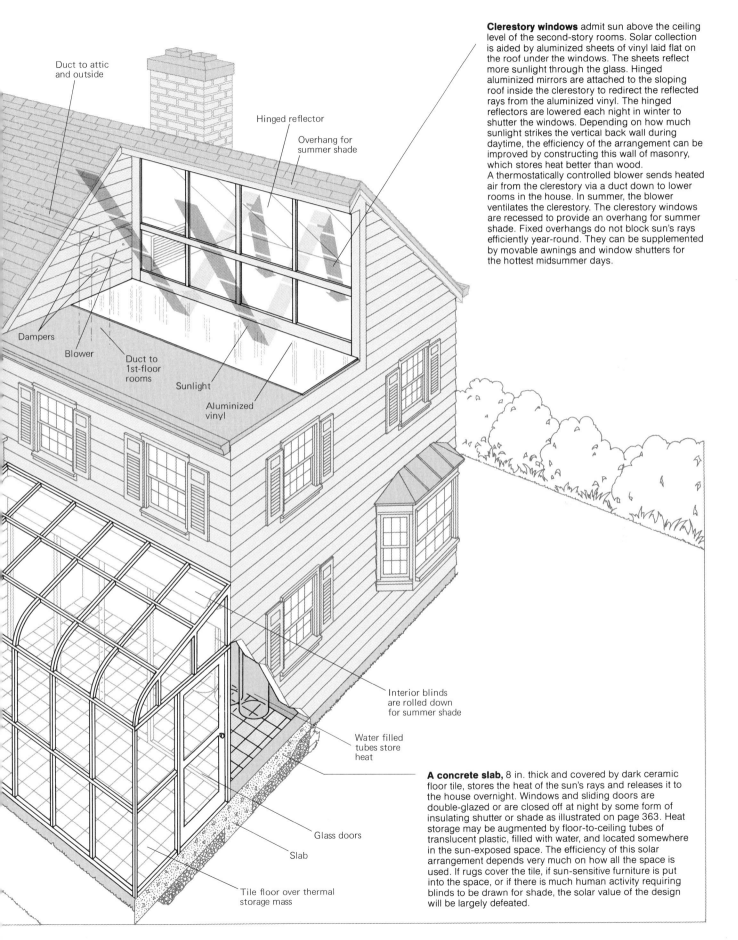

Clerestory windows admit sun above the ceiling level of the second-story rooms. Solar collection is aided by aluminized sheets of vinyl laid flat on the roof under the windows. The sheets reflect more sunlight through the glass. Hinged aluminized mirrors are attached to the sloping roof inside the clerestory to redirect the reflected rays from the aluminized vinyl. The hinged reflectors are lowered each night in winter to shutter the windows. Depending on how much sunlight strikes the vertical back wall during daytime, the efficiency of the arrangement can be improved by constructing this wall of masonry, which stores heat better than wood.

A thermostatically controlled blower sends heated air from the clerestory via a duct down to lower rooms in the house. In summer, the blower ventilates the clerestory. The clerestory windows are recessed to provide an overhang for summer shade. Fixed overhangs do not block sun's rays efficiently year-round. They can be supplemented by movable awnings and window shutters for the hottest midsummer days.

Duct to attic and outside

Hinged reflector

Overhang for summer shade

Dampers

Blower

Duct to 1st-floor rooms

Sunlight

Aluminized vinyl

Interior blinds are rolled down for summer shade

Water filled tubes store heat

Glass doors

Slab

Tile floor over thermal storage mass

A concrete slab, 8 in. thick and covered by dark ceramic floor tile, stores the heat of the sun's rays and releases it to the house overnight. Windows and sliding doors are double-glazed or are closed off at night by some form of insulating shutter or shade as illustrated on page 363. Heat storage may be augmented by floor-to-ceiling tubes of translucent plastic, filled with water, and located somewhere in the sun-exposed space. The efficiency of this solar arrangement depends very much on how all the space is used. If rugs cover the tile, if sun-sensitive furniture is put into the space, or if there is much human activity requiring blinds to be drawn for shade, the solar value of the design will be largely defeated.

Active solar heating

Domestic hot-water systems

Three ways to heat domestic hot water with solar flatplate collectors are illustrated on these pages. The simplest of the three systems, the thermosiphon type, is shown below. In general, the more complex the system, the more versatile it is likely to be, especially in providing adequate amounts of heated water even when outdoor temperatures fall below freezing.

Cost and efficiency: Complexity adds to installation costs and lowers overall system efficiency, however. You will have to pay extra for the electricity to operate whatever pumps you add to assist fluid flow and automatic draining at night or on overcast days in freezing weather. A heat exchanger transfers heat at less than 100 percent efficiency. A second storage tank, which many households need to provide an adequate supply of hot water, adds to losses because heat leaks through the additional walls of the second tank and the plumbing used to move water between tanks, even if insulated.

For these reasons, the cost of the solar heat delivered to your domestic water supply by the two-tank heat exchanger systems shown on the facing page—the drainback and antifreeze systems—is about two and a half times as great as the cost of heat from the simpler ther-

mosiphon system, which must be shut down with the onset of cold weather.

Other systems: Draindown systems (not illustrated) eliminate the need for a heat exchanger, reducing costs. Draindown systems protect against freezing by automatically draining the collector water out of the system into a house drain in severe cold. (The illustrated drainback system drains collector water into the exchanger tank.)

Another type not shown here uses air instead of water as the heat transfer medium. This system delivers heat five to ten times as costly as the thermosiphon system, mostly because air is a poor heat transfer medium when compared to a liquid and because more powerful pumps are required to move enough air to make the system work. The inefficiency of such a system makes it a poor choice, except when integrated into a solar hot-air storage system, such as the one shown on page 378.

Solar collectors: Collectors that use liquid for heat transfer must operate at high temperatures to be effective—normally, 180°F.–200°F. These temperatures can reach 400°F. if the pump fails and flow stagnates.

Caution: Such temperatures char wood; do not mount a liquid collector flush against a wood roof.

The collector glazing best able to withstand such high temperatures without discoloring, breaking, or melting is tempered glass. If double glazing is employed, the two panes should not be bonded because of the widely different rates of expansion each undergoes as the temperature rises. Sealant will have to be applied yearly because of this differential movement.

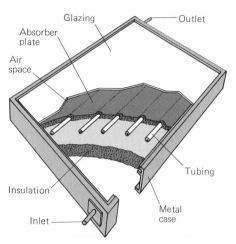

Typical flatplate liquid solar collector consists of: a dark-colored absorber plate with tubing bonded to or embedded in the plate; a transparent cover of glass, glass fiber, or plastic—which can be single- or double-glazed; and insulating backing.

Thermosiphon system

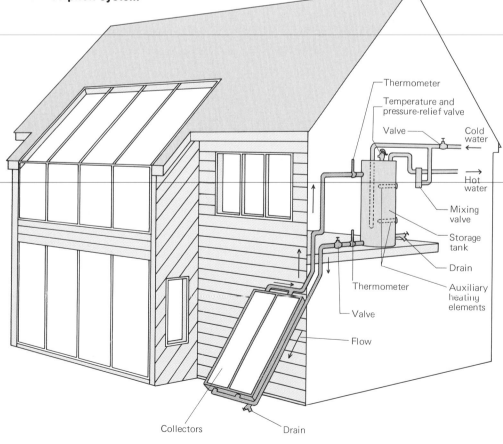

Collectors   Drain

This hot-water system relies on the natural tendency of warm water to rise in moving the water from the collectors to the storage tank. Flow ceases automatically at night or on overcast days. Pumps and electrical controls are not required; their omission makes the system the least costly shown on these pages. This is also the most efficient system, saving more fuel dollars for each dollar invested than the other systems. Unfortunately, this system is not protected against freezing, making it practical only in southern parts of the country or for heating water during summer in colder areas. Cold water is fed to the bottom of the storage tank. From there it descends to the bottom of the collectors, is warmed, and rises through the collectors to the top of the tank. For this thermosiphoning effect to work well, the tank bottom must be positioned at least 2 ft. above the top of the collectors. This generally precludes putting the tank in the basement. When located higher in the house, structural support must be provided for both the tank and more than 1,000 lbs. of water. Thermosiphoning moves water only about one-fifth as fast as pump-operated systems; therefore, lesser amounts of hot water accumulate. So as not to impede flow, the plumbing in the thermosiphon should have few and shallow bends and also be of large diameter.

Drainback system

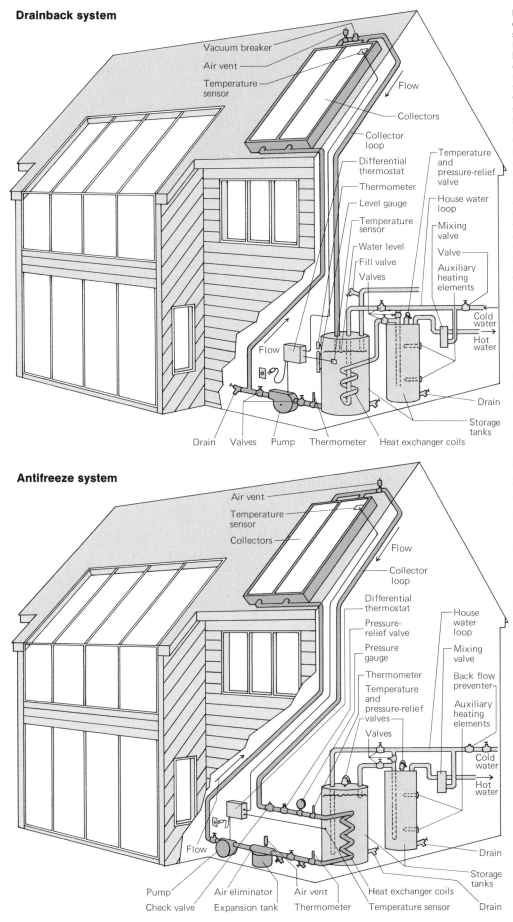

Vacuum breaker
Air vent
Temperature sensor
Flow
Collectors
Collector loop
Differential thermostat
Thermometer
Level gauge
Temperature sensor
Water level
Fill valve
Valves
Temperature and pressure-relief valve
House water loop
Mixing valve
Valve
Auxiliary heating elements
Cold water
Hot water
Flow
Drain
Drain   Valves   Pump   Thermometer   Heat exchanger coils
Storage tanks

Antifreeze system

Air vent
Temperature sensor
Collectors
Flow
Collector loop
Differential thermostat
Pressure-relief valve
Pressure gauge
Thermometer
Temperature and pressure-relief valves
Valves
House water loop
Mixing valve
Back flow preventer
Auxiliary heating elements
Cold water
Hot water
Flow
Drain
Pump
Check valve   Expansion tank   Thermometer   Temperature sensor
Air eliminator   Air vent   Heat exchanger coils
Storage tanks
Drain

In the drainback system (not to be confused with a draindown system, not shown on these pages), house water is kept separate from collector water; the house water is contained in exchanger coils immersed in hot collector water. Collectors are drained when temperatures fall below freezing, and a conventional water heater comes on as a back-up system. In contrast to the thermosiphon system (facing page), this system remains usable during periods when days are warm and nights are cold, because its protection against freezing works automatically. Water is in the collectors only when the pump is active. The pump is a small one, ranging from 1/24 to 1/12 horsepower. It turns off whenever collector temperature—as sensed by a differential thermostat—drops below a pre-set level; the water then drains back into the heat exchanger tank. The freeze protection is fail-safe; in the event of a power failure, the pump turns off. The system must have a heat exchanger, because without one the pressure of the utility water in the collector loop would prevent drainback. Since drainback works by gravity, pipe runs in the collector loop should slope downward. To avoid corrosion, the plumbing can be made of copper throughout and distilled water should be used in loop. If these specifications are not followed, a corrosion inhibitor must be added to the loop water, and the heat exchanger must be a less efficient, double-walled type, as described below.

Protection against cold in this system is accomplished by adding a freeze-resistant fluid such as ethylene glycol to the collector water. The collector does not have to be drained when temperatures drop, and the system can be used year round. Controlled by the differential thermostat, the collector fluid circulates through the collector loop and heat exchanger coils in the house water tank. Since the coils carry collector water rather than house water as in the drainback system, above, you can have one storage tank instead of the two shown. One tank is adequate for small households that do not put heavy, short-term demands on the hot-water system, and is more economical and efficient than two tanks. Collectors, with their small-diameter tubing, are extremely susceptible to blockage by corrosion. Corrosion inhibitors or special oils that are chemically inert can be used in the collector fluid. Some of these fluids, and most antifreeze solutions, are toxic, so precautions to safeguard the house water in the system must be taken. To protect house water from collector fluid leaks, the heat exchanger has to be double-walled—an example, coils that incorporate smaller concentric tubing. Unfortunately, the heat exchanger loses some heat transfer ability in trade-off for this protection. Drain taps in the collector loop should carry a prominent warning label if the loop contents are toxic.

Active solar heating

Heat transfer and storage systems

Solar systems that rely on air rather than water as the heat transfer medium do not have to cope with such problems as winter freezing, leaks, and corrosion. A blower with a ¼- to ½-horsepower motor is included in the ductwork to move the solar heated air from the collectors to the storage bin.

Heat transfer medium: Water is a much more efficient heat transfer medium than air because a given volume of water holds much more heat than the same volume of air. But this advantage is offset by the need for the systems to operate at high temperatures, 180° to 200°F. Below 160°F., hot-water room radiators barely function. A hot-air system, on the other hand, works adequately if the air it delivers is a few degrees above room temperature. The main problem with a high temperature system is that it may be up to four times

as costly to build. About twice as much collector surface is needed, for example, to absorb the solar energy necessary to attain high water temperatures.

Heat storage: In the hot-air heat transfer system illustrated below, water also has a role to play—in the storage part of the system. Vertical tubes of water are arranged in a bin to store the heat transferred by hot air from the collectors. A common alternative is to fill the storage bin with either crushed rock or pebbles from stream beds, instead of containers of water. Whatever the material used, a hefty and insulated foundation must be laid to support the bin and its load since their combined weight is enormous. An 8-x-8-x-30-foot concrete box filled with pebbles, for instance, weighs about 60 tons.

Storage reservoir dimensions are determined by how much heat you will

need from the bin on cold nights and overcast days. An engineering analysis must be made to determine required storage volumes. The 8-x-8-x-30-foot volume given as an example is appropriate for a compact 1,500-square-foot house in an area with moderately cold winters, such as Ohio or Pennsylvania. If water is used as the storage medium instead of pebbles, the box need be only half the volume. But because water transmits heat more readily than rock, more insulation must be placed around the storage bin to keep the heat locked in over protracted periods.

The system has a control panel and operates automatically. The panel receives information from two thermal sensors, and the room thermostat, which you set; it turns the collector blower on and off, and opens and closes dampers in the ducts as indicated.

1. Collectors heat house. Control panel opens direct return dampers. Cool air, drawn by blower from rooms, is forced up to collectors, heated by sun, and returned to rooms via a conventional forced-air system.

2. Collectors heat storage water in bin. When house is warm, room air distribution is turned off, direct return dampers are closed, and the air heated by the roof collectors is pumped by the blower to the storage bin. Sensors in the collector and in the storage bin monitor temperatures at these locations. When the temperature differential drops —that is, when the sun clouds over or night falls—the collector blower is temporarily turned off to retain stored heat in bin.

3. Storage bin heats house. Control panel turns off collector blower and activates air distribution via house system. Heated air is drawn only from storage bin.

4. Furnace heats house. When storage heat is depleted, burner in furnace is ignited and house is then heated in the conventional way. Active solar hot-water systems are described elsewhere.

Typical installation

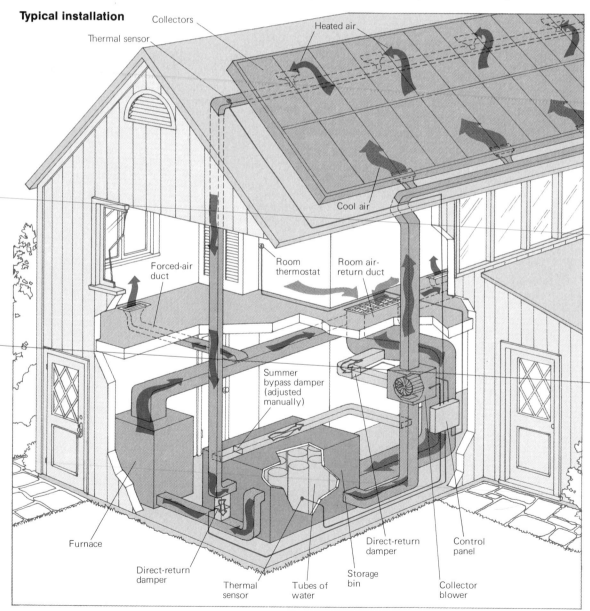

Collectors · Thermal sensor · Heated air · Cool air · Forced-air duct · Room thermostat · Room air-return duct · Summer bypass damper (adjusted manually) · Furnace · Direct-return damper · Thermal sensor · Tubes of water · Storage bin · Direct-return damper · Collector blower · Control panel

Solar electricity

Photovoltaic cells

Photovoltaic cells convert the energy of sunlight directly to electricity. The most common cells are made principally of silicon, which is obtained from the silicon dioxide in sand. Despite the abundance of sand in the world, the cells are expensive because of the great cost of manufacturing the ultra-pure silicon wafers, which are the main components of the cells. At present, it takes four years for a solar cell on your roof to produce electrical energy equal to the energy consumed by the very manufacturing process that made the cell.

Ongoing research: A major research effort is underway to reduce cell cost and improve methods to mass produce cells. Optimistic engineers project a tenfold drop in cost by the mid to late 1980s. Thus solar cells should become common on residential roofs in the 1990s.

A photovoltaic system such as the one illustrated below today costs between $50,000 and $100,000. The system's cost will drop to about $10,000 if the most optimistic forecasts prove correct. At this lower cost, photovoltaic generation will be competitive with power company generation, provided your system includes an effective way to store and retrieve excess electricity produced on sunny days. The best method is selling it to a public utility and buying it back later. Battery storage is another way to absorb excess for later use, but large numbers of batteries are necessary to support the electrical requirements of an ordinary household, adding to the system's expense.

Selling electricity to utilities: Photovoltaic cells covering the roof of every house and building in the country would supply the nation's entire electrical needs—domestic, public, and industrial.

Several laws have already been passed requiring public utilities to accept electricity returned to them by home power plants. The rates to be paid by the utilities for home-generated power will undoubtedly be set by law.

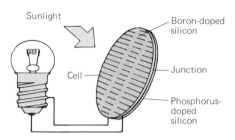

A **photovoltaic cell** is similar to a transistor; it creates an electric potential across junctions between materials impregnated with different impurities. Current flows at junctions when sunlight passes through the wafer.

A system of the future

Photovoltaic system includes a large assembly of panels mounted on south-oriented roof, the panels supporting 30 or more cells each. Panels are wired to each other and to an inverter that converts the DC power from the panels into AC feeds the power into the house electric system, and, as an option, diverts any excess power to the public utility. In lieu of the utility, batteries can be used for storage of the excess power.

Panels have cells packed as close to each other as possible. Cells are wired in tandem. Since each cell provides about ½ volt, 220 of them in series can supply a 110-volt circuit. For more power, groups can be ganged in parallel.

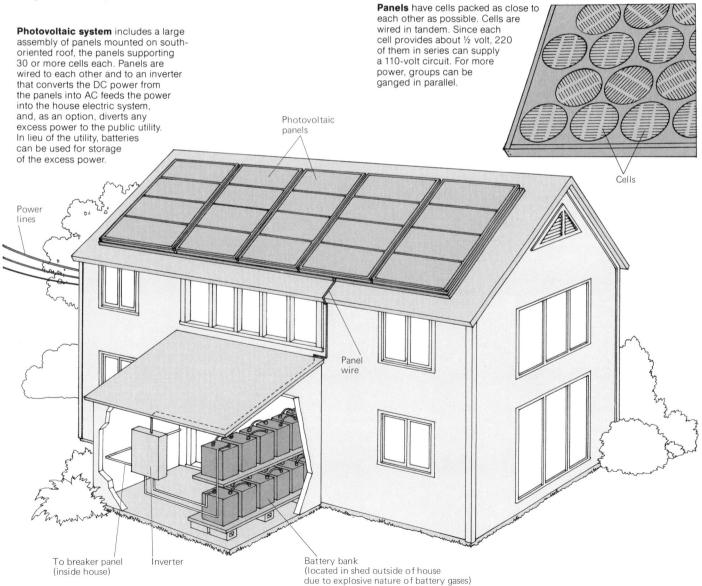

Index

R

S

Ordering concrete

The first step in estimating how much concrete you will need is to calculate the area in square feet that the structure will cover. Measure the dimensions of the space and determine its square footage as explained below. Multiply the square footage you get by the thickness in feet of the planned structure.

The result will be the total volume of concrete required, expressed in cubic feet. To convert this number into cubic yards — the unit by which concrete is calculated and sold — divide by 27, the number of cubic feet in a cubic yard. For example, a 4-inch-thick concrete slab 25 x 15 feet would

require 4.63 cubic yards of concrete: 25 times 15 times 1/3 (4 inches is 1/3 foot) equals 125 cubic feet; this, divided by 27, equals 4.63 cubic yards.

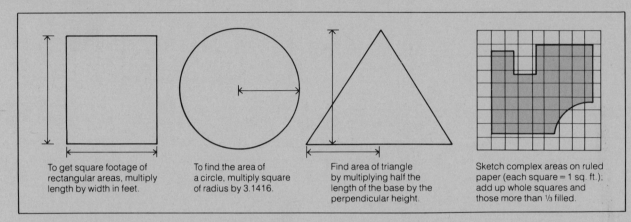

To get square footage of rectangular areas, multiply length by width in feet.

To find the area of a circle, multiply square of radius by 3.1416.

Find area of triangle by multiplying half the length of the base by the perpendicular height.

Sketch complex areas on ruled paper (each square = 1 sq. ft.); add up whole squares and those more than 1/3 filled.

Equivalent mortar mixes

Type of brickwork	Cement-lime mortar	Masonry cement mortar
Retaining walls; sills and copings	1 part cement 1/2 part lime 4 1/2 parts sand	1 part masonry cement 3 parts sand
Freestanding walls; work below moisture line; uncoated parapets	1 part cement 1 part lime 6 parts sand	1 part masonry cement 4 1/2 parts sand
Walls exposed to weather; mortar-coated parapets; inner leaf of cavity wall	1 part cement 1 part lime 6 parts sand	1 part masonry cement 4 1/2 parts sand
Internal non-load-bearing walls	1 part cement 2 parts lime 9 parts sand	1 part masonry cement 6 parts sand

The general-purpose mix (1 part cement, 3 parts sand) is recommended for most repair jobs.

How much mortar?

For 100 square feet of brick wall surface				
Wall thickness	Number of bricks	Cubic feet of mortar	Mix by volume 1:3	
			Masonry cement bags	Cubic feet of sand
3 3/4"	616	9	3	9
8"	1,232	21	7	21

The mortar quantities in this table are approximations. They allow for roughly 20% waste for a 4 in. wall, 12% waste for an 8 in. wall. These allowances are conservative since waste can be higher than 50%, depending on the care and skill of the bricklayer. Table is based on standard building bricks — 2 1/2 x 3 3/4 x 8 in. All mortar joints are assumed to be 1/2 in. thick. A 70-lb. bag of masonry cement holds 1 cu. ft.

Types of molding

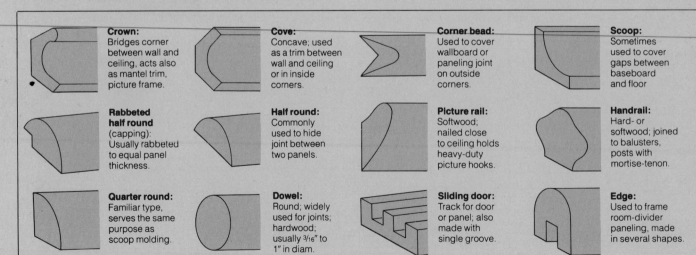

Crown: Bridges corner between wall and ceiling, acts also as mantel trim, picture frame.

Rabbeted half round (capping): Usually rabbeted to equal panel thickness.

Quarter round: Familiar type, serves the same purpose as scoop molding.

Cove: Concave; used as a trim between wall and ceiling or in inside corners.

Half round: Commonly used to hide joint between two panels.

Dowel: Round; widely used for joints; hardwood; usually 3/16" to 1" in diam.

Corner bead: Used to cover wallboard or paneling joint on outside corners.

Picture rail: Softwood; nailed close to ceiling holds heavy-duty picture hooks.

Sliding door: Track for door or panel; also made with single groove.

Scoop: Sometimes used to cover gaps between baseboard and floor

Handrail: Hard- or softwood; joined to balusters, posts with mortise-tenon.

Edge: Used to frame room-divider paneling, made in several shapes.